1981-82 EDITION

THE INSIDER'S GUIDE TO THE COLLEGES

1981–82 EDITION

THE INSIDER'S GUIDE TO THE COLLEGES

Compiled and edited by
the staff of
The Yale Daily News

A PERIGEE BOOK

Perigee Books
are published by
G. P. Putnam's Sons
200 Madison Avenue
New York, New York 10016

Copyright © 1971, 1972, 1973, 1974, 1975, 1978 by *The Yale Daily News*.
Copyright © 1981 by *The Yale Daily News* Company, Inc.

All rights reserved. This book, or parts thereof, may not be reproduced in any form without permission. Published simultaneously in Canada by Academic Press Canada Limited, Toronto.

The Library of Congress Cataloged This Serial as Follows

The Insiders' guide to the colleges. 1st ed.
  [New York] Berkley Pub. Corp. etc., 1970-
v. 20 cm. (-2d- ed.: A Berkley medallion book)
  First ed. compiled and edited by the staff of the Yale Daily News.

  1. Universities and colleges—United States—Directories.
I. Yale daily news.

L901.I 54	378.73	73–161139
ISSN 0093-5220	rev	MARC-S
Library of Congress	73 [r74e2]	

ISBN 0-399-50502-4

First Perigee Printing, 1981
Printed in the United States of America

CONTRIBUTORS

Kathryn Amarante
Dorothy B. Anderson
Nancy Andrews
Tom Arcidiacono
Cindy Bahr
Steve Baker
John Ball
Penny Barker
Peter Barnes
Crystal Bartolovitch
Jeff Barton
Bob Basil
Joel Becker
Jon Bekken
Lucy Bettis
Carol Biby
Larry Biemiller
William Bike
Deborah Binder
Beth Bleisteft
Kate Blumberg
Martin Boles
Ann Bosso
Anne C. Bridgman
Cherry Brieser
Ann Brocklehurst
Claire Burkert
Bobby Byrd
Peter Callaghan
Laura Camozzi
Patrick Carome
Colleen Cattrell
Lisa A. Chung
Gia Cincone
Rachel Cline
Joe Conway
Mark R. Cook
Meg Crager
Edward P. Cypiot III
Marc Davis
Sheila Davis
Steve Diamond
Michael Duffy
Cathy Duncan
Phil Duncan
Jane Dure
Pat Ercolano
Brooks Faurot
Lester Finkle
Jonathan Friedland
Marsha Friedman
Paul Funga
Adam Gaffin
Francesca M. Gany
Ann Gazzerro
Michael Gibson
Gregory L. Goodman
Sara Goodman
Doug Graham
Debbie Graves
Lisa S. Green
Deena Gross
Leslie Gurg
Jock Hatfield
Gary Haubold
Michael Hertz
Robert Holland
Pam Hyde
Dale Ingram
Elizabeth Jacobs
Joe Jolson
Bob Jonason
Andy Kegley
John Keister
Mary Kilzer
Joyce Kruczel
Greg Kuntashian
Gary Langer
Nancy R. Langer
Susan Laubach
Patti Law
Jerry Laws
Tom Lea
Patricia Ledwig
Susan Lehman
Alan Levine
Linda Levine
Gladys Licona
Audrey Liounis
Margaret Liu
Tom Luetkemeyer
Sam Lundquist
Tuan Luu
Cindy McCormick
Robin McCormick
John MacKenna
Ken Mammarella
Regina Maritote
Steve Martarano
Katherine Martin
Claude Marx
Anthony W. Mary
Marc Medoff
Steve Medwid
Kate Meyers
Matthew Miller
Rosemary Mills
Willard Moore
Mary Ruth Moran
Chris Morrill
Deirdre A. Neligan
Pat Nunnally
Peter O'Connor
Martha O'Neill
Ken Palmer
Roxanne Parker
Craig Peters

Edward Petraiuolo
Steve Petranik
Debbie Pines
Bill Porsche
Barbara Rattle
Chip Ray
Judy Reardon
Arie Reinstein
Michael Richards
Nobby Riedy
Kenneth Riesterer
Cathy Robertson
Virginia Marie Rocch
Karen Rogers
David Rosenberg
John Rosenberger
Erin Ross
Brigette Rouson
Julia Rovner
Laurel Rowe

Darlene Rudd
Ellen Ryder
Michael L. Salitan
Cynthia Savage
Gene Schmidt
Philip Shenon
Karen Sherbin
Ann Shillinglaw
Siobhan Silag
Juliette Singer
Mason Snyder
Sarah Snyder
Lorraine Spector
Tracy Staub
Andy Steinberg
Peter Deane Stenzel
Joe Stern
Mickey Strange
Bill Straw
Raymond Swan

Stewart Thompson
Tim Tibbits
David Yandell Todd
Waldemar Turowski
Scott Ulm
Arthur W. Utay
John Veilleux
Jean Walker
Jan Ward
Wayne Wegman
Joel West
Debbie Wilker
Brad Wolbert
Greg Wolf
Llewellyn Young
Nina Young
Elizabeth Miriam Zeidman
Seth Zuckerman

CONTENTS

PUBLISHER'S NOTE	viii
A NOTE TO OUR READERS	ix
PREFACE	xi
GETTING IN: THE ADMISSIONS PROCESS	1
STATISTICS	17
THE COLLEGES	18
INDEX	497

PUBLISHER'S NOTE

The information available in the 1981–82 edition of *The Insider's Guide to the Colleges* has been culled from sources during the 1979–80 school year and is as current as printing schedules allow. We encourage contact with the schools for specific information regarding possible changes in tuition, fees and room and board. All such changes will be incorporated in the next edition.

A NOTE TO OUR READERS

For the past year and a half, the office at *The Yale Daily News* has been deluged with requests for *The Insider's Guide*. We want to extend thanks to Susan Zucker for ably handling all our mail.

We want to thank our contributors for their time, effort, and honesty. We've listed those who asked to be acknowledged and we thank the many others who requested anonymity. To protect our informants from the wrath of administrators or vindictive alumni, we've omitted their college affiliations.

We appreciate your reactions to the descriptions included in this book. Please note that we do not have further information about the colleges in this book, nor do we have any information on colleges not included. Address your comments to: Editors, *The Insider's Guide, The Yale Daily News,* 241–A Yale Station, New Haven, CT., 06520.

Please address all requests for further copies of *The Insider's Guide* to our publisher. We regret that we are not able to distribute copies of *The Insider's Guide*.

Jane E. Allen
Dorian B. Klein
Editors, *The Insider's Guide to the Colleges*

PREFACE

If you're like most applicants, you're probably a little scared about choosing the right college. For those of you who've never been away before, the choice of a new four-year home may be all the more frightening. College is there to be enjoyed, and you'll be paying for that privilege. Consider it an investment. College is a time of choice and change. For some of you, that will mean continuing to plan a career as a musician. For others, college will be the springboard to a career you've never thought of before. Some of the most academic high school students find happiness far from their books while the high school partier finds he likes modern poetry more than he ever thought possible. College is full of discovery and *The Insider's Guide* was put together to help you begin that process. We've given it to you as honestly as we could.

This book is more than student-faculty ratios and admission requirements. It's about things that make college fun and those that might not. It's about life in a town with three traffic lights or four years at a college with three campuses. Whatever the subject, the source is the same: *actual students at the school.* Our college entries come to you from college newspaper editors, friends, strangers, and people whose suggestions help us stay up-to-date. By the time you read this book, some things *may have* changed, others *will have* changed. College presidents will have come and gone, tuition will have risen, male-female ratios will have equalized.

Our guide will give you the taste of the school unavailable in standard guides—genuine reactions from students after years at their school. *The Insider's Guide* is a handbook to student life: one we hope will be all the better for you when you make an informed decision; that is, after you become an insider.

Some words of caution: Don't take the words you read here as gospel. Our correspondents are rarely unanimous. We attempt by judicious editing to give you as broad a picture as possible. Please take our words with more than just a grain of salt. If it's possible, you should try to round out your view of the campuses—talk to students, read the college bulletins, visit the schools if you can. We try to give you a springboard—now you've got to ask the questions. We've already done a little of the homework.

We encourage feedback from our readers and they supply us with more than just polite criticism; we've received some constructive as well as vitriolic commentary on *The Insider's Guide*. We'd like to share a few of these, trimmed under the objective hands of the editors:

From an *Oberlin College* admissions officer: "We members of the Oberlin College Admissions Office have always been fans of *The Insider's Guide*. We keep copies in our waiting room. . . . We've always been pleased with your characterization of us; it has seemed to be both honest and comprehensive. However, we must take exception with one point. . . . We've been thinking about asking for a recall of the current book (à la General Motors), but we'll be charitable and let things stand."

From *Florida State*'s student newspaper: "Yale, fuck off. We don't care to participate in your patronizing *Guide*. The elitism and ungrounded arrogance engendered therein are a trifle annoying. —Much Love, The Florida Flambeau."

From one elated admissions director: "Thank you for the service you provide. . . . We got many a student through your *Guide*."

This new edition of *The Insider's Guide* is especially meaningful to us because we used *The Insider's Guide* in applying to colleges. Needless to say, we both ended up at Yale, so we have gone across the country in search of people who want to help you evaluate their schools. Many of our contributors were themselves enthusiastic readers of *The Insider's Guide* who found it an enjoyable and valuable tool. Our aim in revising it is to make it just as valuable for you. We hope you will join the legacy some day in a future edition of the book.

Jane E. Allen
Dorian B. Klein
New Haven
March, 1980

We are immensely grateful to our numerous contributors, a list of whom appears at the front of this book.

GETTING IN: THE ADMISSIONS PROCESS

If you are reading this book, you are probably thinking about going to college. The other possibility is that you are contemplating a transfer; there is a special section on transfer admissions further down in this introduction.

Sociologists have long maintained that college is a time for experimenting, for breaking away from the restraints imposed by one's parents, and for testing the limits of one's capabilities. But we college students know that college is a respite as well as a challenge.

College, really, is a moratorium. It is a time for you to stick your toe in the Olympic-sized swimming pool of life before taking that final shivering plunge. The "college experience" has only a coincidental relation to the official process of education; even if you never study, you will be a different person when the time for taking that final plunge rolls around. The most significant changes will grow out of the surprises and vagaries of fortune you will inevitably confront, and different surprises await you at different colleges. Remember, there is probably no one "right" college for you—but you want to maximize the chances that the surprises will be good ones. Exactly what you will be four years from now depends largely on which college you pick—and how you go about getting into it once you have picked it. It takes some know-how, and that's why we've written this book.

First, we want to apologize for shattering any illusions. But the fact is that many students, even at the "best" colleges, regard classes and books as annoying details. In their minds, the most important college experiences take place in the clubs, football stadiums, bars, and dormitories. They take place long after the library has closed for the night. They take place during occasional flings of self-indulgent irresponsibility. Too many students think that colleges are only academic institutions and try to choose one on the basis of academic factors alone. Consequently, they end up in the wrong place, and they regret it—unless they're too busy studying to even notice what they're missing. By all means, choose a school that's strong in your academic fields of interest, but remember that you will be in classes for only four or five hours a day, on the average. That leaves about twenty hours for you to spend in the way that suits you best.

As you try to decide which specific colleges interest you, and which might be interested in you, we suggest you consult the rest of this book. We've tried to summarize what is important to know about certain colleges before you apply. The book is one means by which you can narrow down your choices to a manageable list of eight or fewer colleges. The descriptions of the schools may not be all-encompassing, but they are based on our somewhat subjective evaluations of the schools after talking with students all over the country.

The admissions process, we should warn you, is a very emotional experience. For most people, it's the first time in their lives that they've been formally judged and told their supposedly objective worth. Parents have been coddling you for a long time, and teachers may not have had the time or interest to make a rigorous evaluation. The truth is often jarring. Our only advice is to keep a sense of perspective. The admissions process is not a summary judgment on your value as a human being. The most important thing college admissions officers try to measure is your ability to perform at a college level. Even this is likely to be affected by factors outside your control. Some colleges, for example, give a break to students from outside their region, since these students will help the school's regional distribution. State schools, on the other hand, are naturally partial to residents of their state. Your success or failure at this point is likely only to be an indication of your ability to succeed . . . at college admissions.

Before anything else, talk to your guidance counselor and to some friends who have gone through the process. But don't accept what they say unquestioned. There are two kinds of guidance counselors who predominate in the field: the kind who don't want to disappoint anybody, and the kind who want to keep their track record unblemished. Neither of these types will be of much use to you; the first type will assure you that you don't have to worry about getting into the college of your choice, while the other will tell you not to apply to any school whose admissions standards could be considered even slightly competitive.

Your friends at college will be more helpful than your guidance counselors, but not much. Depending upon when you ask them, they may tell you that they really love their school, even though they despise the place. They may tell you that they always study until two in the morning, without telling you that they don't start studying until after midnight and don't wake up before noon. Chances are they won't really think long and hard about how they feel about their school until they graduate. You can still get some good ideas from these people, however, and their advice is a good place to start.

Each university or college has a flavor all its own, and while all will provide an education of sorts, your experiences will be uniquely colored by the school you attend. Trust your instincts in the final decision-making process. You will agonize over details but, in the end, go where you feel most comfortable. You'll find later on that the college is probably different from your pre-admission view, and that your major and intended course of study will change.

Flexibility is a great asset in college. If you can convince admissions officers of a combination of direction and a willingness to experiment academically and live with new people, you've helped convince them of your desirability as a candidate.

Flexibility is a personal asset, especially if your first-choice school doesn't accept you. If you're a believer in making your own happiness, you can make the most of being anywhere.

THE VISIT

After narrowing down your choices, pay a few days' visit to each of the colleges in which you're interested. Nothing, including this book, is a substitute for firsthand experience. Do not take your parents with you when you look at colleges, if it is in any way avoidable. Their advice may be worthwhile at times, but their presence can be distracting, and in the end you are the one who will be attending the school. The best time to look at colleges is early in the fall of your senior year. Summers are not a good time to see a college, and visiting in the spring of your junior year may mean that you'll arrive at the college when the students are in the middle of their final exams.

When visiting colleges, try to live with some undergraduates. Contact them through friends, or ask the admissions office (most will help put you up). Try to get an idea of what the daily life is like, for this is where the real differences among colleges lie. During visits, you should remember that classes are usually not the only important part of college life. Rather, as you visit classes, look around and size up the typical student. Are his eyes glazed and his skin clammy? Does he constantly babble unintelligibly while puffing the wrong end of a filter cigarette? Is his vocabulary limited to the word "intense"? Is he tripping over his own feet, weighed down by a calculator, two slide rules, and the *Handbook of Physics and Chemistry?* If you can identify some sort of common thread running through all the students on the campus, you should be well on your way to evaluating the college.

Also look at dress. If everyone looks like a model for either *Mademoiselle* magazine or *Gentlemen's Quarterly,* you'd better decide whether you're in the market for a college or a fashion show. Check out the food, which is after all a necessity of life. Have many students been known to have prolonged and shattering bouts of heartburn? Does the campus drugstore have more than one shelf of Kaopectate? Check the dorms. Are the rooms just cinderblock cubicles? Try to determine something about the attitude of the administration; if you see campus cops wearing storm trooperish uniforms, that's a bad sign.

Most important, during your visits, you should personally evaluate the spectrum of people. Are they intelligent or vacuous? That is, do you find your conversations with them interesting, or does dining hall talk revolve around who has the most studying to do or who has the cutest date for the prom? Do the people seem far above or below your cultural plane? Don't be fooled by reputations, which often hide more than they reveal. Try to get a sense of where the school is heading. Is the place prospering or declining?

Admissions

By this time we hope that you are thinking in the appropriate terms. Having chosen a college, the next question you should be asking yourself is how to get in—a particularly ticklish question, since admissions offices are the fatal stumbling blocks on the road to higher education. However, it helps to know something about how admissions works.

Most top colleges have five or six times as many applicants as they have room for. Each admissions officer reads several hundred to a thousand applications. As he reads them, he usually rejects about one-quarter and accepts somewhat less than one-quarter to start with. (Figures vary on this, and some colleges are less competitive.) Then he spends additional time on the other half. Most colleges count grades, board scores, and recommendations for only one-half of the total consideration they give you. The other half of your application is your character and personal promise, which means your interview, your past activities, and your application essay. Both sides of your application may be rated on some sort of point scale; many colleges try to get some idea of your possible performance by combining your grades and scores for a composite academic rating.

Whether or not you get in depends on how you, as a total person, rate against other applicants. Good grades alone won't get you in; you have to be an "interesting person." Although it is true that at many large schools (state universities, for example) grades and board scores count for almost everything, at a school like Harvard it's possible to get in with low grades and board scores if you have enough promise in other areas. At most colleges, however, academic and personal promise each count about half. And if your mother or father is an alumnus, or you're a member of a minority group, or you're a top athlete, your chances for admission are almost certain to be increased. Other special considerations vary from school to school.

APPLICATIONS

Your first step in filling out your applications is to remember that they will be the admissions officers' first impression of you. Type them if you can. Don't lay it on too thick; the people reading your applications have very sensitive bullshit detectors. When in doubt, be concise and modest, but let them know the truth about yourself.

There are two other things to remember about your application. First, don't put anything fake on it. If they find out about it, as they probably will, you've kissed your chance for that school good-bye. One prestigious Ivy League school that shall remain unnamed accepted a student who claimed to have made $30,000,000 as an entrepreneur. He forged documents, including his high school transcript and board scores, and even invented an exotic name. Although he was accepted and enrolled, he had to withdraw after the first semester when he was failing his courses and the suspicions of university officials became aroused. There are probably no circumstances in which faking something on an application is worth the risk.

Remember also that the interviewer will be asking you questions about the things you wrote on the application. One student we know wrote on his application that he read *Newsweek* religiously. In the course of his interview, the interviewer asked what he thought about a story in a recent issue of the magazine. The student had no idea what the interviewer was talking about. He was not accepted. Be able to talk intelligently and convincingly about everything you wrote.

The second thing to remember is that by the time the admissions officer gets to your application he will be near nausea with class presidents, student council officers, debate teams, math teams, basketball teams, yearbooks, school newspapers, marshal boards, honor boards, and all of that. These activities won't hurt your chances; Yale takes hundreds of high school editors each year. On the other hand, these high school positions in themselves probably will not help you either, because too many other people have done the same thing. The best way to get into a college is to emphasize something that sets you off from the thousands of other applications.

Too many students try to package themselves as the conventional, well-rounded, all-American student that they think colleges want, and they succeed only in being boring. Let your real self show through, quirks and all. Essays provide a perfect opportunity for you to present yourself as a person instead of a set of facts. One student we know wrote hers about what she considered her great shortcoming—and she was admitted to Harvard, Yale, and Princeton. Remember, the colleges want to admit students who are good people as well as smart people, and a public relations "image" smacks of artificiality and egotism.

Recommendations are the last detail. It frequently helps if you find teachers who know you outside a classroom setting. (By the way, recommendations written by people other than teachers—say, a local bigwig who happens to be your father's best friend—are usually worthless.) Many recommendation forms include, in addition to a space for the teacher's written comments, a series of boxes for a standardized rating. These boxes usually range from "Poor" up through "One of the two or three best students I have ever encountered." By all means, try to get a pair of teachers who will either rate you as "One of the best" or as "Excellent," which is usually the next lower rating. It is generally only a vindictive teacher who will agree to write you a recommendation and then give you a bad one. Most teachers will be flattered that you asked them to write a recommendation and will find something nice to say. Of course, the colleges know this too, and they usually don't attach much importance to the average, bland-praise type of recommendation. A recommendation that is exceptionally good or bad, or one that is written by a teacher whom they know, is regarded with much more care.

THE INTERVIEW

Interviews, like essays, are a good way to communicate what is unique about you.

The most important thing about the interview is to give the other guy a good time. The interviewer sees a half dozen or more people every day, month after month. All of them are in dark suits and red ties or in print dresses. All are well-combed, with stylish but respectable hair and engaging grins. The entire process is like reading twenty *Playboys,* cover to cover, without a break in between. After a while, even the most pleasant of things and people begin to look dismally familiar. If you can make the interviewer laugh or interest him with your unorthodox or forthright views, you have a good chance of success.

The kinds of things the interviewer will ask depend to a considerable extent on the time of the year. For the traditional end-of-summer interview, he is likely to ask you how you spent your summer vacation. Work is a highly creditable answer, whether volunteer or paid, though unique jobs have extra impact. Another very good answer is school, particularly if you attended a National Science Foundation program or a summer session in drama, journalism, history, or some other particular field. School for school's sake, or school to avoid work, does not impress a sharp interviewer, so it is good to be able to tie the study to some real interest.

It is always a superb idea to indicate that you have a special interest in something, but beware: you may wind up with an hour's conversation on the topic, so don't wing it in a field unless you know it cold. Often the interviewer will use your keen interest in some area, rather than your general record and charm, as a yardstick to measure your desirability. If you are really conversant in some applicable field, you can virtually assure your admission. But if not, (and this applies to most applicants), keep the conversation light and moving. Above all, be engaging, funny if you can (but not a bore or a knee-slapping clown), and affable. An open, sensitive, friendly, and direct manner can do much in impressing an interviewer.

One crucial point: keep your parents at least a thousand feet and preferably a thousand miles away from the interview session. When parents come in, interviews tend to be short, fruitless, and often deleterious. The excessive appearance of parents is a clue that an applicant might not survive the pressure, isolation, and uncertainty of the first year of college. All things considered, it is far better for you to hurt your parents' feelings by asking them to stay outside (or better yet to stay home) than it is to destroy your chances by having your parents in the interview with you.

Friends are as bad as parents in this particular situation. Some colleges will offer to interview you with a friend and fellow applicant. Resist this politely. One student irreparably blew his chances at Amherst (where, incidentally, they have an unusually sharp admissions staff) when he and a friend had an interview together and he was completely upstaged by his friend's glibness. At the interview, the last thing you need is competition.

Listen to the interviewer carefully, and read between the lines. The purpose of the interview is not to grill you, but to match you and the school in the best interests of both. Sometimes an interviewer will politely indicate to you, either in his remarks or in a follow-up letter, that you have little chance of getting in. If he says so or implies it, listen, because such remarks are not made lightly. On the other hand, if he is sincerely encouraging, listen to that, too. But remember that his job requires him to seem highly receptive to even the most lukewarm candidates, and do not mistake politeness for enthusiasm.

If an interviewer suggests other schools or other aspects of his school for you to look into, remember that he is a professional and take note. Be as receptive to him as you would have him be to you. An open mind and a capacity to absorb information are traits colleges seek and admire.

The interview is basically an absurd situation. If the interviewer makes you nervous, imagine him sitting there in his underwear, and whatever else happens, don't walk off with his pen. There are no other tricks to making the interview come off successfully. You must tread a thin line, being concise but expressive, relaxed but not blasé, modest but not dull. Even if it gets to the point where a long silence is followed by the interview's point-blank "What books have you read recently?" you've got to stand out. Be prepared for this question, because it is bound to occur somewhere along the way, and be ready to discuss the books you name.

You can direct the conversation. Don't worry about occasional lapses—some interviewers wait to see how you'll react to a potentially awkward situation. Calmly ask a question, or mention something that really interests you. It's your job to present the parts of you and your background that you want noted.

A word on style: too many applicants are afraid to talk confidently about their accomplishments. If the interviewer is impressed by something, don't insist that it wasn't much or he might believe you. And if he isn't impressed by something you think is important, tactfully let him know that he should be. But don't, under penalty of death, be cool and noncommittal; one well-qualified Yale applicant was turned down when the interviewer wrote, "It obviously isn't going to be the end of his world if he doesn't get in. And it won't be the end of our world, either." If there is any quality you want to convey, it is sincere interest—not in everything (because that sort of affectation gets sickening), but in a few carefully selected things. This shows them that you are a selective, earnest, and worthwhile individual.

All of the above refers primarily to interviews with an admissions officer. It's entirely possible that you won't have an interview with an admissions officer, especially if you live halfway across the country and have no way of getting to the college. In this case, you may be asked to have an interview with an alumnus. An alumnus interview is likely to be easier than one with a member of the college admissions staff. Most alumni don't do enough interviewing to be able to ask the really penetrating questions, the ones that make you squirm. Also, because they don't see too many applicants, alumni are more likely to be easily impressed by the more common sorts of activities. Although alumni interviews are easier, they usually carry less weight with the admissions office. One applicant we know of tells of an alumnus interviewer who grills his wintertime candidates from an unheated house, asking them to wear extra sweaters. Don't let characters like this scare you. Their vision of the school may be outdated, so they are not the authorities for all the answers to your questions. But if you're invited, go.

An increasing number of colleges will give you the opportunity to talk to a student about the school. Although you'll be asking him most of the questions, he'll probably ask you a few as well. In many cases, he'll fill out a brief report on you after the interview is over. Although it's hard to say how much weight such an interview will carry, it can be the roughest kind of all. College students are completely indifferent to high school activities, and high school bravado can make them sick. Handle these interviews very, very carefully.

What if you don't have an interview at all? Perhaps you live out in the hinterlands where there aren't any alumni, and you can't get to the school itself. Or perhaps you feel that your lack of poise is so serious that it would jeopardize any interview you had. If your situation is like either of these, talk it over with your guidance counselor or with a friend who goes to the college in which you're interested. Most colleges are willing to make allowances. You can get into even the most competitive school without an interview, although it may be more difficult.

Finally, if after the application and interview are done there is something about you that you don't think has come out, write a letter to the admissions officer and tell him about it. There's no reason for you to limit yourself to the skimpy forms they send you. Make sure that the admissions committee which is going to decide on you has every piece of impressive information about you. Notice that we said *impressive* information; a fat folder alone will not get you in. If you have examples of some outstanding work you've done—outside writing or photography, taped musical recitals, etc. send them. Anything that will enhance the written application will help to give you an edge. The more evidence of talents and abilities you present, the stronger your application becomes. Don't flood the admissions office with mediocre supplements, as they might weaken your application. Quantity without accompanying quality can actually count against you.

Tests

SATs are a real pain. You might argue that they stifle creativity and refuse to take them, but we don't recommend this tactic unless you're really persuasive or are applying to one of the colleges, such as Bowdoin, that don't look at SAT scores. (Incidentally, everything we say about the SAT applies equally to the ACT.)

Some advice on test-taking: Read the practice forms put out by the testing organization completely and thoroughly. The commercially marketed paperback books of practice tests won't work miracles, but they can familiarize you with test-taking technique and thereby help you feel more at ease when it comes time for the real thing. Don't worry about your test scores until you walk out of the testing room. Generally speaking, the better the school you apply to, the less your scores are going to matter. At these schools, tests account for less than a quarter of the weight in your admissions folder. Yale frequently turns away more applicants with 800 board scores than it accepts. Harvard takes many students with scores in the 500s and even the high 400s. You aren't necessarily laying the rest of your life on the line when you walk into a standardized exam.

No one can say, of course, that standardized tests mean nothing at all. If your test scores are considerably below the average, it's going to take a very healthy amount of athletic prowess, high character, and/or "pull" to get you in. Admissions officers have to reserve the limited number of places they can give to candidates without proven potential, and they are likely to seek some exceptional strength to offset the apparent academic weakness.

At the same time, however, remember that you may be judged by other than the usual standards. If you have spent a lot of time abroad or in foreign schools, your English language deficiencies may be debited to lack of exposure to standard English. If you have attended Army dependents' schools or inner-city schools or schools in areas of the country where education is less than high-powered, your apparent lacks may in fact indicate real strength—as long as you have surpassed certain minimal levels.

If you must also take achievement tests for the school, you should do so on a different day from the one on which you take the SAT. Otherwise, you may find that your work level has really tumbled and that you have hurt your chances for admission. Standardized exams are actually quite exhausting no matter how bright you are. The PSAT is good practice for the SAT and can qualify you for National Merit Scholarship honors. The Advanced Placement tests evaluate what you know about specific subjects, and if your school or outside reading has prepared you, take them. Many colleges will allow you to use high scores on the AP exams to place out of introductory courses, which are usually well worth avoiding. AP credits can also enable you to "accelerate" your college career and save money and time. Incidentally, don't hesitate to take other kinds of standardized tests—in math, English, history, etc.—if you think you might do well and can persuade your school to report the results.

THE WAIT

As Joe and Joanna College Applicant anguish from the time of interview and application to the day of the final word (as late as April 15), they build fantasies upon fantasies about the serpentine admissions process. They imagine that small select committees (imbued with divine inspiration, perhaps) reach decisions that determine fates, careers, and lives. If you don't like anguish, avoid it by substituting fact for fantasy.

One way to make things easier on yourself is to apply to colleges that have an "early decision" or "early option" program and exercise it. If you are successful, you'll know several months earlier than regular applicants whether you've made it or are likely to do so. But there are catches. In applying under an early decision plan, you usually must commit yourself upon application to going to the college if they accept you. (This is not true of Ivy League early action plans.) Needless to say, this means that you can apply to only one school on an early decision basis. Sometimes it's more difficult to get in on early decision; sometimes it's easier. The college generally picks only those students it knows it wants to have. On the other hand, if you aren't picked, you regain your choice of options, and you'll usually be considered without prejudice in the regular applicant pool of the school that rejected your early decision application (again, not true in the Ivy League, where you must wait one year to reapply). If there is one school which you know beyond doubt is your first choice and it offers an early decision program, you'd be wise to apply early.

Early decision and early action plans are usually a province of the "prestige" colleges. In most colleges, particularly large state universities, the admissions process is much simpler. For in-state students, certain flat grade and/or college board criteria are set: above, in; below, sorry. For out-of-state students, similar college board and grade cutoffs—usually slightly higher—are set, and extracurricular activities may matter for borderline cases. One warning: If State U is your place (often high academic standards exist even in a computerized environment), apply early. Most large public universities operate on a rolling admissions plan: first come (above the criteria) first admitted, until capacity (or out-of-state quota) is reached. Incidentally, it pays to apply early no matter where you're applying. The earlier they get your application, the fewer other qualified candidates they'll have seen; you'll stick in their minds with less effort on your part. Taking the SAT early will give you a chance to retake it if your score is unusually low. From virtually every standpoint, getting started early is a good thing.

In the smaller, usually private, highly selective colleges, the admissions procedure becomes intense and complex, but it's by no means beyond comprehension. For example, at Yale (in a process similar to that at other highly selective institutions), all the relevant data about a candidate—board scores, grades, alumni and office interviews, teacher and secondary school recommendations, and the student's own application—are put into a folder. Each folder is read separately by two different admissions staffers, who rank the student on academic and personal accomplishments and promise and then render gradations along an "accept" or "reject" axis. Faculty members are becoming involved too, both in the general ranking of applicants and in the evaluation of special work or projects submitted by applicants in support of claims to special talents.

All the information on a candidate (including staffers' evaluations) is transferred to a coded "slate" prepared for use in admissions committee meetings. Candidates from the same secondary school are usually considered together for purposes of comparison.

The admissions committee takes its responsibilities very seriously; meetings run eight hours a day for five, six, and even seven days a week for at least two or three weeks. Although the initial staff recommendations are very important, every case (at least at Yale) is considered and voted on individually. The dean of admissions has a number of "wild cards" that he can use to offer acceptance to particular candidates rejected by the committee as a whole. One note: the college representative (not the local alumnus) who visits your high school is often a member of the admissions committee—*de jure* or *de facto*. His opinion, in either case, is important, so handle him with care.

Admissions officers at most selective colleges vehemently resist any attempt to label how important any one factor is to a candidate's admissions chances. They claim to try to judge a candidate on the whole multidimensional picture delineated by his or her paper qualifications. At one time, college boards seemed to offer an easy and objective comparison of candidates from different schools and states. But the increasing skepticism about the exams—which are skewed toward white, middle-class norms—has made the comparison of candidates from different environments a more subjective and complex process.

Finally, after the admissions machine has ground to a halt, letters fat and thin land in mailboxes across the nation. Making the waiting list, once a booby prize or an honorable mention or a sop to the son of a potentially disgruntled alumnus, has come to have value in this age of overlapping acceptances. If schools miscalculate the number of accepted candidates who will reject them, gaping holes will exist in the incoming freshman class—holes that will be filled from the waiting list.

Decisions at the best schools are often made on subjective impressions. Even if your qualifications seem impeccable, it will pay you to do every single step of the admissions process with as much care as you know how.

Why Bother?

As we said before, there is more to college than academics. College will be the people you meet, the ideas you absorb, the contacts you make. It will probably influence the person you become, may select the person you marry, and will have a strong effect on what you will do for the rest of your life. If you are pretty sure college looks right for you, get busy and get into a good one. Then, if you're not convinced you want to go to college right away, many colleges will permit you to defer matriculation for a year; meanwhile, you have your admissions worries safely behind you. Deferring is preferable to taking a term or a year off once you've started college, because the latter disrupts friendships and course work.

A few final words of caution before we loose you to the fates. Your first year of college can be a wretched thing if you start out with the wrong attitudes and don't watch out for a few things. Meet as many people as you can (stay away from your old high school buddies, and for goodness' sake, don't agree to room with them). Never let yourself sit around and do nothing, and never let yourself sit around and do nothing but study, which is almost as much of a waste. Now that we've told you that there's much more to college than books, we have to admit that many of our own classmates don't realize that. As the competition intensifies for employment and for graduate and professional school admission, the campuses have been gripped by a mood that former Yale President Kingman Brewster dubbed "grim preprofessionalism." You don't have to fall into the trap. Sure, most of the better schools claim that you need to be "well-motivated" to get through, but they wouldn't accept you if they thought you'd flunk out. At most good schools, it takes more effort and planning to flunk out than it does to stay in. Study enough to do well, but don't end up spending all your time in the library or you won't get much out of college. In fact, students who participate in nonacademic activities of any kind usually find that those activities not only are valuable in their own right, but also provide a refreshing change that makes studying more enjoyable and productive.

Society is about to give you four years to play games, be irresponsible, and think about things before you start playing for keeps. You can march, protest, sing, dance, smoke, drink, fool around, waste time, holler, shout, and be as foolhardy as you want, and nobody is going to do anything about it (at the more liberal schools, at least). That's what college is all about, so don't waste your time grinding. If you've taken the trouble to get yourself into a good college, you might as well make the most of your situation. Pack your trunk, wave good-bye to your parents, and set out like Telemachus to see what you can make of yourself. To quote Kingman Brewster, "You probably have not been as free before. You may not be as free again. Enjoy the privilege of doubt."

Transfers

If you're already in college and are trying to transfer to another school, most of the comments above are old hat to you. Either you made the wrong choice, or you simply didn't get into enough schools to have a choice. Theoretically, you know what to do now. Colleges tend to consider a transfer student in a different light from a high school senior, and you should be aware of this. Your college grades will be by far the most important thing in your transfer application folder. High school activities and recommendations are ancient history and hardly figure in the process. Board scores and high school grades are fairly important, but it's your college grades that carry the most weight. Remember this: you will rarely be able to transfer out of a college at which you're getting low grades.

It is usually much harder to enter a college as a transfer than as a freshman. This is particularly true of top colleges with very low attrition rates. It's not only that there is a large number of applicants for the few available places; the colleges expect you to have developed and matured in your previous year or two of college. It helps if the department in which you want to major at the new school is undersubscribed. But no matter how you look at it, it pays to choose your college very carefully the first time around.

STATISTICS

Each college description in this book is preceded by statistical information. The data are supplied for the most part by college administrations and apply to the 1979–80 academic year. Although many are exact, most figures are estimates. Where no figures at all were available, the symbol **NA** has been used. Different schools use different methods to calculate the same figure. It is therefore deceptive to reach conclusions by simply comparing numbers. For the most complete and up-to-date information, you should contact the colleges.

Campus describes the setting of the college; rural, suburban, city outskirts, city center, etc.

Undergraduate enrollment figures give the approximate number of full-time undergraduate day students of each sex for the 1979–80 school year.

Total enrollment figures give the approximate total number of students at campuses that include graduate, professional, and undergraduate students.

The annual **expenses** figure is an estimate of the costs for the 1979–80 school year, including tuition, room, board, and a living allowance. (Travel is not included.) Many colleges figure a very low living allowance, so you may have to add as much as $500 to the figures given. In the case of schools whose costs differ for in-state and out-of-state students, two figures are given, the in-state first. For those colleges for which we did not have 1979–80 figures, we used an estimate based on the previous year's costs.

Financial aid figures represent the approximate percentage of the entering class receiving any type of financial aid. These figures can be misleading, since most schools have a variety of plans combining outright gifts, jobs, loans, and other means to help students pay for their education.

The approximate number of bound volumes in the **library** is included solely to give the prospective applicant a very rough idea of the research facilities available at the school. Comparisons here can be extremely misleading, although differences of large magnitude (five million volumes vs. 150,000) are significant indicators. To help you keep your sense of perspective, remember that a small library might have all the books you'll need, and a huge library might keep many books off-limits to students.

The **student-faculty ratio** is equally likely to be misunderstood. A low number here may be an asset, but it's the attitude and not the number of the faculty that really counts. Also, many colleges count part-time teachers and even researchers as faculty and arrive at a deceptively low student-faculty ratio.

The approximate number of **transfer students** accepted by the college annually is also given. This figure is useful for the student planning to transfer, because it gives some idea of the receptivity of the college to transfer applicants. The figure should not be considered an index of how attractive a college appears to other students, for many schools limit transfer admission to a very small number or simply refuse to admit transfer students on a regular basis.

The **median SAT** scores are for the class entering in September 1979, where available. Where necessary, the scores have been separated for men (**M**) and women (**W**) and for the Verbal (**V**) and Math (**M**) categories. Some colleges use the American College Test (**ACT**) along with or instead of the **SAT**; such information is given where appropriate.

Memberships in **fraternities** and **sororities** are approximate percentages of the student body as reported by university administrations.

The **application deadline** is just that—a deadline. Remember that it's always best to get your application in early; this is particularly true if the school uses rolling admissions. If you do miss the deadline, you might still stand a chance—but not much of one. Even if the admissions committee considers your application, they won't have the time to do it justice.

ADELPHI UNIVERSITY

Location: Garden City, NY 11530
Campus: suburban
Undergraduate enrollment:
   1600 M, 2800 F
Total enrollment: 11,000
Expenses: $6000
Financial aid: 40%
Library: 300,000 volumes

Student-faculty ratio: 15–1
Transfer students: 800
Median SAT: 443 V, 475 M
Fraternities: 10%
Sororities: 8%
Application deadline:
   rolling

Located in the wealthy Long Island suburb of Garden City, Adelphi University mirrors many aspects of the community. The campus is tree-shaded, flat, and occupied by students who are generally happy with the education and life at the school.

Adelphi now boasts a brand-new spacious theater, along with a student center, library and science building, which are already cramped for space. Class sizes are usually small. Only a few courses (general biology, physics, psychology, for example) are larger than forty. Most classes have under thirty students, and classes with fewer than ten are common.

Adelphi's business, social work, and nursing schools are all well known and do a good job of educating their students. In the College of Arts and Sciences, the sciences are probably stronger. A large education department serves to train new crops of teachers.

Some surprises in Adelphi's curriculum are a large and competent biology department, as well as a small but respected and active chemistry department. Adelphi was the first college in the nation to offer a program of suburban studies, and AU has established many innovative programs taking students off campus.

The Long Island area provides a wide variety of entertainment possibilities for those with cars. New York City is forty minutes and a couple of bucks away on the Long Island Railroad (four blocks from campus). There are frequent social and cultural events on campus, but things get quiet on weekends when commuters and many dorm students are at home. Cars are advisable for dorm students. Parking is a problem for all.

Unlike the situation at most schools, women considerably outnumber men at AU. Dating is rarely a problem for dorm students. Commuters who make an effort to meet people and make friends should have no problems, either. A few active fraternities and sororities remain, but membership is by no means necessary. Abuse is restricted to marijuana and alcohol, for the most part.

Adelphi sports a few highly talented intercollegiate teams, both men's and women's. The soccer team in particular is top-flight. Intramural sports are generally well organized and involve a large number of students.

Academically, Adelphi attracts a mixed bag of students. Many prefer to study only when it is absolutely necessary and don't compete for grades. In the sciences, where large numbers of premedical students take the majority of their courses, the competition for grades is keen, and studying is a daily or even a continuous activity. Adelphi has had decent success in getting its top students into medical schools, and a number of students go into other professional and graduate schools.

UNIVERSITY OF ALABAMA

Location: University, AL 35486
Campus: city outskirts
Undergraduate enrollment:
  6576 M, 6304 W
Total enrollment: 16,807
Expenses: $2980 (in-state),
  $3850 (out-of-state)
Financial aid: 33%
Library: 1,219,085 volumes

Student-faculty ratio: 21-1
Transfer students: 2100
Median ACT: 21
Fraternities: 21%
Sororities: 23%
Application deadline:
  two weeks before each term

Football is the main thought at Alabama and not only on Saturday afternoons—it completely dominates student life on campus and it's in the hearts of all Alabamans. It is common knowledge that one of the most popular men in the state is Paul "Bear" Bryant, the "Crimson Tide" coach.

So while the school was busy checking AP polls (the "Tide" rose to number one rankings in recent years more times than any other school), President David Matthews has had great success in improving Alabama's academic image.

Studying, for the most part, takes place in one of the libraries on campus and then only four nights a week (leaving Thursday night for the beginning of weekend festivities). Certainly the most dedicated students are most likely enrolled in Alabama's business, engineering, or premed programs.

But Alabama, like most state schools in the South, is noted more for its living than for its learning. Greek life is predominant, with over forty fraternities and sororities on campus, but it is by no means a must. Both Greeks and independents are active participants in Student Government, sports, honoraries, and other campus-related activities.

Students are from various backgrounds and from various places, but many are native Alabamans, and/or the daughters and sons of alumni. Others are attracted to Alabama by its somewhat conservative traditions or possibly by its rather lenient admissions procedure.

Dorm life is dominated by the women students, with Tutwiler being the choice freshman spot, but men and married students are supplied with ample space. Most men, however, if not living at the fraternity house, choose the off-campus route. Football players are exceptions to the rule, as they receive such preferential treatment as air-conditioned rooms and steak dinners. That's to be expected at Alabama.

The parking problem at the U of A is of growing concern to both students and administrators. Most freshmen should be discouraged from bringing cars to school, unless they enjoy getting little white tickets for improper parking. Cars really aren't necessary as classes are centered around a quadrangle within easy walking distance of all the dorms, and most of the social life is restricted to on-campus fraternity, sorority, or dorm parties and the few local pubs on "the strip," University Boulevard.

Alabama is still the small, conservative state university that it is made out to be. With football, frats, and just plain fun, it still has its serious side toward academics. At this school, you can get just what you want. And as for atmosphere, Alabama has the market cornered on natural beauty and Southern hospitality.

THE AMERICAN UNIVERSITY

Location: Washington, DC 20016
Campus: city outskirts
Undergraduate enrollment:
 2109 M, 2388W
Total enrollment: 16320
Expenses: $8097
Financial aid: 25%
Library: 390,000 volumes

Student-faculty ratio: 17–1
Transfer students: NA
Median SAT: 486 V, 505 M
Fraternities: 5%
Sororities: 6%
Application deadline:
 August 1

American University is probably the best home base for spending a few years in Washington. It is located between the heart of government and business offices and the brick homes and cherry blossoms of the suburbs. A minute's walk puts you at Ward Circle, a fine hitchhiking hub from which you can get to nearly anywhere of interest in Washington with merely the point of a thumb.

American, or AU as it's called by its students, once achieved a high rating in the radical echelon of the East Coast, but those days are long gone. Even so, you can still count on an influx of new and varied people trying to recruit student support around the campus. The students themselves are now what might be called "apathetic liberals." If pressed on an issue, they'll probably take a liberal stand.

What was formerly a Methodist-run school has since been liberated and transformed into a nondenominational institution. However, the school boasts a chapel-in-the-round, crowned by a gold flame. Students in several different campus religious groups congregate here.

Students at American seem to hail mainly from New York, New Jersey, and Pennsylvania. Nevertheless, there are many foreigners from South America, the Middle East, and Africa. They give the campus the required "embassy" atmosphere. In addition, American's "Washington semester" program for government students from other institutions draws a number of Southern and Midwestern representatives. So if the Eastern mystique begins to bore you, there are a lot of other faces to turn to. Unfortunately, not many AU students ever break out of the social circle of their Eastern compatriots.

There seems to have been a shift in students' preoccupation in the last few years. While partying is still a favorite pastime on weekends, and indulgence in alcohol, marijuana, and perhaps other controlled substances is not "out" yet, more students seem to take academics seriously and study accordingly.

Liberal arts courses at AU, like those in many other schools, serve mostly to churn out typical four-year college grads. The school is rather conventional; its method of teaching is not particularly effective. In fact, the school's reputation has more to do with its location than with anything else. As might be expected, the best departments are in government, political science, economics, and history. The standards of advanced courses in these fields are quite high, and most of the students who take them are genuinely satisfied. Occasional innovative sparks help keep students aware and awake. The psychology department is almost uniformly behaviorist. Despite the monolithic Skinnerian approach, the department continues to appeal to many students and is continually instituting new programs.

In the life sciences and chemistry, American trains competent technicians, but neither lab facilities nor faculty are exceptional. Few of the students at American are likely to join the scientific vanguard.

The schools of government and international service continue to uphold their traditionally high academic standards. The school of government offers a variety of opportunities for students to work in Capitol Hill offices or in local city affairs. And the school of international service consistently has more of its graduates accepted into the foreign service than do many of the more prestigious Eastern universities. If history, government, and politics interest you, and if you want to take full advantage of Washington's own resources, AU is a good place to acquire the necessary academic foundations, as well as the essential political jargon.

Not everyone at AU, however, is there for a primer in politics; the arts are thriving as well. A particularly notable example of the school's artistic resources is the dance department, which is the home of the nationally known Wolf Trap Summer Dance Institute. Community aid courses, for which academic credit is given, are also popular among AU students.

The people who attend American are for the most part fairly content. Those who are not satisfied know it right away and usually leave. For the student seeking a cosmopolitan base for his college education, Washington is a superb locale; and for the student looking for a comfortable place in which to grow intellectually, AU is worth investigating. And in these times of patriotic fervor, the name may be inspiring, too.

AMHERST COLLEGE

Location: Amherst, MA 01002
Campus: rural
Undergraduate enrollment:
  1000 M, 500 W
Total enrollment: 1500
Expenses: $7800
Financial aid: 33%
Library: 535,000 volumes

Student-faculty ratio: 10-1
Transfer students: 40-50
Median SAT: 625 V, 650 M
Fraternities: 33%
Sororities: 33%
Application deadline:
  February 1 for freshmen
  March 1 for transfers

Amherst College has been in a state of flux for the past five years, actively examining itself and the meaning of a liberal arts education. The decisions to accept both men and women and create a new curriculum—combined with a new president—illustrates the range and depth of the changes occurring in the fabric of the college. For students, the result is an interesting, dynamic environment in which the education consists as much of being part of the college as attending classes.

In 1974, a special edition of the moderate Amherst *Student* trumpeted "We're Coed!"; only in 1980, however, has coeducation finally become a reality with the graduation of the first class to contain men and women for a full four years. The decision to become coeducational was the result of prolonged study and debate. The school's close relationship with Smith and Mount Holyoke, a more than comfortable endowment, and a large applicant pool insulated Amherst from the pressures faced by other schools in accepting coeducation. Nonetheless, the all-male spirit continues to linger and Amherst women still cringe when asked if they go to Smith or Mount Holyoke.

Amherst has been described and criticized as "euphoric." The combination of a superb faculty, small student body, and idyllic rural setting certainly combine to give that impression. Despite the small college atmosphere, Amherst does have most of the advantages of a large university through the Five College Program (with Hampshire, Smith, Mount Holyoke, and the University of Massachusetts). Students are free to take courses at any of the other colleges, even if something similar is offered at Amherst. The academic departments range from good to excellent. American studies, English, history, and Russian are notable. In the sciences, larger schools have an advantage in facilities, though Amherst's are more than adequate for the average premed (over ninety percent eventually accepted by medical schools). Since there are no graduate students, the emphasis is completely on undergraduate education: all courses are taught by real professors, not the teaching assistants so much in evidence at larger schools.

The new "introduction to liberal studies" curriculum has received mixed reviews in its first year. The requirements are minimal: one of four courses each semester freshman year, plus a program composed of four courses chosen by the student and completed over the remaining three years. The new curriculum has not yet found its true direction, but it does contain some of the more interesting and challenging courses on campus.

The low student-faculty ratio and the liberal office hours of professors help students develop a relationship with their teachers that goes beyond the classroom. The size of the student body assures that fellow student's faces quickly become familiar, allowing friendships to develop easily, but simultaneously creating a lack of privacy. While the well-rounded, preppie-jock is still very much in evidence, the admissions office attempts to incorporate as much diversity as possible in a class of 400. Traditionally, as one of the most selective schools in the country, Amherst students tend to be intellectual, but not to the detriment of enjoying life outside of academics. Extracurricular activities and sports are very popular. Amherst's reputation for producing country clubbers—the proverbial "gentleperson jocks"—is not entirely undeserved. Intramural teams are formed spontaneously and the small size of the school makes intercollegiate sports more accessible to all.

The social scene is still dominated by the fraternities, though they are changing with the college. While all-male fraternities remain strong, several are now coed and others have become nonselective houses. The traditional fraternity party endures, one house or the other is "on tap" every night from Tuesday to Saturday. Free beer, open invitations, and Mount Holyoke and Smith women are the rule, though

Amherst women are as integral a part of the college's social life as the men. The unfortunate structural fact of the social situation is that Mount Holyoke and Smith women far outnumber men in the Five College area. Coeducation is changing the old relationship with these schools, but Amherst is still likely to remain the next best thing to four years in Amsterdam for the men of the college.

The administration's attitude toward anything outside of academics is perhaps best characterized as salutary neglect. Nonetheless, student activism is on the rise and the administration is being forced to take a more active role in bettering race relations and other aspects of student life.

Amherst College is a school that tries to be all things to all students. The education is comprehensive: it consists, as much if not more, of learning what happens outside the curriculum. The school has its shortcomings, some that are built-in mixed blessings (like its size), others that are temporary (like the growing pains of the new curriculum). The surprising thing about the place is that it succeeds remarkably well in being most things to most students.

ANTIOCH COLLEGE

Location: Yellow Springs, OH 45387
Campus: rural
Undergraduate enrollment: 477 M, 533 W
Expenses: $6600
Financial aid: 55%
Library: 250,000 volumes

Student-faculty ratio: 10–1
Transfer students: 80
Median SAT: 540 V, 510 M
Median ACT: 24
Fraternities: 0%
Sororities: 0%
Application deadline: March 1, until class is filled

Antioch College is not the place to go if you're the type who likes cramming for tests, logically ordered tasks, a calm and stable environment, or Chinese food. None of these is readily available at this small campus in southwestern Ohio. Located in the picturesque and very rural Village of Yellow Springs (one movie theater, one grocery, a liquor store, and a host of arts-and-craft shops), Antioch offers just about everything—as long as you're willing to work through the red tape which is necessary in getting things done.

Students who like to do their own learning and have good self-discipline find the courses excellent. The faculty members are accessible and usually quite brilliant in their fields, if sometimes a bit unconventional. Classes are small and informal, and everyone is on a first-name basis. There are few exams, grades are optional, and almost none of the competition common to other schools is found here. This doesn't mean, however, that students spend their hours at leisure. You may find that Antioch structure—or lack of it—demands more than a typical curriculum.

As you might expect, there are no frats or sororities, and the only existing intramural sport is the campus frisbee team. Almost all students live on the premises; off-campus housing is difficult to find, and not encouraged. Social life is loose and friendly. Rarely is a party private, and get-togethers are organized at the slightest excuse. Social events typically include Saturday midnight movies, a variety of speakers and concerts, and periodic oddities, such as bicycle races, costume cabarets, cook-outs, and the like. Campus dances are held twice weekly, with free beer for all. Anything goes at these well-attended functions, and students are known for dancing with themselves, hoola-hoops, beach balls, and stray dogs.

Like the artist Andy Warhol, Antioch College is famous for being famous. For many people, it stands at the vanguard of progressive education, a pioneer in the field of cooperative work-study programs. Under the "cooperative education" plan, students spend half of their college career on "co-op" jobs around the country and the other half on campus. There is a wide variety of available jobs, and students are able to choose from those offered by the college or they can secure them on their own.

The transient nature of Antioch's student body, a result of alternating between study quarters on campus and co-op quarters around the country, provides for an interesting campus environment. Most of the students are well-traveled and can speak knowledgeably about towns and cities from Los Angeles to New York and all points in between. Many are involved with such issues as the antinuclear movement, women's liberation, gay rights, and others. As on other campuses across the country, drug use is less prevalent than in years past. A large segment of the student body are into health foods, vitamins, vegetarian diets, and other organic living habits. Both new wave and punk music are popular. Patti Smith and Elvis Costello can be heard just as often as the ever-popular Rolling Stones. Disco is shunned for the most part.

There are two governing bodies on campus. Community council

("Comcil") is responsible for nearly all aspects of community life, including sponsoring the dances, appropriating money for the various political and social organizations, and ruling on community issues such as a ban on pets, etc. The administrative council ("Adcil"), made up of administrators, faculty members, and students, is charged with the responsibility of advising the college Provost on matters related to academics and the college's governing.

Antioch is committed to trying just about everything at least once. If you're interested in learning the best method for writing haiku while scuba-diving, chances are you'll find a sponsor. The "education abroad" program is considered to be one of the better such foreign study structures.

Financial woes in the past five or six years have hampered Antioch's ability to continue its leadership into new areas of educational endeavor. Despite the fiscal crisis, the lead built up so far is enough to keep Antioch at the top.

It is difficult *not* to become involved at and with Antioch. Few students fade into the woodwork, and few fail to find something which captures their time and attention. Those who don't like the atmosphere soon leave, because things happen very quickly here.

ARIZONA STATE UNIVERSITY

Location: Tempe, AZ 85281
Campus: suburban
Undergraduate enrollment:
   14,590 M, 12,208 W
Total enrollment: 37,122
Expenses: $3400 (in-state),
   $4950 (out-of-state)
Financial aid: NA
Library: 1,500,000 volumes

Student-faculty ratio: 23–1
Transfer students: 10,168
Median ACT: 21
Fraternities: 9%
Sororities: 8%
Application deadline:
   July 31 for fall semester
   December 21 for spring semester

Technically, it's known as student city—a modernistic apartment complex sheltering over ten thousand ASU students. But the ASU matriculants (a largely nontechnical group) know it simply as "Sin City," serving fair warning to straitlaced parents of would-be "Sun Devils" that they have every intention of maintaining ASU's reputation as one of the nation's classiest party schools.

Noted Harvard economist John Kenneth Galbraith would have a

research field day with the Arizona State student body—one of the most affluent of any public (or for that matter, private) institutions. Thorsten Veblen might be interested too, for ASU students certainly constitute a leisure class. Upper-middle-class students proliferate on the attractive and contemporary Phoenix-area campus. Here, possibly more than at any other school, life-style alone provides the key to student life.

And at ASU, life-style centers around off-campus apartments. Parties are the password, and the guideword, and the only word. According to one student there, you can find a party any night, including weekdays, if you want. Many ASU students do. Pot is plentiful despite efforts of the federal and state governments to crack down on the Mexican border traffic.

Like many campus organizations across the country, the Arizona State student government publishes a guide to academic courses. More important (and more widely read) is a student-government-supported guide to off-campus housing. Even the Greeks, on the decline at this campus where individualized fun-seeking is the pattern, have fled their once hallowed on-campus houses for the freedom that apartment dwelling affords. An attempt at coed dormitories was abandoned after even that failed to slow the exodus to the inviting apartment-style living.

Phoenix offers more than enough bars, eating places, concerts, first-run movies, and other entertainment for the fun-loving "Sun Devils." But the city's multifarious offerings do present one problem for ASU students. If a male doesn't have a car, he might as well confine himself to the celibate pleasures of his room. If a female doesn't have a car (and a surprising number do), the situation is not quite as desperate; most ASU women manage very well. The soothing Arizona weather, long a comforter to arthritics and asthmatics, needs no commentary. But ASU students get their kicks from more than their home state deserts, canyons, and even a man-made wave maker named "Big Surf." Phoenix's central location puts the Colorado mountains, the California beaches, and Mexico's south-of-the-border hospitality within hours' traveling time. A long winter break provides ASU students with opportunity to sample the pleasant scenery surrounding Phoenix.

ASU boasts a top-notch athletic program which has increased in strength in recent years. Football (as usual) gets the most support, both financially and from students. The baseball team is a perennial national contender, as is the golf team.

And yes, besides all this, ASU students still find time to go to classes—sometimes. When they do, they can find decent courses. The nursing department is quite good, as are business, education, and anthropology. And partying is among the best in the country.

UNIVERSITY OF ARIZONA

Location: Tucson, AZ 85721
Campus: city center
Undergraduate enrollment:
 9850 M, 8400 W
Total enrollment: 30,826
Expenses: $2220 (in-state),
 $3770 (out-of-state)
Financial aid: 42%
Library: 2,000,000 volumes

Student-faculty ratio: 22–1
Transfer students: 4500
Median ACT: 22
Fraternities: 5%
Sororities: 6%
Application deadline:
 July 1 (fall term),
 December 1 (spring term)

Over the past twenty-five years, the University of Arizona has earned a richly deserved reputation as one of America's party schools. Unlike some of the nation's other hedonistic hideaways, the U of A provides the fixings for a good undergraduate education. Combining fun with education is not unique to the Tucson campus, but it is unusual—and commendable.

A distinguished faculty, a two-million-volume library, a 186-inch telescope, and several other fine research facilities (e.g., the Arizona State Museum and State Historical Society) provide a solid base for U of A studies. Astronomy is the one superdepartment, and students seriously considering stargazing as a career should definitely think about matriculating here. Tucson's clear air and the Kitt Peak National Observatory (which has executive offices on campus and a complex of telescopes nearby) have attracted many of the world's foremost astronomers, most notably lunar and planetary director Dr. Gerard Kuiper (of NASA fame). Journalism is also a top-notch department.

In all honesty, scholastics remain secondary for most students who attend Arizona. The palm trees and spacious lawns of U of A (located just a mile from downtown Tucson) provide a scenic backdrop for the raucous parties of the student body. Whether you are into drugs or alcohol, you will find plenty of company at Arizona. Of course, there is off-campus social action, too, including skiing on nearby Mount Lemmon, extremely popular jaunts to Nogales, Mexico (a hop, skip, and jump to the south), and beer bashes in the surrounding deserts. And for those who get bored easily, the Gulf Coast of California is just three hours away by car.

On-campus activities and clubs are popular. The *Arizona Daily Wildcat*, one of several newspapers put out by U of A (including *El Independiente*, a bilingual publication in English and Spanish for the sizable Chicano community), has the largest circulation in the West.

Sports are on the upswing at Arizona. The recently revamped athletic program has yielded fine teams, especially in the major sports. The football team is routinely in the top ten, while baseball has a history of national championships.

Living accommodations seem good enough, but a prospective enrollee should take heed that at least one of the dorms dates back to territorial days. Off-campus housing is accepted, but it has not become the fashion that it has at other schools, including state rival Arizona State. A car is definitely recommended if you have any interest at all in exploring Tucson, a sprawling city of nearly half a million.

It should also be mentioned that Arizona telescopes have also helped establish the school's optical sciences center as the leading facility of its kind in North America. U of A scientists designed the optics for the Pioneer II spacecraft.

There should be no need for a telescope to discover the opportunities available at University of Arizona, educational and otherwise.

UNIVERSITY OF ARKANSAS

Location: Fayetteville, AR 72701
Campus: rural
Undergraduate enrollment: 6900 M, 4800 W
Total enrollment: 14,421
Expenses: $2700 (in-state), $3330 (out-of-state)
Financial aid: 35%
Library: 900,000 volumes

Student-faculty ratio: 17–1
Transfer students: NA
Median ACT: M: 20 W: 18
Fraternities: 17%
Sororities: 20%
Application deadline: none—last day to register is fifth class day

The most famous and least typical graduate of the University of Arkansas is former Senator J. William Fulbright. As an undergraduate, to be sure, Fulbright was in the mainstream—football hero, student politician, Rhodes scholar. But nowadays, when they brag about Fulbright, they're proudest of the fact that he has never, ever, voted for a civil rights bill. That's what Arkansas is like.

In case you should still cherish an image of Arkansas as a great center of learning, digest just one more point: the national reputation of the University of Arkansas rests to a large extent on the football team's top ranking. The Arkansas "Razorbacks" are rough, tough, and mean, and they make great professional football players.

Arkansas considers itself a peripheral part of the Midwest. In temperament, it's more a part of the South. The University of Arkansas sometimes seems to combine the worst features of both regions.

The most prominent feature of Arkansas—one which is both Southern and Midwestern—is a fraternity system with a surprisingly strong grip on the campus. Only one thing can compete with frats, and that is football. Together, frats and football form the core of a traditional college social life which also incorporates bars, big dances, ostentatious (if not vulgar) spending, and protracted leisure.

To call the admissions policy at Arkansas "rolling" is an understatement; when propounded to the admissions officers of tougher schools, the Arkansas policy "leaves 'em rolling in the aisles." To get in, you need an Arkansas high school diploma (preferably with an average above C); if you're from out of state, a comparable record of mediocrity will do. But this admissions policy isn't so unusual; many state schools admit practically all comers. What's particulary noteworthy about Arkansas is that the school doesn't weed out the deadwood once it arrives. Academic pressures are about as much a threat as a flood in the Gobi Desert.

On the fiscal side, one can go to Arkansas and live in princely style on about $3500 a year, including a fair number of drinks and dates into the bargain. Also, costs of living are lower in Arkansas than in many other states, so nights out on the town aren't too damaging to the purse. (On the other hand, nights out on the town seem a little ludicrous in Fayetteville, Arkansas.)

Other attractions might be the women. During a visit to the U of A a few years ago, Gloria Swanson said that she had never seen a more beautiful collection of women anywhere—or the virtual lack of rules for men and senior women. A few people, certainly not many, may be attracted by the faculty, who are not universally incompetent. In fact, the English and architecture departments are excellent, the vocal music program is second to none, and political science and engineering are both on the upswing. Of course, as a school founded to teach agriculture, Arkansas is also strong in that regard. On the other hand, many departments, especially elementary education and journalism, are terrible. (The school newspaper may be the worst in the nation.) But all of the faculty are receptive and even paternal to bright, interested students—after all, there are so few of them.

Still, on the balance, the University of Arkansas must be capsule-summarized as a conservative state school, deficient in many respects, controlled by tightfisted and illiberal trustees and a backwater legislature. The place is fine to go to if you just need a degree—say, in order to please Dad enough to get him to give you the family business. But if you're seeking an education, rather than simply a pleasant four-year sojourn, think twice before going to Arkansas. Education is a private and almost covert process here, and you'll feel out of step all the while you pursue the studies that a normal university was meant to aid.

AUBURN UNIVERSITY

Location: Auburn, AL 36830
Campus: rural
Undergraduate enrollment:
   8750 M, 6330 W
Total enrollment: 18,000
Expenses: $3000 (in-state),
   $3600 (out-of-state)
Financial aid: 50%
Library: 1,000,000 volumes

Student-faculty ratio: 17–1
Transfer students: 2500
Median SAT: M: 480 V, 560 M;
   W: 480 V, 510 M
Fraternities: 20%
Sororities: 14%
Application deadline:
   three weeks before quarter

Auburn used to be the kind of Southern school where, if you could punt a football and count to one hundred without too many mistakes, the admissions office would welcome you with open arms and steaks for dinner.

But while the football players may still be the "Big Men on Campus," the wheels of change are turning creakily at Auburn, and these days you're likely to find few students among the football fans.

Politically, Auburn is backward and very apathetic. On the political spectrum, the school is somewhere between conservative and reactionary. Ronald Reagan was the choice of a majority in 1980.

Auburn's administration is strictly nineteenth century. They put up with little student input and generally try to impose their morality upon the student body. The trustees who run the university all owe their positions to George C. Wallace, chairman of the board, if that tells you anything.

Blacks are outnumbered on campus by almost forty-to-one and very few black instructors are on the faculty.

The academic atmosphere has improved markedly. There is a good student-run speaker's program which has hosted some unconventional lecturers in the past. But the resident talent, with a few exceptions, does a good imitation of a vacuum. The school was established as a technical institute and offers fine programs in engineering, aerospace mechanics, and architecture. But the liberal arts faculty is generally weak, and the education department, which attracts ninety percent of Auburn women, is downright rinky-dink. Science professors are conservative by Auburn standards, which is saying quite a bit; liberal arts teachers are more progressive.

Despite the deficiencies, both academic and social, Auburn students say they are happy. Women cite the marriage opportunities; men claim a good social life (the spirit of the traditional Southern fraternities is by no means dead, though membership has continued to decline slightly over the past two or three years) and a friendly atmosphere.

Alcohol is the main recreational drug, with beer the most popular drink. Good night-spots are few and far between, so frat parties, private parties, and trips to Columbus, Georgia (thirty miles away), are favorite pastimes. Grass is moderately popular, readily available, and not looked down upon as you might find in much of the South. Harder drugs are rare. Auburn is very Establishment, and alcohol is the Establishment drug.

Housing is inadequate, with overcrowded conditions in dorms, apartments, and trailer courts partially accounting for the highest rental rates in Alabama. Much of the housing is, however, very close to campus and within walking or biking distance, a welcome respite from the citylike traffic problem.

Auburn offers many things—a good climate, quiet surroundings, a friendly campus, the excitement of big football games, and a good concert once every five years. Most of all, it offers a challenge to the student to wake-up the place from its long-standing stupor.

BALL STATE UNIVERSITY

Location: Muncie, IN 47306
Campus: city outskirts
Undergraduate enrollment:
 7200 M, 7800 W
Total enrollment: 17,500
Expenses: $3045 (in-state),
 $4120 (out-of-state)
Financial aid: 60%
Library: 1,000,000 volumes

Student-faculty ratio: 20–1
Transfer students: 940
Median SAT: 410 V, 450 M
Fraternities: 15%
Sororities: 15%
Application deadline:
 none

Ask people in Muncie, Indiana, what "Ball U" means and they'll probably say "Ball State University."

Named after the Ball brothers of canning jar fame, Ball State is a middle-sized, middle-class Midwestern institution located on the outskirts of Middletown, U. S. A. If that sounds like the university smacks of a homogeneous provincialism, then justice has been served. Ninety-five percent of the student body is comprised of Indiana residents. Nearly all of these "Hoosiers" are white, first-generation college students, whose weak SAT scores or meager pocketbooks reduced their chances of enrollment elsewhere.

As a rule, Ball State students are not interested in expanding their cultural horizons. Major pursuits include drinking beer, smoking pot, "skanking," and skipping classes, though not necessarily in that order. The university ranks an unofficial second in the state to Indiana University as far as partying goes.

Ball State also trails pretty far behind in intellectual stimulation. With few exceptions, the university is plagued with an overabundance of underachievers. One such exception is the college of architecture, where "archy majors" can be seen daily with projects under their arms and bags under their eyes. The teachers' college is one of the largest of its kind in the United States, and the college of business, which has been housed in a new building since November 1979, has gained some recognition for excellence. Several other departments demand a better-than-average academic workload, but in general, the going is not too tough. That's fine with the majority of students, who don't really attend Ball State for an education, just a degree.

Faculty at Ball State spans both extremes of the competency spectrum. Every department has one dynamic professor, a few mediocre ones, and the rest. . . . The university has also committed itself to offering refuge to faculty members who previously taught at big-name universities and wish to semiretire in Muncie. But Ball State can't expect to attract the cream of the instructor crop; faculty salaries are the lowest in the Mid-American Conference, and faculty morale is rumored to be scraping the MAC bottom, too.

Problems at Ball State are common to most universities: finding a parking space for your car is like pulling teeth; recreational facilities are limited, even though a good many students partipate in intramural sports; and the university auditorium, partly owned by the community, invites performers who are on the conservative side. Rock enthusiasts, look elsewhere.

Muncie has been called the "armpit of America," and for good reason. The buildings are drab, the street layout is analogous to the inside of a transistor radio, and the nightlife is lacking. Besides a few choice bars and one disco bordering the campus, the only diversion in town is cruising the canning jar factory.

Great anecdotes have centered around the double-entendre of ole "Ball U." While in Chicago for a convention one year, a university journalism professor named Dr. Horney phoned the front desk of a hotel in order to page a friend. After identifying his last name and his place of work, the clerk was flabbergasted. She promptly told the professor where to put his "practical joke" and hung up.

"Ball U" T-shirts are novelty items outside the Midwest, with more than one student partly financing his spring break by selling them in Florida. During football games, the student body chastises the opponent by shouting the school name, "Ball U! Ball U!"

Other positive aspects of Ball State are its library and its housing facilities. Bracken Library, completed at a cost of $14.5 million in 1975, contains almost 500,000 volumes. It is conveniently located in the center of campus. Most of the residence halls were built within the last twenty years, and are therefore still together at the seams (except for Shales, the "animal hall"). Policies in the dorms are fairly liberal.

Physically, the campus is a mixture of old and new. The older buildings, such as the Administration Building and Lucina Hall, abide at the verdant south end of campus known as "the quad." As one moves farther north, the buildings become more modern and the landscaping more tundralike.

The university is conservative, friendly, a bit behind-the-times but complacent. It is the kind of school one would expect in Middletown, U.S.A.

BARD COLLEGE

Location: Annandale-on-Hudson, N.Y. 12504
Campus: rural
Undergraduate enrollment: 340 M, 360 W
Expenses: $7765
Financial aid: 40%
Library: 140,000 volumes
Student-faculty ratio: 11-1
Transfer students: 80
Median SAT: 575 V, 550 M
Fraternities: NA
Sororities: NA
Application deadline:
    March 31 for fall term,
    January 1 for spring term

In the early Seventies, Bard was a very freaky place, and the most unique thing about it, in the words of one student there, was "the absence of straights." Bard, like many other schools of similar size orientation, has changed since then.

The college is a small community, and people take care of each other. Students are, for the most part, friendly, intelligent, socially liberal, politically left, and rich. About a third of the 1976 freshman class came from families with incomes over $50,000 a year. President Botstein, known to all as Leon, insists that the exorbitant cost of a Bard education will not limit enrollment to upper-income families. Hmmm.

Bard does not adhere to one philosophy. Under the presidency of thirty-three-year-old Botstein, the college is in the vanguard of redefining the meaning of a liberal arts education. Freshmen are required to take one "freshman seminar" during each of their first two semesters. The purpose of these seminars is to offer an interdisciplinary approach to usually more specialized areas of study like modern European history or contemporary religious thought. Some students feel that this requirement narrows, rather than broadens their outlook because it limits the number of other academic areas which they may explore. Others, however, are pleased with the direction the seminars have given them.

Bard students have enormous freedom to determine the direction of their education. Social regulations are minimal, and students have the opportunity to slip into whatever niche in the community is right for them. Freedom at Bard goes hand in hand with a minimum of academic competition, although a good number of students are workaholics.

Departments with outstanding faculty are literature and music. The dance department is sometimes criticized for its lack of breadth and the emphasis, as in drama, is on performance. Psychology is oriented toward the experimental, rather than humanistic, approach. The art department is staffed by artists who work in New York City and teach part-time at the school. The fast-growing departments are film and the women's studies program.

The campus is spread over 500 acres of the Hudson River Valley. Its twenty-two dorms (most coed) are scattered over this area, with the exception of the one dormitory located six miles away in Rhinebeck. Some of the dorms are converted mansions, while others are hovels. Fortunately, most of the latter are scheduled for renovation; many have already undergone it. The college is looking for more money to complete the job.

The social life at Bard is somewhat erratic but generally excellent. It is "freewheeling" in the general relaxed mood of the college. The parties are sometimes staid, sometimes really good, occasionally Dionysian. While rock and jazz have a permanent foothold on the musical entertainment scene, disco is becoming increasingly popular. Although marijuana and, to a lesser degree, hallucinogenics play a part in student life, nothing matches the attraction to alcohol. Nevertheless, students remain a highly energized lot. This energy finds its outlets in the biweekly newspaper, the *Observer*, in the campus radio station, WXBC, and in a large variety of more specialized student organizations ranging from the Latin-American Organization to the Cinema Matrix to the Bard Choir.

Frisbee is the recreation of the Bard masses. There are varsity basketball, soccer, cross-country, and tennis teams. Few cuts are made. There is also an intramural sports program. "Sports at Bard exist for enjoyment and recreation in the finest tradition of the New York playground," reports one happy student.

Most Bard students work hard and get their kicks in conventional ways, such as going down the road to Adolph's (the local bar), talking an inordinate amount, or going to New York or Boston. On weekends, the school, while not depopulated, does suffer a certain drop in resident numbers. Boredom with the immediate neighborhood seems to be the major reason for the exodus. The nearest large town is Kingston, across the Hudson River, which is famous for Caldor's, a huge department store with a tremendous record collection. A little north of Kingston is Woodstock, well known for its artistic denizens and its expensively chic shops. Poughkeepsie is about twenty miles south, Albany an hour or so north.

Despite the isolation, Bard is an excellent place in which to spend four years (more or less). The school does not try to make you, the raw meat, into a prefabricated cheeseburger. It lets you cook along in your own fashion. Consequently the Bard student can find out who he really is, and not what someone wants him to be. If he ends up a cheeseburger, well, it was his own choice.

BARNARD COLLEGE

Location: New York, N.Y. 10027
Campus: city center
Undergraduate enrollment: 2300W
Expenses: $8000

Student-faculty ratio: 13–1
Transfer students: NA
Median SAT: 620 V, 600 M
Sororities: 0%
Application deadline:

Financial aid: 40%   **January 15**
Library: 150,000 volumes

Barnard is a sophisticated women's college located in upper Manhattan on the fringe of Spanish Harlem. Many parents tremble at the thought of their daughters' attending a school only five blocks away from 125th Street, the infamous drug capital of the world, and they are not unreasonable in their fears. The area is dangerous. But the campus of Columbia University is well patrolled, and there are usually a lot of people around, so that day-to-day college life is quite safe.

It's Barnard's location in perhaps the greatest city of the world that has most determined its character. For theater, art history, and political science majors, the "Apple" serves as an extension of the classroom, and is for most students the main source of entertainment. Lincoln Center is twenty minutes away by subway, and the theater district, where half-price tickets to Broadway and off-Broadway shows can be bought a few hours before curtain time, is three stops later. The same subway line, which also stops right in front of Columbia/Barnard sweeps one, in about half an hour, to the lively cafes and jazz clubs of Greenwich Village.

Because of the countless sources of entertainment in Manhattan, Columbia's administration has never felt it necessary to offer its students too much in the way of amusements. In the words of many students, "The social life stinks." Students tend to go their own way for diversion, and this problem of social dispersion is compounded by the fact that a large number of students commute, and are often too pressed for time to participate in college activities. There are, however, a wide variety of clubs to join, and good movies to be seen for little money. The West End Cafe, only two blocks south on Broadway, is a traditional gathering place for Columbians, and features live swing jazz nightly.

So, if you think you'd enjoy seeking out the treasures of New York rather than relying on a college council to plan your entertainment, you can have a great time and an excellent education at Barnard. The course requirements are quite structured; a student must know a foreign language, take two semesters of a lab science, "freshman English," sweat through four semesters of gym, and take six courses outside her field of concentration in addition to fulfilling major requirements. Though students may initially complain about this rigidity, most find it interesting to try out courses they might otherwise not have taken. And surprisingly, students often enjoy the well-coached gym courses so much that they opt for fifth and sixth semesters. Squash, racquetball, fencing, volleyball, tennis, and ballet are among the most popular gym courses.

Intellectual standards are high, and competition is rough, especially in science courses. The English department is outstanding, with several of its professors developing something of a cult following among their students (Ulanov, Dalton, and Kurrik). Barnard and Columbia are separate colleges within Columbia University, and as a separate institution, Barnard maintains its own faculty, funds, and administration. While enjoying the benefits of personal attention that a small school can offer, students are free to use the facilities and attend most undergraduate and some graduate courses of the university. Some students do this admittedly to meet the guys across the street. Barnard is a women's college, but there are plenty of men around. Including grad students, the male-female ratio is about eight to one.

There is a good variety of housing available to those students classified as residents. On Barnard's four-acre campus is a complex of three coed dormitories; students living there are obliged to join its meal plan. On 116th Street, Barnard maintains apartments in three buildings for its students. These are shared by up to six women, and include a kitchen. While upperclasswomen like the privacy and independence of living in these suites, freshmen may find them a bit isolating. A number of Barnard students live in Columbia's dorms, and a larger number find apartments independently. In recent years, the housing office has had difficulty in finding an equitable way of distributing its limited dorm space to the growing number of students who want it. As of 1979–80, no commuters will be housed. Commuters will be determined as those whose trip to or from school by public transporataion takes about an hour and fifteen minutes or less. Prospective students who are not sure whether or not they would be classified as commuters can call the housing office to check their status.

Barnard's career placement office is extremely helpful for those approaching graduation. It features opportunities to talk with alumnae about their professions, classes on how to prepare résumés and the best way of looking for a job, and sets up internships for students during intersession. These run the gamut from laboratory aides to TV station assistants to readers for publishing houses. Often these internships lead to paid part-time jobs during the semester. Students "try out" careers, and make contacts which can help them find a permanent job after graduation. This is the kind of opportunity available only at a city school; one of the things that makes Barnard the place to be.

BATES COLLEGE

Location: Lewiston, ME 04240
Campus: city outskirts
Undergraduate enrollment:
 750 M, 650 W
Expenses: $6385
Financial aid: 35%
Library: 250,000 volumes

Student-faculty ratio: 12–1
Transfer students: 100
Median SAT: 580 V, 590 M
Fraternities: 0%
Sororities: 0%
Application deadline:
 February 1

Only one factor separates Bates from the select cadre of out-of-the-way liberal arts colleges in the American Midwest: Bates is set in Lewiston, Maine.

Like the Midwest schools of the ilk of Antioch, Oberlin, and Kenyon—or more particularly of Knox and Carleton—Bates is a superintellectual place, with virtually no social life, dedicated to diligent and thorough, if not brilliant, scholarship and to the production of good citizens, of the solid, concerned middle-class type. And it will probably stay pretty much that way, since the college is shelling out money to grab top professors in every field in line with the president's goal to reach parity with Amherst, Williams, and Wesleyan. Only time will tell, but chances are Bates will succeed. After all, money can't buy love, but it sure can improve faculties.

Bates has both the virtues and the problems of all small liberal arts colleges. With about 1400 students and a good student-faculty ratio, Bates has the opportunities to provide a truly intense intellectual experience. But with the social detritus that is Lewiston, Maine, Bates also has the opportunity to provide virtually unparalleled social boredom.

In addition to acute competition for grades, the Bates student faces the social pressures of a closed community. A very high percentage of Bates students marry within the alumni pool, so the trials of courtship, possible rejection, and the general social awakening of the college years have to be acted out more or less in public. Fewer than ten percent of the students are from Maine, so the men and women have few community ties. Moreover, Lewiston is at best indifferent to life at the college. There is little link, therefore, with the community, and the students find themselves pretty much adrift unless they can fit into college life.

Lewiston is a big city by Maine standards—it has about 75,000 people. But the population (mostly French-Canadian) is not particularly cosmopolitan, and the cultural offerings of the town are slim. There is no art-type movie theater, no noncommercial playhouse. All in all, Lewiston is something of a hole. And Bates's ameliorative effect on the town has been minimal, except for its exceptional theater complex.

One might expect a major weekend exodus of Bates students under these circumstances. But many stay on campus quite consistently. The student union, often a joke at other schools, is the focal point of gatherings at Bates. The typical Bates student, though, isn't looking for a rousing night on the city in some distant metropolis or for a hotshot date, but for a low-key evening with friends.

The drinking age is now twenty, but it doesn't much affect the students, and there is no administration hassle over the use of marijuana and no appreciable student interest in the use of harder drugs.

Social regulations are few, with open dorms and twenty-four hour visitation rights all around, and three coed dorms. The dormitory living is generally intimate and uncontrolled. For the women who don't want to live in the small houses of about thirty, there is a large new women's dorm. Sexual activity does take place on campus and in women's rooms. But despite the close-knit nature of the campus—or perhaps because of it—sexual activity is generally a fairly private matter, and most people don't detail what they're up to, if they acknowledge at all that they're up to anything.

Academics are Bate's forte, and the offerings and demands are extensive. Most seniors are required to complete a senior thesis. The facilities are surprising for so small a college. The programs are similarly good, especially in math, psychology, and studio art; the biology program has won considerable respect at Bates. Languages are a weakness. A "short term" program during the last ten weeks of the school year emphasizes innovation, independent study, and foreign travel.

The campus is still very closed and oblivious to the world outside Lewiston. There is substantial student participation in activities involving community work, but little concern for national politics. Similarly, the administration generally ignores the students (despite the claims to the contrary), and the students are satisfied to return the favor. The student body is almost lily-white, with only about forty American blacks in the college. Most of the campus involvement is purely in the intellectual realm.

Bates is not your average school. It's small and in a small town, but it has a highly qualified faculty and great facilities. Students also feel too big for the shoes Lewiston has to offer them. But on the whole, Bates may be the ideal school for the future; the school is financially secure and the area is underpopulated and unpolluted.

BAYLOR UNIVERSITY

Location: Waco, TX 76706
Campus: city center
Undergraduate enrollment:
 3639 M, 4175 W
Total enrollment: 9000
Expenses: $3600
Financial aid: 84%
Library: 800,000 volumes

Student-faculty ratio: 20-1
Transfer students: 660
Median ACT: 24
Fraternities: 25%
Sororities: 25%
Application deadline:
 rolling

Ever since its founding in 1845 (some claim it was a virgin birth), Baylor University has maintained much of the original spirit of a "Christian institution." Controlled by the Baptist General Convention of Texas, Baylor, despite some recent modifications, is still a bastion of Old South conservatism.

Administrators use the phrase "Baylor Family" to justify the *in loco parentis* policies, which include the standard Baptist prohibitions against gambling, drinking, dancing, and cohabitation. They have relented some: ballet was included in the fall 1979 P. E. curriculum because it is not considered a "social dance." Administrators continue to contend that the strict policies contribute to the overall Christian liberal arts education Baylor seeks to provide.

The school is the stomping grounds for many of the state's socially elite families and good Baylor men and women are notoriously well dressed. Greeks account for about twenty-five percent of the student body but have a disproportionate influence on dress, social customs, and mores. Fraternities and sororities have enjoyed a revival of sorts since a large number of them went national in 1976. Aided by increasing tuition costs at state schools and an aggressive nationwide campaign, the number of out-of-state students is increasing yearly, though Texas Baptists still dominate the campus.

While there have been attempts to put a ceiling on enrollment, the student population continues to grow and competition for admission is stiff. There is no longer a minimum requirement for college board scores but top grades, high scores, and early application are advisable.

Drugs are not big around campus but they can be had if you're willing to look hard and pay the price. The more favored vice is alcohol, and though it's used discreetly in polite society, local clubs do a brisk business with wayward Baylorites.

Tradition is still the guiding influence in many Baylor activities. Each fall, thousands of alumni return to campus for the homecoming bonfire, barricades, parade, and football game. Baylor's is the largest homecoming parade in the country.

Not only does the homecoming football game draw a crowd, but all Baylor athletic competition brings out the fans. Football is, as with all Southwest Conference schools, the most loyally followed sport. Attendance at the games has been steadily increasing for years. Basketball and baseball are also coming into their own at Baylor.

Religion continues to play a key role in Baylor activities. Each Wednesday night, the Baptist Student Union sponsors a gathering called "serendipity," formally the "Baylor religious hour." Ministers, gospel singers, and other practicing Christians talk to the students on a variety of topics. Two semesters of "Forum," formally called "Chapel," are required of all students. The University brings in notable speakers, singers, and media presentations for this thirty-minute noncredit course that meets twice a week.

In the fall, many of the "Forum" speakers are politicians eager to sell themselves to the young voters. Republicans are the favored candidates at Baylor. In fact, it's difficult to find any students who will admit that they are Democrats. And the president of the Baylor Young Democrats gave that organization its last rites in the spring of 1979.

The Republican stronghold is due in large part to the type of families that produce the typical Baylor student—namely moneyed business and professional people. This well-heeled background keeps Baylor students dressed in the latest fashions and driving late-model cars. Finances are not an obvious problem for most Baylor students.

Of course, the limited forms of entertainment in Waco means students don't have much on which to spend their money. In a town with four colleges, Waco caters surprisingly little to college-age adults.

Dating is another item found in limited quantities around campus. There seem to be two categories of romance on campus: the exclusive relationship with that special someone and the nonexistant one. Despite the lack of romance, Baylor has one of the friendliest campuses in the country. This friendly atmosphere is one of the school's strongest drawing points.

Baylor's other drawing card is academics. A growing reputation for academic quality draws a large number of pre-professional students seeking law or medical degrees. The faculty and facilities are growing rapidly to keep pace with the rising enrollment and widening academic offerings. But Baylor must balance the views of the faculty with Christian doctrine. One of the important requirements for a faculty position at Baylor is to be a Southern Baptist, or at least a Christian. This policy rules out a lot of talented people.

Besides the well-known law school, Baylor also has a nursing school in Dallas and a dentistry school in San Antonio.

The Waco campus houses the nation's finest collection of Robert and Elizabeth Barrett Browning's poetry, and many rare documents from the Lone Star State's early history are found in the "Texas collection."

Baylor is a unique place. Traditional and conservative, Baylor is making little effort to assimilate new ideas. The university that prays together manages to stay well out of the mainstream of thought and social consciousness.

BELOIT COLLEGE

Location: Beloit, WI 53511
Campus: city center
Undergraduate enrollment:
  525 M, 480 W
Total enrollment: 1050
Expenses: $6975
Financial aid: 60%
Library: 250,000 volumes

Student-faculty ratio: 12–1
Transfer students: 75
Median SAT: 548 V, 560 M
Median ACT: 25
Fraternities: 25%
Sororities: 10%
Application deadline:
  rolling

Due to financial hardship, which has cramped Beloit's style of innovative academics, the college has undergone some changes that may alter its face forever. The exciting part is that no one really knows what additional changes the future will bring. Despite the recent adoption of a six-term residency requirement and the reemergence of fraternities on campus, Beloit still boasts a fairly innovative program, given its status as a small Midwestern college.

Like all other Midwestern liberal arts colleges, Beloit offers the intimacy of a small student population, a solid academic program, exorbitant tuition, and a quaint rural setting. Unlike other Midwestern colleges, Beloit has a national student body, an anemic but unashamed sports program, and no marching band. Beloit assumes that students attend college as a preparation both for graduate study and for a future of coffee, Camus, and cab driving in the Bronx. To further its (paradoxical) goal of functional intellectualism, Beloit offers its own educational plan, aptly titled the "Beloit Plan."

The "Beloit Plan" is the first and basically the only reason to consider attending Beloit. First developed in 1963, the "plan" features a flexible trimester calendar, a mandatory field-term/work-study term and an advanced foreign study program. All this, and fringe benefits like a free and optional ninth term of study, makes Beloit something of a unique college.

Under the theoretical structure of the Beloit Plan (which the college will readily alter to meet the wants and/or needs of its students), an individual begins with an "underclass year" which consists of three successive fifteen-week semesters, all on campus, all for academic credit, separated only by the briefest of vacations. For students used to heading to sun, surf, or a job in June, the experience of a summer with Milton and molecular equations can be traumatic.

The real fun usually begins in the "middle year," which is close to a year and a half long. The middle year consists of two fifteen-week vacation terms and two fifteen-week on-campus semesters. This second year provides the student the time, based on experience in class and out, to complete serious work in his major. More importantly, the vacation terms allow the matriculant to choose from a highly popular selection of overseas seminars. The seminar is usually conducted in groups of twenty students who are housed with families in whatever country they elect and receive instruction from native profs and in the native foreign language.

Nor does the Beloit student's opportunity for international experience stop with these overseas excursions. The college has an excellent cooperative program set up, with numerous countries allowing students to attend foreign universities for a term. Countries ranging from those located in Europe to Africa to Southeast Asia have been sites for these programs.

The Beloit student rounds out his nontraditional education with a mandatory field term, nearly always in an area related to his or her academic interests and the seminar experience. The school provides the job opportunities and has a broad variety of offerings ranging from working as a General Electric management trainee in the Philippines to anthropology digs in Missouri to secretarial positions in Boston. The work-study programs tend to turn up jobs below the capabilities of the students, but they rarely mind. They figure the job opportunity is a valuable learning tool as a total experience—living off-campus, independence, etc.

The virtues and headaches of the "Beloit Plan" are numerous. On the positive side, the strongest point is the variety and flexibility of the "plan." The "Beloit Plan" stands in refreshing contrast to the standard college structure which decrees that you shall not study in the summer, you shall not work or take a vacation in the winter, and you shall have to drop out or take a leave of absence if you want to order your education differently. Moreover, the regular college year does not provide enough time for real work experience—you are always temporary help. With the freedom built into the "Beloit Plan," you may work up to a full year in the middle of your academic experience, allowing you to hold a worthwhile job. And then there are the advantages of foreign travel.

On the other hand, the "plan" has its flaws. The foremost is financial. In recent years, the college has experienced an overall decline in enrollment. To survive the squeeze, Beloit reduced the funding of its foreign study program, dismissed almost a quarter of its faculty (some of whom were the younger and more progressive teachers), and hired new administrators.

The new administration has chosen to deemphasize the Beloit Plan and concentrate instead on the academic integrity of the institution. Beloit College professors are good, if seldom brilliant. The sciences, most notably physics and geology, have well-justified strong reputations. Many students fear that the decline of the "Beloit Plan" and the new stress on "the academic excellence" of the school will erode the college's nationally distributed student population, and that the bright young stars from sea to sea will enroll in more renowned academic institutions.

Despite all these changes at Beloit, the school still attracts a sizable crowd of intellectual bohemians; the students work hard, wear green T-shirts, smoke dope discreetly, drink Jack Daniels and gallons of cheap Wisconsin beer, and pride themselves on their promiscuity (that's the word they use out there). The "Beloit Plan," with its constant rotation and foreign study programs, accentuates the students' already pronounced individualism.

We think the "Beloit Plan" is good. You might not, so check into it carefully.

BENNINGTON COLLEGE

Location: Bennington, VT 05201
Campus: rural
Undergraduate enrollment:
220 M, 380 W
Expenses: $8420
Financial aid: 30%
Library: 75,000 volumes

Student-faculty ratio: 8–1
Transfer students: 50
Median SAT: NA
Fraternities: NA
Sororities: NA
Application deadline:
March 15

Bennington is a first-rate private college without the traditional procedures of exams and grades, so it is generally free of acadmic competition. If you can live without football games, frat parties, and various other accoutrements normally considered indispensable at the Ivy-covered colleges with which it competes, this may be the school for you.

You don't have to come to Bennington knowing what you want to do, but you should be prepared to meet any undertaking seriously. All students devise their own "plan," their own curriculum and major, with the requirement of the grand finale—the senior project. Most academic majors (literature and social sciences) write a thesis. Performing arts majors usually put on a performance, while art majors present an exhibition. Therefore, something substantial is accomplished before leaving Bennington. The nine-week nonresident term, during which students take jobs all over the country, also helps in the planning of a career. Either you discover what you definitely don't want to do, or you find a job that sets you in a direction. In either case, the NRT helps you build a résumé and makes the outside world seem a little less terrifying.

The NRT is also welcome relief from an intense fall term. Deadlines are flexible and usually only a few papers are required per course. However, what you are expected to do is not limited to what you are assigned. Your teacher may decide to discuss Thoreau and then it is up to you to decide if you are going to read everything that was ever written by Thoreau, or nothing at all. Most people feel obliged to put in their best effort. When classes are so small (the average size is fourteen), you feel uncomfortable not speaking up or meeting with your teacher who is always available outside of class. Comments, instead of grades, are also very revealing about your performance. Achievement, in other words, is not just based on acing a final exam and, in fact, exams are conducted in only a few courses.

You can receive a good education at Bennington if you are self-disciplined and motivated. If you join the prevailing spirit of creativity, you are likely to be satisfied. Everyone at Bennington is creating something, and there is no excuse for the unproductive. The amazing "VAPA" (Visual and Performing Arts Building) is always open and some people work there all night long. Many of the art majors have their own studios. Science majors, of which there are a mighty handful, enjoy the small size of the department which allows for almost private tutorials with superb faculty.

Happiness at Bennington is best sustained by active engagement in academic and creative endeavors. The social life is certainly confusing. Because there are two women to every man, the males are in high demand. And they know it. Most of them love it, although some find the situation rather distracting. Some people believe that the males at Bennington become weak in character because they become absorbed in one beautiful and intelligent woman after another. Most everyone agrees that women at Bennington grow *stronger* in self-confidence and determination. While this fortitude is often painfully attained, the Bennington woman forms strong friendships to support her in her single existence. In general, people at Bennington are individualistic and self-sufficient. Perhaps it is easier to be a loner at a small school—there is usually a familiar face at every meal or party. While this is reassuring, it can also be annoying. People who enjoy more private living can move off campus or hole up in a dorm on the fringe of the campus.

The dorms ("houses") vary widely in character. While some dorms are designated "quiet houses," others blare music at all hours or hold LSD coffee hours. (While sometimes, "big fat reefers" may be sold along with booze at parties, drugs are no more common—possibly less—than at other colleges.) All the dorms are coed, and yes, so are the bathrooms. You get used to it soon enough.

While there are plenty of kids from affluent families, Bennington students, by and large, are not impressed by who is who, or who has what. And to tell the truth, most people look the same. What Salinger wrote in *Franny and Zooey* about Bennington types still holds true: Most people look as if they've been painting or sculpting, or as if they're wearing leotards under their clothes. Bennington does have a few preppies, but on the other extreme it has a number of eye-catching punks.

The one thing you can always count on at Bennington is the Friday night party. These parties take place in the houses or above the café (student-run) and they allow you to dance all night and let off steam from the previous week. They frequently have themes inviting imaginative costumes, such as the infamous annual "Dress to Get Laid" party. Many people prefer the parties that are given after a lecture, concert, or poetry reading, or the socializing that happens while putting together a performance. Gay "teas" held by members of the gay community are open to nonmembers as well. Gatherings which bring together people with common interests are an important part of the "Bennington Experience." There are also foreign films, anthropology films, and Saturday night flicks every week. And nothing will strengthen your faith in the "Bennington way" more than attending student productions, which are often highly professional.

Organized sports are on the upswing. Bennington now has soccer and tennis teams for both men and women and there is even a baseball team, although its members seem to enjoy the before and after beer drinking as much as the game itself. People tend to find some way to be outside, whether it is by jogging or playing frisbee, or painting or dancing. Bennington's setting is splendid. The view from the commons of the "end of the world" (a valley with mountains beyond) is uplifting to any student in need of spiritual replenishment. It is inspiring to work in such an exquisite setting.

Sometimes, however, you need to get away. Bennington is geographically isolated and self-contained. The only mixing most people do with the "townies" is at the favorite local bar, The Villager. Lots of students have cars, so if you don't, it's usually possible to get a ride on a weekend to almost anywhere you'd want to go. Few townspeople come on-campus, except to attend performances in VAPA. The Early Childhood Center on-campus offers students experience in working with preschool-aged or handicapped children, many of whom are local.

Bennington is the place to come if you want to have your way, but with the guidance of professors who often become your good friends. (Everyone, by the way, is on a first-name basis with everyone else.) Bennington has never been just another academic institution. While its reputation for innovation may have been eclipsed, Bennington remains a community of intensely creative and productive individuals.

BOSTON COLLEGE

Location: Chestnut Hill, MA 02167
Campus: suburban

Student-faculty ratio: 17–1
Transfer students: 350
Median SAT: 509 V, 544 M

Undergraduate enrollment:
4000 M, 4500 W
Total enrollment: 13,000
Expenses: $6500
Financial aid: 37%
Library: 1,000,000 volumes

Fraternities: 0%
Sororities: 0%
Application deadline:
January 15

Despite its name, Boston College is not in Boston, nor is it a college. Though bordering on the city of Boston, BC is actually located in the plushy, affluent suburb of Chestnut Hill (which is itself a part of Newton). A full-fledged university, BC is comprised of undergraduate schools of arts and sciences, management, nursing, and education, a broad graduate program, and a law school. Founded by Jesuits in 1863, BC also bears the label of Roman Catholicism. That in reality only affects you if you yourself take the initiative, however, since less than twenty percent of BC's faculty are clerical, the theology requirement is a mere two courses, and non-Catholics form a very large and virtually indistinguishable minority.

Another label which people attach to BC—and one which did fit very well in the early Seventies—heralds BC as a party school. While this is still true for those who make an effort to uphold the tradition (on weekends, crowded keg parties can always be found and the aroma of pot constantly wafts through the dorms), the typical BC student is becoming more and more grade-oriented. Weekends which begin on Thursday are becoming a thing of the past (especially with the new twenty-year-old state drinking age law), grade inflation is rampant, the air of competition is thickening, and studying, although not the "in" thing to do, is what more and more people are doing.

BC is solid academically. Its management and nursing schools are extremely competitive, and the school of education, with its now revamped but somewhat inflexible program, is not far behind. The school of arts and sciences, the largest school in the university, is especially strong in several areas—history and English are standouts—but the university's "freeze" on the total number of faculty members has left a few departments, including "political science" and "communications," pitifully shorthanded in the face of shifting course demands. Although the grad school (except for the reputable social work program) suffers enrollment problems and has not attained a reputation matching that of the college, its presence has helped to attract a number of intelligent and devoted faculty members.

Another one of BC's labels is "Boston's College." Although it was primarily a commuter school during the Sixties and before, BC has rapidly metamorphosed into a primarily (over sixty-five percent) resident school which offers truly fine, although rather expensive, housing options. Qualifying for housing is sometimes a feat in itself—at times, there are a thousand people on the housing waiting list and BC has even resorted to placing students in hotels, other colleges, and, believe it or not, a monastery. Most freshmen live on the beautiful, grass-covered Newton campus, which is located about two miles from the main campus. Junior and senior residents usually qualify for priority housing in BC's spacious, yet costly (over $1300 per person per year), fully furnished apartments. Many students escape both the bustle and the expense of on-campus life by renting apartments in the nearby Allston-Brighton area of Boston.

Right now, BC is changing at an almost frightening pace. Four new buildings (total price tag about $30 million) will be completed in the next four years. University planners hope that this physical expansion will help bring BC closer to its stated goal of becoming one of the country's truly fine universities. A new library will help to alleviate a currently severe lack of on-campus study space and should at the same time address BC's severe need for up-to-date resource materials. A new high-rise dormitory will add 800 beds to BC's housing stock before the end of the 1980–81 school year. A new parking garage will address the troublesome shortage of parking spaces. And, finally, a new theater will hopefully fill a major void by providing BC with a suitable place to hold dramatic performances and other cultural events. While the new buildings may increase BC's prestige, they will most certainly add much more concrete to a campus which is already slightly lacking in the grassy, open-space department.

Athletics are big at Boston College. A huge student sports complex, one that several colleges are now trying to duplicate, is used by a surprisingly large number of students. On the varsity front, BC football is struggling to make the big time, the hockey team is always tough, and the hoopsters more than hold their own.

Despite the individual activism of many BC students, apathy characterizes the student body as a whole. Recent large-scale protests over tuition increases, however, recall a flicker of the not-so-distant past.

BC students often complain that they are faced with a university which is run more like a sterile business than a spirited college. While there are definite weaknesses in how administrators interact with students (in general, they don't), and how well they react to student concerns, BC still manages to serve its students very well. The ever-increasing costs of these services, in the form of hefty increases in tuition, room, and board every year, mean that more and more of BC's students, particularly its noncommuting students, are being drawn from families of higher socioeconomic standing, and of late it seems that a certain homogeneity is settling in over large segments of the BC community. "Preppiness" is common but certainly not overwhelming. Minority students make up less than ten percent of the student body and overall are fairly isolated.

The most important thing to remember about BC is that it is a part of Boston, where the cultural and social resources are almost inexhaustible. With dozens of schools in the area, Boston is the best and most complete college town you're likely to find anywhere.

BOSTON UNIVERSITY

Location: Boston, MA 02215
Campus: city outskirts
Undergraduate enrollment:
  5600 M, 6500 W
Total enrollment: 25,528
Expenses: $7500
Financial aid: 40%
Library: 1,224,000 volumes

Student-faculty ratio: 15-1
Transfer students: 2500
Median SAT: 540 V, 570 M
Fraternities: NA
Sororities: NA
Application deadline:
  open

The initials BU stand for Boston University, not just "Big and Ugly" (even though the two concepts seem to be synonymous to some people). And, as the name implies, BU is in Boston—which, from the student's point of view, is one of the most habitable cities in the United States, that is, provided you are not forced to live in one of BU's worst dorms.

Boston University is a typical big urban university whose true character is as elusive as its campus, which is nonexistent. But it is privileged to have some notable neighbors; MIT, just across the Charles River from BU's dormitories and buildings; and Harvard, farther on the far side of the Charles, deep in the heart of Cambridge. At times, the stench of the polluted river or the cutting winter gales make these schools unreachable (except by MTA), but they are there.

The proximity of these colleges is a tremendous academic advantage but a social disaster, leading to many an inferiority complex, for the male BU student.

Harvard men (and MIT men, to a lesser extent), clothed in their prestige and housed in their supposedly superior intellect, are the bane of a BU man's existence, for they can be found everywhere exercising (usually arrogantly) whatever social prerogative they think they have—which, in Boston, may be considerable. But the situation is not as bad as it sounds, for there is definitely no shortage of the fair sex in Boston, at least during the time of year when schools are in session; in fact, there are at least five junior colleges within walking distance of BU. But, after all, it should not be necessary for a guy at BU to wander off, because BU itself offers a most abundant and varied selection of women. BU women, it goes without saying, have an equally large selection of men at their disposal.

In spite of the distractions of social life at the university and the life of the big city, BU is a place where you can seriously get down to the business of programmed and self-directed learning. Its political science and fine arts departments are particularly strong, offering rigorous professional instruction. BU is large enough to offer sound education in almost every field, from an African language to social work, but this academic mélange also makes BU a place where you can easily become as forgotten as an MTA schedule, and it is up to the individual to make himself seen or heard. One hazard that any academically inclined student will have to contend with is a poor library, which can be supplemented, but not supplanted, by the voluminous collections of Harvard's Widener Library and the Boston Public Library.

Dormitories are what everyone wants to get out of as soon as possible, but if you are an underclassman, good luck. Only recently, with the granting of dorm authority, has there been anything good to say about them. Both alcohol and drugs are fairly easy to come by, and as for the opposite sex—well, we've already mentioned that (we might add that, for those who aren't interested in such statistics, students at BU have started a homophile club). One last note—the food served in the dorms is horrible, but at least it is prepared and one does not have to go to the trouble of cooking and *then* finding out that the food is horrible.

BU's administration, led by president John Silber, has been making drastic moves lately. The emphasis is on economic austerity and academic conservativism. Although these tough policies are strongly supported by the board of trustees, and have resulted in higher numbers of applicants and a higher-quality student body, Silber's measures have encountered disruptive resistance on campus. Most students and many of the faculty members dislike the president and his policies.

No account of life at BU would be complete without a brief description of life in Boston, the home of baked beans, Paul Revere, school busing, and, of course, BC (not to be confused with BU). Not unlike most cities in this country, Boston is growing to the point of being suffocating. Every BU student has had the experience of being trampled by, or of trampling on, other people while commuting on the trolleys to and from school or circulating about the town. For one whose heart is with the serenity and cleanliness of the countryside, Boston is not the place to go; neither is it a place for those who like warm, windless, sunny weather. But if you are not too particular about the weather or the noise and smoky air, and you like traffic, you will love Boston. And Boston is what BU is all about.

BOWDOIN COLLEGE

Location: Brunswick, ME 04011
Campus: rural
Undergraduate enrollment:
  800 M, 500 W
Expenses: $7300
Financial aid: 35%
Library: 550,000 volumes

Student-faculty ratio: 12–1
Transfer students: 20
Median SAT: NA
Fraternities: 50%
Application deadline:
  February 1

Bowdoin College, located in the relative isolation of coastal Maine, continues to provide the finest in the small, liberal arts college experience. Though the size of the student body has increased by one-half over the past decade (without a similar increase in faculty numbers), the college still publicizes (rightly) small classes and concern for the individual.

The academic strengths lie in traditional disciplines—history, government, chemistry—and the tendency towards innovative courses has all but halted with the death of the "senior center program" and its accompanying seminars. An increasing number of students have enrolled in government and economics courses (the number of government majors has skyrocketed of late) causing severe overcrowding of these departments. A loose advisory system and the total absence of distribution requirements leave the student pretty much on his own when it comes to selecting courses. Academic programs can therefore be as tough or as easy as desired, but don't expect to float through four years "under the pines." There simply aren't that many guts to choose from.

Two distinctive features of Bowdoin academia are its four-point grading system (high honors, honors, pass, fail) and a widely-used credit/fail option. Academic pressure at Bowdoin can be intense, especially in the premed or prelaw programs.

Bowdoin's social life or lack thereof is a long-standing complaint among the student body and much of this problem stems from the college's backwoods locale. Brunswick is a typical Maine town—solidly middle-class—and is far from being the entertainment capital of North America. More and more students take advantage of Portland with its many restaurants, Civic Center, and revitalized waterfront district. Perhaps the greatest asset of Bowdoin's northerly location is that it places you within only three or four hours of some of the finest skiing in New England.

Most of the social activites on campus are centered around the ten fraternity houses. Though the frats once provided the major form of weekend entertainment in the form of campus-wide parties, usually consisting of numerous kegs and a live band, the recent change in Maine's drinking age (formerly eighteen, now twenty) has literally turned off the taps. Parties are now smaller and more subdued, occupying only two or three dorm rooms rather than an entire fraternity.

Despite the legislation from Augusta, hard drinking is still one of the favorite Bowdoin pastimes. Beer remains the favorite beverage, though hard liquor, particularly Jack Daniels, gains in popularity during the winter months. The drug scene is much the same as compared to other schools—pot is common and easily available, while cocaine has developed its own more limited following. On the whole, the decision is left to the student; peer pressure is minimal.

Since it is located in a cultural wasteland, Bowdoin attempts to offer its students a variety of lectures, films, dance, and theater. In particular, "the Russwurm Distinguished Lecture Series," sponsored by the Afro-American Society, has brought many excellent speakers to the campus. On weekends, students can choose from several movies and/or a play. Besides, Bowdoin offers a wide array of extracurricular options including publications, music, theater, and interfraternity sports. Although some complain of terminal boredom while awaiting the spring thaw, a little judicious searching can unearth something for almost everyone.

The one thing that keeps most students functional from December to March is not extracurriculars but "Polar Bear" hockey. A perennial Division II power, the hockey team fills Dayton Arena to capacity whenever it plays. Though Bowdoin has recently fielded strong squads in track, field hockey, lacrosse, and swimming, hockey remains by far and away the number one sport in Brunswick.

Because of the steep tuition and fees, Bowdoin is predominantly white, from New England and the Middle Atlantic states, and upper-middle class. There have been efforts to recruit more minority students but Bowdoin's location and the presence of only three black professors have been major drawbacks. Only twenty-seven blacks were enrolled at Bowdoin for the 1979–80 school year, comprising two percent of the student body.

Even with a deteriorating student-faculty ratio, a Bowdoin education is still well worth the high price tag. The college continues to do what it has always done—turn out well-educated, critical individuals. With just a little effort, four years at Bowdoin can be an enlightening and worthwhile experience.

BOWLING GREEN STATE UNIVERSITY

Location: Bowling Green, OH 43403
Campus: city outskirts
Undergraduate enrollment: 6950 M, 8800 W
Total enrollment: 15,886
Expenses: $2467 (in-state), $3754 (out-of-state)
Financial aid: 35%
Library: 622,385 volumes
Student-faculty ratio: 20–1
Transfer students: 525
Median SAT: 442 V, 489 M
Fraternities: 19%
Sororities: 13%
Application deadline: none

Bowling Green, simply put, is the all-American college, the sort of place where even the long-hair malcontents brush after every meal and hold the door open for teachers.

One of Ohio's many state schools, Bowling Green has a fairly good academic reputation in-state, even though most people outside of Ohio have never heard of it. This is easily explained: BG accepts only about six percent of the nonresident applicants each year. Perhaps they are afraid of corrupting their overwhelmingly middle-American, middle-of-the-road student body with the high-falutin' radicalism of the East or the carefree wildness of the West. Interestingly enough, most out-of-state infiltrators hail from New Jersey, which may say more about New Jersey than about Bowling Green.

Though located only twenty-three miles south of Toledo, Bowling Green definitely gives a quiet, isolated impression. Most students attend classes regularly and work conscientiously during the week. It seems many profs prefer short assignments to long, comprehensive studies. This makes for an easy spacing of work time, so that you're never too far behind in your courses. Besides, the quarter system, in which midterms and finals keep hitting you in the face every time you turn around, limits how far you can fall behind.

The largest school on campus is the school of business. The business degree is highly accredited and respected in the business world. The science department and honors seminars are reputed to be the good academic bets, along with a well-known speech and hearing therapy program.

Though half of the students live on campus, some take advantage of the easy traveling distance from hometowns like Cleveland, Columbus, and Toledo. It may seem strange to find such an overwhelming "suitcase school" psychology in a large university, but the fact is that most of the students do not take advantage of the entertainment and activities that are offered to them on weekends (and during the week).

There are over one hundred clubs and organizations for those interested.

Greek life is very prominent and there is a growing number of Christians on campus who join one of two national Christian organizations. The student government association is becoming more involved in the political aspects of the university and the community although they could use more student involvement and support rather than the usual bystander complaints. The Union Activities Organization is responsible for almost all activities on-campus. They program everything from small nonacademic courses and weekend/holiday trips, to major concerts such as Bob Seager, The Doobie Brothers, Jefferson Starship, Jackson Browne, and Chicago, to name a few (there's a wide range of musical taste on campus from disco to jazz to rock and roll). Bar hopping is also a weekend (and Thursday night) activity and drugs are easily available if you know the right people.

For those who enjoy sports, either as a spectator or participant, there are plenty of varsity leagues or intramurals to hold their interest. Football seems to have had its ups and downs over the past year, but the hockey team is nationally known, as they have ranked third and fifth among collegiate teams in the past few years.

In spite of its small-town atmosphere, Bowling Green is a big place. There is a 16,000 enrollment on the main campus, and there are also two-year correlative campuses in Bryan, Fostoria, Fremont, and Sandusky. The main campus itself is large, with lots of free space, but no rolling hills. The distance between dorms and classroom buildings is astounding. This wouldn't be such an inconvenience if the weather were a little more moderate. If there's no monsoon (BG is said to be the bulls-eye of the Midwest monsoon belt), it is either blistering hot or freezing cold.

The dorm rooms aren't what you'd call luxurious, but they are carpeted and each has a phone. Dorm living is a great way to get to know your neighbor, whether or not you want to, and it's a good experience in learning to live with others.

There are a few coed dorms on-campus which seem to be liked by those who reside within. There are also "the Towers," which are air-conditioned and occupied mostly by upperclassmen. The dorms fill up very quickly and in recent years this has pushed many students to off-campus living. The apartments and houses available to student rent are expensive, unkempt, and generally a hassle when it comes to landlords.

To sum it up, BG is a good place to spend four years of your life. Of course, it's not all fun and games socially; a lot of it is continual book grinding, but BG can provide memorable occasions to all who attend.

BRANDEIS UNIVERSITY

Location: Waltham, MA 02154
Campus: suburban
Undergraduate enrollment:
    1450 M, 1350 W
Total enrollment: 3,600
Expenses: $7,900
Financial aid: 46%
Library: 750,000 volumes

Student-faculty ratio: 9–1
Transfer students: 185
Median SAT: 590 V, 630 M
Fraternities: 0%
Sororities: 0%
Application deadline:
    February 1 for freshmen,
    April 1 for transfers

Brandeis has largely recovered from the fiscal difficulties that plagued it in the early Seventies. The number of faculty members is increasing, after several years of losses through firings and resignations, and the administration is once again paying attention to capital improvement of the campus. Nonetheless, some problems still remain.

One aspect of a university that rarely changes is its location, and Brandeis is blessed with one that is excellent: close enough to the attractions of the Boston area (there's a train stop right on campus), yet far from the problems of urban life. This isolation helps to create a world removed from mundane outside problems. Although this may be fine for most people, in such an atmosphere, personal crises such as exams and social relationships, not to mention which dining hall to select, get blown out of proportion. The campus itself is fairly safe (a shuttle van now runs at night) and attractive, with most buildings built so as to blend into the hilly terrain on which Brandeis sits.

The current rush to professional school is in full force at Brandeis. Close to forty percent of each entering class declares itself to be premed, although this number dwindles considerably by the time organic chem rolls around. About two-thirds of those who make it through the "med boards" and apply are accepted. A large percentage of Brandeis graduates also go on to law and business schools. In fact, the sole goal of many Brandeis students seems to be to get into one prestigious Eastern institution or another.

Brandeis's faculty is reputed to be the best in the nation at a university of this size. Professors are usually approachable. The departments of biochemistry, history, and Near-Eastern and Judaic studies are exceptional, and programs in the creative arts are strong. The politics and chemistry departments also have good reputations, but a lack of communication, and at times even hostility, between professors has kept these departments from reaching their full potential.

One advantage that Brandies has over some other schools is that virtually all classes, except for expository writing and some intro math courses, are taught by professors, not graduate students. Course offerings are varied, if not exotic (no "advanced Mongolian" at this school). There are distribution, expository writing, and language requirements, which are easily met, although the language requirement can take up to two years to fulfill if you're starting a language from scratch. A one-semester history requirement was recently instituted. The opportunities for independent study and research in a variety of fields are overwhelming.

Class sizes vary widely, from 250 or so for the intro psychology course (Psych has become Brandeis's most popular major) to ten or less for a seminar class. Competition for top grades is tough, but not cutthroat (even among premeds), although there is some cheating.

Freshmen are guaranteed on-campus housing. Upperclassmen who get low numbers in the housing lottery get to choose from a wide variety of living arrangements, from apartments to coed suites. However, there is a shortage of housing on campus, and many students have to look in Waltham or other nearby areas.

Contrary to popular belief, Brandeis is not made up solely of orthodox Jews, with a sprinkling of radical blacks to provide sociological interest. In fact, Brandeis has a fairly wide variety of students, with a surprisingly large number of foreign students.

Nevertheless, there is a kernel of truth to Brandeis' upper-middle-class suburban Jewish stereotype. A lot more people drive around in Firebirds and Camaros than is common among the general population. Seventy percent of the students come from just three states: New York, Massachusetts, and New Jersey, with an emphasis on areas like Scarsdale, Brookline, and the Five Towns. There are also significant contingents from California, Texas, Illinois, Florida, and increasingly, the English-speaking areas of Quebec. The student population, then, is somewhat homogeneous, and this tends to create an atmosphere that is static and stale.

While there are enough social activities on campus to keep students busy, many seek their entertainment in Boston or Cambridge. Brandeis has its own, erratic, FM station (sometimes you can pick it up and sometimes you can't). The student rag usually manages to get itself accused of slander or yellow journalism at least once a semester.

Brandeis students have liberal attitudes about sex and alcohol and tend to indulge in these vices to a healthy extent, although the recent raising of the state drinking age to twenty has made it a bit (but not much) harder for freshmen and sophomores to get smashed. Pot is easy to find, and is the hardest stuff most people use, although if you look hard enough, you can find all types of chemical stimulants.

Once nationally known as a hotbed of radicalism, Brandeis has cooled off somewhat in recent years. There is even a chapter of the College Republicans on campus now. This is not to say that activism is dead at Brandeis. The administration building was recently occupied by students for several days, making it the first such takeover at Brandeis in several years. Brandeis has become one of the centers of the antidraft movement, and there are political groups on campus working for causes as varied as divestment from corporations operating in South Africa and the overthrow of the U. S. government.

Still, Brandeis is not what it once was, academically, politically, or socially. The library is woefully inadequate for a school of Brandeis's repute and study space is at a premium, mainly because grinding is a favorite pastime. Many students do not seem to care about anything except which pair of designer jeans to wear and getting good grades in the least painful way. All in all, however, Brandeis has a long way to fall before it loses its solid reputation.

BRIGHAM YOUNG UNIVERSITY

Location: Provo, UT 84602
Campus: suburban
Undergraduate enrollment:
  12,000 M, 13,000 W
Expenses: $3000 (LDS),
  $3500 (non-LDS)
Financial aid: 50%
Library: 2,000,000 volumes

Student-faculty ratio: 23–1
Transfer students: 5000
Median ACT: 23.7
Fraternities: NA
Sororities: NA
Application deadline:
  April 30

It's hard to believe. Brigham Young is a large, coeducational institution where students voluntarily comply with dress and moral codes and don't smoke or drink. (Coffee and tea are not even served in the school's cafeterias and dining halls.) At Brigham Young, the national anthem is played twice daily, student devotional assemblies are held every other week, and the main topic of student discussion is religion as a way of life.

No, it's neither a military academy nor a seminary. Brigham Young is a real-life university owned and operated by the Church of Jesus Christ of Latter-Day Saints (known familiarly as the Mormons). Although the image of Mormons as pioneers in wagons trailing a string of twenty-seven wives across the plains is somewhat dated, Mormonism is not a liberal or progressive religion.

Upon hitting the main entrance to the campus, the BYU student can see written proof of the school's goals; a sign there reads: "Enter to learn, go forth to serve." Over ninety percent of the students are Mormons and the university wants them to be both good Mormons and good emissaries of the LDS church.

"Performance scheduling" is a program designed especially to spread the university's name (and beliefs) throughout the world. Nine performing groups (made up entirely of student volunteers) tour the country and the world to "promote good will." These tours are major events: the Young Ambassadors' 1978 European tour, for instance, attracted a live, radio, and TV audience of two hundred million people.

Brigham Young's academic program is tightly tailored to its religious status. All students are required to take religion classes. Theology and family living are popular courses of study and probably the best the school has to offer. Many of the other departments take a narrow and backward approach. Darwin has just barely affected zoology, and

Sartre is regarded as a danger in the literature and philosophy courses.

Campus life is not entirely austere. The school has its own symphony orchestra, one of the largest drama departments in the West, an international cinema, and a nationally renowned jazz group. Art displays, athletic events, symposia, and lectures are scheduled weekly. Much of the social life at BYU revolves around church-sponsored activities. Night life in Provo, Utah, is sorely limited; Salt Lake City, an hour away, is the hub of activity of the intermountain West, but it is still only slightly less provincial than Brigham Young. Women's dorm hours and relations between the sexes are governed by strictly enforced regulations.

To say that the student body is homogeneous is a vast understatement. A rule in the Mormon Church prohibits blacks from joining the priesthood, and despite recent recruiting efforts, there are very, very few blacks on campus. There is, however, an extensive educational program for American Indians. The school's missionary program (in collaboration with the LDS church) assures an international, if not varied, student body.

BYU also fields some of the best teams in the country in all major sports. Football and basketball are traditional powers, while other sports are conscientiously attended (like everything else here).

Located in the Rocky Mountains, the BYU campus is well situated for skiing, hiking, and camping. The school itself boasts excellent facilities for everything from milking cows to making movies to running track. The fact remains, though, that the decidedly unique moral flavor of Brigham Young would stick in most students' throats.

BROWN UNIVERSITY

Location: Providence, RI 02912
Campus: suburban
Undergraduate enrollment: 2838 M, 2312 W
Total enrollment: 6600
Expenses: $7800
Financial aid: 38%
Library: 2,800,000 volumes

Student-faculty ratio: 10–1
Transfer students: 50–100
Median SAT: M: 633 V, 671 M
W: 648 V, 644 M
Fraternities: 18%
Sororities: 0%
Application deadline: January 1

One thing about Brown, the school is about as popular as they come.

Applications have soared twenty-five percent in just three years, meaning that of 11,600 applications received in 1979, only 1290 students finished up at "Camp Bruno" in September. But most argue that the school is worth risking the heavy odds.

Brown is the least typical of the "ancient eight" in the Ivy League. Its innovative curriculum and startlingly relaxed atmosphere set it apart from the more stodgy elite institutions of the Northeast.

The word "university" is practically a misnomer when applied to Brown. Graduate studies are limited to a new medical school and various traditional graduate programs which barely survive from year to year. The big guns among faculty include Nobel laureate Leon Cooper, who commonly uses undergraduates as research assistants; Jacob Neusner, an Ungerleider Scholar who conducts an introductory course on Judaism; and Lyman Kirkpatrick, former executive director of the CIA. Professors are usually readily accessible.

Brown's "new curriculum," founded in 1969 and still its main application drawing-card, eliminated all distribution requirements and made the satisfactory/no-credit grading option available in all courses. In the midst of a national return to the structured "core" curriculum, Brown's faith in its students' responsibility for their own educations is a refreshing commitment.

But the academic freedoms don't mean Brown is easy. The work load is very demanding. So is the grading; Bs are relatively easy to come by, while As seem few and far between.

Brown's quest for academic excellence attracts students from all parts of the country and the world. But one thing all students seem to have in common is pre-professionalism. A little more than fifty percent of the graduates usually go directly into graduate schools; nearly eighty-five percent of those who apply to medical school get accepted, as are about ninety-five percent of those who apply to law school and one hundred percent of the business school applicants. Minorities are actively recruited (although just how actively has long been a subject of campus debate) and the students represent a balance of economic and cultural backgrounds.

Modes of social life are as varied at Brown as its student body. While some students (women and men) are active in fraternities and special interest groups, others find friendships informally in the course of everyday campus life. Nightly films at cut-rate prices and trips to nearby Newport and Boston are among the more popular forms of entertainment.

Extracurricular activities give undergraduates the opportunity to make friends and influence people. The FM radio station, winner of national awards for both its news coverage and music selection, is among the most popular in New England. The daily newspaper (Brown is reputed to be the smallest university in the country with a daily paper) is good, with lots of opportunities for talented writers. *Fresh Fruit Magazine*, a feature weekly, has a readership of 50,000 throughout Rhode Island. Brown's many theatrical and musical organizations are flourishing, especially after the 1979 opening of a new multimillion dollar performing arts complex. The university chorus was the first college performing group in the nation to be invited in the People's Republic of China.

Providence, the capital of Rhode Island, provides interested Brown students with unlimited opportunities in the government and media. Brown's immediate surroundings are placid, and the school is within easy walking distance of downtown. The university is surrounded by intriguing restaurants, shops, and bookstores. The campus rests among some of the best-preserved examples of colonial and Georgian architecture to be found anywhere in the country.

With the inauguration of Howard Swearer as the fifteenth president in its two-hundred-years-plus history, Brown has entered a phase of guarded optimism regarding its financial status. In past years, budget cutbacks resulted in repeated clashes between students and administration. The worst of the retrenchment is now over.

Sports are both a weekday and weekend activity at Brown. Thanks to some energetic recruiting, the football team moved from the gutter to annual contender for the Ivy crown in just a few years. The hockey, soccer, and lacrosse teams are all national powers. Women participate in a fully developed intercollegiate program. Intramural and instructional athletics abound.

Despite their outwardly casual appearance, Brown students live intensely. With a glazed eye always toward the future, they study vigorously, party ruthlessly, and protest actively. For those who can stand the pace, Brown will let you explore the limits of your capabilities.

BRYN MAWR COLLEGE

Location: Bryn Mawr, PA 19010
Campus: suburban
Undergraduate enrollment: 1000 W

Student-faculty ratio: 8–1
Transfer students: 30
Median SAT: 680 V, 650 M
Sororities: NA

Total enrollment: 1600
Expenses: $8000
Financial aid: 42%
Library: 500,000 volumes

Application deadline:
January 15

Bryn Mawr College has a beautiful Gothic campus tucked away on Philadelphia's suburban "Main Line," with easy access both to the city and Haverford College, with which Bryn Mawr is now fully coordinated.

The picture is of an ideal women's college—fashionably located, pretty, and with a full exchange of courses and social life with one of the best small, predominantly male colleges around. Just one salient fact has been left out of the picture: Bryn Mawr is also the most rigorous women's college in the United States. Nearly three-quarters of its alumnae go on to advanced work, and even in their undergraduate days "Bryn Mawrters" are unregenerate grinds, and brilliant to boot.

Bryn Mawr has a distinguished and tough faculty, including some of the nation's finest scholars (especially in the humanities); some even like to teach, while others are learning how, slowly. The teachers are as rigorous with their students as with themselves, demanding not only a huge quantity of work but genuine quality as well. The divisional requirements are stiff—for example, you have to get through a year-long introductory science course, and there are no special courses for nonmajors. If you don't pass a science course—or any other distributional requirement, for that matter—then you have to take another, plus an additional course to make up the lost credit.

The campus is breathtakingly lovely—trees, grass, brooks, ducks, more squirrels than you can count, birds, and lots of wide open space. The architecture, with the exception of Louis Kahn's Erdman Hall, the science buildings, the library, and I. W. Coburn's language complex, is medieval Gothic. The whole thing looks like Merrie England in the time of Arthur, and you'd never guess that the Paoli "local" to Philly is a five-minute walk away.

Moreover, life at Bryn Mawr is as congenial as it is cozy. The dorms are sent up to match English undergraduate colleges, and each houses members of all four classes, plus grad student wardens who function more as big sisters (and brothers, in the coed dorms) than as supervisors. The rooms are generally large singles (some two-roomers for seniors), even larger doubles, and a fair number of two-person suites with living rooms.

Because of the residence exchange with Haverford, four of the dorms at Bryn Mawr, including the language house, are coed. They are coed by room, not by floor, and the bathrooms are used by both sexes, a fact which sometimes causes great consternation among outsiders, but which students accept without a second thought. After her first semester, a "Bryn Mawrter" may live at Haverford; in the past between 150 and 185 students from each school have participated each year in the room exchange.

Through the exchange, "Bryn Mawrters" now have direct access to the Haverford Park Apartments, which come with kitchens, living rooms, and bedrooms, and offer students an opportunity to escape the meal plan, yet remain close to the Haverford campus. Other students may also live off-campus, either in college-owned housing, or in apartments they have found on their own. "Main Line" housing is expensive, however, and students must "draw" into the number of allotted off-campus spaces each year.

The only sterotypes drawn at Bryn Mawr (and they are not always accurate) are based on the dorms. Single-sex residents are considered more industrious, and those living in coed dorms more gregarious. Although not all students identify themselves as purely single-sex or coed women, the campus has been split during room draw time for the past few years over which dorms will be coed. Students of each inclination try to make the other group feel it has no place being at Bryn Mawr; this is perhaps a natural occurance at a college which lures its applicants with the "best of both worlds."

Part of the disputes have concerned keeping one of the college's four dining halls in a single-sex dorm, yet such discussion may soon be moot as Bryn Mawr is in the initial stages of planning for a "campus center" that will consolidate dining. The center is also expected to give the college large meeting rooms, squash courts, improved tennis facilities, and a regulation-sized pool. Current athletic facilities are substandard, despite an ever-increasing interest in women's athletics and a two-year physical education requirement. The tennis courts are in disrepair, the lacrosse field is not regulation size (like the pool), and students wishing to run must use Haverford's track.

Politics at Bryn Mawr finds occasional enthusiasts, and the socialist group (joint with Haverford, of course) is small but vocal. Recent concerns have included investment policy, ERA extension (200-plus "Mawrters" rallied in Washington in September), reinstitution of the draft, nuclear energy, and racism at Haverford.

In many ways, feminism is inherent in the Bryn Mawr mood: equality of women in the academic professions was what the college was once all about. Yet many students feel that the college, without a major or even a concentration in women's studies, and with often minimal professional school application assistance, is not meeting the needs of women in a changing world. Yet the small-but-vocal women's alliance sponsored a very well-attended conference on women's studies last fall, and some faculty are interested in women's issues outside of academia.

A Bryn Mawr woman's prime trait is a determined (and even cussed) individualism. BMC doesn't even want the groupiness of a *Phi Beta Kappa* chapter, so, paradoxically, at this brilliant school there is none.

Yet BMC's cussed individualism doesn't exist within a vacuum. Bryn Mawr and Haverford may be two of the most socially tolerant schools around: every viewpoint and life-style is respected, if only enough to permit its continuation. Part of this reflects the honor codes, separate at each school, but social as well as academic at both. The codes inspire respect for others and sincere sharing of values—along with academic integrity.

Not all is rosy at Bryn Mawr: relationships between students and faculty could be better, if only more human. Most of the faculty live off-campus, and keep a low profile in college life. The administration, too, is not always as receptive as it should be at a college of 1000. It's fortunate that "Bryn Mawrters" do not prefer the hallowed MRS. to the J. D., M. D., M. B. A, and most importantly, Ph.D., for the faculty requires "a lot of rather pointless seriousness invested in the wrong places," according to a past coeditor of *The Bryn Mawr-Haverford News*. They're really not unreceptive—they'd like to reach their students, but they're often not sure how; thus, with some work, valuable and rewarding contacts can be made.

However, the faculty believes in devout, nonstop scholarship, and often induces the guilt that raises a paper to the level of a sword of Damocles—which may not always be good in the long run. So, the general atmosphere at Bryn Mawr is one of working hard all week and most of the weekend, with perhaps—if you're lucky—a Saturday night breather to smoke pot, play bridge, or see a film. And there's plenty of discussion on Kant's *Critique*, or metaphor in Milton, for those interested. There are also traditions: May Day, Lantern Night, class shows, and so on, which provide a link to the past, and are a whole lot of fun.

The most popular departments are classics (particularly the internationally known classical archaeology department), English and art history, with growing interest in the natural sciences and economics. But even the poor departments are complemented by Haverford's (read that entry, too!) and given complete cross-majoring, "Bryn Mawrters" can take any course there without a hassle. And cooperation, as it's called, is here to stay, even though Haverford began admitting freshwomen in the fall of 1980.

Part of the reason is that, in an attempt to eradicate its annual deficit, Bryn Mawr eliminated majors in music and religion; as a result, while interested students must take some courses at Bryn Mawr, they must major at Haverford. Haverford also has majors in fine arts and astronomy, while Bryn Mawr compensates with archaelogy, art history, geology, and urban studies. In case you're wondering about the logistics of cooperation, a "blue (school) bus" runs once each half-hour, each way, during the week, and a smaller, "social bus" runs less frequently on weekends.

Bryn Mawr isn't easy to enter—admissions demands are rigorous. Scholarship money no longer flows as it used to. Once a student is awarded a scholarship, she can feel secure about the next four years, but because the financial aid and admissions offices work separately, many women who are accepted cannot afford to come. Not everyone at Bryn Mawr is a rich preppie with great social connections, but many are. Except for the pressures surrounding its very academic emphasis, the college can be virtually ideal. So consider Bryn Mawr if you're looking for an education—and for a just-forming network of alumnae ready and willing to help you when you're done with your honors thesis in art history. Scholars who don't need the petty assurance of a *Phi Beta Kappa* key can't be faulted in anyone's book, and a Bryn Mawr degree can take you far.

BUCKNELL UNIVERSITY

Location: Lewisburg, PA 17837
Campus: rural
Undergraduate enrollment:
   1600 M, 1400 W
Total enrollment: 3200
Expenses: $6550
Financial aid: 22%
Library: 425,000 volumes

Student-faculty ratio: 14–1
Transfer students: 55–70
Median SAT: 560 V, 630 M
Fraternities: 55%
Sororities: 45%
Application deadline:
   January 1

If you are white, middle-class, professionally and career-oriented, smart, but not particularly interesting or dynamic, then Bucknell is the school for you. Congratulations! You'll have a fine four years here and remember them as the best of your life.

Bucknell is more or less a professional, Establishment school for nice kids from nice families who will do almost anything to land a job with a good company and precious little to do anything else of value. Bucknellians are bright, quick and capable, but on the whole not particularly interested in the finer aspects of life. Go to school, drink lots of beer, and get a job. That's Bucknell.

If you come to Bucknell as part of the active, thinking minority (someone who might stand up in a crowded room and speak out against injustice, for example) be warned that the conservative, limited student body specializes in groupthink and demands conformity. It tends to isolate individualists and independent personalities.

Social life goes along the same lines.

Parties consist mostly of mobbed fraternity affairs (this year over seventy percent of the freshmen men joined fraternities) and doing as much damage to the brain cells as possible. Beer and pot top the list of favorite controlled substances (remember the Pennsylvania drinking age is twenty-one). Cocaine and various forms of speed are next in order of appreciation.

Even some of the most gung-ho "animal house" types admit they are a little bored of the same old frat parties, but that's just about all there is in the Central Susquehanna Valley, except for a flashy new disco called the Great Green Frog that opened last year in nearby Milton (home of Chef Boy-Ar-Dee).

Sex? Well, the stereotype goes that a Bucknell girl thinks anything more than a goodnight kiss is kinky. And most of the time that seems pretty much to be the case. But the student sex information group claims the yearly abortion rate is up in the hundreds. Neither of these extremes is particularly close to the truth, in all likelihood. But don't go looking to Bucknell for a few years of passionate nights in bed, unless you plan on spending them alone.

Moving around to the academic side, students in the sciences, and business and engineering majors work themselves into a frenzy of academic pressure. They work hard and are typically rewarded with good jobs. Liberal arts majors can get by quite nicely with practically no work. The faculty is dedicated and brilliant, but largely wasted on students who don't care.

Bucknell engineering is associated nationwide with prestige, and lots of it. Several psychology professors have national reputations for their work, although it appears that some of the most well known may be seeking positions elsewhere. Biology is also strong.

Michael Payne is probably the school's most loved teacher, known for his popular English course on Shakespeare. He interprets "the Bard" with a touch of historical relevance in addition to literary and psychological aspects, earning the deep respect of almost all his students.

History's favorite is Britain specialist Mark Neuman. His classes and seminars take students far beyond the feared rote of chronological events and enter subtle and revealing aspects of England's culture, society, literature, and people. Neuman's Victorian and Edwardian offerings are particularly rewarding.

The faculty recently approved a new international relations major, which promises to rise quickly to the forefront of education at Bucknell. This program features the juvenile antics of Tom Travis, who manages to convince his students that he is brilliant. A semester's work with Travis should prove to be highly entertaining as well as informative.

Most of the other departments are satisfactory to excellent. Sociology is badly in need of some strong professors and English professors should be chosen with care. (There is said to be a lot of tenured dead weight over in the English wing.) The business department is in shambles, due to a high rate of professor turnover and dissatisfaction.

The main problem at Bucknell is lack of student diversity. The admissions department clearly strives to pick the Bucknell brand of student and so robs each enrolling class of one of the most important aspects of college life: getting to know different types of people.

Some members of the college community go so far as to state that admissions policies discriminate against certain minority groups. But recent studies indicate that people who see the Bucknell stereotype, and realize that they don't fit it, simply choose another school.

Lewisburg's somewhat backward rural atmosphere may be refreshing to urban or suburban freshmen, but the glow of wholesome countryside soons wears off when they realize that they are noplace—in the middle of nowhere. The town offers a movie theater, a car wash, and the campus bowling alley and bar—locally known as Dunkle's. Penn State is the only notable school nearby, one hour to the west.

One of Bucknell's outstanding qualities is its campus. The nickname "Country Club on the Susquehanna" is not unearned. The Georgian buildings and perfect grounds are kept in top condition.

A multi-million dollar field house is the latest addition to campus facilities. Indoor tennis, jogging, racquetball, and other sports are available here. But faculty members and the more astute students notice that Bucknell decided it needed a new gym before a life-sciences building, a theater, or a music and arts center. Of course. Beer before wine. Indeed, beer before food. Bucknell.

BUTLER UNIVERSITY

Location: Indianapolis, IN 46208
Campus: suburban
Undergraduate enrollment:
   950 M, 1150 W
Total Enrollment: 3852
Expenses: $5000
Financial aid: 80%
Library: 190,000 volumes

Student-faculty ratio: 15–1
Transfer students: 150
Median SAT: 513 V, 542 M
Fraternities: 46%
Sororities: 46%
Application deadline:
   August 15

Butler University is located in Indianapolis, Indiana, a few miles from the famous racetrack. Yet its quiet little campus lives up to Indianapolis's reputation as the site of one of the world's most glamorous, most dangerous, most exciting events of all kinds. There are no A. J. Foyts or Mario Andrettis at Butler, and there probably never will be anyone else who is exciting.

Butler is located in the heart of Butler-Tarkington, a widely hailed triumph of integration and nomenclature. But you wouldn't know it to look at the lily-white complexion of Butler students. One student tells us that Butler is a "small, 99.9 percent pure, private institution," and to judge by the middle-class virtues of his colleagues, we would have to agree.

The campus itself covers 286 acres and is bounded on the west and north by the Indianapolis Water Company canal (which keeps the trees flourishing) and the Hinkle Fieldhouse (which keeps the jocks flourishing). Butler's neighborhood is also the site of a former park—Fairvew—which explains the beautifully landscaped gardens that are within walking distance of the school. The buildings are a mixture of architectural types, and Clowes Hall, which is said to resemble Schubert's "Unfinished Symphony" in granite and concrete, serves as the cultural center for Indianapolis.

Academically, Butler offers a mixed bag. Some students claim that the student-to-faculty ratio is higher than the school figures, but this has not been proven. Classes are fairly decent in size, especially if you happen to find an unpopular professor—everyone transfers out.

Butler's pharmacy college is ranked third in the United States. The drama and music departments are also highly regarded and they have brought Butler some acclaim with their annual Romantic Festival. The religion department, on the other hand, boasts a strictly fundamentalist point of view; it still thinks that Roman Catholicism is a little too liberal.

Drugs, mainly marijuana, were once unheard of on the Butler campus, but the Seventies have caught up with the students there. Needless to say, beer is still more popular. Butler's rules and regulations have been a long time in changing, but Butler has come a long way since chaperones were required at parties.

Fraternities and sororities attract a large number of men and women; over forty percent of each. That's only natural considering Butler's traditional leanings. Besides, students under twenty-one are required to live on campus (the reason is unclear).

On occasion, the student assembly has even dared to oppose the university president and board of trustees.

But it is characteristic of Butler that nothing came of it.

CALIFORNIA INSTITUTE OF TECHNOLOGY

Location: Pasadena, CA 91125
Campus: suburban
Undergraduate enrollment: 700 M, 125 W
Total enrollment: 1650
Expenses: $7800
Financial aid: 72%
Library: 350,000 volumes
Student-faculty ratio: 3.5–1
Transfer students: 30
Median SAT: 690 V, 760 M
Fraternities: 0%
Sororities: 0%
Application deadline: January 15

A popular saying at Caltech is that learning at Tech (as it is universally referred to there) is like drinking from a fire hose. This accurately reflects the fact that Caltech has one of the most demanding programs of study in the country.

The list of Caltech faculty is impressive. From Nobel laureates Richard Feynman, Murray Gell-Mann, and Max Delbruck, to Mariner TV innovator Robert Leighton and noted Africa expert Edwin Munger, Caltech abounds with creative, top-notch scholars. The faculty is chosen mainly for its research ability, and although it often seems as if they are more concerned with their research than with their students, Caltech students tell us that they generally do an adequate job of teaching.

At Caltech, classwork does not stop when the student walks out of class. One unit is equal to one hour of work spent on the class each week in some way, and many students take as many as sixty-six units each term. Most Caltech students are intensely dedicated to their academics and spend a great deal of time helping each other with their studies. Although the pressure is high, there is little of the cutthroat competition characteristic of schools of this caliber. However, because Caltech students are required to take heavier loads than students at most other colleges, the school is not a place for someone unwilling to work.

Students list two things responsible for Caltech's standing as one of the best math and science schools in the country: its small size and its opportunities for research. With only a moderate amount of initiative, even a freshman can become involved in a research group in almost any field. Students who choose otherwise often find they've missed out on the best that Tech has to offer.

The literature sent out to prospective applicants notwithstanding, Caltech is still unable to offer a very well-balanced education. Despite recent major efforts at development, the divison of humanities and social sciences is too small to offer a variety of classes. However, Caltech's innovative social science program is being watched with interest by some of the leading universities around the country. About a quarter of the classes a Caltech student takes are required to be in the humanities and social sciences division. Few students major in this division, though, and more than three times as many students exercise their pass/fail option (limited to one course per term) in nonscience courses as compared to science or engineering courses.

Probably the worst aspect of life at Caltech is the social environment. Although not all students are "boy wonders" with slide rules who hole up in their rooms all day, the breed does exist in significant numbers. Most of them take occasional breaks from the drudgery of studying, usually by participating in semiorganized activities in the student houses. (Student houses are a cross between dorms and fraternities.) Students show fierce loyalty to their houses, and are known for their penchant for pranks, usually pulled off by the members of a single house. However, social life at Caltech does not come easily. One has to work for it. It can safely be said that those who are shy and asocial when they enter leave the same way.

Nearly one-third of the undergraduate population lives off-campus, as students increasingly discover that living that way is cheaper, quieter, and a good escape from the notoriously bad college food. Options include joining one of the several student-run co-ops, living in nearby apartments, and commuting from home.

Unfortunately for its students, Caltech is located in the middle of Pasadena, a city that closes at five P.M. However, with a car—a highly recommended amenity—one can take advantage of the myriad social activities available in the greater Los Angeles area.

The Caltech student body organization, ASCIT, is completely independent of the institute, as are all of the student publications. Interest in student affairs is usually meager, and there are many opportunities for advancement in the student body hierarchy.

ASCIT has one of the most successful relationships with administration and faculty of any college in the country. This is typical of the openness of the Caltech administration. The administration is composed largely of faculty members, so red tape is minimal and administrators are usually accessible. Because there are student representatives on all but one faculty committee, students have more of a voice in institute affairs than at most other universities.

One of the most remarkable facets of Caltech life is the honor system, which states simply that "no member of the Caltech community shall take advantage of any other member." The system is run entirely by students, although it also extends to the faculty. Students are intensely serious about the honor code, and it works. Take-home exams are universal, and no one worries about leaving doors unlocked.

Given the peculiar nature of the school, it is not surprising that Caltech has a high transfer rate out. Nearly thirty percent of each entering class leaves in search of a slower-paced or more diversified program. If you're not already set on science as a career, Caltech is best moved down on your list of prospective colleges, for this is no place to weather an identity crisis. But if you are truly interested in science (and have 800-type math achievement scores to prove it), the school can provide some unique opportunities.

CALIFORNIA STATE UNIVERSITY AND COLLEGE SYSTEM

LOCATIONS:
  BAKERSFIELD
  CHICO
  DOMINGUEZ HILLS
  LOS ANGELES
  SACRAMENTO
  SAN BERNADINO
  SAN DIEGO

FRESNO	SAN FERNANDO
FULLERTON	SAN FRANCISCO
HAYWARD	SAN JOSE
HUMBOLDT	SAN LUIS OBISPO
KELLOG-VOORHIS	SONOMA
LONG BEACH	STANISLAUS

(Check with specific locations for more details.)

The California State College system, consisting of nineteen campuses located throughout the state, allows students to attend four-year colleges while remaining in their home areas. For the California student who is concerned with the financial aspects of attending college and who does not mind living at or near home, the state colleges offer an economical solution without necessitating a transfer from a two-year junior college. Even for an out-of-stater, expenses at a California state college need not be exorbitant, and they can provide the opportunity to spend four years on the West Coast—an opportunity which might not be available any other way.

The Cal State colleges do suffer from an illness which plagues many schools today; a desperate shortage of money. Some of the schools don't have dormitories, and the libraries, although fairly large in absolute terms, are less than adequate in view of the number of students they must serve.

Not surprisingly, the nineteen colleges in the system offer a broad variety of academic and social environments. One can choose between the rural boondocks of San Luis Obispo or the smoggy urban sprawl of Cal State/Los Angeles. San Diego State, with its proximity to the finest surfing beaches east of Hawaii, is regarded as one of the top five party schools in the country and is an inviting target for out-of-staters seeking four years of fun in the sun at its best. Long Beach State is best known for its huge size, good art department, and not-quite-as-good-as-UCLA's basketball team. Hayward is renowned for its philosophy courses, while San Francisco draws the nod as the best known of the Cal system schools. Two lesser-known schools, Sonoma and Humboldt State, are emerging as popular transfer havens for in-state students dissatisfied with their own schools. Both are good academically, with Sonoma nestled in the Napa-Sonoma-Mendocino wine country and Humboldt offering a chance for outdoor types to explore the Redwood region.

On the following pages are descriptions of Long Beach State, San Francisco State, and San Jose State, three of the system's better-known schools.

CALIFORNIA STATE UNIVERSITY/LONG BEACH

Location: Long Beach, CA 90840
Campus: suburban
Undergraduate enrollment:
  11,419 M, 12,371 W
Total enrollment: 30,877
Expenses: $2200 (in-state),
  $3900 (out-of-state)
Financial aid: 30%
Library: 701,578 volumes

Student-faculty ratio: 18-1
Transfer students: 5000
Median SAT: 400 V, 400 M
Median ACT: 18
Fraternities: NA
Sororities: NA
Application deadline:
  December 1

If you are twenty-six, married, and plan on commuting to school, you would fit the CSULB student profile very well. The school attracts many students who are employed full-time and have returned to complete unfinished degrees or to earn additional credits. About forty percent of the students are married, and most commute to the campus from home. Those who choose to live at the university must take advantage of the small system of on- and off-campus dormitories. The waiting line to get in is long.

There is not much that would recommend CSULB over many other schools, except perhaps its cost and location. *Changing Times* magazine rated this large university one of sixty-four "good colleges at bargain prices" in the country. The campus is only five minutes from the ocean. Many students take advantage of the location on warm, sunny days to break the tedium of schoolwork with cool waves and UV rays.

The city of Long Beach is situated in a particularly conservative area of California, but the student body is generally liberal. Interest in student politics is negligible; only about ten percent of students vote in student government elections.

Although CSULB is a commuter school, there is a good deal of social activity. The on-campus beer-and-pizza eatery, the Nugget, services many students who drop in for a quick brew or the live music on Friday afternoon. *Genesis* magazine dubbed the university the "horniest" campus in America and said that freewheeling sexual activities of every type are rampant. You might take this characterization with a grain of salt, though, since many students on campus took the survey lightly themselves, and they should know. The Greek system, while active, attracts only a small number of students. Their facilities are adequate but compare poorly with those at other universities.

CSULB boasts good teams in basketball, track, and swimming, and football is on the rise. However, the athletic department has been criticized for shortchanging the minor sports and women's athletics.

Despite the size of the university, student-faculty relationships develop easily. They are generally cordial, and professors are always happy to give advice and talk.

CSULB only gained its university status in 1972, but it is doing well for such a large school. If you live nearby and are considering it for college, you could do worse.

CALIFORNIA STATE UNIVERSITY/SAN FRANCISCO

Location: San Francisco, CA 94132
Campus: city outskirts
Undergraduate enrollment: 5500 M, 5800 W
Total enrollment: NA
Expenses: $1800 (in-state), $3000 (out-of-state)
Financial aid: NA
Library: 500,000 volumes

Student-faculty ratio: 15–1
Transfer students: 5000
Median SAT: 535 V, 525 M
Median ACT: 22
Fraternities: 0%
Sororities: 0%
Application deadline: November 30

In recent years, San Francisco has specialized in teaching chaos as a fine art. Even before the presidency of S. I. Hayakawa, the highly progressive campus was marked by confusion. During the reign of Hayakawa (who resigned about seven years ago and is now a U. S. senator), the confusion became institutionalized. Depending on how you look at it, this can mean utter disaster or stimulating freedom. SF State continues to attract the kind of faculty and students that make it an exciting place—and we think it remains the best of the California State College system.

Students are extremely liberal but peace-loving. With visions of busted heads still carrying over from the demonstrations of the Sixties, the campus has quieted down. As one student said, "Students are very discouraged. During the Sixties, they were active and mobilized. Now it's gone." The only real source of campus controversy now is the student government, a half-million-dollar corporation that loosens its purse strings often and without much thought. Though less than ten percent of the student body usually participates in campus elections, griping about the way each student's $20 fee is spent is more audible than ever.

The students come from widely diverse backgrounds, but most are not from wealthy families. Many are considerably older than the average college student (average age here is twenty-five). Many blacks, foreigners, Vietnam vets, and older working people (the latter usually attend night classes) come together at SF State. The one thing that most have in common is that they work; the school is only a part of their lives, unlike most students for whom college is their life.

SF has a solid academic image; it generally draws the B-average high school student. Although very few of the students are career-oriented, they usually maintain a self-motivated interest in studies. The driving competition of the top name colleges is not a problem here. If anything, the opposite problem—an overly unacademic approach—sometimes crops up at SF State.

The school's "meaningful discussion seminars" can be transformed into "pooled ignorance" quite easily.

SF State tends to attract young, enthusiastic instructors who do not face a "publish-or-perish" ultimatum. Consequently, they are eager to teach, which can make all the difference in the world. Sometimes they bend over backward to prove they are "progressive educators," which can lead to open-minded bull sessions or "specialized topics appealing to the contemporary interests" (e.g., courses in the occult or in vampires in literature). However, the SF State faculty does welcome unbridled student initiative, and the serious student can often learn best in this environment. Arts, English, and literature are SF State's best departments, with an abundance of special courses for the aspiring writer, painter, or jazz musician. The largest department, though, is business.

The campus itself, located in an upper-middle-class residential area, is compact and easy to get around in. It is not within walking distance of downtown, North Beach, Haight-Ashbury, or any place where it's happening (or used to happen). Buses and trolleys are handy, and there's a large pay parking lot on campus. There is very little on-campus housing, and most students must scramble for the exceedingly expensive city apartments.

A new student could well be disappointed by the unstructured social life at SF. Because most people are into individualized interests, there's scarcely any school cohesion, no "rah-rah" togetherness, and little extra-academic rapping. Weekends on campus are dead, but administrators have tried to promote some two-bit flick nights for those who do live on campus. Of course, with any effort at all, you shouldn't be bored in San Francisco, a city full of avant-garde cultural treats as well as the usual big city entertainments.

CALIFORNIA STATE UNIVERSITY/SAN JOSE

Location: San Jose, CA 95192
Campus: city center
Undergraduate enrollment:
 7400 M, 7100 W
Total enrollment: 26,950
Expenses: $2900 (in-state),
 $4800 (out-of-state)
Financial aid: 21%
Library: 700,000 volumes

Student-faculty ratio: 18–1
Transfer students: 4517
Median SAT: NA
Fraternities: 1%
Sororities: 1%
Application deadline:
 until quota is filled

Transferring from one university to another, once relatively uncommon, has become acceptable among the "try it, you'll like it" crowd. San Jose State, with beautiful weather and a party school reputation, has been one of the nation's most popular sanctuaries for the university nomads and freshmen as well. Upwards of 5000 transfer students try their luck here annually; few are disappointed.

Riding the crest of enrollment increases, San Jose has become the second largest school in the California State University system, surpassed only by Los Angeles State. San Jose's modern campus, an easygoing place for both fun and learning, is a far cry from the original teacher's college which was constructed way back in 1857. Although smoggier than San Francisco (located fifty miles to the north), San Jose is a few degrees warmer and still gets moderating breezes from the ocean most of the time.

The college is large enough to accommodate the social and academic desires of most students, but the number of scholastic offerings has taken a slight nose-dive recently (not necessarily to the chagrin of the student body). Diversity reigns; there are a goodly number of hippies and radicals in addition to many jocks, partygoers, and plain old clean-cut American kids.

Fraternities are unimportant, as the bountiful entertainment opportunities available both locally and in nearby San Francisco make the social security of group society unnessecary. There is always something to do no matter what your pleasure is: football games, films, gourmet food, beaches, or museums. And it's easy to meet members of the opposite sex. The SJS dorm system does not impede the search for companionship in the least; the dorms are all coed with practically zero restrictions.

Unfortunately, good teachers are becoming scarce at the San Jose campus, according to some student sources. New students, both freshmen and transfers, might do well to check out *The Tower List,* a student guide aimed at evaluating instructors. In general, steer clear of the profs who have the proclivity to read the same lectures year after year with a minimal interest in enhancing the learning experience. The SJS art department remains one of the best in the state. Another "best" is the journalism lab paper, the *Spartan Daily.*

San Jose's strong Chicano population plays a major role in student politics, and women's voices have also been consistently making themselves heard in the past few years. The town of San Jose has even constructed a women's center on the campus, and the student council recently allocated money for a university birth control clinic.

San Jose State is definitely a fun place to go to school. And with luck, you might pick up an education on the side.

THE UNIVERSITY OF CALIFORNIA SYSTEM

The University of California has alternately been described as monolithic, fragmented, bureaucratic, and creative. It is all of these things, yet only a few generalizations fit the eight undergraduate campuses; Berkeley, UCLA, Santa Cruz, Santa Barbara, Irvine, Riverside, San Diego, and Davis all have their separate identities. All of them, however, have been subject to severe budget cuts which have crippled a number of worthwhile programs. The Cal system has been referred to as "the house that Reagan wrecked," and Jerry Brown's austerity program has not helped the schools. All too often the good people of California have been trying to eliminate the campuses themselves. Although bloodbaths have been infrequent in recent years, don't say we didn't warn you if the repression changes from fiscal to physical again.

From metropolitan UCLA to bucolic Santa Cruz (located in a national park), from party-school San Diego to world-famous Berkeley, the eight schools provide everything for everybody. For surfing, there's San Diego or Irvine. For wine tasting, Davis has a 100,000-bottle cellar. For basketball fans, UCLA has the best tradition in the country. For premeds, there's Riverside. Finally, partying is rampant at all eight, but Santa Barbara may be the one which sets the norm. So if you're from California, you need go no further.

Individual reviews of the eight campuses follow.

UNIVERSITY OF CALIFORNIA/BERKELEY

Location: Berkeley, CA 94720
Campus: suburban
Undergraduate enrollment:
    12,000 M, 8000 W
Total enrollment: 30,000
Expenses: $4514 (in-state),
    $6914 (out-of-state)
Financial aid: 10%
Library: 5,500,000 volumes

Student-faculty ratio: 18-1
Transfer students: 2200
Median SAT: NA
Fraternities: 10%
Sororities: 10%
Application deadline:
    November 30

Everybody in California assumed that when Ronald Reagan left office, the days of Berkeley's academic deterioration would be over. No one could conceive that the university's budget would get tighter than it was under Reagan. It couldn't help but get better.

Nobody had reckoned on Jerry Brown, Jr., though. Brown succeeded in giving the university its smallest budget increase in history: a mere four percent. Department cuts were necessary to fit the new budget.

Berkeley is not what it was ten years ago. To be sure, radical groups still set up their tables in Sproul Plaza, rallies for various causes are held not infrequently, and surveys show that the average Berkeley student is still more liberal than his or her national counterpart.

But the mass demonstrations are gone, at least temporarily, and skyrocketing library attendance and lab use figures indicate students are concentrating more on finding their respective niches (hopefully well-paying niches), which Plato assures them are there if they can only find them.

If one must find one's niche, Berkeley is a good place to do it. The university offers a vast selection of courses, and groups and organizations of every type abound. Moreover, the campus community is not isolated from the rest of the city as is the case at many schools. Much interaction between students and "citizens" exists, both politically and socially. For this reason, the environment is not as strictly academic as at some schools. (It is not yet, however, the "real world." For that, one must travel down to Oakland or across the Bay to San Francisco.)

Perhaps the main problem facing students is housing. Rents in Berkeley are sky-high, to the extent that the past few years have seen a steady exodus of students from the campus area. South of the campus, rents are high, the population is dense, and the area is dirty and fairly noisy. North is physically much nicer, but rents are higher still. North Oakland is perhaps the best alternative. Rents are substantially lower, and it's only a short bus ride (bus service is excellent) or, in nice weather, a bike ride from campus.

Within Berkeley, several living alternatives are available. The dorms are one, but unless you're some sort of masochist, they're also the worst. Bad food, poorly maintained buildings, noise, and lack of privacy render them unlivable for most people.

The university-owned co-ops are somewhat better. They are semi-communal to the extent that members share responsibilities for cooking and maintenance; they are also cheaper and provide a good environment for meeting people.

Before too long, most students end up in an apartment or house rented with a group of friends. Enough alternatives exist for everybody; the main problem is finding something suitable in the right price range.

Despite the problems of living in urban Berkeley, the benefits usually outweigh the detriments. Social and cultural activities abound, offering opportunities to escape from schoolwork. There is no excuse to remain isolated if you don't want to.

On the other hand, isolation is certainly possible, if you so choose. Many classes are huge, and the university's bureaucracy can often be formidable, reaching the point of complete impersonality.

Nevertheless, Berkeley has the potential to provide as good an education as anywhere. The graduate division, which is frequently considered the best in the country, often takes priority over undergraduate teaching. With a little perserverance, though, it is usually possible to get what you're after, whether it's a book or an audience with the dean.

Although Berkeley's population of Nobel laureates and other distinguished personnel is among the highest in the country, don't expect to meet them. They're usually involved in research and take little time to teach classes. This does not mean students get stuck with bad teachers. Some of the best instructors are in the lowest rank in their departments, and the most decorated profs are frequently poor teachers.

There are no bad departments, and many, including English history, languages, and practically all the physical sciences, consistently rank among the best in the nation. Although some of the instructors are still of the "tell 'em and test 'em" breed, many others are open to student suggestions and innovations regarding teaching methods and assignments.

A number of years ago the idea of a resurgence of beer, football, and stereotyped sex at Berkeley campus would have been pretty remote. But in fact this onetime hotbed of radical social change is acting a lot like many other schools: it is not taking itself so seriously anymore.

The students are quieter, more studious, and more polite than their predecessors. They are still independent and individualistic, though. There is a decided lack of social order around campus; people pretty much have to find their own entertainment (which is not hard to do in the pleasant San Francisco Bay area). Many students develop into nature lovers in the mild climate, and cutting classes in the spring is *de rigueur*.

Looking at the new chancellor of the Berkeley campus and the new president of the nine-campus university, both of whom are stodgy, tedious, low-profile people, one could get the impression that Berkeley has become very traditional, conventional, and acquiescent; on several levels that opinion is probably justified. But the institution remains an exciting place to study with a wide range of competitive intellectual bases, in very stimulating and enjoyable environs. It's a good place to search, and often, even to discover.

UNIVERSITY OF CALIFORNIA/DAVIS

Location: Davis, CA 95616
Campus: small city
Undergraduate enrollment:
   6400 M, 6300 W
Total enrollment: 17,580
Expenses: $3380 (in-state),
   $5400 (out-of-state)
Financial aid: 35%
Library: 1,375,000 volumes

Student-faculty ratio: 19–1
Transfer students: 1806
Median SAT: 468 V, 518 M
Fraternities: 3%
Sororities: 1%
Application deadline:
   until quota is filled

The town of Davis, California, might have remained as unheralded and forgettable as its sleepy Sacramento Valley neighbors Dixon, Woodland, and Winters. But at the turn of the last century, the University of California established an agricultural station at Davis as a branch of its Berkeley campus, and life in Davis hasn't been the same since.

The campus, for years called "the University Farm," or simply "the Cow College," is set on what was once hayfield and stock range. The landscape surrounding it is a tedious, flat patchwork of rice and tomato fields, walnut groves, vineyards, and acres of hay and alfalfa. Needless to say, the setting is less than ideal for hayfever sufferers. Even so, Davis is only fifteen miles west of a decent meal and movie in Sacramento, seventy-two miles northeast of dinner and a play in San Francisco and about 150 miles from a weekend of skiing and gambling at Lake Tahoe or a tan on the coastal areas of Mendocino and Santa Cruz. For students without cars, the local buses, Regional Transit, Greyhound, and Amtrak provide adequate means of transportation into and out of Davis.

The architecture at UCD varies from wood-shingle Victorian buildings to multistory concrete modernstrosities. The buildings are interspersed with century-old oaks and elms. Outah Creek oozes through the campus and invites moonlight strolling, sailing, and canoeing, but don't swim in the stuff.

The outdoors is big at Davis. Nearly everyone takes part in intramural sports, especially softball in the spring, when teams try to outraunch each other with pornographic team names.

The main focus of social interaction is "the quad," a broad, grassy expanse in the center of campus that attracts speakers, student rallies, noon-hour concerts, brown-baggers, and frisbee flingers. Grass is popular—both kinds.

Fraternities are not well thought of, but they have good, noisy parties. About 3000 students survive in campus residence halls, eating food from the Gulag Archipelago. Nearly all students live in the dorms their first year or two, make some friends, adjust, then move to off-campus houses or overpriced apartments.

Except for those going through rush during fall quarter, dress is very casual at Davis. Many resort to just about anything that will keep them dry en route to campus by bike during the winter. For those who refuse to wear rain pants and put on fenders, well, they just have to live with wet thighs and a nice streak up their back.

Political activism lingers on at UC Davis. Davis is a college town, and the students wield real power in city elections. The Davis housing task force and city-student lobby watch out for student interests. The city itself is progressive and liberal. The emphasis on pedal-power (there are about twice as many bikes registered as cars) and solar-heated homes are just two ways the town of Davis has done something about the energy crisis.

The academic atmosphere at Davis is tense. The many manic prelaw, prevet, and premed students seem out of sync with the placid, countrylike campus. The ten-week quarter demands that nearly everyone study hard. In the main library it's difficult to find a seat, even on weekends. Still, most people are ready to have a good time, if it doesn't interfere with their studies.

After fifty years as a strictly agricultural school, UCD became a general campus in 1951. Now the third largest of the nine UC campuses, Davis offers courses in everything from agronomy to zoology. The viticulture and enology department, probably tops in the U. S., has a cellar of over 100,000 bottles of wine which may never touch human lips—the license is for winemaking but not for wine drinking. The food science and technology department examines every aspect of edibles from taste and preparation to packaging and consumer acceptance. Humanities departments such as art, design, English, political science, and history all offer first-rate programs. UCD also boasts very competitive grad schools in law, veterinary medicine, and medicine.

If you live in the sprawl and cement of a big city, Davis is a great place to find a little breathing space but still be close to civilization. The campus is modern, but there is a sense of tradition and a feeling of permanence. Most of the people who go to Davis complain about its lack of nightlife and its bucolic setting, but they come to appreciate the fact that, in many ways, Davis belongs to the student community. How important that is is something you have to decide.

UNIVERSITY OF CALIFORNIA/IRVINE

Location: Irvine, CA 92717
Campus: rural
Undergraduate enrollment:
  4104 M, 3564 W
Total enrollment: 9920
Expenses: $4000 (in-state),
  $6400 (out-of-state)
Financial aid: 35%
Library: 900,000 volumes

Student-faculty ratio: 19–1
Transfer students: 1080
Median SAT: 515 V, 563 M
Fraternities: 0%
Sororities: 0%
Application deadline:
  none

The University of California campus at Irvine is located in Orange County—which says a lot. For Orange County, one of the most conservative counties outside the Deep South, is the home of Disneyland, San Clemente, and the John Birch Society. Although Irvine does not fit in any way, shape, or form, between the poles of Walt Disney and Richard Nixon, it is also a long way intellectually and ideologically from Berkeley. Irvine's superficial liberalism is one reason why Irvine students are not exactly *persona grata* in the surrounding community.

Academically, Irvine is an interesting and exciting place with a host of young professors who are often more innovative than their students. The anthro and social science departments attempted a unique experiment that set off a little plot from the rest of the campus (called "the farm") and imported a Colombian family to live on it in their natural habitat.

Most of Irvine's academic alternatives are far less offbeat. By building up outstanding biology and psychobiology (neurochemistry, neuroanatomy, and neurophysiology) faculties, the school has become a gathering place for premed types of late. The schools of social science and social ecology have also maintained "progressive and innovative" reputations.

The campus, three miles from Corona del Mar, covers over 1500 acres of beautiful southern California coastal land. Among the many facilities are thirty residence halls and units for married students.

Undeniably, Irvine has its disadvantages. A whopping eighty-seven percent of its students commute. Little organized community social life exists, and a car is a must to escape Irvine on the weekends. For entertainment, many go to Balboa Island, which is far from being a peanuts-and-crackerjack sort of place. Of course, some of the best surfing beaches in the southland are only miles and minutes away.

UNIVERSITY OF CALIFORNIA/LOS ANGELES

Location: Los Angeles, CA 90024
Campus: city center
Undergraduate enrollment:
  9650 M, 9550 W
Total enrollment: 30,545
Expenses: $3400 (in-state),
  $5800 (out-of-state)
Financial aid: 40%
Library: 4,000,000 volumes

Student-faculty ratio: 17–1
Transfer students: 2500
Median SAT: 490 V, 554 M
Fraternities: 17%
Sororities: 14%
Application deadline:
  none

Don't expect to meet the next Bill Walton in any of your UCLA classes. Don't expect to meet anyone, for that matter. UCLA may be the only school in the country with more parking structures than classroom buildings.

An exaggeration, of course, but you get the idea. UCLA is huge and was probably the original inspiration for the notion that large universities are impersonal. Most undergraduates are from Los Angeles (with the exception, naturally, of the football and basketball teams). Those who still live at home, and a great many do, tend to remain faithful to their high school cliques with very little wandering afield. Some, in desperation, move on-campus, into dorms or fraternities, just so they can meet some new people.

Classes are huge, with popular courses drawing over 500, with still more students unable to register. Upperclassmen enjoy smaller numbers (seventy to one hundred), while special seminars or obscure classes may only have six students. This further contributes to the lost feeling of the average student.

As if size wasn't enough of a disadvantage, the atmosphere itself is highly impersonal. Some students, knowing what they are in for, apply to UCLA just so they will never have to come face-to-face with a professor. Because of the number of students, the anonymity will not be challenged. Many students are frightened to consult a mumbling professor who has just lectured to 800 students. Partly as a result of this attitude, the professors are not nearly as busy seeing students personally as they should be, and as many assume they are.

If the undergraduate feels lost amidst a maze of activity and purpose that seems not to concern him, it is probably because he is. UCLA is remarkably active in the community. Far more goes on there than mere undergraduate education. The graduate schools, particularly law, business, and medicine are well respected and attract most of the attention and funding of the administration. University Extension offers many highly worthwhile and innovative courses open to the entire community. The theater arts department may be the best in the nation; excellent film festivals and dramatic presentations are the result. Top-name concert series, the justly famous athletic teams, an excellent hospital, extensive science facilities, an experimental elementary school, and community-related projects in the social sciences serve more than the student community.

These opportunities are all available to the undergrad, as is the city of Los Angeles; which, despite its never-ending freeways and ugly smog, receives more criticism than it deserves. Theaters, museums, skiing, beaches, and peeks of the stars are all within relatively easy driving distance of UCLA.

With more students planning to attend graduate schools and more professors and departments cracking down on grade inflation, high grades are becoming difficult to achieve at UCLA. Students generally study seriously; science majors and law school hopefuls work very hard. French, anthropology, history, and, of course, theater arts are all well regarded.

Music, political science, biology, and chemistry are considered among the twenty best in the country, and UCLA was ranked behind only Berkeley and Michigan by the authoritative *Gournan Report* among public universities.

Sports are a way of life at a school that dominated NCAA basketball for fifteen years before the recent decline. Football, track and field, swimming, tennis, and just about every other major sport fields a nationally-ranked team. But due to UCLA's size, there is plenty of room for the student who doesn't know a zone defense from a viral attack.

Some of the dorms are fairly decent versions of the high-rise, claustrophobic apartment life-style. Westwood rent is notoriously high, and the immediate campus community is rather frat-jock-rich-kid oriented. Many students prefer to live within driving distance of campus and out of its sphere of influence, thus ignoring the university as much as possible and taking advantage of the city itself. At UCLA, that's not such a bad idea.

UNIVERSITY OF CALIFORNIA/RIVERSIDE

Location: Riverside, CA 92502
Campus: suburban
Undergraduate enrollment: 1700 M, 1570 W
Total enrollment: 4500
Expenses: $3475 (in-state), $5880 (out-of-state)
Financial aid: 25%
Library: 915,000 volumes

Student-faculty ratio: 15-1
Transfer students: 650
Median SAT: 505 V, 547 M
Fraternities: 6%
Sororities: 7%
Application deadline: as soon as possible after November 1

If UCR has any obvious problem, it is one of image. Largely because of its reputation for smog, Riverside has been seen as the ugly sister of all UC campuses. The climate is actually delightful in winter (in the summer, there aren't too many students around, anyway), but the negative image has stuck, and UCR's enrollment leveled off a few years ago.

To some students, UCR's reputation for dirty air is a blessing in disguise. They'd like to keep the campus's small size a secret so they can have the advantage of a friendly atmosphere and informal student-faculty relationships to themselves. And for a campus with a fair number of "re-directs"—students who would have preferred another UC campus, but were sent to UCR because their first choice was closed to further admissions—it's surprising that few people transfer out of UCR. So, while the school may lack the glamour of the "beach campuses" like San Diego and Santa Barbara, there seems to be something keeping students at UCR. We think it's probably the academics.

All the sciences are good. It would be hard to pick out one or two and not do an injustice to the others. The most popular majors on campus are biology and psychology, followed by more sciences like biochemistry, chemistry, and physics. UCR offers a unique intensive biomed program which enables a student to go through the premed obstacle course in a year less than the regular route requires. The "finalists," twenty-five students who survive the first four years and a final qualifying exam at UCR, go on to enter the *second* year class of medical school at UCLA.

Outside of the sciences, both the political science and history departments have excellent reputations. Francis Carney of the former and Carlos Cortes of the latter are examples of professors who are admired by their colleagues and students alike. Along the lines of UCR's "small, but good" quality are the theater, art (especially photography), and art history departments.

Even in lower division courses, classes are generally small. Preregistering for classes is loosely structured—students shop around a bit before settling on their schedule.

The cost of living at UCR is low, at least compared with the other UC campuses. Apartments are cheap and plentiful within walking distance. Inexpensive parking lots are located close to the center of campus. Bikes are very popular. The dormitories, unimaginatively based on the standard design of little cubbyholes lining an endless corridor, have experienced a surge in popularity recently. Again they are reasonably priced, and they offer French, Spanish, and German language halls.

The UCR football program, dropped in 1976, has not yet been reinstated, and this seems to suit most people just fine. Most UCR sports have trouble drawing a crowd, although the baseball, basketball, and women's volleyball teams all have impressive records. The lack of excitement over spectator sports is compensated for by UCR's strong intramural sports program, where dozens of informally arranged teams compete against each other for glory and T-shirts.

UCR's small size has some drawbacks. The campus is financially unable to support large rock concerts, although the performances in dance, theater, and classical music and the speakers series have attained an unusual level of sophistication. The Barn Coffeehouse consistently brings top-notch performers of country-folk-jazz to campus every Saturday night.

The relationship between students and the UCR administration is very relaxed. Red tape, usually associated with student dealings with the administration, is proportional to the campus's small size. And that can make a difference.

UNIVERSITY OF CALIFORNIA/SAN DIEGO

Location: La Jolla, CA 92093
Campus: suburban
Undergraduate enrollment:
  4954 M, 3864 W
Total enrollment: 11,183
Expenses: $3800 (in-state),
  $6200 (out-of-state)
Financial aid: 25%
Library: 1,300,000 volumes

Student-faculty ratio: 18–1
Transfer students: 1500
Median SAT: 510 V, 580 M
Fraternities: 1%
Sororities: 1%
Application deadline: NA

Superficially, the greatest advantage of the UC campus at San Diego is one of the best beaches in the world. The water is clear, for California, and the surfing is unbeatable. However, a word to the wise: San Diego is not intended for the surfer who can't or won't think. Academics take a high priority there.

San Diego was originally set up as a graduate school for Riverside, and like Riverside it is superb in physics, math, and biology. The teachers are rated from good to excellent. Linus Pauling (and some other Nobel laureates) once taught here, as did radical philosopher Herbert Marcuse.

The UCSD communications program has some of the top names in the field, most notably Herbert Schiller. Other departments of particular merit include the history department (which has some outstanding junior faculty, like Robert Edelman in Russian history), and the music department, which concentrates heavily on avante garde music.

The four colleges (Muir, Revelle, Third, and Warren) are academically segregated. Though a student can elect any major in any college, distributional requirements are very different. Whereas a Revelle student will take advanced courses in all areas covered by requirements, a Warren student will only take those classes that are related to his proposed career. Muir has a highly flexible requirement choice and the Third college strives to find students "real-world" situations through internships and special programs.

What keeps people here is not academics but such features as the intramural program, in which over fifty percent of the students participate. The program is organized on an anticompetitive basis (one of the few things here that is), and features both traditional and nontraditional sports. On the other hand, intercollegiates are really played down. There is no football, and the other teams compete primarily on a local, small-school basis. In fact, most students view intercollegiates as an adjunct to the more important intramural program.

Other things people do here include hanging out at the pub, a recently opened complex featuring overpriced food and moderately priced beer, attending smoke-ins on the plaza, organizing Fungus Festivals, and partying. Jazz is really in, and there is a large subculture that is into rock and/or folk music. In addition, a string quartet series sells out every year. This year, such acts as Count Basie are appearing on campus.

UCSD has one of the best critical campus newspapers in the country, the *New Indicator*. This paper, which has been around (under various names) since 1966, is UCSD's oldest paper and it offers a radical socialist/anarchist perspective. Anarchists are big here; they sponsor smoke-ins, Fungus Festivals, study groups, and at one time they ran the print co-op. They were instrumental in the success of the recent sit-in at the chancellor's office by 500 students who demanded the maintenance and expansion of the campus daycare center.

Things are happening here! Last spring, there was a rally on tenure which succeeded in saving two of its target professors; five years ago, the CIA was kicked off campus in a movement that included rallies of over 2000 people; and there exists a popular, long-standing political film series concentrating on people's liberation struggles and community control.

The most important thing to remember about San Diego is that you can get a sure grounding in the sciences, that in some ways rivals nearby CAL tech. And the San Diego beaches beat smoggy Pasadena any day.

UNIVERSITY OF CALIFORNIA/SANTA BARBARA

Location: Santa Barbara, CA 93106
Campus: suburban
Undergraduate enrollment: 6394 M, 5926 W
Total enrollment: 14,250
Expenses: $4265 (in-state), $6665 (out-of-state)
Financial aid: 50%
Library: 1,325,000
Student-faculty ratio: 17–1
Transfer students: 3000
Median SAT: M: 496 V, 576 M; W: 491 V, 519 M
Fraternities: 5%
Sororities: 8%
Application deadline: July 1

The most salient characteristic of UC/Santa Barbara is that it has reduced every student to a computer card, and many people wonder if a more proper name for the school would be University of California, Sacred Bureaucracy. The school is big, and that is probably the first thing you should know about UCSB. You should also know that its location is idyllic, with blue California waters on three sides of the campus.

Academics at UCSB are important. Although the administration emphasizes publishing over teaching, there are many profs who defy the old "publish-or-perish" dictum and prevail as good teachers. The professors in the English department are always eager to lend assistance to students whenever needed, and all go out of their way to arrange conference times. Within this department, there is a tremendous emphasis on long reading assignments and careful analyses, but most students agree that they come out of the classes knowing more than when they went in.

In all departments, stress is placed on writing. The economics department is popular and requires a large amount of work in most classes. The classics department is similar in its requirements, with a great emphasis placed on testing. Professor Clarke in the classics department is one example of the dedicated classroom teacher at UCSB; he insisted on correcting each student's five essays in a class of nearly 300 and even wrote comments in the margins.

Since the opening of the National Physics Institute on-campus, there seems to be more research of all kinds going on. A rare "speech and hearing" major is the only one of its kind in the UC system. The psychology, engineering, and computer science departments are highly regarded, and music is also quite good.

Parties abound on campus and the nights with no such occurrences can be counted on the fingers of one hand. People drink incessantly, and it is not uncommon to find small, private dorm room herbariums growing pot. There is no visible supervision of any kind in the dorms (although head residents do exist in each dorm). The only authority figures are the maids.

Dorm life is a study in itself. Stereos and TVs go full-blast nearly twenty-four hours a day. If you like noise, look no further.

For those who don't like noise, off-campus housing is generally better than dorm life. Right next door to the campus is the college community of Isla Vista. Some people love living there, while others will not walk around unarmed. There are a lot of street bums, a lot of drugs, and a lot of violence. The rents are usually pretty good, although the housing conditions are steadily deteriorating. Dogs and bicycles rule the streets.

For those who hate the idea of dorm life only less than they hate the prospect of living in Isla Vista, there are usually apartments available in Santa Barbara, Goleta, and Carpinteria. The apartment vacancy rate is very low (about one percent) and rents are correspondingly high.

The university provides a lot of entertainment for the students. Small concerts, dance groups, recitals, and plays are all available at no or low cost. Movies are shown just about every week, and most students are able to find something they would like to watch either on campus or off.

The litany of campus groups and organizations is predictably long. There are racially oriented groups, department groups, folk dance clubs, Gay People's Union, and many more. About 13,000 students participate in intramurals and there are seventeen intercollegiate sports for the more serious jocks. The men's water polo team is ranked first in the country.

UCSB, like all the schools in the UC system, is good, both academically and socially. The workload is definitely heavy, but you can count on the partying and California way of life to temper it.

UNIVERSITY OF CALIFORNIA/SANTA CRUZ

Location: Santa Cruz, CA 95064 **Student-faculty ratio: 18–1**
Campus: rural **Transfer students: 1400**
Undergraduate enrollment: **Median SAT: 537 V, 551 M**
** 2624 M, 2910 W** **Fraternities: NA**

Total enrollment: 5880
Expenses: $3900 (in-state),
 $6300 (out-of-state)
Financial aid: 63%
Library: 568,000 volumes

Sororities: NA
Application deadline: none

Santa Cruz is geographically the largest of the California campuses, and aesthetically it is far and away the most pleasing. Situated in a national park region overlooking the somewhat polluted but still beautiful Pacific, the campus provides outlets aplenty for the nature worshipper.

Despite its environment, Santa Cruz is by no means a primitive school. It was designed as the most experimental of the California universities, and it lives up to its reputation both in the style of education it offers and the type of people it attracts. Santa Cruz is divided into colleges—in the tradition of Oxford and Cambridge, Yale and Harvard—which specialize in the social sciences, humanities, or natural sciences.

There are problems, of course, as with any experimental system. Theoretically, an instructor is supposed to write out an evaluation of each student in a class numbering less than thirty (although this occasionally happens in large lecture classes as well). Some teachers, however, have used the evaluation as an excuse for instituting a covert grading system, and others actually rank their classes. By and large, however, the faculty is extraordinarily receptive to the students—so much so that in recent years a number of them lost their jobs because they did not publish. The regulations of the UC system, in fact, have temporarily crippled Santa Cruz's economics department, which was filled with devoted, but perishable, teachers. Other departments have retained their strength, though—the chemistry, physics, and mathematics departments have solid reputations, as do many of the social sciences.

The experimentality of Santa Cruz made it a very attractive campus in the Sixties. But with the decline of the hippie movement in the Seventies and general economic downturn, the administration set about the task of "rationalizing" UCSC into a more traditional world.

One result has been a gradual loss of power on the part of the colleges to a stronger centralized administration. Chancellor Robert Sinsheiurer's recent "reorganization" placed virtually all academic decisionmaking in the hands of the three UCSC deans, leaving the colleges with neither distinction nor import.

This transformation has indeed attracted more students, though they are of a different variety from the ones who made the school popular ten to fifteen years ago—more conservative, less willing to take chances (academically and socially), and more inclined to the "practical" and "applied" programs. Most come from upper-middle-class families and are generally at the top of their class.

The social life at SC, like everything else, is very untraditional. When asked whether he had any conventional dates, one Santa Cruz student replied, "No, we just do things together." It goes without saying that liberation in sexual relationships and drug usage is widespread. Most of the students either like the place a great deal (and stay) or dislike it a great deal (and leave for one of the other Cal campuses). A surprising number travel to San Francisco on the weekends, but others are content merely to curl up under a tree.

If there are any criticisms to be made of this "Nirvana on the Pacific," it is that it is too isolated, too far removed from the anguish of the real world. But if nature is your thing, and you're interested in getting a fine education to boot, Santa Cruz is the place for you. Even if you aren't Henry David Thoreau.

CARLETON COLLEGE

Location: Northfield, MN 55057
Campus: rural
Undergraduate enrollment: 950 M, 870 W
Expenses: $6175
Financial aid: 75%
Library: 390,000 volumes
Student-faculty ratio: 11-1
Transfer students: 20-30
Median SAT: 600 V, 630 M
Fraternities: 0%
Sororities: 0%
Application deadline: March 1

The best thing about Carleton is that it's not what people perceive it to be. Though in a rural setting, it's cosmopolitan in student background and administration attitude. Despite its small student body, Carleton attracts the big-name professors and the student variety it needs to maintain its high reputation. Although in the midst of "Winterland" (Minnesota), "Carls" care more about literary movements than about hockey.

Locally referred to as the "Harvard of the West" (or, to set the records straight, Harvard would be the "Carleton of the East"), Carleton is a top-quality undergraduate liberal arts school vying for academic recognition. Admissions standards are very high and the work load is understandably heavy. Most professors have doctorates and maintain high visibility in their areas of research, while still devoting much of their time to instructing undergraduates—that seems to be one of the selection criteria. By most professional surveys, Carleton is also ranked among the best in the country at what it does: providing a fine undergraduate education.

Northfield's claim to fame is a couple of plaques commemorating Jesse James shoot-outs and the fact that it's one of the few towns with more colleges than movie theaters (St. Olaf, a Lutheran school conforming perfectly to out-of-staters' perceptions about Minnesota colleges, is located on the other side of town). Students make up most of the clientele at the local shops, restaurants, and bars, so their patronage is appreciated.

The "Twin Cities" (Minneapolis-St. Paul) are only forty miles away, however, and as cities go they offer an excellent assortment of culture and entertainment. Carleton students can take one of the twice-daily shuttle buses and catch a play at the Guthrie Theater or see an exhibit at Walker Art Center or perhaps watch a hockey game.

Private cars are prohibited on campus (surprisingly, yearly student referendums show strong support), yet it seems that everyone knows someone who has a friend who knows someone with a car (and this may even be illegal). This rule, besides insuring compliance with one of many Northfield ordinances, also keeps much of the student body on-campus at all times. Students are housed in nine residential halls (all but two coed), as well as in several so-called "special interest houses," inhabited by groups with common interests (such as "environmental studies," "Jewish studies," etc.).

Carletonians say they study hard, but it may be that they only think so. The trimester system means that tests are only a couple of weeks apart. And competition for grades keeps a fair segment of the population in the library.

Biology, chemistry, economics, and English are superior departments. History, geology, philosophy, and religion are not far behind, featuring some of the most energetic professors. Outside of regular academics, however, students are encouraged to experiment with semesters abroad, internships, and other programs with an orientation different from Carleton's.

Social life was drastically improved with the conversion of an old gymnasium into the Sayles Hill Student Center. It features a snack bar, a bookstore, and a game room, all potential (and real) hang-outs and meeting places, within a large open structure speckled with tables and couches. This is also where most campus affairs take place.

Intramural sports are big (basketball draws over 500) as is the theater group. Varsity teams have not excelled, but judging by recent performances against bigger arch-rival St. Olaf (still losses, but not by the usual fifty-point margin), football is improving. Gay and women's lib is on the rise and out of the closet, with open debate, in the editorial pages of the *Carletonian*. Last, but certainly not least, are "Rottbat" and "Wombat," the softball leagues in which skill or sobriety are regarded as flukes and incompetence has become legendary.

In Minnesota, winter can make you wish the fifty states were somewhere in Latin America. It does get cold and snowdrifts can be a problem. But look at the bright side: you get to cross-country ski to class.

CARNEGIE-MELLON UNIVERSITY

Location: Pittsburgh, PA 15213
Campus: city outskirts
Undergraduate enrollment:
 2691 M, 1247 W
Total enrollment: 5351
Expenses: $7205
Financial aid: 67%
Library: 550,000 volumes

Student-faculty ratio: 10–1
Transfer students: 300
Median SAT: 568 V, 663 M
Fraternities: 11%
Sororities: 6%
Application deadline:
 March 1

In theory, Carnegie-Mellon University offers a unique combination of programs, with an emphasis on the fine arts, engineering, and science. The result is an educational philosophy very different from the traditional liberal arts perspective; the university calls it "the professional approach." In practice, however, this hodgepodge combination of arts and technology is not completely successful.

The problem is that fine arts and engineering students just don't mix. This dichotomy has become popularly recognized on campus as the "fruits" (fine arts people) versus "vegetables" (engineers) issue. Students' lives tend to revolve around their academic departments, and everyone could benefit from more contact with people from other parts of the university.

CMU consists of six colleges: the college of fine arts, the college of humanities and social sciences, the Carnegie Institute of Technology, the Mellon Institute of Science, the graduate school of industrial administration, and the school of urban and public affairs. CFA, H &

SS, CIT, and MIS all offer both undergraduate and graduate degree programs. GSIA and SUPA offer only graduate programs.

The college of fine arts includes architecture, art, design, drama, and music. In the past few years, almost all of these departments have received considerable criticism from students, who protest the lack of a quality education. Architecture has been attacked most often. The music department has always been good, but because of poor facilities, mediocre instructors, and little encouragement (and money) from the rest of the university, many music students transfer to better places. The design department offers a two-segment program which first gives the student basic skills and then offers the opportunity to specialize. The department is heavily oriented toward graphic design, with few offerings in industrial design. Politically, art is the most placid of the fine arts departments, even though it produced Andy Warhol.

The drama department is a pleasant exception. It is arguably the university's best, and over the years it produced many of the top stage and screen performers of today. Dramats, understandably, tend to be cliqueish and snobby about the legacy left to them.

The Carnegie Institute of Technology houses the engineering departments: chemical, civil, electrical, mechanical, metallurgy, and materials science, and the newly formed department of engineering and public policy. "Chem E" and "EE," with the most students, are probably what the school is famous for. The whole college is oriented toward finding employment for the student after graduation. CIT students have been very successful at getting high-paying jobs but have had trouble getting into the better graduate schools.

The Mellon Institute of Science embraces biology, chemistry, mathematics, physics, and computer science. The biology department was only started in the early Seventies and is still quite small. The chemistry department has a few professors who are unquestionably leaders in their fields, but on the whole it is hampered by too much deadwood. John Pople, a theoretical chemist, is probably the most outstanding scientist in the university. The math department has recently developed a curriculum emphasizing applied mathematics, in the hopes of making its majors more employable. The physics department specializes in high-energy physics (and high-energy majors).

The computer science department is one of the best in the country, featuring such prominent names in the field as Herb Simon and Alan Newell. There is no undergraduate degree program, but the course offering is extensive.

GSIA, the graduate business school, staffs an administration and management science department for undergrads. Although GSIA is one of the top business schools in the country, its undergraduate subsidiary is often criticized for unqualified lecturers (namely grad students).

Somewhere in the gulf between the fine arts people and the engineers, students of the college of humanities and social sciences flounder. The college comprises the departments of economics, English, history and philosophy, modern languages, psychology, and social relations, as well as a fledgling department of social sciences. Psychology is the best of these, strong in cognitive psych but weak in the clinical area. In English, the creative writing staff is good. Excellent teachers are scattered here and there throughout the college—it's a matter of finding one to suit your taste.

The library system is woefully inadequate. If you're looking for something you need, chances are they don't have it. President Richard Cyert has promised to spend a large sum of money in order to improve the three libraries—(the Engineering Library, the Science Library, and the "everything else" library).

Just about everyone on campus is heavily committed to academic work. Studying is a popular pastime, even on weekends. Most students want to get into grad school or find a good job, and they are willing to make the necessary effort. There are many relaxed moments (it's impossible to grind *all* the time), but be prepared to spend a lot of time with your books when you get here.

Sex is available for all persuasions. CMU is much more liberal toward the gay community than most campuses, probably because the gay population is large here (don't be misled, though—straights are still in the majority).

Marijuana and other drugs can be found easily (prices are average), but alcohol is the biggie, even though the Pennsylvania drinking age is twenty-one. In line with students' obsession with their work, No-Doz is the most popular drug on campus.

The university sponsors a large number of activities. Students can attend movies, lectures, concerts, dances, and student-produced plays. Most of them are free, except for concerts, and movies, which still cost a fraction of the commercial box office price. The University of Pittsburgh is right down the block, and other colleges are close by, so CMU students take advantage of their offerings too.

The dormitories are miserable and poorly maintained, and everyone complains about how awful the food is in the cafeterias. Most people move out of the dorms by the end of sophomore year. Apartments are readily available within walking distance of the campus, and several good shopping areas are located nearby.

In general, Pittsburgh isn't as bad as you might have heard. Air quality has improved dramatically since the smoky 1940s. Pittsburgh has big-city assets (culture, a variety of ethnic groups), without big-city liabilities (crime). There is a good variety of entertainment, restaurants, stores, services, and residential districts within the city limits.

The Carnegie-Mellon administration doesn't do enough to bring the students and teachers in the different colleges together. But if you're lucky enough to be majoring in one of the school's strong departments, you'll probably be glad you went there.

CASE-WESTERN RESERVE UNIVERSITY

Location: Cleveland, OH 44106
Campus: city center
Undergraduate enrollment:
   1900 M, 780 W
Total enrollment: 8,185
Expenses: $7000
Financial aid: 67%
Library: 1,600,000 volumes

Student-faculty ratio: 9–1
Transfer students: 220
Median SAT: 563 V, 641 M
Fraternities: 25%
Sororities: 3%
Application deadline:
   March 15

Case-Western Reserve sounds a bit like a corporation manufacturing rifles, or just about anything but a school. Despite the unlikely moniker, Case-Western Reserve *is* a school—or more precisely two schools, and therein lies the idiosyncrasy of the Cleveland institution.

In 1967, Western Reserve, a well-known liberal arts school, merged with the Case Institute of Technology, an excellent engineering school with a solid national reputation. Even from the start the marriage was not made in heaven, but rather at the bargaining tables of fiscal and administrative convenience. Beset with dwindling funds, combination seemed logical. After all, the two colleges were more or less across the street from each other on the east side of Cleveland.

The blueprint, however, never quite worked out. Administrative, geographic, social, and temperamental divisions persist, and the two student bodies retain their separate identities.

A typical Case student, according to the popular image, leaves high school with SAT scores of 800 math and 300 verbal. "Casies" are clearly recognizable on campus by their white socks, black shoes, pants ending four inches above the ankles, and scientific calculator strapped to the belt. This garb changes, though, for recreation, as warm weather finds the "Casie" in dark Bermuda shorts, black socks, and green (or orange) tennis shoes.

A "Casie" is never without his briefcase and never with a girl.

The stereotypical "Reservie" belongs to quite a different breed. His wardrobe consists of two pairs of faded Levi's jeans, Earth shoes, and a variety of printed T-shirts bearing slogans such as "Ohio State University" or "UCLA." He spends his time either in extracurricular activities or in cramming for tomorrow's exam. His favorite time of the year is the end, for only then can he sell his textbooks for that new bong that he wants.

One-half of the "Reservie" freshmen call themselves premeds, fifteen percent of the seniors do. Unlike his Case counterpart, the "Reservie" is never seen with a book or without a girl.

For both groups of students, opportunities for extracurricular activities are almost unlimited. So are opportunities for diversion. The campus offers a club with live entertainment, a bar and game room, restaurants, film societies, free athletic events, several lecture series, and an active theater department. University Circle, the cultural area where the school is located, also boasts such nationally acclaimed institutions as the Cleveland Museum of Art and Museum of Natural History which offer specialized courses in conjunction with the university in areas such as art history and field biology. Their collections and libraries offer additional depth to the university's own resources.

Probably Cleveland's best-kept secret is the abundance of diverse, quality music available in and around University Circle. Intimate clubs and large concert halls offer everything from classical to New Wave, bluegrass to jazz, and everything between and beyond. Bus and Rapid Transit lines provide transportation to those social and cultural events not easily reached on foot.

Despite these attractions, though, Case-Western Reserve students tend to concentrate on their studies, and the academic strengths of the school make that a not altogether unwise choice. Graduate schools are also aware of these strengths: ninety percent of premeds graduating in 1979 with a cumulative and science grade point average of 3.3 were accepted to U. S. medical schools. Even more impressive, all of the thirty predents graduating in 1979 were accepted to U. S. dental schools. The university offers unique pre-professional programs that grant entering freshman conditional acceptance into the excellent nursing, law, medicine, and dentistry schools. Through the department of anesthesiology in the school of medicine, students may pursue a baccalaureate program that prepares them for employment as anesthesiologist's assistants. This is one of only two such programs available in the U. S. The Bachelor of Science major in accounting allows students to obtain a broad liberal arts background as well as accounting skills.

Case-Western Reserve is a university for the above-average student. The engineering student currently fares better than the English major, but a fund drive to endow new chairs in the humanities will probably help to equalize the situation.

CATHOLIC UNIVERSITY OF AMERICA

Location: Washington, DC 20064
Campus: city outskirts
Undergraduate enrollment: 1300 M, 1300 W
Total enrollment: 7,726
Expenses: $6000
Financial aid: 45%
Library: 998,000 volumes

Student-faculty ratio: 10–1
Transfer students: NA
Median SAT: 504 V, 531 M
Fraternities: 10%
Sororities: 5%
Application deadline: June 1

With a student body that consists almost entirely of Catholic parochial school graduates who are in the middle of the political road, Catholic University does not exactly offer an environment pulsing with diversity. Yet CU is noted for its junior faculty's liberal stance on Church issues, and many students are strongly opposed to the Roman Catholic establishment—partly because of the architectural deformity known as the "National Shrine of the Immaculate Conception" that imposes on an otherwise attractive campus.

An important thing to consider is CU's location, which is both a blessing and a curse. The fact that the school is in Washington is a drawing card; the political and cultural life of the city is enormously exciting. But while Georgetown enjoys a bohemian setting near M Street, and while the American University is nestled comfortably near embassies and suburbs, CU is in a fairly boring northeast Washington residential area once known as the Little Vatican because of the many religious institutions clustered there. The neighborhood has never been a place to roam around after dark.

Dormitories are divided into three widely distanced areas, one for graduate students and two for undergraduates. The result is a "ghetto effect" for the undergrads who live in the area farthest from the main campus. The college dorms look handsome from the outside, but a monk's cell atmosphere pervades within. Off-campus housing is not hard to find although the best spots are over a mile away.

Students who have access to cars manage to flee to Georgetown or Pennsylvania Avenue for some nightlife. Beer bashes are the main form of entertainment on campus. Hard drugs are practically nonexistent at CU, although the International Bong Association has probably the largest enrollment of any student organization. The sports program has declined in recent years.

CU began as a graduate school, and as *the* home of Catholic higher learning in the country, it is forced to emphasize its graduate departments. Liberal arts undergraduate programs are frequently neglected and underfinanced, especially as the school faces increasing financial problems. On the other hand, the grad school makes a wide range of graduate courses and top-level professors available to undergrads.

CU's academic life is traditional, with requirements in philosophy, religion, humanities, science, and language. Comprehensive exams are required for most majors at the end of senior year. Although the atmosphere is not particularly intellectually stimulating, there are some standout teachers and departments. Greek, Latin, Hebrew and other Biblical studies, French, and the sciences are all strong. Relations among students, faculty, and administration are informal and friendly.

Most graduates of Catholic University are generally satisfied with the school, but few would have named it as their first choice four years before. CU allows the student to set the pace of his own education, with little pressure from the institution as a religious or intellectual entity. If Washington is the chief attraction for you, rest assured that there are better schools in that city.

UNIVERSITY OF CHICAGO

Location: Chicago, IL 60637
Campus: city center
Undergraduate enrollment: 1700 M, 1000W
Total enrollment: 8000
Expenses: $7925
Financial aid: 65%
Library: 3,500,000 volumes

Student-faculty ratio: 8–1
Transfer students: 100–125
Median SAT: 617 V, 644 M
Median ACT: 28.5
Fraternities: 5%
Sororities: 0%
Application deadline: January 15

The University of Chicago ranks as one of the nation's foremost private schools, and its reputation is well deserved. Long a bastion of the spirit of "the liberal education," the school has found itself in the past few years confronted with the same issues troubling all major colleges. The school's record in meeting these disturbances has shown its reputation is neither outdated nor exaggerated.

Several virtues stand out immediately: the school has remained small amid growing pressures toward expansion; the faculty has refused to give up control to the administration (as has happened elsewhere with increasing frequency); the university has maintained its lofty academic standards despite a tightening monetary belt.

As long ago as 1891, the University of Chicago pioneered in educational technique when it elected to combine university and college facilities. Its attempts to combine the best of the English system of education (teaching) with that of Germany (research) were viewed with skepticism at the time, but have formed a model for the development of the American educational structure.

In keeping with Chicago's liberal education traditions, all entering students must fulfill common core requirements in the humanities, social sciences, physical sciences, and biological sciences before concentrating in their majors. This process generally requires two years, although the specific requirements vary among divisions. The common core requirement can be very frustrating for those who know what they want to do. On the other hand, many find it a broadening experience, and students at Chicago may change majors two or three times.

The academic opportunities at U of C are comparable with any school in the country; its small size enables a distinguished faculty to interact with students, and the course offerings are extremely diverse. Of particular note are the social science departments; outstanding scholars have been attracted to the faculties of the history, political science, psychology, anthropology, and philosophy departments. Nobel laureate Milton Friedman heads a top-notch conservative economics department, which has become known as the Chicago School. The graduate schools rank among the best in the nation, with special consideration to business, law, medicine, and social service administration. The university ushered in early admissions practices some thirty years ago, and it still dares to take some high school students before graduation if they are well qualified.

Chicago is organized on a quarter system, beginning in late September or early October. The quarters are about eleven weeks long (with a good summer program also offered) and enable students to take more courses than at most schools. The drawback, of course, is that there is considerably less time for the student to involve himself in his courses.

But judging from student habits across the country, this isn't too serious a problem.

It is mandatory that first-year students live in the housing system and take meal contracts, a requirement that is not always to the student's advantage. Once one gets out of the dorms, the scarcity of apartments can be a significant but not insurmountable problem.

Extracurricular life at Chicago now is not as limited as in previous years; it is even slowly improving, we are told. The limited athletic facilities, notably the Field House, are being renovated and expanded and do not suffer from underuse. Participation in intramural sports is wide-ranging and spirited. Social life, although by no means thrust on the student, is not utterly elusive. There are a large number of clubs and organizations, and with some effort you can find almost anything to suit your interests.

The city of Chicago offers many things in addition to miserable winters: ethnic restaurants, the Art Institute, the world-famous Symphony, sports, and much more. Unfortunately, most of these diversions are found on the affluent north side of the city, and the university is situated on the less affluent south side. Traveling can be a problem in the neighborhood, and walking in the middle- and low-income residential areas which surround the campus is not always safe. Fortunately, most of Chicago's attractions that we mentioned above are accessible by public transportation, although an automobile is hardly a liability. Fraternities still exist on campus but are virtually impotent—socially and politically.

The provincialism which sometimes besets the Midwest is not to be found at the U of C. With a national student body, the school is ideal for a student who wants a top-flight education but doesn't care for Eastern ways. No one who can bear up under great academic pressure should ignore Chicago when contemplating colleges.

UNIVERSITY OF CINCINNATI

Location: Cincinnati, OH 45221
Campus: city outskirts
Undergraduate enrollment:
  11,000 M, 8800 W
Total enrollment: 38,239
Expenses: $2724 (in-state),
  $4044 (out-of-state)
Financial aid: 62%
Library: 1,500,000 volumes

Student-faculty ratio: 17–1
Transfer students: 1100
Median SAT: 478 V, 541 M
Median ACT: 22.5
Fraternities: 8%
Sororities: 6%
Application deadline:
  none

The students at the University of Cincinnati are sincere. They take themselves and their responsibilities seriously. They are well-meaning and forthright. They are, in fact, the kind of people who should be Young Republicans regardless of their politics (and after all, Cincinnati was the home of "Mr. Republican," the late Senator Robert A. Taft). This heavy-handed approach extends into their scholarship. A lot of infinitives have been split at Cincinnati since its founding in 1819.

When it comes right down to it, what can you expect of a large urban university which is primarily interested in the professional training of its students and is located in a city which prides itself on a combination of midwestern mores and Southern gentility? Eleven undergraduate colleges (including journalism, pharmacy, architecture, and business administration), a graduate school, and colleges of law and medicine make up the university. Liberal arts get little attention; the main emphasis is on engineering, and Cincinnati offers seven kinds of training in this area (aerospace, metallurgical, chemical, civil, electrical, materials science, and locomotive).

The library is better than average, and so is the professional training. In business administration and engineering, students follow alternate periods of classroom study and professional practice assignments, described by the school as "a dynamic system of total education designed to provide the most comprehensive professional preparation possible." In less fastidious circles, this is known as on-the-job training.

Situated in the hilltop suburb of Clifton, two miles from the downtown area, Cincinnati is not exactly what you'd call an exciting campus, especially since about half the students are commuters. As a result, social life is centered on a thriving fraternity system. The fraternities are beer-oriented; there is much hearty goodfellowship. The women are wholesome, and male-female relationships tend to be straight-from-the-shoulder.

Cincinnati's best claim to fame (besides some of the professional education techniques developed by Dr. Herman Schneider in 1906) is its basketball team, which won several national championships in the early Sixties under coach Ed Jucker. In keeping with the character of the institution, these teams were known for their deliberate, methodical style of play. "Watching Cincinnati play basketball," said one rival coach, "is as exciting as preparing your income tax return." Since then, the team changed its style of play and has even been involved in a recruiting scandal. The university, however, maintains its traditional, conservative atmosphere.

THE CITY COLLEGE/CITY UNIVERSITY OF NEW YORK

Location: New York, NY 10031
Campus: city center
Undergraduate enrollment:
 6300 M, 5700 W
Total enrollment: 14,360
Expenses: $1000 (in-state),
 $1500 (out-of-state)
Financial aid: 85%
Library: 1,000,000 volumes

Student-faculty ratio: 15-1
Transfer students: NA
Median SAT: not required
Fraternities: NA
Sororities: NA
Application deadline:
 January 15

The City College of New York is precisely what its name implies, it is a city-run institution, with free tuition for city residents, and its purpose is very simply to get as many New York City students as possible through some sort of college education.

City College, or CCNY, as it is known to the cognoscenti of Queens and the Bronx, is not fancy. Far from it. Its facilities are old, and many are literally crumbling. Its social and extracurricular provisions are minimal. Its student body is enormous, amorphous, and distinctly not a community; every single student is a commuter.

Despite its noticeable flaws, CCNY is a worthy and worthwhile institution. After all, its purpose is to send thousands and thousands of New York City kids to school cheaply. These students then become small merchants, neighborhood lawyers, dentists (if they make it big), and, most often, public school teachers. Moreover, the availability of City College has provided an education to some of the most prominent people in America, people who otherwise might not have gone to college at all. The managing editor of *The New York Times,* for example, and the former dean of Yale Law School are both products of City College's mass inexpensive education.

Within the college, open enrollment is a fiery subject. Students seem to agree that social conditions are not going to change in New York until more nonwhites are educated. But many of them fear that the worth of their own degrees is being jeopardized as enrollment standards drop in order to accommodate the educationally disadvantaged. Their fears are not unfounded.

CCNY's troubles, however, are only one part of the institution. The school is, after all, one of the major colleges in New York, even in these days of turmoil. Moreover, it continues to offer, at least on paper, a solid education.

City College houses some of the brightest students, and some of the best faculty, of any public institution in the United States. It's not so much that CCNY students are brilliant—more than a few are, though many are quite middling in their talents—but they are reasonably bright, diligent, and fairly well-read before they enter. The faculty, moreover, includes several outstanding scholars and more than a few outstanding teachers, all of whom are dedicated to public education. The academic climate is one of enthusiasm for learning because learning in itself is desirable and because learning opens doors to useful roles in society. Thus everyone is pretty serious about his work.

As for the nonacademic side of things, the campus of City College is the city. Radicalism and fraternities both exist, but they are minor, and other extracurricular activities also prove highly secondary in the face of the daily outflow of students when classes are over. Students most often live at home, and their lives generally revolve around their families and their high school friends and sweethearts. We won't say there's no CCNY community, but the most important fact about the school in every regard is that it is New York's city college.

THE CLAREMONT COLLEGES

CLAREMONT MEN'S COLLEGE

Campus: suburban
Undergraduate enrollment:
   620 M, 200 W
Expenses: $7782
Financial aid: 60%
Library: 1,300,000 volumes

Student-faculty ratio: 11.5–1
Transfer students: 45
Median SAT: NA
Fraternities: 0%
Sororities: 0%
Application deadline:
   March 1

HARVEY MUDD COLLEGE

Campus: suburban
Undergraduate enrollment:
   410 M, 80 W
Expenses: $7860
Financial aid: 65%
Library: 1,300,000 volumes

Student-faculty ratio: 8–1
Transfer students: 12
Median SAT: NA
Fraternities: 0%
Sororities: 0%
Application deadline:
   March 1

PITZER COLLEGE

Campus: suburban
Undergraduate enrollment:
 290 M, 435 W
Expenses: $6830
Financial aid: 50%
Library: 1,300,000 volumes

Student-faculty ratio: 13-1
Transfer students: 25
Median SAT: 550 V, 550 M
Fraternities: 0%
Sororities: 0%
Application deadline:
 February 1

POMONA COLLEGE

Campus: suburban
Undergraduate enrollment:
 690 M, 640 W
Expenses: $8000
Financial aid: 45%
Library: 1,300,000 volumes

Student-faculty ratio: 10-1
Median SAT: M: 590 V, 650 M;
 W: 620 V, 610 M
Fraternities: NA
Sororities: NA
Application deadline:
 February 1

SCRIPPS COLLEGE

Campus: suburban
Undergraduate enrollment: 567 W
Expenses: $8550
Financial aid: 50%
Library: 1,300,000

Student-faculty ratio: 11-1
Transfer students: 25
Median SAT: 520 V, 505 M
Sororities: 0%
Application deadline:
 February 15;
 May 1 for transfers

It is misleading to speak of the "Claremont Colleges," since each of the five undergraduate institutions and the graduate school has a very definite and unique identity, and their commonalities are primarily physical in nature.

The colleges are located in the pleasantly quiet community of Claremont, at the base of Mt. Wilson. For those with a car, Hollywood and downtown L. A., with concerts, theaters, and restaurants galore are about thirty-five minutes away. The good beaches are a little further—

from forty-five minutes to one hour. Thus, a car is a very handy thing to have, but rides are not hard to find for those without one.

One of the bigger disadvantages to the colleges' location is the intensity of L. A.'s famous smog during the warmer months at the beginning and end of each academic year. Despite the smog, most students enjoy the climate. Winter seemingly does not exist here, yet there is occasionally snow and some skiing up on Mt. Wilson.

The colleges share common dining and library facilities, so that meeting students from each of the schools is easy for those who so desire. The undergraduate schools all encourage cross-registration, and the graduate school opens some of its courses to undergrads. However, intercollege unity is not particularly strong, and each school tends to retreat into its stereotypical image as the year wears on.

Pomona, the oldest of the five, is perhaps the most isolationist. It approaches the Ivy League in appearance, academic atmosphere, and, its students might claim, stature. Pomona features a broadly based liberal arts curriculum, with strong natural sciences and humanities programs. Some very good programs are available for those who want to spend some time abroad, and there is also an exchange program with Colby College in Maine. Pomona's students are probably the most intellectually aggressive of the five student bodies, and are quick to tell you how serious they are about academics. They tend to be comparatively liberal and are stereotyped as preppies. Pomona College appears to function smoothly in the face of the problems that beset the other colleges.

Claremont Men's College is very much coeducational. Barely thirty years old, it faces the problem of what to do with its name, in addition to the usual problems faced by young colleges like CMC. Considering its age, it appears as if CMC has done quite well. It features a stellar economics department, and is also quite strong in political science. The college supports several public affairs institutes, and as such is an excellent breeding grounds for future politicians and businessmen. CMC does suffer from a lack of diversity among both students and courses, a condition which is mollified to some degree by easy access to the other colleges. Its students are seen as jocks and dull business types, but there are enough exceptions to that rule to make CMC an attractive choice for whomever is interested in its strong points.

Scripps has long been regarded as the female half of a social marriage with CMC. Recent years have seen the demise of most of the rules associated with life at an all-women's college; yet Scripps retains a strong sense of tradition. Second oldest to Pomona, Scripps has a beautiful campus and several elegant old dormitories. Many students come from fairly affluent families, and the stereotypical "Scrippsie" is always well dressed. The curriculum is centered around the humanities and fine arts, and courses in these areas are of consistently high quality, especially in literature. Scripps offers a successfully conservative response to women's education today.

Barely coeducated, Harvey Mudd is the most specialized of the schools. Its superb physical science and engineering courses compete with those of MIT and Caltech. The workload is rigorous and demanding, and students consequently have little time for much else. The students are looked upon as being a little eccentric, and their stereotype is easily recognized—unkempt, badly dressed, with the everpresent calculator dangling from their belt. The campus is modern, and HMC shares sports facilities with CMC. Harvey Mudd lacks diversity, and students desirous of a traditional liberal arts education should be wary.

Last, and perhaps least, is Pitzer, a child of the Sixties which appears anachronistic beside the other colleges. It is the most liberal and experimental of the institutions, and faces serious problems ahead. A lack of direction, and financial problems resulted in the appointment of a new president in 1979. The rather unstructured curriculum emphasizes the social and behavioral sciences. Pitzer's students are stereotyped as freakish. Drug use is fairly heavy, and students appear to place a great deal of importance on both the quality and the quantity of their social life. The only things Pitzer has in common with Pomona are athletic facilities.

The social environment at all five colleges is informal. The city of Claremont rolls up its sidewalks at dusk, but there is always a myriad of lectures, dances, concerts, and parties on campus. The student body has a large California contingent, ranging from conservative San Gabriel Valley natives to privileged-class children from L. A.

All in all, the Claremont Colleges and their students are quite diverse. Knowing the specialty of each school, deciding which of the five is best for you is not difficult. In general, the colleges provide as good a private education as money can buy in southern California—and that's pretty good.

CLARK UNIVERSITY

Location: Worcester, MA 01610   **Student-faculty ratio: 14–1**
Campus: urban/residential   **Transfer students: 150–200**

Undergraduate enrollment:
900 M, 900 W
Total enrollment: 2800
Expenses: $7700
Financial aid: 40%
Library: 400,000 volumes

Median SAT: 550 V, 570 M
Fraternities: NA
Sororities: 0%
Application deadline:
February 15

The Clark admissions department, one of the most fastidious in the country, does a unique job in picking extremely individualistic people. And, if one can hazard a rash generalization, the foremost concern of most "Clarkies" seems to be the zealous protection of their own egos. As a result, Clark is an anomaly among colleges: a small college without much unity.

Its social flaws aside, Clark richly deserves its excellent reputation in at least two departments: psychology and geography. Sigmund Freud once lectured at Clark, and his influence is still felt there. The school's Heinz Werner Institute is one of the nation's finest research facilities for developmental psychology.

But geography? At first mention, it sounds as though Clark is attempting to provide a second chance for junior high school students. But no, geography is a serious discipline and an important one at Clark. Most of the courses are stimulating and are taught by some of the leading scholars in their field.

Most of the other departments at Clark are small but relatively strong, especially the sciences and history. Departments are small, so students can coordinate their research with professors.

It should not be forgotten that this is true in geography and psychology as well. Although the faculty is accessible at Clark, it is often the student who must take the initiative in establishing contact.

Unfortunately, the geography department at Clark is in no position to change Clark's own geography, a fact frequently bemoaned by its students. Worcester cannot simply be swept under a rug, a latent desire of many Clark students. Since Boston is only an hour away by car or by bus, it provides an outlet for anyone who wants to escape. Within Worcester there are a few cultural diversions, such as the very fine Worcester Museum and the Higgins Armory. There are also eleven other colleges in the city, including The College of Holy Cross. Social contact between the schools is minimal, but academic contact is fostered by a consortium that permits students at one institution to take courses at another.

Socially, Clark is far from ideal, but it is by no means a wasteland. Social activities quickly fall into a routine, but if one takes the time to look, there are interesting things to do. There is a social activities board which plans weekend coffee houses and sporadic concerts, but it does not seem capable of satisfying the entire student body. An active film society sponsors about three movies a week. A "fine arts series" has attracted such artists as Misha Dichter and Pepe Romero. There is also a nightly pub on campus. An activities center provides the Clark community with modern gym facilities of all sorts. There are a limited number of intercollegiate sports on the varsity and club levels, and intramural sports are popular.

The library is one of the most impressive buildings on campus, but some students find the resources inadequate. In conjunction with the other consortium colleges, Clark has developed an efficient interlibrary loan service.

The school provides on-campus housing for those who desire it. A large number, particularly upperclassmen, don't desire it. The privacy and comfort of off-campus living is available in the nearby three-story houses, many of which are owned by Worcester slum lords. Clark has both coed and single-sex dorms, as well as foreign language houses in French, German, and Spanish.

Clark offers the motivated student opportunities for self-defined majors, special projects, and internships. It also offers the unmotivated student a fairly painless route to a respectable college diploma.

COLBY COLLEGE

Location: Waterville, ME 04901
Campus: rural
Undergraduate enrollment:
  850 M, 750 W
Expenses: $6760
Financial aid: 35%
Library: 340,000 volumes

Student-faculty ratio: 13–1
Transfer students: 30
Median SAT: 580 V, 610 M
Fraternities: 25%
Sororities: 10%
Application deadline:
  February 1

Colby College happens to be in Maine, and that is one fact which no Colby student can ever quite forget. Maine is cold in winter, beautiful, little heard of, and little heard from. Some Maine folks around here are rumored to speak as much as seven or eight times a day when they have something on their minds. But these brief bursts of loquacity are infrequent. The Colby experience may well stimulate the student to develop his skills of nonverbal communication, such as fighting and drinking, to the fullest.

Located on Mayflower Hill, the picturesque 900-acre campus overlooks Waterville, the seventh largest "city" in Maine. Though small and not particularly exciting, Waterville offers a full complement of small town amenities. There is an Opera House (it converts into a community theater in the winter), a community symphony, seven restaurants, and two movie theaters. Metropolis it's not, but quiet and pleasant it is.

Colby's main emphasis is on providing a broad liberal arts education. The "January program of independent studies" (popularly called the "Jan Plan") allows students to devote a month to the pursuit of a topic of interest not covered in the curriculum. Some students do take advantage of the program, but the results are unclear. "Jan Plan" has been described as "twenty-nine days of skiing and two days of unbelievable cramming."

Colby's faculty is well paid, well qualified, relatively free from administrative pressure, but nonetheless dissatisfied. Some of the dissatisfaction seems to stem from the apathy of the students, but apathy, even in Maine, is fading, and it is hoped that the professors will soon become less dissatisfied. If they do, they should bolster Colby's already strong reputation in English and languages.

Despite a vaunted nationwide recruiting program, Colby's students are still predominantly New Englanders and New Yorkers, including a high percentage of alumni sons and daughters. Contrary to some trends in today's universities and colleges, Colby still gives some preferential treatment to alumni offspring applications for admission.

The limited social life of Colby centers, predictably enough, elsewhere. There are only three weekends when widespread social gatherings occur at Colby. For the rest of the year there are junkets to Boston (all year round), the ski slopes (in winter), and the southern coast of Maine (in spring). The beaches on the coast are only an hour or so away down one of Maine's infamous back roads, renowned for their soft shoulders and softer speed restrictions. The University of Maine, farther up the Maine Thruway, is also a popular destination. Freshmen are obliged to hitch rides, since cars are only permitted for upperclassmen.

President Robert E. L. Strider retired after nineteen years, and William Cotter, his successor, is looking to enhance the school's attractiveness. In the last few years, Colby built a new art gallery, a theater, a health services building, a radio station, and a converted student center.

Social life on campus centers mainly on informal gatherings, concerts, film festivals, art shows, and student-constructed happenings. The nine fraternities play a significant role in hosting all campus parties and other activities that help bring Colby students together. Several communal dwellings exist off-campus, often to the chagrin of local townspeople but to the betterment of Colby.

COLGATE UNIVERSITY

Location: Hamilton, NY 13346
Campus: rural
Undergraduate enrollment:
 1400 M, 1100 W
Total enrollment: 2650
Expenses: $6770
Financial aid: 80%
Library: 320,000 volumes

Student-faculty ratio: 15-1
Transfer students: 50
Median SAT: 610 V, 640 M
Median ACT: 29
Fraternities: 65%
Sororities: 0%
Application deadline:
 January 15

Colgate University is an oasis in the cultural desert of rural upstate New York. The serenely beautiful campus is surrounded by fields, hills and a town which boasts one stoplight, six gas stations, and five bars.

The small, isolated school (nearest major "city" is Syracuse—thirty-eight miles away) is noted for its personal approach, and most students choose Colgate because of its attention to the individual. The faculty provides ample hours for student discussion, and administrators often make themselves available to talk with students as well.

Most of the freshman class lives and eats together, although some freshmen may live in upperclass housing. Students can usually recognize most of the people in their class by the end of freshmen year. Upperclassmen may choose to move out of the dorms, and the opportunities are many; special interest housing such as "ecology house," "Spanish and French" houses, and "Peace house" are popular alternatives. There are two all-female houses, and eleven fraternities. The university sponsors a sizable number of off-campus apartments (fourteen buildings' worth), and getting one's own house or apartment in town is not particularly difficult.

Academically, Colgate is quite traditional, and many programs in the humanities and sciences are superb. The English, chemistry, biology, and history departments are all first-rate and very popular. The philosophy and religion department is reputedly one of the best in the country. A required course in philosophy and religion (one of five "area core requirements" designed to provide a wide liberal arts basis for all students) introduces freshmen to the department. In addition to the core requirements, most students are required to spend one summer on campus (thus freeing a fall or a spring semester as vacation in recompense). Exemption from summer term is possible but not common. Three or four "January projects," usually independent study, as well as eight physical education credits are required for graduation. The language and fine arts departments are adequate but not broad enough to constitute a reason for coming to Colgate, though the latter is presently upgrading facilities and offerings to a large degree. Economics, sociology, and political science are all uneven departments at best.

Academics consume a large part of student energy, and the library is almost always packed, often resulting in an all-too social atmosphere which sends the serious studier fleeing to other venues. Colgate students lead Jekyll-Hyde lives, however, and the epithet "work hard . . . party hard" is particularly applicable. Friday afternoons and weekends are earmarked (in good weather) by an abundance of frisbee, softball, jogging, and stereo broadcasting out of dorm windows. Spring and fall party weekends feature nonstop craziness, and an evening at the campus pub is always popular after a session of studying.

Colgate earned the "professional" rating in *Playboy*'s 1972 article on beer-consuming schools and has striven to maintain that rating ever since. Fraternity parties are a main center of the social life, and all houses have tap systems. The alternative to the frats or the student run pub is a night drinking in downtown Hamilton, a town that makes Hanover, New Hampshire, seem cosmopolitan by comparison!

Drugs have their place at Colgate. Pot is ever-present, as is hash. Speed is popular during exams, and acid is usually available. Rock and roll is here to stay at Colgate. The student-run social committee is exemplary. Recent concerts have featured Billy Joel, the Grateful Dead, Renaissance, Jorma Kaukonen, NRBQ, and the Pousette-Dart Band.

There are two student weeklies, the *News* and the *Maroon*, as well as WRCU-FM (1000 stereo watts of mainly progressive rock) and a myriad of student-run publications and organizations available to fill any extra hours. Student government is well organized, although recent years have seen an onset of general apathy towards students' abilities and determinations to have their collective voice heard. Student theater is popular, as is the orchestra and the jazz band. The university chapel pipe organ is a wonder to behold, and the music department sponsors a wide range of recitals and concerts.

The central role in the extracurricular world belongs to sports. Spectating is an integral part of the social life. Although Colgate is not well known for football, the "Red Raiders" play and win against schools ten times its size (. . . and even if the team has not made it to the Super Bowl, the Colgate Thirteen choral group has, singing the National Anthem at Super Bowl XIII). The football schedule is semi-Ivy, and the popular support of the team is tremendous throughout the entire season.

Hockey is as popular as football. Basketball and swimming rate high in student interest as well. The women's sports program is one of the strongest in the state; the tennis team is state champion.

Women as a group play a large part in student affairs, and after roughly a decade of coeducation, relations between men and women have stabilized and are generally free of condescension on either part. Dating, however, is more or less kept at a bare minimum.

The student body at Colgate is drawn from many states and countries. Nonetheless, the odds are fifty-fifty that someone you meet is from Long Island, Westchester, or New York City. Minorities are well represented, though the WASP element predominates.

The town of Hamilton is charming, but offers limited weekend excitement other than drinking and the town cinema (one bar downtown recently has taken to sponsoring local bands on occasion). The university makes a strong attempt to provide social alternatives. Cars are nice additions, and those who have them will tend to take a road trip or three during the course of a given semester. Skiing is popular during the winter; bicycling, sailing, and jogging in the summer. The relative remoteness of the campus tends to cause students to create their own entertainment.

Colgate is cold, small, sheltered, and usually covered with snow. But the people are warm and open, and the education is good, basic liberal arts.

COLORADO COLLEGE

Location: Colorado Springs, CO 80903
Campus: city center
Student-faculty ratio: 14–1
Transfer students: 150
Median SAT: 600V, 600M

Undergraduate enrollment:
  925 M, 925 W
Total enrollment: 1865
Expenses: $6350
Financial aid: 33%
Library: 287,000 volumes

Median ACT: 25
Fraternities: NA
Sororities: NA
Application deadline:
  February 15 for freshmen;
  April 1 for fall transfers;
  November 1 for spring transfers

Some giant steps in liberalizing educational procedures have made Colorado College more than just the ski or party school it once was.

CC instituted an experimental program for all students a few years back, and it's more than an educational novelty. Students take one course at a time for a three-and-a-half week period, followed by a half-week break. Each of these four-week units is called a "block," and nine blocks constitute one school year. All grades are on an optional A-B-C or pass-fail basis: the choice is yours.

The students were so ecstatic about the program when it was first introduced that they tied up the registration facilities the spring before it began. But the fun is still there at Colorado College.

Though fraternities and sororities are not the havens they used to be, social activities still center on these housing units. The beauty of the Rocky Mountains gives an inspiration to any student, and the skiing resorts of Vail and Aspen are not far away. In addition, Colorado College's nationally ranked hockey team provides weekend thrills and spills during the season for students, faculty, and staff.

After floundering for a good many years, Colorado College is making a strong, and for the most part successful, effort to recover the prestige it once held as one of the foremost private institutions in the country. The struggle is made difficult by its distance from large urban areas, but the flexibility of the college's block plan enables it to bring in excellent guest lecturers and professors to supplement its outstanding faculty. The peaceful atmosphere and updated facilities are features that not every college can offer.

Though the college is attempting to provide ethnic diversity by wooing minority students, most of the students are from upper-middle-class white homes. Yet the college has a pleasant diversity among its students, with an infinite number of interests and goals represented.

While the block plan calls for a generally intense academic environment, CC students live a large part of their lives outside their books as well.

COLORADO STATE UNIVERSITY

Location: Fort Collins, CO 80523
Campus: suburban
Undergraduate enrollment:
   9050 M, 8400 W
Total enrollment: 18,000
Expenses: $3167 (in-state),
   $4962 (out-of-state)
Financial aid: 31%
Library: 1,000,000 volumes

Student-faculty ratio: 18–1
Transfer students: 1760
Median SAT: 480 V, 520 M
Median ACT: 22.1
Fraternities: 0.5%
Sororities: 0.5%
Application deadline:
   sixty days prior to term

If you don't mind enduring endless, and most often unflattering, comparisons to the University of Colorado/Boulder, Colorado State can be quite a lot of fun.

The school is highly attractive, ultramodern, and a superb spot for sports and some partying. Skiing is big, and the year-round climate is pleasant. Located in Fort Collins, a town of 60,000 at the feet of the Rocky Mountains, the school has two other campuses, including the Pingree Park campus, fifty miles into the Rockies.

Moreover, Colorado State is one of the very few large public universities in the country which is undercrowded. There is more than enough dormitory space available—if such a thing is possible. The reason, as usual with state schools, is an intransigent legislature—which voted the funds for more dorms, then withheld the money for expanded faculty and facilities, boosting community colleges instead. As a result, Colorado State students have nothing if not space.

Academically, Colorado State is not quite so breathtaking. The largest college, or division, of the university is humanities and social science—but only thirty-five percent of the students are enrolled in it. For those who do take the liberal arts program, the offerings are decidedly unspectacular. About the only strong department is business. In the other colleges, however, things do get a bit better. The school of veterinary medicine is one of the best and most sought-after in the country. The forestry and engineering departments are strong, and agriculture still enjoys a top billing. The latter three programs are all benefited considerably by the university's extensive branches on farms and foothills, which provide many opportunities for practical observation and experimentation.

Colorado State is largely a "silent majority" school. Some seventy-five percent of the students are from Colorado (all in-state students who rank in the top half of their high school classes are welcome). The urban-rural split seems to be a close sixty-to-forty. Only a few liberal types attend the school, we are told, and most of them are in the liberal arts program, where they remain pretty much isolated from everyone else.

Still, Colorado State's excellent facilities and heavenly location make it a hard-to-beat value for state residents. And even with the double expense, out-of-staters may find the school good quality for the money—especially if you want to do some skiing.

UNIVERSITY OF COLORADO/BOULDER

Location: Boulder, CO 80302
Campus: city center
Undergraduate enrollment:
  9793 M, 8074 W
Total enrollment: 21,727
Expenses: $3000 (in-state),
  $4600 (out-of-state)
Financial aid: 25%
Library: 1,800,000 volumes

Student-faculty ratio: 17–1
Transfer students: 1500
Median SAT: 516 V, 568 M
Median ACT: 25
Fraternities: NA
Sororities: NA
Application deadline:
  none

The atmosphere surrounding Boulder, the home of the University of Colorado, is perhaps the most enjoyable in the country. The college town of 80,000 is located right where the Rocky Mountains interrupt the Great Plains. Although Boulder's air is often affected by the same exhaust fumes that have polluted Denver's, which is only twenty-five miles away, the days are bright and sunny all year-round, and the low humidity means that extremes at either end of the thermometer are rarely reached, no matter what the season.

The people and students who live in Boulder like the out-of-doors. Hiking and driving into the mountains are common pastimes. And of course, there's skiing, and more skiing. In fact, it's almost impossible to find someone who doesn't ski. Dozens of some of the world's finest ski areas are within a few hours' drive.

Academically, CU maintains its reputation as the best school in the Mountain states. Traditionally, it has been excellent in the sciences—and only in the sciences. Physics is superb and is closely followed in excellence by chemistry and psychology. History and philosophy are good but not exceptional. The fine arts are blossoming into popularity along with sociology, but neither could be described as better than mediocre at present.

Unfortunately, the university has recently come under attack by the joint budget committee of the state. The ordered financial cuts have resulted in teacher layoffs, decreased student enrollment, and losses in funding for graduate and other programs. These cuts have hurt; even before, there was concern over the size of lecture classes, which usually led to little or no personal contact with faculty members. The school tried to alleviate the problem by increasing the number of seminars in the dorms, but even these are reportedly overcrowded.

The student body is a melting pot of sorts; there are a lot of out-of-staters and a lot of foreigners, although not many blacks. Wealthy New Yorkers seem to have discovered that Boulder is not a bad place to go to escape the megalopolis for three or four years. Yet, they, too, can feel right at home in the Downtown Mall—the site of the now-famous New York Deli where Mork and Mindy work. On the whole, the student body is very active and vocal.

Housing at Colorado can be a hassle if you aren't rich. Seventy-five percent of the student body lives off-campus—not because the dorms are unpopular, but because there is only enough room for 5000 out of the roughly 20,000 students, and many of these are reserved for freshmen, who are required to live on campus. There are virtually no social regulations in the dormitories; twenty-four-hour visitation is the vogue in all.

Even apartment space is really tight, and therefore expensive—often as high as $350 a month for a two-bedroom place. The cheapest way to live is in a house; it is not uncommon for several people to split the costs down to about $125 per person!

In sports, skiing is tops, along with football (despite recent losing seasons, Chuck Fairbanks will make a difference). The new Events Conference Center will hopefully pave the way for a competitive basketball team. Over half the student body participates in at least one intramural sport.

As for student life, there's plenty of partying to be found. Not everyone at CU is into the books, so students like to make the most of their weekends. They do. There are several bars to go to and let loose to any kind of music from rock to disco to country and western. The Greek system is not very big, but growing—over ten percent of the men and women join a fraternity or sorority. There are some heavy drinkers (the drinking age is twenty-one, but eighteen-year-olds can drink 3.2% beer). And there are *very* heavy pot smokers. The evil weed and other forms of contraband can easily be found and the price, although not cheap, is reasonable.

If you're looking for a place to get away from it all, but still be within reach of the trappings of society, then Boulder is the ideal place. There is enough to see and do, and enough people to meet, for anyone to enjoy this Rocky Mountain paradise. Better bring your skis.

COLUMBIA COLLEGE OF COLUMBIA UNIVERSITY

Location: New York, NY 10027
Campus: city center
Undergraduate enrollment: 2800 M
Total enrollment: 16,000
Expenses: $8400
Financial aid: 60%
Library: 5,000,000 volumes

Student-faculty ratio: 5–1
Transfer students: 50
Median SAT: 640 V, 650 M
Fraternities: 10%
Application deadline: January 15

If there's one thing that affects Columbia University's character, it's New York City. Columbia is the quintessential urban institution in the quintessential urban center. Like the city it's in, Columbia is big, impersonal, at times alienating, and lacking community. Columbia is by no means a four-year vacation from real life. But its liabilities are more than matched by its assets. Columbia offers a tremendous variety of courses, opportunities, and facilities. "The city" gives it a kind of urbane sophistication that few other environments can offer. The student body reflects a wide range of backgrounds, abilities, and interests. If there's no overall sense of community here, there are enough niches for nearly everyone to find their own. For an incoming freshman from Peoria, Illinois, it can all seem somewhat overwhelming, but in the end it will be well worth it.

Another factor that looms large over Columbia is the 1968 strike. After twelve years, it's difficult to place it in perspective. In some ways, Columbia was profoundly affected by the strike and police action that resulted in 700 student arrests and nationwide publicity. The strike and subsequent events swept most of the pre-'68 administrators out of office, and the trustees and current administration remain very cautious of student activism. Relatively speaking, Columbia students remain very political. Hardly a spring goes by without large demonstrations and an occasional sit-in. But unlike in '68, the number of students who participate in campus politics (or even tacitly support them) constitute a small minority. And while the administration takes activists very seriously, their responses tend to be more public relations efforts than substantive action.

But there's a great deal more to Columbia than New York City and student activism. Columbia offers a first-rate academic program, if one knows his way around. Columbia has the usual arts and sciences offerings, with a few hard-to-find programs such as Middle East studies and philosophy-economics. But the most distinctive part of Columbia academics is its general education program—a series of courses required of all undergraduates. The centerpiece of the program is "contemporary civilization," a year-long course that's something equivalent to philosopher-of-the-week. The long list of requirements also includes "literature humanities" (a year-long survey of western literature), a semester of "art humanities" (art history), "music humanities" (music appreciation), two years of a foreign language (everything from Arabic to Urdu), one year of science, and the always-popular "freshman composition."

Like most of the Columbia academic experience, these courses are good if you know who and what to choose. The wide range of instructors and courses gives you a great deal of leeway, but it also makes choosing more difficult. Highly recommended instructors include Robert Murphy and Marvin Harris (anthropology), Alexander Erlich and C. Lowell Harriss (economics), Wallace Gray, Edward Said, and Ann Douglas (English), Eugene Rice and James Shenton (history), Gerald Feinberg (physics), and Karl Ludwig-Selig (Spanish and Portuguese).

But if academics are first-rate, "student life" is not. Columbia has fortunately never staked its reputation on providing students with the best creature-comforts. The dorms are cramped and in need of renovations (though a major dormitory is scheduled to be completed in 1981 and renovation of older buildings has been promised). Because there's so little in the dorms worth preserving, however, Columbia gives residents a good deal of freedom to do what they want with their rooms. The food situation compliments housing very well; it's also pretty bad. But here again, Columbia allows students to go their own way; there are no mandatory meal plans. Instead, many students cook in their rooms (albeit illegally), and Columbia, in typical fashion, is slowly installing floor kitchens in the dorms. Moreover, Morningside Heights—a neighborhood which has little else to offer—has a wide variety of conveniently located restaurants.

The Columbia man's social life to a large extent revolves around sister school Barnard College. A few words about that. Barnard is technically independent of Columbia, but affiliated with it. What that means is that Barnard has its own campus, faculty, dormitories, course requirements, and pretty much everything else. But for all practical purposes, they may as well be the same school. Almost all Columbia dormitories are effectively coed, as are nearly all classes and extracurricular organizations. For freshmen, this is still not exactly an ideal arrangement. Carman Hall, the *de facto* freshman dorm, has few girls and most general education courses are all-male classes, since Barnard has its own set of requirements. This may change in the near future, however. Columbia has been pressing Barnard to make freshman dorms coed. Barnard has yet to knuckle under, but the trend of past events is on Columbia's side.

New York also plays a major role in Columbia's social scene. A great many students depend on the city for all their entertainment and have little to do with activities on campus. As a result the number of on-campus parties are fewer and more sparsely attended than at other campuses.

Morningside Heights is probably one of New York's least charming neighborhoods. It's not a bad neighborhood; just not the kind of place you'd want to call home, either. But what it lacks in charm, it makes up in convenience. It's less than twenty minutes from midtown by subway. There's lots of shopping in the area catering to students, and many places stay open late at night. Riverside Park (a block away from campus) and the campus itself provide the area with some green space, something not to be taken for granted in this part of the world. The crime-rate (contrary to what you might have heard) is not at all bad by New York standards—people freely walk around at nights and ride the subways.

Columbia is by no means the ideal school for everyone; there's a lot to contend with for four years. But for students looking for a first-rate education and an opportunity to explore new ideas, people, and experiences, Columbia has a great deal to offer.

CONNECTICUT COLLEGE

Location: New London, CT 06320
Campus: suburban
Undergraduate enrollment: 650 M, 950 W
Total enrollment: 1800
Expenses: $7140
Financial aid: 35%
Library: 370,000 volumes

Student-faculty ratio: 12–1
Transfer students: 120
Median SAT: 560 V, 570 M
Fraternities: 0%
Sororities: 0%
Application deadline:
    February 1 regular,
    January 1 early

Connecticut College enjoys a somewhat ambiguous reputation. It is generally known to be a "good" school with many departments and numerous opportunities for high-quality education in a variety of academic disciplines. Yet it still lacks the prestige of the Ivy League schools and the original "Seven Sisters." Formerly known as Connecticut College for Women until men were admitted to the freshman class in 1969, the college held a tradition of highly selective admissions.

In 1979–80, Connecticut served as first choice to forty-seven percent of the freshman class. The rest used Connecticut as a "safe" school while waiting to hear from Yale or Harvard. But even students bypassed by these top schools can be a highly qualified group.

The decade of transition to coeducation saw much change and new stability. Men not only choked the "suitcase school" image but also brought about an increase in school spirit and morale. This was achieved, to a large degree, by the addition of a strong sports program. Sports have grown from a single-sex pastime to strong teams showing well in major national and local events. The new ice hockey rink complex has quickened the school's heart rate to an exciting level, adding new blood to all aspects of college life, from student government to living space and on through academics. The school has passed through the seventies and that decade's link to apathy and has evolved as a new community with awareness and continuity as its primary goals.

The geographic distribution of students is limited. While the majority come from Connecticut, New York, Massachusetts, and New Jersey, minority and even overseas students are well represented.

As for the kind of student one finds here, there is considerable diversity. Depending on whom you encounter, it is possible to get widely disparate views of the college. Some students are truly gifted in their particular fields of study, while others are barely getting through. There are the "grinders" who study virtually nonstop throughout the semester, along with the "bar crowd" who are most often found in Conn's own campus drinking spot in the student activities center. At Connecticut, the differences between the truly academically inclined students and those who are taking it very easy seem particularly pronounced. Perhaps the best judgment one can make of the school is that an excellent undergraduate education is available for those who want it, but it's not difficult to coast through and obtain a B. A. without a great expenditure of time and effort.

Academically, the college is strong in both the liberal arts and science departments. Philosophy and psychology are particularly outstanding. The studio art and dance programs enjoy spacious facilities and creative faculty. The psychology and education departments include a great deal of laboratory and field work. The 415 acres surrounding the campus are an excellent resource in the environmental sciences. The other departments' strength comes from quality faculty and large course selection. By far the strongest feature of the school is the smallness of class size, which allows greater contact between professors and students and freedom from the strictly lecture format during class. The faculty is approachable and receptive to students, although too often these opportunities are not fully exploited. While the college, like any other, has its weak departments, the range of academic offerings is impressive.

With over ninety percent of the students living on campus, there is a great need for recreational activities—this need is satisfied by numerous intramural teams in football, volleyball, basketball, and water polo. In addition, there is a wide variety of club activities including a radio station, sailing club, political organizations, and student-faculty committees which range across the spectrum of campus and academic life. There is also an impressive array of cultural events for a college of this size, including current, classic, and vintage movies, and lectures related to current affairs, departments, or life in general. The weakness at Connecticut stems from a general perception of student apathy. There is always that period in the semester around finals when students have a semester's worth of work to deal with and the interest in outside activities is at a low.

Relations between students and the administration are normally placid, with the exception of an occasional controversy that breaks out now and then over some aspect of academic or social policy. Students do have a considerable say in college affairs through their participation in the student-faculty committees.

Now that coeducation is here to stay (the male-female ratio stands at two-to-three), Connecticut faces new challenges. In the face of rising costs, Connecticut will be hard-pressed to maintain the academic standards to which it is accustomed. The foundation is there.

UNIVERSITY OF CONNECTICUT

Location: Storrs, CT 06268
Campus: rural
Undergrad enrollment:
  6,250 M, 6081 W
Total enrollment: 25,677

Student-faculty ratio: 10–1
Transfer students: 878
Median SAT: M: 500 V, 583 M;
  W: 507 V, 530 M
Fraternities: 9%

Expenses: $4300 (in-state), $5640 (out-of-state)
Financial aid: 50%
Library: 1,700,000 volumes

Sororities: 7%
Application deadline: February 15

From a small agricultural school, UConn, Connecticut's land grant university, has become an active and bustling center for social and academic learning. And it's still growing. New additions include a large Battlestar *Galactica*-looking library, a fine arts center, and the cooperative bookstore presently under construction.

Besides a top-notch honors program, many other departments are widely recognized for quality. The math, music, biology, psychology, and agriculture departments are among the favorites here on campus, as well as being well known outside of Storrs. The academic competition these days is especially stiff in such vocationally oriented areas as pharmacy and physical therapy, but the result is usually a good output of top-quality professionals.

A wide scope of academics is offered, with majors ranging from acting to zoology. If you are interested in acting, you can make the scene in productions of Shakespeare, Molière, Albee, presently unknown fellow students' plays, and contemporary musicals like *Hair*; and if you're interested in zoology, the variety of animals on campus, domestic and otherwise, will surely help along the way.

Most of the approximately 25,000 students enrolled at Storrs live on campus to avoid the hassle of finding or maintaining an apartment. Campus living also allows them to be closer to what goes on throughout the student community. The course of the week may offer dorm-sponsored movies, faculty and student recitals of all kinds, guest speakers, guest performers at Jorgensen Auditorium, and sports. Sports seem to be a very important part of most students' lives at UConn. Apart from participating as spectators (UConn students go bananas about soccer and basketball), students can be seen jogging, keeping fit and trim on the weight-lifting equipment, or playing a good game of racquetball.

Thursday night, however, seems to be the night when forgetting the week's worries is the thing to do. It's a fifty-fifty split on whether to unburden by attending a dorm party or one of the occasional school-wide affairs sponsored by the board of governors at the ROTC hangar.

Many people leave the campus for the weekend, giving UConn a distinctive "suitcase school" atmosphere. Those who remain wind up going to the movies, the bars, or the local Dairy Bar; then, for a change, they feed the ducks at Mirror Lake. Storrs, Connecticut, offers little else. Occasionally, the school arranges concerts with such groups as The Little River Band, the Poussette-Dart Band, and America.

The student body itself tends to vary quite a bit. Students come from quite different domestic socioeconomic backgrounds and other countries as well. There are rich and not-so-rich kids, partiers and bookworms. With such diversity, it is not difficult to make friends.

Students have a wide choice of living arrangements, single-sex or coeducational dorms, a small dorm with close-knit associations, or high rise dorms with the opportunity to meet a wider variety of people. There are also special interest houses, such as the "romance language house," where people speak the language they are studying, and "IDC," where students run everything from the house government to the kitchen.

As far as radical social conflicts go, there is no denying UConn was once one of the more heated campuses. Now, however, the school is quiet, except for occasional demonstrations in front of Gulley Hall, which houses the administrative offices, in protest of budget cuts, fee hikes, and dismissal of nontenured professors. Opportunities exist for those who want to express their feelings on how the school, or the dorm, is run.

From small agricultural community to academic city, the Storrs campus has come a long way in a hundred years. In these days of high tuitions and early vocational concerns, it has become an increasingly popular place to be. You may not appreciate cows, but at UConn it doesn't matter. You'll eventually find something of interest socially, culturally, or academically.

CORNELL UNIVERSITY

Location: Ithaca, NY 14853
Campus: small city
Undergraduate enrollment:
  6700 M, 5000 W
Total enrollment: 16,433
Expenses: $8000
Financial aid: 75%
Library: 4,000,000 volumes

Student-faculty ratio: NA
Transfer students: 00
Median SAT: 584 V, 649 M
Fraternities: 40%
Sororities: 15%
Application deadline:
  January 15

Cornell is a remarkable study in contrasts. Combined in one university at the undergraduate level are a college of arts and sciences; a college of architecture, art, and planning; a college of engineering; a school of hotel administration; New York State colleges of agriculture and human ecology (neé home economics); and a state school of industrial and labor relations.

Because Cornell is both a public and private institution with widely divergent standards of admission, it has an extremely varied student body. The radical and the reactionary, the city slicker and the country bumpkin—they're all there.

This offers terribly exciting opportunities and terrible tendencies toward divisiveness. In fact, the various schools within the university seem to exhibit antagonism toward one another. Allegiances are usually to the student's own division; each division has its own stereotype ranging from the jocks or jet-setters of the hotel school to the engineering grinds strapped to their pocket calculators to the human ecology students researching prospective husbands.

The one common factor at Cornell, though, is the campus, one of the most impressive in the country. Sprawling over some 700 rugged acres, Cornell is not only blessed with an awesome abundance of natural beauty on its own land, but is also within fifteen miles of spectacular state parks that served as silent movie sets when Ithaca was the "Hollywood of the East."

Yet even this feature can be divisive. Because Cornell is so rustic and isolated, the student body is easily lulled into apathy. Notorious as a hotbed of campus unrest during the Sixties, Cornell has settled into a state of complacency. The student body has accepted with extraordinary equanimity the dismantling of its once-powerful government by the trustees of the school. While some students discuss and apparently care about campus and world affairs, the majority seems more interested in grade point averages and securing jobs after graduation than in toppling the pillars of imperialism.

Cornell does have a history of racial problems, brought to national attention in 1969 by the armed takeover of its central union by black students. More recently, protests have arisen over proposed changes in the minority financial aid program, university involvement in South Africa, and alleged abuse of minority students' civil rights. The administration seems to be listening and trying to increase minority enrollment and input.

Socially, Cornell was one of the leaders in the liberalization of campus life-styles. Back in the fussy Sixties, women were only allowed in men's rooms on certain evenings at certain times, and then only if the room had a light on and the door was open at least a book's width.

Now, almost all dorms are coed, often by room or shower stall. Myth has it that whenever a virgin walks at midnight on the "arts Quad" between the statues of Ezra Cornell and Andrew White, Cornell's founders, the men walk to the center and shake hands. In recent years, the two haven't budged an inch.

In spite of this, the social scene at Cornell is far from ideal, particularly for freshman men. The male-female ratio is still lopsided. Many men take their frustrations to neighboring universities more noted for their women, particularly Wells College and Ithaca College, where Cornell men can boast about being Ivy Leaguers, if nothing else.

Housing is also a problem at Cornell. Dorms are filled to capacity, and most upperclassmen live off-campus. Many join fraternities or sororities, often opulent places with tennis courts or swimming pools. There has been an increase in the number of frats and sororities in the past five years, and much of the campus's organized social activity is centered around the Greeks.

Those upperclassmen who can't stomach formal dinners and pledge raids often opt to share the simple farm life with sheep and goats in outlying communities. Otherwise, off-campus housing is concentrated in Collegetown, the popular student ghetto of overpriced, poorly maintained apartments owned by a handful of landlord barons.

Some students think Cornell is culturally deficient. Ithaca (whose own offerings are a couple of movie theaters) is an afternoon's drive from many major cities, but the university does try to provide a modicum of culture. Most impressive is the new art museum, which looks like a five-story sewing machine and houses a fine collection of Asian works. Rock concerts are infrequent; many students travel to Syracuse and Binghamton to see the big names.

The community is heavily dependent on the college. Cornell students form a large share of the consuming public for area businesses, the *Cornell Daily Sun* is Ithaca's only morning newspaper and students are visible in all branches of local arts and government.

Academically, Cornell is "pseudo-Ivy League," says one of its graduates. This description is a bit harsh. Cornell offers excellent programs in engineering, biology, history, English, and philosophy. Noted professors like Carl Sagan, Theodore Lowi, and L. Pearce Williams teach introductory level courses. The work and competition are often so demanding that they foster the unfortunate pastime of "gorging out," but the claim that Cornell has the highest suicide rate of any college in the nation is (we think) unsubstantiated.

A lot of people are talking about "general education" these days. Although there are still relatively few university requirements, a trend toward more coherent, interdisciplinary programs is developing, particularly in the arts school.

Cornellians have long suffered an inferiority complex next to students from Yale, Harvard, and Princeton. An old college song notes:

If you were a preppie, you were probably rejected
From each and every Ivy League school but Cornell.

There's a large grain of truth to this. Cornell is the third or fourth choice of many of its students; even the football team lately has been the doormat of the Ivies. But once you're there, its easy to fall in love with the place. Cornell is rugged and unpretentious. Because many feel they haven't quite reached the top yet, students overcompensate by spending long hours slaving away in the library. Unpampered and isolated, many Cornellians innocently perceive the outside world as a place that can still be conquered by hard work.

Incidentally, with Bob Blackman (the winningest Ivy coach ever) at the helm, Cornell football is on the rise. Can the rest of the school follow suit?

CREIGHTON UNIVERSITY

Location: Omaha, NE 68178
Campus: city center
Undergraduate enrollment:
 1600 M, 1400 W
Total enrollment: 5027
Expenses: $5000
Financial aid: 51%
Library: 467,140 volumes

Student-faculty ratio: 11–1
Transfer students: 234
Median ACT: 23
Fraternities: 20%
Sororities: 20%
Application deadline:
 one month before term

If you were to blend the Midwestern and Roman Catholic traditions, you would not end up with the most liberal atmosphere in the world. That, unfortunately, is what has happened at Creighton University in Omaha, Nebraska.

A Jesuit school founded in a stockyard city, it has been something less than an excellent-but-restless liberal arts college. In the past, it has drawn primarily from the sons and daughters of Omaha's Catholic lower-middle class, and despite the large influx of out-of-staters and minority groups, Creighton is still too close to being a commuter university. And, unlike the streetcar colleges found in more exotic spots, Creighton is at the mercy of Omaha, a vast urban sprawl that nearly demands a car. Those students unfortunate or foolish enough not to have wheels are usually confined to the dull expanses of the campus, interrupted only by an occasional venture on Omaha's bus system (a story best left to itself).

Although the large majority of students enjoy their normal sleepy conservatism, more and more students are beginning to question the value of a traditional Catholic education, and more and more are beginning to be dissatisfied with the answers. The administration, they claim, is only interested in building more facilities and maintaining Creighton's "pure" image in the Omaha community. To remedy the situation, they have founded their own experimental university, where the more liberal faculty members offer noncredit courses on subjects as diverse as astrology, the use of rhetoric, and melodrama. The experimental university provides an opportunity for the ordinarily shy student to present papers and give speeches.

The typical Creighton student seems to be more curious than serious about change, more ready to look at innovation than to embrace it. Depth of outrage has never been a symptom of the average (or perhaps even of the extreme) Creighton student.

Socially, of course, Creighton is just emerging from its Catholic cocoon. Creighton girls are always homey, occasionally comely, and generally virgins. Creighton men, despite their "Don Juan" stereotypes, are not much more promiscuous, and if they are, they don't really have too many places to go—the only women's college in Omaha is the College of St. Mary, which is about as far from being a Bennington or a Sarah Lawrence as the Virgin Mary was from being Mary Magdalene. Fraternities still predominate at the Jesuit school, much as the original monks might disapprove of them. They would, however, approve of the generally tight regulations which govern female dorms.

In the academic galaxy, Creighton is distinguished for its strong professional schools. And in other realms, a Black Cultural Center has been opened on campus to house the offices of the Creighton Afro-American Students Association, which has plans for a community teaching tutorial program employing voluntary instructors. The house includes a library of black literature and reading and meeting rooms which should one day host the school.

The fact that Creighton is both Midwestern and Catholic cannot be changed, of course. But the traditional definition of a Catholic (or

Midwesterner) is breaking down rapidly, and we can only hope that Creighton changes with it.

After all, who would have thought that the Pope would be Polish?

DARTMOUTH COLLEGE

Location: Hanover, NH 03755
Campus: rural
Undergraduate enrollment: 2412 M, 1067 W
Total enrollment: 4174
Expenses: $7725
Financial aid: 34%
Library: 1,200,000 volumes

Student-faculty ratio: 11–1
Transfer students: 20
Median SAT: 625 V, 665 M
Fraternities: 40%
Sororities: 10%
Application deadline: January 1

Daniel Webster once said of Dartmouth, "It is a small school, but there are those who love it." Dartmouth students would agree with both points. Outsiders would agree that it is small.

Founded as a humble missionary school to tame and civilize the savage Indians, Dartmouth has grown into one of the nation's most famous (or infamous) institutions. Along the way, it picked up the stereotype of an "animal school" isolated in the New Hampshire wilds. Although it is no longer the predominant species, the traditional Dartmouth animal has had sufficient influence on the school and will never die out.

The fraternities are the major stronghold of all the old college traditions. One of the traditions that is nearest and dearest to the hearts of the students, particularly—though by no means exclusively—those in fraternities, is the consumption of copious quantities of beer. On "sink" night, for example, when fraternities induct new members, it is not at all unusual for one fraternity to consume more than a dozen half-kegs of beer, though it must be admitted that a good portion of it is used for bathing and swimming rather than drinking. While discussing fraternities, it is only fair to mention that two sororities and a nonexclusive women's social organization have helped to balance the formerly male-oriented social life.

Which brings us to the subject of the "Dartmouth Ratio," the ratio of men to women at the college. Since coeducation began at Dartmouth, the number of women has been slowly increasing each year, and this has been and continues to be the major issue on campus. Most students and faculty have been promoting sex-blind admissions, while alumni have wanted to keep a higher number of men for fear of a deterioration in the quality of sports, and the present compromise is to increase the number of women by about fifteen each year until equality is reached. Activism for immediate sex-blind admissions increased greatly in the past year and the feeling on campus is that the quota system is on its way out.

The alumni fears about the quality of sport seem so far to be unfounded, at least if student enthusiasm is any indication. This is particularly true of football, the biggest sport at Dartmouth, and the "Big Green" still attracts its share of talent. Both football and hockey won Ivy League championships in 1978. Despite its fraternities and football emphasis, however, Dartmouth is far from the stereotyped "rah-rah" school. Dartmouth is much closer in spirit to Amherst than it is to the Big Ten. Women's teams have also excelled in their brief history, with several individuals named to national teams every year.

At three-to-one, though, the ratio does make the social life at Dartmouth difficult, both for the men and the women. Some feel that the student body is less cohesive than it could be, and some women, though not all, feel it is difficult to be a woman at Dartmouth. The college's unusual academic calendar, which is based on quarters, also contributes to the lack of cohesiveness. While the "Dartmouth Plan" does provide unique opportunities for foreign study and leave-term jobs, it all too often results in a situation where good friends freshman year may not see each other again until senior spring.

This situation isn't helped by Dartmouth's geographical isolation, which makes it difficult for the men to make up for the lack of women. It is only fair to point out, however, that Dartmouth's picture-postcard campus is in an ideal location for skiing, hiking, climbing, bicycling, and canoeing, and fanatics of any of these pastimes will find more than adequate compensation for the social isolation.

Despite this isolation, however, the social life is relatively active and includes several gigantic, candy-colored, streamlined, orgiastic weekends, including the granddaddy of all college weekends, the Dartmouth Winter Carnival. Furthermore, Dartmouth students are allowed to have cars, and Dartmouth is located near I-91, so that some frustrated Dartmouth males find roadtripping (particularly to Smith, Mount Holyoke, or Wellesley) to be a viable social alternative.

We haven't mentioned academics yet, which really counts as an oversight. The academic opportunities are superb, and some departments, such as math, are reputed to be the best in the country.

Dartmouth has a fantastic Honeywell 6600 computer system which offers terminals and time to any student who wants to use it. John Kemeny, the president of the college, created the "BASIC" language. (The computer even has a program that purports to check your compatibility with your date.) The romance languages department is also widely known, especially for its Rassias teaching method, developed by a Dartmouth professor, and features an extremely popular "language study abroad" program. Other strong areas are English, chemistry, geology, and history.

Dartmouth is small enough to allow for small classes, many seminars, and a good deal of contact between students and faculty members. Even President Kemeny teaches freshmen and holds weekly office hours for students, a rarity at larger schools.

Academic requirements for distribution are limited (students must take four courses in each of three divisions). There are few departmental requirements, and Dartmouth has an excellent pass-fail option. The general freewheeling attitude of the students extends into the classroom, where classes are often animated and interesting.

In short, the "Big Green" has a lot to offer a student who can accept the drawbacks of Hanover (Hangover, to the rest of the Ivy League): a lack of commercial entertainment and a relative lack of women. But if you like the outdoors and a generally hearty campus, Dartmouth may be the place for you. There are worse places to get a good education.

DAVIDSON COLLEGE

Location: Davidson, NC 28036
Campus: rural
Undergraduate enrollment:
  900 M, 400 W
Expenses: $5540
Financial aid: 40%
Library: 250,000

Student-faculty ratio: 13–1
Transfer students: 20
Median SAT: 570 V, 620 M
Fraternities: 3
Sororities: NA
Application deadline:
  February 1

Davidson College may be Presbyterian and provincial, but it's still a good place to go to school. There's a myth that Davidson is the South's answer to the Ivy League, but nobody at the college except starry-eyed alumni and the admissions officials believe it. The fact is, many of the students have never been north of the Mason-Dixon line, and occasionally those in the administration and faculty act as if they haven't, either—and what's more, they don't care. If it's a small, Southern, casual, academically tough college you're after, Davidson is the best place you'll find. Otherwise, you'd be a fool to go there.

Life at Davidson is really rather mundane. The school is twenty miles from anything of significance, and that's no accident. Back in 1837, when those "hardy Scotch-Irish Presbyterians" were looking for a place to put their college, they wanted it away from worldly temptations, and that's what they got. The 1300 Davidson students have only fifteen stores and the 1300 people of the town where they can look for sin.

Given this immediate environment, it is not surprising that nightlife at Davidson borders on the nonexistent. But come the weekend, it's a different story. There are an increasing number of coeds, as well as several women's colleges within striking distance—and if a male student wants a date, the wherewithal is usually available. Needless to say, female students have an even better deal, socially.

Three times a year, Davidson itself is where it's at. For on the happy occasions of the three major dance weekends, the residents of the two newest dorms pull down their pinups and move out to make room for some 700 female guests, (even though these days residents don't necessarily move out . . .). The dance weekend scene usually follows a pattern: concerts on Friday and Saturday nights followed by parties until the wee hours at various spots within a twenty-or thirty-mile radius of the school. Daytime activities include picnics, long walks, and side trips to the mountains.

The social scene at Davidson is relatively loose for a church-affiliated school. Since the adoption of a code of responsibility in 1968, the college is no longer cast in the role of the student's mother and handholder; the responsibility for conduct rests with the student.

Specifically, it means that tightly restricted parietal hours and a ban on campus drinking are no more.

Academically, liberalization came in the form of a device known as the "blue sky" curriculum, which went into effect simultaneously with the new social regulations. In brief, this new curriculum includes a three-two-two calendar in place of the traditional two-semester format, more emphasis on independent study, an honors college, a non-Western studies program, a pass fail option, and no Saturday classes.

The academic program at the college is good and is becoming even better with the liberalization of college requirements. The student is now bound to pursue studies in four broad areas: language, literature, and the arts; religion and philosophy; math and the sciences; and social sciences. The average sensate being can dredge up a fairly good liberal arts education and go on to graduate work, as about half the students do.

On the religious side, 1965 saw the abolition of the hated Sunday night vespers, and 1969 saw the end of mandatory weekly chapels. Many still feel the college is too chummy with the church, however, and there are unconfirmed rumors that faculty tenure hinges on a professor's religious commitment.

With the seven dorms in sad shape, the slack in social life is taken up by the eating houses on the north side of campus. Students join one of the dozen or so clubs in their sophomore year, but most of the clubs' social activities are open to all.

There is little interest in politics, perhaps because all the power centers are so far away. Students would rather support charitable organizations such as the Muscular Dystrophy Association, the Heart Fund, groups representing city poor, through discos, dance-a-thons, and fund-raising campaigns.

Davidson has seen major changes in the last ten years (fortunately unnoticed by alumni), but one relic from the past has survived: a strong sense of community.

A lot can be said for going to college at Davidson, not the least of which is that the school offers a good, solid liberal arts education.

UNIVERSITY OF DAYTON

Location: Dayton, OH 45469
Campus: city outskirts
Undergraduate enrollment:
   3600 M, 2400 W
Total enrollment: 10,000
Expenses: $4400
Financial aid: 73%
Library: 500,000 volumes

Student-faculty ratio: 18–1
Transfer students: 300
Median ACT: 22
Fraternities: less than 30%
Sororities: less than 30%
Application deadline:
   rolling

Despite its location—Dayton is a straitlaced Midwestern city which is proud to proclaim itself the home of Roller Derby—the University of Dayton is well known in Ohio for its blooming social life. The atmosphere is easygoing and wholesome, with most students (even those from New York and Iran) fitting the conservative, traditional mold of the state.

UD, a Catholic Marianist school of 6,000 undergraduate students offers a well-above-average academic program with engineering and business being the strongest course offerings.

In a move away from traditional education, UD has implemented programs such as independent study, self-directed learning, a pass-fail grading option, four- and five-year M. A. programs. There are few Catholic clerics still teaching, except perhaps in the science and theology courses. The great majority of teachers have Ph.Ds and due to the relatively small size of the school, are accessible in times of need.

Service organizations such as Circle K and the Appalachia Club offer students with something to give an opportunity to contact those persons less fortunate and spend time teaching, learning, and experiencing. Other organizations on campus are directly related to particular majors such as for the "advancement of management," and the "American home economics association."

Social life abounds at UD; it is considered one of the top party schools in Ohio. With university-sponsored affairs, numerous nearby bars and street parties drawing 600–700 students and one hundred kegs of beer, there is never a lack of something to do. The majority of sororities and fraternities are local organizations and do not greatly influence student life.

UD athletics center around the basketball team which, until star Jim Paxson graduated and was drafted by the Portland "Trailblazers," was worth being centered around. Other sports include a Division III football team, a soccer team with a losing record the past three years, and a top-ranked women's basketball team—all of which are wholeheartedly supported by students and Dayton area sports fans.

Living accommodations range from the typical dormitory to semi-rundown houses making up the nearby "ghetto" area. In the middle, you will find the new university-owned apartments featuring wall-to-wall carpeting and air-conditioning. Housing at the university is arranged by hierarchy, so seniors get the preferred locations—mostly in the ghetto where life is never dull with occasional couch burnings (only on special occasions, such as a basketball victory over Notre Dame), and steak barbecues in mid-January.

The most recent political uprisings on campus are a far cry from the sit-ins of the Sixties, but are enough to warrant coverage by the local Dayton television station. Demonstrations of the Iranian students demanding the return of the Shah coupled with demonstrations against registration and the draft have kept even sheltered students abreast of world developments.

UD offers students the opportunity to discover and develop their own individual life-styles. From a student's viewpoint, "UD is a real good time."

UNIVERSITY OF DELAWARE

Location: Newark, DE 19711
Campus: suburban
Undergraduate enrollment:
  6000 M, 6600 W
Total enrollment: 18,712
Expenses: $3000 (in-state),
  $4500 (out-of-state)
Financial aid: 17%
Library: 1,500,000 volumes

Student-faculty ratio: 18-1
Transfer students: 500
Median SAT: 480 V, 529 M
Fraternities: 6%
Sororities: NA
Application deadline:
  March 1

Delawareans have spent the last few years trying to offset an image created by Allen Funt in a classic segment of "Candid Camera." Funt placed a road sign leading into the state with a notice that Delaware was closed for the day. Despite the state's reputation for being small, quaint, and usually dull, the University of Delaware has remained one of the strongholds in countering the boredom that residents and nonresidents alike are so inclined to believe about the "First State."

The University of Delaware stands on about 1000 acres in the middle of Newark, a quiet college town of 26,000 people. Newark is in the northwestern corner of the state, only a few miles from Maryland's Eastern Shore and the Pennsylvania mushroom country. Local bus service connects the town to Wilmington, fifteen miles away. Interstate 95 passes just south of town. After the university, the second biggest employer is the Chrysler assembly plant, located across from the university's agricultural college and athletic complex.

On campus, the most distinctive and beautiful feature is the grassy, elmlined mall that fronts a dozen Georgian-style classroom and administrative buildings. But many university buildings were designed with only the whims of current architecture in mind and not in any overall scheme. Some offices were converted from houses, an apartment building and an automobile showroom. The other campus landmark is "Christiana Towers," sixteen- and seventeen-story towers of extremely popular university-owned apartments for undergraduates. Nearby are the "Pencader dormitories," where all the rooms have private outside entrances. About half of the students at the university live in these and other more traditional dormitories. All are presided over by the comprehensive "residence life" staff, who have won national acclaim for programming. Many other students live in the apartment complexes that ring the town.

Financially, a lot of influence is held by the du Pont family and friends. As *The New York Times* said of Wilmington: "It is impossible to drive far in any direction without passing streets, highways, schools, office buildings and museums named for or endowed by the oldest and biggest of American billionaire families." This support places the university's endowment near the top among public institutions. With a third of its funding coming from the state, the university is one of a rare breed of "state-related" institutions that are neither public nor private. The in-state tuition rate is one of the highest among public universities. Delaware (or, more accurately, du Pont) puts most of its money into the natural sciences and engineering, leaving the social sciences and humanities unsure of what their support will be. For example, geography and communication, two of the newer departments here, are only grudgingly funded despite proven interest. But the situation has improved greatly since the late Sixties, when *Science* magazine described the school as coming "close to being a du Pont-directed enterprise," known only for engineering and chemistry. Noted programs now also include art conservation, biology, ornamental horticulture, and marine studies.

Academically, most administrative decisions are made very slowly, with several years' trends necessary for a major change—which is unfortunately too long for the student who is here for only four short years. But this conservative, far-sighted policy is expected to pay off when enrollments decline across the country in the Eighties.

The student body hasn't flared up in demonstrations about anything since the early Seventies, when freedom of speech and religion and restrictive administrative policies were hot issues. The campus is now quiet, with fun immediately following studying. Beer, marijuana, and partying in general are still the favorite forms of weekend entertainment here. The university's policy on responsible drinking seems to forget the official drinking age of twenty, but the administration has cracked down on large, rowdy, outdoor affairs known as "open campus parties." The Deer Park and the Stone Balloon are Main Street's most popular night spots. Parties in "Christiana Towers" are campus classics. Rock music is popular, with George Thorogood hailed as a hometown hero. Philadelphia is close enough (via 1-95) for regular activities. The administration doesn't support much entertainment outside of extensive film series and popular lectures.

The university instead concentrates on athletic and specialty programming. Sports include intramurals and collegiate competition (with free entry for students) led by the financially and morally successful Division II football team. The academic side is headed by the honors program. Begun for gifted high school students, it now lends a scholarly air to campus. Specialty programs for women, minorities and Greeks are all highlighted by activities weeks. About one hundred clubs are registered here, with a generally weak student government spending most of its time policing these groups.

Reams of regulations spell out nearly every situation, with most being made possible by the university's self-styled schizophrenia. But most students protest more about parking tickets than they do about university policies. Political activism is handled by the same small number of students who each year create another group for a new social cause.

Like those at most state schools, the students are largely middle-class residents, but Delaware is getting increasingly popular among out-of-state students. It seems they are attracted by the ambiguous combination of large and small: in a small town, but near a big city; with small classes but large numbers of them; small enough to know people, but large enough to meet new ones.

DENISON UNIVERSITY

Location: Granville, OH 43023
Campus: rural
Undergraduate enrollment:
　1040 M, 960 W
Expenses: $6960
Financial aid: 20%
Library: 235,000 volumes

Student-faculty ratio: 14–1
Transfer students: 25
Median SAT: 480 V, 530 M
Fraternities: 60%
Sororities: 46%
Application deadline:
　February 15

On top of an Ohio hill flourishes Denison University, a four-year liberal arts college for men and women. As of 1978–1979, Denison has adopted coed housing, with only four dorms still all-female and one all-male. The student body represents the upper-middle-class values of its parents, embracing their conservative outlook on most things. Summer vacations are spent either camp-counseling or waitressing in Nantucket, Martha's Vineyard, Newport, or the Jersey shore.

Granville is a typical New England town transplanted in Ohio, complete with cobblestone streets and quaint shops. No longer completely dry, there are now two bars plus Fuller's (the local market that sells beer and wine). The closest "city" is Newark. Students drive there for liquor runs, car repairs, fast food joints, and tacky shopping malls. This typical factory town offers nothing in the way of intellectual or social stimulation. Columbus, however, twenty-five miles away, does offer some good museums, concerts, and similar vestiges of a cosmopolitan city. The restaurants are great, able to satisfy even the most discerning of palates.

Denison's recent implementation of coed dorms has opened the eyes of the traditionally conservative trustees. They are seeing that coed living does not necessarily mean "sex in the hallways." The new attractiveness of the dorm life has hit the frat system hard. Students are finding that living with members of the opposite sex is more pleasant than crowding into a dirty frat house. Denison is unique in that all of its residence halls are student managed. Decisions concerning dorm policy are made by the students.

The frats and sororities are the center of social activities on the DU hill. Fall, Christmas, and Pledge Formals always manage to bring about new romances. Wednesday night is party night and a good many students journey to Newark to the Manor house, Tony's (known for their red dogs), or Mac's Disco to tie one on or simply cop a light buzz.

A substantial group of students have totally rejected this system and either spend their time studying or become part of the "downhill" crowd. This group is so named because most of its members live in dormitories or apartments off the campus hill. The downhiller majors in one of the fine arts, writes an occasional poem for *Exile*, the Denison literary magazine, likes to smoke Colombian at least as much as the next guy, and goes to the uphill academic quad only to check his mailbox or play some Friz.

Weekdays, eleven-thirty marks the height of "face time" in the Union, when students come en masse to get their mail. Women are ogled by the frat rats who perch on permanent seats (*Beta* and *Phi Delt* Benches, *Sig* Landing, etc.).

The intellectual atmosphere has increased in intensity since Robert Good became president in 1976.

It is certainly not the faculty's fault if partying dominates learning. An unsuccessful faculty proposal to limit and deemphasize fraternity and sorority rush sparked the recent controversy over the role of intellectualism at Denison. Generally young and enthusiastic, the faculty includes nationally known scholars in the philosophy, religion, and modern languages departments. The history and English departments are strong, and the premed program is well respected.

Partly due to faculty concern over grade inflation, the school now uses a plus-minus 4.0 grading system. While it is not difficult to receive Cs, As and Bs demand conscientious studying and little deviation from the course syllabus. A final word of caution: don't visit Denison on a nice day. The verdant beauty of College Hill and the quaint village of Granville have been known to cloud the minds of even the most cynical urbanites.

UNIVERSITY OF DENVER

Location: Denver, CO 80208
Campus: suburban
Undergraduate enrollment: 2250 M, 1750 W
Total enrollment: 7875
Expenses: $6100
Financial aid: 52%
Library: 1,200,000 volumes

Student-faculty ratio: 14-1
Transfer students: 525
Median SAT: 510 V, 540 M
Median ACT: 24
Fraternities: 15%
Sororities: 17%
Application deadline: April 1

If you're under the impression that the University of Denver is a party school in mellow Colorado, you're probably mistaken. Though it's true that UD may have once been a scenic outlet for the East Coast rich collegiate fond of a good time, we are told that this is certainly no longer the case. Many students are on financial aid, and although UD still boasts an active social atmosphere, academics are quite important.

The university has a highly liberal academic outlook and offers considerable opportunity for fashioning one's own curriculum. There is an extensive work-study program involving 200 students. UD was recently one of very few institutions to receive a National Science Foundation grant for the improvement of undergraduate science education. Freshmen and sophomore humanities courses are benefiting from a similar substantial grant at a time when most other colleges must pinch pennies.

The psychology department at UD is considered by many to have one of the most outstanding programs of its size in the country. The physics and English departments are also strong. About thirty percent of the undergraduate class is enrolled in the UD College of Business Administration, which has received national press acclaim. (The large enrollment in this division should tell you something about the student body at UD.)

Surprising for any school, a recent survey has indicated that an overwhelming percentage of students consider their education at UD good or very good. Even more surprising, students at UD don't spend all their time grinding away in the library, either. Intramural sports are very big, as is fraternity life. Interest in the Greek way of life has been steadily increasing over the past few years.

Chances are good that Denver will give you that "Rocky Mountain high." It is a modern, progressive place, a cultural oasis between Chicago and San Francisco. And (you guessed it) the ski slopes are only minutes away.

Colorado's only private university, UD is bound not by state legislators' incessant demands for preferential treatment for local students (either in granting admission or in total expenses). This means that UD attracts a pretty varied student body, even if most applicants are from the higher economic echelon.

If you like the locale, want a good education, and are heading into business (or even if you're not), Denver is a decent place to crack your books.

DE PAUL UNIVERSITY

Location: Chicago, IL 60604
Campus: city center
Undergraduate enrollment:
   2542 M, 2220 W
Total enrollment: 12,149
Expenses: $4940
Financial aid: 65%
Library: 168,710 volumes
Student-faculty ratio: 19–1
Transfer students: 1200
Median ACT: 23.5
Fraternities: 5%
Sororities: 4%
Application deadline:
   July 1

Chicago's local press likes to describe DePaul University as "the little school under the elevated tracks." As it continues to grow in national recognition, however, DePaul has emerged from the El's shadow for good.

An urban university, DePaul's two campuses exemplify the diversity of city dwelling. The downtown campus, situated in the seventeen-story Frank J. Lewis Center, lies in the heart of Chicago's "Loop" business district. Uptown, DePaul maintains a twenty-five-acre facility in Chicago's historical Lincoln Park area which includes all the residential halls.

The Chicago Board of Trade, the Mid-American Commodity Exchange, and many of the city's major banks and insurance companies are all within a few blocks of DePaul's downtown campus. The

Lewis Center, located at Wabash and Jackson, also houses the university's law school and commerce schools.

Dorm students uptown are within a few blocks of the Lincoln, Clark, and Diversey strip of restaurants and bars. However, the drinking age in Chicago has recently been raised to twenty-one so only juniors and seniors are usually allowed to bring alcohol into university buildings. Campus social activities are dominated by dorm students who lack a ride into the suburbs where drinking restrictions are more lenient. Marijuana is a popular alternative to drinking.

Most DePaul students are middle-class commuter students who live in the Chicago metropolitan area. They attend classes and then leave to work either in the "Loop" or the suburbs. Most students are grade-conscious: they must adhere to a tight work-school schedule to allow for adequate class and test preparation. Commuter students are virtually immune to university political activity. However, university organizations have been involved in city mayoral and aldermanic campaigns. Recently, a few DePaul undergraduates have run for political office in the suburbs.

On-campus organizations cater to a wide variety of student needs. Many of the national fraternities and sororities are represented; these groups alone organize many of the university's formal and informal dances. The university-sponsored "program council," managed by a student board, presents movies, musical groups, and individual performers at both campuses for student entertainment. *The DePaulia*, the student newspaper, offers undergraduates the opportunity to write and edit a weekly publication. DePaul's student organizations provide an alternative to draining work-study routines.

Academically, best known are the college of commerce and the school of music and fine arts. Both faculties are prominent in the business and arts communities. In addition, the college of liberal arts and sciences has a reputation for quality education in both graduate and undergraduate divisions. The Goodman School of Drama, famous for its dramatic excellence, offers the theater-oriented student a rare educational experience. Traditionally a prominent professional college, the university's law school is fighting to maintain its academic standards while undergoing an administrative transition.

But most of the national attention focussed on DePaul recently is due to the prowess of the basketball team. Led by Ray Meyer, the dean of college basketball coaches, the "Blue Demons" have been invited to the NCAA playoffs four of the last five years and were ranked first in the country in 1980.

Although men's basketball is DePaul's major sport, other good intercollegiate teams include both men's and women's tennis, men's track, men's golf, women's volleyball, women's basketball, and women's softball. The average student has the opportunity to compete in a variety of intramural sports, most of which are played in DePaul's two gymnasiums: Hayes-Healy and Alumni Hall.

While the board of trustees is responsible for the governance of the university, the university senate serves as a deliberative body through which educational and administrative policies, in accordance with the fundamental policies of the board of trustees, are made. The senate contains sixty-five members, thirty-six of whom are faculty, thirteen students, twelve administrators, and two of whom are drawn from the staff. The senate deals with academic freedom and tenure, student affairs, appointments, public relations, and physical and general financing plans. Most of the work is done in standing committees and subcommittees.

A balance of political and academic activity provides a comfortable university environment. DePaul attracts a wide variety of students from Chicago's diverse neighborhoods and suburbs who come to learn, or play, or both. But whatever reason they come for, they usually stay in Chicago and go into business or law. And that's their right.

DE PAUW UNIVERSITY

Location: Greencastle, IN 46135
Campus: suburban
Undergraduate enrollment:
　1050 M, 1150 W
Total enrollment: 2350
Expenses: $6500
Financial aid: 54%
Library: 360,000 volumes

Student-faculty ratio: 14–1
Transfer students: 60
Median SAT: 500 V, 540 M
Fraternities: 65%
Sororities: 70%
Application deadline:
　April 1

Several years ago the civic-minded city fathers of Greencastle, Indiana, constructed a small sign and stuck it like a chastity belt on the southern edge of town. It read, "Welcome to Greencastle—Protect our Children." Since 1837, "protecting our children" has been a time-honored aim at this small, church-related liberal arts institution. Happily, they've never really succeeded.

The Good Lord knows they've tried. For instance, possession of alcoholic beverages can be grounds for expulsion from the school (even if you're twenty-one), any student who marries must report the marriage to his dean, and cars are denied to nearly everyone except second semester seniors and student pastors.

Or at least that's what the De Pauw handbook says. The students who fought for social liberalization during the past decade attained the abolition of all visiting hours as early as 1969. Students have subsequently ignored all the conditional requirements (like visiting hours for freshman women) that the university's administrators have attached to the innovations. Booze flows freely, and sexual activity has been known to occur without the knowledge of the administrators (that's the official version, anyway). De Pauw enjoys social freedom—in fact, if not in theory. Long-range prospects are even better, so there's definitely hope.

Academic reforms have also shown a progressive trend of late. Independent study terms between semesters, cross-departmental offerings known as the "experimental division," a successful four-one-four setup, and an increasing number of pass-fail options have all become realities. The liberal studies program, in which fifty freshmen selected at random chance their academic careers without the hindrance of normal course requirements, got off to a promising start several years ago. Also, a remarkably active foreign study program gives scores of De Pauwites the opportunity to gleefully escape Greencastle's Middle America confines for other destinations—Europe, Africa, South America, and the Far East. Overall, music, nursing, and just plain old liberal arts remain the best scholastic bets at De Pauw.

A brand-new arts center has just been completed and has increased the cultural possibilities in Greencastle.

Enough of the Middle American consciousness (which spawns most of the student body) remains on campus to keep Greeks in the center of the social mainstream. With three-quarters of the students going the fraternity-sorority route, dances and pledge parties are definitely "in."

Traditionally, De Pauw graduates have followed up on their middle-class background to become Midwestern leaders, turning up with regularity in state legislatures and chambers of commerce in the area.

Although the realization of the "American dream" has generally been the goal of most De Pauwites, many are beginning to question that dream.

De Pauw is better for it.

UNIVERSITY OF DETROIT

Location: Detroit, MI 48221
Campus: city outskirts
Undergraduate enrollment:
 1400 M, 1730 W
Total Enrollment: 9307
Expenses: $5500
Financial aid: 75%
Library: 500,000 volumes

Student-faculty ratio: 17–1
Transfer students: NA
Median SAT: 442 V, 491 M
Median ACT: 20
Fraternities: NA
Sororities: NA
Application deadline:
 August 15

The University of Detroit is surrounded by all the sights, sounds, culture, and problems of Detroit. The university itself is a landmark in the city, with over 25,000 alumni living in the metropolitan area.

The Jesuits founded UD in 1877 as a liberal arts college; over half the student body is Catholic. The school participates in a consortium program that enables its students to attend classes at seven other local Catholic colleges.

The University of Detroit, it is important to note, is a commuter college; most students live in the tricounty metropolitan Detroit area. However, the school's enrollment does include students from forty states and thirty foreign countries. (UD has dormitories for its noncommuting students.)

The dormitories are situated on the seventy-acre main campus in residential northwest Detroit along with the school of liberal arts, the school of science and engineering, the school of architecture, and the school of business and administration. The other two campuses are located in downtown Detroit near the new nationally acclaimed Renaissance Center.

Students at UD tend to be just that: studious students. Each year, the administration attempts to recruit top scholars in the region. The relationship between the school and the city in which it is found is more than geographical. The university boasts the largest black population for a Jesuit university: approximately twenty-five percent.

The university is currently facing a serious financial crisis which led to extensive cutbacks. Programs in social work and black studies have been reduced, the School of Education lost its national accreditation in 1979, and budgets have been trimmed all over the campus. Some students decide they've had enough and transfer (mostly to Central Michigan University).

Even with the fiscal crunch, some departments remain strong. The communications department offers good experience and the schools of architecture and engineering are among the best in the nation.

Other facts that might be important to know about UD are that "long hair is 'out' on campus, and drinking and short hair are 'in,' " according to one student there. Students are quite conservative. They are job-oriented and many justify their presence at the university in that context. Most students hold part-time jobs or are in work-study programs. An overwhelming number of guys at UD were jocks in high school, and the sight of old high school letter sweaters and jackets is not uncommon.

Sports and social life at UD are what would be expected at a university of its size with a mainly commuter population. The campus sponsors many special nights and social weeks that involve commuter and noncommuter alike.

If you are from Detroit or the vicinity, chances are you already know about UD. If you are not, pay close attention to what UD can offer and make sure you're not requiring a school with a diverse student body.

DICKINSON COLLEGE

Location: Carlisle, PA 17013
Campus: rural
Undergraduate enrollment:
  850 M, 800 W
Expenses: $6285
Financial aid: 30%
Library: 250,000 volumes

Student-faculty ratio: 14–1
Transfer students: 30
Median SAT: 540 V, 572 M
Fraternities: 68%
Sororities: 40%
Application deadline:
  March 1

For a small city of 20,000, Carlisle boasts of several immortal names: Masland Carpets, the U.S. Army War College, Jim Thorpe, the Frog Switch and Manufacturing Company, Molly Pitcher, Bixler's Hardware Store, and Dickinson College. By no stretch of the imagination is Carlisle a hot (or even tepid) cultural center, but the historical seat of Cumberland County imparts an atmosphere to Dickinson College that might best be described as intimate.

The setting of the college is almost idyllic—rustic without big city hustle—and garners admiration from parents and applicants arriving for interviews. Although boredom can eventually overcome the admiration, the college provides the active, interested student with enough academic, social, and extracurricular activities to keep him busy for four years.

Since its founding in 1773, Dickinson continues its strong tradition of, and commitment to, small size and quality undergraduate education. A staunch supporter of the liberal arts, the college maintains high standards: it is considered selective and academic pressure is keen. Although the existence of several huge introductory classes seems to contradict the benefits of small size, the student still has the unique opportunity to get to know and work closely with his professors. In fact, it is not uncommon that seminars and small classes are held at the professor's home. Administrators as well as accessible and genuinely interested in students; at Dickinson, a student is never a number.

Academically, the college is especially strong in English, languages, biology, and the social sciences, with the exception of psychology and sociology. In addition, independent study and "self-developed" majors are encouraged.

There exists a strong internship program in which students combine classroom theory with practical experience by working off-campus at a job in their area of interest. Students are awarded academic credit for internships and find them to be excellent ways to explore career possibilities. Most internships are designed by the student, although Dickinson sponsors several of them. Moreover, an active off-campus study program sends students all over the world.

Living accommodations vary in quality depending on the circumstances. Even in these times of decreasing application rates, Dickinson has a tendency to overenroll slightly, but the college purchases or leases small houses close to campus to meet housing needs. In addition to this coveted option, other living arrangements include one dormitory of four-bedroom suites, two of two-bedroom quads, and one upperclass dorm consisting primarily of singles. (Singles aren't extra and are available on a first-come, first-served basis.)

The opportunity for coeducational housing by dorm section or floor is increasing, and special-interest small houses for foreign language and black students are also available. Most Greek men live in the fraternity quadrangle and off-campus living is seeing a substantial rise, in spite of the scarcity and expense of apartments. The four sororities, however, provide no living quarters.

Reflecting the fact that more than half the men belong to fraternities, social life is limited to and centers around the quadrangle—a major complaint among independent students. However, several independent social organizations sponsor activities during the year and offer increasingly viable alternatives to the Greek-letter societies.

Whether "geek" or Greek, Dickinson is a heavy drinking school. Although local tavern owners may be hesitant to sell to minors (drinking age is twenty-one in Pennsylvania) and liquor stores are run by the state, students have no trouble procuring alcohol of all kinds. Dope is also available for those who partake.

A focal point of the campus is the adequate library, which has an effective interlibrary loan system to supplement and enlarge its offerings. Moreover, the state library in Harrisburg is only twenty miles away from Carlisle.

There is little political activity on campus. Politicos make their moves in the student senate, which has a strong voice in college affairs and controls a $100,000 budget to fund student organizations. Of perhaps greater importance is the all-college governance structure, which consists of seven major committees comprised of elected students, faculty, and administrators. These committees play a prominent role in recommending policy to the faculty. Social-help organizations, music, dramatics, religious groups, the radio station, the yearbook, and the newspaper help to round out the extracurricular picture.

The emphasis on interscholastic sports is much lower at Dickinson than at many other small colleges. The college grants no athletic scholarships. Nonetheless, the school has fielded some outstanding individual athletes, and there is a strong intramural program. At present, the biggest dissatisfaction is with the antiquated gym and the poor facilities it provides. However, Dickinson recently broke ground for construction of a multimillion-dollar life/sports learning center which will include a 200-meter indoor track, squash, racquetball and basketball courts, indoor pool, weight room, and more. Classrooms are also provided for in the plans for the new gymnasium, which is scheduled to be completed by the spring of 1981.

It is fairly easy to fit in at Dickinson and, despite the strong Greek orientation, no one group truly dominates on campus. A friendly, if complacent, campus, students find comfortable niches from which to pick and choose. Even though the emphasis is on academics, students still manage to find ways to party as hard as they work. For the money, Dickinson offers a first-rate liberal arts education with all the frills, but admittedly with few of the thrills.

DRAKE UNIVERSITY

Location: Des Moines, IA 50311
Campus: city outskirts
Undergraduate enrollment:
   3600 M, 1400 W
Total enrollment: 7200

Student-faculty ratio: 17–1
Transfer students: 650
Median SAT: 510 V, 550 M
Median ACT: 24.8
Fraternities: 19%

Expenses: $5500
Financial aid: 44%
Library: 470,000 volumes

Sororities: 20%
Application deadline: May 1

If you know now that you want to be a pharmacist, you should consider applying to Drake University, as their five-year pharmacy program is very good, albeit highly selective. If you are not sure that pharmacy is the thing for you, Drake may still be a mellow place to spend your undergraduate years. It is a small nonsectarian school in the residential part of Des Moines, Iowa. Eighty percent of the students come from the north central states, most of them from the Chicago area.

From the point of view of academic opportunities, Drake is uneven. The college of liberal arts is the largest college at Drake. It is considered good in foreign languages and political science. The poli sci department, though, is more oriented toward abstract concepts than toward practical application. The sociology department is good; most of its curriculum is modeled after the department at Iowa State University, one of the best in the country. The geology department is very small. The psychology program is weak and consists mainly of self-paced courses. English has been criticized by some for not being well organized. Fred Adams and Charles Nelson are popular history professors. Other popular instructors include William Francois at the journalism school, Francis Wilhoit in poli sci, and Rodney Rogers in biology.

The college of fine arts offers majors in art, music, and theater. Artwork is frequently displayed in the student center and symphony concerts and plays are common. The college has good facilities and faculty. However, there is a stated bias in the music department for applied music majors as distinct from music education majors.

One last note about academics: the business school, with about 900 students, claims one of the best actuary science departments in the country, and its placement rate is very high.

The academic atmosphere at Drake is only mildly competitive. Students do a lot of cramming before tests, and residence halls are not study-oriented.

The university senate is a student government body that has potential for power in school policies, but it is ignored by most students. Life in the residence halls is governed by the students themselves. Students publish a school paper and magazine. Interest clubs and fraternities are also present on campus but are not very conspicuous. A women's center and a black student's organization are funded by the university, but few students are involved in them. The residence halls at Drake sponsor parties, community speakers, and tournaments. It isn't necessary to join a fraternity or sorority to have an active social life. Drake Relays Week-end is the most exciting time of the year, and people come from all over the United States to participate in and watch the events.

Freshmen are required to live in the residence halls unless they choose to live at home. About one-third of the full-time students live in residence halls. They are becoming increasingly crowded, though, and lotteries are being used to mete out the available spaces to upperclassmen.

Students in sororities and fraternities can live in the Greek houses. Off-campus housing near the school is difficult to find. The campus itself is somewhat restricting for students without cars, but there is daytime bus service to downtown Des Moines and to some other main areas of interest. Des Moines is the state capital and is home to many large parks and an art center.

Nightlife on weekends revolves around alcohol. Drugs are used by some students, but they are discouraged by the strict surveillance of the university. Movies are shown in the student center on weekends, and students often perform in the center's bar. Many students go off-campus for entertainment, but the majority do not frequently leave Des Moines for the weekend.

The student body at Drake is complacent. Unless you have a specific reason for wanting to go there, though, you might look elsewhere.

DREW UNIVERSITY

Location: Madison, NJ 07940
Campus: suburban
Undergraduate enrollment:
 650 M, 770 W
Total enrollment: 2205
Expenses: $6600
Financial aid: 44%
Library: 400,000 volumes

Student-faculty ratio: 15–1
Transfer students: 100
Median SAT: 530 V, 540 M
Fraternities: 0%
Sororities: 0%
Application deadline:
 March 1

Drew University is about half an hour from both Newark, New Jersey, and New York City. Being so close to Newark is not one of Drew's biggest advantages. Being so close to New York is. Students continually take advantage of "the city" alone or through Drew programs such as the Art Semester, which lets students spend two days a week in art studios and museums, and the UN Semester, which lets them spend two days a week at the United Nations Building.

Other off-campus programs are also popular, including semesters in London, Brussels, and Washington, D.C., and arrangements with many other schools for easy transfers of credit. Drew also has cross-registration with nearby all-female St. Elizabeth's College.

But what happens on Drew's own Madison campus? Some very good things, we are told. Political science is the largest department, followed by economics, English, psychology, history, and zoology. All of these departments are strong. Among the many popular professors are Julius Mastro and Frank Wolf in poli sci; Joan Weimar, Inez Nelbach, and Robert Ready in English; Jim Mills, Ed Domber, and Sylvia Pollock in psychology; and Lee Pollock in zoology. In addition to the college of liberal arts, Drew offers a grad school and a renowned theology school.

Drew is the current home of the New Jersey Shakespeare Festival, headed by Paul Barry, and Drew students are accepted as interns in the company, whose season starts in June and extends into the fall semester. A new theater professor, Robert (Buzz) McLaughlin, has completely revitalized the whole theater arts major. There is no specialization within the major, which emphasizes the production of new works written, directed by, and starring Drew students. The music major is not specialized either and consists of a basic overall approach to theory, history, and composition.

The academic load here averages fifteen credits a semester, enough to keep the students plenty busy. There is a predominant pub-study-pub-study atmosphere among an unusually apathetic student body. The campus pub and the pinball machines in the university center have a virtual stranglehold on the college social life. All the same, Drew has come a long way since its "suitcase school" days a few years ago. There are free movies every weekend, as well as on Wednesday nights. Semiformal affairs are organized by various clubs, and there is generally a dance in the UC every weekend. The dances, all of which are free, are sponsored by the social committee, which also sponsors good rock concerts for a few bucks.

Drew is not a jock college, but it has interscholastic teams in soccer (a pretty good one), basketball, baseball, rugby, tennis, cross-country, fencing, and lacrosse. Admission to all athletic events is free for Drew students. There is also a fine intramural program in all sports for both men and women. Women's sports are on an upswing, and student interest in them is high.

WERD is the radio station at Drew (closed carrier, broadcasting only on campus). Very few people listen to it. There is also a student-run weekly newspaper. The student government is inexcusably weak, especially considering the strength of the political science department.

The college of liberal arts enrolls both residential students and students who commute from their homes in nearby communities. Finding an apartment off-campus is not encouraged. Living facilities on campus range from singles to suites, with doubles predominating. The meal plan—not gourmet quality, but bearable—is mandatory for residential students.

Drew has a sprinkling of students from many states and even foreign countries, but most are from the Massachusetts-down-to-Virginia area of the Eastern seaboard. "Ruggers" tend to hang together, as do baseball and soccer players. There are no fraternities or sororities (and no football team, for that matter), but cliques and factions are not unknown.

Drew is a good place for someone who likes very liberal rules. Twenty-four hour visitation is taken for granted, and students serve on the security force. Security officers do not carry guns or stage surprise visits to student rooms.

Drew is *not* a good place for someone who likes very liberal politics. It's not easy to get people up off their asses over an issue when everyone is preoccupied with five tough courses. Many students come to Drew just for academics, and it shows.

Finally, as the catalog says, the semirural Drew campus is beautiful. It rains more than it should, and the ground is like a sponge, but on those days when there's a warm breeze and the trees are in bloom, it's wonderful. And the bright lights of New York are never far away.

DUKE UNIVERSITY

Location: Durham, NC 27706
Campus: city outskirts
Undergraduate enrollment:
   3100 M, 2600W
Total enrollment: 9000
Expenses: $7450
Financial aid: 31%
Library: 3,000,000 volumes

Student-faculty ratio: 9–1
Transfer students: 75
Median SAT: 620 V, 650 M
Fraternities: 45%
Sororities: 33%
Application deadline:
   January 15

In deep night, when Durham's modest skyline is buried in darkness, the gothic spire of the Duke Chapel hovers disembodied over the forested outskirts of the city. Such magic is produced by a powerful light trained on the campus's central tourist attraction. But daytime reveals the entire 200-foot structure, and before it, the statue of a very unmagical man—tobacco baron James B. Duke—whose imprint has been slow to fade in the fifty years since Trinity College became Duke University.

"Buck" Duke built his university in the verdant North Carolina piedmont to train hard-nosed ministers, lawyers, and doctors. The numbers of premedical and prelaw students on campus attest to his legacy. But then, so does the depressing state of the fine arts.

Nevertheless, Duke has taken amazing strides forward in the last fifteen years. In 1965, freshmen were subjected to a humiliating "traditions test" and had to wear "Blue Devil" beanies; disgusted students of that era often referred to Duke as "the hardest high school in America." Four years later, the stodgy curriculum was entirely revamped. Virtually all requirements were tossed out, and a four-year independent study option was created.

Whereas most students used to come from the South, Duke has become a national institution, with Northerners who seek intellectual challenge without the academic intensity of Yale or Swarthmore making up sixty percent of the student body. And in the early Seventies, the stilted "weekend date" social system deteriorated, as coed dorms brought Dukies together at last, eighty years after women were first admitted to Trinity. Today Duke offers, with the possible exception of Rice, the finest undergraduate education in the South.

And the South may not be a bad place to get your education. A relaxed life-style and lush, gauzy springs belie the area's rapid changes, and Duke, at the top of a "research triangle," which includes the University of North Carolina and N. C. State, plays a leading role. The Institute of Policy Sciences and Public Affairs draws frequent speakers from all over the country, and undergraduate policy majors are envied for their summer internships in Raleigh and Washington, D. C. The school is branching out and is a good example of the "New South."

But something of an older South lingers more than a decade after blacks (and hundreds of white supporters) were teargassed in a takeover of the administration building, the number of black students at Duke remains small, and in 1973 a black administrator quit after the school refused to increase minority financial aid and recruitment. Fraternities declined in the Sixties but are now enjoying a revival. During the mild winter months, a venerable Southern obsession—

big-time basketball—brings everyone together in mammoth Cameron Indoor Stadium to scream "Go t'hell, Kerlina, go t'hell!" at nationally ranked Maryland, N. C. State, and, of course, Carolina. Duke has been in the top few in the country the last four years and made it to the NCAA finals in 1979.

It is a measure of Duke's diversity that you may well trudge back to the Cambridge Inn Café, hoarse (it is inevitable) after a close game, and sit down to a raspy discussion with a professor. The campus is loose and open, and professors are accessible if you are willing to approach them (although some grade-grubbing students abuse this opportunity in search of a higher grade point average). Construction began in 1979 on a $16 million university center, a welcome addition to the campus.

Fraternities and sororities are active and growing at Duke. For many, they provide the answer to the entire question of social life. But there are other ways to meet people outside of the at times sovereign Greek system—for instance, most students take advantage of the extensive variety of extracurricular organizations. Duke is also becoming a livelier campus, politically. Controversy is created by such issues as funding for campus publications, unionization of Duke Hospital, race relations, nuclear power, and Chancellor A. Kenneth Pye's "Planning for the Eighties".

On warm weekends, a good many Dukies roadtrip, although Duke is by no means a "suitcase school." Their destination these days is likely to be the Great Smoky Mountains or the ghostly Outer Banks beaches, rather than the Greensboro College for Women. An ever-increasing number of students have cars, freshmen included, which makes getting away easier. Durham's nightlife is scant. Interaction between Dukies and the town is increasing, however. Social life centers on campus (main attractions are concerts in the "Indoor Stadium" and the film series) but long lines can be found in front of Daryl's, a popular local restaurant.

Most Duke students live on-campus. Housing is fast becoming an issue, as the four-year on-campus housing which has traditionally been available is becoming scarce because of enrollment increases. Dorms vary from sex-segregated to coed to special-interest living groups.

Duke has two campuses, both of which are coed. The Gothic west campus is the former men's college, while the brick buildings of the east campus housed the college for women until just a few years ago. Free buses run regularly between them, although many prefer to walk or ride the mile-and-a-half to get to and from classes. The west campus has most of the major facilities, and many students choose to live there because they feel it is more convenient. The smaller east campus is more peaceful, and many students find that returning to the quieter campus at the end of the day is an advantage.

Duke is a magnificent place, a fairytale mixture of Gothic and Georgian architecture on the edge of an 8000-acre forest. Buildings range from a gargantuan new medical center to a converted garage and a tiny, warehouselike structure for art and drama. A new music center, however, may be the phoenix, around which the fine arts will blossom. Duke has always relied heavily on suitcase visits from dance companies, orchestras, and New York theater directors; now, however, there is a commitment (and even some money) to hire top faculty and expand undergraduate programs in the arts. With time, the least magical of Buck Duke's legacies are disappearing, and the baron's heirs may soon achieve first-rate excellence at Duke without sacrificing the school's distinctive Southern charm.

DUQUESNE UNIVERSITY

Location: Pittsburgh, PA 15219
Campus: city center
Undergraduate enrollment:
  500 M, 500W
Total enrollment: 7188
Expenses: $5300
Financial aid: 70%
Library: 367,000 volumes

Student-faculty ratio: 18–1
Transfer students: 500
Median SAT: M: 460 V, 520 M;
  W: 465 V, 485 M
Median ACT: 21
Fraternities: 10%
Sororities: 8%
Application deadline:
  July 1

Duquesne University is a Roman Catholic school located between Pittsburgh's largest ghetto, a superhighway complex, and the Monongahela River. The school considers these its advantages. Enough said. We should note, however, that downtown Pittsburgh (within walking distance) does provide diversions, and the ghetto offers volunteer social work opportunities. But, otherwise, the Duquesne campus is tightly self-contained on a hilltop.

The school offers a complete range of departments and majors leading to a B. S. or B. A. degree. Nursing and pharmacy programs have the heaviest enrollments. Interest in education courses at Duquesne, formerly very intense, has waned over the past several years. Students tend more toward specific career training, showing greater interest in those programs which lead into some job market. Duqesne's graduate schools are large for a university of its size and include a sizable law school.

Duquesne has surprisingly few rules and regulations and considerably more freedom than most Catholic schools. Then again, Duquesne students aren't the kind who break the few existing rules. There are no rules on class attendance, and the only religious requirements are theology and philosophy courses for Catholic students. Parietal hours and sign-in and sign-out rules persist, but students have a voice in determining them.

Duquesne's social life suffers because fewer than half its students are residents. Others commute or live off-campus. The school has little identity or collegiate atmosphere, while its downtown, hilltop location keeps it far removed from Pittsburgh's lively cultural-university area, Oakland. Duquesne's fraternities and sororities function, but just barely, and the university hosts few all-school events. The ones that do take place, are in the form of major dances, such as Greek Week and Fall Carnival.

Attempting to construct a university identity, Duquesne built a comfortable triple-towered dormitory to house 1200 students, and invested $3.5 million in a lavishly equipped student union. But the dormitory failed to attract enough of its own students, and the university has been forced to recruit as residents the student overflow from nearby schools. Despite the luxurious activity center, Duquesne remains a commuter school.

Duquesne's primary claim to fame is still its basketball team, which has been consistently nationally ranked (certainly not typical of the school's other sports). The school also pumps considerable sums into a music group called the "Tamburitzans," which has gained worldwide renown. Being confused with Duke University in North Carolina is Duquesne's ("Duque's," locally) next closest brush with fame. Still, the school's free atmosphere is impressive enough compared with other church-affiliated colleges, and if you're interested in a career in music, nursing, pharmacy, or religion, you could do much worse.

EARLHAM COLLEGE

Location: Richmond IN 47374
Campus: city outskirts
Undergraduate enrollment:

Student-faculty ratio: 12–1
Transfer students: 50
Median SAT: 520 V, 530M

500 M, 500W
Total enrollment: 1050
Expenses: $6200
Financial aid: 60%
Library: 230,000 volumes

Fraternities: 0%
Sororities: 0%
Application deadline:
March 15

Earlham College is small, diversified, and, no pun intended for the eighteen percent Quaker student body, friendly. It's the kind of place where everyone is on a first-name basis, where everyone smiles at everyone else. Some of the old, somewhat whimsical traditions remain—such as the age-old welcome upperclassmen extend to entering freshpersons. The night before "new student week," they scour the area motels and decorate luggage-laden cars with crepe paper and "Welcome to Earlham" signs. The next five days are filled with an extensive orientation including discussion of topics ranging from the concept of community to Quakerism and the developing of interpersonal trust. But intimacy is sincere, and friendships don't come any easier than at Earlham.

Nonetheless, Earlham's academics are intensive and rewarding. Course requirements are numerous, somewhat traditional, and cover all areas of liberal arts studies. The new humanities sequence, a four-course interdisciplinary requirement, integrates history and English. Four trimesters of science, including two laboratory courses, are also required. Student response to requirements varies, but one thing is clear: by their inclusion the humanities and hard sciences are stronger and more diverse than one would expect for a college of this size.

The college's support of integral education strenthens small departments to the advantage of both students and faculty. Innovative departments—such as "human development and social relations," and "peace and conflict studies"—typify some of the efforts made to stimulate learning through different perspectives. Courses like "philosophy of natural science" and other integrations of two or more fields pervade the curriculum. Independent, interdepartmental, and self-designed majors gain support from this orientation as well as from professors' attitudes.

The languages at Earlham have become much stronger recently through the "intensive language" programs in Spanish, French, and German. Students study a given language four to five hours a day on campus one term, and then travel to Mexico, France, or Germany for the other term. Other opportunities for off-campus study are numerous and, in many students' views, one of the best learning experiences available. From Colombia, South America, to Kenya, Africa, to "southwest field studies," possibilities abound. As the Great Lakes College Association Center for Japanese Studies, Earlham students can study the Japanese language and culture here and in Japan.

Domestic programs are not quite as popular but just as available. The small student-faculty ratios in these programs make classes rewarding, although they often lapse into simple exhuberance rather than critical study.

If the thought of writing papers and discussing Thucydides in the freshperson humanities sequence is simply too much, "pre term" is an excellent break-in for wide-eyed wilderness seekers. Canoeing, backpacking, and bicycling trips are all offered in combination with nightly lectures in geology, history, environmental studies, and others given by accompanying professors. Eighty percent of the student body participates on one or more of the variety of special programs offered.

Back at home, Earlham provides a unique atmosphere of quietness and reflectiveness. Although it seems safe to say that most of the students share "liberal" views, there are no traces of Sixties-type activism. Quaker nonviolent philosophy is a unifying factor among most of the community, but without prominent social causes Earlham students are thinking more of themselves than the outside world. "Community," an overused word at Earlham, does carry weight although it is as ambiguous as overused.

With few social opportunities in the culturally insignificant town of Richmond, students tend to center their attention almost exclusively on campus. Big-name performers pass by without raising an eyebrow, but "Earlhamites" seem content with what is offered.

What sets Earlham apart from other small colleges, however, is its peculiar social atmosphere. Formal dating is unusual. Friendship often gets in the way of romantic inclinations amid an overly wholesome atmosphere. The feeling that students are either friends or heavily involved is surprisingly true. The friendly atmosphere has a unique benefit: student-faculty rapport is unusually good, so students never hesitate to approach professors.

EMORY UNIVERSITY

Location: Atlanta, GA 30322
Campus: suburban
Undergraduate enrollment:

Student-faculty ratio: 12–1
Transfer students: 150
Median SAT: 550 V, 600 M

1622 M, 1328 W
Total enrollment: 7500
Expenses: $6,300
Financial aid: 25%
Library: 1,700,000 volumes

Fraternities: 50%
Sororities: 40%
Application deadline:
March 1

If you're looking for the excitement of a rib-bruising college football game, Athens (the University of Georgia) is sixty-five miles to the northeast; if you're looking for a hard-fought, hair-raising debate (possibly with your girl or boyfriend), Emory is the right place.

One of the most intellectual of the Southern schools, Emory offers athletics consisting of tennis, frisbee-throwing, track, or skateboarding (the new library has a beautiful graded ramp).

And Emory has something no other school can boast—"Wonderful Wednesday." Emory students live for 'Wonderful Wednesday,' " one undergraduate confessed. Like the doctors and dentists most of them are planning to become, students at the college take Wednesday off. An experiment started several years ago to see if a break in the middle of the week would help class attendance and concentration. "WW" has now become the best-loved thing on-campus, the only exception being a water tower in the shape of a huge tee with a giant golf ball atop that stands high above most of the buildings and brings on thoughts of Saturday night.

Academically, Emory is one of the soundest schools in the South. Almost ninety percent of the full-time faculty members hold doctorates. Faculty salaries are above average, and the student-faculty ratio is a healthy twelve-to-one. The premed, predent, and prelaw programs are especially good, and a large number of graduates would prefer never to leave their Atlanta base until they're ready to hang out a shingle. A recent bequest of $100 million (three million shares of Coca-Cola) will increase Emory's endowment by fifty percent and insure its high academics stability. Renovations of older dorms and the construction of new ones are already starting.

Most black students seem to be satisfied (there is a "black house" on campus) and are just as settled into the preprofessional rut as their white counterparts. Recently, Emory gained a black fraternity and a black sorority.

Dress is extremely casual, there are no limits on class cuts, and the weather (except in the dead of winter) is generally mild or hot.

It was on Emory's hallowed grounds that God first died in the South a few years ago under the teachings of professor of religion Dr. William Hamilton. Hamilton was followed by Dr. Thomas Altizer, who has since departed voluntarily for SUNY Stony Brook. The irreverent post was then taken by Dr. Eugene Bianchi, a former priest married to a former nun, who is nationwide head of Priests for a Free Ministry.

Social life on campus can still be found in abundance on fraternity row, although with open visitation the dorms can lay claim to their share of hanky-panky. Some of the frats, in fact, have become quite freaky—the word on campus is that if there were a raid, *Alpha Epsilon Pi* might be the first to be busted. With Atlanta near, however, the independent need not suffer from underexposure to social life.

Atlanta is Emory's biggest drawing card. A big city that hasn't quite lost its sense of Southern easygoingness, Atlanta can be quiet or bustling and is one of the most enlightened and liberal-minded metropolises in the country, let alone the South. Every spring, Atlanta's Piedmont Park Arts Festival offers a variety of food and entertainment.

Only a minuscule proportion of students find it necessary to leave the area on weekends, and they generally head toward Athens. The school's two party weekends—Greek Week and Dooley's (the latter being named after Emory's patron saint, a skeleton)—have gone the way of other weekend extravaganzas and were severely cut back in recent years. During Dooley's week, there are free movies, beer parties, semiformals, and classes are dismissed if Dooley happens to shoot your professor (with a water pistol).

But fraternity parties are wet and wild and stoned. The school was founded by Asa Candler (of Coca-Cola fame), and bourbon and Coke is the main drink. Formerly women were not allowed in a frat room, but all that is gone now (in fact, it was gone before—as one blonde said, she had never been denied entrance yet). There is no housing in the sororities, and most women live in dormitories.

Cars are permitted for all students, though freshmen and sophomores with cars are frowned upon. Note that ownership of a car leads to suspension of financial aid.

A quiet, rolling campus is Emory's strength, and many students go in for quiet rolling. But academics are foremost at Emory. God would have liked it that way.

FAIRLEIGH DICKINSON UNIVERSITY

Location: Rutherford, NJ 07110   **Student-faculty ratio: 13–1**
Campus: suburban   **Transfer students: 1300**

Undergraduate enrollment:
3919 M, 3259 W
Total enrollment: 19,796
Expenses: $5300
Financial aid: 55%
Library: 522,000 volumes

Median SAT: NA
Fraternities: NA
Sororities: NA
Application deadline:
rolling

Students who go to Fairleigh Dickinson University seldom have good reasons for attending FDU. Rather, they have great excuses.
"It's close to home."
"My mother teaches here."
"I couldn't get into Rutgers."
"They accepted me."

FDU has all the classic characteristics of a large diploma mill. It's easy to get into, virtually impossible to flunk out of, and almost everyone you talk to bad-mouths the place.

Admission material for the Teaneck campus likes to point out that FDU is nestled in a suburban community while only being a short drive from New York City. For many at the school, that geographical quirk takes on added significance: escape.

The seventh largest private school in the United States, boasting five campuses (including two overseas), FDU despite its diversity, has become a refugee camp for wayward high school graduates. Students don't call the school "Fairly Ridiculous" for nothing.

Students don't seem to choose Fairleigh as much as they seem to "wind up" there. Most are seeking diplomas and well-paying jobs. Others simply aren't ready to give up high school yet. The school is hardly a hotbed of intellectualism. Yet if the students seem careless, FDU's academics are sound.

Several departments are deemed more than respectable, some even outstanding. FDU's business program is regarded as top-notch, while the Dental School remains a great source of pride as the "Harvard on the Hackensack." And the graduate institute of international studies, chaired by Dr. Nasarollah Fatemi, is one of the most respected in the area and the site of guest lectures by well-known international figures.

But by and large, hitting the books is not a popular pastime for FDUers, which is surprising, since aside from the school pub, the social scene can be described in one word: dull.

Primarily a commuter school, most students rush home after classes on Friday and are not seen again until sometime Monday afternoon. Those left in the dorms soon find out that Teaneck is not Collegetown,

U. S. A. Drugs are readily available, but hardly a mainstay of student life. Fraternities are also around, but do not constitute a powerful social force.

Politically, FDU is the school that pops up every year in a local newspaper article on how "apathetic and apolitical" today's students are. A small knot of students operate a "government," but are generally ignored by the administration and laughed at by their peers. Still, some issues have sparked reactions. A tuition increase two years ago set off demonstrations on two campuses. But when an even larger increase was announced last year, the student government voted to support it.

Physically, the campus is cramped and in sore need of repair. The school, which only several years ago was in serious financial difficulty, has put off numerous maintenance projects to save cash. Last year, it managed to balance its budget, but by then students were complaining that the campus was falling apart.

If you don't have 690 SAT scores, aren't interested in becoming another Einstein, and can't get into Rutgers, you might wind up here. And, oh yes, you can get good grades. Not long ago the university senate sent out a letter admonishing the faculty for giving out too many As and Bs. The letter was reportedly ignored.

RUTHERFORD CAMPUS

The school's second largest campus is distinguishable from its big sister in Teaneck only by its location. It's a longer drive to New York City. Adding to that depressing fact is the massive publicity the small town received a year ago when health officials said it had one of the highest cancer rates in the state. One more? It's also one of the few "dry" towns left in New Jersey. No bars.

MADISON CAMPUS

Madison is the campus always talked about at Teaneck and Rutherford as being a cross between "Shangri-La" and heaven. Located on 180 sprawling acres in rural New Jersey, the campus is beautiful. There's a swimming pool, lots of woods to get lost in, and snow that stays white after it hits the ground. The grades reportedly come just as easily. Why isn't the whole university there? Well, Madison is a long way from everywhere, which keeps the jokes going on campus that it's not really part of FDU. In fact, its distance from Rutherford and

Teaneck has resulted in a certain amount of isolation, but no one at Madison seems to care.

If it's distance you want, your best bets are the school's Wroton College campus in England (liberal arts program for one semester) and its biology lab in St. Croix. Now that's where you'll really feel like you're not going to FDU.

FLORIDA STATE UNIVERSITY

Location: Tallahassee, FL 32306
Campus: city outskirts
Undergraduate enrollment:
  6501 M, 7795 W
Total enrollment: 21,735
Expenses: $2700
Financial aid: 60%
Library: 1,100,000 volumes

Student-faculty ratio: 17–1
Transfer students: 8000
Median ACT: 24
Fraternities and Sororities:
  25%
Application deadline:
  rolling

One of Florida State University's biggest boasts in recent years is that one hundred percent of its first two law classes passed the bar exam. That may say more about the Florida bar than about Florida State.

Ever since the Twenties, Florida has been pretending to be another California, and Florida State is presumably masquerading as another UCLA. Neither makes it. FSU's situation is the more hopeless, because it is located in Tallahassee. Tallahassee, a long way from Los Angeles both literally and figuratively, is a synonym for Hicksville. Although the city is the capital of Florida, only a rash of motels and drive-in banks testify to its modernity. Few students have anything to do with the town.

Florida State is definitely behind the times. Long hair finally arrived here just about the same time it was going out of style in the rest of the nation. At FSU, even the longhairs are rednecks. In Tallahassee, the center of the state's backwater and backwash, little else could be expected. FSU has not quite caught up with the rest of the country, let alone California.

If mass protest is looked down upon at FSU, so are fraternities and sororities. Social life is pretty much left up to individual initiative, which generally means off-campus parties, beach orgies, or treks to Florida's more hospitable cities, such as Miami or Fort Lauderdale.

With plenty of sun and surf all year round, nearly everyone at Florida State manages to have fun.

Florida State is something of a trade school, especially when compared to its sister school, the University of Florida. Its finest department is elementary education, and its speech department ranks among the nation's top ten. Home economics is also passable if you're into a domestic life-style. Most of the rest of FSU's scholastic offerings are mediocre at best.

But not everyone is out to make it as a scholar. If you're looking for four unhassled years of fun in the sun and are prepared to put up with the multifarious drawbacks of Hicksville, you'll probably enjoy FSU. You could do a lot better, though.

UNIVERSITY OF FLORIDA

Location: Gainesville, FL 32611
Campus: city center
Undergraduate enrollment: 15,000 M, 10,000 W
Total enrollment: 31,000
Expenses: $3250 (in-state), $4280 (out-of-state)
Financial aid: NA
Library: 1,800,000 volumes

Student-faculty ratio: 20–1
Transfer students: 4000
Median SAT: 498 V, 553 M
Fraternities: 30%
Sororities: 30%
Application deadline: March 1 for freshmen; seven weeks before each quarter begins for transfers

You've probably heard about the "New South." Well, most Southern schools haven't. The University of Florida, however, is one that has.

For starters, UF is one of the few state institutions in the South which one needn't feel embarrassed to identify with, academically. Florida's sound scholastic curricula make it peculiar in Florida, where party schools for the nation's rich are the rule. UF is particularly strong in math, zoology, and botany. The English department is considered good by many. Undergraduate engineering, however, is a bit overrated. Although UF does not feature the rigorous academic pressure-cooker atmosphere common to the country's top scholastic institutions, it does have a low-key competitive spirit of its own. Freshmen and sophomores must maintain a C-minus average or face probation and possible suspension, while upperclassmen are required to hold a C average or better. Over a third of UF's graduates continue on to grad-level work.

UF also has more stringent entrance requirements than many state schools. Not all Floridians can matriculate here—applicants must maintain a C-minus average in high school and score reasonably well on the statewide twelfth grade placement tests. Out-of-state applicants must have performed even better in high school, as UF requires them to have a B average and a rank in the top quarter of their graduating class. Florida rejects some one-third of its total applicants each year, but does accept transfer students annually to help handle the migration to the "Sunshine State." If not an academic giant, Florida ranks well above the "Tom Thumb" status.

Politically, the UF student body is significantly more progressive than Florida as a whole. Greeks have never been particularly vibrant at Florida, but their popularity has decreased even more in the past decade. Social life now centers around parties in off-campus apartments, although nearly all freshmen are required to live in university dorms. The male-female ratio is decent and well exploited.

At least one tradition from the "Old South" has been carried over in force at UF—the football weekend. With "Gator" football teams reaching national prominence in the last few years, the weekly fall blasts have become even more important and tumultuous of late. The annual game against arch-rival Florida State has become legendary in scope and popularity. Track and swimming are also natural fortes at this sports-conscious school.

The last thing one notices about UF is Gainesville. Once avoided by the students, the city has gone a long way toward shaking off its sleepy atmosphere, and now ranks as one of the more progressive municipalities in the state. Although lacking the cultural advantages of a bigger city, Gainesville is pleasant enough, but many students still only notice it on the way to the beach.

The University of Florida may be one of the schools which has made it into the "New South" era, but there is still a place for the mint julep and four years of relaxation for the student who is so inclined.

FORDHAM UNIVERSITY

Location: Bronx, NY 10458
Campus: city outskirts
Undergraduate enrollment:
   3531 M, 2747 W

Student-faculty ratio: 16–1
Transfer students: 500
Median SAT: 530 V, 551 M
Fraternities: 0%

Total enrollment: 14,865
Expenses: $5000
Financial aid: 50%
Library: 1,209,289 volumes

Sororities: 0%
Application deadline:
February 15

Fordham University is a Roman Catholic institution, and therein lies its problem. Like most Catholic colleges, it is increasingly pressed for funds, students, and faculty in an era of secular educational tastes. Fordham is fortunate in its coed student body and its location in New York. Its heavily Jesuit-dominated nonprogressive administration, though, is hardly a blessing. But the school's assets are likely to prolong the college's life long after the demise of less flexible Catholic colleges.

Probably Fordham's greatest strength is its student body. Many students come from the solid background of New York-area public and parochial schools. Many also possess the intellectual and social sophistication of the area, although by and large the students come from the Catholic bourgeoisie and are, therefore, rather conservative in their politics and apathetic in general. In the past, Fordham was the preeminent college for the children of the dedicated, literate, affluent Catholic middle class. Despite the advent of better faculties at other private schools, much of Fordham's onetime prominence still lingers.

Moreover, a number of experimental efforts on the part of the Fordham administration may well reverse the decline and restore the university to its former spot in the first rank of educational institutions. By far the most impressive is an effort to construct a complete educational experience, from junior high school through college, for extremely bright adolescents who are capable of considerable acceleration. Although it is hard to tell if the particular program can really pan out (it may be a quarter of a century before the project can be evaluated fairly), the spirit of quest and the focus on educational contemporaneity and reform bode well for Fordham's future. Similarly, an administration receptive to new course programs and a lack of insistence on the most dogmatic kind of Catholicism make the intellectual environment of Fordham acceptable to keen students.

There are still the limitations one might expect of a Catholic college: a heavy emphasis on theology and philosophy, a pervasive Catholicism in much of the curriculum, and a Romanist view of the Western world and its cultural history. But Fordham will not purge nonconforming faculty. The administrators realize that Fordham is a part of the twentieth century, and that the Catholic Church does not and cannot sit at the centers of the lives of all contemporary Americans.

Socially as well as academically, Fordham is a livable place. Social restrictions don't count for much, because virtually everyone dwells off-campus, in the heart of one of the great social centers of the world.

Fordham's main facilities are in downtown Manhattan, housed in a complex in Lincoln Center, right next door to the Metropolitan Opera. There are no residence dormitories on the Manhattan campus, and most of the Manhattan students are either permanent city residents or occupants of apartments nearby. A few live on the Rose Hill campus in the Bronx, just twenty minutes away by subway. The urban cultural opportunities of New York are in reach of every Fordham student if he is willing to contend with "twenty harrowing minutes on the most degrading transportation system (he) has ever had the displeasure to encounter," according to one student.

The general atmosphere is less social than at a Big Ten school, less intellectual than at a New England college with comparable average board scores, less lively than at a more representative New York school (the eclectic NYU, for example, or Columbia). In fact, the combination of diligent studiousness, rather than genuine scholarship, and of ultracasual personal life is somewhat reminiscent of a fairly hip high school.

Alcohol is always permissible and readily obtainable (New York has had eighteen-year-old drinking age laws for as long as anyone can remember).

In an exercise in hyperbole, one Fordhamite suggested that "alcohol makes up seventy-five percent of the bloodstream of the average Fordham male." Pot is smoked frequently now, and acid and cocaine are not unheard of. Dorm regulations permit the Rose Hill campus women and other lovelies to visit the Rose Hill men on a liberal basis.

Margaret Mead and Marshall McLuhan have been among the visiting faculty, and there is a free school, with no costs, requirements, or, alas, credits, but with a fairly responsive curriculum providing a real chance to study nontraditional topics.

Despite all its virtues, however, Fordham is still no Yale or Harvard, no Amherst or Bowdoin. It is not even a Columbia or an NYU, for those who feel they must study in New York.

FRANKLIN AND MARSHALL COLLEGE

Location: Lancaster, PA 17604 **Student-faculty ratio: 15–1**
Campus: suburban **Transfer students: 60**

Undergraduate enrollment: 1166 M, 908 W
Total enrollment: NA
Expenses: $6700
Financial aid: 65%
Library: 275,000 volumes

Median SAT: 570 V, 600 M
Fraternities: 45%
Sororities: 25%
Application deadline:
February 10
May 1 for transfers

In general, three types of students populate F and M: those who are there to get into graduate school, those who are there to get a good liberal arts education, and those who don't know what they want and just enjoy themselves for four years. In recent years the number of freaks has drastically dwindled, while the number of grad-school grinds has increased as competition for grad school space has become tougher.

F and M's premed and prelaw programs are renowned, as far as survival is concerned. The psychology department takes a completely experimental approach, which leads to some unhappiness when majors apply to clinically-oriented grad schools and suffer from the department's reputation in other areas of the science.

Strengths in the humanities are varied. The government, English, economics, religious studies, philosophy, and drama departments are strong; art, music, and history are unreliable. The removal of a language requirement has weakened the language programs, although French and Spanish are surviving well.

The trend in the past few years has been toward a more conservative academic environment. The college's expectations of students have grown as the quality of students admitted has increased, and there is talk of strengthening the now-light distribution requirements.

Everyone who is not attached to another person or to a fraternity complains of the lack of on-campus social life. The weekend film series is excellent, and there are occasional midweek films as well as unending lectures, but other than that there is little collegewide organized social activity. For social life, the school is almost entirely dependent on fraternities, who have been attracting increasing numbers of pledges in the recent past. There is also one sorority with about twenty-five members. The college has trouble with major concerts and is unwilling to take risks in that area, so concert-oriented students often travel to Philadelphia, Baltimore, or Washington.

Clubs and organizations seem to be recovering after a rough period, but many of the smaller ones floundered for good. The radio station, dance club, and campus theater are strong.

Sports are important at F and M, despite the school's small size.

Football and basketball are very good, while wrestling and lacrosse are respectable. On the whole, though, students are reluctant to join any activity that will require their time without giving them a negotiable return—they just don't want to take time away from studying.

The student population is primarily middle to upper-middle class, but as tuition rises, the number of BMWs and 280Zs in the parking lot also increases. Minority students are few, and the college is not always successful in holding on to those who enroll.

Despite almost constant complaining, most students seem to respect the college and the education they receive. But they are working pretty hard to get it.

GEORGETOWN UNIVERSITY

Location: Washington, DC 20057
Campus: city outskirts
Undergraduate enrollment:
 2600 M, 2600 W
Total enrollment: 10,500
Expenses: $7600
Financial aid: 50%
Library: 1,000,000 volumes

Student-faculty ratio: 15–1
Transfer students: 300
Median SAT: 620 V, 630 M
Fraternities: 0%
Sororities: 0%
Application deadline:
 January 15

Why did Ralph Nader, Jerry Brown, Carol Burnett and other personalities come to Georgetown last year? Sure, because they happened to be in Washington and Georgetown is in Washington, but things would be different if Georgetown wasn't the first-rate school it is.

Georgetown is a Catholic school, considered by many the best in the D. C. area. Especially for the three-fourths of the students who aren't from Washington in the first place, the city is an excellent setting for a college. The offices of the federal government, swarms of *Who's Who* citizens, and some beautiful surrounding vistas—Washington has much to offer. The sprawling ghettos and huge government agencies are playgrounds, or workgrounds, for budding social scientists of whatever persuasion or inclination. And Georgetown's Federal style townhouses and palatial homes, along with the campus of Gothic and greensward, provide a nice place to escape to for more purely academic pursuits.

For the latter, Georgetown has a wide offering of solid departments and a high reputation as a whole. The foreign service and government programs are particularly fine, and well known. English, history, philosophy, theology—the core subjects of a Jesuit liberal arts education—are also good, as are the American studies, chemistry, and psychology departments. Requirements are pretty stiff as compared to most universities. Everyone must take two semesters of both philosophy and theology, for example.

Georgetown has a good faculty behind these programs. The administration likes to boast about GU's big guns (e.g. Arthur Burns and Henry Kissinger, although they teach only about twenty students apiece per semester). GU's real strength lies in its less well-known, but dedicated, teaching staff. Most of the faculty are published scholars, but they usually come to Georgetown to teach. As a result, professors (not their grad students) religiously observe their office hours. Most are accessible, even amiable, and it's better than even money that the professor himself will riddle your paper with red ink or grade your test. Even the administration is responsive, if not receptive to the students' gripes.

Unfortunately, recent years have brought increasing enrollment, worsening the already severe housing shortage. Up until now, the annual room lottery was virtually an exercise in futility; only about one-third of the upperclassmen can be accommodated in the older university housing. The rest find, or try to find, housing in the neighborhood, which is costly and of varying quality. A side note: it takes about forty-five minutes to walk to Capitol Hill from Georgetown. The public transportation system is very good, and the university operates its own bus line to strategic points throughout the city and Virginia suburbs where many students have apartments.

"Hoyas" do have fun, in large and small groups. Besides going out on the town (the D. C. beer drinking age is eighteen), Georgetown has a pub on campus. Pot and other drugs seem to multiply of late, although use varies among groups.

Perhaps the most exciting activity at Georgetown in the past has been to watch how things go with the school's inadequate facilities. Since the student union only exists on paper, the already overcrowded library must often serve as a meeting place. The library itself is not too hot, although one may argue that GU's proximity to the Library of Congress makes a large native library unnecessary. Still, even the few books at G. U. are often old and obsolete. The new "Rec Plex" will ease the shortage of athletic space on campus and bring to GU the pool it has not had for a long time.

There are other things to Georgetown besides its location, its academics, and its lack of facilities. John Thompson's basketball team is annually nationally ranked. The cross country and track teams are also strong, boasting a world record holder (in the women's mile walk). The debate team is indisputably one of the top four in the country.

The average "Hoya" though, is career-oriented: highly motivated academically, and active (at one time or another) in some career-related off-campus activity. Many feel, and with good reason, that they will be the Jerry Browns of the future.

GEORGE WASHINGTON UNIVERSITY

Location: Washington, DC 20052
Campus: city center
Undergraduate enrollment:
  3350 M, 2750 W
Total enrollment: 17,000
Expenses: $5800
Financial aid: 18%
Library: 900,000 volumes

Student-faculty ratio: 14–1
Transfer students: 2000
Median SAT: 550 V, 580 M
Fraternities: 5%
Sororities: 1%
Application deadline:
  March 1,
  May 1 for transfers

Radical leader Rennie Davis once called George Washington University the most strategically placed college in the nation, and with the White House a scant four blocks away, one has to agree. The State Department and many other Establishment edifices are within easy walking distance as well. Unfortunately, being so close to the White House also means being surrounded by office buildings, stores, and wicked traffic. The George Washington campus has merged into its urban milieu so well that if it were not for the groups of students on the sidewalks, one might not recognize the place as a university.

Many of America's most distinguished cultural centers and collections are within a walk or short drive. Constitution Hall, home of the DAR, is a brief stroll away, as are the Kennedy Center for the Performing Arts and the Corcoran Gallery of Art. Farther off, but accessible, are the National Gallery of Art, the Smithsonian Institution, and the Library of Congress (the biggest and best there is). Being a mile from the Library of Congress was considered by some students to be a handicap, since the university could use it as a substitute for the development of its own collections, but the school's new $10 million library has put that concern to rest.

The most dramatic aspect of the campus is the palatial student center. The $9 million modernistic structure is the physical and social center of the university. Along with a plush cafeteria more reminiscent of a State Department ballroom than a restaurant, it sports a twelve-lane bowling alley and a bar on the top floor. The bar is open until midnight but is usually crowded by early evening. Its popularity is partly due to the fine view of the southern end of the city and its reasonable prices for wine and beer. Altogether, the center has proven a big step toward making George Washington a comfortable place to spend four years. The rest of the university is more conventional, however, perhaps because of the rush to build; the last seven years have seen $100 million worth of building on the campus. The dorms are still a bit crowded, and many of the classroom buildings are undistinguished; courtyards and quiet nooks are at a minimum.

There is no residency requirement, and most students move off-campus when they have a chance. There has been some trouble with students allegedly skipping out on final utility and phone bills at the end of the year, and many of the less expensive apartment complexes will not rent to students as a result. But even without student blacklisting, cheap housing is nearly nonexistent. Not living within walking distance of the campus is a problem because parking is difficult and the bus system is barely tolerable.

George Washington students are generally upper-middle-class. Only about twenty percent are native to the Washington area, and well over a quarter come from New York and New Jersey. In the past, the undergrads have been liberal but generally complacent toward events in the surrounding community and the nation, although the law students have a national reputation in the area of consumer protection. One student told us that if the White House were 1000 miles away, the university would be exactly the same.

The social life is good. There are numerous theaters and restaurants in the campus area, and, of course, many students just wander over to the student center or the University Club for beer and talk. But Georgetown is deservedly the campus favorite for anything beyond the most informal social event. It is packed with small shops, a large collection of great bars, and has the city's best youth-oriented nightclub, The Cellar Door.

The new athletic center is used mostly for friendly games of hoops and for "a few hours at the gym to keep in shape." GWU varsity teams are understandably weak.

George Washington is fair to good as an academic institution. It is probably better than most, but not as good as rival Georgetown University, a mile away. Most students seem to come to GW for the fun of living in Washington, not for the university's academic attributes. However, several departments are noteworthy, including political science, history, and philosophy. The school is increasing its use of nearby federal government resources, and eminent politicos and ex-politicos stop off to give courses for a semester or so. The faculty, however, is relatively conservative.

Another reason why students come to GWU is that they need to find a school at the last minute, either because they were rejected from their other choices or for any other of a variety of reasons. GWU accepts freshmen and transfers into all semesters and its application deadlines are about as rigid as a rubber band.

The university administration is usually considered hard-line and unsympathetic toward the students, but there is no longer any enforcement whatever of class attendance. The penalty for possession of grass or hash is likely to be only a reprimand. Drugs, by the way, are easy to get, although not as popular as they used to be.

George Washington's big plus is Washington, D. C. It's by no means a bad place to go to school, but there are other universities in the city, and some of them, like Georgetown University, have campuses.

GEORGIA INSTITUTE OF TECHNOLOGY

Location: Atlanta, GA 30332
Campus: city center
Undergraduate enrollment:
   7689 M, 1606 W
Expenses: $3100 (in-state),
   $4200 (out-of-state)
Financial aid: 20%
Library: 875,000 volumes

Student-faculty ratio: 16–1
Transfer students: 930
Median SAT: 523 V, 618 M
Fraternities: 22%
Sororities: 18%
Application deadline:
   April 1
   January 1 for out-of-state

Georgia Tech is hardly your average state university. On the other hand, it's national reputation is primarily attributable to its old athletic tradition and its famous symbol—a car fondly known as the "Rambling Wreck."

Unfortunately, the car isn't the only thing that's a wreck lately. If the recently sagging football program isn't turned around soon, its former glory may never be restored. Alumni are grumbling and game attendance is tumbling.

The direction of the whole school is also somewhat up in the air. For instance, Tech has the largest university-based solar energy research program in the nation, yet a stingy state legislature has chiseled away faculty salaries over the past years, and they are now among the lowest in the nation; several good faculty members have already left. To compensate for the paucity of state funding, recent freshman classes have set records: class sizes have increased, and a severe shortage of on-campus housing has resulted.

Still, Georgia Tech has a few good points going for it. It is in the heart of Atlanta, one of America's most dynamic cities. While the area lacks the cultural offerings of many Northern cities, its relaxed atmosphere and bright social life make getting away from school easy. According to one national magazine, Southern women are the loosest in the nation. Whether Southern men can rise to this opportunity is unclear.

Tech also boasts a diverse student body that represents virtually every state and numerous foreign countries. Almost half the students are from outside Georgia—an extremely high percentage for a state school and a constant sore point with the state legislature. However, most students are from the Southeast, and a strong provincial air pervades the school.

Many are from places like Rome, Valdosta, and Americus. Their goal at Tech is to get a degree, find a wife at one of the women's schools in the area, and settle down.

Black students tend to socialize at Morehouse or Spelman, black colleges only a short distance a way.

On campus, social and recreational life is not great but it's improving. A new intramural athletic complex recently opened (seventy percent of the school participates in intramurals), and the thirty-three fraternities and sororities are enjoying a resurgence.

Life on campus is not cushy, and by no means is Tech a party school. Freshman dorms, the WPA variety, bear a striking resemblance to prisons. They lack air-conditioning, but do have metal furniture. Most students find themselves studying on at least a few weekend nights during the year. Tech's on-campus food is expensive, and the trend in quality has run from bad to worse. But fear not. The Varsity, said to be the world's largest drive-in restaurant, is just across the expressway. It is a longtime Tech tradition.

Student government at Tech is inconsequential, and student participation in many academic decisions is limited. Drug use is limited to pot, and alcohol is a popular means of diversion.

Finally, you might note that the Tech catalog boasts of a five-megawatt nuclear reactor, electron microscopes, large microwave experimental stations, and a lot of other neat gadgets, but most undergraduates never see them except in the catalog.

GEORGIA STATE UNIVERSITY

Location: Atlanta, GA 30303
Campus: city center
Undergraduate enrollment:
    4500 M, 6500 W
Total enrollment: 20,500
Expenses: $4000 (in-state),
    $6500 (out-of-state)
Financial aid: 15%
Library: 650,000 volumes

Student-faculty ratio: 26-1
Transfer students: 7500
Median SAT: 466 V, 479 M
Fraternities: 10%
Sororities: 10%
Application deadline:
    August 1

Every day, in the late afternoon, Georgia State University undergoes a metamorphosis. It's as though GSU were two different schools.

Thirteen thousand students, mostly young undergraduates, populate the campus during the morning and early afternoon. By dusk, an older crowd (the 8500 evening students, many of whom are graduates) crawls out of the woodwork (or actually, Atlanta office buildings) and takes over until the end of classes at 10:00 P.M.

GSU is a business-minded school, and more than eighty percent of the students hold full- or part-time jobs. Few GSU students are here continuously for four years. Often married and hassled by job responsibilities, they enroll every few quarters, as time and money allow.

As you might expect, GSU is not equipped for the college antics and social activities of the younger students, many of whom are transfers, refugees from more famous "party" schools. With an average age of twenty-seven (undergraduate twenty-five, graduate thirty-one), the GSU student is more interested in graduation and career advancement. The typical student is on campus just long enough to attend classes, go to the library, and hop on a bus home.

Located two blocks from "Five Points" in downtown Atlanta, GSU is a totally commuter college with no dormitories. The campus has its attractions, however, if you like a five-square-block maze of bland, modern architecture.

GSU's social life is limited, largely because over half its students are married. About ten percent join fraternities, sororities, student activities, and student government. Most of these are housed in the antiquated student center (built in 1964 with a 1950 blueprint).

There are few concerts, dances, or speakers, so the best bet is to leave the campus behind and seek Atlanta's more promising social environment.

With a completely paved-over campus, GSU has never emphasized athletics. Intercollegiate basketball is the biggest sport at the school, although the team, which is a charter member of the new Sunbelt Conference, is just now becoming average in quality.

Academically, GSU has little to offer. As one might expect at a multipurpose state university, the facilities and faculty are, for the most part, mediocre. Founded in 1913 as a business college, GSU didn't get its university charter until 1969, and the business influence still dominates. GSU's six academic colleges cover a wide variety of subjects from business administration to liberal arts to education. But only the business school is recognized as outstanding (it was voted among the country's top twenty in a poll of business school deans). Psychology is the only other above-average department at GSU.

There are 800 teaching faculty members at GSU, seventy-five percent of whom hold doctorates, and their average age is forty. Unfortunately, except for the business administration faculty, most of the better professors move on to schools where the salaries are higher than the state-subsidized pay at GSU.

GSU may not be the most scintillating name in higher education, but it is an inexpensive way to an average, no-frills education.

UNIVERSITY OF GEORGIA

Location: Athens, GA 30605
Campus: suburban
Undergraduate enrollment:
 7464 M, 7506 W
Total enrollment: 22,946
Expenses: $3000 (in-state),
 $4000 (out-of-state)
Financial aid: 35–40%
Library: 1,900,000

Student-faculty ratio: 16–1
Transfer students: 3100
Median SAT: M: 489 V, 552 M;
 W: 497 V, 518 M
Fraternities: 18%
Sororities: 20%
Application deadline:
 twenty days prior to
 registration

Some years ago, a national magazine published a list of the top twenty social schools in the country. A footnote at the bottom of the page states, "If you're wondering why the University of Georgia was not listed, it's because we consider it not a college, but a twenty-four-hour-a-day nightclub." That description still holds today, but it is only partially correct. Partying is rampant at Georgia, but not in the tradition of massive campuswide affairs. More often, the social events consist of four friends and a case of beer.

You won't find large soirees except in the fraternity houses. Georgia is blessed with a large, obnoxious Greek community—3000 walking, talking, living, breathing stereotypes of everything bad brought to mind by the term "frat boy."

For eleven weeks in the fall, the primary form of entertainment is the football team, ranked annually among the powers of the Southeastern Conference. Each November, thousands of students flee the campus at midweek for the trip to Jacksonville for the world's largest cocktail party, ostensibly known as the "Florida game," while the Georgia Tech game is the biggest event of the year.

Students at Georgia do enroll in classes, and most even know where the library is. Several of the graduate schools enjoy reputations of national excellence. The agriculture and journalism schools are among the finest in the country, and the excellent veterinary medicine school is nearing completion of a new $6 million facility. Lumpkin Law School turns out more lawyers yearly than any other school, (perhaps because it admits more) and most are well prepared and successful.

The journalism school has spawned a thriving campus media, including the Southeast's best four-day-a-week daily collegiate newspaper (*The Red and Black*) and the Southeast's weirdest radio station, run largely by jazz-addled hacks and nonstudent holdovers from past generations.

The university union's eight divisions provide diverse and generally tolerable entertainment, including two or three "major" shows a quarter (often leaning toward Southern rock) and a number of smaller acts. The nationally ranked Cinematic Arts division books different movies each night. The student center was built sometime around the Civil War, but construction has begun on a new $12 million complex.

Politically, it's apathy time down South. The most vocal (and offensive) group on campus is the Young Americans for Freedom (the Reaganites). There is no student government association. Stripped of all pretenses of power years ago by the tyrannical administration, it was voted out by the student body in April, 1979.

Socially, Athens is a typical college town (population: 45,000) deep in the Bible belt: the bars close at midnight on Saturday, and you can't buy anything alcoholic on Sundays. However, Atlanta's nightlife is only an hour and a half away.

A great many students have sports cars—a chief status symbol next to having a good-looking and slightly inebriated date.

The housing situation is adequate, even though all rooms are small doubles. No wild dorm parties go on, due to a law prohibiting the expenditure of "state funds" on booze. However, keg parties at $1.00 a pop often spring up. A shocking number of dorm residents head home on weekends (usually to Atlanta).

The university requires several standardized tests, including "rising junior" and "senior exit" exams. Graduation from any of its schools hinges on passing an examination on the constitutions of the United States and Georgia. Appropriately enough, the tests are given the Thursday following George Washington's birthday or the Fourth of July. Also appropriately enough, to suit the university's atmosphere, many frats and sororities hire persons to take the tests for all their graduating members.

GOUCHER COLLEGE

Location: Towson, MD 21204
Campus: suburban
Undergraduate enrollment: 910 W
Total enrollment: 1053
Expenses: $7100
Financial aid: 48%
Library: 202,300 volumes

Student-faculty ratio: 10-1
Transfer students: 75
Median SAT: 520 V, 530 M
Sororities: 0%
Application deadline:
   none

Goucher is not the country club for rich girls that it used to be. Of course, it still looks like a country club; Goucher's 330 acres in suburban Towson, Maryland, are beautiful in the fall and spring, and almost tolerable in the wet and miserable Baltimore area winters. But the important point is that you do not have to wear white gloves and drink tea to attend Goucher. Most people here do neither of these things. In fact, about half of the student body receives some type of financial aid.

What you *do* have to be is a serious student. Four years at Goucher are not an academic hayride. Professors expect you to work—hard, and students do a lot of researching and studying on their own.

Because of the intense drain on the student body wrought by academics, however, the campus is rather quiet politically and socially. Many students find it difficult to squeeze in a quick glance at a newspaper between classes, much less get involved in "real world" issues. Despite this fact all the seats on the student government are filled, the campus newspaper has never missed a deadline, and a small but dedicated woman's issues group, Goucher ERA, keeps the student body informed of how things fare for women outside the gates of Goucher.

But back to basics. With a thrust toward what the dean calls a "literate and competent" student body, Goucher has retained its foreign language and distribution requirements, and a "core" course in the humanities at a time when many other institutions junked requirements as unnecessary clutter in the curriculum. And while Goucher has always had a reputation for being a "paper school," concern for an even greater emphasis in writing across the departments has grown.

Strong programs in science have always been one of Goucher's claims to fame. The success rate for premeds is high for those with the stamina to complete the grueling requirements. And the English, historic preservation, and political science departments are also noteworthy. Economics is in a flux presently but the administration maintains that it is strengthening and regrouping it to meet the needs of the large number of majors.

An internship or an off-campus experience is required of all students and is considered by many to be one of the most valuable segments of their education. The possibilities are countless, with students being placed in government offices, newspapers, museums, hospitals, and a wide variety of other institutions with offerings sponsored by every department of the college.

One reason that internships are so popular may be that they give students the opportunity to get off-campus. There is a residency requirement which extends over all four years, except for a small number of seniors and Baltimore residents who acquire "commuter" status. Students on campus are scattered among 16 autonomous houses, each of which sets its own rules for quiet hours and other house legislation. Parietals are unknown and underclasswomen can get singles. All students are required to join the College Food Service, which is, as most institutional food services, of dubious quality.

The dorms are quiet, which is great for studying, but not so great for partying. While there are many who would like to see this changed, social life at present revolves around Johns Hopkins University, a twenty-minute college-provided shuttle ride away, with their numerous fraternity parties, speakers, films, and the disco-oriented Rathskeller. Hopkins is also utilized by Goucher students for research in their excellent library facilities, while for additional course work, Goucher has an exchange program with Hopkins and several other local colleges and universities.

What then, do Goucher women do for fun when Hopkins fails them? Well . . . there is the Greenhouse, a sort of poor excuse for a student center on campus—which consists of a snackbar, pinball machines, and lots of modular furniture—in what was once a dining hall. Its redeeming qualities are two-fold: the food is better than that served in the cafeteria, and beer and wine can be purchased for a reasonable price. The houses are the actual social units, each giving several parties yearly.

Towson sports an interesting diversity in nightlife with restaurants, bars, and the usual disco scene. More students than ever before have shifted their social pursuits into Towson with its greater opportunity for meeting different kinds of people and its switch from the usual college atmosphere.

The administrative concern for social life on campus stops short of building a student center. However, there are indications that the climate is changing. Despite the usual quiet, Goucher parties are drawing larger crowds now.

But the core of Goucher is still highly academic. The atmosphere favors the intellectually venturesome, free-spirited individual, who won't miss the extraneous hoopla of college life that Goucher lacks. Perhaps one of its assets is this lack of "rah-rah" collegiate partying, because it keeps academics in the center ring.

The faculty is, of course, the main attraction. Freed from excessive pressure to publish, they have more time to give to students, and they do. Goucher is not a research-oriented institution: the faculty members are here to teach, and their abilities are almost unanimously fine. Several have made significant contributions to their field of study, but most have made a significant impression in the classroom.

Add on to Goucher's sincere and capable faculty an unyielding dedication to the education of women and you have the whole story of what makes Goucher so special. It takes women seriously, and encourages them to explore all the avenues opening before them. Goucher seeks to help the "brave new woman" in each of her students. It is a place to grow.

GRINNELL COLLEGE

Location: Grinnell, IO 50112
Campus: rural
Undergraduate enrollment:
 600 M, 600 W
Total enrollment: 1243
Expenses: $6595
Financial aid: 49%
Library: 250,000 volumes

Student-faculty ratio: 11–1
Transfer students: 90–120
Median SAT: M: 580 V, 630 M;
 W: 590 V, 580 M
Median ACT: 27
Fraternities: NA
Sororities: NA
Application deadline:
 February 15

An out-of-town visitor to Grinnell, Iowa, might expect a sleepy Midwestern community of conservative farmers, a community where the corn harvest was the year's most exciting event. By and large he (or she) would be right, except for the fact that Grinnell harbors one of the most enlightened, progressive colleges in the Midwest—or the entire country, for that matter.

Grinnell College just doesn't fit with any of its surroundings. Its students are generally liberal in all respects—academic, political, social, and personal. The faculty, heavily laden with PH.Ds, seems to belong more in the Ivy League than in the cornfields of Iowa. No one seems fully capable of explaining this, but no one denies that it exists, and so Grinnell College must go on record as one of the biggest anomalies in the midst of Middle America. Perhaps part of the explanation lies in the diversified student body attracted to Grinnell. Many students come from the East—predominantly New York—while Illinois and Iowa add large numbers to the population.

Academic interests of the freshman class usually tend toward premed and prelaw, but as students progress through Grinnell the liberal arts curriculum distracts many from their original goal. The curriculum is traditional liberal arts, but the lack of required courses allows students a great deal of flexibility. Independent projects in which students design their own courses are encouraged. Strong departments include history, political science, and English. With the heavy emphasis on medicine, the biology and chemistry departments are particularly good. The anthropology department is growing by leaps and bounds, and Spanish and Russian are small, but excellent.

Learning is not solely relegated to the classroom. The number of symposia and lectures the college sponsors is startling, and it is conceivable that a Grinnell student could get every bit as good a formal education if he dropped all his classes and just attended the extra lectures.

However, intellectual stimulation, as all students will admit, is not the only kind. Because the town of Grinnell does not exactly offer a plethora of activities, the college is generally self-sufficient, socially. Every weekend, a lengthy calendar is handed out, listing plays, concerts, movies, and art exhibitions. Though the college provides ample opportunity for both a satisfying academic and social life, many students find it difficult to do justice to both, opting in favor of the academic. Friends are many times more readily located in the library than in their rooms.

The burden of the social life is placed on the students themselves as there are no fraternities or sororities. The majority of the residence halls are coed by alternating room or by floor. The exceptions are two single-sex dorms.

Because the campus is both small and relatively isolated, personal relationships tend to be informal and close. All campus parties and activities draw the community together, although the college's diversity encourages many people and groups to go their own way. The size of the campus, however, can become a drawback. Many complain about claustrophobia, especially around finals time, when academic pressure becomes more intense than usual. Privacy is often at a premium.

Despite its isolation, Grinnell has not escaped the conservative trend sweeping all college campuses. Bizarre clothes and habits are not as common as in the past, although a small hard core of eccentrics keeps alive the antiestablishment mood of past decades. Tolerance is still the rule; it is not unheard of for a jock and a "deadhead" to be close friends. Activism has all but disappeared, although small groups such as the antinuclear Mobilization for Survival retain loyal followings. And there's always student government.

"Winning isn't everything" is the cliché used in reference to sports, but Grinnell's athletics are better described by the phrase "Winning isn't anything." Athletics takes a back seat to academics—Knute Rockne would not be comfortable here. An impressive revival of intercollegiate athletics has occurred recently, however, especially for women. For those who care to become involved, intercollegiate sports can be an important element of life at Grinnell—both for the athletics and for the social outlet.

If you are not overly concerned with the prestigious name of the school you attend, Grinnell deserves more than a spot as a safety school. Grinnell is a mature place for mature people and costs considerably less than the majority of academically excellent schools to which it is compared. If you're interested in either placidity or tremendous "rah-rah" spirit, you'd better not apply. But if you're somewhere in the middle and intellectually inclined, this school in Middle America is well worth your consideration.

HAMILTON COLLEGE
(WITH KIRKLAND COLLEGE)

Location: Clinton, NY 13323
Campus: rural
Undergraduate enrollment:
 1000 M, 600 W
Total enrollment: 1600
Expenses: $7025
Financial aid: 38%
Library: 350,000 volumes

Student-faculty ratio: 12–1
Transfer students: 30
Median SAT: 600 V, 630 M
Fraternities: 47%
Sororities: 0%
Application deadline:
 February 1

In a film several years ago, *The Sterile Cuckoo*, a young man at an isolated woodsy college was socially dependent on the comings and goings of his eccentric weekend girlfriend.

The college was Hamilton. It's changed. A lot.

Hamilton has undergone a real regeneration: Long known as a preppie, conservative, rather washed-out finishing school for future doctors, lawyers, and executives, Hamilton has been transformed from isolated and isolationist to involved, from celibate to coeducational.

The key to the transformation lies in that latter innovation—the addition of Kirkland College, the women's school. After nine years of coexistence as separate but entirely coordinate colleges, Hamilton decided to take over Kirkland College, lock, stock and barrel in 1978. The move was prompted in part by financial necessity (Kirkland's endowment had dropped dangerously low), and it was met with opposition from students and faculty alike. Today, Hamilton is coeducational, and much of Kirkland has fallen by the wayside. Kirkland's unstructured, experimental approach has been sacrificed in favor of the more traditional and conservative Hamilton education.

Another significant change at Hamilton has been the liberalization of fraternity life, once a closed and crucial circuit. Not that the frats are in danger of folding; the decline in membership has been considerable but by no means crippling to the frat houses. What has changed is the usual scene of despair at rejection, for the nonfrat minority is no longer so tiny; moreover, everyone who rushes has his admission to some house guaranteed. The more appalling aspects of rush week have been eliminated, and the atmosphere of untouchability around nonfrat men has evaporated.

Perhaps the only good thing about Kirkland's demise is that the administration finally opened all dorms to both sexes. From the dark halls of the Hamilton campus dorms, to the modern and gray concrete housing units at Kirkland, coeducation living has changed the whole character of the campus. No longer must the lonely student trudge to the Pub or the frat which happens to be on tap that night. Fun is to be found at home, right next door to you.

There's not much to be said for Clinton or nearby Utica. There's no avoiding it, you're five hours away from civilized life. But Hamiltonians don't despair too much. When the weather is not twenty or thirty degrees below zero, outdoor sports (cross-country skiing) or walking are favorite pastimes. But spring is best. When the temperature is fifty or fifty-five, and there's still snow on the ground, Hamilton is the only place in the world where you'll find students playing frisbee in shorts while dodging snowballs.

Similarly, the time-honored road trip, once the other pole of the axis of Hamilton social life, is losing much of its popularity. An increasing number of "Hamiltonians" (perhaps now a majority) find it ludicrous to spend a couple of hours along high-speed highways in a cramped car in search of young lovelies when an acceptable product is visible right at home. Better a road trip with someone by your side—Clinton is all right for making a movie or for the scholarly pursuits of Alexander Woolcott, whose library is housed at the *Theta Delta Chi* house. But high drama and dazzling adventure are not to be found in the somnolent serenity of the upper New York State town. The alternatives, of course, are hardly more promising—Ithaca and Binghamton to the south, Albany to the east, Syracuse in the west. We recommend a trip to Paris, New York, or across the trickling Erie Canal to Rome. Then, bundle down in the back seat and plan a trip to Niagara Falls.

The school's principle curricular advantage has always been its size. Just as SDSers and YAF-types were once forced to meet face to face here, rather than bullhorn to bullhorn, so students and professors have been thrust together in intimacy rather than confrontation in search of excellence in education. Of course, the kind of close encounter Hamilton's size generates has its drawbacks of sorts; the pressures on the student to know what he wants and to go after it are considerable.

But perhaps this very pressure to decide and to achieve has resulted in Hamilton's large number of professionally oriented students. Future doctors abound, though they are rarely visible outside the library. Future lawyers, tycoons, and bureaucrats gravitate toward economics, government, and political science, and future scholars, few though they may be, are nurtured like early orchids in such small, paternal departments as French, German, and biology.

James Michener once wrote that Hamilton's athletic program is ideal. Last year, the school acquired a $6 million athletic center, equipped with an indoor track, several basketball courts, and squash and handball courts. The athletics at Hamilton are not on the wane as some suggest. Once low-key about sports, Hamilton is now thrusting itself into the big-time leagues with its eyes closed, it seems. The students feel this, too. Already, there are plans to dot the Kirkland campus with playing fields and tennis courts.

Preppie or not, Hamilton has one of the country's best offerings in core subjects like English, history, political science, and natural science, complemented by Kirkland's emphasis on the arts and the social sciences. And the isolation and peace of the campus, with raw natural beauty heightened by the Colonial, Romanesque, collegiate Gothic, and modern buildings can provide a truly vibrant and vital alternative to study in dirty, albeit lively, cities.

HAMPSHIRE COLLEGE

Location: Amherst, MA 01002
Campus: rural
Undergraduate enrollment:
  555 M, 645 W
Expenses: $8000
Financial aid: 30%
Library: 50,000 volumes

Student-faculty ratio: 12–1
Transfer students: 150
Median SAT; 590 V, 560 M
Fraternities: 0%
Sororities: 0%
Application deadline:
  February 15
  March 1 for transfers

Although occasionally described by cynics as a haven for the "find yourself" crowd, Hampshire College nevertheless commands respect as a legitimate educational experiment. In fact, the entire program of studies is extremely innovative. The credit system maintained by traditional colleges is nonexistent at Hampshire. Instead, a series of divisional exams which are designed by the individual student, in collaboration with faculty and advisors, paves the way toward graduation.

The classes at the school are largely in the form of small seminars, so a freshman may find himself leading a discussion on "freudian views of humor" after a mere six weeks at college. This obviously has drawbacks: weak lectures, shallow coverage of topics, or too narrow a view of a given subject. The advantage of this method is that students, we are told, learn by doing. In the words of one student, "Imitation soon leads to improvisation." You know, like in kindergarten.

But there are professors at Hampshire, and they don't hide at home or in the library. It is not uncommon to have coffee with the school dean or to meet with a faculty member on a regular basis outside of class to discuss topics of mutual interest.

Students progress through Hampshire by completing divisional exams. There are four Division I exams designed to give the student a general knowledge of the mode of inquiry of a particular school—humanities and arts, language and communication, social science, and natural science. For example, the student must understand the differences between a natural sciences approach to a problem and the approach taken in the humanities. The method and length of the exam are determined by the student and his faculty sponsor, who also evaluates the project. It may be a presentation, paper, discussion, or experiment.

Division II is a deeper concentration, usually in one of the four schools. It is similar to a junior thesis, and the work is evaluated by three members of the faculty. Division III is very similar to a senior thesis. Again, three faculty people evaluate the work.

Despite the absence of grades at Hampshire, student work is carefully assessed. Course work and exams are judged by written evaluations from the instructor. While students often compete through grades at more traditional schools, the high pressure at Hampshire is generated in more subtle ways. It's not so much who got the A as who wrote the best essay or poem, who is working with the better faculty person, or who passed the most Division I exams.

All dormitories at Hampshire are coed. Most students live in singles. A great advantage to Hampshire residential life is the on-campus apartments. Each module, as it is called, has a living room and kitchen. Students living in these apartments usually cook their own meals, although they have the option of eating at Saga, the Hampshire dining service.

For those who choose the former, there is a good food co-op that provides inexpensive and fresh food on a weekly basis.

Housing at Hampshire is very modern. Dakin and Merrill Houses, the only real dormitories on campus, don't differ much from the typical college dorms at other schools. Enfield House is a series of apartment dwellings in a townhouse complex. Greenwich House, also known as "the Donuts" because of its circular construction, is nestled in the woods facing the library. It is the quietest of all the residences.

The campus itself is situated on one of the most beautiful landscapes anywhere in the country. One hundred yards behind the campus are rushing brooks, a pine forest, fields of corn, and pastures. To the south is the Holyoke range, a mass of small mountains replete with streams and trails.

Social life at Hampshire is largely the responsibility of the student. There are no social organizations like frats, drama club, or the like. There are, however, informal communities such as students in "the outdoors program," those who work on the humor magazine, those who frequent the tavern, or the students who work in dining commons. The well-attended social events on campus are dances, private parties, gallery openings, movies, or rallies of one sort or another.

A better defined social life is gradually evolving at Hampshire with the new tavern as a base. The Robert Crown Center, a new athletic facility, has a pool, game room, basketball court, and nude coed sauna. While many students smoke pot, drinking and dancing are the more popular pastimes.

One of Hampshire's greatest assets is its participation in the Five College consortium that includes Amherst, Mount Holyoke, Smith, and the University of Massachusetts. Students at Hampshire can take courses at any of these college at no extra expense. Transportation is facilitated by free shuttle buses which run every half hour. The consortium compensates for the weakness of one school with the strengths another has to offer. Thus, about 600 students came to Hampshire last year to study film and photography, environmental studies, writing, television, and electronic music.

Hampshire is best characterized by its experimental approach to academics, its great flexibility, and its placing of the burden for a sound education on the shoulders of the student. Perhaps the most attractive thing about Hampshire is that it is a school of potential rather than a school of tradition.

UNIVERSITY OF HARTFORD

Location: West Hartford, CT 06117
Campus: suburban

Student-faculty ratio: 14–1
Transfer Students: 600
Median SAT: 454 V, 492 M

Undergraduate enrollment:
 2200 M, 1800 W
Total enrollment: 9274
Expenses: $6300
Financial aid: 38%
Library: 260,000 volumes

Fraternities: 5%
Sororities: 5%
Application deadline:
 February 1 suggested

"Surburban" seems to be the best way to describe the University of Hartford. Located in West Hartford, one of the wealthiest suburbs in the country, U-Har is surrounded by three golf courses and numerous one-family residences with station wagons in the driveways.

This is the ideal school at which to pursue that cherished vision of a best-of-all-worlds version of the "Great American Dream": good background, college degree, family business, eat out every Thursday night.

Not all students come from Long Island and New Jersey and the Connecticut suburbs of New York City, but enough do to give the college a distinctly bourgeois air. U-Har has expanded the geographical scope of the student body but has hardly increased its diversity, because the school, which is a private nonsectarian institution (as they say in the catalogs), merely pulls students from more distant suburbs.

The university grew out of the consolidation of several Hartford colleges which had been struggling along separately through the Fifties. It engaged in a massive building program on land that was acquired in the early Sixties, and the quality of the architecture is relatively high considering the haste with which the buildings were constructed. One student commented, however, that "the whole campus was designed to inspire apathy and an air of unreality."

The school, which has almost as many part-time students as full-time ones, suffers somewhat from a split personality. Little community feeling has developed, even among the full-time students, and perhaps as a consequence, social "good times" are rare. The quality of the students, rising for awhile, has plateaued at mediocrity.

The university hit a gold mine by establishing evening classes, used mainly by businessmen intent on advancing themselves. The rates for the evening school are exorbitant, leading many more academically elitist residents to question the color of the parchment.

The Hartt School of Music is probably the outstanding academic feature of the university, but other departments are improving. Though nothing to write home about, a U-Har education is good enough for the students who come here.

As for social life, well, the difference between U-Har and other schools is the same as that between a wealthy suburb and a bustling metropolis. . . .

HARVARD UNIVERSITY
(WITH RADCLIFFE COLLEGE)

Location: Cambridge, MA 02138
Campus: city outskirts
Undergraduate enrollment:
   4300 M, 2200 W
Total enrollment: 15,000
Expenses: $8130
Financial aid: 65%
Library: 9,000,000 volumes

Student-faculty ratio: 6–1
Transfer students: 30–70
Median SAT: NA
Fraternities: NA
Sororities: NA
Application deadline:
   January 1

If it's a name you're after, you can't do much better than Harvard (although students at an Ivy League school in Connecticut would sometimes disagree). The Harvard insignia is associated with power, prestige, and wealth. And on the whole, the association is accurate; in most surveys of social, professional, and political achievement, graduates of the Cambridge school always rank first. On the other hand, the end result is not always directly due to a Harvard diploma: it is frequently a reflection of the student's background before he came here.

This leads us to the obvious conclusion that Harvard is an elitist university for the elite (intellectual, for the most part, but also social, athletic, etc.). If you consider yourself one of the privileged few, there are some things we think you should know.

Harvard is not everyone's dream come true; twenty-five percent of those who are accepted decide not to enroll. The reasons range from fear of a big city like Boston to fear of competition within a highly qualified student body. While all of the students are smart and most professors are brilliant some of the time, it is not true that all of your education is tops as compared to all of the other schools.

First things first: Harvard is located in Cambridge, a bustling city within a city with pleasant little cafés, quaint little restaurants, and numerous little shops (on "this" side of the river, anyway). Boston is all around and is perhaps the best city in the country to go to school. Museums, theaters, and operas combine with lots of nightlife, Cape

Cod, and Vermont skiing within a couple of hours to make Boston a college student's ideal.

Not everything is this rosy. Boston's pollution is no better than that of the other major cities. Though tempered by the city's proximity to the ocean (and the Gulfstream), Boston's winters are by no means mild. The cold, wet winds blowing in from the sea are not likely to make for pleasant promenades around town. Cambridge's almost exclusive eighteen-to-twenty-three population is a curse in disguise and it can get very boring. And the major construction project undertaken in Harvard Square (a major traffic bottleneck even before) can only be a nuisance for the students of the early Eighties.

An education is still why people go to college, and Harvard made quite a reputation for itself in this area. Though most knowledgeable sources agree that Yale is a little better at the undergraduate level, Harvard has undisputably the strongest, most complete graduate program. The business and medical schools are reputed worldwide, and the law school (again challenged by Yale's) is just as famous. The Fletcher School of Diplomacy (run in tandem with Tufts) and other special schools and programs attract and maintain an incredible faculty. Nobel laureates are as common as Ph.Ds at lesser schools. Not so in the undergraduate classrooms, however; given the extent of research and graduate instruction to which they are committed, "star" faculty members are seldom available for "bio 110" or "introduction to medieval poli sci." They are also less accessible, which is understandable; it's difficult to spend time with your students when there is a weekly meeting in Washington to attend.

The administration made headlines in 1979 with the announcement of a new, more liberal arts-minded distribution requirement. Stemming from fear (shared nationally) that, in their quest for pre-professionalism, students bypass the coveted ideals of a broad liberal education, the requirement is supposed to sprinkle the prelaw or premed curriculum with a few philosophy and French courses.

Students are always intelligent and ambitious, but a recent shift towards a more broadly based group has resulted in more variety (more jocks, minority and foreign students) at the expense of outstanding ability. The principle is that anyone who is very special in some area will add diversity to the student body and will make for a better environment. But the feeling that there are basically three types of students on campus (wonks, jocks, and preppies) seems to be as accurate as ever. Wonks are the nerds who, given a choice between a night in the library and a pair of tickets to the World Series, select the former. Jocks are those who would give up eleven term credits for tickets to a game in the American Soccer League (with a few beers thrown in). Preppies are just that, the Exeter and St. Paul graduates who walk around in Brooks Brothers cords and L. L. Bean hunting boots.

The problem with all students here is that they are taught to think, talk and act in a certain way: obnoxious, superior, and self-confident. So they do.

The social division is made worse by the famous clubs (such as Porcellian), which are joined by an ever-decreasing number of students (the current figure is ten percent). They are very WASPish, prepish, and rich, and nonclubbies claim that they are wombs of sorts, into the exclusiveness of which people retreat who are afraid to compete for status in the open community of Harvard (where the competition is fierce, indeed). There is probably some truth to this, although clubbies will, of course, deny it vehemently. We hear that the really talented people at Harvard spend their time at public activities, such as publications and drama (which is extremely popular at Harvard). So don't worry too much about clubs.

Harvard admission officers have a particular affinity to athletes and the school tries its best to provide them with top facilities. The new Blodgett pool has brought instant success to the swimming program (in the form of Montreal medalist Bobby Hackett and the staging of the NCAA championships) while a new indoor track is considered among the fastest ever built. Basketball is not rated highly, and the football team hasn't won an Ivy championship in years. The team did manage, however, to upset Yale's "Elis" several times in "The Game," like in 1979, when it spoiled Yale's undefeated, untied season.

Women students are now completely integrated in the Harvard community. The full name of the school is actually Harvard-Radcliffe University and all women graduates receive diplomas from Harvard. They are still somewhat physically separated from the men by virtue of separate housing on the Radcliffe campus. Most dorms, however, are coed. Coeducation has become so complete that most women wouldn't be caught dead calling themselves "Cliffies." They clearly tell anyone who asks that "I go to Harvard" (or "Hah-vahd," as most locals call the school).

Students live in "houses" (the equivalent of residential colleges at Yale, Oxford, and Cambridge), donated by the same Yalie who funded the colleges in New Haven. Each house has a dining hall, but the food is usually bad. House intramural teams and activities abound.

In part due to the enormous success of its graduate schools, in part due to the decision *not* to invest in stocks in the Sixties, Harvard managed an impressive growth in its endowment, the largest in the country at over a billion and a half. But despite its unique facilities (huge endowment, largest library, star-studded faculty), Harvard is not as outstanding as it should be. There are better educations to be found for the money, and it's unclear whether the mold to which most Harvard students must accommodate is desirable, or even acceptable. But if it's a prestigious alma mater you're after, nothing should discourage you from applying.

HAVERFORD COLLEGE

Location: Haverford, PA 19041
Campus: suburban
Undergraduate enrollment:
  950 M, 50W
Expenses: $8100
Financial aid: 40%
Library: 350,000 volumes

Student-faculty ratio: 12–1
Transfer students: 30
Median SAT: 650 V, 690 M
Fraternities: 0%
Sororities: 0%
Application deadline:
  January 31

If you were asked to design a small, academically oriented college that approximated the ideal conception of such an institution, a good place to go for the blueprints would be Haverford, Pennsylvania. Haverford College is located on an impressive, pastoral campus twenty minutes by train from Philadelphia. Quietly prestigious, it boasts an excellent faculty, a first-rate student body, and a top-notch nearby women's college (Bryn Mawr) with which it is coordinated.

After years of heated debate, Haverford's board of managers decided to admit women as freshmen on an equal basis with men, starting with the class of 1984 (entering in September, 1980). This followed an interim move in 1977, when the college began admitting women as transfers only. At the same time, Haverford is making efforts to strengthen its ties with Bryn Mawr. Both schools value their separate identities and traditions, but students at each college take an average of one course a semester at the other school, and students can now major in any department at either college. Between 150 and 180 students from each school participate in a dormitory exchange, so well over half the students in the bicollege community (and virtually all "Haverfordians") lived in coed dorms. Most extracurricular activities (newspaper, yearbook, drama and music groups of all sorts, etc.) are combined. A free shuttle bus runs regularly between the two campuses.

Bryn Mawr has in the past resisted Haverford's desire to go coed, fearing that potential Bryn Mawr applicants would be less attracted by cooperation with a coed school than by the same program with an all-male institution. However, Haverford's faculty, administration, and students have almost unanimously agreed that coeducation is a "good thing," because a school with a strong Quaker tradition should not have a sexist admissions policy and because the present cooperative arrangement does not produce an environment as fully coed as most people want. No one is quite sure how full coeducation will affect cooperation between the colleges, but Bryn Mawr's opposition to coeducation at Haverford has given way to grudging acceptance.

In any event, Bryn Mawr is and will remain for some time the salient fact of social life at Haverford. Social activities include campuswide dances, parties, movies, concerts, and plays. Though the variety is less than one might find at a large university, there are usually several major events every weekend. Downtown Philly is nearby, and it provides many different types of entertainment and cultural events, but surprisingly few students take advantage of the city.

Hard drugs are almost nonexistent at Haverford. Dope, beer, and liquor are quite common, though. The Quaker state of Pennsylvania is one of the few with a twenty-one-year-old drinking age, and this makes it difficult for many students to imbibe legally off campus. Nonetheless, there's almost always a cooperative twenty-one-year-old senior, or someone who looks like it, to make a quick trip to the state-owned liquor stores. Pennsylvania's liquor control board has been cracking down recently, but mostly at larger schools like nearby Villanova, where social events are more wide open.

Academically, Haverford is among the best. The chemistry department is outstanding. *Change* magazine recently selected the philosophy department as one of the success stories of the year, and it rated Haverford philosophy prof Richard Bernstein as one of the top ten professors in the country. In general, sciences are very strong, while languages lag behind. But note that Bryn Mawr is usually very good in areas in which Haverford is weak (e.g. languages and classics). Introductory courses have gotten somewhat larger since the college reached its expansion goal of 1000 students. Nevertheless, enrollment rarely exceeds one hundred for popular lecture courses; most classes are seminar or discussion-sized, and some have five or fewer students.

Despite the number of very bright, very motivated students, there is very little competitive tension at Haverford. Five years ago, the college instituted distribution requirements involving "dimension points" in seven academic areas, a system in some ways similar to the one adopted recently by Harvard. In addition, there are requirements for gym and a foreign language. Over half the members of recent graduating classes have applied to graduate or professional schools; almost everyone got in and most went to top-notch institutions. Med and law school admissions are particularly high, in 1978 every law applicant and every med applicant but one got in somewhere. Getting credit for off-campus, not-very-academic work is very difficult these days at Haverford, but the college recently started a volunteer service program coordinated with social agencies, and over a hundred students are taking part. Students can "bankroll" credits one term in order to take a reduced load during another. And taking a semester off is a cinch, thanks in part to then-President Jack Coleman's much-publicized 1973 sabbatical as a ditch digger, garbageman, and salad maker, which he detailed in the book *Blue Collar Journal*. A student-enforced honor code governs both academic and nonacademic conduct and it seems to be effective in preventing cheating; here there is no such thing as a proctored exam, nor is there the need for one.

Almost all students live on-campus, or in the college-owned Haverford Park Apartments, located next to the campus and purchased to accomodate the increased number of students. While students sometimes grumble about it, housing at Haverford is among the best in the nation. Though financial pressures have forced a greater number of students into doubles, almost all upperclassmen—and the majority of freshmen—have their own rooms. Most of the rooms are in suite groups, with from two to six bedrooms and sometimes a common living room.

Although the college dropped intercollegiate football a few years back, athletics are gaining popularity at Haverford. Soccer, basketball, and track are particularly good, winning or coming close to winning district titles each year. Haverford also has what was at last report the only collegiate cricket team in the country. Not all teams are consistent winners, but campus spirit is high. Interest in intramural sports, particularly basketball, softball, and volleyball, is on the rise. Rivalry is sometimes fierce but always fun, particularly when it comes to archrival Swarthmore.

One sour note is diversity. There's too little of it at Haverford. Although the number of Puerto Ricans, particularly those from the island itself, has grown, the proportion of black students plummeted in the Seventies. During the last few years, minority students have staged a series of small demonstrations protesting a campus atmosphere many of them find alienating. The college is, however, attempting to make minority students more comfortable. The number of blacks on campus has been increasing in 1979 and 1980 (coeducation should help here, since more minority women take the SATs and go to college than men), and a concerted program to attract minority faculty is just starting to succeed. The "minorities coalition" and campus radicals (of a sort) have also lobbied for plans to diversify the curriculum; student government and the faculty are looking into variations on these, but here again work is just beginning. And so there is good reason to hope that Haverford will not become an upper-middle-class white ghetto, although increasing financial pressures may make the college's recently expanded efforts to recruit minority students more difficult.

HOBART AND WILLIAM SMITH COLLEGES

HOBART COLLEGE

Location: Geneva, NY 14456
Campus: rural
Undergraduate enrollment: 1100 M
Expenses: $6900
Financial aid: 35%
Library: 201,000 volumes

Student-faculty ratio: 14–1
Transfer students: 40
Median SAT: 532 V, 591 M
Median ACT: 26
Fraternities: 35%
Application deadline: February 15

WILLIAM SMITH COLLEGE

Location: Geneva, NY 14456
Campus: rural
Undergraduate enrollment: 680 W
Expenses: $6900
Financial aid: 35%
Library: 201,000 volumes

Student-faculty ratio: 13–1
Transfer students: NA
Median SAT: 539 V, 550 M
Sororities: 0%
Application deadline: February 15

Hobart and William Smith are coordinate liberal arts colleges situated on a picturesque campus high above the waters of Lake Seneca. They share a board of trustees, central administration, faculty, classrooms, and libraries. At the same time, they have separate deans, admissions offices, physical education programs, housing, student governments, and alumni-alumnae governments. It is a rather unique and sometimes troublesome arrangement.

The quality of education at HWS, according to its students, is near-Ivy. The strongest departments are in the social and natural sciences. Future lawyers are attracted to the political science department, which most students regard as the colleges' best. History and economics are also quite good. Unfortunately, the economics department is understaffed, and graduate students from other colleges and universities are imported to teach lower-level courses.

Premeds receive excellent preparation in chemistry and biology. Of the students who survive the rigorous program, almost one hundred per cent get into medical school. Most aspirants, however, never get through "biology 110"; in the fall term twenty-to-twenty-five per cent of the class fails.

The English department is also very strong but hurting from the expected retirement of John Lydenburg. The weakest department is probably modern languages, although there are several chances for travel in Europe to supplement the rather inadequate instruction.

One of the best things about HWS is that faculty members are very accessible. Whether in their offices, at the gym, or even at the pub, most are more than willing to help students. It's quite easy to establish close personal ties with most profs.

There really isn't a typical HWS student. Jocks, freaks, scholars, and average "Joes" and "Joannas" can be found all over campus. Yet most people are upper-middle class, as demonstrated by the plethora of stereos, down jackets, and sports cars, and the "preppie" breed is far from dying out.

As far as scholarship goes, the colleges have their share of "blow-offs" (a term we think particular to HWS, at least in this context). This kind of student is able to exist because of the school policy of recording only A, B, or C grades on transcripts. Anyone who does below C work receives a "/", known as a "slash."

Freshmen have to slash three out of nine courses before they are reviewed by the dean's committee. Sophomores and juniors are "only" allowed two before they are reviewed. Despite these apparently lax standards, five to ten percent of the students flunk out annually.

For those who do want to work, and there are a good deal of them, the challenge is certainly there. You won't hear pre-professionals calling HWS "Camp HO-ho," as so many of the blowoffs do. As are hard to come by in most courses. For those who graduate with good averages, the rewards can be great. Recent HWS graduates have been accepted to some of the best grad schools in the country.

To become a senior, however, the student has to complete an academic exercise called the "baccalaureate essay," an interdisciplinary paper that all students must successfully complete by the spring of junior year. The "baccalaureate essay" *can* be one of the biggest hassles at the colleges. It drives some to transfer.

One thing to be aware of is that HWS is not a coed institution. There are definite barriers between the Hobart men and William Smith women on campus. The most obvious barrier is the physical distance between the "quad" where most "Hobies" live, and the "hill" where most "Smithies" live. There is only one coed dorm, but there has been pressure for more coed living. While all underclassmen live on-campus, most seniors live in off-campus apartments.

Since men outnumber women, many "Hobies" travel to nearby Keuka and Wells for female companionship. This is certainly the biggest drawback in the coordinate college system.

Going to frat parties, movies, or hanging out at the Oaks (a bar located a block from campus) are the usual weekend activities. In the spring, people hang out on the quad, throwing frisbees and lacrosse balls, or watching everyone else. There is usually a stereo or two blaring music from a nearby dorm. There are only two or three concerts a year, basically small-name groups. For the bigger names, Cornell, Syracuse, and Rochester are only an hour away. The drug scene is definitely apparent at HWS. Almost everyone has smoked pot, and a few are into cocaine. Speed is also known, but primarily around finals time.

Hobart's nationally ranked lacrosse team draws more spectators than any other sport, although hockey and basketball are also very popular.

Most students come to Hobart seeking, and finding, an excellent education at a small liberal arts institution with one of the finest small-college libraries in the country. But you have to put up with the coordinate college system, the relative seclusion of Geneva, and the "blowoffs".

HOFSTRA UNIVERSITY

Location: Hempstead, NY 11550 **Student-faculty ratio: 17–1**
Campus: suburban **Transfer students: 1100**

Undergraduate enrollment:　　Median SAT: 520 V, 565 M
2500 M 2050 W　　Fraternities: 10%
Total enrollment: 10,000　　Sororities: 10%
Expenses: $5600　　Application deadline:
Library: 750,000 volumes　　May 15

Located in arch-suburban Long Island, Hofstra is predominantly a commuter school, charging high fees, maintaining a mediocre faculty, and attracting a good, if disappointed-about-not-getting-into-first-choice-school, student body.

Of the various departments, the ones in the social sciences are probably best, led by good faculties in anthropology and sociology. The political science department is good, although balanced a bit toward the Establishment in its staff and curriculum. And the enormous English department is considered weak. Just about the only true positive aspect of the life of the mind at Hofstra is a strong speaker program, although the roster of guests tends to be overly shaded toward politicos.

The school's predicament is student apathy. The major exception is "New College," an academic niche in the university. Superior students enrolled in "New College" can take advantage of several intensive programs of study, including an accelerated three-year degree program.

Faced with a group of often unthinking students, the administration is extraordinarily soothing. The campus officials are willing to engage in debate until everyone drops prostrate in exhaustion. Now and then the administrators do crack down, but not often. A number of extremely young administrators have been appointed, and two students sit on the college board of trustees. In addition, many students are involved in decision-making through governance committees (most of which are impotent).

On the extracurricular side, the campus newspaper, *The Chronicle*, is an award-winner (which has both its good and bad sides). A literary magazine called *The Word* appears very sporadically. But more popular with students are community projects—tutoring, etc.—to supplement the officially sponsored social help programs. Town-gown relations, however, remain poor, although the university fits in well with most of middle-class Long Island.

Probably the best thing to be said about Hofstra is that it's expanding—in some good directions, and in some not so good ones. The tuition (Hofstra is known as "tuition land") is always going up (the price is phenomenal for a commuter school)—but the school has good financial aid programs. The grad school has grown, and a law school has been open for about eight years. And the university is perennially seeking more territory.

HOLLINS COLLEGE

Location: Hollins, VA 24020
Campus: suburban
Undergraduate enrollment: 900 W
Total enrollment: 1000
Expenses: $6920
Financial aid: 40%
Library: 180,000 volumes

Student-faculty ratio: 11-1
Transfer students: 60
Median SAT: 479 V, 484 M
Sororities: NA
Application deadline: March 1

It is a little hard to imagine 1000 women studying in the mountains of Virginia. Still, the president of Hollins College says that the students constitute a "community of scholars," and most "Hollie Collies" seem to love their community in the hills.

So it's fair to conclude that they are actually doing something worthwhile up there, including studying. There are excellent programs in psychology, English, and American studies. Nevertheless, one of the finest programs available at Hollins takes you away from the place—to the Sorbonne—from the middle of the sophomore year to the middle of the junior year. (Other special programs include a "London abroad" program, "United Nations semester," and "Washington semester." Hollins also participates in the Seven College exchange program.)

On the home front, Hollins students have obtained a fair degree of power. The student senate is empowered to change any social regulation, subject to approval by the president. Students are full voting members of the college legislature and all its committees, including academic policy and tenure and promotion of faculty. Students also administer the independent exam system and community trust system, which includes trying and determining penalties for breaches of social regulations and the honor code (lying, cheating, and stealing).

Almost all of the students (ninety-five percent) live on campus and are accommodated by a variety of housing options. Each hall in each dormitory votes on its visitation and quiet hours, according to guidelines set by the college. Dorms are locked at six P.M. but all students have keys which allows for a self-regulating curfew. Living options range from the hill houses (small houses occupied by ten-to-nineteen women) to large dorms. Seniors and some juniors may opt for the apartments located across the street, which are owned by the college. They have twenty-three-hour visitation (the maximum allowed by Virginia law). Drinking regulations follow Virginia law throughout the campus (eighteen for beer, twenty-one for wine and liquor).

For the average Southern belle, college is just a step on the way to marriage. And before wedding bells comes dating and other assorted social games. A "Holly Honey" feels encouraged by the atmosphere at the school to seek the protective custody of men at often distant schools. But with increasing feminism on campus, the "suitcase school" syndrome is slowly disappearing. And if women don't come to men, men must come to Hollins.

The men that visit come from various nearby schools. Washington and Lee is fifty miles north of Hollins. The University of Virginia is two-and-a-half hours away by car. Hampden-Sydney, Virginia Military Institute, and Virginia Tech are also nearby. Several dances are held at Hollins throughout the year, and space is available to rent for private parties.

All students may now have cars, which is helpful because Roanoke, Hollins's home, has only one airline.

A favorite campus activity is Tinker Day, a surprise day in October when classes are canceled and the entire student body and most of the faculty and administration climb to the top of nearby Tinker Mountain for a picnic, skits, and songs.

On the academic front, Hollins has a four-one-four calendar, with the month of January reserved as a short term. Options for the month include a variety of classes offered on campus, independent studies, internships in Roanoke, organized trips, or anything else that can be arranged.

After the studying and the dating, Hollins students become alumnae and then usually either rich matrons or fancy career women. What is notable is that most Hollins graduates known how to think. They may not always see fit to employ the ability, but at least they have it.

THE COLLEGE OF THE HOLY CROSS

Location: Worcester, MA 01610
Campus: city outskirts
Undergraduate enrollment:
   1400 M, 1100 W

Student-faculty ratio: 15–1
Transfer students: 20–25
Median SAT: 580 V, 600M
Fraternities: NA

Total enrollment: 2565
Expenses: $6100
Financial aid: 45%
Library: 362,965 volumes

Sororities: NA
Application deadline:
February 1

It's been said that Holy Cross is the Jesuit college built on a bluff and operated on the same principle ever since. That's not altogether a fallacy. Located atop Mount Saint James (the Romanized name given to Mount Packachoag), Holy Cross claims the dubious distinction of being the best small, liberal arts Catholic college located in the largest New England inland city which is not a port. So much for superlatives.

The seminary atmosphere of Holy Cross remains only as a memory, with booze and drugs common enough. In fact, the only visible reminder of the Christian Spartan tradition is dormitory accommodations. Two students generally share a room the size of a matchbox, so you have to like your roommate, no matter what. But that should be no problem, since the student body is fairly honogeneous. Freaks are "out," and the student body is pretty collegiate, although hardly in a stifling sense. Academics are increasingly important, but "geeks" (local term for "eggheads") can be easily avoided—they politely confine themselves to the library stacks, so that the rest of the students don't feel guilty about goofing off.

However, even the geeks can take a Saturday night head-on—literally. Beer is the staple of life, and "the Cross" is renowned for its consumption of Schlitz (although, since Irish Catholicism is on its way out, Michelob and even [gasp!] Heineken are on their way in). Bars used to operate in every dorm—unfortunately, none of them were licensed, so they were shut down. A successful pub has replaced them all.

"The Cross" graduated its first fully coeducational class in May 1976. For those high school girls who are trembling in their knee socks at the sordid tales of coeducation in formerly all-male colleges, there need be no fear where Holy Cross is concerned. The first full-fledged female "'Saders" (short for "Crusaders," the school symbol) have fared well. Both the yearbook and newspaper have been edited by women, and a woman was named as a Fenwick Scholar, a prestigious academic honor awarded to one student yearly in the senior class.

Regulations at "the Cross" are lax, with twenty-four-hour visitation for both sexes. Few Jesuits live on the dorm corridors; most were rounded up and relegated to a Jesuit residence attached, appropriately enough, to the infirmary. Since the median age in Worcester hovers somewhere around forty, and the major industry is furniture store "fire sales," students tend to rely on Boston for diversions. It's a forty-minute ride by car; bus service isn't bad (although the last bus out of "the Hub" for Worcester leaves around midnight), and it's an easy hitch down Route 9.

Holy Cross has an academic program and workload rivaling the undergraduate sections of some of the best universities. In fact, only its small size and religious affiliation combine to prevent Holy Cross from gaining wider recognition. The philosophy department is one of the best in the East. History and math are strong. The English department, suffering from a series of bad tenure decisions, is rebuilding, with the best of the old guard forming a solid base. Fine arts is a growing department, although music suffers. In addition, the area colleges joined with Holy Cross to form a consortium, pooling resources and facilities. No one coming out of Holy Cross has a right to complain about a second-rate education.

Student-administration relations are hurting. Unfortunately, the current administration is concerned with financial stability at the expense of student and faculty morale. On the other hand, faculty-student relations are more open and casual than at nearly any other place. A group of amiable, easygoing Jesuits lives near the campus and constantly invites students over for dinner and/or booze. Even married faculty members keep long office hours and make a point of hosting students at their homes once or twice a semester.

Sports are an important part of the Holy Cross culture. The new athletic complex, scheduled for opening this September, will provide a home for the burgeoning hockey team, the championship basketball team, and various minor sports, as well as providing numerous indoor sports facilities for the average, physically unfit students.

Dining is a horror at Holy Cross. Unfortunately, it is impossible to pay room and board separately, so the resident student is stuck. However, Worcester has some excellent options in both pizza and VCs with red sauce (a veal parmigiana sandwich). Just be sure you have a friend with a car.

Finally, there is the traditional question—is Holy Cross still a Catholic college? The administration always assures the alumni that it is, but don't be fooled. Even the remaining Jesuits eat meat on Fridays during Lent, and few still wear clericals. Why, the theology department even changed its name to "religious studies"! How ecumenical can you get?

So don't take your high school guidance counselor too seriously when he or she recommends the Cross as a sobering experience. If these are to be the four most exciting years of your life, sobriety will have nothing to do with them.

UNIVERSITY OF HOUSTON/CENTRAL CAMPUS

Location: Houston, TX 77004
Campus: city center
Undergraduate enrollment: 6709 M, 5501 W
Total enrollment: 29,666
Expenses: $1924 (in-state), $2784 (out-of-state)
Financial aid: 4%
Library: 1,161,482 volumes
Student-faculty ratio: 19–1
Transfer students: 5500
Median SAT: 975 combined
Fraternities: 4%
Sororities: 5%
Application deadline: July 20

The country's fifth largest city, with 500-plus miles of freeways, petrochemical industry, and smog, Houston is *hot* in summer and mild and wet in winter. Not terribly pleasant. This is probably one reason the University of Houston attracts few students from outside Harris County; about eighty to eighty-five percent are metro commuters. It is also the reason for Houston's lack of a cohesive university community like Austin's "drag" or Cambridge's Harvard Square.

Academic orientation is largely pre-vocational, though recent administration bids for new faculty show an increasing shift toward scholarship/research and pursuit of higher aesthetic and intellectual questions. But in Houston, officially classified as "boomtown," immediate student concerns are still of great importance.

The faculty is large and teachers range from excellent (UH has been "raiding" academe) to poor in ability. The consensus is that there are few good lecturers; this is unfortunate, since the school relies heavily upon the large lecture format for introductory and intermediate level courses in most disciplines.

Cultural focal points for most students are spread across the city, though completion of an expanded University Center building with cafeterias, a bar, amusement arcades, and bookstore have brought more cohesion to the campus. Fraternities and sororities are growing in impact.

The two main residence complexes on central campus offer two distinctly different environments: students bent on the modern are generally attracted to the Moody Towers, the more expensive dorms. Rooms are relatively small, with few single-student rooms. Though

Moody is segregated, with men in the south tower and women in the north tower, liberal visitation prevails. The removal of curfews is a major change from the *in loco parentis* attitude of years past.

Students who prefer less status-oriented housing opt for the Quadrangle, a group of low-rise dorms in the most heavily wooded area on campus. Three of the five buildings are coed, and the only building with specified visiting hours is the women's dorm.

For the handicapped, UH is perhaps the most accessible campus in the nation. Except for two residence halls, every building on campus is equipped with ramps and elevators. Special parking areas are provided next to almost every building, and a minibus makes special runs between the campus and downtown Houston.

Choosing UH over UT/Austin depends largely on economics, including proximity to Houston's mushrooming growth and five percent unemployment rate. Blacks and Chicanos usually find more and friendlier companions here than at almost any other Texas state school. A very large international student population has been recruited, which affords cultural and political diversity of opinion and attitudes.

Pot has withered in popularity, while beer and booze flourish (the University Center is wet, with tap and "longnecks," and mixed drinks available after five P.M.). Uppers and downers are scarce, while "snorting" at UH is indicative of the common cold.

Rodeos and knee-walking drunks are "out;" disco and designer jeans, mod hair and clean-shaven faces are "in." In the past three years, live theater, art, and music events, in addition to nightly film and concert events, have livened an erstwhile sleepy campus.

Engineering, law, and natural sciences form the cream of the thirteen colleges and schools, with national ranking common in these areas. Drama, music, and architecture form an avant-garde, on- and off-campus, with career still the major goal of area majors. Liberal arts have not yet found a niche in a pre-professional and vocational curriculum.

If you can stomach the weather, if a broad education is not essential, and if you want the security of a job-laden community, there is no reason not to try University of Houston.

HOWARD UNIVERSITY

Location: Washington, DC 20059 **Student-faculty ratio: 10–1**
Campus: city center **Transfer students: 1400**
Undergraduate enrollment: **Median SAT: 397 V, 412 M**

3050 M, 3300 W
Total enrollment: 10,150
Expenses: $4051
Financial aid: NA
Library: 1,012,493 volumes

Fraternities: 4%
Sororities: 4%
Application deadline:
April 1

Howard University has come a long way since the early Sixties when it was a sleepy, backwater university training black teachers, social workers, and an occasional doctor or lawyer to take their places among the nation's black bourgeoisie. The university has shown a steady march to the left educationally in the past fifteen years, and now stands on the verge of becoming the country's first consummate "black university." Its most prominent graduate of late is former UN Ambassador Andrew Young.

Articulate and widely respected on- and off-campus, university president James M. Cheek triggered Howard's attempt to transform all scholastic disciplines into modes of expression for the black experience. In a revolutionary move, Howard University has come to define education as fundamentally political—knowledge is to be gained as a tool for liberating blacks from exploitation. The ghost of Booker T. Washington has been irrevocably buried.

The ultimate goal of Howard's academic reform is to make Afro-American studies (established now at many campuses, both black and white) superfluous. The black experience should be inherent in all curricula, not set off as a separate area of study, according to Cheek. Already, sixty-five percent of the Howard history department deals with the black experience. The school of business and public administration aids struggling black businessmen in the Washington community—a sign of the school's improving interaction with the predominantly black city. Political science students concentrate on questions of political strategy, such as how a minority group asserts pressure on a nonresponsive system. Engineers receive training in the problems of urban living from transportation to ecology. And Howard has quadrupled course offerings in Afro-American and African art and produced a unique "institute of jazz studies."

Besides reforming the school's academic direction, administrators have bolstered Howard academically in recent years. The monetary struggle to maintain top-notch teachers continues, with Howard claiming some victories while incurring several costly losses. Many of the students at Howard are serious about their work, and a great number go on to graduate school. The most popular majors are still psychology and business, but the fine arts have grown prodigiously, and the sprinkling of musicians and artists has added depth to Howard's extracurricular life.

Financing at the private, nearly all-black (ninety-nine percent) institution has long been a major concern. Cheek has done well in getting money from D. C. bureaucrats of late; Howard's federal subsidy is large, although the administrators claim that Howard is autonomous. From the school's revolutionary revisions, the claim appears justified.

So far we've painted Howard a pretty sober place, but it has its light side, too. Parties are the rule rather than the exception on weekends, while the D. C. area swings every night of the week. Frats and sororities are on the upswing. One of the aims of many Howard students is to have fun, and they make no bones about it.

Howard is well on its way to becoming *the* institution in America to study the black experience (whether you are black or white). Stokely Carmichael graduated from Howard before it started its push to become a "black university." Many more Carmichaels, at least in spirit, are likely to follow.

HUNTER COLLEGE/CITY UNIVERSITY OF NEW YORK

Location: New York, NY 10021
Campus: city center
Undergraduate enrollment:
 3765 M, 11,107 W
Total enrollment: 18,000
Expenses: $800 (in-state),
 $1500 (out-of-state)
Financial aid: NA
Library: 450,000 volumes

Student-faculty ratio: 17.5–1
Transfer students: 2400
Median SAT: NA
Fraternities: NA
Sororities: NA
Application deadline:
 January 15 for freshmen,
 March 1 for transfers

Time was when Hunter was the largest women's college in the world, and one of the best. Now, like most city universities, particularly in New York, it's fallen on somewhat harder times.

Hunter still retains a reputation for academic rigor and, more often than not, excellence. There is evidence to suggest, though, that open enrollment hurt the school academically.

Hunter has developed distinct, if small-scale, difficulties. The problems are rooted in the fact that Hunter is a city-supported public school, with only nominal costs. But because of its financial accessibility, Hunter tends to attract the less-affluent (and, because of New

York's decentralized school system, less-prepared) students. Many of the Hunter women (and now, men) are extremely diligent, and more than a few are talented, but many of the students from the underprivileged sectors of the city are more inclined toward job training than academic pursuits, and quite a few are extremely disenchanted with the predominantly white middle-class values which Hunter's administration has traditionally espoused. For most students, reform is now achieved through mutual discussion rather than confrontation.

Hunter started as a teacher's training college for women, and it only evolved into a full-scale liberal arts college in 1950. At the same time, it began admitting men.

Nonetheless, Hunter offers a number of fine programs in the traditional arts and sciences. The mathematics and education departments have always been good, and history, philosophy, and English are highly respected. The advent of coeducation has led to a beefing up of the science courses, and in general Hunter can hold its own with most public universities.

In terms of facilities, however, Hunter may not be in the same league with newer, better-equipped schools. Almost all classes are held in one big building, and when necessary, an FBI center next door is used. This is to be expected from a mid-Manhattan campus.

The Hunter student body is fragmented, both geographically, because people live at home, and ethnically (the major groups these days are Jews, blacks, and Puerto Ricans, with a sprinkling of Irish). There is one local hangout, the somewhat grimy Donohue's Cafe. Most students cannot afford the other offerings in Hunter's rather well-to-do neighborhood. Some frequent local pickup bars, but these establishments cater primarily to working people in their middle-to-late twenties.

The Hunter scene, already chaotic, is further complicated by the presence of a fine elementary school and an excellent high school, both in the same building as the college. Like Hunter College, these schools have traditionally served bright, talented, but unmonied city youth. In addition to the small fry, a large contingent of old people—some using the library, some just looking for a place to go—hover around Hunter. And to top it off, Hunter runs both a day college and a night college, with vastly different student bodies, all using the same overtaxed facilities.

But if life at Hunter is crowded and confusing, it is also educationally solid. For those who live in New York City—or plan to—Hunter is certainly a school to consider, although out-of-staters have to do some fudging on residency requirements. After all, like many other colleges, Hunter offers New York City as your campus. But unlike a great many of the other schools in the city, Hunter also offers a very inexpensive and quite intensive education.

IDAHO STATE UNIVERSITY

Location: Pocatello, Idaho 23209
Campus: city outskirts
Undergraduate enrollment:
 1787 M, 1689 W
Total enrollment: 10, 804
Expenses: $2000 (in-state),
 $3300 (out-of-state)
Financial aid: 60%
Library: 289,080 volumes

Student-faculty ratio: 18–1
Transfer students: 750
Median ACT: 18–19
Fraternities: 5%
Sororities: 5%
Application deadline:
 August 1

Idaho State University is a university with a personality. It is small enough to allow students and staff the chance to seek their individuality, yet it is big enough to offer some creditable programs.

The first and last things to remember about ISU are the skiing and its minidome (a smaller version of the Houston affair). Academics fall a distant third in the hearts and minds of ISU students.

And perhaps with good reason. Idaho State is located in the midst of the finest skiing in the West—the "Skyline" area is only twelve miles away, and Sun Valley, Alta, and the Grand Tetons form a larger circle about 150 miles distant. Idaho State offers everything a skier could hope for—uncrowded, powdery, and challenging slopes. But should he or she feel the urge for big-city life, Salt Lake City is a distant 160 miles away.

As for the fully enclosed $2,500,000 stadium, it comes complete with Astroturf and inside lighting and has vaulted Idaho State into athletic prominence in the Sky Conference. Presumably, the athletes feel spurred on to greater efforts when playing in such a magnificent arena—in fact, ISU beat its archrival, the University of Idaho, for the first time in football the first time they played there.

Aside from these two prominent features, life in Pocatello, Idaho, is rather dead. Although it is the second largest city in Idaho (pop. 40,000), Pocatello is no hot spot for entertainment. ISU students, in the fall, tend to drink beer for leisure (drinking age is twenty) and then watch the football team lose. Sound dreary? You decide.

The competition between ISU and the University of Idaho is more athletic than academic, but the U of I is a bit better. Idaho State started out as an agriculture school and has maintained a relative superiority in the sciences. What Pocatello lacks academically, it makes up for in its proximity to the numerous ski areas and greater geographic accessibility to out-of-state matriculants. A surprising number of outdoor-minded Californians forsake their native sunshine to come to ISU each year, giving the school a slightly more diversified makeup.

Social fraternities and sororities are not big at ISU, but they are growing. Probably the most powerful fraternity is a non-Greek organization called the "Intercollegiate knights." The Greeks are starting to grow as they take themselves more seriously.

The student "program board," which is expected to come up with things to do for bored college students, does an excellent job. The few concerts include name bands. Fleetwood Mac, Marshall Tucker, Chuck Mangione, and Jethro Tull have all visited ISU in the last two years. Many movies make it on-campus before they are named as Academy Award-winners, and there is also a foreign film program. The university offers quite a few diversions for the student, he just needs to look around.

Academically, ISU is the image of its hometown. Although classes are small and teachers available after hours, the student never gets the feeling he's getting a quality education. Idaho, a state with less than a million people, supports three major universities, including ISU. Aside from little concern on the part of state legislature for higher education, there may arise a problem when Idaho's version of Proposition 13 is implemented.

It is unclear how much longer Idahoans will be willing to fund three state schools and what the future will bring to ISU.

ILLINOIS STATE UNIVERSITY

Location: Normal, IL 61761
Campus: small town
Undergraduate enrollment:
 7007 M, 9069W
Total enrollment: 19,576
Expenses: $3499 (in-state),
 $4700 (out-of-state)
Financial aid: 60%
Library: 1,089,000 volumes

Student-faculty ratio: 18–1
Transfer students: 1787
Median ACT: 20
Fraternities: NA
Sororities: NA
Application deadline:
 March 1

It's a strange sight when one first comes within viewing range of Illinois State University. Towering dormitories and educational facilities seem to rise out of the middle of cornfields and the small, sleepy town surrounding the university. It's a striking contrast, but the contrast also extends to the personality of the region, where ISU remains something of a cultural oasis.

Located in the conservative heartland of Illinois, the university tends to dominate the life of the community. The town of Normal has never had a reputation for exciting nightlife or extra-curricular activities. Subtracting the student population, about 25,000 people live in Normal. The university divides the city in all directions, being more or less in the middle of things. The larger community of Bloomington (population 46,000) is only a mile to the south and contains Illinois Wesleyan, a small private institution.

In the late Sixties, a columnist for the student newspaper ventured his opinion that the most exciting thing to do on a Friday night in Normal was to take your date down to a local grocery store and watch milk trucks unloading. But times have changed. In recent years, the university has built a new bowling and billiards center and a new union. The campus recreation program is excellent, featuring a progressive intramural program, canoeing, camping, access to sports equipment, and gym facilities. The university maintains an eighteen-hole golf course which students may use for a small charge.

Until recent years, students bitterly complained that the university cared more about "culture" entertainment than the pop-rock diversions more popular with the student body. But it now appears that the university is having its cake and eating it, too, as a strong balance has developed between the two varieties of entertainment. The Union Auditorium, a very plush facility, regularly books symphony orchestras and other cultural productions, in addition to frequent performances by pop-rock groups. The student entertainment committee has brought in so many well-known groups that the institution has developed a reputation as one of the best places in the state for popular entertainment.

But the most dramatic change in the social environment has been the introduction of alcohol. One of those rare towns which learned to like prohibition, Normal finally threw in the towel in 1973, and demon rum has since been available to the withered tongue. A handful of watering holes have opened, attracting a predominantly student clientele. But, for those desiring more variety in their drinking locale, Bloomington remains a popular place to relax.

In short, ISU has progressed from one of the most depressingly dull places to go to school to a place that has considerable recreational opportunities.

The fact that drugs, especially marijuana, are easily accessible to those who want them has brought cries from townspeople for more stringent action by the university. So far the administration has moved cautiously to explore the situation, and it appears ISU officials may resist the temptation to put on hardhats and stock the university farm with dope-sniffing canines.

While statistics are not complete, indications are that the student body has a solid middle-class background. Statistics also show a fairly even division between students from urban backgrounds and those from more rural areas. Also, more minorities are entering the university. Almost eight percent of the student body is black, and figures on Oriental-American and Spanish-American students are about the same. About nine percent of students are from foreign countries.

Academically, ISU is a little different from most large universities. Faculty members are less concerned with graduate students and research and more with providing an undergraduate education. It is not unusual to find the best professors in the school teaching introductory courses.

ISU students give high ratings to the quality of instruction. Surveys of student opinion showed that a high percentage of the student body rated courses in their major or minor as being either good or excellent. On the negative side, the surveys found only half the students rated the general education courses as good or excellent.

ISU is known primarily for its teacher education program, which is one of the largest producers of teachers in the nation. About one of every two students receives a teaching degree, but that figure is diminishing as teachers are no longer in great demand.

Other programs of note include special education, which has long been known as an outstanding department; the theater department (which is one of the most active in the Midwest), psychology, English, mathematics, history, and biology.

In general, ISU retains many characteristics from the not-so-distant days when it was a small teachers' college. There is very little snobbery within the student body, and the Greeks do not hold great sway over the social life of the campus as is sometimes the case at Midwestern universities. Even administrators usually come across as being unpretentious.

All in all, four years surrounded by cornfields can be a comfortable if not overly demanding life for the prospective college student.

UNIVERSITY OF ILLINOIS/CHAMPAIGN-URBANA

Location: Urbana, IL 61801
Campus: city center
Undergraduate enrollment:
   14,900 M, 11,100 W
Total enrollment: 34,000
Expenses: $3850
Financial aid: 50%
Library: 5,500,000 volumes

Student-faculty ratio: 15–1
Transfer students: 2550
Median ACT: 26
Fraternities: 20%
Sororities: 12%
Application deadline:
   March 18

In the heartland of America—Champaign-Urbana, Illinois—are assembled 34,000 graduate and undergraduate men and women at the eighth-largest collegiate institution in the U. S.: the University of Illinois. The twin cities, sometimes called "Chambana" by people in a hurry, are located in the midst of Illinois's fertile farmland, 150 miles (a short three-hour drive) from Chicago. The center strip of activity, Campustown, with its delis, bars, stereo shops, banks, pizza parlors, movie theaters, and expensively dressed students, provides a stark contrast to Champaign's ghetto, a short walk to the north.

Rated in the league of public universities, which, in all truthfulness, is the fairest way to rate it, Illinois is academically fourth (according to a survey published in the *Chronicle of Higher Education*), behind Big Ten rivals Michigan and Wisconsin and the University of California at Berkeley.

Despite some lean years of funding, UI still ranks as one of the nation's outstanding educational bargains. Although tuition is rising for the current academic year, the school is still a haven for the sons and daughters of well-to-do families that don't qualify for the state's generous tuition assistance program.

While enrollments at other universities have been on the decline, UI is still turning away many applicants. Competition for admission has sent admission standards soaring, although complaints about the inability of students to read and write effectively are heard as often here as at other, less prestigious institutions.

Everything and everyone revolves around the campus. Movie theaters are built around the most frequented student hangouts; merchants jockey for position in Campustown, making the land more valuable than prime Illinois farmland; and politicians, both state and Chicago, remember that UI's 34,000 are all eligible to vote, and make sure their campaign stops include Champaign-Urbana, though most students are politically apathetic or conservative.

The resurgence of the middle class is exemplified in the Greek system, a strong organization that proclaims to be filled with "pride and brotherhood." It reminds one of a large Rotary chapter. With fifty-four fraternities and twenty-two sororities, the Greeks are powerful and fraternally conservative. Though some of the degrading aspects of hazing and initiation rites have been abolished through internal and external intervention, there are still excesses. Drinking is naturally very big among fraternity members, often at bars such as Kam's and Dooley's. In the past, during football weekends, when proud alumni would visit and drink, Dooley's would sell more beer than any other bar in a fourteen-state area in the Midwest. Unfortunately, Dooley's has gone the way of popular culture and has lately yielded to the disco craze.

Drinking is not limited to the Greek way of life. Oh, no. Peer pressure and academic pressure have raised the intake of alcohol to 12,500 gallons of beer a week in the campus bar areas. Drugs, too, are popular, but not as much as in years past. A Midwestern campus that didn't latch onto the protest and demonstrations of the Sixties until the early Seventies is not one to remain high. It is alcohol, not drugs, that is the opium of UI students.

Illinois is a practical school. Agriculture and engineering are the school's strong points, along with architecture, business, law, math, and psychology. Art, and education for education's sake, are also good. Krannert Art Museum is the second-largest public art museum in Illinois, next to Chicago's Art Institute; yet Krannert's collection is not extraordinarily extensive.

The practicality of the university even stretches to its music. Though there are a few die-hards and seers, the majority of UI goes along with the national norm. When rock and roll was popular, the students loved it. As the disco craze spread, Illinois adopted it as its own. So, each new wave of freshmen bring their disco 45s, while the outgoing seniors fondly cherish their sophisticated rock albums.

The highlight of social life at UI is the football season. The "Fighting Illini" usually establish their mediocrity in the first few games, but they still attract thousands of real and would-be alumni from all over the state. Watching the "Illini" play is not nearly as much fun as watching the inebriated alumni lust after young coeds and stumble from bar to bar with their orange "I" lids rakishly covering their pates.

Beyond basketball and football, interest in university athletics wanes. Gymnastics and swimming field good teams, but spectator interest and support is virtually nonexistent, which is strange since UI has an excellent and widespread informal athletics program. The intramural and physical education complex includes nine full-length basketball courts, two pools, weight-lifting rooms, skating rink, five tennis courts, archery range . . . well, you get the idea.

Life at UI is not all drinking and entertainment. A decent, cheap place to live is harder to find than a good ten-cent cigar. Students are required to live in university-approved housing until they have accumulated sixty credit hours, though each year the possibility of lowering the requirement to thirty is discussed. Private housing is relatively cheap, with rent hovering somewhere around a hundred dollars a month for the average student. Finding an apartment, however, is the hard part, since the vacancy rate in student housing areas is only one percent. Cheap housing means cheap landlords, remember, so usually apartments will remain in perpetual disrepair, and damage deposits are not always returned promptly.

Illinois and other state universities have only recently begun to approach academic excellence, and they do not want to lose their foothold in the area traditionally dominated only by the elite private universities. Illinois has the third-largest library among American colleges, behind Harvard and Yale. It is the national leader in facilities for the handicapped, fully equipped to accommodate students with all types of disabilities. It has one of the finest graduate schools in the country. A majority of its graduates go on to graduate or professional study.

If you think you can make it in a school the size of a small city, and if you do not feel restricted living for four years in the cultural capital of the cornfields, the University of Illinois is one of the best places of its breed.

INDIANA UNIVERSITY

Location: Bloomington, IN 47401
Campus: rural
Undergraduate enrollment:
   11,456 M, 11,360 W
Total enrollment: 31,526
Expenses: $2300 (in-state),
   $3600 (out-of-state)
Financial aid: 55%
Library: 4,600,000 volumes

Student-Faculty ratio: 19–1
Transfer students: 1800
Median SAT: 461 V, 500 M
Fraternities: 20%
Sororities: 15%
Application deadline:
   July 1

Indiana University is probably the closest thing to a storybook romance among American colleges. Amid a wholesome atmosphere characteristic of the region, the Greek way of life assures that the clean-cut Midwestern student body is caught up in a constant whirl of parties and activities and a long chain of love stories.

The beauty of the campus is purely a little girl's dream of college come to life. IU's rolling acres feature verdant forests replete with lush green grass and babbling brooks (which by legal dictum cannot be cluttered with construction). Modern facilities (including a plush new library housing over four million volumes, a recently finished auditorium, up-to-date science buildings, and a rambling, ivy-entwined student union reputed to be the largest in the country) complement IU's countrified charm nicely. "Sunnybrook Farm" couldn't have offered Rebecca more.

Forgive us if we reiterate the preeminence of the Greek system on the IU campus, but it bears repeating at Bloomington, where the high point of a coed's collegiate career is to be "pinned" or "lavaliered" by a frat man. Nineteen sororities and thirty-five fraternities act as the social centers of the university life, sponsoring everything from beer blasts (known as "keggers" at IU) and dinner dances to lectures and films. Thanks to the Greek system, there is something going on every weekend. And although the cliquish frat rats still tend to view non-Greeks as "goddamn independents," they have been opening their parties to the general campus after eleven P.M. in a spirit of benign ecumenicism.

Students usually lead active social lives, too. For if nothing else, the hugeness of Indiana University offers diversity. Although some students feel lost, no one need get bored on the IU campus—and few do, as this is a highly social school.

Thursday night finds everyone down in Bloomington's lively nightspots, as that is IU's traditional "bar night." In keeping with the Big Ten stereotype, Indiana is a notorious drinking school. Most kids say booze is preferred to pot (which is available and acceptable). Although Indiana's drinking laws say you must be twenty-one, getting liquor is no problem at all.

The dormitories, modern and pretty, reinforce the campus's beauty. Though some of the old, bug-ridden variety are still in use, most are ultrahigh-rises with plenty of room and maid service. Each dorm has its own governing council which decides parietals and other regulations by a democratic vote of residents. Forty-three percent of the students elect to live in dorms.

Male chauvinists will note with pleasure that skirts predominate over the jeans worn by women at most schools. This is in keeping with the generally conservative nature of both the student body and the administration. IU is the type of campus parents, if not necessarily kids, are pleased to walk around.

Bloomington, a large city by southern Indiana standards (pop. 40,000), caters to its student population. The town may well have more cheap eateries per capita than any other U. S. city—and they all deliver to campus, even Burger Chef.

In addition to the good times and beauty of IU, the school offers a decent if unpretentious education. Students tend to be average, and courses are of good quality as far as state schools go. Unfortunately, the course of study is rigidly structured, even for a state school. Facilities are up-to-date, but classes are usually large, impersonal lectures, with smaller classes closing out quickly at registration. Many students complain that extensive use of graduate students as teachers creates inequities within large lectures and that the TA has more to do with shaping a course than the professor.

Although most of Indiana's offerings are typical of a large state university, it does excell in some departments. The music school is rightfully renowned as one of the finest in the country, and the publication of *The Kinsey Report* put IU's research psychology department on the map. Importantly, Indiana has the money to boost these and other academic programs. The school gets ample state funds and has a very active network of alumni called "the student foundation" that is extremely efficient in fund-raising.

A picture of IU is not complete without mentioning its claim to Big Ten athletic prowess. Sports are an integral part of Indiana life, and the university goes all out in support and recruitment of its jocks. Fairly big in all sports, Indiana's real pride is its unmatched swimming circus. Led by numerous Olympic stars, most notably Long Beach refugee Mark Spitz, the "Hoosiers" had won, at one point, five consecutive NCAA titles. The basketball team is still talked about for its amazing undefeated championship season in 1976. IU's swimming squad, like so much of the rest of the university, hinges on storybook-style incredibility.

It's no wonder that Indiana University was chosen as the setting for the recent film, *Breaking Away*—in which the campus was depicted as the natural habitat of iron-jawed preppies driving sports cars, with voluptuous coeds by their sides. If you liked what you saw in the movie, why not try it out in real life?

IOWA STATE UNIVERSITY

Location: Ames, IA 50011
Campus: small city
Undergraduate enrollment:
  12,072 M, 8048 W
Total enrollment: 23,052
Expenses: $2900 (in-state),
  $3965 (out-of-state)
Financial aid: 25.7%
Library: 1,263,738 volumes

Student-faculty ratio: 17–1
Transfer students: 1550
Median ACT: 24
Fraternities: 5%
Sororities: 5%
Application deadline:
  none

Iowa State University's in-state image is of the conservative ag school variety. And in Iowa, a state where there are as many pigs as people, that's saying something. Many a farmer's daughter has taken up home economics, while many of pa's sons still matriculate here to learn the latest farming tricks. On the other hand, there are some unexpected bright spots.

Located in Ames, Iowa, a not-so-bustling community of 35,000, Iowa State does not have any of the problems of a metropolitan campus: no awful crush of people, no major pollution problem, and no ghetto-like environment. Ames is strictly a college-oriented town and it does its best to cater to the student's desires. If you're from the big city, this might not be enough. On the other hand, Ames does offer some unusual cultural events, such as the International Orchestra Festival, which has featured the London Symphony, the Cleveland Symphony, and the Royal Swedish Ballet.

The college of science and technology used to be just that—a great school to learn to be an engineer, and little else. It remains a great school in which to get a degree in engineering in particular and the physical sciences in general. ISU's architecture department also merits a laudable rating. And, of course, we can't forget agriculture and home economics. Although the school has made efforts to upgrade the humanities and social sciences, ISU is still far from the poet's paradise.

The school may, however, be heaven for aspiring television reporters. The journalism department is reputed to be excellent and maintains strong ties with ABC-affiliated WOI-TV in Ames. Students constitute a quarter of the station's staff. As opposed to schools specializing in print journalism (which many professional editors have told us are overrated), ISU's hands-on approach to broadcast journalism seems worthwhile.

On a campus where men outnumber women two-to-one, a viable social life can be hard to find—if you're male. Sources maintain, however, that the diligent adventurer can find plenty of illicit activities both on- and off-campus. But most ISU students are into the marriage-two-tractor-barn syndrome by the time they graduate.

The student body is not particularly diversified; over ninety percent come from around Iowa. There are, however, 1200 foreign students on campus. Less well-represented are minorities, with blacks comprising one-percent and other groups a little over two percent.

Iowa State does have at least two things going for it: a beautiful campus and a top wrestling team. New and attractive buildings span the spacious Ames campus, a far cry from the smog-infested scholastic settings dotting the Eastern seaboard.

If you can be happy with a nice campus, solid science courses, a TV station to work at, a good wrestling team, or marriage, ISU just might be the place.

UNIVERSITY OF IOWA

Location: Iowa City, IA 52242
Campus: suburban
Undergraduate enrollment:
    7800 M, 7500 W
Total enrollment: 22,990
Expenses: $3093 (in-state),
    $4153 (out-of-state)
Financial aid: 68%
Library: 2,000,000 volumes

Student-faculty ratio: 20–1
Transfer students: 1600
Median ACT: M: 24, W: 23
Fraternities: 5%
Sororities: 5%
Application deadline:
    Ten days before session
    begins

Most people, if pressed, envision Iowa as an extended cornfield, interrupted here and there by gas stations and diners where farmers (the Iowans who grow the corn) congregate. Consequently, the general impression of Iowa state schools is that of farms elevated to university status by some popular agricultural program.

University of Iowa, however, deserves a closer look. It seems Iowans, more than some of their fellow Americans, "take educatin' their young'uns seriously." Iowa City, for example, is the base for the Iowa Basic Skills Tests (the achievement tests you took in elementary and junior high schools). But the most important thing in Iowa City is the University of Iowa, which gets its lion's share of the numerous tax dollars the state's citizens invest in higher learning. The result is a solid academic outlook with a promising future.

Science and premed courses are probably Iowa's best bets academically, due primarily to a superlarge medical complex on-campus which includes a 1700-bed hospital, plus separate children's and veterans' hospitals. Literature, English, and music are also good (surprise!). With the aid of generous Iowans, several new buildings have been built, including a $2 million music complex, a computer center, a school of nursing, a dental school, numerous science labs, and a three-story addition to the library.

Of course, the University of Iowa is still far from challenging Grinnell as the state's top scholastic institution. The problems of the megaversity crop up contantly here, with student's biggest complaints centering around the ironhanded requirements (particularly those regarding physical education). Sources indicate that the languages (also a requirement) are painfully poor.

One of the biggest problems with the U of Iowa is the social environment. There simply isn't much to do in Iowa City. The drinking age was lowered to nineteen a few years ago, so Iowa City may become a bit more congenial in the future, but it will never rival Chicago or even Des Moines. Most students presently are content to stay on-campus with the customary fare of movies, music, and parties. You can have fun here, but you have to show a little initiative.

So much for sterotypes, but there might be some truth in the part about being surrounded by cornfields. . . .

JACKSONVILLE UNIVERSITY

Location: Jacksonville, FL 32211
Campus: suburban
Undergraduate enrollment:
 1160 M, 840 W
Total enrollment: 2104
Expenses: $4790
Financial aid: 42%
Library: 230,000 volumes
Student-faculty ratio: 18–1
Transfer students: 350
Median SAT: 444 V, 487 M
Median ACT: 22
Fraternities: 20%
Sororities: 20%
Application deadline:
 Thirty days prior to matriculation

Jacksonville U is trying its best to outgrow its community college image. The student body boasts representatives of thirty-eight states and twenty foreign countries, and while only a few years ago ninety-eight percent of the students were Floridians, now only about fifty percent are. JU has also expanded its academic and social horizons, although the former still have a long way to go. There are special programs in urban studies and prelaw as well as three-two engineering studies cooperative with Columbia University and nearby University of Florida (Gainesville is seventy-five miles away). The majority of degrees are granted in business administration, and JU is definitely a place for the incipient capitalist. Physical education majors also abound, and if you can play basketball, you may not have to worry about majoring at all.

For social life there are five fraternities and five sororities, but only about twenty percent of the undergraduate body belongs. Life on campus holds a few spellbound on weekends, with the rest scampering to see the oldest jail in America in St. Augustine or to well-known night spots. Cars abound on campus to make such treks possible, and all students are allowed to have one. There are several nice beaches in the area, though there are no cities of note for many miles beyond Jacksonville's limits.

Jacksonville itself is a fast-growing community of over a half-million and provides ample social prospects, plus one of the finest pop radio stations in the South (WAPE) for those who just like to listen.

But back to the university—and most of the students do return after the weekend; how else could they meet all the required courses and graduate? To do so takes a 2.0 average and 128 semester hours. Included in the hours must be two years of science (one lab), English, two math courses, four semesters of P. E., two social sciences, and two years of a foreign language. Teaching these courses is a mediocre-to-good faculty, nearly fifty percent of whom have doctorates. Library facilities are still fairly small, although the addition of a new wing has added additional space. There is an independent study program available for those with a 3.0 average or better who want to work outside the classroom.

Admission, though selective, is comparatively easy. About sixty percent of the male applicants and over seventy percent of the females were accepted in a recent freshman class. Most accepted were in the top half of their classes with a C average or better.

But overshadowing everything else at JU is the basketball squad, which vaulted Jacksonville into the big college ranks and the NCAA finals seven years ago and ensured that JU, for better or for worse, isn't planning to be a small college ever again.

JOHNS HOPKINS UNIVERSITY

Location: Baltimore, MD 21218
Campus: city outskirts
Undergraduate enrollment:
   1600 M, 630 W
Total enrollment: 3000
Expenses: $7055
Financial aid: 55%
Library: 1,800,000 volumes

Student-faculty ratio: 10-1
Transfer students: 60
Median SAT: 614 V, 668 M
Fraternities: 25%
Sororities: 0%
Application deadline:
   February 1

Just as McDonald's is famous for its hamburgers, Hopkins is renowned for its premeds. Fortunately, the notion of Hopkins-as-premed-factory is changing. With the passing of each year, the distribution of area majors is becoming more evenly balanced. Yes, premeds and engineering majors still lead the parade and probably will as long as there is a JHU; but, happily, the number of humanities and social science majors is on the increase.

The academic atmosphere at "the Hop" is rather intense, and that applies to the English major as well as to the premed. Actually (and this is one of the nice things about the school), you can "nerd out" and be a "throat"—someone who spends twenty-five hours a day studying in the bowels of the excellent Hopkins library—or you can set your own laid-back pace if you choose. Despite the abundance of "throats" at Hopkins, there is really no pressure to follow suit and likewise become chained to the books. Though there is a tendency to malign certain groups on campus ("Why did the premed cross the road?" "Because it was required."), the general feeling is, "You do your thing, and I'll do mine."

But alas, most "Hoppies" spend too much time on their studies, and not enough time on extracurriculars. Students complain that there are too few interesting activities and groups to join. That's fifty percent truth and fifty percent alibi. Rather than spend some time with the school paper or the fencing club, most students would rather devote their energy to setting themselves up for a good job or graduate school

The professors at Hopkins are brilliant and dedicated to the pursuit of knowledge. Hopkins is a research/graduate-student-oriented institution, and while some professors may seem distant in lectures, they are readily approachable outside the classroom. Many students become involved in individual research or reading projects under the direction of a faculty member.

An extra attraction of Hopkins is that students can take courses at other Baltimore colleges, including the Peabody Conservatory of Music, the Maryland Institute College of Art, Towson State College, and others.

The housing situation is unique among top-rated universities. Many schools feed and house their students for four years. At "the Hop," dormitory living is mandatory for freshmen, but after that, because Hopkins does not own enough housing facilities, most people take up residence in apartments and houses within a one-mile radius of the campus. This set-up has its disadvantages (for instance, unfriendly landlords and neighbors who aren't too crazy about Elvis Costello at ten decibels), but it acquaints the student with the important art of apartment-hunting and -living.

If you're looking for a wild party school, then avoid Hopkins. The social scene here is quiet, but not so quiet that everyone can't find a way to unwind. Students throw parties in their dorms and apartments, and of course there are the occasional blow-outs at your friendly neighborhood frats. The student council sponsors weekend dances and beer blasts, and the Rathskellar provides a nice place to listen to live music and relax with a brew or a glass of wine. The Chester's Place Coffee House, a JHU tradition, takes place every Wednesday night. On Thursday nights, the Rathskellar becomes the home of "Disco Nite"—Hopkins students, plus busloads of love-crazed females from the local women's colleges, crowd "the Rat" in what is often called "the Thursday night meat market."

Drugs are not a big thing at Hopkins. If anyone indulges in drugs, he does so in the privacy of his own little room and rarely goes around bragging about it. Drinking—everything from beer to the hard stuff—is the most popular way of getting "buzzed."

The male-female ratio at Hopkins (about six-to-three) is bad news if you happen to be a male of the species, but lately the administration has been making an effort to even the score by admitting more women. If a Hopkins guy has trouble winning the heart of some Hopkins lass, then he simply takes his act on the road and tries his luck at one of the local women's colleges (Notre Dame or Goucher) or at the nearby coed school, Loyola College.

Student-administration relations are distant at best. Not many students are aware of the university's extensive defense research and weighty stock portfolio, and those who do know don't give much thought to them. The administration maintains the upper hand in most campus issues, but they are surprisingly willing to back down whenever threatened with student uprisings or bad publicity.

Though not known as a school with great athletic teams, Hopkins, in 1978–79, was the only college in the nation to win NCAA national championships in two sports: Division III swimming and, of course, Division I lacrosse. Other Hopkins teams do well, considering that few of the athletes were recruited. Still, lacrosse remains *the* sport at "the Hop." The "Blue Jay" lacrosse squad is always a contender and has many times been national champion.

A few comments should be made about Baltimore. The city is currently undergoing a sort of renaissance. The downtown area is being revitalized, and by the early 1980s, Baltimore's beautiful "Inner Harbor" will have one aquarium and a mall of shops and restaurants called Harborplace. The city boasts countless movie houses, several fine museums, a few excellent play houses, many first-rate restaurants, Memorial Stadium (home of the "Orioles" and "Colts"), concert arenas, symphony halls, parks, and much more, all within a short bus ride from Hopkins. Students who say that Baltimore has nothing to offer in the way of culture just ain't looking. Also, Washington, D. C., with all its cultural and historical goodies, is an hour away by car or train.

Hopkins doesn't pretend to be an ivy-covered utopia. It has its share of small annoyances, but then what school doesn't? If you have a good mind and are willing to take the initiative in running your life, you can get an education as good as any, and have fun doing it.

KALAMAZOO COLLEGE

Location: Kalamazoo, MI 49007
Campus: city outskirts
Undergraudate enrollment:
　725 M, 700W
Expenses: $5949
Financial aid: 40%
Library: 200,000 volumes

Student-faculty ratio: 18–1
Transfer students: 60
Median SAT: 565 V, 610 M
Median ACT: 26.7
Fraternities: 0%
Application deadline:
　May 1

Kalamazoo College is a small liberal arts school in Michigan offering a nontraditional education to its students, many of whom go on to graduate or professional schools. The college's greatest asset is its progressive educational policy; its greatest drawback is its increasingly homogeneous student population of Michiganders from white, middle- to upper-middle-class families.

Kalamazoo offers an educational plan which is naturally (if unimaginatively) named the "Kalamazoo Plan." The school year is divided into quarters so that the schedule of on-campus, academic quarters is broken up by off-campus quarters. Students spend two or three quarters on-campus, followed by a quarter working, traveling, or studying at various places in the country under the auspices of the college.

Under the "Kalamazoo Plan," the majority of students spend the fall and/or winter quarters of their junior year studying in Europe, Africa, or Asia. Most of the students in the program elect one of the European Centers. Since the "Kalamazoo Plan" is geared toward the individual, there are several directions to choose from. How interesting or educational your four years at Kalamazoo are depends on the curiosity and motivation of the student.

The highlight of academic life at Kalamazoo is the SIP—the "senior individualized project." The intent of the project is to "allow" students to justify their going to college for four years. Credit is awarded for the projects and they can be completed anywhere in the world!

The faculty is good, liberal, and well educated. Classes are small and usually interesting. Kalamazoo's strong departments are in the physical sciences and in the pre-professional programs, but not at the expense of more traditional disciplines such as English, history, and the social sciences.

Some students at K College think that the school has tried to combine the best of two worlds—Midwestern virtue and progressive education. A senior at Kalamazoo told us that students' grandmothers think the school is a "lovely place." Not surprising. Not so long ago, alcohol was forbidden on campus, everyone went to chapel, and the boys and girls didn't go into each other's dorms. So much for Midwestern virtue.

But as we said, Kalamazoo is a progressive institution, and it attracts progressive students who seem to like the school a great deal. On occasion, these progressive students have been known to engage in the nasty college habits of drugs, drink, and sex, but they do so discreetly. Overall, Kalamazoo social life is relatively stable, and certainly not the best reason to pick Kalamazoo.

The K College campus is only a ten-minute walk from the city's downtown area. Kalamazoo, with a metropolitan population of about 200,000, is located about three hours east of Chicago and two-and-a-half hours west of Detroit.

Kalamazoo offers a good, varied education with heavy emphasis on off-campus self-discovery missions. If study abroad is a criterion for selecting a college, Kalamazoo has an extensive offering. And if you come here, just think of the fun you'll have telling people where you go to school

KANSAS STATE UNIVERSITY

Location: Manhattan, KS 66506
Campus: rural
Undergraduate enrollment:
  8750 M, 7250 W
Total enrollment: 19,000
Expenses: $3400 (in-state),
  $4400 (out-of-state)
Financial aid: 40%
Library: 900,000 volumes

Student-faculty ratio: 20–1
Transfer students: 1000
Median SAT: 500 V, 500 M
Median ACT: 23
Fraternities: 15%
Sororities: 10%
Application deadline:
  August 15

One drunken University of Kansas alumnus recently commented, "The thing I can't stand about those people from K State is that they're all like Alf Landon." (The statement probably says as much about KU's "Snob Hill" image as it does about K State's "Silo Tech" image.) Really now, no one is like Alf Landon—not even the students at K State. They do, however, pretty much live up to their reputation as "K Straight."

Admittedly, there is an Alf Landon lecture series on campus (purely coincidental, we are told), and when Richard Nixon spoke at KSU nine years ago as part of the series, he was well received. But the K State student is much closer to Eisenhower (a home state boy) do-nothingness than Nixon Republicanism—KSU students would probably also receive Bobby Seale, Moshe Dayan, or Santa Claus without disgruntlement, for they simply don't care who is speaking, usually.

If you're going to knock KSU, "Silo Tech" is as good an epithet as any to hurl. For Kansas State is the premier university in the whole world at which to learn to be a farmer. The ag department is extensive (everything from agriculture journalism to poultry science and then some) and top-notch. Moreover, KSU is the only school in the U. S. offering degrees in feed and milling technology. If your heart's greatest desire is to slop hogs or harvest wheat, this is the place for you.

Predictably, K State is also strong in the natural sciences which serve to complement the agricultural offerings. KSU's veterinary medicine is good, especially with its relatively new $3 million vet building. A new biological science building and gym have just been completed. Engineering and math are solid, but humanities and social sciences takes a definite backseat. KSU is no place for a poet. It is important to note that funding shortages have hurt K State's overall program of late, with many teachers leaving the school for more lucrative paychecks elsewhere.

Kansas State is "Purple Pride" country, which means, among other things, that everyone wears purple to the all-important fall football contests. A relative newcomer to big-time football, K State has gone in for the hoopla in a big way— a 30,000 seat stadium, astroturf, and gung-ho school spirit. How long K State students will continue to let sports teams have more expensive and better facilities than the school of education (to cite one important curriculum) remains to be seen.

Football schools are drinking schools, and K State is no exception. A minitown only blocks from campus (called "Aggieville," fittingly enough) provides students with all the bars (and sundry other items) they will need in their four-year stay in Manhattan. Manhattan, the city, is extremely dull and will never be confused with Manhattan, the island. Drugs can be found, thanks primarily to the proximity of the Army at Fort Riley, but alcohol is undisputed king at KSU.

Overall, the life-style is rather staid. With the sex ratio slowly approaching parity, there's hope; but the school has a reputation for providing a better atmosphere for harvesting a husband than sowing wild oats. Greeks remain active, but independents are becoming increasingly antagonistic toward the "snobbish" "Sorority Sals." The feeling is mutual.

One of the school's biggest immediate problems is an incredible housing shortage, caused ironically by luring state students from archrival (and more liberal) Kansas University.

Off-campus living is still the choice of many, although finding an apartment can be difficult. The cost of apartments around Manhattan is high by frugal Kansas standards.

In closing, we should probably reiterate that Eisenhower isn't Landon, but he's equally far away from the McGovern or the Kennedy family. K State is changing, but more slowly than most. If you're apolitical, rural (or at least folksy), a prospective farmer or engineer, and don't mind becoming the butt of Kansas jokes yourself for four years, KSU may well be for you.

UNIVERSITY OF KANSAS

Location: Lawrence, KS 66045
Campus: city center
Undergraduate enrollment:
   9400 M, 8800 W
Total enrollment: 23,915

Student-faculty ratio: 16–1
Transfer students: 5392
Median ACT: 23
Fraternities: 19%
Sororities: 11%

Expenses: $2800 (in-state),
$3800 (out-of-state)
Financial aid: 33%
Library: 2,100,000 volumes

Application deadline:
none

It may be difficult for you to believe that the University of Kansas enjoyed, at least for a time, and at least in Kansas, the reputation of being "radical." That was in 1970, after a visit by Abbie Hoffman. Freshman enrollment dropped sharply after that, but has since more than recovered.

Even so, students have been forced to deal with problems which have lingered. State officials have watched the Lawrence campus with a hawklike eye, hoping to nip leftist activities in the bud. The state attorney general's office and the state police conducted drug raids on the campus, with limited success. As one *Daily Kansas* spokesman said, "Drug usage didn't actually decrease, but people were a lot more paranoid when they smoked."

Kansas continues to be a sound school academically, particularly in the social sciences. Outside the social sciences KU boasts a top-notch chemistry department strengthened by its ties with KU's college of health sciences and hospital (one of the few in that part of the country). The William Allen White School of Jounalism also stands out as exceptional, reflected by the student paper's ability to merit top recognition in its class. KU continues to score highly in fellowship competitions, despite the traditional problems of the behemoth university— overly large classes, impersonal instruction, and overuse of graduate students in the classroom. An unhealthy high percentage of degrees continues to be granted in fringe areas, such as education and business and commerce.

The student body as a whole is intelligent enough, but KU is a state school and must take the bad along with the good. The students are nearly all Midwestern, although the number of in-state matriculants has dropped in recent years (Kansans now compromise a reasonable sixty percent of the student body). To its credit, KU pioneered the people-to-people program and works hard to attract foreign students to Lawrence.

Fraternities and sororities, dominated by the upper-middle-class bourgeoisie from Wichita and Kansas City, are on the wane at the Midwest campus. The student senate even voted to cut off activities funds earmarked for athletics—a surprising move at the traditionally jock-oriented school which has given us Wilt Chamberlain (who didn't graduate) and Jim Ryun (who did). Athletically, KU remains competitive in the increasingly powerful Big Eight.

While support of athletic teams has declined slightly, possibly in reaction to the gung-ho school spirit emerging across the state at Kansas State University, most fall afternoons find a majority of the students at the weekly football contest. Dating at the campus remains traditional.

Off-campus living, a national trend, is becoming increasingly popular at KU. Unlike some towns, Lawrence provides fairly adequate off-campus housing in both inexpensive and "luxury" price spread. Coed dorms, which in Kansas means males and females living in the same building, not in the same room (or even the same floor), is also catching on at KU.

KU appears to be stabilizing. It is not, and probably never was, the hotbed of student activism which some Kansans feared. It is also not the archconservative, backward academic institution which effete Easterners all too often associate with the state. It's a sound school, scholastically stocked with down-to-earth Midwesterners who know how to enjoy Lawrence's unpressured environment.

KENT STATE UNIVERSITY

Location: Kent, OH 44242
Campus: rural
Undergraduate enrollment:
 7500 M, 8500 W
Total enrollment: 18,500
Expenses: $2745 (in-state),
 $3945 (out-of-state)
Financial aid: 55%
Library: 1,500,000 volumes

Student-faculty ratio: 20–1
Transfer students: 1500
Median SAT: M: 438 V, 501 M;
 W: 446 V, 460 M
Median ACT: M: 19.8, W: 18.4
Fraternities: 7%
Sororities: 7%
Application deadline:
 August 15

The image of a Kent State coed huddled over the bloodstained body of a fallen classmate was indelibly engraved on the American consciousness when the wire services flashed the photograph across the country following the cataclysmic shooting by Ohio National Guardsmen on May 4, 1970. The four deaths on this usually quiet campus touched off the first national student strike in U.S. history.

Many of the campuses that erupted in 1970 have returned to the tranquility that has traditionally dominated the nation's colleges. At first glance, Kent State seems to be an exception. Only three years ago, close to a hundred protestors were arrested and evicted from Blanket Hill, the site of the shootings ten years ago, where many of them had been camping for two months. The protestors' goal had been to block construction of a $6 million gymnasium that the university planned to build on the hill. The importance of the Kent State killings merited the preservation of the area as a "national monument," the protestors maintained.

This demonstration of idealism was strikingly incongruous with the predominant apathetic spirit of the late Seventies. It was also strikingly incongruous with the predominant apathetic spirit of the rest of Kent State. The student body did not flock to the support of the protestors, many of whom were nonstudents. In 1970, the radical activities (including the burning of the ROTC building even before the shootings took place) had been widespread. In 1977, a few students participated in the nonviolent protest; thousands of others were content to continue with life as usual. And in 1980, the life-as-usual at Kent State is that of an average school for the average Midwestern student.

Always humble scholastically, Kent focuses on training teachers. Both its elementary education offerings (including special courses on the pre- and early-school child) and secondary education selections are highly acclaimed. Music, art, and architecture are also popular. The school's speech therapy program is unusual and considered good. Nevertheless, entrance requirements for Kent State are not demanding, and the students themselves generally tend towards mediocrity. The university provides a new fourteen-floor library and an honors program, but it still has a long way to go to attain any measure of academic distinction.

Minor changes have occurred in the social situation, but the feeling is still basically for the great middle. Nightlife continues to center around bars; the fraternities are dying. Students find the town social life stomachable but are reportedly making more weekend trips into surrounding cities, such as Columbus, in search of a more gala dating scene. Pot has joined alcohol as the most popular means of intoxication on campus, and the traditional animosity between the Greek drinkers and freak smokers has evaported.

Housing is a bone of contention between students and administrators. Disgruntled with housing conditions and university regulations, many students have been moving off-campus. In an attempt to soothe dissatisfied students (and maintain the university's room and board income), the administration opened coed dorms and even abandoned a long-standing ban on alcohol in student rooms. These carrots failed to have the desired effect, so officials brought out the stick: all freshmen and sophomores are now required to live on campus.

The country will never be the same after what happened at Kent

State on May 4, 1970. But the school's administrators are doing a good job of pretending that the shootings, and the activism that led to them, never happened—and only a few of the students are trying to prove them wrong.

UNIVERSITY OF KENTUCKY

Location: Lexington, KY 40506
Campus: city center
Undergraduate enrollment:
  8250 M, 6590 W
Total enrollment: 21,000
Expenses: $2900 (in-state),
  $4000 (out-of-state)
Financial aid: 75%
Library: 1,720,000 volumes

Student-faculty ratio: 17-1
Transfer students: NA
Median ACT: M: 20.7; W: 20
Fraternities: 18%
Sororities: 12%
Application deadline:
  June 1

The University of Kentucky is like the state itself—confused about whether it is Southern rural, vaguely aristocratic and gentlemanly, or an essentially Midwestern entity seeking to be progressive. The confusion may not be resolved soon. But the fact that such uncertainty exists at all makes the University of Kentucky, mediocre though it may be, one of the better state universities south of the Mason-Dixon line.

The University of Kentucky is a small state university—its undergraduate student body is about 15,000, about two-thirds the size of the freshman class at Ohio State. As a result, things are a lot folksier and less high-pressure than at other state schools. This isn't any computer-card university, "no, suh." Despite the superficial appearance of efficiency and order, Kentucky is as relaxed and undemanding as one could wish. The days are lazy, the weather fine, and everybody goes to the basketball games.

Academically (and it is almost ludicrous to speak of the University of Kentucky in this context), pressures are minimal. There are honors programs for those who seek them, and there are some real scholars among both faculty and student body. But admission to the university is open to all Kentucky high school graduates, and the reception given out-of-state applicants is generous, to say the least. As a result, scholarship is a strictly voluntary pursuit. Of course, for those who are eager to learn, there are exciting courses like "household appliances" and "research in swine husbandry" (which you can take three times). In addition there are all the traditional studies, although the vast majority of Kentucky students major in a trade-school subject like education, engineering, or business.

Socially, Kentucky is social. While there isn't much competition for grades, Lexington is known for its equine competitions. Traditions like the Avenue of Champions, the Memorial Coliseum, big weekends, sports spectaculars, and all the trappings of old-time state universities abound. Dating, parties, and occasional debauchery are the major pastimes of the students, and they pursue these ends with requisite glee. The reasonably close male-female ratio makes for lots of mingling.

Perhaps, after all we've said, you're wondering why we think Kentucky is better than most Southern state universities. It, like the rest, is easy to get into, almost equally easy to stay at, congenial, undemanding, socially oriented, not particularly intellectual, and with a few discreetly hidden academic virtues. Well, we'll admit that save for a slightly better faculty than most, Kentucky as a university is similar to the institutions in, say, Georgia, Mississippi, and South Carolina. But there is a difference—the state of Kentucky. Its schools, and therefore the students they produce, are better than those in the South; further, its lower level of racial tension keeps such political issues from dominating the classroom. Both of these advantages make Kentucky more of a relaxed place to attend college, rather than simply a head-in-the-sand insitution which fails to fulfill the university's classic function of probing and evaluating what it sees all around.

So if you want the social life and academic ease of a state university, and either want (or for admissions reasons, have) to find some place in the less-demanding South, Kentucky is among the best of a not overly impressive lot.

KENYON COLLEGE

Location: Gambien, OH 43022
Campus: rural
Undergraduate enrollment:
    800 M, 650 W
Expenses: $6600
Financial aid: 30%
Library: 250,000 volumes

Student-faculty ratio: 12–1
Transfer students: 25–30
Median SAT: 625 V, 575 M
Median ACT: 27
Fraternities: 35%
Sororities: NA
Application deadline:
    March 1

Got your Ohio map with you? Good. Now, we want you to draw a circle around Ohio State—that shouldn't be too hard. Now find Kenyon. In the town of Gambier. That's right, *G-A-M-B-I-E-R*. All right, we'll give you a hint: look about fifty miles north of Columbus. Mt. Vernon? Yeah, that's pretty close, it's about eight miles from there. . . . It's a little college town on top of a hill, way out in the farmlands. . . . Still can't find it, huh?

Well, if you are addicted to city life, Kenyon will be a shock for you. The closest big city, Columbus, is fifty miles away, and no one who has ever been there would dare call it a cultural center. But things aren't as bad as they might sound; the college attempts to bring in good lecturers, movies, and classical and rock concerts. In general, though, Kenyon's pleasures—like the beautiful campus—are subtle.

Most people come to Kenyon for the academics. The college is the alma mater of many top-notch writers and critics and the home of the soon-to-be-revived *Kenyon Review*. The English department is still strong, although not as exciting as during its heyday in the 1940s. Religion, history, and the sciences are outstanding departments, and the premed program is well respected. The religion department includes a full-time Jewish faculty member, a first for a Protestant institution.

A recent addition to the campus is the $2 million Bolton Theater. For its opening play, Kenyon invited famous alumnus Paul Newman to direct it.

Another reason people come to Kenyon is for the school's small size. All faculty are required to live within ten miles of campus, and it's not usual for students to babysit for, play softball against, or drink beer with their professors. Kenyon prides itself on being a residential college. Everyone must live in a college-owned dorm or apartment and eat in the dining commons. Although this arrangement engenders a feeling of community, it can be stifling and makes a relaxed social atmosphere nearly impossible. Miniscule Gambier cannot offer the student a temporary escape from the familiar Kenyon community. As one upperclassman lamented, "By the end of two years, I knew everyone in the school. By the end of three years, I knew everyone all too well."

Students are generally conservative and white middle-class, which accounts for the apparent homogeneity of the college. But they are also an impressive group of students in terms of academic potential and achievement.

Kenyon is not entirely a grind school, though. Students study hard all week but party hard on weekends—with the same familiar faces they've seen all week. Occasionally, there are organized coffeehouses and dances. Nonresidential fraternities provide most of the school's social life. Many are now actively recruiting women as members.

Because of the limited access to outside diversions, there is a lot of emphasis on extracurricular activities. Almost half the campus participates in intramural sports, forming volleyball or frisbee teams at the drop of a book and giving rise to the sobriquet "Kamp Kenyon." A children's theater and sailing club are among the fifty other activities.

Kenyon is small and isolated, but it is ideal for the serious student who wants a good education, likes fresh air, and can handle the social liabilities of Gambier.

KNOX COLLEGE

Location: Galesburg, IL 61401
Campus: rural
Undergraduate enrollment:
  595 M, 455 W
Expenses: $6024
Financial aid: 70%
Library: 168,000 volumes

Student-faculty ratio: 11.5–1
Transfer students: 40–50
Median SAT: 520 V, 565 M
Median ACT: 26
Fraternities: 25%
Sororities: 25%
Application Deadline:
  April 1

Knox is bred in the mold of a bunch of small Midwestern schools with high aspirations of academic excellence (Kenyon, Carleton, Oberlin, etc.). Like the rest of them, it likes to compare itself with Harvard (in Knox lingo, "the Knox of the East"). Also, like the rest of them, it boasts few students, many good teachers, adequate facilities, and a beautiful rural campus.

Knox is indeed one of the best colleges in the Midwest, keenly competitive and academic, with an outstanding record of graduate-school placements and fellowships. The Illinois school is particularly strong in the fields of math and science. A couple of years ago, a joint program was launched with the Rush Medical School in Chicago which enables students to complete their last year at Knox and their first year of med school simultaneously, using the facilities of Knox's newly completed math-science center.

The scholastic grind at Knox is distinctly challenging, and the student body's general level of interest is high. Besides the math department, the political science and history departments are strong and popular. Knox has taken advantage of its location to build up its Midwest studies program.

As a member of the Associated Colleges of the Midwest, Knox affords specialized opportunities to its students, such as study in Colorado for future geologists, or in Florence for art students, or in Japan, or in a ghetto, for budding sociologists. The college has its own language programs in Barcelona and Besançon and has had success placing students in a program for study in Leningrad.

The tendency for conservative Galesburg to ignore Knox (and vice versa) has continued in recent years, and though there is some communication (the Knox-Galesburg Symphony is one joint effort), serious interaction is nonexistent.

A few students live in the town in off-campus apartments, but the school is increasingly reluctant to grant off-campus housing privileges. The administration has made an effort to make dorm life more attractive. The number of students living in single rooms has increased, and a number of college-owned houses and a co-op provide alternatives to dormitory living.

The college still has an outdated visitation policy on the books, but it generates little opposition as restrictions are not enforced. Most dorms are coed.

The student-run union board is responsible for organizing most activities. Movies and dances are frequent on weekends, and speakers often visit the campus. Students who want to get away for a day often take a drive through the nearby Spoon River Valley. Chicago and St. Louis are about three hours away, and Bradley University and Western Illinois are both about an hour's drive away.

Most Knox students are upper-middle-class types from suburban Chicago, but the social nature of the school is not monolithic—students from downstate Illinois are well represented, and New York ranks first in out-of-state student population. The sports program is extensive but unheralded; being a jock carries little prestige. Fraternities attract about twenty-five percent of the male population, and being a frat man carries the same nonprestige as being a jock, although there is no social stigma attached to either jocks or Greeks.

Hard drug usage has decreased markedly in the past several years, though smoking remains popular, with little hassle from authorities. Most student complaints center around the college food service, and most find the administration willing to at least listen to gripes and problems.

Knox students are generally satisfied with their life at the college. If you are from the Midwest and considering the exodus to the coasts in search of academic excellence, you might be happier scholastically and socially with the opportunities at Knox. And, if you are from the East and interested in a taste of the Midwest, Knox may well fit into your plans.

LAFAYETTE COLLEGE

Location: Easton, PA 18042
Campus: suburban
Undergraduate enrollment:
1300 M, 700 W
Expenses: $7095
Financial aid: 30%
Library: 335,000 volumes

Student-faculty ratio: 13–1
Transfer students: 70
Median SAT: 556 V, 626 M
Fraternities: 60%
Sororities: 10%
Application deadline:
March 1

Lafayette does not seem to possess the grandeur or the flair of its namesake, the young French soldier who quickened American independence. In fact, the college seems determined to be a model of suburban, upper-middle-class America.

At worst, four years at Lafayette will mean a good dose of boredom with little, if any, academic achievement. At best, a four-year stint on "the Hill" will provide a great deal of meaningful campus involvement, coupled with one of the best undergraduate educations to be found in a small college. The key to which one it will be (even if it could fall somewhere in the middle, and usually does) lies with the student. You can learn to love Lafayette ardently or hate it passionately.

The Lafayette campus is extremely isolated, sitting on a hill overlooking the poor, small town of Easton. The town is dead as far as nightlife is concerned, thanks to Pennsylvania's drinking age of twenty-one. The hour-and-a-half bus ride to New York City or Philadelphia is the only diversion that prevents a total edge-of-civilization atmosphere from swallowing the innocent, unsuspecting student.

Since food is something that concerns most incoming students, let it suffice to say that Lafayette's is no worse than anyone else's—in the freshman year, that is. After that, the fraternities take charge, with their own meal plans. Most of the fraternity cooks can actually come close to Mom's home cooking. And the Lehigh Valley offers a good number of surprisingly exquisite restaurants.

Housing has greatly improved over the last few years. As a freshman, the student will find himself with either one or two roommates, with both first-year students and upperclassmen on the same floor. There are coed and single-sex dorms, although the college has not gone as far as Wesleyan has with coed bathrooms. The sophomore year is the one to worry about, as far as rooms are concerned, because sophomores get last pick in the housing lottery. Be prepared to live in a double again. Junior and senior year, the crunch is no longer on, and most students not living off-campus get singles.

Social life (oh! that magic word) revolves around frats, although sororities are trying to nudge their way in. The Greek way of life is here to stay, so sit back and enjoy it. The brothers and sisters pay social dues at the beginning of each semester, and the elected officers see to it that these funds are dispersed by year-end. This is done in a variety of ways. "Pubnights" abound, so that anyone who so wants can get beer any night of the week. Hard liquor is usually restricted to weekends.

Ah, yes, the weekends. Imagination is the key to social life on Friday and Saturday nights, as long as alcohol is included. There are, however, two staple social functions that are almost as solidly based as the college itself. First and most elegant are the cocktail parties. These are jacket-and-tie affairs that come up whenever anyone can find a good reason to have one. In the fall, after the football games, virtually every fraternity puts out a lavish display of liquid nutriment. In the winter, they follow basketball games, and in the spring, it's a whole new ball game. "Band parties" are evening escapades that include beer, bands, and sometimes grain. In-between are "theme nights," which includes pajama night, sunglass night, toga parties, preppie night, and anything else that your devious little mind can think of. While drugs are available, they aren't prevalent.

Once the spring hits, however, the campus turns country club. Frisbees, tennis, and sunbathing replace classes, and the social life shifts into high gear. This is also the time for Lafayette's unique variation of the senior prom, "I. F.s." It consists of cocktails at the man's fraternity, dinner and dancing on Friday, and more partying over the rest of the weekend. Of course, any good fraternity will have grain at this function. And so life goes on. But what happened to academics?

Unfortunately, not enough students take school seriously at Lafayette. Too wrapped up in the social scene, most students will miss some of the great educational opportunities that "Laf Col" has to offer. Biology, engineering, history, and English are all highly regarded departments. Foreign languages (except German), music, and art are weaker. Although the performing arts have been sorely neglected in the past, construction of a fine arts center is on the drawing board.

Because there is a strong feeling among the faculty that Lafayette should train people to think independently, not just so they get a job, there are no pre-vocational majors besides the engineering program. Journalism and accounting majors are nonexistent, although the student newspaper, the oldest college paper in Pennsylvania, offers an excellent testing ground. Also on the rise are internships offered with area businesses to English and economics majors.

The faculty is accessible and friendly. The administration, under new President David Ellis, tries its best to keep its doors open to students. Most of the time you can just walk into a dean's office without an appointment.

Lafayette's most successful athletic teams belong to the women. The field hockey, basketball, and lacrosse teams rarely lose, and each has participated in a major Eastern tournament. Most students actively support the men's football and basketball teams. The football program is generally weak, but a win in the yearly contest with Lehigh, the most-played rivalry in college football, keeps the fans content until the following year. Basketball attracts a large group of devoted fans who boisterously root on their beloved "Leopards." And the "'Pards" are on the verge of entering big-time basketball, with contests against top schools now being arranged.

If you don't mind the idea of being stuck for four years on top of a hill with no major city around, Lafayette is as good a small college as any.

LAKE FOREST COLLEGE

Location: Lake Forest, IL 60045
Campus: suburban
Undergraduate enrollment:
 560 M, 520 W
Expenses: $6425
Financial aid: 50%
Library: 225,000 volumes

Student-faculty ratio: 12–1
Transfer students: 75–85
Median SAT: 520 V, 540 M
Median ACT: 26
Fraternities: 10%
Sororities: NA
Application deadline:
 none

It usually takes a long time for a small private college to earn a reputation, and even longer for that reputation, once established, to change. The days are over when Lake Forest College was a rich man's party school composed of and controlled by East Coast preppies with enough Chicagoland natives to field a football team. The image, however, hasn't disappeared.

LFC's academic quality has improved a great deal over the past five years or so, thanks to a strong and aggressive admissions staff and some unique academic innovations. The highlight of these innovations is the three-two-three academic calendar. Students take three courses in each of the fall and spring terms, and two courses in the seven-week winter term. While allowing students more time to participate in nonacademic activities, the calendar's primary advantage is that it allows students to participate in the college's extensive internship program.

This extremely popular program gives a student two course credits for working for various public and private institutions, usually but not always in the Chicago area. The new interdisciplinary social science major, the Robert E. Wood Institute for Local and Regional Studies, relies heavily on the school's location in metropolitan Chicago. The seven-week, two-course-credit "term in America" combines classroom study of community and urban history with a three-and-a-half-week field trip along the East Coast from Boston to South Carolina. A health services major is currently being organized and will probably be offered soon.

Practically everyone on-campus agrees that LFC's faculty is its outstanding feature. The history, politics, English, and economics departments are excellent, filled with highly qualified and highly regarded professors. Outside of those departments, Frank Schulze of the art department is the widely read art critic for the *Chicago Sun-Times*. George Speros, the head of the language department, went to school with the King of Spain (Juan Carlos). Talented as they are, the professors are not intimidating. It is easy to get to know them on a personal basis. LFC's size makes it possible for you to find yourself in a class of, say, ten people. So be prepared for small classes.

The lack of academic competition is an overlooked gem. Few seem to realize how good it is to not hear students comparing grades. Although most students drink or smoke pot at least on the weekends, hard drugs aren't looked upon too highly. Not many students are interested in it. Those who are show it. There even is room at LFC for those who drink nothing harder than Pepsi. LFC is liberal in that there aren't many pushy peers or nosy neighbors. You are left to your own business, if you like. But with all of the interesting and off-beat students, you won't want to just mind your own business.

With thirty-six different states represented, and an unusually high number of working class and minority students, there is some pressure for people to retreat into small groups. As a result, adjustment to

LFC's environment isn't always easy. Once in a clique, it's hard to get out.

LFC gives its students considerable freedom. Housing, though one of the school's weaknesses, has no restrictions on curfews or cohabitation. Students also control the allocation of their activity fees, about $60,000, and they have a significant voice in the school's administration system. While more conservative than their predecessors of this decade, the students are generally taking a more active role in college affairs. Fraternity membership has not reached the high levels of many other schools, though the members of one frat, *Phi Pi Epsilon,* exert a considerable influence on the college's atmosphere. The tightly knit black student group has formed a housing unit called the "House of Soul."

Lake Forest itself is a pleasant town with little more than a movie theater and clothing shops. Everyone makes the one-hour train ride into Chicago at least once a term. Some would like to go every weekend. Chicago's Art Institute is fantastic. People who have never been there tend to miss the fact that Chicago is a full-fledged metropolis that many consider to be the "Big Apple" of the U. S. They might not be wrong. Athletics have always been big on campus, with football and basketball getting top billing.

Lots of students transfer out of LFC. Their complaint is usually that the school turned out to be smaller than they had expected. But after a year at a big university, the size and intimacy of LFC doesn't seem to be such a bad thing.

LAWRENCE UNIVERSITY

Location: Appleton, WI 54911
Campus: city center
Undergraduate enrollment:
  600 M, 600 W
Total enrollment: 2500
Expenses: $6180
Financial aid: 51%
Library: 220,000 volumes

Student-faculty ratio: 11–1
Transfer students: 35–40
Median SAT: 535 V, 565 M
Median ACT: 25
Fraternities: 25%
Sororities: 25%
Application deadline:
  March 1

Lawrence University is actually a misnomer, for the "university" consists of Lawrence College, the Conservatory of Music, and the Milwaukee Downer College for Women, which merged with Lawrence in the mid-Sixties. Depending upon your perspective, the school's major drawback or asset is the town of Appleton (pop. 60,000) in which it is located. After four years at Lawrence, chances are that the graduating senior will have gotten reasonably tired of the favorite campus joke: "Question: 'What was Houdini's greatest escape?' Answer: 'From Appleton, Wisconsin.' " Appleton itself has gained notoriety as the home of the late Senator Joseph McCarthy.

Cultural events in the area are usually sponsored by Lawrence. The Conservatory of Music serves as a major cultural resource for the university; student and faculty recitals are numerous, well publicized, and best of all, free. The Lawrence Symphony Orchestra is first-rate.

Students may earn a B. A. from the college or a B. Mus. from the conservatory—or both, in a demanding five-year program. Lawrence provides a basic education with no gimmicks or frills. Prospective students interested in film editing or business administration are advised to look elsewhere, as Lawrence is sincerely dedicated to a rigorous, traditional liberal arts education. The university requires only two core "freshman seminar courses." Because of the low student-faculty ratio, tutorials are relatively easy to obtain, although this may vary from department to department.

At LU, the science departments such as biology, chemistry, and physics are particularly strong. In the humanities and social sciences, history, Slavic languages, economics, government, and philosophy are the better departments.

Probably the strongest selling point of the Lawrence experience is the availability of diverse foreign and off-campus study programs. Students may study in Chicago (in an urban studies program) and in nine foreign countries, from Hong Kong to Italy (Florence). The most unique plan that Lawrence offers is its Eastern European camping trip—a fourteen-week VW van trip across Russia and Eastern Europe—headed by Slavic department chairman George Smalley, who is one of the great cult figures on campus.

The students at LU are quite "independent." Only a quarter of the student body belongs to frats and sororities. With the exception of one dormitory exclusively reserved for women, all dorms are coed with no restrictions on visitation hours. Students are allowed to drink in their rooms, which (according to one student there) reflects the general attitude of tolerance toward booze and drugs.

Lawrence is expensive, and about half the school is on some form of financial aid. It is difficult for the student on financial aid to move off-campus. The atmosphere, while admittedly WASPish, is not necessarily rich or jocky. A majority of students come from Wisconsin and the northern suburbs of Chicago. A major concern of the university recently has been the recruitment of blacks.

Students are generally into academics, but booking does not necessarily transform students into introverts.

Outside of the theater (which presents mainly traditional works), the campus newspaper, and the radio station, extra-curricular activities are not very exciting or abundant, largely due to budget constraints. However, the university does sponsor more lectures and recitals than most students have time to attend. For those who want to get away from the beautiful campus, the University of Wisconsin/Madison is approximately two hours away; Milwaukee, two hours; Minneapolis, five-and-a-half; and Chicago, four hours away.

Both intramural and intercollegiate sports are available, with the emphasis on the former. Frequent competitors include the other small, prestigious schools in the Midwest (Carleton, Kenyon, etc.)

You've heard this before: "College is what you make it." At Lawrence, you have a lot to work with.

LEHIGH UNIVERSITY

Location: Bethlehem, PA 18015
Campus: city outskirts
Undergraduate enrollment:
   3000 M, 1000 W
Total enrollment: 6000
Expenses: $7230
Financial aid: 40%
Library: 700,000 volumes

Student-faculty ratio: 14-1
Transfer students: 100
Median SAT: 550 V, 650 M
Fraternities: 50%
Sororities: 15%
Application deadline:
   March 1

Lehigh used to be synonomous with engineering and men. Not anymore. After going coed in 1971, and making a genuine effort to improve its arts and business colleges, Lehigh University is finally coming of age.

For the chemically, electrically, industrially, mechanically, or metallurgically inclined (in roughly that order), Lehigh was and still is one of the best engineering schools in the country. But no one comes to Lehigh to major in the humanities unless his first two or three choices fall through. And for those who choose Lehigh as a back-up school and who aren't too serious about engineering, beware: it could be a dismal form of insurance.

The break of Lehigh's engineering preoccupation came hand in hand with coeducation at the school. The ratio is now four men to one woman, and despite the men's initial fears of having to share a Lehigh date with her pocket calculator, almost all the women reportedly ended up as hunamities majors. So the periodic table is not the big topic of social conversation.

Engineering is still what Lehigh is about from an academic standpoint (although we should mention that accounting is also very strong). The engineering courses are sensible and well taught, and student regard for the school is high. Grading is tough. But in flexibility of curriculum, Lehigh administrators are receptive, with options such as a semester of paid work for credit or combined graduate and undergraduate work available.

Professors are readily available and easy to get to know on a personal basis. Having dinner at the prof's house is not an unusual experience for a Lehigh student.

For the seriously inclined engineer, the college has attractive facilities. Its compression-testing machine, for instance, weighs in at about five million pounds. Squating elsewhere on campus are a CDC 6400 computer and the Printing Ink Institute. The gadgetry is impressive.

Bethlehem, Pennsylvania, is not. Home of a five-mile-long steel mill and a skid-row main street, Bethlehem's most exciting color is brown, and the whole picture looks like a Soviet painter's impression of drabness. In short, you wouldn't send even your mother-in-law there for a vacation. A nearby water tower rates as a cultural attraction for the students.

Despite coeducation, there are also definite social limitations. Journeys to nearby Cedar Crest College are frequent, but the competition for the social-register honeys often forces the men elsewhere. Road trips in the Porsche or other gift from Daddy are the rule when one of the thirty-one fraternities hasn't brought in the women and beer, and the society at more distant Wilson College Centenary College for Women, or various Pennsylvania state teachers' colleges is ever present.

With thirty-three fraternities and three sororities, Greeks rule the social life at Lehigh. Weekends begin with Thursday pubnight and continue until Sunday morning hangover. Frat parties are open and beer is on the house. Drugs are around, but not openly visible—you've got to make the effort to find them.

The majority of students live on-campus, though some upperclassmen opt for nearby off-campus housing. About half the men choose the Greek way of life, and sororities are becoming increasingly popular with women. Dorms range from the good, to the bad, to the ugly.

Unfortunately, the food cannot be spoken of as highly. Home is most sorely missed at mealtimes.

Yet another of Lehigh's drawbacks is that its students form a very uniform group. Practically all are upwardly mobile middle-class and from the surrounding Pennsylvania, New York, New Jersey, Maryland, and Connecticut countryside. It is unlikely that your roommate will be a surfer or an amateur harpsichordist; more probably, he'll be a member of the Air Force ROTC, a wrestler (Lehigh is athletic-plus), or, most of the time, a grind. If you stare at your pocket calculator long enough, though, you won't care.

LOUISIANA STATE UNIVERSITY/BATON ROUGE

Location: Baton Rouge, LA 70803
Campus: city outskirts
Undergraduate enrollment: 10,440 M, 8096 W
Total enrollment: 24,952
Expenses: $3210 (in-state), $4140 (out-of-state)
Financial aid: 52%
Library: 1,659,954 volumes
Student-faculty ratio: 27–1
Transfer students: 2500
Median ACT: M: 20, W: 19
Fraternities: 17%
Sororities: 22%
Application deadline: thirty days prior to semester

LSU students used to live for two things—the "Ole Miss" football game and to see Peter Maravich score almost fifty points a game on the basketball court. You might say that when Pete dropped out, the school lost its right arm.

But football still flourishes, and so do the parties. Academics fall a distant third (or maybe fourth, or fifth, etc.) down the list.

For the student able to get up Monday mornings after a football weekend socializing in one of the university's twenty-one fraternities or sixteen sororities, weekdays can promise especially good classes in chemistry, physics, mathematics, and geology.

There is approximately one professor for every twenty-seven undergraduates, an unreasonably low ratio. More than fifty percent of the profs hold doctorates, but only thirty-five percent of the students take advantage of their instruction for four years and graduate from the institution.

But back to those mainstays of life at LSU. The week before the "Ole Miss" game is the wildest in the South, where this sort of wildness seems a way of life. Several years ago, overzealous fans even trampled one student to death during the festivities.

Unfortunately, "Pistol Pete" isn't around any longer to exercise his magic on the courts, but his father-coach is still there, and he is promising better teams for the future.

Life in Baton Rouge interests only about half of the students each weekend, and the other half heads for New Orleans (one-and-a-half hours away) or searches for treasure or fish in the Louisiana bayous. The school grounds themselves are dotted by huge expanses of water and forests. There is an eighteen-hole golf course, and the university's teams are always challengers for the SEC golf crown.

LSU can provide all the joys of life, but not of learning. But after all, most of its students are looking for the former, anyway.

UNIVERSITY OF LOUISVILLE

Location: Louisville, KY 40208
Campus: city center
Undergraduate enrollment:
   10,025 M, 8950 W
Total enrollment: 18,975
Expenses: $2825 (in-state),
   $4255 (out-of-state)
Financial aid: 35%
Library: 1,100,000 volumes

Student-faculty ratio: 18–1
Transfer students: 1120
Median ACT: 21
Fraternities: NA
Sororities: NA
Application deadline:
   rolling

In the middle of tobacco, bourbon, and horse-racing country lie the four campuses that make up the University of Louisville, a typical, mostly commuter, overcrowded, impersonal state school. The same problems are common to most schools of its kind, so don't hold this against U of L alone.

Over eighty percent of the students are from the Louisville metropolitan area. Most of them head home after classes. There is little chance—or desire, it seems—to meet other students. Most U of L undergrads associate with their high school friends. Out-of-town students would be well advised not to show up alone, if at all.

U of L is still recovering from the main result of its entry into the state system of higher education: the university's enrollment has nearly doubled since 1970. Tuition for state residents fell drastically, and the university, already short on facilities, found itself with more people than it was really ready to handle. Few programs are financially sound, and it will be several years before even a majority of them are on good footing.

The quality of student life is generally poor. Student activities is the area in the best shape, offering a wide variety of movies, small concerts, and sundry other goodies. However, few commuter students venture back to campus after hours, so attendance at most student activities is limited to the small dormitory population.

The renovated "Red Barn" is the site of periodic dances, while a University Student Center has a cafeteria, game room, and bookstore. The problem with these facilities is that they are too small for such a large university.

U of L does offer ample opportunity for involvement in nonacademic affairs. Since few students do much of anything other than going to classes and going home, leadership positions in student government, publications, and other activities open up regularly. Most student organizations enjoy some degree of autonomy.

Community involvement is encouraged by the administration, but it is usually limited to faculty members or special individual students. The university is instrumental in supporting the city's solid performing arts repertoire, for example.

The dormitories are about par for the course—dirty, noisy, crowded, and unpleasant. The visitation policy is more liberal than at other Kentucky universities, and there is no curfew. Many residents spend more evenings out of the dorms than in them. Drugs and alcohol are prohibited on campus; one student tells us that this translates as "Don't get caught."

Most students prefer to live off-campus, which offers more privacy and more quiet and might even be cheaper. Apartments are fairly easy to find in the Old Louisville district, only a few blocks from the main U of L campus. Maintaining an apartment also allows students to do their own cooking, which is prohibited in the dorms. Campus food is, well, campus food. Restaurants near campus are either just as bad or very expensive or both.

The city of Louisville has been called everything from the strategic city of the Seventies and Eighties to a two-bit tanktown on the Ohio River. The truth, predictably, is somewhere in between, unless it happens to be Kentucky Derby Week, in which case Louisville is the greatest city in the world.

Nightlife is improving. A variety of clubs and bars (none near the main campus) is available, and one can usually find something to one's liking. Bluegrass and light rock are big at the clubs. The drinking age in Kentucky is twenty-one, although that little obstacle can be circumvented. Alcohol is the poison of choice at U of L. Grass runs a distant second, and use of hard drugs is negligible. Just about anything can be obtained by anyone who wants it badly enough.

Louisville also has the standard offerings of films, restaurants, and concerts. More of the latter are likely with the opening of two new concert halls in Louisville and Lexington (one-and-a-half hours away).

Academically, U of L has suffered from its transition to a large-enrollment university. Among the better offerings are English (including linguistics), history, political science, chemistry, and engineering. Among the turkeys are physics, communications, sociology, geology, and art.

Academic counseling is poor, and interaction with faculty is declining as the school grows. Fellow students, mostly job-minded, apathetic, and rather conservative, are also of little help. Anyone expecting to drift into a major at U of L is more likely just to drift.

On the other hand, it is not overly difficult to breeze through the courses. You can pick up Bs with a modicum of work and an A average with a little more effort. Large amounts of research are rarely necessary, which is fortunate since the university's library is obsolete. Nearly half of the library's already meager holdings are in storage and available only on twenty-four-hour recall. The library has no other place to put them.

Intramural sports and women's athletics are similarly cramped, being housed in two small gymnasiums that are frequently commandeered by the men's athletic teams. As far as athletics in general go, basketball is by far the big moneymaker and helps keep the minor sports operating. It's also the most popular sport on campus, despite what some claim is poor student seating in cavernous Freedom Hall. The Darrell Griffith-led teams of the late Seventies were known as the "Doctors of Dunk" for their crowd-pleasing displays of playground-style basketball antics.

Louisville is suffering from growing pains. A decade after joining the state university system, it is still trying to settle into its new role. In the future, U of L may well become a top-caliber institution. For now, the situation is confused.

LOYOLA UNIVERSITY OF CHICAGO

Location: Chicago, IL 60611
Campus: city center
Undergraduate enrollment:

Student-faculty ratio: 14–1
Transfer students: 900
Median SAT: 485 V, 510 M

3381 M, 2886 W
Total enrollment: 14,909
Expenses: $5100
Financial aid: 75%
Library: 750,000 volumes

Median ACT: 23
Fraternities: 5%
Sororities: 3%
Application deadline: August 15

Loyola University has always been in the dubious position of being referred to as "that private university between Northwestern and Chicago." But while the two educational Goliaths may be resting on their laurels, little David-Loyola is doing the building and the academic expansion.

A new law school was recently added to the downtown campus and two dormitories were acquired. A new Humanities Building is just around the corner. It's about time, since most facilities are well past their prime.

Loyola also has Chicago. While Chicago is neither the cleanest nor the most liberal town in the Midwest, and since 1968 has been something of a dirty word among college students, Chicago is a real city, with culture and people and several other universities. Including the University of Chicago and Northwestern, which are two of the most distinguished institutions in the land. Chicago offers more than enough for any one person to deal with.

Loyola students in particular like the city—after all, most of them are residents. For the seventy-five percent who do not live in Loyola dormitories, there are large student ghettos around other universities and a variety of appealing downtown living areas. Many of these neighborhoods are a bit scruffy, but they are citified and lively.

Loyola can boast of its fine theater department, which continually furnishes the Chicago area with high-quality amateur actors and actresses. Another feather in Loyola's cap is its political science department, especially its theory division. The clinical psych, premed, and nursing programs are other bright spots. One definite plus for Loyola is the fact that senior professors often teach freshman introductory courses, an impossibility at most other schools. Students planning to study fine arts, engineering, or environmental studies will find Loyola highly inadequate, however, since the school has few or no programs in these fields.

As a Jesuit institution, Loyola is bound by strict Jesuit ideals of acquiring a "well-balanced" education. The so-called "core curriculum" is quite extensive and students are required to spend many hours in the study of philosophy, theology, history, English, and social sciences.

At the North Shore campus where there are dormitories, student apartments, and grass, there is more the semblance of a university, with its usual coterie of reformers and diehards. But for the presence of a sizable (for Loyola) contingent of minority students—ten percent at last count—even this modest agitation might get lost in Lake Michigan.

The faculty is not as clerical as one would expect. Most of the teachers are young Ph.D.s from reputable schools or Ph.D.-minus-dissertation types, particularly from the Universities of Chicago or Northwestern. Also, more than a few of the faculty are wives of Chicago or Northwestern profs, barred from teaching at the same school by antinepotism rules.

Though making progress, little David-Loyola is still no threat to its rivals for academic superiority in the Windy City.

MACALESTER COLLEGE

Location: St. Paul, MN 55105
Campus: city outskirts
Undergraduate enrollment
  825 M, 825 W
Expenses: $6325
Financial aid: NA
Library: 280,000 volumes

Student-faculty ratio: 13–1
Transfer students: 90
Median SAT: 540 V, 540 M
Median ACT: 24
Fraternities: 0%
Sororities: 0%
Application deadline:
  March 15

If you are a person who is ready to take advantage of your situation, then Macalester will suit you well. Small, strong academic departments are more the rule than the exception. Personal friendships with teachers are also very commonplace. A trek to a downtown St. Paul bar to see anthro professor David McCurdy jamming on banjo in a Dixieland band or playing intramural softball with English professor Bob Warde is required of all "Mac" students before graduation.

If you can learn from your own mistakes, then Macalester with its academic and social freedom offers a good learning atmosphere.

Operating on a four-one-four calender, "Mac" (as it is affectionately called by students) has few major or graduation requirements; professors are glad to help students design individual majors. Internships under the "community involvement program," and independent studies are easy to get. Administrators boast that eighty percent of each graduating class spends a month, a summer, a semester, or an entire academic year abroad. The Macalester alternatives, some of the most diverse in the nation, include January interterm trips to Florida or Mexico with college-sponsored study groups; the "student work abroad" project, which enables students to get jobs in Europe, Latin America, and elsewhere; and the more customary academic programs, which allow students to spend time at a foreign university as part of a college-related exchange program.

Socially, the administration watches (from a distance) student organization-sponsored events where alcohol is served. Otherwise, marijuana usage is widespread; students are known to smoke in and outside the dorms without fear of being harassed. All dorms are coed, with no restrictions or "visiting hours."

Besides the freedom, "Mac" offers unusual diversity for a college of its size. More than forty states and forty nations make up the student body. Unfortunately, a large number of students are from Minnesota and large Midwest cities (Chicago, Cleveland, and St. Louis). There is no average student, but a menagerie of liberals, rich preppies. premed students, and a few jocks.

Chemistry, geography, economics, and anthropology are the best departments. The science facilities are outstanding. Bob Warde of the English department, David White in philosophy, and Sung Kim of physics are the most respected profs.

Relations with administrators are strained now. The college president, John Davis, is respected by the faculty, liked by the students, and well known for his fundraising abilities. Administrators are accessible, and there are town hall meetings every month in which the college president, top administrators, and students get together and voice their concerns.

The social life is what you make it. Some traditions are still part of the fun, though they sometimes tend to the decadent. The annual North-South snowball fight with a third team being unofficially formed by the St. Paul Police is expected every year in late winter on the night of the first above-freezing day. As for more informal get-togethers, students tend to party relatively often. The "Eleven O'Clock Club" and the (room) "411 Club" are more noteworthy examples. A yearly celebration of the end of winter, known as Springfest, is not to be missed. Who can pass up two pounds of dope, over eighty-five kegs of beer, frisbees, balloons, and music from noon until two A.M. all free? There are no fraternities or sororities, but there is a good variety of campus activity each weekend. Although you won't get bored, a car is advisable. The "Twin Cities" have an excellent bar scene, the Walker

Fine Arts Center, the Minnesota Institute of Art, the Guild for Performing Arts, and numerous other cultural possibilities.

The school fondly boasts (along with about five other schools) of being the "Harvard of the Midwest," or, on less presumptuous occasions, the "Princeton of the Prairies." To the best of our knowledge, it has never been called the Yale of anything, which we must admit doesn't bother us all that much. Overall, "Mac" is solid, but not outstanding. It does offer the dual advantage of small classroom settings with a strict emphasis on the undergraduate education. Campus organizations are varied and strong, though a losing athletic tradition seems to be the rule.

If you enjoy freedom and diversity and can stand cold Minnesota winters, then applying to "Mac" is a good idea. The phrase "College is what you make it" is applicable to all schools, but it was written about Macalester.

UNIVERSITY OF MAINE/ORONO

Location: Orono, ME 04473
Campus: rural
Undergraduate enrollment: 4799 M, 3659 W
Total enrollment: 11,574
Expenses: $3500 (in-state), $5300 (out-of-state)
Financial aid: 63%
Library: 544,400 volumes

Student-faculty ratio: 19–1
Transfer students: 700
Median SAT: 476 V, 530 M
Fraternities: 23%
Sororities: 20%
Application deadline: March 1

Most outdoorsmen and preppies have heard of Maine. The L. L. Bean Company makes its home there. So does another bastion of conservatism: the University of Maine. But liberalization has been underway; you can now drink legally on campus, and parietals have all but disappeared. It will still be a while before Maine loses its conservative reputation. The State Song remains appropriate and Richard Nixon was a campus hero right up until the final days of Watergate.

Fraternities provide the most dramatic example of UMO's lingering conservatism. Just a few years ago, only a small percentage belonged or even wanted to; their two basic goals: sex and beer. Even though dorms have liberalized and the legal drinking age has dropped to eighteen, fraternities today enjoy high popularity.

Located in the town of Orono (pop. 10,000), the university can hardly offer much nightlife, and weekends often drag, especially during winter. Frat parties help keep them from dragging to a complete halt. Another common recreation is athletics, which are an integral part of winter weekends; those who prefer more intellectual pursuits might want to think twice before choosing UMO. Drinking and skiing (in that order) linger as the most popular student activities, and gala social events are out.

The students form a fairly representative cross-section of the state, a fact which, alas, does not speak for their cosmopolitanism. The image that most out-of-staters hold, not altogether unjustly, is that Maine residents are either potato farmers, fishermen, or trappers. Most Maine students seem content to let this stereotype pass unchallenged; after all, they do enjoy their solitude. Strangely, though, out-of-state students frequently like Maine better than natives, perhaps because they are more excited by beaches and skiing, both of which are within an hour's drive. The spacious campus is also appealing and remote from smog and noise, except for the growl of an occasional bear.

Drugs were slow to hit the Maine campus, were never really accepted, and are on their way out. The Maine climate is hardly conducive to weed horticulture.

Living accommodations typically mean university dorms, which range in quality from excellent to poor. Off-campus sites are scarce and generally unsatisfactory. The food situation is a little better. There's always plenty because no one will eat it, goes the old joke. But nearly everyone praises the local pizza places and hamburger joints, most of which will deliver.

Academically, UMO rates as respectable but is certainly no match for Maine's excellent private schools (Colby, Bates, Bowdoin). Classes range in size from two to 600, following the typical pattern of large introductory courses and smaller advanced sections. The library draws frequent complaints. The technology and agricultural schools, deviating from the mediocre mean, are among the best in the country. Obviously, however, not everyone is interested in hoes.

Distribution requirements for the Bachelor of Arts degree include four courses in social science, two in the natural sciences and math, two semesters in humanities, a public speaking course, foreign language proficiency, and phys. ed. Entering freshmen must take an English proficiency placement exam.

Athletics lie at the center of campus recreation, with participation and spectating sharing equal billing. Interestingly, though, Maine teams haven't fared too well in recent years, largely because they've been unable to attract top prospects from out-of-state. Baseball is an exception, and basketball improved somewhat in recent years. But football is the big sport, and it's been all downhill for the gridmen since a Tangerine Bowl appearance more than a decade ago.

If you like a woodsy setting and are a confirmed outdoor enthusiast, then the University of Maine/Orono is for you. Otherwise, you can put on your L. L. Bean boots, look like a Maine type, and go elsewhere.

MANHATTANVILLE COLLEGE

Location: Purchase, NY 10577
Campus: suburban
Undergraduate enrollment:
    300 M, 600 W
Total enrollment: 1800
Expenses: $7240
Financial aid: 50%
Library: 230,000 volumes

Student-faculty ratio: 10–1
Transfer students: 90
Median SAT: 521 V, 533 M
Fraternities: NA
Sororities: NA
Application deadline:
    March 1

Once upon a time, in posh Purchase, New York, there was a sort of playground for nuns and nuns-to-be called Manhattanville College of the Sacred Heart. Several years ago, the "Sacred Heart" was dropped, the nuns started to be replaced by lay people and even non-Catholics, and the college began a curriculum reform designed to take better advantage of students who were notably bright and notably nonproductive. The school became coeducational and dropped virtually all of its ties with the Roman Catholic Church.

The epithet "parochial," is by now almost ludicrously inaccurate. On the other hand, "liberated" and "democratic" don't quite fit, either. The school has changed enormously, and in many cases Manhattanville is similar to a number of other small, private schools that cater to the spoiled children of the nation's rich. Most of the students are Catholic (although this is changing), most are rather bright and rather well prepared, and many are intending to pursue high-level careers.

The ratio of females to males is still about two-to-one, despite efforts to reach a more equitable balance. Commuting students are increasing in number, as are continuing education students. The Manhattanville women vary from pure to prurient in morals, and from devout to disaffected in religious fervor. Manhattanville men share approximately the same qualities. The student body is a varied mixture of all sorts, with rich snobs outnumbering other species of student life. The preppie look is worn and adored by many.

Most of the staff is non-Catholic, and many are Jewish. Thus the faculty isn't pushing a single point of view, and its own theological and ideological eclecticism provides a pleasant balance. Moreover, the administration is following a progressive route; changes were made several years ago which led to the elimination of credits, graduation requirements, and traditional course structures. A portfolio system was adopted—by senior year, each student is expected to fill a portfolio with samples of his or her best work. The relevance and utility of the portfolio system are now being reevaluated, and graduation requirements are slowly beginning to reappear.

There are practically no campus rules. Only one floor in one residence hall has parietals, and no one has ever called the cops to complain about marijuana smokers. Students are expected to be responsible for their own "moral development."

The most noted departments on campus are music and education; most of the other departments range from fair to excellent. In addition to programs on the Manhattanville campus, itself, the school also offers diverse programs in Europe, exchanges with other American colleges, interdepartmental study, and combined programs in law and business with other schools.

As far as sports go, the college's swimming and basketball squads are first-rate and nationally ranked. But if you're fond of spending fall afternoons cheering at football games, don't come to Manhattanville. The closest substitute is a soccer team—and a poor substitute at that.

Manhattanville's chief asset—as well as its chief liability—is its location. Purchase is delightfully near New York City (thirty-five minutes by train), but the campus is precisely three-and-one-half miles from the nearest convenient public transportation. Moreover, many students find it depressing and inconvenient to leave school every weekend. "Suitcase schools" necessarily lack social morale. Many students have begun to find reasons to spend more of their weekends on campus: the campus bar has its regulars, and a new attraction is a group of New York Medical College students who now board at Manhattanville (due to the excessive cost of living on their own campus, supposedly). The arrival of the self-assured "meds" has induced many women to remain within reach. SUNY Purchase is only two miles down the road and offers a change of scenery.

Dorm life (except perhaps for the food) is pleasant, commodious, and sometimes even attractive, especially in Dammann and Tenney halls, which feature spacious suites. And the curriculum is flexible and increasingly "relevant."

Perhaps the best idea of what life at Manhattanville is like is given by the students' own pet names for their school: "The Country Club," "Manlessville," and "Manhuntingville."

MARLBORO COLLEGE

Location: Marlboro, VT 05344
Campus: rural
Undergraduate enrollment:
110 M, 110 W
Expenses: $6600
Financial aid: 35%
Library: 40,000 volumes

Student-faculty ratio: 8–1
Transfer students: 25
Median SAT: 513 V, 506 M
Fraternities: NA
Sororities: NA
Application deadline: rolling

Marlboro College is a unique educational and living experience. *Totally* unique.

Two hundred and twenty students live together on the 300-acre Marlboro campus in rural Vermont. They are housed in coed dorms, cottages, cabins, and married-student housing. The dorms are centrally located on the immediate campus. The cottages and cabins, which house four and two students respectively, are off a dirt road just below the campus. The nearest town is twelve miles away. If you're a confirmed city slicker, you'd better forget Marlboro.

The "outdoor program" is an important aspect of the Marlboro community. Both students and faculty are involved in various outdoors activities like rock and ice climbing, canoeing, camping, kayaking, and cross-country skiing. There is no sports program as such (nor is there a gym), but students play soccer and basketball and, in the spring, softball—complete with a keg of beer. Both men and women play these sports.

Social activities depend entirely on student initiative. There are a few formal dinners and various impromptu parties. Fall, Winter, and Spring Rites weekends are the major social events of the year, complete with dinners, dances, movies, cocktail parties, and sporting events suited to the season. In addition to these and other minor events organized by the social committee, there is a series of weekly lectures and concerts by outside speakers and musicians, as well as productions by the theater workshop. For much of Marlboro's social activity, students are still up to their own devices.

The town meeting convenes regularly three times during the academic year and whenever called for by the board of selectpersons or community petition. Marlboro is not politically active. However, students and professors are concerned with issues within the community and in the state of Vermont.

Marlboro has a long-term goal of becoming self-sufficient. With the help of National Science Foundation grants, Marlboro has been able to study solar energy possibilities for the college. The first solar energy experiment five summers ago consisted of equipping one of the student cottages with solar heating. Marlboro has built a solar heated greenhouse which will house, in addition to vegetables, an aquaculture project.

Quite apart from the intense social and political scene, Marlboro is a high-pressure academic institution. Classes are informal, but expectations are high. There are no required classes, but each student must pass the English requirement (or an equivalent exam) by the end of sophomore year. Because of the school's size, most classes are small, and tutorials are easily arranged.

The "plan of concentration" is the hallmark of the Marlboro academic experience. The final two years are spent researching one particular problem or subject. The student's work is closely supervised by a member of the faculty. A "plan" usually results in a thesis, a performance, or an exhibit. All plans must be defended in an oral examination; written exams are optional. The plan is intended to allow for comparatively independent work in an area of particular interest to the student. It is a demanding experience—some feel it's too demanding—in terms of both time and energy.

Marlboro has a fine, dedicated faculty that works well with each other and with the students. The literature, music, philosophy, and science departments are outstanding. The art department could stand some improvement, and may be receiving some in the future in the form of a new arts building. A new theater was built four years ago, and aspiring actors and actresses may choose to become involved in the Summer Guild Theater Company.

Being a student at Marlboro means being self-motivated, serious, and diligent. Each student is largely responsible for charting the course of his or her education and social life. You have to make things happen at Marlboro. Many students do. Those who don't, transfer—but even they appreciate the uniqueness of Marlboro.

MARQUETTE UNIVERSITY

Location: Milwaukee, WI 53233
Campus: city center
Undergraduate enrollment:
4200 M, 3400 W
Total enrollment: 13,000
Expenses: $5830
Financial aid: 60%
Library: 600,000 volumes

Student-faculty ratio: 18–1
Transfer students: 460
Median SAT: M: 480 V, 560 M;
W: 482 V, 508 M
Median ACT: M: 24.7, W: 23.4
Fraternities: 2%
Sororities: 1%
Application deadline: none

Marquette is a Catholic, urban, middle-sized Midwestern university located in the heart of Milwaukee, Wisconsin. It's difficult to ascertain whether it prides itself more on being a solid (if unsensational) educational institution or a national basketball powerhouse.

Marquette is a workingman's school in a workingman's town. Although the university has always welcomed minorities and students from other religious denominations, the fact remains that the majority of students are white, Catholic, and come from middle-income families. Most students come from urban areas in the Midwest such as Milwaukee or Chicago, some hail from Ohio, but a significant number are imported from Eastern cities in Massachusetts, New York, and New Jersey.

Students come to Marquette not so much for its Catholic tradition but for the Jesuit tradition of excellence in education. Even so, Marquette is far from being the hub of academia and its academic reputation rests largely on past laurels. Though it often tries to bill itself as intellectual, Marquette is not often mentioned in the same breath as Harvard. Nevertheless, its faculty is better than average. As at any other college or university, some professors are good; others help you catch up on your shut-eye. The professional schools, especially law and dentistry, are well respected. For undergrads, political science, history, philosophy, theology, and the physical sciences (especially nursing) are the best offerings. Departments like physical therapy and the college of journalism are improving. Foreign languages, fine arts, social work, and education have seen better days—vast improvements are needed here.

Perhaps the greatest change in Marquette over the past decade has affected the campus itself. The university recently completed a major remodeling and redevelopment program which has seen over a dozen old buildings torn down or remodeled; new buildings have also been constructed. The university has a new theater and a sports and recreation center that the students have gone crazy over. In addition, the colleges of journalism and speech have moved into new facilities in an effort to bring those departments out of the Dark Ages. Alumni return to the campus with surprised gasps and "omigods." The "1990 Plan" for expansion to accomodate ever-increasing enrollments and to upgrade academic programs and living conditions is already being implemented and several funding drives for the plan have been launched.

Basketball is king at Marquette. In fact, some say that Marquette would not exist except for NCAA rules that clearly state college sports teams must be part of a college. Al McGuire, who resigned just a few years ago as coach, was treated with godlike respect, and some say he's the man responsible for putting Marquette on the map. Since McGuire's departure, coach Hank Raymonds has carried on the basketball tradition. In fact, the "Warriors" finished the '79 season by gaining their third consecutive bid to postseason tournament play. And each year, basketball tickets are a scarce and prized possession.

The only physical object more beloved and treasured than season basketball tickets is a can of beer. The drinking age in Wisconsin is eighteen and students spend their weekends in area bars trying to prove that Milwaukee is the beer capital of the world. Marijuana is plentiful, but hard drugs have never found a real hold at Marquette. While the university will never secure itself a reputation as a genuine party school, the social life is active and enjoyable. Downtown Milwaukee is offering better and more diversified entertainment than ever before. Only a few blocks away, the lakefront and a wide assortment of concerts, discos, and restaurants offer Marquette students who are looking for more than just a brew at the corner tap a lot to do.

Marquette students are generally middle-of-the-road, semiintellectual, and semijock. But political and social consciousness is increasing from a former dormant state. Two current issues on Marquette's campus involve students demanding divestiture of investments in South Africa and demanding adjustment of student rights policies following a violation of these rights in a dormitory.

The administration has opened up to student needs in other ways. Student representation on university committees is increasing.

Marquette is not located in a posh neighborhood by any means. A semighetto is located north of the campus, and walking alone is not recommended. A sea of industrial poison rests south of Marquette, cleverly disguised as a giant garbage dump for the Milwaukee Road. Downtown Milwaukee lies to the east, bringing the congestion of a large metropolitan area through the campus. A variety of odors, including roasting hops, processing yeast, and fumes from the chocolate and tannery factories are present year-round.

The most depressing factor about Marquette and Milwaukee is the weather, which ranges from poor to outright horrendous. There are a few weeks of warm weather in September and May, but the interim period is filled with snow, rain, and cloudy skies. Modes of dress vary. It is not unusual to see students dressed up, but dressing down is commonplace—often out of necessity to combat the elements.

Students are forced to live in on-campus housing during their freshmen and sophomore years. The rooms resemble breadboxes in size. Coeducational housing is available, but members of the opposite sex are still ushered out of the dorms before the wee hours of the morning. On- and off-campus housing is becoming crowded due to increasing enrollment. And, on the whole, off-campus housing is of low quality.

Marquette is slowly catching up with the rest of liberal education and gradually emerging into the twentieth century. While a social revolution will never take place here, the university is gradually loosening its restrictions on students and recognizing their maturity and independence. And then there's basketball—if you can get the tickets, you can always let loose during basketball season.

UNIVERSITY OF MARYLAND/COLLEGE PARK

Location: College Park, MD 20742
Campus: suburban
Undergraduate enrollment 15,583 M, 13, 839 W
Total enrollment: 36,905
Expenses: $3628 (in-state), $5387 (out-of-state)
Financial aid: 37%
Library: 1,500,000 volumes

Student-faculty ratio: 17–1
Transfer students: 5000
Median SAT: M: 460 V, 540 M; W: 450 V, 470 M
Fraternities: 9%
Sororities: 9%
Application deadline:
June 15 for freshmen,
August 1 for transfers

The official school symbol of the University of Maryland is a large, sluggish freshwater turtle called a terrapin. Many students and observers of the College Park campus feel the emblem is most appropriate. UM, after all, is large—with a student body of over 36,000, it is one of the ten largest universities in the United States—and its progress into the modern age has certainly been slow and awkward.

UM is large, perhaps even ungainly. Students seem to get easily swallowed up by it. Faculty and administration are remote and lectures do little to improve the impersonality of the system.

For the time being, the school's academic weaknesses are legion. There are, to be sure, a few scattered strengths. As at almost any state university, the engineering and physics departments are sound if overly practical in approach, and the research equipment includes one of the largest cyclotrons in the world. Journalism and agriculture are offered in abundance, with lots of practical experience available. But virtually all of the liberal arts departments, which should be the core of any good university, are seriously lacking; in history, government, and especially in foreign languages the programs and faculty are almost uniformly weak. With 300 majors in twelve "schools," or divisions, Maryland is truly remarkable in having so much in the classroom that is so bad. Fortunately, there is a general honors program which offers accelerated courses and special seminars for highly motivated students. But such students are rare; although the library is usually crowded, many UM students don't set foot in it for four years.

Many in-state students are at the university because they were turned down at private out-of-state schools. Most of the rest of the students are not sure why there're there.

The campus is a small city in itself, offering plays, movies, lectures, night spots, and fraternity parties. The student union is a mammoth affair with bowling, ballrooms, conference rooms, lounges, stores, restaurants, and a mind-frying game room. There is enough debauching to cause a fifty-three percent attrition rate for each class by the time it graduates.

The student body is socially fragmented, largely because of a sizable commuter population that contributes little to the school other than an insoluble parking problem. Even many of the on-campus residents take off for their Maryland homes on the weekends. At other times, they flee to nearby shabby Route 1 for booze (if they're twenty-one or equipped with a phony ID), or to Washington, D. C. (eight miles away) for the culture and the eighteen-year-old drinking age. Extracurricular activities hold a few people on campus, but only a few. However, the relative lack of competition makes for good opportunities if you're interested. The daily newspaper has a reputation that eclipses the school's.

It's hard to blame people for running away from UM, though. The 1300-acre campus is huge and confusing. And when you finally do master the art of picking classes in adjacent buildings, you are likely to discover on registration day that enrollment is filled in every course you have chosen. The perils of a large university are acute at Maryland:

students are identified by social security numbers, and early in the semester the bookstores are mobbed. But there are also many excellent facilities that only a large university can offer, such as the extensive radio and TV workshop, large theater, astronomical observatory, and animal science stables.

UM is not our conception of an ideal school. It's far too easy to get lost in the 36,000-student shuffle. But if you're sure where you're going, UM just might have the facilities to get you there.

MASSACHUSETTS INSTITUTE OF TECHNOLOGY

Location: Cambridge, MA 02139
Campus: city center
Undergraduate enrollment:
  3550 M, 750 W
Total enrollment: 8800
Expenses: $8900
Financial aid: 50%
Library: 1,500,000 volumes

Student-faculty ratio: 8–1
Transfer students: 150
Median SAT: 640 V, 735 M
Fraternities: 33%
Sororities: 0%
Application deadline:
  January 1

There's no doubt in the mind of any MIT student that "the 'Tute" (as it is fondly called) is the premier science and engineering school in the country. While Caltech and other institutions may challenge the school in specific fields, MIT *is* technology: apocryphal stories abound about the impact of the MIT name, or recognition of one's brass rat (MIT's distinctive class ring) by an influential alumnus.

This technological orientation manifests itself in the general degree requirements: all students must take one year of calculus and physics, one semester of chemistry or biology, three sophomore-level courses in different sciences, and a lab. This applies equally to the physicist and to the philosopher. The only other Institute requirement is eight semesters of humanities-social sciences.

In spite of these and other unifying pressures, the campus has a diverse character that sometimes borders on schizophrenia. MIT students were active in the formation of the Clamshell Alliance; the dean's office was nice enough to arrange make-up finals for the many students who were arrested for protesting at Seabrook, N. H. in May 1977. On the other hand, an informal poll in the wake of the Harrisburg nuclear accident showed that MIT students were still overwhelmingly in favor of nuclear power. In an age when it has become fashionable to regard technology per se and its pioneers as cold-blooded monsters, there is a growing emphasis on the personal and human side at the Institute, which extends from environmental protection studies to letting freshmen have a lot to say about what they learn and how they learn it.

Politically, MIT students are by and large more conservative than their counterparts at other universities. Antiapartheid protests have been poorly attended and ineffectual; the Sixties' counterculture paper recently folded due to apathy, while the libertarian weekly remains strong. In general, engineering students (as elsewhere) tend to be primarily concerned with their future careers in industry, careers that are virtually assured by the MIT name. The government does have an exceptionally large effect on the undergraduate at MIT. Like it or not, a large plurality of the jobs that will be held by students are on Uncle Sam's payroll. Some of the nasty allegations made about the nature of the research done at MIT may be true; the fact is, the students choose their own life's work, and for many fields, peaceful and otherwise, MIT is the place to learn it. In fact, most people at MIT are involved in learning a trade, and they spend their spare time much as people at any college do, except that their pranks are more sophisticated.

Student-faculty contact is frequent and often enthusiastic. Professor Victor Weisskopf, for example, one of the world's leading physicists (his fans rank him with Fermi and Einstein), insists on teaching freshman physics. "I always find," he says in explanation, "that there is something I have forgotten."

There is a strong faculty in areas other than science, too, including economist Paul Samuelson and Noam Chomsky, the well-known radical hardhead linguist, who proves by his mere continuing presence on the MIT faculty that neither the U. S. government nor the stuffy alumni run the school.

Architecture, urban studies, economics, management, and political science are all strong departments, and draw substantial numbers of undergraduate and graduate majors. The other humanities are good, with some exceptional individuals, but lack the depth and diversity provided by a major program: music, literature, and history combined graduate less than a dozen students every year.

To hear some MIT admissions staffers talk, you might think that this already prestigious school is on the verge of having one of the best liberal arts programs in the country. Indeed, it is now possible to construct an excellent major in several nonscientific fields at MIT. The scientific requirements for even an architecture major are stiff, however, and the degree offered is a Bachelor of Science. Technology is the name of the game at MIT.

Most students agree that anyone who is admitted is capable of doing the work. With proper planning and no bad luck, the demands of obtaining a B.S. are not terribly difficult. Active social lives, double majors, three-year majors, student activities, or difficult departments chosen by the student tend to make the task less than "trivial."

Most students take their studying very seriously; "tooling," as it is called, takes precedence over other activities. Popular topics of conversation among tools is how much class work they have to do, how many times they have "pulled an all-nighter," and how little sleep they have had recently.

When one tires of studying, however, the attractions of Boston beckon. In some ways, MIT's location is close to ideal. It is within easy walking distance of many of Boston's historical and cultural attractions, such as Harvard University, the Museum of Fine Arts, Symphony Hall (home of the Boston Symphony), Fenway Park (home of the Red Sox), and Boston Garden (home of the Celtics and Bruins). Good transportation makes theaters, movies, and concerts accessible.

Intramural and varsity sports at MIT are very popular. It is *de rigueur* for an article dealing with the subject to mention that despite its lack of a football team, "MIT has more varsity sports than any other university in the country." Over a thousand students participate in intramurals. Tiddlywinks, one of the more unusual sports, fields a good team. One year of phys. ed. is required, but just about everyone can find something tolerable.

Socially, things are a bit awkward. MIT freshwomen are barraged with attention from the moment they arrive, and most have boyfriends within a month. As the undergraduate population is twenty percent female, many men are left out in the cold. For more determined individuals, the fifty-odd women's colleges in the area offer the best pickings, though coed Boston University and Harvard are also popular. The image of the calculator-toting "Tech Tool" is partially justified, enough so that MIT men often find themselves scorned by college women. Fraternity men, with a reputation and big-brother introductions working for them, seem to fare better.

Dormitories are overcrowded, though singles are available to almost any upperclassman who wants one. The dorms are fairly rowdy, with loud stereos and water fights used to vent off steam. The food is considered terrible; many students cook with hot plates and broiler ovens.

Fraternities are an alternative place to eat. But to eat there, you usually have to be a member. The frats are small, autonomous groups with systems of pledging that minimize snobbery. They own their own houses, mostly across the Charles River, in winter a long, cold walk from the rest of the campus. The Greeks make their own rules and hire their own kitchen staff. Each fraternity has its own flavor, of course. There are jock frats, "meatball" (bookworm) frats, a sci-fi-fan frat, and one or two that live like nobility. The one thing they all have in common are excellent bars. There are no sororities, but a small "women's independent living group" started recently in an MIT-owned Cambridge building.

Living off-campus has lost much of its attraction in light of the current rental shortage in the Boston-Cambridge area; in addition to physical isolation, one can easily become socially cut-off, lacking the intramural sports and late-night bull-sessions that bind living group residents together. The best bet is to share an apartment; cooperative cooking and housing can be cheaper while providing better food in more spacious surroundings. Freshmen can't live off-campus (except at home), while transfer students have virtually no other choice.

Despite its many failings, MIT does have some unique advantages for the technically oriented student. Undergraduate opportunities to do research and take graduate courses are taken for granted, while the MIT name opens up vistas for employment or graduate study. Academically, the school is as much of a challenge as one wants to make it, and freshmen pass-no credit enables almost anyone to survive the first year. Finally, the collection of the best minds, coupled with a unifying interest in science, makes for a sense of community that shouldn't be passed up by anyone who has the opportunity of experiencing it.

MASSACHUSETTS STATE COLLEGE SYSTEM

Locations:
Boston
Bridgewater
Fitchburg
Framingham
Lowell
North Adams
Salem

(Check with specific locations for more details.)

Sound, secluded, white, and straight, the Massachusetts state college system seems like a refugee from the modern world. But if you're a Massachusetts resident, if you'd like to be a teacher, and if you have no particular expectations of finding college either interesting or fun, then one of the seven state college centers may be for you.

Most of the schools are set in pastoral lands—if you'd like to be near a state correctional center, take Bridgewater; Framingham is semisuburban, semirural, and near Boston; Fitchburg and North Adams have a small-town flavor; Salem and Lowell offer glimpses of once-wealthy cities in decay; and for those who demand the big city, the Boston campus is convenient to that great college town, though it is a commuter school.

Despite their general remove from the outside world, the schools are academically good and aesthetically varied. They offer a variety of sizes—2000 undergrads at North Adams, up to 5000 at Boston—and a few have many modern facilities. Salem State College is constructing a new library and physical fitness center. Yet in all their differences, the Massachusetts state colleges have a consistency: all are highly competent in the training of teachers.

None of these schools is what you'd call experimental, or even particularly inventive. But the faculty-student ratio is a reasonable one-to-seventeen, and almost all faculty teach full loads. And if somewhat limited in their breadth of perception, the faculty knows what it's doing when it comes to teaching education. Most of them, after all, have been teaching at these schools for years, and very recently most of the state colleges had only two majors—elementary and secondary education. Although the schools have branched out somewhat, none offers more than eight majors, and most don't offer that many. However, the students don't seem to mind; more than ninety percent of them major in education. For the few who do seek other majors, the experience is generally disappointing, since most of the newer departments are pretty weak.

Outside the classroom, however, the satisfaction to be garnered from the "Bay State's" state colleges drops sharply. Massachusetts was the original Puritan colony, and blue laws of every description still linger. As a consequence, the state college administrators seem to operate under the delusion that they, too, are guardians of chastity. Perhaps their maxim is "Freedom corrupts."

Yet even if campus rules were to loosen, things would still be dull. Many of the state colleges used to be all-female institutions, and men are still in a minority at most. This would be fine for the men, if it weren't for the fact that the colleges are basically commuter-oriented, rather than residential. The constant efflux of students at the end of the day drastically reduces what little social life might occur. The atmosphere is bland to the point of being soporific in some.

Yet another factor cutting down on both socializing and activism is the fact that more than half of the students at the state colleges hold full- or part-time jobs throughout their terms as students. Most are much too busy to become involved in politics, and even fraternities and sororities, by far the most successful activities, enlist only ten percent of the student population. (That figure, however, is somewhat misleading, as it reflects substantially greater participation on some campuses and virtually none at all at others.)

Drugs are not popular at the state colleges any more than radical politics or long locks. The students tend to accept traditional values in every respect, even socially, and most regard an extended beer blast as the best possible fun.

Sports, traditionally a strong activity at state colleges because so many of the male students aspire to coaching, is beginning to boom on the various campuses. Nearly all boast respectable hockey teams, and several compete quite well in basketball, baseball, and soccer, though football has yet to find much of a berth. The women play field hockey and basketball.

Despite the limited curriculum and lack of intellectualism, academic pressures are fairly intense. The students are generally competent. Yet ten to twenty percent (figures vary from school to school) drop out at the end of freshman year, most on the invitation of the college because of poor grades. A fairly high level of classroom performance is expected, as Massachusetts schools are fairly good, and up to ninety-nine percent of the students are state residents.

On the whole, though, the Massachusetts state colleges are distinctly pedestrian places to go to school. The courses and activities are humdrum, the students are generally boring, and there is a plodding sameness and a general degree-hungry orientation among students. But, then, these traits are not unique to the Massachusetts state colleges. Nearly all state systems are so afflicted, and the Massachusetts units are among the best of the lot.

UNIVERSITY OF MASSACHUSETTS/AMHERST

Location: Amherst, MA 01002
Campus: rural
Undergraduate enrollment: 9620 M, 8880 W
Total enrollment: 23,500
Expenses: $3000 (in-state), $4650 (out-of-state)
Financial aid: NA
Library: 1,500,000 volumes

Student-faculty ratio: 18–1
Transfer students: 1600–1800
Median SAT: M: 472 V, 533 M; W: 476 V, 503 M
Fraternities: 6.3%
Sororities: 3.7%
Application deadline: March 1

UMass is a state school located in an area full of private schools. Amherst, Massachusetts, is a pretty town with beautiful scenery and a lot of students milling around. The Five College student population and exchange programs provide some very good opportunities for the UMass student to explore offerings at Amherst, Hampshire, Mount Holyoke, and Smith Colleges.

Students at UMass run the gamut from boring to interesting, from hard-working out-of-staters who passed by some tough competition to be admitted, to in-staters who didn't work hard enough in high school to get into a better college or who couldn't afford a more expensive college. Consequently, there is a large subculture at UMass that is as sophisticated and interesting as the best of any college. Many students live off-campus and do all sorts of interesting things, such as painting, writing poetry, and smoking dope (which is present in both quality and quantity). There seems to be a remnant from the counterculture hanging on at the campus; with their presence, UMass is hardly a haven for bores.

For those who are not academically inclined, many classrooms, labs, and dorms face the beautiful Connecticut Valley and offer great natural diversions from attention to classes.

UMass does offer several very strong programs, notably in chemistry, which is a top-rated department. Special programs also exist, such as the "university without walls," independent study, and January interterm.

Recreation facilities of UMass are notably lacking, though intramural sports are popular. Publications, music, and drama are among the encouraged extracurriculars.

UMass is full of bright students, though not all are hard-working. For someone who doesn't have the money or the grades to go someplace better, U Mass is a very viable alternative. With the available facilities, it need not be a compromise.

MCGILL UNIVERSITY

Location: Montreal, Quebec, Canada, H3A 2T5
Campus: city center
Undergraduate enrollment: 5875 M, 5875 W
Total enrollment: 17,800
Student-faculty ratio: NA
Transfer students: NA
Median SAT: NA
Fraternities: NA
Sororities: NA
Application deadline:

Expenses: $6000
Financial aid: NA
Library: 1,800,000 volumes

March 1 for September,
November 1 for January

McGill used to be considered the "Harvard of Canada." Some people still think it is. In fact, one of the first intercollegiate football games ever played pitted McGill against Harvard in the 1800s. Though admission standards are more lax today than in the past, the university still offers students a quality education.

Located in downtown Montreal, the second-largest French speaking city in the world, McGill has a fairly heterogeneous student population: twenty percent of McGill's 17,800 students are French Canadians, seven percent are foreign (seventy-one percent of the foreigners are American) and the rest are Canadian, many of whom commute from their Montreal homes.

Academic life at McGill is pretty much what you make of it. McGill today is still a fine university. Its psychology department is internationally acclaimed, and its biology department is also very strong. This might reflect the presence of the prestigious McGill Medical School. Political science is a small, good department that is oriented toward Canadian politics. The French department is also very strong, in part because of the heavy French influence in Montreal. A student-produced course guide is available to arts and science students to help steer them away from the clinkers and into the better courses.

McGill is not an "animal house"-type university. Only hard-core jocks go to football games (including homecoming), cheerleading is frowned upon, frats are definitely not *de rigueur*, and freshmen are not subjected to any "fun" orientation activities.

This is not to say that McGill is a dull place. *Au contraire.* The residences, four coed and one women's only, are constantly humming, and the student-run University Center is another hotbed of campus entertainment.

We are told that life among the students in residence consists of one party after another. And if the environs of the dorms get stifling, the revelry spills over into the many bistros, bars, and pubs five minutes away by foot.

For students who grew up on football and cheerleaders, McGill might be something of a disappointment. College sports are not a big deal. During the winter, though, one can catch "Les Canadiens" at the Forum (also close to campus).

Montreal is probably McGill's greatest nonacademic asset. Although most of the students are commuters who live at home and tend to socialize with their high school friends, foreign students who live in-residence or off-campus lead a totally different life. They have the advantage of virtually living on top of the city. The coed residence halls, four high-rise buildings, are situated on Mount Royal, overlooking downtown. The view itself is exhilarating. Many rundown and some nicer apartments are available at the foot of the mountain, but they are generally costly. Despite its size (three million), Montreal has none of the crime problems that afflict U. S. cities of comparable size.

For those who might hesitate about living in a foreign country, fear not. Many of the faculty members are American or American-trained. The ratio of Canadian to American students, we are told, is about eight-to-one. And of course, the cosmopolitan flavor of Montreal should make even the most Mom-and-apple-pie American feel at home.

With the Canadian dollar at its current value under the American, McGill is looking like an education bargain. (A little less of a bargain since the differential fee for non-Canadians went into effect in January of 1979.) It's a quality university in a cosmopolitan city.

If you like to party, ski (the Laurentians are an hour away and Vermont, two hours), want a decent education, and would like to spend four years in one of the most lively cities in North America, get out your passport and head north. Pack a warm coat. The winters get cold.

One final note. In September 1979, McGill's new president, David L. Johnston, took office in the midst of a new era in Canadian internal affairs and academic crises. McGill's enrollment is competing with that of other major Canadian universities, but even more critical is the increasingly assertive French-speaking majority in a province that may decide on possible separation from Canada. If so, McGill's funding could be threatened.

MIAMI UNIVERSITY

Location: Oxford, OH 45056
Campus: rural
Undergraduate enrollment:
  6186 M, 6685 W
Total enrollment: 14,758
Expenses $3260 (in-state),
  $4860 (out-of-state)
Financial aid: 50%
Library: 1,000,000 volumes

Student-faculty ratio: 18–1
Transfer students: 600
Median SAT: 504 V, 558 M
Median ACT: 24.2
Fraternities: 25.3%
Sororities: 25.3%
Application deadline:
  March 1

Nestled in the hills of southwestern Ohio and replete with the red brick and ivy-covered walls of many Eastern schools, Miami University has become a satisfactory Ivy League substitute for many students, another "Yale of the Midwest."

The psuedo Ivy League status is supported by high admission standards and a generally excellent educational reputation, but severely diminished by antiquated restrictions on social life which place Miami squarely in the Midwest.

The best educational program offered at Miami is probably the accounting major in the business school. The only problem with the business school is its overcrowded state, which only grows worse. More than thirty percent of 1979 freshmen opted for business majors. This has in part resulted in a stifled curriculum of mandatory courses with room for few electives.

The schools of education and arts and science are regarded highly within Midwest circles, but some programs have lost their luster in the last decade. Enrollment is down in education, in some programs by almost thirty percent.

In the school of arts and science, social programs have fared worst. The natural sciences—in particular, chemistry, microbiology, and botany—are among some of the finest in the country. But social work programs have seen some cuts, and there are limits in other people-related fields.

In applied science, system and paper technology graduates sell better than imported cars—the placement rate for graduates is near one hundred percent, and salaries start at an average $18,000 per year.

Fine arts is not what it could be, unless you're in the excellent architecture program, which limits its enrollment every year to fifty.

Socially, Miami students find red brick walls confining. A no-car rule not only prohibits students from having cars on campus, but in the city of Oxford as well. In recent years, however, many students have ignored the restriction because of the administration's reluctance to enforce the rule off-campus.

Miami residence halls accommodate only 7800 of the total enrollment, forcing many off-campus without choice. Oxford landlords have prospered in light of the situation. Students have also helped laundries, groceries, and other home-related businesses survive and expand.

Those in residence halls face a lack of coeducational opportunities, with only four coed halls, and no twenty-four-hour visitation. However, surveys conducted by students and university staff indicate that the students favor round-the-clock visitation and more coed halls.

In the larger sense, Miami students find four bars and a lack of liquor (3.2 beer only) in Oxford. "Uptown," as it is called, has its problems. In the past two years, one bar has burned, another has become a plasma bank, and a third is now part of a bookstore-clothes outlet.

Miami students have always turned to Greek life for social involvement and the town situation has only helped swell the rolls of Miami's twenty-six fraternities and twenty sororities. Approximately twenty-five percent of all students choose Greek life at Miami. Even during the lean protest years of the late Sixties and early Seventies, Greek participation at Miami was high. The formation of four national frats at Miami earned the school the title "mother of fraternities."

Despite problems, Miami social life is usually fast and furious. Students take social opportunities almost as seriously as their studies, and reflect this attitude even in their dress. The Ivy League image is reflected in the topsiders, straight-leg designer jeans, and button-down collars many students wear. Women in particular seem to enjoy dressing well.

Athletics are as important to alumni as they are to students; Miami consistently leads the Mid-American Conference in most sports. Its football team often embarrasses Big Ten schools with upset wins and close losses. Miami sports training has produced coaching greats, including Ara Parseghian, Weeb Ewbank, Bill Mallory, Woody Hayes, and Bo Schembechler.

In general, the student choosing Miami finds a well-respected educational program, a beautiful campus of red brick and ivy, but restrictive social regulations.

The Miami life-style, though it provides few options, is a comfortable niche for those expecting a conservative, unchallenging environment during their college years. If a student is searching for a pseudo-Yale or Harvard, Miami may just be the place, at a much lower cost and with a less-challenging academic environment.

UNIVERSITY OF MIAMI

Location: Coral Gables, FL 33124
Campus: suburban
Undergraduate enrollment: 5430 M, 4178 W
Total enrollment: 19,235

Student-faculty ratio: 22–1
Transfer students: 2000
Median SAT: M: 467 V, 526 M; W: 455 V, 476 M
Median ACT: 21
Fraternities: 10%

Expenses: $6500
Financial aid: 40%
Library: 1,100,000 volumes

Sororities: 10%
Application deadline: rolling

Suntan lotion and Corvettes, lavish consumption, and all the paraphernalia of suburbia characterize this university among the palm trees. Long known as "Sun Tan U," the University of Miami, located in the plush suburb of Coral Gables, still remains a rare opportunity for Northerners to preserve the atmosphere of a spring vacation all year 'round en route to a college degree.

However, if you're planning a four year schedule of "suntan 101," and "underwater-basket-weaving," you had better think again. University officials are constantly making efforts to bolster the school into the ranks of the first-rate academic institutions. While no one will pretend that UM is as tough as Cornell, it is certainly on a par (if not above) most middle-of-the-road schools, like Syracuse, GW, and Boston University. On the basis of large federal research grants, UM has amassed a respectable faculty and some very fine facilities. And because of its geographical location, UM has also become one of the prime institutions in the country for marine sciences and Latin American studies.

Yet what the school has gained in quality it still lacks in quantity. The student-faculty ratio, usually a good indicator of the extent of academic opportunity at a school, has been falling but is still fairly high at around 22-1. However, there are many overcrowded lectures taught by nameless instructors where you will be nothing more than a social security number. Success in most courses depends on how well one can learn by rote, but if the method of teaching suggests Paris's Sorbonne, the attitude of the student does not. Although there are many diligent, hard-working students at UM, just as many are more preoccupied with the weather report than with the lack of qualified instructors in the English department. Course outlines usually outsell the required texts, and a depleted stock of Monarch notes at the campus bookstore could create a minor panic.

It is generally acknowledged that a student interested in learning should enroll early in the honors program, which provides approximately 500 relatively intelligent men and women the opportunity to avail themselves of the best of the faculty, interesting seminars, a host of courses of an interdisciplinary nature, and preferred housing on campus. However, UM has traditionally been weak in the humanities and social sciences, and a student wishing to concentrate in these areas might do better to apply elsewhere.

But what the students lack in academics they make up for in consumption. It is not uncommon for a freshman or sophomore to have a loaded luxury car (Firebirds are *"in"* at UM) or for a young lady to have a wardrobe requiring six closets to house it. Stereo systems abound and the range of music emanating from them starts with Mangione and runs the gauntlet from Donna Summer to The Knack and the Beatles to Ramsey Lewis. A good many students come to UM expecting a four-year party, and since marijuana is a cultural necessity, a good many of them find it. It is generally conceded that some women enroll at UM strictly for their MRS., a situation which has caused a bit of chagrin for the males on campus and which has lead cynical observers to dub UM the "Syracuse of the South." Syracuse it may be, but Parsons it is not.

Although the attrition rate has dropped, only one out of every three or four students who enters as a freshman remains to graduate with his class. If you select Miami solely on the basis of its climate, you will no doubt become restless and transfer before your junior year.

UM has a lovely, spread-out campus nestled underneath sun, palms, and coconuts. The double-sized olympic pool is open all year 'round and a slight fee takes care of its pseudo-country club membership. The pool is a great place to catch rays and *zzz*s before your next class. Most logical people use the tropical climate to their advantage. Those who enroll at UM only for a tan usually don't make it past freshman English. UM has the potential to accommodate anyone and like any other school it is only what you make of it.

The dorm situation at UM is not bright right now but efforts are being made to upgrade it. If you are expecting the dorms to match the quality of the Diplomat Hotel, you will be in for a rude shock. If you are lucky enough to get an on-campus apartment, it won't be air-conditioned unless you are a student of "special status". (Honor students, football players, and graduate students qualify). The other housing facilities are run-down and in need of many renovations. Of late, UM policy-makers and administrators have been grappling with the warfare between the athletic deficits and academic needs. Most educational facilities and departments have been going begging while dollar after dollar has been poured into the football team.

Whatever your interests, you can probably accommodate them at UM. It has the largest music program in the country and a vast selection of academic and nonacademic courses. As one student told us, you can "Look at it this way. If you are going to subject yourself to the torture of college, you might as well do it in Miami."

MICHIGAN STATE UNIVERSITY

Location: East Lansing, MI 48824
Campus: city outskirts
Undergraduate enrollment: 18,000 M, 17,700 W
Total enrollment: 43,744
Expenses: $3540 (in-state), $4820 (out-of-state)
Financial aid: 50%
Library: 2,500,000 volumes

Student-faculty ratio: 14–1
Transfer students: 5500
Median SAT: 470 V, 530 M
Median ACT: 22.3
Fraternities: 6%
Sororities: 5%
Application deadline: thirty days before term begins

Founded in 1855 among cow pastures and peaceful barns, Michigan State University, long derided as "Moo U" by its more sophisticated detractors in Ann Arbor, has recently and successfully shed its second-class image as the state's former agricultural college. Granted, MSU still retains vestigial farming remnants—including a college of agriculture and natural resources with courses from animal husbandry to crop science—but new priorities have resulted in top-flight science programs and a budding school of liberal arts and social sciences.

MSU attracts more than 40,000 students per term with its parklike atmosphere, agricultural program, and sciences.

State has retained its emphasis on specialized training and offers a variety of genuinely capable undergraduate majors in business, education, home economics, human and veterinary medicines, etc. Course requirements are now less rigid for freshmen. MSU has gone far to provide students with the chance to obtain a first-class education; unfortunately (or fortunately, depending on one's academic wants) the work load is unoppressively light, and one so tempted may survive the four years in good stead having invested little sweat. An additional and oft-heard grievance involves calendar structure: operating on quarters, MSU holds its scholars until the second week in June, making summer job or travel plans difficult at best.

Despite its gargantuan undergraduate population, MSU has laudably managed to avoid totally dehumanizing its students. Incoming freshmen are assigned an orientation group which meets in East Lansing (a nice, unobtrusive place to live, really) during the summer to plan schedules, meet with advisors, and otherwise become familiar with the sprawling, potentially fearsome, campus. The entire university is split into fifteen coordinate colleges usually entered during junior year, although some—such as Lyman Briggs College for prospective science people—admit frosh.

Class size is frequently atrocious, both in upper-level as well as lower-level courses, but discussion groups and TV monitors help minimize impersonality somewhat. Students rate the faculty both competent and accessible, although one must recognize that even an innovative and well-intentioned administration cannot surmount overpopulation problems endemic to a school of MSU's size. One can easily feel lost and overwhelmed at State.

Admissions requirements have toughened with State's new image, and the university is no longer strictly a haven for wayward jocks, party people, and ne'er-do-wells turned down at Michigan. There is no "typical" MSU student—the university accommodates the whole gamut of student types from freaks to jocks and intellectuals to hardhats. We're even told that MSU enrolls the most Merit Scholars at any public university. The school's "Come one, come all" admissions philosophy brings diversity.

Socially, MSU students have no complaints. Put bluntly, MSU is considered a party school and despite a knee-jerk public referendum in 1978 which returned the drinking age to twenty-one, booze and hallucinogenics are in bountiful supply to needy consumers. For those over twenty-one, or who at least look twenty-one, there exist plentiful watering-holes in the neighboring city of East Lansing. Party stores outnumber parking meters. Grass abounds, and the penalties for possession (a $5 fine by city council edict—minor offenders rarely face worse) promise the weed a thriving campus future.

Sports are a biggie at MSU. Football games, especially of the Big Ten variety, consume all thought and motion during the fall term. The outcome of the MSU-U Michigan football game determines the rise and fall of MSU's fortunes. Basketball, since MSU's emergence as a national power, has grown so large that the expensive tickets are hard to find. Fraternities are not as strong as they once were. Of the ninety-five percent not in frats or sororities, half live off campus in less than desirable East Lansing, student-ghetto housing. Dorms are crowded and new students risk being forced into triples in two-person rooms.

While MSU's student activism has been seemingly dormant, there are signs that some of the verve of earlier students may be returning. But not from student government. Students have independently organized to protest police practices, university investments in foreign nations, minority discrimination, and nude sunbathing.

If you're only looking for an education, go to Harvard. But for a good time, wild weekends, a beautiful campus, and a smattering of old-fashioned book learning, MSU is the place to come. You've got to push to get past the graduate teaching assistants and professors, but if you do, a solid education can be part of the good times.

UNIVERSITY OF MICHIGAN

Location: Ann Arbor, MI 48104
Campus: suburban
Undergraduate enrollment:
 10,500 M, 9500 W
Total enrollment: 35,000
Expenses: $4200 (in-state),
 $6500 (out-of-state)
Financial aid: 50%
Library: 5,000,000 volumes

Student-faculty ratio: NA
Transfer students: 1200
Median SAT: 530 V, 600 M
Fraternities: 10%
Sororities: 12%
Application deadline:
 March 1

Contrary to what admissions officers say, Michigan is NOT a large university. Rather, it is a number of small universities with the student bodies all occupying the same campus. UM has studiers, partiers, freaks, jocks, frat rats, and activists all managing somehow to coexist. In short, if you don't feel you fit in anywhere, you're bound to fit in here.

Essentially, these small groups have only two things in common: they live in Ann Arbor, a not-so-small small town of 100,000 (including the university), and they all go to football games. After football season ends, though, the various groups tend to divide up and do what comes naturally.

If football is king at Michigan, then academics are surely queen. Michigan competes only with the University of California/Berkeley for the title of the nation's best state institution. Unfortunately, labels such as these tend only to reflect graduate departments and big-name faculty, which may have little or nothing to do with what kind of an education the typical undergrad will get in four years.

The good thing about Michigan, though, is that a superior education is there to be had—at a price, though, of initiative on the part of the student. The faculty is ranked among the nation's top five, and opportunity for a student to work closely, even individually, with a nationally known professor does exist, if the student is willing to make an effort.

Especially strong are the social science departments—political science, psychology, and anthropology. But though these are the departments that really shine, there are few departments in the university that are not at least good.

It must be stressed, though, that one must work to get a good education at Michigan, and that it doesn't come easily. Degree requirements have recently been tightened, and while every large university has its gut courses, they tend to be few and far between at Michigan. But this is not to imply that every class is good. Many professors, in the old college game of "publish-or-perish," extend little time or effort in their undergraduate courses, and many courses are not even taught by professors at all, but by graduate student teaching assistants who may not even have any teaching training. Furthermore, it is not uncommon to find large lecture classes with five or six hundred students, or to come across a student who graduates without ever having been in a class taught by a professor with less than fifty students.

Another graduation requirement not listed in any of the catalogs is called "learning to live with the bureaucracy 101." A school with 40,000 students hardly has time or staff enough to deal with anyone on an individual basis. In fact, students in this computer-run university are not names, but simply numbers printed on a plastic yellow card. One of the worst hassles a student can encounter is trying to replace a lost ID card, a necessity for everything from registering to checking out library books to gaining admission to some university buildings. Registration for classes, known as "CRISP," is an experience in and of itself, and a nightmare which binds together the entire student body twice a year. The ever-present computer is the be-all and end-all of the process, and some students actually find themselves selecting classes by taking whatever the computer says is still open. The computer always needs somebody for an eight o'clock chemistry lecture.

Ann Arbor is still coming to grips with the fact that not only are the Sixties over, but they're not coming back. Student activists, in the honorable tradition of SDS, are still as loud as ever, but their noise doesn't make up for their dwindling numbers. There is considerable interest in having the university divest itself from companies doing business in South Africa, but the overwhelming majority of the student body is far more concerned with grades than with social injustice across the ocean. In addition, the university itself is run like a corporation, with the state-elected board of regents sweeping in and out of Ann Arbor once a month, hardly allowing the students any input at all into decisions which may affect them.

Student life extends far beyond the main drag, though, and the overall quality of life in Ann Arbor must be given a very high rating. Most freshmen and many sophomores opt for the dorms, most of which are coed, and many of which offer such inviting amenities as darkrooms, music rooms, art studios, and libraries. Dorm fare is slightly above average, and the city has an enormous variety of good and cheap restaurants for those who just can't take another night in the cafeteria.

Dorm life is optional and, after the first year or two, many students decide to move off campus into private rental housing. The university's reluctance to build any new and much-needed housing, and Ann Arbor's tight housing market has forced students to start looking for fall housing as early as January. Rents near campus tend to be on the high side, but you get what you pay for. Students willing to live in residential neighborhoods further from campus find rents that border on the reasonable.

Fraternities and sororities are on the rise again, with some houses being expanded and some chapters being revived for the first time since the Fifties. Greek life, though, is still predominately for the jocks, the jock admirers, and those who desire a ready-made social life and lots of beer.

For those who would rather make their own social lives, Ann Arbor is hardly lacking in things to do. Its deceptively small size, by large city standards, is misleading. Bars and restaurants abound, and although the drinking age was recently raised from eighteen to twenty-one, the city council quickly passed an ordinance to reduce the penalty to a $5 ticket similar to its revolutionary dope law.

The arts are particularly well represented. Both the university and the city have distinguished theater and dance groups, and national touring companies often pass up nearby Detroit to come to Ann Arbor. A student-run jazz group brings nationally known jazz acts every year, and the university's professional concert promoters have little trouble attracting major acts to the 14,000-seat Crisler arena and the nearly acoustically perfect Hill Auditorium. Finally, no fewer than four film co-ops operate on campus.

Ann Arbor is also a good place for the sports enthusiast. Spectators can take advantage of the nationally ranked football and basketball teams, but the student body benefits most from the teams because the money they bring in funds a first-class intramural sports program, offering everything from paddleball to figure skating to indoor track, tennis, and swimming.

For those few who really can't find anything to interest them in Ann Arbor, Detroit is less than an hour away, and Canada just across the river from there.

In short, Michigan can be a lot of things to a lot of people. But it isn't the place for the person looking for an individually oriented atmosphere where all the students and faculty know each other. Nor is it for the noncompetitive. But for the person who wants a good education and a good time, and is willing to work for it, UM certainly fills the bill.

MIDDLEBURY COLLEGE

Location: Middlebury, VT 05753
Campus: rural
Undergraduate enrollment:
 1000 M, 800 W
Total enrollment: 1900
Expenses: $7650
Financial aid: 20%
Library: 300,000 volumes

Student-faculty ratio: 13–1
Transfer students: 20
Median SAT: 585 V, 615 M
Fraternities: 20%
Sororities: NA
Application deadline:
 January 15

The founding fathers of Middlebury College wanted to build a school far from the centers of civilization, in a setting which would provide as little distraction as possible for the future thinkers of society. One hundred and eighty years later, Middlebury is still in the boondocks. The campus is rural, with mountains looming on its eastern and western horizons. It is spread out over enough area to make getting anywhere very inconvenient when the snows settle in for the winter (and spring and fall). The campus is surrounded by woods, farmland, and the town of Middlebury, which is not, in the strictest sense, a college town. The college remains, nevertheless, the center of attention.

Academics at Middlebury virtually control undergraduate life. Academic responsibility assumes priority over most other activities. The faculty takes a traditional, no-nonsense attitude toward its work, and most students are equally serious about their studies. While Middlebury's honor code has recently come under attack for its specific wording, it is generally appreciated and taken seriously. Grinding into the wee hours is commonplace, as most courses require a steady level of effort even for marginal grades. Those few who can satisfy themselves by partying for four years with a minimum of work can succeed in doing so, but they tend to stand out.

Introductory courses are often as large as those in urban universities, although professors still attempt to be easily accessible. Student-faculty relations range from cordial to heavy, but the ivory tower doors are opened widely as a rule.

One of Middlebury's strongest features is the opportunity it provides for a first-rate education. The departments of history and English are as good as any in the country. Professors William Catton and Pardon Tillinghast (history), and John Gavin, Robert Pack, and Edward Martin (English) are renowned in their fields. Recently instituted programs in "Asian studies," and particularly "northern studies" are rapidly gaining notoriety. The departments of psychology and sociology-anthropology are terrible. The scientific and laboratory facilities are reasonably good, but the language facilities are great. Middlebury's reputation in the foreign languages comes from its summer schools, and schools abroad in which a large number of undergraduates participate. Over the regular academic year, these departments remain quite good (especially Russian and Chinese) but lack the fanatic attitude which is characteristic of the summer programs. The "junior year abroad" program is *very* popular, but there simply aren't as many language majors here as most people believe.

The college has recently begun to reemphasize the liberal arts background as a necessity for classical education, and for graduation. The Sixties' "do your own thing" method of curriculum planning has been eliminated. The school's size and more importantly, its philosophy, limit both diversity of departmental course offerings, and the freedom to explore beyond certain intellectual boundaries. Even winter term, which had previously been an opportunity to wander from the beaten intellectual path, has fallen victim to "Let's get serious" muckraking on the part of the faculty. Courses are becoming perhaps, too serious, and too classical. Majors must be declared by the end of the freshman year, presumably to prevent any academic aimlessness.

Middlebury students are not homogeneous, but a majority are from upper-middle-class families and a plurality are WASPs. The college has made attempts at recruiting black and minority students, but many find themselves unprepared to compete successfully in what is basically another universe. The student body is small enough, however, that most people are able to meet and become comfortable with each other in spite of any such boundaries. The college carries out low-profile recruiting of skiers and a minute number of male athletes who would otherwise be unacceptable candidates for admission.

Yet, by and large, the student body reflects diverse interests and talents. Preppies are fairly common, and some treat the campus as an extension of their prep schools. They aren't the norm. Many outdoorsy types are attracted to Middlebury because of its location, and the attitude toward nature which Vermont as a state exemplifies. Jocks (mainly male) can feel at home. Top-notch football, hockey, and ski teams are perennial. The elements manage to somehow interact on a more or less common level with only occasional problems.

Life in the sticks makes extracurricular activities a necessity. There is enough ability and enthusiasm floating about that the activities are well participated in, and surprisingly variable for a small college. Anyone who looks for a position of importance within an organization can find it. Many of the activities are geared to the community—Big Brother programs, a Mountain Club, and an Environmental Quality group have been highly successful.

The town of Middlebury is able to appeal to only a narrow range of social needs and interests. A few freshmen arrive here each year expecting all the social stimulation of a large city to appear on their first Saturday night. No so. Deeply disillusioned and disappointed, they are unable to adjust, and transfer to larger colleges or universities. This lack of entertainment is often unfairly mistaken for a lack of intellectual stimulation—the two should not be confused. Darwinian laws apply here. Those who are unsatisfied and bored by what the college and town have to offer in the way of entertainment simply leave. The ones who remain are willing and able to make the most of what exists. This is an important consideration for anyone who is thinking of applying. Middlebury students must generate their own entertainment and enthusiasm, rather than rely on being passively entertained by the activities going on around them.

Concerts are frequent, usually featuring smaller groups. Recently Weather Report and Pat Metheny have performed here. Generally, few of them find the road trip to Middlebury a profitable enough venture, and opt instead for Burlington, forty-five miles away. Aside from college-sponsored social events (dances, parties, etc.) which are of a predictable consistency, there are fraternity parties which are even more predictable and of late, expensive. An abundance of movies are shown on-campus, including avant-garde, foreign, cult, and classic, but the first-run material must be sought at the town theater. Drinking is carried on at a "collegiate" level, probably no more heavily than at any other institution, perhaps even less. Pot has become more available and less expensive, as have Quaaludes, psilociben mushrooms, and acid. The hard drugs are a good deal less prevalent, however, and good old American booze is still first on the drug abuse list.

Living options on campus are nearly nonexistent. Freshmen dormitories are single sex by floor, and all other dorms are coed. There have been efforts by the administration over the past few years to consolidate the college community back onto the campus proper. Very few students are permitted to live off-campus and dining rebates for them are mysteriously low. Fraternities used to be an appealing living option for a few, but the trustees have voted to end fraternity dining as of 1980. The college operates its own dining service and doesn't hold itself accountable to the students, since it is a monopoly. The quality of college food has noticeably decreased over the past few years, but is still palatable if not inspiring. Attempts have been made to doll up the dining atmosphere by having more candlelight dinners and special functions, but these are still in the awkward stage.

Only in the past year or so have Middlebury students raised protests over anything at all, and even then over internal issues such as fraternity dining and unpopular tenure decisions. Much of this activity has been initiated by irate fraternity members, with whom few students are inclined to argue. The administration and fraternities are currently at war over the fate of fraternities at Middlebury, which looks dismal. At a recent (and rare) meeting of the student body with President Robison (whose reputation for contact with the students is meager at best), the students found themselves evenly divided on issues which had been assumed unanimous. All that anyone could agree upon was that there is a growing lack of communication between all the elements of the college community. The noise which is now being made for the first time in years is obviously a sign of life, and a definite asset at a school which has been criticized as being "safely ensconced in the torpor of the Seventies."

Middlebury College has all the drawbacks of a small New England school, plus the drawbacks of a school situated in the middle of nowhere. These drawbacks are, for many, what makes Middlebury a less than attractive choice among the selective New England schools. Ironically, they are also what can make it a very exciting place to spend four very important years.

MILLS COLLEGE

Location: Oakland, CA 94613
Campus: city outskirts
Undergraduate enrollment: 850 W
Total enrollment: 987
Expenses: $6885
Financial aid: 35%
Library: 180,000 volumes

Student-faculty ratio: 13–1
Transfer students: 200
Median SAT: 550 V, 540 M
Sororities: NA
Application deadline:
February 1

In the predominantly coeducational West when a Mills student is asked, "Mills? Isn't that an all *girls*' school?" more likely than not, she will respond with, "You mean a WOMEN'S COLLEGE? Yes, it is." Unlike her predecessors, a Mills student no longer espouses pretensions of adopted sisterhood among the socially elite seven sisters. Instead, it is clear that in attending a women's college in the West, she is one who takes herself seriously.

Academically, Mills has always been strong in the humanities; French, art, music, and dance faculties are among the finest in California. Mills houses the Center for Contemporary Music, one of the best-equipped electronic music centers in the country. Mills has also developed an excellent program for bringing women into the mathematics and computer science fields, under the guidance of professors Lenore Blum and Carol Lennox. Med school applicants here are more cooperative than competitive—those who have successfully been accepted have, in the past, held coaching workshops to encourage hopeful underclasswomen. Mills has just approved a "communications" major, and the last new major, "administration and legal processes," is probably the largest major on campus.

The small size of Mills affords many advantages in class size, and the proximity of larger institutions—UC/Berkeley and Stanford are twenty minutes and forty-five minutes away, respectively—offsets some of the disadvantages of being small. A regularly scheduled jitney service from Mills to Berkeley makes it easier to use library facilities there and an exchange program enables Mills students to take courses for credit at Stanford and U.C./Berkeley. Other exchange programs and the "junior year abroad" offer alternatives to four years on the Mills campus.

Faculty-student rapport is also a strong point. Most classes are small and faculty members take personal interest in students. Professors are easily accessible both in and out of the classroom, and it is not unusual for close and lasting friendships to develop. Academic excellence is pursued for its stimulation rather than for competitive satisfaction, and the faculty is more concerned with reaching the student than graduating her.

Participation in student and hall government is also more easily accessible; many women consider it a plus to have the opportunity to explore and develop leadership skills here for the first time.

Mills is primarily a residential college; the school strongly encourages students to live on-campus in one of the six very comfortable residential halls or in the campus apartments. For the student who wants to live off-campus, Berkeley, Oakland, and San Francisco offer limited accommodations, due to the housing crunch in the area. Most students seem content to live on-campus, however, and close and lasting friendships are nurtured in the halls. Twenty-four-hour visiting privileges enable boyfriends to stay overnight and many do.

Though the academic bent at Mills is strong, most people have a good time. Most are Californians who went to public schools, and come from upper-middle to upper class backgrounds. However, there are large foreign, Asian, and black groups at Mills; the student body is diversified for its size. "Resuming students" have also been credited for adding a certain maturity of perception to the classroom, by increasing the age range beyond the traditional eighteen-to-twenty-two span. Like many of the "laid-back" California campuses, Mills is characterized by a generally easygoing atmosphere. There is less class-consciousness here than in other areas; a scholarship student will find herself accepted as easily as a full-tuition student.

Despite the intimacy and quiet of Mills's beautiful tree-lined grounds, most students flee its confines for the lure of Bay Area nightlife. With its dominant Spanish-style architecture of red-tiled roofs and its huge eucalyptus trees, Mills is an oasis in the middle of an otherwise bleak East Oakland. Nevertheless, San Francisco is a mere twenty minutes across the Bay bridge, Oakland Airport only fifteen, and the ski slopes of Tahoe or Mills's own lodge at Sugar Bowl, a four-to-five hour drive away.

Although coeducation might improve social life, Mills women have indicated they want to remain a women's institution. Not all Mills students would classify themselves as feminists, though some have formed a Women's Resource Center, and the "women's studies" major developed some years ago continues to thrive. The common denominator is that Mills women have a healthy sense of their own capabilities developed in an atmosphere where their aspirations are encouraged.

UNIVERSITY OF MINNESOTA

Location: Minneapolis, MN 55455
Campus: city center
Undergraduate enrollment: 14,476 M, 12, 201 W
Total enrollment: 45,765
Expenses: $4005 (in-state), $5319 (out-of-state)
Financial aid: 47%
Library: 3,738,168 volumes

Student-faculty ratio: 15–1
Transfer students: 4207
Median ACT: 22.4
Fraternities: NA
Sororities: NA
Application deadline: July 15

The University of Minnesota is just another large state school. Academically, it has a number of plusses; socially, it has all the usual amenities; athletically, it has teams highly rated often enough. In short, there is little to recommend Minnesota above most other big land-grant colleges.

But there are strengths. For example, the school is located in a metropolitan area, a situation unique in the Big Ten. The cultural opportunities in the Minneapolis/St. Paul area are impressive: The Guthrie Theater, a wide range of smaller theaters, the Minnesota Orchestra, the St. Paul Chamber Orchestra, the Minneapolis Institute of Arts, the Walker Art Center, etc.

Scholastically, one can find one of the nation's top two or three journalism schools, a highly rated psychology department, and lots of noted economists, including Walter Heller, an adviser to Presidents Kennedy and Johnson. (At least he's prestige, if you don't care about his politics.) Another strength is political science, which along with history boasts several government-accused and spied-on Communists (so-called) actually teaching day-to-day with no apparent detriment to students.

Engineering is highly rated at Minnesota in several specialities, although faculty problems prevent the departments from being as strong as they might be. A special four-year intern program is offered giving a student alternate three-month blocks of time spent in school and on the job.

But with few exceptions, academic programs are merely good, which is to say that they are average. It's best to check the reputations of individual programs.

Geographically, the "Twin Cities" campus (there are four other campuses across the state, but none is significant) is divided in two—part in Minneapolis and part in St. Paul. Agriculture, biological sciences, forestry, and some other programs are in St. Paul, as are most of the students and activities.

Physically, U of M is crowded, but the campus is slowly expanding. Having used up the available space on the east bank of the Mississippi River, the university some years ago began to construct a major addition on the west bank. The two campuses are connected by a covered pedestrian bridge. A large dormitory, a new performing arts center (including extensive television studios), a large library, sizable classroom facilities, and most of the social science instruction are on the west bank now.

Now for the minuses. Non-Minnesota tuition is relatively high. And, remember, we're talking about Minnesota. Although the "Twin Cities" long ago lost its collective Swedish accent, the annual snowfall remains, and you'll have a number of wind-chill stories to write home about. Cold. Very cold. But there is a spring and an autumn; sometimes they are short, but there are lakes galore for typically hot summers in the area. Just remember to bring a heavy wrap for winter.

Minnesota is a commuter campus, with over sixty percent driving or busing or whatever to school each day from home. Only about five percent live in dorms, although most dorms are coed. A conduct code was passed and dorm students can determine hours of visitation. Housing close to campus is a hassle, as is parking everywhere.

Students at Minnesota are nothing special. Student government is a farce, but then that is largely a result of mass apathy about such things on campus, which indicates only that student government at Minnesota historically has had little to offer. Greeks, after a decline in the early Seventies, are on the upswing.

Extracurriculars range from clubs, drama, and music to professional fraternities and sororities that recognize particular talents and abilities. Varsity and recreational sports are popular.

All in all, Minnesota is very normal. You'll find a little of just about everything, much that is good, but very little of the best. You could do worse—or better.

MISSISSIPPI STATE UNIVERSITY

Location: Mississippi State, MS 39762
Campus: rural
Undergraduate enrollment: 5901 M, 3764 W
Total enrollment: 11,374
Expenses: $3380 (in-state), $4230 (out-of-state)
Financial aid: NA
Library: 126,100 volumes
Student-faculty ratio: 19–1
Transfer students: 1354
Median ACT: 21
Fraternities: 76%
Sororities: 64%
Application deadline: 20 days before term begins

Mississippi State University has long been known as a "cow college" and snickeringly referred to in terms of cowboy boots, livestock prices, and fertilizer. Today, in an era of sweeping and intense moral and social change, Mississippi State University is still known as a "cow college" and is snickeringly referred to in terms of cowboy boots, livestock prices, and fertilizer.

The student population of Mississippi State, ninety-six percent Southern, is still very largely what it's been all along: conservative and more interested in beer than in student government. The faculty is the "Dixiest" of any major Mississippi college, and the administration is "Dixier" than the faculty. Mississippi State attracts many agricultural types, and there are great numbers of bona fide cowboys who, along with the ever-present jocks and clean-cut fratmen, create a rural "Southern Comfort-type" atmosphere which permeates most of the student activities and organizations.

The fraternities and sororities, although relatively small in number, have a large influence on social life and a firm stranglehold on student government. The associate student body has little say-so, and their most significant accomplishment in recent years was obtaining cigarette machines in the dorms. The student government's major function each year is to serve as arena for the fraternity power struggles, with a lot of prestige being at stake in the election of the major officers.

Most of the students at State go to class and do very little else. A new student union is nice and clean but lifeless. The adjoining town of Starkville offers little more than a movie or two, and brighter lights are as far away as Memphis and New Orleans.

Starkville and the surrounding area is wet, but only for liquor—not for beer. This interesting situation leads to many a late-night trip to nearby counties where beer is readily available. The nearest legal bar is a veritable mecca of State students.

The curriculum leans heavily toward engineering and agricultural courses (agribusiness is big) and, in these particular areas, is surprisingly good. Teaching techniques are high-schoolish, and the liberal arts courses are sparse, but there are chances for a wide variety of studies if the student doesn't mind sacrificing quality for that variety.

Most State students who aren't in a fraternity or playing football for a living are really concerned with academics and do most of their fooling around on weekends. However, classes are not hard, and there are "guts" galore. Despite the relatively large amount of money State spends on facilities, classes suffer because in most cases the faculty lags far behind the equipment.

State gives few academic scholarships each year, and these are usually on the skimpy side. As at all Southern schools, the athletic program is strong and presently trying to catch its upstate rival, "Ole Miss," in prestige and success. In athletic scholarships, money flows a bit more freely.

The polarization between black and white is beginning to break down, although the enrollment of black and other minority groups is still quite small. And while the open friction between the races has largely disappeared, blacks keep mostly to themselves socially and are excluded from the lily-white fraternities.

Mississippi State is an agriculturally-oriented institution set in a backward state with students from its rural countryside. The state is still so poor and so bigoted and so incredibly depressed that some people have suggested it should qualify for the foreign-aid program. Mississippi is still the sort of place where a member of the state's college board will say that he fears "the influx of foreign ideologies, maybe city slickers" because of the moderate changes which have helped to make State livable. Despite some of the moderation, though, the students are to a large extent simply dull, and the curriculum and faculty have adjusted to this dullness with corresponding rigidity. Football reigns, and if you're not a jock and don't belong to a fraternity, Mississippi State soon becomes a very boring place. And New Orleans is almost as far away geographically as it is philosophically and culturally.

UNIVERSITY OF MISSISSIPPI

Location: University, MS 38677
Campus: rural
Undergraduate enrollment:
    4250 M, 3600 W
Total enrollment: 9655
Expenses: $2452 (in-state),
    $3252 (out-of-state)
Financial aid: 51%
Library: 875,000 volumes

Student-faculty ratio: 17–1
Transfer students: 800
Median ACT: 21
Fraternities: 42%
Sororities: 48%
Application deadline:
    twenty days before
    registration date

"Good things are happening at 'Ole Miss'" is the latest public relations theme, and it must seem that way to the administration and alumni. A dorm visitation proposal was brushed aside, students now get their cars towed away for $15 and a parking fine, and administrators have perfected the technique of politely ignoring inquisitive students who are concerned about the future of the university. But some good things are happening.

"Ole Miss" is coming up with some very strong and innovative programs. A two-year-old Center for the Study of Southern Culture, established in part with an NEH grant is attracting affiliates, speakers, and supporters from around the nation. The program focuses on some of the great Southern writers, musical forms, and regional history of the confederacy.

But aside from what the P.R. releases tell you about academics, we hear that "Ole Miss" students still know how to have a good time. Dixie Week in the spring and Homecoming in the fall are unmatched in the nation for total commitment to bands, booze, and bed. Five good bars give students five good reasons for sleeping through those eight A.M. classes.

The campus is located near William Faulkner's Oxford in the rolling farmland of northern Mississippi. The scenic countryside is nice, but students wish Memphis were less than an hour-and-a-half away.

Everybody remembers the integration of "Ole Miss" in 1962, but the integration hasn't progressed much. Only nine percent of the students are black (two percent are of other races) and blacks and whites seem to prefer to stick with their own kind. The social classes at "Ole Miss" are also still fairly well defined, with the Greeks struggling to maintain control while the independents are the jocks.

The frat man is easily recognized because he will look like half the other guys on campus. Faded jeans with just enough of that worn look and a bushy moustache, make him one of the crowd. The fratman's counterpart, his sorority sister, thinks moustaches are "cute" and smiles whenever she sees one. She reads *Bride* (choke!) and *Glamour* and dates a lot.

The Greeks who aren't into beer usually like politicking, and they spend their time making contacts, talking on the phone, and filling out law school applications. "Ole Miss" is recognized as the breeding ground for the state's political leaders.

A bare majority of students don't join the Greek system and remain, shall we say, independent. Many hold responsible positions in student government, academics, and student publications, but it is unusual for an independent to hold the very highest offices. Many find that off-campus living, although more expensive, is lots of fun. After all, a little drinking and messing around never hurt anyone, and besides they save money on food.

There are no coed dorms, and freshmen must live on-campus. The dorms for women lock up at midnight, but a security guard allows residents through.

For the academically inclined, "Ole Miss" does have something to offer. The school prides itself on the number of Rhodes Scholars it has graduated, as well as on the nationally ranked Pharmacy School, the Law School, which is the fourth oldest in the nation, and on a strong liberal arts program.

"Ole Miss" is now grappling with the problem of offering degrees in more scientific pursuits, while still maintaining a strong arts program. There are now degrees in forensic science, radio/TV, and computer science, as well as training programs in medical technology and medical records, physical therapy, and premed and predent.

Academics for the majority here can be summed up by the two all-important concerns: how many cuts are allowed and the final grade. For the average student, "Ole Miss" offers a prestigious name (prestigious in the South, anyway) with academic standards which allow him to slide by.

UNIVERSITY OF MISSOURI/COLUMBIA

Location: Columbia, MO 65201
Campus: city outskirts
Undergraduate enrollment: 16,540
Total enrollment: 23,064
Expenses: $2300 (in-state), $3700 (out-of-state)
Financial aid: 35%
Library: 1,930,000 volumes

Student-faculty ratio: NA
Transfer students: NA
Median SAT: 510 V, 545 M
Median ACT: 23
Fraternities and Sororities: 15%
Application deadline: NA

There is no justification for the location of the University of Missouri's Columbia campus. The town is small and dull, literally in the middle of nowhere.

Nevertheless, Columbia is the largest of the University's four campuses, and it picks up the lion's share of whatever money the Missouri legislature is willing to distribute to the whole system.

Money has been a big topic here lately. UMC's new chancellor, Barbara Uehling, began an ambitious reorganization program when she arrived last spring, only to find herself caught in the middle of a seemingly endless series of budget hassles with the legislature.

Unfortunately, the school must play catch-up with the funds it does wrestle free. UMC's power plant is years behind in conforming to federal pollution standards. The main library has overflowed into a small building several blocks away. Faculty salaries rank no better than sixteenth among Big Eight and Big Ten schools.

With priorities like those, the UMC administration has little time to deal with students. That's not so bad, though: students here don't seem to want to be bothered. The student block could easily have flexed its political muscle last fall when two young, liberal candidates for the city council ran in student-dominated districts. The pair lost by a combined total of sixty-odd votes.

The "ho-hum" climate here is typical of schools this large, and the students cherish their beer-swilling days. Moreover, the student body includes more than a few deadheads, as enrollment is open to any Missouri high school graduate (though the policy is to flunk out about half the class at the end of the freshman year). All told, the atmosphere is not conducive to scholarship.

Missouri has begun to acquire a decent reputation, but it still has a long way to go. As might be expected, agriculture is very strong. But so is journalism, and, surprisingly, so is art history. Dr. Uehling is trying to improve every department's faculty, but the task if difficult. Some, like chemistry, have no untenured faculty members. Barring death or resignation, there is no way to clean out complacent profs. Many of the scientific departments, where strong efforts to revamp dusty programs are underway, have shelled out extra bucks to get outside department heads. The idea is that these new people will ignore departmental politics and "persuade" unwanted faculty members to pack their bags. It's too early to tell how well this is working.

The principal problem for the serious student is not a lack of opportunity but simply coping with the administrative morass. Following one's desired program can get sticky unless you are well into your department early in the game. Most of the teachers are responsive to the minority of students who are serious about learning, because scholars are a welcome relief from the masses. But big-name faculty members are rare. Facilities in agriculture and science (the university does research worth hundreds of millions of dollars annually for the federal government and maintains its own research reactor south of town) surpass all.

Socially, Missouri is not the big party school it once was. There are nearly forty fraternities and sororities, and they keep pretty much to themselves. The university's women are often shunned, the college men preferring females from nearby Stephens College and Columbia (formerly Christian) College. The university's regulations on drinking have tightened in recent months, and the frats feel the pinch. Most glaring are racial relations—they are nonexistent. The only black woman to participate in last fall's sorority rush was harassed and refused a bid. Blacks here are justifiably resentful.

Town-gown relations are notably poor, with Columbia residents likely to be hostile to students. Prices in all local shops are very high. Students generally find the best thing about Columbia is leaving for

Kansas City or St. Louis, both two hours away in opposite directions.

Unless you want to be a kingpin in the major daily newspaper of Columbia, there are serious reasons to question going to the University of Missouri/Columbia. The school is, if anything, a little below the average state university—scarcely a school to go out of your way to attend.

UNIVERSITY OF MONTANA

Location: Missoula, MT 59812
Campus: city outskirts
Undergraduate enrollment:
   3626 M, 3346 W
Total enrollment: 8376
Expenses: $2900 (in-state),
   $4300 (out-of-state)
Financial aid: 40%
Library: 600,000 volumes

Student-faculty ratio: 19–1
Transfer students: 1350
Median ACT: 21.3
Fraternities: 2%
Sororities: 2%
Application deadline:
   one month before
   beginning of term

If you're fairly straight, not overly intellectual, and wild about ecology, the University of Montana could be a great place to go to school. The university's main branch is located in Missoula, a bustling and progressive metropolis (by Montana standards, anyway) of 50,000 located just west of the Continental Divide in a semi-arid region surrounded by picturesque mountains.

The undeniable natural beauty of Montana has spurred the interests of countless students in forestry, wildlife management, and general ecology. The university owns 20,850 acres in nearby Lubrecht Forest and another 167 acres on Flathead Lake, and it has taken advantage of both locales to initiate programs in wildlife research and forestry science. The UM School of Forestry works closely with the U. S. government, but thus far their purposes have been benign, in sharp contrast to the defense orientation at some campuses.

UM is a liberal arts-based institution, offering some strong undergraduate programs in business administration, education, fine arts, forestry, journalism, and pharmacy. The Graduate School offers master degrees in forty program areas and the doctoral degree is offered by eleven departments and professional schools.

Missoula is more than mountains. The arts are supported and there are cultural events to attend. Missoula offers some good restaurants, bars, and theaters. Among some of the advantages of living in country as pretty as Montana are campus-sponsored backpacking trips, river floats, and skiing.

On campus, student interests range from football to politics. Excellent recreational facilities are provided. University of Montana students can choose between comfortable dorm rooms, sorority and fraternity housing, or off-campus housing, if they can find it.

For the most part, the faculty is student-oriented. A new interdisciplinary writing program has been initiated to ensure good writing training.

The university has been battling with the state legislature over funding for the past few years. As a result, faculty and student morale has declined. A decline in enrollment and larger class sections has occurred, but the situation should improve with the increased efforts of the administration to attract new students to the university. Both financial aid and academic counseling are easier to find than they used to be.

But the premier advantage of Montana, we repeat, is the physical locale. If you're from New York City and want a completely different way of life, you ought to consider it; a good quarter of the student body comes from out of state.

MORGAN STATE UNIVERSITY

Location: Baltimore, MD 21239
Campus: suburban
Undergraduate enrollment:
  2400 M, 2600 W
Total enrollment: 6000
Expenses: $3000 (in-state),
  $4000 (out-of-state)
Financial aid: 85%
Library: 100,000 volumes

Student-faculty ratio: 24-1
Transfer students: 350
Median SAT: 375 V, 375 M
Fraternities: 3%
Sororities: 4%
Application deadline:
  rolling

Morgan State University was founded in 1867 as an all-black school. Today, Morgan State is one of the bigger and better examples of a traditionally black university. It is gifted with an intelligent administration, a capable faculty, a serious, nondisruptive, and somewhat integrated student body, and a solid pre-professional curriculum, particularly in education.

But Morgan State, like virtually every major American college, has begun to feel a pinch, engendered by the increasing wave of social consciousness. Morgan's problems, moreover, are especially acute because its difficulties result from the social awareness far afield rather than any specific awakening at home. Major prestige universities have of late undertaken a rush program of integration, in order to serve minority groups and prove good intentions. As a result, the best black administrators, faculty, and students have all but abandoned black colleges, and those who remain are competent, but probably not the cream.

A number of black colleges have been forced to close their doors. Morgan State, however, because it is a public college and because it enjoys academic and social strength, is far from ready to fold up under competition, even from the likes of Harvard and Yale. Instead, it is doing a successful job of replacing talent with more talent. And it is conducting an integration program of its own. A series of advertisements stressing that "Morgan is not just for blacks" have increased the school's very small white enrollment to some extent.

The focus at Morgan State is on-the-job training, and the two biggest departments are education for teachers-to-be and sociology for future social workers (although the latter subject is not held in the highest esteem by most students). Few students enroll in political science or history, traditionally large departments at white liberal arts colleges, and the two departments have been combined. Music enjoys a considerable popularity, however. The academic demands are not overly rigorous—to which the nonstop round of partying in some sectors of the campus attests. But there are many distributional requirements, which are now just in the process of reduction. Because of the fairly substantial size of the school—over six thousand students—many freshman courses are large, even oversubscribed. But upper-level courses, particularly in more obscure departments, provide individual attention.

Socially, Morgan State is not very lively. The bulk of the student body consists of Baltimore commuters, and their ties are to their families or to downtown neighborhoods. Most students disappear at five P.M., and for those who remain, there are only six dormitories, forcing even more of the student populace off campus. Food, we are told, is awful, so many students drive to restaurants. Cars are permitted, and half the students have them. Thus, although Morgan State is stuck in Baltimore, which inevitably has an impact on one's feelings about the college, it is possible to escape to Washington, less than an hour away. The D. C. area is particularly attractive for its beverages.

Fraternities, surprisingly enough, do exist. In fact, even though they draw only a very few members, the frats have power out of proportion to their size. But competition for the frat system is offered by parties every night of the week, particularly house parties in the city, which are reportedly extremely swinging affairs. Indeed, the frats are probably better known for their do-gooder leanings, like the distribution of Thanksgiving baskets to the poor, than they are for social importance.

Politically, Morgan State is attempting change through social action. Tutoring projects in South Baltimore are largely conducted by out-of-state students who live on-campus.

On the extracurricular side, football is very big. The campus newspaper is also becoming more popular and more respected. Many students would like to write for it, but space is limited, as it appears only weekly.

The future looks healthy for Morgan State, which is growing in both its academics and its extracurricular activities.

MOUNT HOLYOKE COLLEGE

Location: South Hadley, MA 01075
Campus: suburban
Undergraduate enrollment: 1850 W
Total enrollment: 1948
Expenses: $6820
Financial aid: 50%
Library: 422,175 volumes

Student-faculty ratio: 11–1
Transfer students: 60–70
Median SAT: NA
Sororities: NA
Application deadline: February 1

Mount Holyoke College, originally founded as a women's seminary in 1837, is located in South Hadley, Massachusetts, a quiet town in the Connecticut River Valley. A few years after its founding, the seminary became an all-women's college. Mount Holyoke remains a liberal arts college for women today. There is no pressure for coeducation.

Like many other colleges, Mount Holyoke was changed by the Sixties and the Seventies. The college has a new, more modern outlook. Women are in control here, and are encouraged to succeed in their academics.

At Mount Holyoke, academics follow a traditional liberal arts route, and yet the chemistry department is outstanding. Although the college is able to offer a variety of courses, there are limitations. Students seeking courses which Mount Holyoke does not offer are free to take a shuttle bus to one or more of the other cooperating colleges (Amherst, Hampshire, Smith, or the University of Massachusetts) in the Five College program. Courses taken at one of the other colleges are considered part of a student's regular schedule. The Five College exchange program provides seemingly limitless course offerings and a chance to meet other students in an academic setting.

Mount Holyoke is strong academically with several distinguished professors on campus. Prior to the publication of his latest novel, *The World According to Garp*, John Irving was teaching at Mount Holyoke. The college's small size allows for friendly relations between students and faculty, who are frequently seen having dinner in the dorms with their students and their families. The students are generally very serious about their work and interested in exchanging ideas. (Preweds are frowned upon). Holyoke offers some flexible and challenging programs: a twelve college exchange, independent study, undergrad research, and Washington political internships.

The great interest in academics does not imply that "MHTs" (Mount Holyoke-types) are grinds; they do come out of the library fairly often. (But they also go in fairly often). Activities and events are popular and usually well supported. The location and atmosphere brings out the outdoorsiness of many students: many go jogging, biking, and cross-country skiing. Unfortunately, Mount Holyoke does not offer the finest physical education facilities for more serious athletes. Though the crew team recently purchased a new shell designed for women and organized a major regatta, the annual National Invitational Women's Regatta, students must endure a gym without bleachers for basketball games.

The 800-acre campus is rural, peaceful and beautifully landscaped. The dorms house between sixty and 130 students each. Since each dorm has its own dining room, living room, and lounges, the result is very homey. Housing arrangements are on a yearly basis, providing the opportunity for both a change in surrounding and exposure to more students.

Holyoke's social life is not manless. There are mixers and casino nights which are often, though not always, well attended by both sexes. During weekends, the campus can empty out. Some women choose to visit other campuses. Dartmouth is a particular favorite, just as men (and often whole fraternities, particularly from Dartmouth) visit Mount Holyoke. The tradition of roadtripping still lives. Even Princeton men are known to make the trek.

There are usually four movies a week. The local ski area, Mount Tom, isn't Aspen, but it is always crowded with students. Better snow and major resorts are less than an hour away. The towns of Northampton and Amherst are a free bus ride away, both of which offer the expected night life of college towns. After all, over 20,000 students attend college in Amherst.

On campus, student involvement in government sometimes wanes, but student interest in college governing committees is strong with most major seats on committees, departments, and legislative groups open to student members. Students take responsibility for how Mount Holyoke is run.

Students also take the honor code seriously. Mount Holyoke rarely enforces a code of conduct and there are no student informers. However, students' respect for the honor code has allowed the college to institute a policy of self-scheduled exams.

Mount Holyoke is a woman's college, and as such it is not for everybody. However, Mount Holyoke women take their college seriously, and in return the faculty and administration are serious about encouraging their women students.

MUHLENBERG COLLEGE

Location: Allentown, PA 18104
Campus: suburban
Undergraduate enrollment: 846 M, 665 W
Expenses: $6200
Financial aid: 52%
Library: 176,000 volumes

Student-faculty ratio: 14–1
Transfer students: 24
Median SAT: M: 525 V, 613 M; W: 547 V, 570 M
Fraternities: 40%
Sororities: NA
Application deadline: February 15

Muhlenberg College maintains high academic standards while providing an individualized education. It has a well-earned reputation in pre-professional programs (especially premedical), and it is one of the few small, private colleges to have a nationally accredited education program. It is a liberal arts school which, through its general academic requirements, emphasizes a broad education to complement a concentration in one field.

Muhlenberg boasts one of the finest art facilities in any small college. The Center for the Arts, designed by Philip Johnson, exhibits and houses workrooms for painting, sculpture, drawing, literature, music, and drama.

Muhlenberg is partially supported by the Lutheran Church of America and is named after a Lutheran minister who was one of the first German settlers in the Allentown area. Although it is a church-related school, its student body is diverse.

The campus is located within a fifteen-mile radius of Lehigh, Lafayette, Moravian, and Cedar Crest colleges, which creates a university atmosphere and much cross-traffic on the weekends. The cities of New York and Philadelphia are also accessible. The educational climate is not confined to the classroom. Teachers and administrators share insights and enthusiasm with students on a personal level.

The Muhlenberg community encourages freedom of expression and welcomes suggestions for change. The college is, in fact, continually changing as the student body forms interest groups to reexamine academic requirements, codes, and calendars.

Dorm living at Muhlenberg is unrestricted, safe, and for the most part orderly. There is a combination of fraternity, coed, and single-sex dorms. Each residence hall has its own personality and periodically sponsors progressive dinners, casino nights, tension breaks, in addition to joint activities and competition.

There are five fraternities (and a sixth on the way) which take turns providing the student population with pub nights, band parties, and happy hours on the weekends. Their members fill the varsity athletic ranks, while the remainder fill the stands. Women's athletics at Muhlenberg are being increased under pressure.

Student resident advisors, trained in counseling and first-aid, provide general tips about how to succeed at Muhlenberg and still have a good time. They are also, we are told, responsible during "fire drills, panty raids, and blackouts."

The campus includes a "quad," which is a secluded lawn reserved for parties and folkfests, a student center, a chapel, and a versatile library with some floors designated for study and others for socializing. Each dorm also has a "pit" or study lounge and a TV lounge.

In recent years, Muhlenberg has been visited by the Doobie Brothers, and Vincent Price—a wide variety of cultural entertainment.

For a small college atmosphere, a chance to participate in outstanding pre-professional programs and open opportunities for self-designed study abroad or college exchange, you might want to look further into Muhlenberg College.

UNIVERSITY OF NEBRASKA/LINCOLN

Location: Lincoln, NE 68508
Campus: city center
Undergraduate enrollment:
 9200 M, 7000 W
Total enrollment: 22,477
Expenses: $2900 (in-state),
 $4200 (out-of-state)
Financial aid: 35%
Library: 1,500,000 volumes

Student-faculty ratio: 17-1
Transfer students: 1650
Median ACT: 21.1
Fraternities: 15-20%
Sororities: 15%
Application deadline:
 August 15

The University of Nebraska/Lincoln is just about No. 1 in football—and vice-versa. The senior member of the University of Nebraska system (comprised of UNL, the Medical Center, and commuter student-oriented UN/Omaha), UNL is still trying to become a university that the football team can be proud of.

Of course, football is not everything. As a state-supported school, UNL's main duty is to train students in skills needed by the state, such as agriculture, business, engineering, and teaching. Over ninety percent of the student body is from in-state, making this a school of, by, and for Nebraskans, complete with old-fashioned pep rallies, the world's largest tractor-testing laboratory, and a rock festival that had to be named "Cornstalk."

Academically, UNL is a typical large state university, and its size means that a few diamonds do exist among the heaps of coal. The schools of agriculture and journalism are among the nation's best, while most other departments are respectable, albeit mediocre. Large classes and so-so teachers are common, and the schools of engineering and business turned a number of students away in 1978 because there wasn't enough money to hire enough professors. Outstanding professors can be found, however, if a student takes the time to look for them.

And things are getting worse. State financial support has not kept pace with inflation, and, thanks to the perennially stingy state legislature (the nation's only unicameral), major budget cuts are expected soon. Compared with other Big Eight universities, UNL falls within the middle in terms of teacher's salaries and lowest amount of state financial support, and (you guessed it!) the conference's highest tuition rate. During the fall of 1979, *all* computer research was halted for lack of funds, and only an irate student government prevented the library from closing on Saturdays to save money.

Then again, there's always football. Memorial Stadium is the state's third-largest city, and its 76,000 seats have been sold out for every home game in the last fourteen years. The men's gymnastics team ranks as national champion, and the new Bob Devaney Sports Complex (named equally after UNL's winningest football coach and the state's mental condition) combines with a beautiful women's phys. ed. building to give UNL outstanding sports facilities. Unfortunately, football players have first claim on virtually everything; UNL's recreational facilities rank seventh in the Big Eight.

Life in Lincoln is not unpleasant, however. Lincoln is the state's capital and most progressive city, with a newly renovated downtown, a good mass transit system, and numerous parks. While many students life off-campus, a large number find residence hall life so inexpensive and convenient that the dorms have been at one hundred percent occupancy since 1976. The Greek system is also popular.

Social life revolves around football games and beer parties. Alcohol is banned on campus (and marijuana is uncommon), but heavy drinking can be found to some extent in the dorms (which also suffer from a fourteen-hour visitation rule), and to a greater extent in Greek houses and off-campus haunts. The latter are few, for while UNL's main campus is in downtown Lincoln, the few decent bars are bedecked with "Big Red" memorabilia. The east campus, which houses the agriculture, law, and dentistry schools, is two miles from the main campus, but right next to the state's best pizza restaurant.

Politically, UNL is conservative, pragmatic, and often apathetic. Both students and faculty are more concerned with tuition rates, budget cuts, and educational quality than with nuclear power. Despite valiant and moderately successful efforts by UNL's strongest student government bodies, student input is still largely ignored by an ultraconservative board of regents. As one regent said in 1975, "Students are children and we ought to treat them like children."

If you're a Nebraskan, if your car's horn toots the "Cornhusker" fight song, or if you're interested in a specific program such as agriculture, journalism, or chemistry, then UNL is for you. If not, bear in mind that many observers don't consider UNL to be one of the top institutions in the Big Eight. The "Cornhuskers" may be the best defensive football team in the country, but UNL is not one of the three top educational institutions in the western world—or even the western "Cornbelt."

UNIVERSITY OF NEVADA/RENO

Location: Reno, NV 89557
Campus: city outskirts
Undergraduate enrollment:
 2742 M, 2278 W
Total enrollment: 7700
Expenses: $2600 (in-state),
 $4100 (out-of-state)
Financial aid: 30%
Library: 594,885 volumes

Student-faculty ratio: 18-1
Transfer students: 2000
Median ACT: 19
Fraternities: NA
Sororities: NA
Application deadline:
 July 15 for fall,
 January 2 for spring

With the distractions of Reno, it's a wonder anybody actually graduates from the University of Nevada/Reno.

The school's image of being one of the country's biggest party schools has diminished somewhat, but the nonacademic atmosphere has not. Many activities are easily accessible around the UNR campus, activities that are virtually unthinkable anywhere else.

"Keeping the mind strictly on books is tough to do," we were told by one student, "when such things as legal prostitution are fifteen minutes away, there are absolutely no drinking or liquor-peddling curfews, and fantastic skiing is within an hour of the city limits."

The campus is still one of the most traditionally beautiful in the West, with tree-lined Manzanita Lake dominating the middle of campus and the old-fashioned quadrangle still the favorite spot of fall touch football games.

It is a quiet, noncontroversial campus to the point of apathy. It reflects a widespread trend, although UNR has never been know for its campus radicals.

Athletics were something that students didn't think about very much until 1976. But with the acquisition of a new football and basketball coach, the program has risen into the national spotlight.

The football team was undefeated in the 1978 Division I–AA season and was ranked No. 1 most of the year until the playoffs. Basketball rolled to a 20-win season in 1979 and won the opening round of the NIT playoffs.

The city has responded to this success, with one of the most proficient and hard-core booster programs in the country. The booster monetary intake has reached the point where student funding is not needed, but still tokenly accepted.

Outside of student participation at sporting events, it is tough for them to get excited over anything else. Fighting a losing battle to educate the university are the campus publications, which are run without faculty supervisors. The *Sagebrush*, the prize-winning campus paper, is openly in rebellion against the university's Neanderthal journalism department. The literary magazine, *Brushfire*, was revived in 1973, and within two years it had published works by, or interviews with, Norman Mailer, Joyce Carol Oates, William Stafford, Nikki Giovanni, Richard Armour, Jesse Stuart, Walter Van Tilburg Clark, and others. Fraternities seem to carry most of the party load these days. After the nationally publicized drinking death in 1975 of a student during initiation rites into the Sundowner Club, a nonrecognized university drinking organization, the campus mellowed into a sedate state that alumni of ten years ago would never have thought possible.

With the recent boomtown growth of the past two years in Reno, housing inflation has risen to unaffordable student rates. As a result, the six on-campus dormitories are full.

Fraternities and sororities are also relatively healthy. The seven on-campus fraternities and five sororities still reflect the 1950s, "animal house" syndrome with frequent beer busts, panty raids, and other hi-jinks that only Greeks could get away with.

Academically, it is safe to say that UNR is pretty run-of-the-mill. It does boast lots of good Ph.D. programs, though. The once-famous Mackay School of Mines has slipped dramatically and had a tough time getting its accreditation the last go-round. Professional schools on campus are still trying to build a reputation. The Desert Research Institute is one of the best in the country.

Problems were finally worked out last December. Nevada has plans for a law school and vet school. The senate seems to favor neighboring sister school Las Vegas.

If a student is clever, he can make the most out of his nonacademic college experience by staying away from gambling downtown and using the clubs for their cheaper offerings, such as liquor and food. To lure people into the casinos, the clubs feature the cheapest quality meals anywhere. Steak and eggs for ninety-nine cents, great buffets for under $4 all come in handy for the tight-budgeted college student. And availability of free drinks is remarkable. Casinos are more than willing to give them away on the premise that a drunk tourist is a spend-happy toursit.

The good citizens of Reno are not opposed to culture. They like art, literature, and music just as much as the next person. They just want all artists, writers, and longhair musicians to keep the hell away. The lack of creativity in the "Biggest Little City" has rubbed off on the university as well. Professors specialize in aborting all traces of creativity in their students. UNR has had but two artists of note. Walter Van Tilburg Clark, author of *The Ox-Bow Incident*, quit the university once in protest and is now ridiculed posthumously by his unpublished former colleagues in the English department. Painter Robert Cole Caples has since fled to the sanctuary of the Connecticut Berkshires.

If the college is hard on creative people, it is death on minorities. Reno's populace thinks a Chicano is a delicacy sold in one of the city's countless taco stands. Blacks, moreover, are still called "colored folk" by the enlightened Nevadans. Women are welcomed with open arms—as long as they put out and keep their mouths shut.

The city boasts one of the most repressive police forces in the country, and the UNR campus police certainly aren't much better. UNR gendarmes handed out 15,000 parking tickets during a recent year. Not bad for a school with about half that many students.

In short, Reno's university is as intellectually arid as the nearby desert. The city is not a nice place to visit, and you certainly won't want to live there. Besides, anyone who enrolls in one of the nearby California state colleges qualifies automatically for free admission to UNR parties—he knows the reality of UNR—a school whose extras outweigh the academics.

NEW COLLEGE OF THE UNIVERSITY OF SOUTH FLORIDA

Location: Sarasota, FL 33580
Campus: suburban
Undergraduate enrollment: 237 M, 250 W
Total enrollment: 509
Expenses: $2800 (in-state), $4600 (out-of-state)
Financial aid: 60%
Library: 127,000 volumes

Student-faculty ratio: 12-1
Transfer students: 80
Median SAT: 607 V, 609 M
Fraternities: 0%
Sororities: 0%
Application deadline: rolling

New College merged with the University of South Florida (in Tampa) in 1975, and is part of a branch campus of USF. Its existence since then has depended on the raising of $750,000 a year by the New College Foundation—essentially, making up the difference between the student-faculty ratio of USF at twenty to one and the student-faculty ratio at New College of ten to one. Raising three-quarters of a million was not always easy; New College came close to defaulting several times in its first two years as New College of USF. In June of 1979, however, the state legislature approved a bill that would grant New College three million dollars in matching funds if the New College Foundation could raise the same amount by 1983. The signing of this bill into law has given New College a good shot at the financial security it has been lacking ever since its creation.

There are few organized social groups at New College; cliques and factions, however, abound. There is an expanding schism between new (mainly first-year) students and older students. First-year students live in the dorms, are primarily carrer-oriented, more conservative, less tolerant, and like disco. Older students live off-campus, are artists, poets, anarchists, and like to consider themselves radical, freaky, or beat. As the older students graduate, drop-out, or fade away, and as the new students come in (mostly from Florida), New College is becoming more traditional. Older students are "gettin' itchy by all this"; waiting in the wings are the high school graduates of the 1980s. New College's conservative block (which it has always had—some considered it a refuge from the campus riots during the Sixties) may begin asserting itself in the next few years.

For the time being, though, things are still pretty relaxed; the weather, we are told, will mellow "any neo-fascist first-class mind." New Yorkers unused to the sun, surf, and sand can lose themselves in the climate, but most count themselves lucky if they can swing a few hours of rays. The pool is a popular mixing spot, for faculty and student alike. Individual sports like racquetball are popular, but intercollegiate athletics are nonexistent. There are a few intramural and city-league teams—the New College "Devos" came in second in 1979 basketball. If New College becomes any more mellow, they may build a jacuzzi.

The social life is feast or famine: lots of parties, films and concerts, or beer and pinball. The film series in consistently good. Drugs of most kinds are not too hard to come by. Marijuana is widely used, mushrooms are easily obtained (in season, pick your cow pasture), and the more esoteric recreational devices are available. Alcohol is still the drug of choice. The drinking age in Florida is eighteen. There are several popular bars near the school, including a gay disco.

Politics at New College is a constant (and continuing) struggle to maintain the New College identity. Current administration changes (all the way to the president of USF) have brought about a positive commitment to the New College ideal. USF Sarasota has been given more local autonomy over campus policy, and the results have been positive. A successful boycott of the food service has brought a reexamination of the local food operation. All of the administrators involved have given a lot of lip service to keeping New College alive. Most are hopeful.

The architecture of New College is basically Mediterranean. The west campus is the former estate of Charles Ringling, brother of John, and is located on Sarasota Bay. It houses the Palmer dormitories, now used for classrooms and office space, and the newly reopened B Dorm, which provides singles.

The east campus, designed by I. M. Pei (who resigned from the project out of dissatisfaction with the administrators) most notably contains the Pei dorms—luxurious motel rooms with private entrances, balconies, and baths, which offer isolation but no privacy, and can be maddening to live in. The east campus is built on airport land (the Sarasota Bradentar airport is right across the street), and contains some tacky Army barracks left over from WWII days. Crossing from the east campus to the west campus involves some risk, since U. S. 41 is right between the two.

Most students move off campus after they have served their compulsory first three terms on campus. Housing in Sarasota is becoming scarce. Many of the professors and staff live in the immediate area as well, so if you do find housing off-campus you may possibly be your lit professor's neighbor.

Student government at NC is like that of a New England Congregational church: representatives are so concerned about getting a consensus that they sometimes fail to get anything done. Minor decisions can take two weeks to decide, and major decisions, such as revising and adopting a new constitution, have taken as long as seven years. The chief political air of student government is maintaining the New College identity, and to stop any encroachment of NC by the University of South Florida. To their credit, they've been successful.

Academics alone can occupy most of your time, so people who do more than study often find themselves burned-out after a term or two. Most students who take an interest in New College other than in academics find themselves finishing in four or five years, instead of the usual three.

The academic environment is rigorous. Some departments are superb, others mediocre, and others nonexistent. The faculty is friendly, easily accessible, and devoted. Mapping a course of study generally revolves around choosing a congenial professor and establishing an apprentice relationship with him. A student and his faculty sponsor get together to devise an overall educational plan or "contract" for each term and often work together in independent study and tutorials. The major field of study is not restricted; the areas run from traditional "departmental majors" to general studies. The exam required to receive a degree is a defense of the mandatory senior thesis.

History, philosophy, physics, and math are excellent departments, and the natural sciences program is surprisingly good. Literature and political science are strong areas, and the environmental studies program, which emphasizes involvement in the preservation and protection of the ecology of southwest Florida, is very popular with students and has had an appreciable impact on recent local developments. Psychology and sociology are weak departments.

New College is a challenging, invigorating, captivating place. It can get under your skin and refuse to let you go—graduates often talk of the "New College mafia." It is possible to hide in your room for three years, do your work, write a thesis, and graduate before anyone notices your existence. No one minds. New College will get you into a good graduate school, prepare you for a professional school, and give you a solid education. It's an experience you'll never forget.

UNIVERSITY OF NEW HAMPSHIRE

Location: Durham NH 03824
Campus: suburban
Undergraduate enrollment:
   3049 M, 2869 W
Total enrollment: 12,386
Expenses: $2855 (in-state),
   $5400 (out-of-state)
Financial aid: 50%
Library: 760,000 volumes

Student-faculty ratio: 20–1
Transfer students: 1200
Median SAT: 485 V, 545 M
Fraternities: 3%
Sororities: 3%
Application deadline:
   February 15 for out-of-state
   March 1 for in-state

If you're looking for a laid-back country setting and like the idea of being fifteen minutes from the ocean, a half-hour from the mountains, and an hour from Boston, the University of New Hampshire may be your place.

But if it's a cosmopolitan environment, ready-made entertainment, or top-notch academics you want, look further.

The university's biggest asset is its natural surroundings—virgin New England countryside abounds, replete with rolling hills and wooded vales. And the cities of Dover and Portsmouth are close enough to provide some relief from the scenery.

Despite its settings, UNH is not without troubles. The school ranks last in the nation in terms of state funding for a state university—and that means the students bear the brunt of the costs.

With the ousting last November of archconservative Governor Meldrim Thomson, however, things are looking up for UNH. The new governor, Hugh Gallen, has pledged support for the university—and the school has carried on admirably despite its financial difficulties.

One way the school maintains its programs is through rising tuition, especially for out-of-staters, of which there are thirty-five to forty percent. Besides providing big bucks, those out-of-staters also give UNH an interesting mix of city slickers among the hayseeds—and everyone seems to get along rather well.

UNH is a pleasant, down-to-earth place. Town-gown relations between the university and Durham, a stereotypical college town, are good. The university itself comprises most of the town, with a 500-yard long, thirty-five-store Main Street tacked on. Eight of those establishments are popular beer halls.

The environment is sylvan and pretty; the college is architecturally simple in a quiet New England sort of way. Town and campus blend well with the natural setting.

Academics at UNH are uneven. Some departments are abominable, others are great, and most are average. The philosophy and English departments are outstanding. The English department is led by Pulitzer Prize-winning journalist Don Murray and National Book Award-winner Tom Williams. Unfortunately, none of the other liberal arts departments are nearly as strong.

Outside liberal arts, biology and chemistry are solid, with good facilities that include a marine biology station on the nearby coast. A federally funded "sea grant" program is in full swing.

There are strong programs in engineering and agriculture and the Whittemore School of Business and Economics has a highly rated hotel administration program.

Most of the teaching at UNH is done by professors with PH.D.s, and though an interdepartmental squabble in the political science department has tempers high, student-faculty relations remain better than at most universities.

Campus organizations are strong and well-staffed. The twice-weekly student newspaper regularly wins top national honors. Two student organizations provide popular concerts and entertainment, including Bruce Springsteen, Little Feat, and Bonnie Raitt in past years. The

Outing Club boasts more than 500 members and a stock of canoes, cross-country skis, and even a cabin in the mountains.

Varsity and club sports are equally popular. The UNH hockey team finished first in the east and fourth in the nation in 1979. The football team, though less consistent, is a regular contender in the Yankee Conference.

Another sport, probably unequaled in popularity, is drinking. A 1974 *Playboy* magazine survey on college drinking placed UNH in a class by itself. Fraternities and sororities have a large following for their renowned beer blasts. Drugs, except for marijuana and small quantities of speed around finals, have generally remained in the background, although cocaine seems to be catching on.

More than half the students live off-campus, in dwellings ranging from one-room apartments to luxury homes on nearby Rye Beach. Rents, though inflated in Durham, are more reasonable in the nearby student centers of Newmarket and Dover.

Many in-state students head home for weekends. Others, including out-of-staters, take off for the skiing or the shore. Weekend binges in Boston are common, as well.

If four years surrounded by a beautiful snow-covered countryside sounds good to you, just follow your nose north to New Hampshire.

NEW MEXICO STATE UNIVERSITY

Location: Las Cruces, NM 88003
Campus: city outskirts
Undergraduate enrollment: 5586 M, 3987 W
Total enrollment: 11,864
Expenses: $2900 (in-state), $4100 (out-of-state)
Financial aid: NA
Library: 556,619 volumes

Student-faculty ratio: 21–1
Transfer students: 950
Median ACT: 17.2
Fraternities: 2.5%
Sororities: 1.7%
Application deadline: one month before beginning of semester

You don't see many cowboy hats at NMSU any more. They've all been replaced by the familiar golf-style caps with the product emblems or witty slogans. Unfortunately, the athletes as well as the fraternity men have adopted the caps, as have the various species of engineers, business majors, ROTC members (on nonuniformed days), sports fans, and staff employees.

Yes, this desert is certainly a land of variety!

The surrounding community mirrors this; persons live fairly conventional middle- to lower-middle-income lives. Though the area is predominantly conventional in values and life-styles, the presence of Hispanic and Indian peoples and their cultural influences contribute to the unique character of the area. Las Cruces has a black mayor, and aside from isolated high school gang fights, New Mexico is really quite racially harmonious.

There are all sorts of characters here: left-over hippies; disco royalty; ranchers and ranchettes; UFO cultists; people who live way out in the desert; hot-air balloon fanatics; profiteers and mafioso; lots of charismatic and noncharismatic Christians, Jews, atheists, Moonies, artists, poets, and writers—you name it. There is still real comformity, nevertheless; an overwhelming majority wear those big, quilted, goosedown vests and jeans.

The university isn't one of those ivy-covered, brick institutions with creaky wooden floors; in fact, it has only been a full-fledged university for about twenty years. It was built out from the Agriculture College's stock pens. By working like crazy over the last two decades, NMSU has produced a downright modern campus.

About 2500 students live on-campus in fairly decent dorms, except one, Wells Hall; some with terrific views of the beautiful Organ Mountains at sunrise, or of the city, overlooked by the Corralitos mountains and the placid Picacho Peak, at sunset. Nearby mountains, desert, wilderness, and other open spaces foster outdoor activities.

Cruces has bars (Country and Western, disco, and short doses of rock) but the drinking age is twenty-one. If you aren't twenty-one, there are adeuqate numbers of movie theaters, a great classic film theater, community theater dramas, and musicals. There are several good restaurants in town, as well as a California-style selection of fast food.

El Paso is only about forty miles away, and the Mexican city of Juarez borders that. El Paso has plenty of nightlife, a few good restaurants, and the drinking age is only eighteen. Juarez has lots of nightlife, plenty of fabulous restaurants, and a friendly population. The Texas border itself is only about twenty-two miles from campus, and the town on the border, Anthony, has a fine Country and Western/country rock bar.

As for academics, agriculture and ag research are big and reportedly good. The engineering college, which conducts extensive solar, geothermal, and wind energy research is highly respected. The sciences are fair, the education program is mediocre, the liberal arts are average, and the business college is good.

And as for life in general at NMSU—well, the students don't object to very much—except the smell of cattle manure after it rains.

UNIVERSITY OF NEW MEXICO

Location: Albuquerque, NM 87131
Campus: city center
Undergraduate enrollment: 6300 M, 5800 W
Total enrollment: 21,600
Expenses: $3000 (in-state), $4000 (out-of-state)
Financial aid: 60%
Library: 900,000 volumes

Student-faculty ratio: 22–1
Transfer students: 2650
Median ACT: 18.5
Fraternities: 3%
Sororities: 2%
Application deadline: one week before first week of classes

In a state that is fifty percent Hispanic by ethnic count, it is no wonder the dorms here offer green chili alongside your scrambled eggs.

The University of New Mexico boasts having the largest percentage of Hispanic students (twenty-five percent) of any state-supported university, and the evidence is everywhere: from bilingual conversations in the Student Union Building to mariachi music on Saturday night.

The school also is proud to point out that it enrolls the largest number of Native American students (750) of any university anywhere. This is all fine and especially good for public relations, until one discovers that the drop-out rate hovers around sixty percent, with minorities being the largest groups to leave the university.

But no matter how many students come and go, the atmosphere at UNM, like that of the entire Southwest, remains unhurried. Albuquerque's mellow climate engenders a mild-mannered populace with strong ties to church and family. Low-key individuals can feel right at home in the state—that is, if they don't admit their out-of-state origins.

As can be found all along the exclusive Rocky Mountain Range, gringos coming in from out-of-state are overtly despised. And, as can also be found along the Rocky Mountain sierras, the more hostile "natives" are often those who have most recently acquired state citizenship. At any rate, New Mexico is not the place to brag about your Westchester County upbringing.

Academically, UNM can provide most anyone with an adequate

college education. Departments worth considering are anthropology, history, and art.

Scholastically, the students at UNM are in trouble. Recent statistics show that the average male freshman, with a grade point average of 1.89 on a 4.0 scale, was on academic probation after his first semester. The average female freshman tallied a remarkable 2.14 on the same scale.

For all practical purposes, there are no admission requirements. An entering freshman must have completed some form of high school, and must have taken a college entrance exam. That's about all.

The dean of the College of Arts and Sciences has been quoted as saying that roughly one-third of the incoming freshmen are not prepared for college work. And a university administrator has said that if the school raised admission requirements, there wouldn't be enough qualified students to keep the place going. So the depressing scholastic picture isn't all the fault of the institution.

In the past, the university offered remedial courses in basic English grammar and mathematics. These courses, once taken only as college preparatory work, are now offered for academic credit to incoming freshmen with poor ACT and SAT scores.

Ignoring scholastic problems, the school itself is quite pleasant to look at. The buildings are all the same sandstone color, built in a style reminiscent of local Indian pueblos.

The social life at UNM beats at a slow, steady pace. The "evil weed" is still the staple source of social misadventure, and there are the requisite number of coeducational living arrangements. But life itself is really rather dull.

The average UNM student rises in the morning to a brilliant sun, attends a few classes, leisurely chews a burrito for lunch, and returns home to a small, decrepit apartment located somewhere in Albuquerque's "student ghetto." If this overly mellow existence appeals to you, then UNM might be the place to locate your next four years.

STATE UNIVERSITY OF NEW YORK/ALBANY

Location: Albany, NY 12222
Campus: city outskirts
Undergraduate enrollment:
  5433 M, 5401 W
Total enrollment: 15,391

Student-faculty ratio: 17–1
Transfer students: 1200
Median SAT: 530 V, 580 M
Fraternities: 12%
Sororities: 5%

Expenses: $3300 (in-state), $3900 (out-of-state)
Financial aid: 85%
Library: 950,000 volumes

Application deadline: April 15

The State University of New York/Albany (SUNYA) has a student body among the smartest in the nation but lacks a nationally recognized faculty and is suffering state budget cutbacks of a number of its programs and services.

SUNYA has two locations: an older downtown facility and an isolated, compact suburban campus. Students take advantage of the school's proximity to the state legislature by securing internships and jobs with various agencies and groups associated with the state government.

The school is architecturally imposing. Classes are held on an "academic podium" which has symmetrically placed buildings on a concrete base. All the basements are attached. The podium is surrounded by four living "quads," each with a twenty-one story tower at its center. The architecture lends an impersonal feeling to the SUNYA experience. It doesn't help either, to be one in a lecture-center sea of 550, though most big courses enroll about 200 people.

SUNYA's resemblance to a factory can be misleading, though. There are annual spring and fall party weekends, free daylong concerts and picnics, movies, a large speakers' forum, and many coffeehouses. Students may indulge in drinking beer with friends at "the rat," the campus snackbar that provides weekend entertainment, or at the many area bars. Nightlife in Albany includes six or seven downtown bars close to off-campus life which remain open until four A.M. Some people drive to Saratoga Springs or Colonie for off-campus diversion.

Student activism at SUNYA may be an anomaly: it is not dead. Two thousand students marched to protest recent budget cutbacks. A number of students were also arrested as they held a sit-in to block construction of a parking lot on a recreation field. Admittedly, the motivation of this activism pales considerably when compared to the antiwar protests of a decade ago, but at least SUNYA does not share the apathy of the Seventies.

On the other hand, there is a strong "grinding" trend at SUNYA. Many freshmen enter as premed or prelaw and continue that way. But many students are also entering the business school program, which requires a separate application in sophomore year. An increasing proportion of students are accounting or business administration majors, and large firms actively recruit them on campus.

Albany has an international reputation for the departments of criminal justice, atmospheric science, and geology, and it is also strong in political science, biology, and business. Physical sciences are highly regarded, and the school has been improving its mediocre social science programs. "Social welfare" is now strong and the "rhetoric and communications" program is growing quickly. The previously extensive offerings of English, languages, and art have been trimmed, though, because of financial cutbacks.

The student body is evenly divided between students from the New York metropolitan area and from the rest of the state. There are active Jewish and Christian groups on-campus, and a kosher kitchen operates out of one campus cafeteria.

Tuition at SUNYA is low. About half of the students choose the school because they couldn't afford not to, and the other half because they didn't think a private school was worth the money.

Forty percent of the students live off-campus along a free school bus line that runs from the campus through downtown shopping areas. Many grads, freshmen, and international students live on the downtown collegiate-looking, ivy-covered campus. Uptown, there is a dorm oriented toward academics and a recreation dorm. Most students live in four- and six-person suites with double bedrooms attached to a common room. Each dorm has different living arrangements.

The usual extracurricular activities abound. Students also participate in the faculty-run university senate that decides campus academic issues.

All in all, SUNYA has a solid academic program, good extracurricular offerings, and opportunities for a good social life. And you can't beat the cost and SUNYA's proximity to the seat of New York State power (and jobs).

STATE UNIVERSITY OF NEW YORK/BINGHAMTON

Location: Binghamton, NY 13701
Campus: suburban
Undergraduate enrollment:
 3490 M, 3560 W
Total enrollment: 10,000
Expenses: $3510 (in-state),
 $4110 (out-of-state)
Financial aid: 80–85%
Library: 790,000 volumes

Student-faculty ratio: 19-1
Transfer students: 700
Median SAT: 543 V, 592 M
Fraternities: 0%
Sororities: 0%
Application deadline:
 January 15

SUNY/Binghamton is the haven for many a hard-working metro-New York kid. While fun may be had at many SUNY schools, Binghamton is by no means a party school. Even though people do take drugs and drink, these are not the sort of things to do during study hours, and due to recent busts, drugs are becoming harder to find. Students here are pretty liberal in their sexual attitudes. So no matter what you are into (so to speak), you can do it here, that is, if you can find the time.

Grades are the name of the game for the Binghamton-goer. If you are not into competition, do not plant your feet on the Binghamton campus, which is a stepping-stone for grad school. The greater percentage of the students are premeds or prelaws who expect to go to the best professional schools.

When these students are thrown into this superficial environment, primarily because private schools were too expensive, they live among four residential college complexes. Actually five, because if you are a transfer student and have the unfortunate circumstances of getting locked out of on-campus housing, the university makes an effort to house you at a motel just up the road. On-campus living is divided into Hinman, College-in-the-Woods, Newing, and Dickinson, each with its own distinctive personality. Of those that live on-campus, the majority are freshmen and sophomores, who usually escape to off-campus housing by their third year.

Off-campus living does not pose a great problem, since the county and the university provide good mass-transportation. Recently, the largest amount of student involvement was due to a possible cutback in the off-campus college (OCC) bus budget.

Most students would rather go off-campus to a bar than stay on-campus on the weekends and hit the pub. The only bar on campus, the Pub, is fun, but it gets hot and crowded. Various clubs and organizations show weekly movies and you can usually find a floor party or dorm party somewhwere. Off-campus, there are bars, restaurants, and even a shopping mall with many big-city stores. Binghamton is basically a small city with its suburbs; a mixture of a city and a country all mixed up in one. Most students here do not plan to stay in the area once they graduate, primarily because there are few job opportunities, and secondly, because of the weather. The sun never shines and it has been said that the Binghamton area is second only to Seattle, Washington, for treatment of skin cancer patients. It either rains or snows most of the year.

For these kids to get out of their depression from overwork, lack of social life, and crummy weather, there are sports activities. In addition to intramurals, "Co-rec" teams, usually made up of guys and girls from the same dorm floor, compete.

Most students enjoy getting involved in one sport or another, although guys seem to get more involved than girls. In fact, more money is allocated to intramurals than to the varsity sports program. This is not a "rah-rah" school with mascots and giant stadiums, and rarely is the participation overwhelming. At one basketball game, the winning team was quoted as saying "Binghamton, Binghamton, go back to your books."

A main "gala" event is spring carnival weekend, when you can see Binghamton at its best and rowdiest.

The guy-gal ratio is fairly even but that does not mean that this is the "Dating Game" by any means. People enjoy "hanging out." Hanging out consists of anything from going out with a bunch of people to going back to someone's room or apartment. And then there is "pigging out." This event consists of stuffing your face with crackers and peanut butter stolen from the dining hall. But don't worry, the extra weight that you might put on protects you during the long cold winter.

STATE UNIVERSITY OF NEW YORK/BUFFALO

Location: Buffalo, NY 14214
Campus: suburban
Undergraduate enrollment: 8072 M, 5799 W
Total enrollment: 25,100
Expenses: $3800 (in-state), $4250 (out-of-state)
Financial aid: 85%
Library: 1,700,000 volumes
Student-faculty ratio: 22-1
Transfer students: 1800
Median SAT: 485 V, 553 M
Median ACT: 24
Fraternities: 0%
Sororities: 0%
Application deadline: January 5 for fall, December 15 for spring

Surrounded by a sea of reactionary Bethlehem Steel workers in a town whose mayor hates students, it's a miracle that any education goes on at all at UB. This is a large university in the State University of New York system which has an identity crisis.

Once a bastion of liberal thought and radical activities in the late Sixties, UB is now a nest of conservatism. Today, the typical student carries a programmable looped into his belt rather than a gas mask or baseball bat. The radical English and political science professors have gone to Berkeley and the university administration is eagerly replacing them with foreign-born civil engineers. Curriculum changes reflect this trend. This swing to conservatism was inspired by volatile unrest a few years ago and the state trustees and the Buffalo police department seem intent on "keeping control."

The other real bummer about UB that contributes to its identity crisis is that it is split into two campuses, five miles apart. Since the course schedules are not coordinated either by department or time, a student here can spend as much as an hour-and-a-half a day riding back and forth on the intracampus Bluebird buses.

However, all is not Henry Fonda and Richard Nixon. Culturally, Buffalo is not desolate. Buffalo sports reams of concerts (often sponsored by the UB student association), is endowed with a fine orchestra for the classical scene, and features the Albright-Knox Art Gallery, which has one of the most extensive modern art collections in North America.

Most students are interested in little more than getting Bs in their courses and partying. There are, however, a few student organizations like the student paper and a public interest advocacy group which have acquired sturdy local reputations and have become an effective student voice.

The innovative and radical course offerings have been largely curtailed and humanities departments trimmed while the resources and faculty of management and computer science have been tremendously expanded. This curriculum switch has changed Buffalo's atmosphere to one of terminal "pre-job."

But there are some good points about UB. The course selection is extensive. UB has its own observatory. It has a nuclear reactor which leaked short-lived particles into the Buffalo sewer system last year. It has a small group of students and professors who don't kiss political or administrative ass for tenure or research grants. It has several local cafés where poets speak and amateurs play the harmonica. (As a matter of fact, the bar situation in Buffalo is not bad if you have a car. Most of them usually have some pretty good New Wave or jazz bands. . . .) As far as drugs go, pot's the norm, and only the richer students can afford coke. Rumor has it that some biochemistry grad students make their own acid.

In short, it is easy to get lost in such a large university. But there are a few active clubs and activities which offer some creative and challenging companionship and extracurricular learning.

One more thing, it's cheap, with an appealing price tag especially if you are an in-stater. Except for the large number of foreign students, almost all the students are from New York State with a good portion from downstate and "the city" (who like to go to discos or imitate Woody Allen).

Buffalo is in all honesty an ugly city with unbearable weather. But escape to Canada offers relief.

If you're psyched for a good four years, even the weather won't matter.

STATE UNIVERSITY OF NEW YORK/STONY BROOK

Location: Stony Brook, NY 11794
Campus: suburban
Undergraduate enrollment: 5800 M, 4700 W
Total enrollment: 16,000
Expenses: $3200 (in-state), $3600 (out-of-state)
Financial aid: 60%
Library: 1,500,000 volumes

Student-faculty ratio: 17–1
Transfer students: 1100
Median SAT: NA
Fraternities: 1%
Sororities: 0%
Application deadline: January 1 for fall, December 1 for spring

The sprawling State University of New York/Stony Brook, constantly in the midst of construction and change, starkly contrasts the quaint waterfront village on the Long Island Sound which surrounds it. Opened in 1962, it has grown from a small campus for the arts and sciences to a major cultural, medical, and economic center for Long Island with about 16,000 undergraduates and graduates.

The physics department, which maintains its own Van de Graaf accelerator and stars Nobel Prize-winner C. N. Yang, has been widely respected for more than a decade. More recent additions include a Fine Arts Center, which has hosted several of the world's finest musicians, and a Health Sciences Center, which boasts a highly sophisticated 540-bed teaching hospital for tertiary care that is being opened in stages throughout the 1980s. Several upper division (junior and senior) medical-related programs are offered in the fields of allied health professions, social welfare, and nursing.

A major complaint, that the university has little regard for the undergraduate, is borne out by an unusually high attrition rate (about forty percent in 1979) among freshmen and sophomores. Lower-division classes are generally large lecture courses which tend to be graded on a straight C curve with no pluses or minuses. Academically, the school is highly rated in fields such as physics, engineering, chemistry, biology, and applied math, but it is also extremely competitive.

Many on-campus residents are forced to live as triples in two-person occupancies. Freshman and sophomore residents can't bring cars on campus and those studdnts with cars find parking tight. A decent intramural sports program exists for residents, although the facilities are rundown and outdated. The varsity athletic student-funded program receives negligible state assistance.

Social life is virtually nonexistent for commuters, who generally feel like outsiders. Both residents and commuters may take advantage of the largest library facility on the island and a small, usually understaffed, all-purpose "student union." Residents, however, usually have small, student-run coffeehouses or bars in their buildings, which administrators are constantly looking for excuses to close. Dorm cooking facilities are inadequate, so without your own hotplate and broiler oven, the optional twice-daily meal plan is not a bad alternative.

Other than the dormitories, most facilities are closed by midnight. On the weekends, a large portion of the campus community goes home. Most people who go to Stony Brook come from Long Island or Manhattan and to get to campus, a car is practically a necessity. Although the local roads are overburdened, a car is more effective than the erratic bus service or pathetic train service.

Despite its modernistic appearance, the university has avoided complete urbanization. Several scattered wooded areas over its 1100-acre expanse tend to take away from its coldness and impersonality. The surrounding towns of Stony Brook, Setauket, and Port Jefferson contain both the aspects of a seventeenth-century colonial village and the advantages of Long Island's numerous parks, beaches, restaurants, and bars not far (about fifty miles) from New York City. The town of Stony Brook was restored to fit the image of Williamsburg, Virginia, by philanthropist Ward Melville, who donated the parcel of land where the university now stands.

The campus itself, offers more than fifty different clubs and organizations. Though things tend to be slow on weekends, there are parties most nights, including a campuswide Quad Fest with live bands and beer.

All in all, Stony Brook offers something for everyone and lots of future opportunities as the university continues to grow and expand.

NEW YORK UNIVERSITY

Location: New York, NY 10003
Campus: city center
Undergraduate enrollment:
  5000 M, 5000 W
Total enrollment: 48,000
Expenses: $7500
Financial aid: 70%
Library: 2,100,000 volumes

Student-faculty ratio: 13-1
Transfer students: 2000
Median SAT: NA
Fraternities: 1%
Sororities: 3-5%
Application deadline:
  February 1

NYU is a well-known, high-quality university in Greenwich Village, one of the more attractive parts of New York City. Among its more famous alumni or near-alumni is Woody Allen, who flunked out in his first year there. Allen's personality aside, it's not surprising that he couldn't hack it. The work load at NYU is relatively heavy, and the challenges of functioning in a large city university shouldn't be underestimated.

NYU is in the process of upgrading itself both academically and financially. The university is trying to attract a better student and increase its reputation across the country. Thus, competition at NYU is somewhat tighter than it used to be.

Premed students at NYU are notoriously ruthless in their competition. Ruining each other's biology experiments, stealing each other's notes, and other pranks are not uncommon.

The school is in the process of instituting general education requirements that become effective for the class entering in the fall, 1981. Distribution requirements in social sciences, humanities, and literature will then go into effect. The university already requires two terms of composition and a course in mathematics.

Threatened by financial crises in the mid-Seventies, NYU is now pouring money into its arts and sciences, thanks in part to $115 million realized from its sale of the C. F. Mueller Spaghetti Company. This injection of vitality means new faculty positions, and with it a growing university enrollment. NYU is looking forward to brighter days ahead with a $1 million grant from Warner Communications, Inc. The school of the arts is developing a new facility for its institute of "film and television," and new programs in dramatic writing and telecommunications.

NYU professors are quite demanding. It is hard to find the proverbial "easy A" among the many course offerings. Most professors stress creative thinking in order to balance the large quantities of memorization or intensive study required in many courses. Among the best departments are psychology, classics, philosophy, Spanish, and art history.

The university has a pass/fail option, much to the delight of students who want to take difficult or specialized courses outside their major just for the sake of exposure to different areas of knowledge. Unfortunately, the option can be used only once per semester and is irrevocable several weeks after course registration. Aside from the requirements, the freedom to choose your courses and the resultant feeling that you are being treated as an adult capable of making your own decisions are two of the very positive aspects of NYU academic life. Skilled advisors who have taken many of the courses themselves are available for consultation.

The social life at NYU is inseparable from that of New York City itself. None of the students, including those living in the dormitories, restrict themselves to the activities organized by the university. These include the usual concerts (mostly rock and jazz), parties, movies, and lectures. But within blocks of the complex of buildings that make up NYU are nightclubs, off-Broadway theaters, innumerable restaurants, parks, boutiques, and all the allure of "Fun City."

Most of the students live off-campus. NYU is experiencing a serious housing shortage, but with Manhattan's one percent apartment vacancy rate apartments are also becoming harder to get. According to some people living in the dorms, the atmosphere on-campus is also like that of having your own apartment. There is a lot of privacy, and most dorm residents keep to themselves. There is a group of students who organize occasional get-togethers and parties in the dorms, but don't expect to be able just to drift along with organized social activities. NYU is not the kind of place where people will take you under their wing and introduce you to all their friends. If you're not the kind of person who is willing or able to actively seek out friendships on your own, you are likely to spend a very lonely four years.

We are told that the three regular student school papers provide open forums for the venting of student grievances. None of them is under any supervision by the school other than in their budget guidelines. NYU also has a radio station, WNYU-FM that broadcasts from four P.M. to one A.M. Monday through Friday, and an AM band broadcast in the dorms from ten A.M. to three P.M.

NYU attracts all types of people and with them all sorts of talents and interests. Many students come to NYU just to experience life in

New York, and the city provides incredible resources for the school, if one takes the initiative to use them. Internships with galleries, museums, and artists are all available. NYU also draws prominent speakers and lecturers from the New York community. Away from campus, the university has programs abroad as well as in the city. It maintains its own facilities in various European cities.

If you have always fantasized about living in "the Village," NYU is the obvious choice for you. Come prepared to make the most of it, for it offers you experiences and facilities you might not find elsewhere. But you'd better be willing to work, for both your academic life and your social life.

UNIVERSITY OF NORTH CAROLINA/CHAPEL HILL

Location: Chapel Hill, NC 27514
Campus: rural
Undergraduate enrollment:
 6900 M, 7100 W
Total enrollment: 20,000
Expenses: $3100 (in-state),
 $5200 (out-of-state)
Financial aid: 35%
Library: 2,800,000 volumes

Student-faculty ratio: 14–1
Transfer students: 750
Median SAT: 525 V, 560 M
Fraternities: 19%
Sororities: 19%
Application deadline:
 February 1

Images of an idyllic existence hang over the University of North Carolina. "Blue Heaven," they call it. "A town touched by strange magic." "The Southern Part of Heaven." But it was an ultraconservative state senator who captured its most distinctive characteristic. During a session of the legislature, he suggested that a fenced-in Chapel Hill would serve well as the new State zoo.

If a zoo is an exotic collection of animal life, then Chapel Hill may well qualify. For it is a sanctuary for a wide spectrum of life-styles. Living in peaceful coexistence are the Greeks and freaks, Southern belles and women's libbers, dorm rats and apartment dwellers, downhomers and out-of-staters, homos and heteros, activists and passivists, whites and blacks, and conservatives and liberals.

The problem in Chapel Hill—if it can be called a problem—is that the environment can often be as titillating as the academics. Chapel Hill is a total living and learning experience, and many students prefer to live and learn outside of the classroom and the library. Still, enough students are into steady "booking" that UNC consistently turns out its share of Rhodes Scholars and other prestigious graduates.

Academics can be extremely challenging for those who seek out the right professors and courses, but they can be equally dull for those who wait for such professors and courses to come along. And whether or not one's course of study is interesting and demanding, there are always plenty of social and extracurricular distractions waiting to lure one away from the books. The student union does a good job providing current as well as tried and true films (for free); the Playmakers Repertory Company opens several full-scale productions a year, while the Laboratory Theater presents many less-elaborate but high-quality productions. The Union Forum, the Carolina Colloquium, and the Carolina Symposium bring a number of top-notch and occasionally controversial speakers to campus each year. There are numerous other activities available including *The Daily Tar Heel,* yearbook, student radio, the Association for Women Students, and the Black Student Movement, to name a few. The Southeastern Gay Conference has met at UNC for the past few years.

In addition to the "enriching" activities that can eat up one's time, there's a lot of partying going on. On weeknights, studying for a couple of hours and then going downtown for a beer (or two or three) is not at all uncommon. In fact, all of the many local bars are usually crowded. On weekends they're jammed. The drinking age is eighteen for beer (3.2 is all that's sold) and twenty-one for hard liquor (which is not sold by the drink, but everyone makes do).

UNC definitely offers the raw material for a superior education. The school of journalism and the classics department are among the top in the nation. Drama, English, and psychology are particularly strong departments. The school offers increasingly popular courses in American and Afro-American studies. Art history is good; studio art isn't. An individualized interdisciplinary major is available to the student who wants to create his own program. A freshman and sophomore honors program, as well as the option of reading and writing for honors as a senior, provides the opportunity to go beyond the standard requirements and rewards. And the student who can't hack four years in Chapel Hill can spend junior year on an exchange in such far away haunts as Spain, Germany, Columbia, Toronto, or even beach-bumming in Puerto Rico. If one is more grimly pre-professional, UNC provides political internships in Raleigh and Washington, D. C.

UNC's reputation extends well beyond the state borders, and the school is a popular choice for non-Carolinians. Admission for out-of-state students is highly competitive, since the number of places for them is limited. There are always srong contingents of Northeasterners, Virginians, and Georgians.

Athletics at UNC are big-time. Football weekends are major social events in the fall, and in the winter the ever-powerful basketball team is the toast of the town. Students are always willing to camp out for twenty-four hours to get tickets for the big games, a fact of life necessitated by the lack of a major coliseum.

Many upperclassmen live off-campus; freshmen are required to live in dorms. Apartments or small houses are not hard to come by if the student begins the search long enough in advance. Most dorms make a good effort toward social planning, and a few even offer academic courses to their residents. Restrictive quotas unfortunately force many juniors out of university housing.

Almost everyone who spends any time at UNC ends up loving it. UNC is the oldest and the best state university in the South and offers a chance to meet an interesting variety of people and to get an excellent education in a low-pressure environment.

NORTHEASTERN UNIVERSITY

Location: Boston, MA 02115
Campus: city center
Undergraduate enrollment: 9000 M, 6000 W
Total enrollment: 40,000
Expenses: $5600
Financial aid: 62%
Library: 8,000,000 volumes

Student-faculty ratio: 18–1
Transfer students: 800
Median SAT: M: 440 V, 510 M; W: 440 V, 490 M
Fraternities: 8%
Sororities: 4%
Application deadline: April 1

Many unkind words have been spoken about Northeastern University, most having to do with the fact that the school offers very little personal contact. First of all, Northeastern is large. It's the largest private university in the United States, and it has a library absurdly small in proportion to its number of students. But Northeastern has its assets and they are notable.

One of the best things about Northeastern is its location—Boston. No student (and we really mean *no* student) wants to leave the "Hub of the Universe" once he is here. Boston is the student center of the country, with more than fifty colleges located within a thirty-mile radius. With its numerous museums, historical sites, and cultural aspects, Boston is called home by many after graduation.

If extracurricular activities are your thing, Northeastern may be for you. There's something for everyone, from Ping-Pong to billiards to swimming to football. Whatever it is you like, you'll find it at Northeastern.

And then, of course, there is Northeastern's main attraction—"co-op," a plan that attracts over ninety percent of the school's upperclassmen. The "co-op" program, if followed to the fullest extent, requires a student to spend five years accumulating the credits for a B. A. Under a trimester plan, students spend eight to fifteen four-month blocks on campus, with the seven intersticed four-month blocks on the job. But many students choose to modify the program in order to complete the B. A. in four years or even less. The results for the program, as one might imagine, are confusion, alienation, and disunity. Friendships form, break, and reform with a rapidity that plays havoc with emotions. The splitting of all studies into neatly handled semester courses eliminates depth and precise focus in most of the classroom work. And unless they stay in Boston at all times, and in all probability unless they stay in the same general neighborhood, and unless they forgo dormitory living, students have to endure the constant harassment of moving in and out.

Nothing is perfect, and "co-op" is no exception. There are times students are stuck with jobs unrelated to their majors. It is hard for students not living at home to make decent money. Many students complain about low salaries and high tuition.

But, as the old saw goes, every dark cloud has a silver lining. The major benefit from "co-op" jobs is not money—it's experience. The difference, we are told, between a Northeastern graduate and a grad from any other four-year college is noticeable in the "real world." Northeastern grads settle in much faster and, in many cases, are hired right out of college by their "co-op" employers. A large majority of Northeastern students like their jobs and find them a rewarding experience.

Freshmen are required to attend classes from September to June. If students don't like their particular job, they can always change if another is available. Sometimes "co-op" sends students over to Europe in exchange programs.

Despite its enrollment, Northeastern is a remarkably concentrated campus. You can walk from one end to the other in ten minutes. If you're not fussy about parking in the nearest space to the heart of the campus, you're all set—there are six parking lots with plenty of room for everyone.

Northeastern has improved dramatically over the past ten to fifteen years in both quality of education and physical appearance. The faculty is becoming more in-tune with the students. Fund-raising efforts have proven to be an enormous success in erecting new buildings.

Northeastern is not for everyone. If you like a grassy spread-out campus, stay way. Although many programs offer a regular four-year course sans "co-op," few take advantage of it because they can get that anywhere else. Northeastern borders on a ghetto, and a few edges around the campus are definitely labeled "unsafe." Some may find the vocational orientation distinctly not to their liking.

But if you come to Northeastern (with these caveats in mind), get involved and meet people, study (a little goes a long way), and take advantage of what Boston has to offer, you probably won't be disappointed.

NORTHWESTERN UNIVERSITY

Location: Evanston, IL 60201
Campus: suburban
Undergraduate enrollment:
 3500 M, 3000 W
Total enrollment: 12,500
Expenses: $8215
Financial aid: 58%
Library: 2,800,000 volumes
Student-faculty ratio: 10–1
Transfer students: 200
Median SAT: 620 V, 640M
Median ACT: 29
Fraternities: 24%
Sororities: 29%
Application deadline:
 February 15

The typical Northwestern student—if there is such an animal—is a serious, career-minded, relatively conservative individual.

But there really is no typical student at NU. Although the largest percentage of students come from the Midwest, the 12,500-member student body is drawn from all over the United States, with sizable portions from the East and South. They range in political orientation from extreme left to extreme right, but political activism is usually limited to writing letters to the editor of the school newspaper. Most wear jeans and T-shirts to class (and, of course, several layers of wool in the winter), but even this cannot hide their well-bred, well-dressed suburban backgrounds.

If Northwestern students share one thing in common it is a strong—even fierce—desire to suceed in the field of their choice. Grinding premeds and prelaws abound and "grade grubbing" is a favorite pastime. Many NU students came to Evanston for the specialized career-oriented schools. The faculties in the music and business schools are ranked in the top ten in the country. The journalism and theater schools are nationally renowned.

On the whole, the university tends to favor its graduate programs over its undergraduate schools. This has caused much concern recently among undergraduates, but most claim to be too busy with schoolwork to get involved with university politics.

This does not mean that campus politics have been put to sleep. Indeed, the students and faculty constantly grumble about the university administration. The faculty recently branded the administration "unapproachable." The university president often scoffs at the student government. Nevertheless, the faculty won its fight with the administration last year over improved salaries, and even students seem to be making small, but steady gains in influencing university policy.

But Northwestern students don't spend all their time studying and fighting with professors, administrators, and each other. Sometimes they argue for fun—NU's debate team is consistently ranked with the best in the nation.

Though the social life may be considered subdued, especially compared to nearby state schools, it does exist. Fraternity and dormitory band parties are frequent favorites. Liquor, though, is a sore point on campus. The spirits have flowed profusely at NU for years, but because of obscure laws the campus itself lacks a student pub. And in contrast to most college towns, Evanston has almost no bars. Liquor can only be bought in a restaurant with a meal. Still, the whole point could soon become moot: the state is expected to push the drinking age back to twenty-one.

The beautiful lakefront campus in suburban Evanston, just twelve miles from downtown Chicago, is one of NU's premier attractions to high school seniors. There is a good mix of old-time, Gothiclike architecture and modern abstractism, though recent construction threatens to turn the campus into a series of concrete boxes. Nevertheless, Northwestern springs are gorgeous. When the weather warms up, students spend a lot of time on the campus beaches, sailing on Lake Michigan, and playing intramural sports.

Winters, however, are notoriously obnoxious and may well be NU's biggest drawback. Blizzards are not unknown and neither are subzero temperatures.

Many undergraduates complain of a lack of cohesiveness in the student body, despite its relatively small size. One place they do unite is in their rivalry with the University of Chicago. But this is only by tradition. About a third of all students belong to fraternities or sororities, and Greek/non-Greek tensions still exist. The student body is similarly divided between north and south campus, and off-campus, science and liberal arts. But everyone agrees on one thing: the tuition is sky high.

One other thing students agree on—Northwestern's men's athletic teams are predictably miserable. The NU "Wilcats" are consistently the doormats of the Big Ten in football and basketball. Women's teams are generally better. But frankly, most Northwestern students don't care, because most Northwestern students consider themselves first and foremost serious students and not athletes—including the athletes. It's a tough place.

UNIVERSITY OF NOTRE DAME

Location: Notre Dame, IN 46556
Campus: city outskirts
Undergraduate enrollment: 5250 M, 1550 W
Total enrollment: 8000
Expenses: $6580
Financial aid: 56%
Library: 1,350,000 volumes
Student-faculty ratio: 13–1
Transfer students: 200
Median SAT: 580 V, 660 M
Fraternities: NA
Sororities: NA
Application deadline:
  March 1 for freshmen,
  June 1 for transfers

The typical Notre Dame student is upper-middle class, from a Catholic background (family and schooling), in the upper realm of the high school graduating class, and, most likely, a high school student leader. The current trend, however, shows that fewer people are taking on a majority of the available positions of responsibility around campus.

The pressure for a high grade point average at Notre Dame is extremely intense. The most rigorous programs are in the college of science and engineering. The college of business, in accordance with the national trend, is gaining in popularity and is also experiencing intense competition. Serious students do a great deal of work, although liberal arts is often considered a "jock" major. A high number of students are interested in attending graduate school, and many of their efforts are aimed toward this goal. The typical Notre Dame student is achievement-oriented. A sense of competition pervades academic life, and this is a source of complaint to many students, particularly those in the liberal arts. Because of Notre Dame's fight to gain national prestige in the academic world, administrators have helped to foster this atmosphere through stringent admission requirements (only eighteen percent of the applications for this year's freshmen class were accepted) and the wholesale hiring of well-known academic personalities with little regard for their teaching skills. A quote from an April, 1979, issue of *Notre Dame Magazine* gives the sales pitch that reflects this attitude: "Notre Dame—no longer the provincial school it once was, not yet the great university it intends to be."

It is very possible to get a good education here, in the sense of an education that is both well-rounded and somewhat suited to the needs of the individual. But you'll have to work for it—not only in the classroom, but within the administrative structure. It is easy to get lost in and frustrated by requirements and the structure of academic programs, forgetting what you really want to learn.

Many advantageous programs are available, but not widely publicized. Many professors are willing to take time and explain these programs to you: in general, most professors are genuinely interested in the students. The faculty-student ratio varies in each college and within each department. Notre Dame emphasizes its undergraduate program, so it is not unlikely that a student will have a Ph.D. as his professor quite a few times in his academic career.

Notre Dame is in its sixth year of coeducation and recently completed an evaluation of the first five. The report shows room for a lot of growth and greater awareness, but the vast majority of female students feel "comfortable" at Notre Dame. The uneven ratio of men to women is partly compensated for by the proximity of St. Mary's College for Women. The naturally sociable will encounter few difficulties in meeting and dating the opposite sex.

Unfortunately, Notre Dame has a low percentage of minority students. Some of those who are at the school have trouble adjusting. The questions of minority recruiting and counseling, and the problem of discrimination are being discussed with increasing frequency. In 1978, Dr. Hesburgh, university president, appointed a director of "minority student affairs."

Most students live in the dorms. Surprisingly for a Midwestern university, Notre Dame has no fraternities or sororities; the dorm life fills that social gap to a degree. The dorms are sex-segregated, and visitation regulations linger on.

Statistics show off-campus living is decreasing in popularity. Many reasons are given for this. Among them are the inadequacy of decent housing, lack of transportation, lack of security, and high cost of living. South Bend has an ordinance restricting the number of nonrelated residents in a building, which tends to exclude students from many of the safer neighborhoods. Over the past few years, however, a neighborhood society has tried to work with the students and the university to improve the quality of life in student neighborhoods and the surrounding areas. Student government is also working with the university to make off-campus life more attractive and alleviate the overcrowding problem on campus.

South Bend is far from anyone's idea of a college town. There are a number of bars within walking distance of campus, but the drinking age in Indiana is twenty-one (a barrier easily circumvented in some of these bars.) There are no theaters or places of entertainment off-campus within walking distance. South Bend relies heavily on Notre Dame/Saint Mary's, and Indiana University of South Bend for much of its cultural life. Many of these cultural events are, for some unknown reason, not patronized by students. Chicago is ninety miles away; buses and trains leave daily.

What do people do to have fun? Drink beer, play sports, throw small parties in their rooms. The drug scene is minimal, but growing. A good number of students smoke dope, but few are into anything harder. Sporting events are big at Notre Dame; many feel that the football weekends are the high point of the social calendar. The concert schedule is better than at most schools situated away from a large city. There are three or four major concerts a semester, with recent appearances by Boston, Bruce Springsteen, Yes, and Billy Joel. There is also a collegiate jazz festival and blues festival each year. Mixer-type dances are extremely rare, but most dorms sponsor at least one semiformal or formal dance a year, as do the various classes. The usual film series, student-union sponsored events, and dorm activities complete the social calendar.

Most students are involved in some sort of activity organized either by the dorm or by the university. There are four major publications: a daily newspaper, a biweekly magazine, a biannual "journal of the arts," and the yearbook. There is a large number of small sporting clubs, and there are extensive interhall and intramural sports programs. Notre Dame has many service organizations, such as "Big Brother" and "Big Sister," tutoring programs for disadvantaged children, and the Notre Dame Hunger Coalition."

Notre Dame life can be an extreme hassle at times. The big finger points most often at the administration. Many of its decisions come down from on high, with the implication that the infallible and omniscient has spoken. The school is run on the Roman Catholic model—as if it were a family, with the administration playing the lead role of

"Father Knows Best." Often a complete disregard for student input accompanies decisions which directly affect student life.

Notre Dame has many good people and provides the opportunity for a good education. And if you're willing to do a little searching, a good social life is not as elusive as many claim.

OBERLIN COLLEGE

Location: Oberlin, OH 44074
Campus: rural
Undergraduate enrollment:
 1380 M, 1380 W
Total enrollment: 2815
Expenses: $7600
Financial aid: 43%
Library: 800,000 volumes

Student-faculty ratio: 13–1
Transfer students: 80–100
Median SAT: 602 V, 610M
Median ACT: 26
Fraternities: 0%
Sororities: 0%
Application deadline:
 February 15

Though the motto on the Oberlin College seal is not in Latin, students here are often unsure just what "Learning and Labor" means. Which is not to say they don't know how to apply it. It's hard to imagine 2700 people (of whom thirty percent are Jewish and/or from greater New York) getting together to practice some kind of educational Calvinism in Northern Ohio, but here they are. And when they're not learning and laboring, they're congratulating themselves for not having "gone Ivy."

Oberlin, though a very good and difficult school, is not the haven of pre-professionalism one might expect. Almost everyone here works hard at something, but that something often has more to do with learning for its own sake than with any foreseen end.

Nearly all the departments are good. Sociology, communications, modern languages, and psychology (for those interested in anything but rats) are the only obvious exceptions. English, art history, chemistry, history, and biology are superb. World-renowned scholars are scarce in all fields but excellent lecturers abound, and best of all, they tend to have time for students.

The college is currently going through a phase of interdisciplinary fever in an effort to consolidate weak departments, cut costs, and present better course offerings. For example, a recently instituted "public service studies" program has grafted math and economics professors into a weak government department and brought political science courses up to date with student interest. Similar combinations have spawned programs in "environmental studies," "urban studies," and "women's studies."

The Conservatory of Music (the only thing your next door neighbor has ever heard about Oberlin) is and isn't part of the average student's experience here. There are undoubtedly students at the college who have never set foot inside the "Con." But then that is also true of the gym.

In general, there is a healthy kinship between college and "Con." Daily free concerts are well-attended and introductory music courses for the uninitiated are among the most popular on-campus. College students learn to recognize that in the midst of their happy abstractions a small core of professionals *are* preparing themselves for the job market.

Oberlin has a reputation as a peculiarly liberal place. This reputation, based largely on the past, though still viable, began with Oberlin's beginnings as a Christian Missionary training ground and frequent shelter for runaway slaves, continued with the school's landmark admissions of blacks (1835) and women (1837), and was rekindled by the educational reforms of the last decade.

Since the horrific arrival of the Seventies most of Oberlin's liberalism consists of the common conviction among students that they're going to that school with the peace sign in the "O." Over and above that, the school maintains an aggressive minority recruitment program and very adequate advising and special services for blacks and Asian-Americans in particular.

Oberlin has also held onto a number of educational reforms though their value is frequently debated. These options include, credit/no entry grading, a fairly lax probation system, private reading courses, an experimental college, winter term, and distribution guidelines (as opposed to requirements).

Oberlin's single greatest attraction may be its diversity. The ratio of students enrolled to courses offered is unusually high, and if the breadth of the curriculum is not enough to satisfy you, the option to major in two departments, to create your own major, or even to go somewhere else for a while, is all yours. There is also a five-year program through which you can graduate with degrees from both college and the Conservatory.

Even with this diversity, newly arrived city-dwellers tend to complain about Oberlin's small size and relative isolation. On the other hand, many come to savor this intimacy. Oberlin is small enough so that anyone can have a significant "place" here, whether it be in the

Computer Center or on the dance floor. It is so small that one may get the feeling that one's friends are being recycled. You end up sharing things you never thought you would have and though it makes it hard to leave, this is one of the best things about Oberlin.

Which doesn't altogether eliminate certain logistical problems. For example, what's to share in a town that doesn't serve alcohol in any form other than 3.2 beer, that only has one movie theater, and one half-decent restaurant? Moreover, Oberlin students are actively discouraged from owning cars, there is nothing but Oberlin in Oberlin and Cleveland isn't really worth the thirty-minute trip.

Making the most of life in Oberlin is a major activity here for the reasons just mentioned. The college bends over backward to import speakers, artists, and bands for students, and students, for their own part, know how to make a party when one seems appropriate.

Another aspect of this concern with campus life is the plethora of housing options. Some cater to races and languages, some to pursuits. ("creative writing," "organic farming"), some to inclinations (all women, quiet floors, Quakers), and some to life-style (co-ops).

Even off-campus houses (of which there are generally fewer than one would like) have been known to take names for themselves.

There are six cooperative dining halls at Oberlin where students plan, buy, cook, and clean-up their own meals. And whereas cynical onlookers force the inevitable comparison to fraternities, the fact that membership is governed by lottery, and that co-ops are coed, make them primarily a good place to learn through labor. And make friends.

Friends can be very important in a school as intense as this one.

OCCIDENTAL COLLEGE

Location: Los Angeles, CA 90041
Campus: city outskirts
Undergraduate enrollment: 800 M, 800W
Total enrollment: 1650
Expenses: $6200
Financial aid: 52%
Library: 330,000 volumes

Student-faculty ratio: 19-1
Transfer students: 120
Median SAT: 550 V, 600 M
Fraternities: 10%
Sororities: 10%
Application deadline: February 1

Occidental is a small, academic-minded college caught in the big city of Los Angeles. "Oxy," as it is affectionately called, prides itself on the paradox. The college administration has characterized Occidental as "a green place in the city," meaning that one can enjoy the playground of L. A. while insulated from its urban blight.

Indeed, this description seems apt in reference to "Oxy's" appearance. Although small, the campus is spacious, its grounds meticulously and beautifully kept. "Oxy" looks classically collegiate; Hollywood frequents the campus whenever it needs a college setting. The "ivory tower" metaphor takes on meaning here.

Despite its attractiveness, however, Occidental is not insulated from Los Angeles. The campus is stuck in the northeast Eagle Rock district, whose slum sprawl threatens to engulf the college. Occasionally, a neighborhood flasher or mugger pays the school a visit.

And to enjoy Occidental, one must enjoy Los Angeles, with its smog and stiffness as well as its playground potential. To enjoy Los Angeles, one must have transportation. L. A. still lacks a decent mass-transit system, and the school offers only meager bus service. A car, or access to a car, is a virtual necessity.

Two thirds of "Oxy's" residents live on-campus, and dormitory living comprises a large part of what is called "the Occidental experience." Fortunately, students are mostly tolerant; one is largely free to choose one's vices and pleasures without pressure or sanction. Students at Occidental come from a variety of backgrounds, and diversity is a key feature of the campus community. It has "Jesus freaks" and atheists, radicals and conservatives, and a significant element who don't really give a damn. Students dance in the quad, hit the beaches in the spring, and hike in the nearby Sierra backcountry. Intramural athletics are far more popular than the collegiate teams.

Most of Oxy's students are passive, serious-minded, here-to-study types. About half of them go on to some kind of graduate school. There's a lot of pre-everything.

The academic program caters to these students. It is rigorous, demanding, and liberal-artsy. The emphasis is on exposure to diverse subjects and opinions. The student is generally free to draft his own program of study. Although there is growing concern at Occidental about "standards," student independence is too large a part of the Occidental tradition to permit much restricting. A "free university," run completely by students, supplements the regular curriculum with offerings ranging from gourmet cooking to auto mechanics.

And planning ahead for your post-"Oxy" years, the college has several joint programs of study with other universities. Among these are a law program whereby qualified students may attend Occidental for three years and get a B. A. and then attend Columbia Law School for three years and get a J. D. Similar programs exist in engineering with both Columbia and Caltech.

Easily the best part of "Oxy's" educational program is its faculty. The professors—most of them young—are hired to teach, and they are expected to teach well.

The college professes an egalitarian campus atmosphere and to a certain extent attains it. A fairly small student-faculty ratio yields a lot of student-professor interaction. It is virtually impossible not to get to know professors at Oxy, and it is quite easy to establish good relationships with most. A common sight is a student and his professor meandering to a nearby hamburger joint, or ruggedly jostling each other in a pick-up basketball game, or sitting on the lawn discussing issues of grave importance and the "Dodgers."

Although the president of the college is never seen—except at the opening convocation—and rarely heard from, other administrators are almost as accessible as the faculty. Student opinion is sought and listened to.

The admissions office at Occidental considers the personal qualities of applicants more than most. Interviews are important and sometimes decisive. The college strives for a diverse undergraduate population. Minority applicants are encouraged, as well as out-of-staters. Financial aid is relatively easy to come by.

If you are admitted, visit the campus, even if you've already seen it once. Occidental is not the right place for everyone. You have to like Los Angeles, and you have to like serious academic work. It you fit both of those descriptions, Occidental is a pleasant place to be while getting an excellent education.

OHIO STATE UNIVERSITY

Location: Columbus, OH 43210
Campus: city center
Undergraduate enrollment: 31,200
Total enrollment: 52,100
Expenses: $3172 (in-state),
$4357 (out-of-state)
Financial aid: 39%
Library: 3,407,699 volumes

Student-faculty ratio: 20–1
Transfer students: 8700
Median ACT: 20.3
Fraternities: 9%
Sororities: 9%
Application deadline:
August 15

If you've ever spent Easter vacation on the beaches of Ft. Lauderdale, you've no doubt felt the dominant presence of the landlocked students of OSU. But there are more of them back in Ohio. Almost 40,000 at last count, and that doesn't include the grad students. OSU is a city in itself, with dorms twice as large as many entire colleges. An individual can feel hopelessly insignificant there.

Jokes about computer-card schools and "degree factories," which are made about lesser institutions, cease to be funny at Ohio State. The main campus alone stretches over 1700 acres and has 275 buildings. The curriculum offered at this behemoth of a college includes a staggering 5000 courses in some 250 programs of study.

There are a lot of other things to say about Ohio State, and we'll get to them shortly. But we're still awed by the size of the place. All of the traditional bugbears of college life—a freshman identity crisis, an acute sense of loneliness and dislocation, a feeling of utter frustration and inability to cope with one's environment—are bound to be accentuated by the oppressive vastness of OSU. We particularly want to forewarn you if you're an out-of-stater thinking about going to OSU, for many Ohioans are soothed amid the enormousness of it all by the presence of half their high school classes on the same campus. A New Jerseyan or a Californian is going to have a rough time adjusting to inner demands for independence and individualized life-style at this megaversity. You may seriously want to consider joining a fraternity or sorority if you opt for the Columbus campus—we practically guarantee it will be the only place at OSU where people will know your name.

If we haven't dissuaded you from going to State—either because you're an Ohioan with 300 friends already on the campus or because you can picture yourself surviving satisfactorily as a goldfish in the ocean—we do have other things to tell you about the school.

For one thing, Ohio State does not unanimously share the Taft Republicanism which has dominated home-state politics in recent decades. There is occasional evidence that liberal elements still exist, but moderate voices definitely tend to dominate student opinion at the school.

Clearly the long, popular stereotype of the Ohio Stater as the wholesome, handsome, easygoing, ass-slapping, beer-gulping jock no longer applies to everyone. And the legendary Woody Hayes's "clouds of dust" no longer pollute Columbus air, either—not since the perennially powerful "Buckeyes" began playing in their newly Astroturfed stadium in 1972. Enough of the avid Midwest sports enthusiasts (both fans and athletes) matriculate at OSU to keep the stadium overflowing and the teams winning.

When OSU students are not attending athletic events, they can choose from diverse activities in their own Columbus—or in Cleveland or Cincinnati for the more adventurous. A city of 600,000, Columbus offers the normal array of bars and fast-food joints, plus the concerts and other amusements that go with a growing urban center. Within the confines of the campus, moreover, are a number of theaters and two student unions.

Fraternities wield considerable influence in campus politics, but relatively little in social affairs, because of the sheer size of OSU. For dating, etc., it's pretty much "make your own," because social events on OSU's scale are impossible to schedule.

Dormitory life can be satisfactory, particularly if you live in one of the relatively new facilities, which are often roomy, pretty, and airconditioned. The on-campus meals, mass-produced for the swarms of humanity, are execrable, and force upperclassmen off the campus in droves. Friendly Columbus affords OSU exiles ample off-campus apartment space.

All told, Ohio State isn't such a bad place. The school is not costly, and for the Ohio student body it services, it may not be a bad bargain. "After a period of adjustment," we are told, "life becomes routine, and not at all unpleasant." Alcohol is permitted in rooms, and cars are allowed, but can only be parked on the campus perimeter. Once you get the hang of it, OSU offers a lot. But then, that initial period of adjustment can be a real killer.

OHIO UNIVERSITY

Location: Athens, OH 45701
Campus: rural
Undergraduate enrollment:
  5026 M, 4289 W
Total enrollment: 13,656
Expenses: $3471 (in-state),
  $4815 (out-of-state)
Financial aid: 46%
Library: 1,000,000 volumes

Student-faculty ratio: 16–1
Transfer students: 1000
Median SAT: 448 V, 463 M
Median ACT: 18.8
Fraternities: 7.8%
Sororities: 7.8%
Application deadline:
  May 1

Ohio University is not to be confused with Ohio State University. For although the names of the two schools are similar, one is a huge, training-school-oriented, extremely easy party school, while the other is a slightly less huge, distinctly nonscholarly, rather undemanding school, with much less partying.

Ohio U is the latter of the two educational giants maligned above, and the bigger in-state preference. Valhalla it's not, but because it is smaller and more progressive, it is probably the better of the two mammoth universities which provide the bulk of Ohio's dentists, sales executives, and PTA presidents. While Ohio U could not be called rigorous in anybody's parlance, it is blessed with a progressive administration and with at least some pretense at academic pursuits for the few students who are interested in such things. Moreover, the general run of its students, is of slightly higher caliber than the mass of Ohio State-types (both schools, however, are open to virtually any Ohio high school graduate).

Ohio University, located amid the rolling hills of southeastern Ohio, has a distinctly small town atmosphere unique for an institution of its size. The city of Athens grew around the university, which was the first to be established in the northwest territory. Many of the original buildings still remain, surrounded by tree-lined brick walkways.

The moderately large student body at OU can best be described as diverse, although about eighty percent are Ohio residents. Ohio University has one of the largest international student populations in the nation, with students from as far as Nigeria, Turkey, and, most recently, China.

The surrounding area, with all its offerings, provides OU with a special advantage over the many schools that are crammed into large downtown areas. There are twelve state parks and thousands of acres of national forest within forty miles of campus. Stroud's Run is a favorite swimming hole of many students when spring fever strikes and classroom desks sit empty. For winter sports enthusiasts, the hilly terrain offers the opportunity for both downhill and cross-country skiing (Ohio-style).

Ohio University is not a tough academic institution. Admission is open to just about any in-state student with a high school diploma. Out-of-state enrollment is limited, however, and the requirements are a bit stricter. OU offers top-ranked programs in communications, engineering, fine arts, and hearing and speech, as well as solid programs in several other areas. There are special certification programs including such areas as international studies, black studies and women's studies.

The general atmosphere of the campus, as well as the surrounding community, is rather relaxed and easy-going. Athen's nightlife is centered around the many bars within a block or two of campus. Fraternities and sororities offer alternative social activities for a relatively small but growing segment of the student body. Athens will probably never be a cultural hub, but the university does a decent job of attracting top performers, dance companies, singers, and guest lecturers. The theater, dance, and art departments also sponsor frequent campus events.

One of OU's major problems is housing. Many of the dormitories are old and poorly maintained. Crowding is a particular problem at the beginning of fall quarter, when large numbers of walk-on students arrive. All unmarried freshmen and sophomores, except veterans and commuters, are required to live in "university approved-housing," meaning the dorms or Greek houses. The residence halls ideally provide the students with a pleasant living environment offering special opportunities for social and educational activities. For the most part, though, dorms fall short of this expectation due to lack of student and staff support. The majority of upperclass students opt to live off-campus, though the living conditions and landlord problems tend to discourage some.

A relatively large university in a relatively small town, Ohio University has a lot to offer. In a time of declining enrollment among most institutions, OU has in the past few years seen an increase in both incoming freshman classes and transfer students. The financial situation, shaky during the early Seventies, has stabilized. The university has been able to put more money into much-needed improvements around campus. The academic offerings have recently been expanded to include the colleges of osteopathic medicine, and health and human services. With enrollment figures expected to remain close to present numbers, Ohio University's future looks stable.

OHIO WESLEYAN UNIVERSITY

Location: Delaware, Oh 43015
Campus: suburban
Undergraduate enrollment:
 1150 M. 1100 W
Expenses: $6150
Financial aid: 35%
Library: 400,000 volumes

Student-faculty ratio: 13–1
Transfer students: 100
Median SAT: M: 500 V, 520 M;
 W: 510 V, 510 M
Median ACT: M: 22, W: 24
Fraternities: 55%
Sororities: 45%
Application deadline:
 March 1

The first thing to know about Ohio Wesleyan University is that it is not a university. It is a small, private liberal arts college, full of many out-of-staters, usually bright, wealthy, and protected, who find themselves spending four years and quite a bit of money in slow, rainy Delaware, Ohio.

Before you dump Ohio Wesleyan because you don't have an umbrella, note that somehow its students find something to keep them content until graduation—usually. So why the apprehension?

Like most colleges of its kind, OWU hasn't had much room to breathe in the last few years. Money has been tight. But OWU managed to come out better than most by coasting modestly down the middle of the road. There is no flashiness and no frills—just straight-ahead schooling interrupted frequently by fraternity parties. Consequently, it's easy to accept things the way they are and come out with a respected degree with few questions asked along the way.

But if you want to go your own way, you'll probably get tired to swimming against the current. As a rule, happiness at Ohio Wesleyan is found in conformity, and those who hear a different drummer may be in for some hard times.

From the standpoint of academics, the college is strong but traditional. Professors, generally excellent, like to lecture, students like to take notes, papers are written, labs are recorded, and exams are taken. That's that.

There is no problem in getting individual attention from professors and a host of special programs can make one's education at OWU very individual. Semester study in selected fields in such cities as New York, Philadelphia, and Chicago can add some variety to one's program. Credit/no entry is among the more useful, though not widespread, options.

OWU can be the friendliest place you'll ever find. Students, faculty, and administrators are genuninely cordial and make you feel right at home. The administrators, however, are rarely seen outside their offices.

According to the OWU men, their female classmates are "among the most beautiful and foxy to be found anywhere." We have no reports of the opinions of OWU women. So much for prospects among the opposite sex. As for what you do once you find somebody, OWU has virtually no visitation restrictions. OWU has a good weekend social life.

The most common student complaints revolve around OWU's location. One student put it pretty well: "Delaware's a nice place to live—if you don't care where you live." The town of about 20,000 has a few bars, a movie theater, some decent stores, and quite a few "townies" driving jacked-up cars. Columbus, in some ways only slightly better, is twenty-five miles away, while more wordly Cleveland and Cincinnati are both two-and-a-half hour drives. Even if you don't have a car (juniors, seniors, and some sophomores may have them), transportation out of Delaware isn't hard to find. The town leaves OWU students pretty much alone, and neither Delaware nor campus police seem to get down on students for smoking strange-smelling things in their rooms, which most students do.

An excellent lecture-artist series and good concerts spotlight OWU weekends. In the past, Bonnie Raitt, Stephen Stills, and Chick Corea have all performed at the school. But these big nights happen at most only two or three times a term. The rest of the time, OWU students are likely to be sliding on the beer-covered floors, during a fraternity party.

Many students feel that frat parties are forced upon them as the only type of social life available. The administration has been indifferent to sponsoring any kind of social activity. The Memorial Union Building, created as a student gathering place, has not proved very inviting. Frat alternatives are needed.

Although the school maintains a quality liberal arts program, OWU is sincerely trying to respond to the job-hunting needs of today's students. Internships and off-campus programs are encouraged, and with a new career counseling center, OWU is hoping to maintain its good placement record.

The work load can be as hard or as easy as you choose, but one thing is for sure: the ten-week term conveniently enables you to do a whole term's work in the last two weeks. Most do just that.

After four years of having no classes on Wednesday, the administration decided to reinstate them to eliminate Tuesday night parties. Still, most classes meet only four days a week. Students take three courses each of the three terms. The six-week Christmas break is great if you can keep busy, but you may turn into a vegetable if you choose to lie around. School's out in early June.

OWU's food is okay, but that's not saying much. Start saving pizza delivery coupons as soon as you come to OWU.

Athletic participation is strong, thanks to the modern phys. ed. center. Nearly everyone uses it for one thing or another. Track and basketball look brighter in the coming years, and the soccer, lacrosse, and sailing teams are consistently nationally ranked.

At OWU students are conservative and life is mundane. Amid a petty social life and a lot of complaining, the school can definitely grow stale. But add to that a good academic program and it almost becomes worth the money. Students at OWU will tell you that in the end it's not all bad.

OKLAHOMA STATE UNIVERSITY

Location: Stillwater, OK 74074
Campus: rural
Undergraduate enrollment:
 12,649 M, 9354 W
Total enrollment: 22,003
Expenses: $2200 (in-state),
 $3100 (out-of-state)
Financial aid: 50%
Library: 1,200,000 volumes

Student-faculty ratio: 30–1
Transfer students: 2378
Median ACT: 17
Fraternities: NA
Sororities: NA
Application deadline:
 August 22

In 1890, Oklahoma A & M was founded as a land-grant institution with an emphasis on agriculture and applied sciences. The school's name has since been changed to Oklahoma State University, but its priorities have remained intact.

Programs in agriculture, veterinary medicine, engineering, and business administration continue to be the strongest areas in terms of student and faculty quality, and receive priority funding.

The school's largest college, arts and sciences, has a reputation of being a "sprawling program of low quality." Its lack of top-notch faculty and facilities has been blamed on lack of funding.

Capital improvements have been getting the lion's share of the funds. Construction of a veterinary medicine-teaching hospital is underway, while major renovation is either in the works or being planned for the Student Union, athletic facilities, and other buildings. This work has enhanced OSU's reputation of having the most attractive college campus in the state.

Everyone at OSU seems obsessed with sports; many equate athletic success with quality education. New administrators and coaches in the athletic department are trying to overcome a tarnished image left by recruitment violations and NCAA probation. OSU retains some prestige with Big Eight conference competition in most sports. The wrestling and golf squads have winning traditions and boast several national championship trophies.

Still, it is a source of frustration for many alumni that the football squad rarely managed a victory over arch rival University of Oklahoma. There is fierce competitive spirit between OSU and OU, with OU often gaining the upper hand.

For the most part, the student body seems as content as the cows which graze in the pastures outside this northcentral Oklahoma community. A few antinukes and vocal students make waves, but most seem reluctant to challenge authority or seek change. Student government is largely token with no real power.

The fraternity-sorority system remains strong. To the dismay of independent students, it is the hub of much student activity. But, the system was embarrassed by recent allegations of racial discrimination; one sorority was found guilty of such practice. The system has adopted a policy designed to combat discrimination.

The residence hall organization offers both high-rise modern facilities, and older, traditional dormitories. The residence hall system has gained an excellent record of service and organization, but students eternally grumble about food quality and small living space.

About half the students live off-campus and have been labeled apathetic. Most of them don't care enough to argue. Town-gown rapport is poor. City officials didn't gain many student friends when they banned open alcoholic containers on city streets, and held an election between semesters to approve a one-cent sales tax increase this year.

OSU students pride themselves on per capita consumption of beer and their ability to party with the best. Taverns and local movie theaters remain the "hot spots" of Stillwater (pop. 35,000) social life. The only question is: Are the students celebrating or drowning their sorrows? Stillwater holds no magical allure for most students, many who travel home, often to Oklahoma City or Tulsa, for the weekends. As for escapism, well, there's the ever-present drug scene that is gaining student acceptance.

The administration, faculty, and students are aware of the school's problems and are working in some ways to improve its overall quality and attract more top-quality students. Budgetary constraints make this process a tedious one at best. Politicians maintain a tight control of the purse strings.

However, since most of the money currently being spent is directed toward the agricultural and mechanical aspects of the curricula, a student with highly specific academic aspirations (i.e., veterinary medicine) may find OSU to his or her liking. It may also seem appealing to many more students but it seems that education quality takes a backseat to other things. For a majority of students considering an academic career at OSU, perhaps the best advice is contained in the old Indian adage: "Still water breeds still minds."

UNIVERSITY OF OKLAHOMA

Location: Norman, OK 73019
Campus: city center
Undergraduate enrollment:
  9000 M, 6500 W
Total enrollment: 20,357
Expenses: $2800 (in-state),
  $3700 (out-of-state)
Financial aid: 28%
Library: 1,500,000 volumes

Student-faculty ratio: 20-1
Transfer students: 2000
Median ACT: M: 21.9, W: 20.2
Fraternities: 18%
Sororities: 20%
Application deadline:
  September 1

The University of Oklahoma may be the best college in Oklahoma, which reveals more about Oklahoma than it does about OU.

Administrators are quick to point out that many of the entering freshmen score extremely well on the ACT test and that almost all of these freshmen have directed majors and goals for their college careers. The school also has a newly developed, limited-enrollment honors program designed for students who have the ability to achieve academic excellence. But dedication hardly infuses the OU campus. For the majority of students, OU remains the "gut" school it has traditionally been. Actually, the football program, another long-standing tradition, commands more interest than anything else on campus. In fact, the "Sooners'" return to national gridiron prominence may be one of the best reasons to consider enrollment at OU. Two athletic dorms (both equipped with color TV and special dining facilities) and curriculum stalwarts like "theory of handball" and "beginning tennis" testify to the athletic department's powerful influence in many areas of university life.

Football cannot be mentioned, however, without recognizing the "Pride of Oklahoma." The OU band, exhibiting both skill and showmanship, has become a large attraction at each football game. It, too, signifies OU tradition at each football game and it celebrated its seventy-fifth birthday this past year. The band, directed by Gene Thraikill, leads the students and fans supporting the football team and is another beneficial reason for coming to OU.

The quality of the curriculum can be quite high in many areas. The university has always been strong in the natural sciences at the undergraduate level, and the medical school advances steadily in quality and reputation. The history and English departments are the strongest outside the sciences, though teaching is likely to be weaker at the lower levels where graduate assistants have full class control. Class size averages around twenty-five in nonlecture courses.

At least one school official believes the university has recently undergone a "profound metamorphosis" in its social and political thinking. And indeed, change has permeated even the most basic aspect of OU existence. For one thing, striped shirts and short hair are no longer required for Saturday afternoon admission to Owen Stadium. For another, students are likely to celebrate the latest "Big Red" triumph by smoking pot instead of the more traditional sojourn to local beer joints. Dope, along with a light sprinkling of harder drugs, has become quite a strong campus influence in recent years. In fact, CBS reports that Norman, Oklahoma, is a regional center for the distribution of drugs throughout the country (a stopping point from Mexico). This dismays city and school officials, who manage to arrest a substantial number of students on charges of trafficking and sales each year. Simple possession (now reduced to a misdemeanor in Oklahoma) is, however, better tolerated, and for the most part safe either on or off-campus.

Despite OU's ostensible metamorphosis, the frats and sororities have withstood the heat of change and remain defenders of OU's more conservative traditions. Few blacks, for example, are members, and they have instead traditionally maintained their own social organizations.

Though some students live in dormitories or the on-campus Greek houses, the majority now live in nearby off-campus buildings. On-campus living is required only for athletes and freshmen, the former being strictly supervised in all cases, the latter only at parental request.

All in all, the living conditions are tolerable if not stimulating, a description applicable to campus conditions as well. Academic quality is high in certain areas and selective judgment and a little luck can turn four years at OU into a rewarding experience. And you might get to see the "Sooners" beat Nebraska!

ORAL ROBERTS UNIVERSITY

Location: Tulsa, OK 74171 **Student-faculty ratio: 13–1**
Campus: suburban **Transfer students: 240**

Undergraduate enrollment:
1850 M, 1850 W
Total enrollment: 4000
Expenses: $4025
Financial aid: 50%
Library: 250,000 volumes

Median SAT: M: 485 V, 545 M;
W: 492 V, 513 M
Fraternities: 0%
Sororities: 0%
Application deadline:
rolling

Oral Roberts University, in its commitment to the historic Christian faith, is geared to assisting the student in his quest for knowledge of his relationship to God, man, and the universe. Roberts, the Methodist minister whose soap-box oratory and alleged healing powers have earned him a national reputation, long dreamed of a university fashioned in his own image. And some Tulsans, particularly businessmen who are more impressed with saving money than saving grace, think rapid development of Oral Roberts U may well be the fiery preacher's greatest miracle ever.

We are told Roberts's accomplishments "could not have been done by him but through God." They certainly hint of the divine. In less than seven years, 500 rolling, suburban acres south of Tulsa were built into a modernistic $125-million campus. Full academic accreditation was achieved in less than six years with a first student body of 400 students. To top it off (literally), a 200-foot blue-and-gold-mirrored prayer tower rises inspirationally from the heart of the ORU campus. The legendary structure is just that, for in it dwells a twenty-four-hour on-call board which receives prayer requests from around the world. The tower is the chief attraction of Tulsa.

The educational facilities are well-advanced and ultramodern. The Learning Resources Center, which houses four and a half acres of library, laboratory, and classrooms, was called by the Ford Foundation "one of the most creative facilities on the American campus today." The building is equipped throughout with the "Dial Access and Information Retrieval System" that, with closed-circuit television, permits professors to make lectures and films available for student viewing. With the requirement of viewing "DAIRS," students are expected to attend classes alongside in order to have the maximum amount of educational growth and benefit from the "personal touch" of more traditional class situations.

It is the conviction of ORU's students and administration that the purpose of God for each person is to help him become a complete individual, a "whole man." This is the nucleus of the life-style and trend-setting pace on campus. All regulations stem from a fundamental criterion of conduct at ORU—"the code of honor." Acceptance to ORU is not complete until students have formally signed the "code of honor" pledge in Chapel. Along with the "code of honor," university regulations include required biweekly Chapel attendance, ladies curfew, neck-ties, and modest-length dresses. No drinking, smoking, or dancing is allowed on-campus. As President Roberts appropriately said, "Wholeness will be a way of life here."

In an attempt to strengthen "wholeness," the institution has channeled much of its religious zeal into a burgeoning sports program. In its first season of major college competition, the basketball team went in search of an eventual NIT berth. And ORU has climbed to the top in sports. In 1978, it was ranked fifth nationally in overall sports in the NCAA. All students are required to take a phys. ed. course every semester (complemented by personally planned health-education programs), and to participate in an aerobic fitness program.

The "City of Faith," which will be opened in 1981 is a testimonial to ORU's biblical belief of "going out into every man's world, where the light is dim." But ORU's biblical beliefs are also incorporated into its extracurriculum activities, and grad schools. The student association has affected not only the campus, but Tulsa and Oklahoma as well with its actions. The ORU music department's World Action Singers and Richard Roberts and Soul's A'Fire Groups "have sung their messages into the hearts of their spectators." The *Oracle* newspaper staff has refined the professionalism of the paper. Involvement and interaction is part of each student's life. The motley crew at ORU is woven together despite different backgrounds. Student unity is a key; President Roberts addresses the "family." With the opening of the schools of business, dentistry, medicine, and law, ORU has grown not only numerically but also in effect with human lives. Unfortunately, it also suffers from tenacious expansionism.

The school's theology department is nationally respected, but don't go to ORU just for a liberal arts education. Administrators and President Roberts are interested in the experience of the "whole person education," stressing the mind, the body, and the spirit. And at "Miracle U," "Something good does happen to you," for "the whole experience is life-challenging and life-changing."

OREGON STATE UNIVERSITY

Location: Corvallis, OR 97331
Campus: suburban
Undergraduate enrollment:
  7987 M, 5717 W
Student-faculty ratio: 17–1
Transfer students: 2192
Median SAT: M: 457 V, 534 M;
W: 440 V, 465 M

Total enrollment: 17,181
Expenses: $3850 (in-state),
$5800 (out-of-state)
Financial aid: NA
Library: 850,663 volumes

Median ACT: M: 22, W: 19.5
Fraternities: 10%
Sororities: 7%
Application deadline:
thirty days before
term begins

Like many states, Oregon possesses two major state-affiliated universities: Oregon State University and University of Oregon. Like many states, Oregon's dual system tends to produce a conservative-liberal dichotomy with the science-oriented OSU sporting the former image and liberal arts-minded OU the latter.

Oregon State University, located in Corvallis, is one of the few schools in the nation which is both a land-grant and sea-grant university. Originally an agricultural college, OSU's strong point lies in the studies of agriculture and agricultural engineering.

The university is made up of twelve colleges and schools: the colleges of science and liberal arts, and the schools of agriculture, business, education, engineering, forestry, home economics, health and physical education, oceanography, pharmacy, and veterinary medicine. Academic inclinations tend to the practical. Agriculture, science, and speech departments are among OSU's best.

Marine biology and oceanography research is conducted at the Marine Science Center in the coastal town of Newport, fifty-five miles from the OSU campus. Research facilities include two cruise vessels which conduct worldwide expeditions.

Because of its popularity, the school of engineering recently raised its admission requirements and limited enrollment.

Students in OSU's excellent forestry department have a tremendous resource at their disposal: McDonald Forest, an 11,000-acre tract curving around the northern and western edges of Corvallis. Agriculture, engineering, and biology students also use the forest for research work.

The school of veterinary medicine officially opened in the fall of 1979. A part of the cooperative Washington-Oregon-Idaho program with Washington State and Idaho State, the curriculum coordinates study at all three schools. An eight-and-a-half-million veterinary clinical and teaching hall houses the new program.

OSU offers some strong student activities and special programs. Student government, made up of executive officers and a representative senate, plays an influential role in university decisionmaking. Task force directors head programs in volunteer services; the experimental college; student, state, and city affairs; and environmental studies.

Housing options include a strong residence hall system, cooperative living, sororities and fraternities, and off-campus living. The Greek system at OSU is alive and well—in fact, it's one of the strongest on the west coast. In October, 1979, the Panhellenic Council was recognized as leading one of the top three sorority systems in the country.

For the independents, there is always "the commons," but sooner or later that becomes mundane. While traditional socioeconomic patterns linger at Corvallis more than at many other schools, pot intake among both Greeks and independents has climbed significantly in the past few years. Student sources indicate that McDonald, one of OSU's own forests, has proved quite fertile for harvesting the smokable weed, although imported grass is more potent. Alcohol is forbidden in dorms.

Besides Corvallis's size limitations, which prohibit a thriving social milieu, the town's weather often puts a damper on students' plans. It rains in the Willamette Valley from September to May every year. As one student noted, sometimes the spring rains don't end before the winter rains begin again. OSU students have found the nearby Cascades (with its skiing opportunities) one inviting way of escaping inclement Corvallis. The university even offers a ski class winter term, which includes weekly trips to the mountains for a full day on the slopes.

The emphasis at OSU occasionally fails to fulfill student needs, as in the case a few years back, of the state building a $425,000 horse barn when a new gym and updated classrooms were more sorely needed. However, new black studies, urban and women's studies programs are beginning to serve more current issues. Unfortunately, Corvallis may still be far from the sources of cultural change.

UNIVERSITY OF OREGON

Location: Eugene, OR 97403
Campus: suburban
Undergraduate enrollment: 6200 M, 5800 W
Total enrollment: 16,500
Expenses: $3500 (in-state), $5500 (out-of-state)
Financial aid: 40%
Library: 1,300,000 volumes

Student-faculty ratio: 19-1
Transfer students: 2500
Median SAT: M: 461 V, 522 M; W: 454 V, 467 M
Fraternities: 3%
Sororities: 3%
Application deadline: September 15

Few schools can make the transition from playboy school to radical mecca. But the party-oriented University of Oregon, long one of Californians' few reasons for venturing north of their own state border, emerged in the Seventies as a liberal bulwark of the state and of the entire Pacific Northwest. Today, we're told that students are still balancing that line between activist and playboy. "We may be tilting toward the latter. We still vibrate with activism, though given the choice between promoting human rights, saving a whale, and going to a function, eighty percent choose the function and twenty percent choose the whale."

Frats and independents coexist here, with low-key, high-quality fun the general rule. But the Greeks "love nothing better than low-key, high-quality fun when there is an independent around to have it on. Rush provides a perfect opportunity for this. Activities such as picking up olives off ice blocks with butt cheeks and jumping nude into the Millrace rank high on the list." The student union provides a popular gathering place for OU students. Sports remains a popular extracurricular activity of the Pacific Eight school, which is challenging California and Kansas as the track capital of the world. Eugene was the site for the U. S. Olympic trials in 1972, and the late Olympian Steve Prefontaine got his collegiate experience at OU.

Intellectual awareness has coincided with increased social concern. Journalism, business, and speech are appealing, and OU has prestigious departments in art history, architecture, and allied arts. Strengths also lie in the standard State U collection of liberal arts, technology, and pre-professional fields, with the best faculties operating in the education and economics departments.

A recently completed construction program has also served to boost OU's arts and sciences.

All that glitters is not gold, however, and OU still has some academic shortcomings alongside its improvements. A once-high faculty turnover has slowed down. Said one cryptic Oregon *Daily Emerald* editor, "The average age in certain departments is seventy-five, and we are lucky if they move at all." OU still falls short in many areas, including such standard fields as anthropology and sociology.

A definite cosmopolitan touch has developed in less-than-cosmopolitan Eugene. The university attracts out-of-staters, minority students, and a high percentage of foreign students. But tuition has been rising, threatening to price foreigners, out-of-staters, and the poverty-stricken out of the education market.

In sum, OU remains a bit disuniform. Some departments are outstanding, others respectable, several deficient, and a couple execrable.

Socially, a hodgepodge of tradition, trivia, and genuine progressivism can be found. In the Sixties and Seventies, radical politics helped to change the university for the better. But, today, says one student, "the influx of new ideas has dried up. In its place, we have stability and permanence."

PENNSYLVANIA STATE UNIVERSITY

Location: University Park, PA 16802
Campus: suburban
Undergraduate enrollment: 15,016 M, 11,503 W
Total enrollment: 35,093
Expenses: $4775 (in-state), $6270 (out-of-state)
Financial aid: 60%
Library: 1,500,000 volumes

Student-faculty ratio: 19–1
Transfer students: 1050
Median SAT: 501 V, 563 M
Fraternities: 14%
Sororities: 7%
Application deadline: none—November 30 recommended

The most important thing to remember about Penn State is that it's not called "Happy Valley" for nothing. Nestled in the mountains of central Pennsylvania, it is a three-and-a-half-hour drive from the nearest metropolitan center, Pittsburgh; Philadelphia is a four-hour drive in the other direction. The campus is isolated from the harsh realities of the "real world"—there is no pollution, little crime, and a general good time for anyone who wants it.

The campus makes up about half the town, State College, and lies in the shadow of old Mt. Nittany. The university community is self-sufficient for the most part; local merchants take advantage of the great amount of student money that flows into the town. There are sixteen bars, scores of fast-food restaurants and pizza places, and lots of little knick-knack shops where visiting parents can drop their money.

About sixty percent of the students live off-campus in apartments and single houses. Yet despite their number, students have been apathetic politically in local government. Only one student has ever sat on municipal council—that was in 1972 when eighteen-year-olds got the vote. Students remain apathetic in other politics as well; voter turnout rarely reaches fifteen percent of all registered students in any given election. The political mood on campus, though, seems to be conservative of late.

The student body is diverse academically. There are many who come to Penn State to party for four years; to them, a good time is more important than a good education. But recently, the competition for grades among students has increased, especially in business and sciences. Students seem to have an underlying concern about their futures; many students seem worried about inflation, jobs, and graduate school.

The faculty is equally diverse. There are few big-name professors. Young professors find opportunity here; in some cases, it is their first time teaching, and they take it on with enthusiasm and a genuine concern for students. But as professors get older and more concerned about research and tenure, they become less and less accessible to students, shuffling them off to graduate assistants.

For many freshman and introductory courses, class sizes are out of sight—400 students jammed into one lecture hall, for example. Consequently, tests are computerized and multiple choice. There are a variety of "cake courses" to choose from, that is, a minimum of studying will get you an A. Upper-level courses can be tough, though, especially in the sciences and in business.

Each type of housing is unique. The majority of students live downtown, with three or four students to one apartment. Apartments are expensive; landlords can charge just about whatever they want because of the lack of competition. Competition for apartments is strong, primarily because many students from the university's branch campuses—eighteen across the state—transfer from the main campus in their junior year and aren't required to live in the dorms. (Freshmen must live in the dorms. Unless you start apartment-hunting early, you may find yourself in a bind.

Dorm life can be crazy. "No-alcohol" policies are strictly enforced, but you can get away with it if you are sneaky. Security in women's dorms is especially tight; unescorted males are given warnings and fines.

Fraternities have come on strong in the last few years, due partly to the strict "no-alcohol" policies in the dorms. The campus boasts fifty fraternities and twenty sororities, most of them national. Three houses won their respective "best chapter in the nation" awards in 1978. The Greeks are very active in fund-raising and charity events, and help orgnaize many activities like Homecoming and Spring Week.

As for the social scene in general: sometimes, somewhere, every day of the week, someone is partying. In the fall, the center of social activity, of course, is football. For each home game, thousands of alumni and fans pour into the town for a weekend of drinking and tailgating. In the winter, the partying is kept alive in bars, apartments and fraternities. When the warm weather returns, it's back outside again.

If Penn State sounds like a Midwest school, say, one of the Big Ten giants, perhaps the comparison is apt. Football, drinking, dating, and fun are highly rated in both sectors. The Penn State student body, moreover, includes many people of Midwestern leanings, and western Pennsylvania is generally considered the beginning of the Midwest, anyway. But many Eastern influences remain. Life at "Happy Valley" can be more than just fun—it can also be full of academic rewards and hard work.

UNIVERSITY OF PENNSYLVANIA

Location: Philadelphia, PA 19104
Campus: city outskirts
Undergraduate enrollment:
  5051 M, 3135 W
Total enrollment: 15,637
Expenses: $8600
Financial aid: 50%
Library: 2,600,000 volumes
Student-faculty ratio: 7–1
Transfer students: 500
Median SAT: 620 V, 660 M
Fraternities: 10%
Sororities: 3%
Application deadline:
  January 1

Ask any Penn student what he thinks of the school, and he will probably tell you it stinks, but take this opinion with a grain of salt. Penn students have a habit of self-deprecation. Somehow they have gotten it into their minds that being successful means going to Harvard or Yale. Attending Penn was only a last resort after being rejected by "quality" schools.

As if to compound this inferiority complex, the so-called weak sister of the Ivies had the misfortune of being placed in W. C. Fields' favorite town—the butt of everyone's humor, Philadelphia. The school's founder, Ben Franklin, is cursed for ever having left Boston. Of course, Philadelphia makes up for a lot of things. If you dig gritty city life, West Philadelphia past 45th Street is your kind of place. For the rest, downtown Philly has decent shopping and entertainment, Chinatown, and Society Hill cobblestone streets. For those willing to risk the city's public transportation, the discovery awaits that Philly isn't really that bad a place.

Penn social life, we hear, is pretty good, and many freshmen come back feeling like they're at a very social Ivy League college. Movies, concerts, dances, and private parties are regularly scheduled. And then there are always frats, over twenty-five of them, which regularly provide their own forms of entertainment.

Many students move off-campus, often to pursue life in Philadelphia. A city with great restaurants, night spots, theaters, the Academy of Music, and the Pennsylvania Academy of Fine Arts, Philly leaves few big-city plusses lacking.

The Penn campus is politically quiet, and 1979 publicity over Penn women posing for *Playboy's* "Women of the Ivy League" issue put the student body in a spotlight over which the university had no full control.

While Penn has become yet another bastion of pre-professionalism, it offers a general, broad-based liberal arts curriculum. The reputed heavy work load owes more to the weight of premeds, prelaws, and others who add their own pressures of achievement than to a faculty-inspired burden. Even so, the format of most classes does little to alleviate the competitive and potentially impersonal nature of the school. Largely following a two-lecture-one-discussion-period-per-week pattern, about half of the courses come to depend upon the teaching assistants, who are usually graduate students. Individual professors, for those students brave enough, are usually more than willing to meet with students outside of the usual class hours.

Penn, however, fits very much into the mold of conventional academia. University profs all too often concentrate on forcing students to assimilate large quantities of factual material, rather than encouraging creative, dynamic thought. Reputed to have a larger-than-usual work load, Penn often emphasizes mere *quantity* of work and grades at the expense of what could be gotten, in terms of *quality*, out of many courses.

Despite certain academic weak points, Penn is by no means a bad school. In many areas, it can match and in some it can surpass any American university. Undergraduate science programs all excel, along with a revitalized liberal arts program. The nationally acclaimed Annenberg School of Communications and the influential Foreign Policy Research Institute are just an indication of Penn's various strengths. For those primed early for financial success, Penn's Wharton School offers one of the nation's most highly regarded programs in business.

A new building program (seventy-eight separate projects) has added architectural diversity to the once-staid campus. While accommodations in the new "Superblock" dorms are uniformly sterile, rooms in the tradition-bound Quad have "character," and (if you like a long walk to class) off-campus housing can be a pleasure.

There have been nonarchitectural innovations, too. In an effort to overcome the impersonality of the old two-lectures-and-a-discussion format, "freshman" and "thematic" seminars were introduced. The small classes (usually around twenty) tend to promote intimacy. Penn has decided to move to a "residential college" set-up for dorms, which stresses house activities and development of a house spirit. The beginnings of this move are seen in several "house projects" on campus: a language house for Spanish- and French-speaking students of American origin, and a house devoted to students interested in the arts.

From preps, "Jewish-American Princesses" (JAPS), and jocks to laid-back partiers; reclusive academics to political activists, there is little real pressure to conform at Penn. Although the majority enrolled are from the New York-New Jersey-Pennsylvania area, there is a sizable population of foreign students and ethnic groups as well.

It has been fashionable in recent years to deride Penn as being the "bottom of the Ivy League, an alternative for those rejected from Harvard or Yale." But to speak of Penn as a mere compromise is deceiving at best. It's a place for a student who has the nerve to go out and get what he wants. And he can have a pretty good time while he's at it.

UNIVERSITY OF PITTSBURGH

Location: Pittsburgh, PA 15213
Campus: city center
Undergraduate enrollment:
  6627 M, 5648 W
Total enrollment: 29,743
Expenses: $3900 (in-state),
  $5300 (out-of-state)
Financial aid: 65%
Library: 1,700,000 volumes

Student-faculty ratio: 17–1
Transfer students: 650
Median SAT: 520 V, 540 M
Median ACT: 23
Fraternities: 35%
Sororities: 35%
Application deadline:
  July 1

The University of Pittsburgh has been around since 1787, but few people outside Pittsburgh have noticed. Back in the early Sixties, though, some real waves were being made. Chancellor Edward Litchfield ruled the university and put Pitt on a crash program to achieve national prominence and publicity. His educational plans and building schemes were just short of fantastic, and the whole university was riding high. Then a sudden financial crisis shot it all down, and when the dust settled and Litchfield had blown away, the state legislature was the only entity with enough money to put together the pieces. Pitt became a state-related university in the late Sixties. No one knew if this would doom Pitt to the mediocrity of the state, or allow it to realize some of its grandiose plans.

The school is located three miles from downtown in Oakland, Pittsburgh's center of culture (usually pronounced "coilchur" in Pittsburgh). The location really is quite good: large parks, the Carnegie Museum and Library, professional theater, the Pittsburgh Symphony and Opera, shops and restaurants are all right on campus. Full of students (Carnegie-Mellon University is nearby), this university-cultural center is easily the most lively and interesting area for hundreds and hundreds of miles. The sometimes-opulent campus facilities reveal that Pitt was the recipient of gifts from the Carnegies, Mellons, and Fricks long before the rest of the country found out what soft touches they all were. With the future closing of a few busy streets, the Pitt campus could actually become quite pleasant—a rarity for an urban university.

Academically, the school boasts several graduate departments which are rated with the best in the country. While these add to the undergrad curriculum, senior professors do not teach many undergrads. Pitt has all the courses, majors, departments, and degrees you'll find at any large university. It also features an honors program with independent study and self-designed majors, a junior year abroad, and a three-year B. A. in English and psychology that seems sound and solid.

Pitt has distribution requirements in the natural sciences, humanities and social sciences. Credit/no grade options are offered in many courses.

When the state stepped in, tuition (for Pennsylvanians) immediately dropped. This resulted in much greater competition for admissions (virtually all students are from the top two-fifths of high school classes). But it also caused instant crowding by Pennsylvania students. More than half the student body is nonresident or commutes, and nearly ninety percent comes from in-state. Fortunately, the school is attempting to remedy its provincialism. The football team, for example, truly remarkable for its masochism, annually faces the nation's toughest teams, with devastating results. But the large commuter population guarantees that political involvement will be kept to a minimum, except among a hard core of student leaders who take advantage of the administration's encouragement of student participation.

If you're looking for the kind of four years offered by the big urban university, definitely add Pitt to your list. It's every bit as good as

Boston University, for example, only Pittsburgh, unlike Boston, would never (ever, ever) claim itself to be the center of the universe.

C. W. POST CENTER OF LONG ISLAND UNIVERSITY

Location: Greenvale, NY 11548
Campus: suburban
Undergraduate enrollment:
 2776 M, 2683 W
Total enrollment: 12,927
Expenses: $6000
Financial aid: 75%
Library: 550,000 volumes

Student-faculty ratio: 12–1
Transfer students: 1800
Median SAT: 452 V, 488 M
Fraternities: NA
Sororities: NA
Application deadline:
 rolling

For the kid who was weaned on Grape Nuts Flakes, C. W. Post is a natural choice.

The campus is the former Marjorie Merriweather Post estate on the North Shore of Long Island, and the college is named for Mrs. Post's father, Charles William Post, the breakfast-foods pioneer.

Much of the splendor of the old Post estate remains—the formal gardens, the meticulously maintained grounds, and the riding range, where horse shows are still held every year. Several new structures have been added, however, and their modern brick-box style marks them as dormitories and classrooms. Post has a beautiful Student Union Building, which is connected to a multipurpose concert/ lecture facility, known to students as "The Dome." Unfortunately, "The Dome's" roof collapsed in 1978 and has yet to be repaired. Predictably, the students prefer the woods to the buildings, and one could hardly blame them, for the rustic beauty of the sprawling, 315-acre campus is not easily surpassed.

Unfortunately, C. W. Post's academic quality is easily surpassed, although a fine education is still obtained by a hardy few. Post's academic offerings are a mixed bag, ranging from a decent English department to a mediocre foreign-language program. Music and theater arts are solid, the social sciences are good, and the natural sciences include a well-recommended psychology department and a tiny group of geologists. In the past, Post has been business-oriented, largely owing to the presence of the Roth School of Business as one of its graduate schools. Another growing program is the "weekend college," a popular program for adults.

All in all, though, you would be hard-pressed to find students at Post who think that the relatively high tuition is worth it. This problem is somewhat alleviated by a rather generous scholarship policy, but Post's improvement has not matched the exorbitant upswing in tuition in recent years.

Socially, Post does not offer that much. The majority of the students are commuters (only 1500 students live in the dorms) and by Friday, the school is deserted. If you are stuck on campus, a car is a necessity. New York City is only thirty minutes away and the Nassau Coliseum, with its sports, concerts, and entertainment, is just fifteen minutes from school. The college does have shuttle buses running to two of the nearby train stations but their service is sometimes questionable. Because of the "Dome" collapse, there is only a tiny lecture hall and concerts are few and of poor quality. There are plans for a new facility. Unfortunately, when plans were made for this new building, the students really didn't have a say in the final decisionmaking. As for Saturday nights, the people who are stuck on campus can go down to the Rathskeller, which usually has a band. Most students become bored with this after their freshman year, but it is still packed on Saturday night. Because of Post's beautiful grounds, jogging has become a favorite pastime for everyone. However, if you are looking for indoor recreation, Post has the ugliest and tiniest gym around. It hardly suits the needs of the athletic teams, the intramural program (which is a favorite among residents), and the students themselves. There has been talk of a new gym for years, but no construction.

As to why people would come and live here, the answer is usually the pretty campus. It has a way of capturing just what a college should look like. Too bad they don't cater the facilities better to the students.

PRINCETON UNIVERSITY

Location: Princeton, NJ 08540
Campus: suburban
Undergraduate enrollment:
   2895 M, 1550 W
Total enrollment: 6000
Expenses: $8661
Financial aid: 42%
Library: 3,000,000 volumes

Student-faculty ratio: 7–1
Transfer students: 30
Median SAT: 630 V, 670 M
Fraternities: NA
Sororities: NA
Application deadline:
   January 1

Princeton University's reputation for social exclusiveness, largely undeserved, is dying a slow and welcome death. Lodged halfway between New York and Philadelphia, in one of the nation's most attractive country club settings, Princeton today attracts its share of women (first admitted a decade ago), minority students, and political radicals. And, because of changes in undergraduate residential and social life being considered by the university, Princeton's century-old, unique upperclass eating club system may soon be drastically altered.

Social life varies greatly between underclass and upperclass years. Most underclassmen at Princeton eat either at Commons—five large dining halls whose food accounts for the popularity of eating clubs—or live and eat at one of two residential colleges. There is also a kosher dining facility, as well as other, smaller university-run eating halls, generally frequented by sophomores.

At the end of the fall term of their sophomore year, Princeton students choose among the diverse options for living and dining as juniors: a majority of about seventy percent joins the clubs; some, generally minority students, choose to join or remain in residential colleges; others, more courageous, stick with university eating facilities; a substantial minority decide to be independent altogether of university or club eating halls.

The thirteen eating clubs lining Prospect Avenue have experienced over the last few years a collective surge in popularity, after declining in the Sixties, and serve almost the entire gamut of Princeton students: from the Brooks Brothers-type to the radical chic. (Minority students, by and large, choose to do their socializing at the Third World Center or in the residential colleges.) Eight of the clubs have open memberships, but the remaining five practice a controversial membership selection process known as "Bicker" (similar to fraternity rush)—three admit men only, while two are coed.

If all this sounds confusing, don't worry; it's easy to move from one dining "option" to another, and many people do. Freshmen, by the way, are assigned, in groups of about twenty, to resident advisors-upperclassmen, living near the freshmen in their dorms, who help to counsel them and organize social events.

Housing at Princeton is crowded, but by no means unbearable. The school's philosophy is that dorm life enhances undergraduate life and, consequently, virtually no one lives off-campus for any one of the four years, in contrast to other universities. Freshmen are assigned the worst rooms, seniors the best. (A large number of seniors are able to obtain coveted four-man suites in Spelman Halls, which feature a living room, four bedrooms, a kitchen, and a bathroom).

As for the composition of Princeton's student body, about sixty percent are from public schools, the rest from private. Most students come from the Northeast, although there are a large number from California, and many foreign students. About twenty percent of the students are from minority groups.

Fortunately, Princeton's main strength remains in academics. Although the assertion that Princeton offers the finest undergraduate education in America is debatable, certain aspects of that education and certain departments are surpassed nowhere. There is a considerable amount of contact between faculty and students, and, in any case, there is less emphasis on graduate education—Princeton has no professional schools—as compared to Yale or Harvard. In a poll conducted by Ivy League schools, Princetonians gave their faculty significantly better grades for interest and accessibility than did students at other institutions. Academic pressure, though intense, is not overpowering, and many seniors called the rigorous independent research required in the upperclass years their most fulfilling academic experience.

Princeton is particularly good for students interested in mathematics, physics, philosophy, and history. The English and politics departments are also strong, and the Woodrow Wilson School of Public and International Affairs is a near must for the budding politico or bumbling bureaucrat. Creative and studio arts programs have a very long way to go, but are growing. The weakest departments include the newer of the social sciences—psychology, anthropology, and sociology. Finally, there is the freedom to roll-your-own if the traditional structure proves imperfect, as students can design independent majors.

If academic distinction is Princeton's major strength, coeducation has been its major change. Some 1500 women are currently enrolled, pulling the male-female ratio to about two to one. The effects of coeducation have been far-reaching, and mostly positive. Fewer students now leave on weekends and mixers are dead, although some men continue to date women from as far away as Vassar, Smith, and Wellesley. However, in and out of the classroom at Princeton, a good deal of tension exists between men and women. Some men apparently resent what they perceive to be a greater academic drive possessed by their female counterparts, as well as the women's advantage in social life. But many women indicate their social lives are unsatisfactory.

Princeton is politically conservative. Activity on the left is well organized and vocal but divorced from the rest of campus life. In the past few years, the most prominent issue has been the university's reluctance to get rid of stockholdings in companies doing business in South Africa. The administration is quiet, more intent on keeping the school solvent and following federal regulations than on taking political stands.

The campus atmosphere remains peaceful and often lazy. Princeton, New Jersey, is far from a major urban center and, rather, basks in self-imposed isolation. The town itself with its quaint and overpriced stores, caters to a rich suburban clientele, not students. There are few bars and no clubs—and the "night spots" in town close at one A.M., before the library. But, then again, New York and Philadelphia are easily accessible in about an hour through public transportation.

There is a myriad of extracurricular activities at Princeton—from a cricket club to a daily newspaper—which are largely easy to break into, and most students become connected with one or more organizations. All told, Princeton is well up among the top ten universities in the country and has a bigger name than most of the others. And as for prestige, nothing can beat being part of the Ivy League's "Big Three."

PURDUE UNIVERSITY

Location: West Lafayette, IN 47907
Campus: suburban
Undergraduate enrollment: 14,500 M, 10,000 W
Total enrollment: 30,445
Expenses: $3400 (in-state), $4700 (out-of-state)
Financial aid: 40%
Library: 1,265,000 volumes

Student-faculty ration: 12–1
Transfer students: 1000
Median SAT: 464 V, 541 M
Fraternities: 20%
Sororities: 20%
Application deadline: none

Purdue University, located in West Lafayette, sixty miles northwest of Indianapolis, is a school renowned for its academics—and conservatism.

The academics of this "land-grant" public institution are well known, with strong departments in engineering, agriculture, pharmacy, and veterinary science. Especially respected are the engineering schools, which are continually highly ranked and heavily recruited by industry; and the agriculture school, which advises and consults numerous agencies in government and industry, in addition to performing basic research to improve farm technology.

Courses at the upperclass levels in most curricula are taught by professors. Freshman lectures are led by professors and are often accompanied by smaller "recitations" taught by teaching assistants.

The campus is ideally suited for only half of the 30,000 students it now supports. The strain on facilities necessitates the class day to stretch from seven-thirty A.M. to five-twenty P.M. during the week, with Saturday classes from seven-thirty A.M. to twelve-twenty P.M., and some night classes. Night exams are scheduled for freshman and some upperclass courses.

The student body is seventy-five percent "home-grown" "Hoosiers," with the remainder composed of students representing all fifty states and thirty-seven foreign countries. The ratio of guys to girls has been approaching parity in recent years with a current proportion of about one-and-a-half to one. With all the diversity of the student body, however, the attitude here is one of general apathy toward campus, national, and international issues.

Almost half of the student body lives off-campus, with the dorms housing about 12,000 students, and the Greek and "co-op" systems sheltering under 5000 students.

Of the three housing options, the residence halls are least admired. Purdue still has restricted visitation hours for men and women in its dorm system, with men allowed in women's living areas (and vice versa) only between the hours of twelve-thirty P.M. to eleven-thirty P.M. Monday through Thursday. The weekend hours are extended to one A.M. on Friday and Saturday, with corresponding rollback of the morning hours to ten-thirty A.M. on Saturday and Sunday.

Visitation is heavily enforced on the female side by matrons, who guard the entrances after hours, and by the counseling staff, which "writes up" offenders. Sanctions against the offenders by the dorm or dean of students may result.

Six of the thirteen dorms are coed; however, this means only that meals are eaten with members of the opposite sex. Living areas for males and females are in separate buildings.

The administration has fought successfully against open-visitation proposals, claiming alumni support and academic intergrity as reasons to maintain the status quo.

Greek life is big on campus—at least for Greeks. Many sororities are as strict as the dorms, but fraternities are largely unsupervised. Forty-one frats and fifteen sororities have houses here, and a general animosity between dormies and Greeks exists, as can be evidenced by the annual scuffles on the opinion page of the *Purdue Exponent*.

Off-campus housing is popular, although some of the older sections of West Lafayette have been termed "slums" by locals. Even with declining enrollments, off-campus housing is tight, and apartment-hunting season begins around spring break.

No "college town" atmosphere exists here, as the land around the university is almost exclusively residential, with only a few eateries at opposite ends of campus. About six miles due east, on the U. S. 52 bypass, almost every national franchise is available, as are a few places a half-mile east of campus on the "levee."

There are a few bars and liquor stores between campus and the levee, though a recent crackdown on underage drinking has resulted in the only under-twenty-one drinkers being those with fake IDs. Parties are mostly off-campus or at frats, since restrictions against alcohol consumption are rarely, if ever, enforced. Some parties happen in the dorms, but only behind closed doors so as not to attract the attention of the counseling staff.

Drug busts occur whenever authorities become aware of drug consumption, regardless of the location. Dormies are especially vulnerable under the watchful eyes of counselors.

Frequent concert appearances by top-name groups draw many students, as do numerous films shown on-campus each week. Students are fanatical supporters of "Boilermaker" football and basketball teams, selling out almost every home game. Grand Prix, an annual go-cart race, is a popular student attraction, as are the evangelists, who entertain students on the malls when the weather becomes warm.

QUINNIPIAC COLLEGE

Location: Hamden, CT 05618
Campus: suburban
Undergraduate enrollment:
  810 M, 1507 W
Total enrollment: 3801
Expenses: $5940
Financial aid: 31%
Library: 125,000 volumes

Student-faculty ratio: 16–1
Transfer students: 100
Median SAT: 500 V, 550 M
Median ACT: 24
Fraternities: 1%
Sororities: 1%
Application deadline:
  June 1

"Quinnipiac" sounds like it should have been the name of a children's summer camp. Once a junior college, fifty-year-old Quinnipiac has grown up; it is now a four-year college that includes schools of business, allied health and natural sciences, and liberal arts, and also offers two-year degrees.

During 1979, the anniversary celebration year, the college dedicated a new academic center. This uniquely designed round building features a center lecture hall, with windows that look out onto two small courtyards. A wheel of classrooms and laboratories is built along the outer wall, while the inner wheel is composed of faculty offices. The new facilities include chemistry, biology, and physics labs, as well as a radiology room, medical technology suite, and carpeted conference room.

The largest number of students enroll in the allied health sciences and applied sciences. Many complain that too little attention is given to pure sciences and to courses in liberal arts. For a student who wants training in his specific field, Quinnipiac offers internships in most of the health science majors (and frequently in other majors).

The faculty of Quinnipiac's business school consists of a large number of Ph.D.s who seem to be both well liked and well respected by their students. Business offerings include hospital administration, a major which combines offerings in the school of allied health and natural sciences. Quinnipiac offers an occupational therapy program, is one of the few schools to have a B. S. in clinical chemistry and clinical microbiology, and was the first to offer an associate's degree in cytotechnology.

Its school of liberal arts has recently introduced theater arts and mass communications majors.

The school of liberal arts provides opportunities with the yearbook, the newspaper, the radio station, and a video magazine, which are also open to those in other divisions. The student government has some pull in collegewide decisions. Students are also elected to represent their peers on the all-college senate, board of trustees, and can sit on an all-student judicial court.

Hamden, Connecticut, may not be a cultural hot-spot. However, the annual Jazz Festival takes place there each April, featuring competing jazz bands, invited from schools all over the country. Honored guests have included Benny Goodman and Eubie Blake.

If Hamden life becomes all too mundane, one can always head to New Haven to experiment with the offerings of both the larger city and the Yale campus. Excellent theater and concerts are a constant there.

The Quinnipiac campus is nestled beneath Sleeping Giant Mountain, with its trails and outdoor activities. Other than that, however, the campus is very secluded. Students begin to feel themselves quite cut off from the rest of the world. Even though they live in the town of Hamden, most resident students are ill-informed about local politics.

About half the students live on-campus, in traditional dorms, suite-style dorms, or apartments. Another type of dormitory is currently in the planning stages, to alleviate a serious overcrowding problem.

Students at Quinnipiac come from all walks of life and all backgrounds. Even though the undergraduate enrollment totals less than 2500, you can find some real variety here.

RANDOLPH-MACON WOMEN'S COLLEGE

Location: Lynchburg, VA 24503
Campus: suburban
Undergraduate enrollment: 750 W
Expenses: $6000
Financial aid: 50%
Library: 130,000 volumes

Student-faculty ratio: 10–1
Transfer students: 30
Median SAT: 550 V, 550 M
Sororities: NA
Application deadline: March 1

Nestled in the foothills of the Blue Ridge Mountains lies a small women's school that prides itself on changing with the times.

Randolph-Macon Women's College is a school where the odd- and even-year classes serenade each other in an effort to bolster school spirit. Some traditions, like the seniors' Pumpkin Parade, make RM seem like it was cut out of the summer camp mold, but this brings a healthy balance to a college where the academics are taken seriously. The college is a blend of old and new, of a Southern finishing school (although they're defensive about this) and a progressive educational institution. It is at once steeped in tradition and responsive to change.

While freshwomen fulfill a distribution requirement of courses from at least four departments each semester, only guidelines direct upper-class course choices. Twelve semester courses must be chosen in areas outside the declared concentration. Most classes meet for one hour on Mondays and Thursdays, or on Tuesdays and Fridays. Wednesday mornings are left free for study. Attitudes toward the midweek break from class vary. While some find class time lacking, others enjoy the Tuesday-Wednesday or Wednesday-Thursday "miniweekend."

After the Pine Houses were closed due to damage suffered at a party, the social life has become more stifled than ever. Fraternity men from Washington & Lee and UVa still do roll down, but not as frequently as they used to. So, for some, the social life is oriented around the suitcase. Other women spend most weekends on campus in sisterly fellowship. Evenings can find them partying with friends in the dorms or in a bar (three are within walking distance). Also, RM's social committee plans a variety of weekend social events.

The honor system is an integral part of life behind RM's red brick walls. Enforced by a student judiciary committee, the code states that the student will not lie, cheat, or steal, nor tolerate others doing so. Under this system, students pledge their take-home tests and have organized a self-scheduling exam procedure.

If the small campus size and rural setting begin to make the world seem isolated, RM offers some great ways to see the world. Study at the classical center in Athens, participation in a near-Eastern archaeological seminar, and a "junior year abroad" program with the University of Reading in Reading, England, are among RM's eye-openers. Approximately thirty juniors take an interdisciplinary seminar and study two subjects in the British tutorial method. Extensive travel is possible during the four- and five-week vacations at Christmas and in the spring. Study is possible in special cooperative programs with UVa and Vanderbilt, while exchanges with Lynchburg, Sweet Briar, and the Seven Colleges are also available to escape from campus.

There have been rumblings for coeducation, but the trustees and most of the students seem content with things the way they are. Except for a few individuals and the articles in the student newspaper, there is little questioning of administrative authority. The faculty takes a sincere interest in the students, and communication between the two groups is probably better than at many other schools.

In any event, those women who do hang on for four years are perfectly able to hold their own in the "outside" world. About half go on to further schooling, many doing independent work on fellowships. Others, of course, join the suburban hairdresser-and-stove set, but they know what they're about—and are perfectly ready to let their husbands know as well.

REED COLLEGE

Location: Portland, OR 97202
Campus: city outskirts
Undergraduate enrollment:
Student-faculty ratio: 10–1
Transfer students: 160
Median SAT: 630 V, 640 M

700 M, 500 W
Total enrollment: NA
Expenses: $7200
Financial aid: 50%
Library: 250,000 volumes

Fraternities: 0%
Sororities: 0%
Application deadline: March 1

"Reedies" are a strange bunch of people, and they know it. Insanity—or lack of normal behavior—is the norm at this small liberal arts college tucked away in Portland, Oregon.

Casually referred to as the "Brandeis of the West," Reed has traditionally attracted a liberal, intellectual student body. Standards for acceptance seem higher than the statistical averages, and many students actually get into their work. Academic pressure is intense, and students are given extensive comments on their papers and exams, rather than semester grades. Letter grades are filed, though, for future reference, and students are informed if they are doing unsatisfactory work (C-minus or below).

The student-faculty ratio is good, and large lecture courses are rare. The fact that the president signs all of his memoranda "Paul" is indicative of the informality of student-teacher relations. There is a good deal of encouragement for one-to-one conferences, tutorials, and independent study programs from both faculty and administration. This personally oriented style of learning fosters a self-investigative approach to most subjects and also exposes students to various points of view in discussions. Academically as well as socially, "Reedies" are taught the value of individuality and self-expression. The science and history departments are particularly strong, while the art courses reportedly leave much to be desired.

It's ironic to note that, for all its liberal traditions, Reed does have requirements which tend to be quite limiting the first two years (including a freshman humanities course, which the students try unsuccessfully each year to vote out of existence, and a gym requirement). Perhaps the emphasis on academia can account for at least part of the high attrition rate. Out of a freshman class of about four hundred, Reed usually only graduates half that number.

In spite of the highly diversified student body, the sense of community at Reed is so strong it is almost overpowering. It is a common belief among students that life at Reed is incestuous in every sense of the word. "If you want to know anything about anybody in the Reed community, just ask the person next to you," one student explained. People seem to lack any true privacy. Though located in the southeast section of Portland, a fairly large city, Reed remains its own tremendously insular world.

As a result, Reedies spend much of their time "relating" to each other, or at least trying to. Though this constant analysis may cause a few tense people to seek shelter, the security of such a close-knit community can also have a positive effect.

Social life at Reed has as many different sides as the academic. There is no set life-style, and hardly any prescribed, organized activities. There are only a few interspersed campus-sponsored concerts and movies. Many good times grow out of spontaneous gatherings, all kinds of parties, or drinking beer at Lutz's Tavern. However, the drinking age in Oregon is officially twenty-one.

Fraternities and sororities do not exist on the Reed campus, and there is no effort to revive them. "Reedies" tend toward "relationships," rather than any traditional forms of dating. Since most people know each other, this often makes for complex involvements, but that's what Reed is all about.

Most varsity sports are played just for fun; there is simply no enthusiasm for squealing cheerleaders or heavily dated football weekends in the fall. "Reedies" are not lacking in other extracurricular interests. Some are into music, some into political action, and some into drugs (all kinds easily available). Some even manage to find escape in the academic field—a spring term course in outdoor body-painting elicited quite a response one year.

The unwritten honor code, which allows Reed students to take tests anywhere, also applies to general living—doors in dorms are left unlocked without worry, and the old idea of parietals has been abandoned. Students are expected not to act in any way injurious to the Reed community or any of its members. A rule so vague is difficult to enforce, and punishment for honor code offenders is rare.

Though living in the dorms is relatively unhassled, many students are forced to move off-campus due to a housing shortage. Not all move under duress, though. Large houses in the country are easy to find, and rental is cheap. In fact, overall, living in Oregon is inexpensive. Aside from the rain, which can get to be a drag, Portland is clean, pretty, and close to the West Coast—all factors making Reed an appealing place to spend four years.

Essentially, Reed College provides an opportunity to learn about yourself in the process of learning about others. A community that gives birth to many good thoughts and good people, Reed is an experience that stays with you for the rest of your life.

RENSSELAER POLYTECHNIC INSTITUTE

Location: Troy, NY 12180
Campus: city outskirts
Undergraduate enrollment:
 3500 M, 600 W
Total enrollment: 5106
Expenses: $7900
Financial aid: 60%
Library: 300,000 volumes

Student-faculty ratio: 11–1
Transfer students: 120
Median SAT: 565 V, 695 M
Fraternities: 32%
Sororities: 10%
Application deadline:
 January 1

RPI, like Avis and Lafayette, tries harder, and what it is second to is the twin domination of relatively nearby MIT and definitely faraway Caltech over the teaching of engineering to undergraduates in America. There is little question that RPI can offer several excellent programs in mathematics and the sciences, but its students seem to lack the aura of genius and the 800 scores on the math SATs which so characterize the students at MIT or Caltech. The RPI man is more likely to be a determined and hard-working student who got Cs in English and As in physics in high school, though a new infusion of life into the humanities and social sciences is changing that trend and contributing to a more balanced curriculum. Students in most RPI programs take courses in math, physics, chemistry, humanities, social sciences, and phys. ed.

When RPI programs aren't enough, cross-listings with Union, Albany Medical College, Skidmore, and Russell Sage take up the slack. In its own right, RPI provides some excellent undergraduate/ professional programs. Among them a six-year B. S./M. D., B. S./J. D. and B. S./D. M. D. are especially well-known.

Pressures on campus for academic achievement are great, but students do find time to channel their energy into other avenues. Although the extent of student participation in extracurricular affairs is not overwhelming, the newspaper, student handbook, and yearbook have consistently won awards for excellence. The FM radio station may be the best upstate.

For future politicos, RPI is burgeoning with student-student, student-faculty, and student-administration committees. There are varsity athletic teams, but there, too, RPI is not exactly a league power, as can be seen from a glance at the "Engineers' " football record over the past few campaigns. Hockey seems to be the favorite sport at both an intercollegiate and intramural level.

However, the sport which most RPI men would like to boast proficiency in is drinking. While cocktails and martinis may be quietly sipped at Princeton, RPI men prefer noise and beer, despite the fact that neither is greatly condoned on campus. Students, moreover, will point out that, while Rensselaer's football squad has never been known to be included in *Playboy* magazine's predictions for the top twenty, it has been rumored that RPI received an asterisk rating (too professional to be ranked) on the same magazine's listing of the top ten drinking schools.

On top of beer, there is the pursuit of women as another favorite pastime. Although there are some six hundred undergraduates of the female sex enrolled at RPI, students prefer to try nearby Russell Sage, Skidmore, Green Mountain ("The Groin"), and Albany State as hunting grounds. Once a year, the students manage to combine their love for engineering and their interest in the opposite sex in an activity which seems both natural and representative of the school: the Computer Mixer.

If you've somehow got the impression that RPI students spend too much time drinking and socializing, you're right. But any diversion which helps students keep their mind off Troy, New York, a particularly dull and ugly city, can only be excused.

One final note to women: women at RPI often find themselves competing with men academically and with other women socially, which combined with a past tradition of male domination in engineering and science, may account for the male-female imbalance. Things are looking up, though; sixty-one percent of RPI women live in coed dormitories and there are three coed fraternities. Then again, you'd better like science a lot. With the ugliness of Troy and men oriented toward off-campus social outlets, you'll need a good reason to go out of your way to come here.

UNIVERSITY OF RHODE ISLAND

Location: Kingston, RI 02881
Campus: semirural
Undergraduate enrollment: 4465 M, 4183 W
Total enrollment: 11,255
Expenses: $4050 (in-state), $4183 (out-of-state)
Financial aid: 43%
Library: 600,000 volumes

Student-faculty ratio: 18–1
Transfer students: 850
Median SAT: 452 V, 505 M
Fraternities: 19%
Sororities: 19%
Application deadline: March 1

Out-of-staters learn to howl with the best of the natives about the seemingly habitual put-down of the college by the state's largest newspaper, the *Providence Journal*. URI is beset with its "annual problem." One year, it was the drug bust at High Noon (a small weekly gathering of congenial folks); the next year, it was the highlighting of the Halloween food fights (a ten-year tradition that seems to have ended this year); this year, it was a media blitz on the first faculty strike. The heartbreaker this year came when two women charged some fellow students with rape, and the *Journal* developed it into a story with a headline reading "Harassment, Verbal Abuse All Routine, URI Women Assert." Despite the notoriety, the university is a quiet place, in spite of the reputation it garnered somewhere along the line when *Playboy* magazine tabbed it one of the top ten party schools in the nation.

Still, the school suffers from an inferiority complex. The University of Rhode Island, like its home state, is in many ways one of the most provincial places in the Northeast. A thousand students recently showed up for a Greek-sponsored "Gong Show," but only a couple of hundred bothered to come listen to Nikki Giovanni read her poetry.

URI has followed the trend at most campuses, partially due to a small influx of business-type majors. The biggest campus issues in the last three years have revolved around a lack of student parking spaces close to classrooms.

Frank Newman, president of the university since late 1974 and a former public relations honcho at Stanford, is a good-looking, intelligent smoothie, and he is constantly talking up the university to anyone who will listen, especially the R. I. general assembly. The assembly is apparently not impressed; they cut recently $1.6 million from URI's budget request.

Like most state schools, URI has trouble turning down in-state applicants. Admission standards for out-of-staters are predictably more stringent, and it shows; there are more of them proportionally (and sometimes numerically) in almost every phase of student leadership and nonathletic extracurricular activities.

Dorm life has improved over the last few years. There are few rules, and most of the dorms are coed. There are dorm councils that plan social activities, and some of them run their own co-ops for food and supplies. Unfortunately, the dorms are noisy and are abused by their occupants, so that even the recently built ones have deteriorated considerably. Many students move "down the line" to vacant summer houses along Narragansett Bay. Off-campus life is cheap, and the beach is a nice place to live.

The Kingston area is in the middle of nowhere but affords a pleasant, semirural environment. Hitchhiking is very easy. There are several local bars catering to the college crowd, and those dissatisfied with the cultural offerings at the school (there is quite a bit offered) may opt for nearby Providence. Boston is only one-and-a-half hours away. Thursday night is party night, and on weekends the campus is almost barren.

URI students are generally middle-minded, middle class, and of middling ability. But if you look past the provincialism of many of the students, it's not difficult to get a quality education at URI. The faculty is generally good, if undemanding, and well-motivated students have no trouble getting extra help and attention. The library suffers from theft and mutilation problems and is criticized by everyone because it is next to impossible to find whatever book you happen to be looking for there.

URI is fairly strong in the natural sciences, with a good engineering school and a nationally known graduate school of oceanography. The humanities, though, are hurting. One history prof, whose department has suffered an enrollment decline of fifty percent, caused a minor uproar when he advertised one of his courses in the campus newspaper.

Fraternities and sororities are experiencing a minor resurgence. Most of their activities are usually excuses to drink beer, raise money for charity, or both. Some students pledge not because they are particularly enamored of the Greek system but because they dislike the dorms and the dining halls and are too poor to buy a car and move off-campus.

Basketball is the biggest sport at URI, both in terms of spectators and intramural participants. The big-name sports teams generally do not fare as well as their lesser-known counterparts; while the football team struggles to reach .500, the sailing team is ranked in the top three in the nation.

Rhode Islanders who go to URI generally do so because it's cheaper than private schools. It has yet to be completely determined why out-of-staters do. One reason why many New England students apply is because of URI programs in pharmacy, journalism, oceanography, and other fields that are not offered in their home states. Under the New England Board of Education "Apple Book" program they pay in-state tuition rates.

It is easy enough to get swallowed up at URI, but it is not so huge that dealings with the administration are completely impersonal. The student body is diverse enough so that you can find people of your own mindset if you look hard enough. If you have an intellectual bent, your search will be hard, indeed.

RICE UNIVERSITY

Location: Houston, TX 77001
Campus: suburban
Undergraduate enrollment:
 1700 M, 900 W
Total enrollment: 3500
Expenses: $5700
Financial aid: 60%
Library: 920,000 volumes

Student-faculty ratio: 9-1
Transfer students: 60
Median SAT: 635 V, 685 M
Fraternities: 0%
Sororities: 0%
Application deadline:
 February 1

Rice is sometimes called the "Harvard of the South." Although many Ivy League-types might take offense at the presumption, Rice *is* the foremost school in the South—and one of the better schools in the nation. Despite budgetary squeezes brought on by the energy crunch, Rice continues to strive to maintain its national prominence, particularly as a science-engineering school.

Academics at Rice can be tough. Five-course loads are required for graduation. Although a total of four courses may be designated pass/fail, grading is strict. In most cases grades are curved, but grade inflation is not a practice among professors. Competition, universally self-imposed, is intense, especially in the science-engineering ("S-E") courses. Although two out of three students enter Rice as "S-E" majors, only half wind up graduating with "S-E" degrees. The rest are divided between the highly rated architecture curriculum, and the humanities, which vary in quality. Recent much acclaimed additions to the humanities program include the Shepherd School of Music and the Jones Graduate School of Administration.

Student-faculty relations are excellent; professors are generally very accessible outside class for additional information and special help. And the faculty actually teaches—teaching assistants are uncommon except in labs and some tutorials.

Most students consider Rice's social life inadequate. Nonacademic life revolves around the student pub on campus and the eight semi-autonomous residential colleges. These colleges have their own governments, social and academic programs, and living and dining facilities. Since Rice allows no social fraternities or sororities, students develop strong loyalties to their respective colleges. Each college has about two hundred residents, and off-campus students are also affiliated with them, though not integrated into them. Many students are obsessive-compulsive about academics, preferring to study or "weenie," rather than socialize. However, there are alternative forms of entertainment offered on campus. Avant-garde, soft-porn, and Hollywood pictures are screened daily, and highbrow theatricals are staged six times a year. In the winter, intercollegiate basketball games are a popular diversion. Otherwise, people sit around the colleges and gripe about courses.

As a rule, Houston police don't come on campus. Dope smoking is widespread, and other drugs are fairly common, but beer is the most popular intoxicant.

The food at all meals is universally disliked. Even so, the colleges maintain a high occupancy. Following a successful coed living experiment in two colleges in 1973, a third college became coed in 1978. In spite of a recommendation to the president of the university that the remaining colleges (three male and two female) become coed, their future status remains uncertain. Even if all the colleges do go coed, however, Rice will remain predominantly male—the ratio of men to women is about two to one. All the colleges are air-conditioned (the need for which you may not appreciate until you arrive in Houston).

Considering the size of the student body, the campus itself is very large—300 acres, with buildings well spaced and more trees than students. The architecture covers the whole range from modern to Italian Renaissance, with red-brick-and-tile the unifying element.

Rice has an unusual problem: each winter, more than a million blackbirds take up residence. Although tree-trimming efforts have forced the feathered creatures into unpopulated areas of the campus, their presence (and smell) is still an annoyance.

Surrounded on three sides by quiet, established neighborhoods, Rice is adjacent to the Texas Medical Center, site of several large hospitals, medical schools, and famous heart surgeons Michael DeBakey and Denton Cooley. Downtown is only three miles away, and the city zoo is across the street.

Even though Rice is located three miles from the center of Houston—the nation's fifth-largest and fastest-growing major city—the campus remains secluded. This is not to say, however, that Rice students never take advantage of their urban surroundings. Houston offers opera, symphony, ballet, and theater for the culturally minded, and a large number of night-spots (both straight and gay) for those seeking a little fun. The legal age in Texas is eighteen, which allows the majority of the student body the chance to enjoy the nightlife. Fifty miles to the south lie Galveston and the Gulf—a suitable retreat from the demands of university curricula. Houston's adequacy as an urban center is relative—to the student from a middle-sized community, Houston is exciting; to the New Yorker or Chicagoan, it's a disappointment.

Recreation is readily available. Three major Gulf beaches, Austin and its Country Western music, and the largely unspoiled Big Thicket wilderness are only several hours away. For the more ambitious, New Orleans and Mexico are within an afternoon's drive.

Big-time Southwest Conference athletics are losing the grip they once held on Rice. In fact, many students show up at football games merely to see the Marching Owl Band (MOB) perform its satirical halftime shows. Often off-key and out-of-step, the MOB once paid halftime tribute to the banana. Another show poked fun at a more serious-minded neighbor school's hallowed traditions; the MOB wound up being held captive inside the stadium until police could escort them to safety.

Rice is unique and somewhat out of place in the South. To many, though, that difference is worth all the study and extra cost.

UNIVERSITY OF ROCHESTER

Location: Rochester, NY 14627
Campus: suburban
Undergraduate enrollment:
  2561 M, 1707 W
Total enrollment: 7881
Expenses: $7800
Financial aid: 52%
Library: 1,700,000 volumes

Student-faculty ratio: 11–1
Transfer students: 100
Median SAT: 560 V, 625 M
Median ACT: 27
Fraternities: 17%
Sororities: 6%
Application deadline:
  January 15

The University of Rochester has, in some quarters, a reputation for being a school for Ivy rejects. The character of the UR student body is not so much shaped by their not having gone to the Ivies, however, as much as by the fact that the student body is very homogeneous. A high percentage of the student body originates from the New York metropolitan area. This seems fine to a large portion of those students, while at the same time it annoys those who came to the school expecting to broaden their social and intellectual horizons. It is quite possible to spend four years here and speak only to New Yorkers.

The student body is also limited in that it sees college as an advanced trade school, the trades being law and medicine. At the beginning of the freshman year, about one-quarter of the class indicates a desire to become doctors. By the time application time comes around, this number has dropped. Unfortunately the desire to add the "M. D." to the end of the name is a hopeless goal for some students. Because Rochester, like most liberal universities, frowns on most mandatory academic guidance, these students can spend their time in a premed track, ignoring the bountiful intellectual opportunities present at the university.

The school's river campus houses the college of arts and sciences. Students spend the first two years there and can then continue there or in one of the professional schools. For some students, this two-year stint in the liberal arts can be a rushed experiment in an otherwise professionally oriented path.

The school's atmosphere favors studying. Those who expect to spend a large amount of their time squirreled away in the library will feel right at home at the university. There are a substantial number of undergraduates who frown on such antisocial behavior, but the pervasive work ethic can be a drag for the less studious.

The university's "X-period" is one of its unique and positive qualities. The period includes the months between the end of the spring term and the start of the fall semester. Participation is totally voluntary, and in most cases no academic credit is given for "X-period" studies. The program is, however, an excellent opportunity to work one-to-one with a professor and pursue some in-depth research or intellectual problem which appeals to the student. The university insists that the individual student have a large degree of responsibility for setting up his "X-period" activity, but the school makes sure that the facilities and faculty are available.

Any discussion of the University of Rochester must deal with the school's location. It is located, not surprisingly, in Rochester, New York. The city has a population of approximately 300,000. Culturally, the city is well endowed for its size. Most of this is directly provided by UR, however. The Eastman School of Music, one of the top schools of its kind in the world, is part of the university. As such, there is always a good deal of concert activity, most of which is free. The city has its own philharmonic orchestra, along with several theatrical groups. There is a good planetarium in the city and one fine art museum, the Memorial Art Gallery, which is also a part of the University.

Unfortunately, Rochester is located in an area of the country which receives a very limited amount of sunlight. It is not unusual to go for weeks without having a sunny day. The seasons in Rochester are strong, since winter seems to last from the beginning of October to the middle of April. The city is capable of putting out some beautiful days, but overall the climate is depressing. Some say the sun only shines on the Fourth of July.

The school itself is isolated from the community. It is surrounded on three sides by the Genessee River, and on the fourth by a large cemetery. This makes for some beautiful scenery around campus—cemetery walks are a springtime favorite—but it does present problems to the UR undergraduate. What has happened as a result of this isolation is that there is no "college town" feeling near the campus. The city, however, is not large or varied enough to make up for this. Without a car, transportation is difficult, and the frustration of being stuck on campus can be great.

The university facilities are excellent. The recently completed chem-bio and psychology buildings are some of the best buildings of their kind to be found at any university. The medical school facilities are only a few years old; and the university has its own cyclotron.

The quality of the library's humanities holdings has been criticized, and it does not appear that there will be any substantial improvements in the near future. Some students supplement them with the "fine arts" semester in Sussex, "british politics" semester in London, or through the on-campus center for special degree programs that cater to individualized interdepartmental majors.

The scientific libraries, especially the medical school's, are excellent. The university has several outstanding undergraduate departments, along with its excellent medical and music schools. In general, the sciences are strong. There are several "name" professors, and it is general university policy to have professors, rather than graduate students, teach courses. The university has an excellent optics program and has a small but good engineering department. The political science department is excellent.

The university's pride and joy is the medical school. It has been placed near the top of virtually every rating of medical schools in the nation, but the diversion of an inordinate amount of money to support it tends to make the various other departments feel cheated. There are always internal dissents over the sacrifice of the humanities at the university to the sciences. For a large part, this is true, so students interested in going to UR should carefully examine the departments with which they will have the most contact.

In general, the University of Rochester is a good school in terms of faculty and facilities. Its major weaknesses lie in the lack of a varied student body, both in geographical distribution and interests, the highly competitive attitude of many of the students, and the inescapable fact that the school is in an isolated area of the city of Rochester.

RUTGERS COLLEGE OF RUTGERS UNIVERSITY

Location: New Brunswick, NJ 08903
Campus: suburban
Undergrad enrollment: 4590 M, 3660 W
Total enrollment: 33,665
Expenses: $3065 (in-state), $3895 (out-of-state)
Financial aid: 52%
Library: 2,000,000 volumes

Student-faculty ratio: 17–1
Transfer students: 1180
Median SAT: 500 V, 540 M
Fraternities: 12%
Sororities 12%
Application deadline: February 1, March 15 for transfers

The New Jersey student finds Rutgers University a small consolation to the general dearth of top New Jersey educational institutions. Jealousy of nearby New York State's fine and substantial university system runs at high levels among Jersey students. Rutgers College, along with Douglass College, Cook College, and Livingston College, bears the burden of being the Garden State's one strong facility.

New Brunswick, which houses Rutgers, Cook, Livingston, and Douglass Colleges, four of the state university's eleven undergraduate divisions, is thirty miles from New York City. Rutgers College, the oldest of the state university system, adopted coeducation in 1972.

The Rutgers student has a particularly acute case of the state university Scylla and Charybdis complex: he can't knock the place because competition is tough and his less-than-perfect grades have to be defended, and he can't praise the school because, after all, It's Only the State University.

New Jersey is the most densely populated state in the nation and sends the majority of its college students out-of-state while still turning down a solid half to two-thirds of applicants to all state schools. There are a number of Ivy League rejects, but the state is not doing much to assuage many wounded egos.

Rutgers facilities are improving and are even excellent in many cases. Unfortunately, courses are often rinky-dink in content, though not in grading, and a lingering anti-intellectualism makes attempts to upgrade the difficult atmosphere. In fact, the red-brick-and-gleaming-chrome look is more than a bit galling to students at one of the oldest (seventh established college in America) schools in the country.

Rutgers's virtues are many. Students are studious, if not always brilliant or sensitive; competition is keen, and the epithet "throat" (grind) is common if not beloved. The newspaper is a daily, and the radio station a good one.

The student government is active and students have made strides in earning the attention of administrators and faculty members. Extracurricular offerings include a full program of intramural and varsity sports, many cultural organizations and religious groups, and a slew of clubs.

There are some good academic reasons for going to Rutgers. The English department, generally recognized as the school's best, has been brightened by such luminaries as John Ciardi, and even lesser lecturers are as well respected. The Microbiology Institute, founded by Nobel Prize-winner Selman Waksman, ranks among the top centers in its field nationally. The other science departments and the engineering staff are solid, and the biology and chemistry departments are better than at many prestige schools.

Some of the faculty are concerned with trying to teach and produce an atmosphere of intellectual curiosity and concern for the student. However, too much of the faculty, especially in the sciences (and chemistry, in particular) show little concern for the students as students and even less concern for them as individuals. Many professors seem too preoccupied with their own reputations and the reputations of their departments to provide any more than a bare minimum of help to the student. Many professors are also concerned that they are giving too many high grades, and not with how well they are teaching or how much the students are learning. It is obvious that in such a situation the frustrations of the student hinder both his academic learning and intellectual curiosity.

Rutgers's prelaw and premedical programs pay off in good graduate school placement, and good grades at Rutgers are a strong recommendation as indicators of diligence and solid background. One top opportunity is the Henry Rutgers Scholar program, which substitutes independent research for half a senior course load (unfortunately, the number of participants is normally limited to one or two per major).

The freshman drop-out (and flunk-out) rate is rather frightening—it can skyrocket up to a quarter of the class. And some freshman courses—notably, calculus—are a terror. But few applicants accepted will find themselves unable to do the work. In most cases, a failure means that the often-mammoth reading load proved a bit more than the flunkie had bargained for. A majority of the students take their work seriously—many, if not most, come from noncollege-graduate parents of middle-class means and are at college to become "somebodies." And there is a small but growing colony of literate thinkers, although it will take a while to overcome the prevailing utilitarian outlook toward education.

Socially, Rutgers students have a new student center in which to play together. Beer and wine are permitted on campus, and dorms have complete intervisitation. New Brunswick is close enough to New York by train that the city's great cultural, gastronomic, and other offerings can be had with little difficulty.

Rutgers has its problems, but for a solid education in New Jersey, you can't beat it. Unless you go to Princeton, and that's another ballgame.

ST. BONAVENTURE UNIVERSITY

Location: St. Bonaventure, NY 14778
Campus: rural
Undergraduate enrollment: 1200 M, 1050 W
Total enrollment: 2550
Expenses: $5495
Financial aid: 43%
Library: 300,000 volumes

Student-faculty ratio: 15-1
Transfer students: 140
Median SAT: 489 V, 535 M
Median ACT: 24
Fraternities: NA
Sororities: NA
Application deadline: rolling—usually closes January 1

St. Bonaventure University is a small, coeducational, Catholic college in the "Heart of the Enchanted Mountains." The way you can tell that the mountains are enchanted—or perhaps sanctified, considering the general prevalence of religion—is that they are covered with snow from early October to late April or even May.

If you don't mind being unable to venture outside for several months of the year, and if you don't mind being expected to genuflect every few feet when you do get outdoors, St. Bonaventure can be a genial enough place. The setting is beautiful, if somewhat isolated (the nearest metropolis is bustling Olean, New York). The faculty is good, if rigid, and the program is solid, if overly structured and overly religious.

St. Bonaventure is the sort of school where the raging controversy is whether the school is a university first or a Catholic institution first.

Despite the dilemma of dogma vs. didactics, St. Bonaventure is much liberalized in comparison to bygone days. The dress code has been dropped, and curfews don't exist—except for freshman women. The advent of coeducation has, slowly, over a quarter of a century, eroded much of the sternest aspect of the religious administration, and coed dormitory living is now a fact.

For the moment, the major pursuits on-campus continue to be drinking and skiing. St. Bonaventure long maintained an "animal" reputation—women used to fear entering the men's dining halls, where they were likely to be pelted with food or worse. The men, apparently terrified of retaliation, decline to enter women's dorms. Instead, the most popular meeting place is the campus rathskeller, which serves beer. People are also likely to meet over drinks on boating trips down the Allegheny River (after the ice melts).

Academically, St. Bonaventure both benefits and suffers from its small size and closed environment. The faculty is accessible, but the course offerings are limited. Moreover, the churchly inclination to rules has led to requirements of fifteen hours each in theology and philosophy, and twelve hours each in natural sciences, social sciences, and humanities. Little time, therefore, is left for electives, although there are choices of courses within each distributional requirement.

In general, the academic rating of the school is fairly good. Philosophy has a genuine reputation, and the English staff is competent. Journalism is well regarded, although possibly living off its reputation, and the science offerings are palatable, despite execrable facilities. Even sociology, not a favorite Catholic subject, is improving.

But despite such recent improvements, St. Bonaventure is by no means even a first-class Catholic institution yet. Probably the key to its trouble, of course, is that it still thinks of itself as a Catholic institution first and thus negates its responsibilities as a secular learning center as well.

ST. JOHN'S COLLEGE

Location: Annapolis, MD 21404
   Santa Fe, NM 87501
Campuses: city outskirts
Undergraduate enrollment:
   200 M, 180 W (Annapolis)
   150 M, 150 W (Santa Fe)

Student-faculty ratio: 8–1
Transfer students: 50
Median SAT: 620 V, 610 M
Median ACT: 28
Fraternities: 0%
Sororities: 0%

Total enrollment:
  380 (Annapolis)
  300 (Santa Fe)
Expenses: $7000
Financial aid: 50%
Library: 72,000 volumes
  (Annapolis)
  50,000 volumes
  (Santa Fe)

Application deadline:
rolling

St. John's is a four-year, nondenominational, coeducational liberal arts college. The Sante Fe campus, in operation since 1964, is a twin of St. John's College in Annapolis, Maryland, established in 1696. The faculty is shared by both campuses, and the students are granted open transfer privileges. There are no majors and no electives; the curriculum is all required. Transfer students are accepted only as freshmen. Enrollment at each campus is limited to a small number of motivated students.

The present curriculum was established 1937 under the direction of Scott Buchanan and Stringfellow Barr, two of the most influential and inspiring "Mr. Chipses" of the century. They believed that men could only be free who had been educated in the "higher, and exclusively human arts," the liberal arts of "apprehending, understanding, and knowing." The result of this belief has an experimental curriculum based on the traditional liberal arts of grammar, rhetoric, logic, arithmetic, geometry, music, and astronomy, and molded around a core of one hundred great books in the Western tradition—from Homer and Plato to Einstein and Whitehead. The didactic method of this curriculum was the seminar. Two seminars a week were held in which the books were discussed, in roughly chronological order, over the four years. In addition, more intensive study was provided for in daily tutorials (professors are called tutors, regardless of degrees, and students and tutors always address each other by their proper names) in language and mathematics. The latter covered Euclid, Ptolemy, and Copernicus, and went up to Newton and Lobachevsky. The four years of language study consisted of a year each of Greek, Latin, German, and French. In addition to these two tutorials, biweekly laboratories were established in which the history of scientific thought, from measurement to the atomic theory, was traced. None of these classes were lectures; all of them depended upon student participation. A series of weekly formal lectures, given on diverse subjects by members of the faculty or visiting authors, scholars, poets, and scientists, was started, always followed by a long and often severe question period. The college itself was kept mostly residential in the hope that it would become a "community of learning."

The experimental atmosphere of the college remains. Since the new program began, many changes have been made on the basis of experience and innovation. A music tutorial has been added to the sophomore year, Latin and German have been dropped from the language program, and, of course, the list of the great books that are read is being constantly questioned, supplemented, and revised. "Preceptorials" replace the seminars for a few weeks during the junior and senior years in an attempt to stabilize the extremely rapid pace in which the books are covered. In these "preceptorials," usually held at the tutor's home, the pace is relaxed and informal. The students are thus given the opportunity to look more closely at a single book or a single concept in several books. Recently, St. John's has added classes in crafts, dance, and karate.

In short, St. John's is a four-year exploration of beauty—the beauty of our tradition. The path of this exploration is limited only by time; there simply isn't time to explore the entire territory, to encounter the whole of tradition. But that isn't the goal. The intention of the college is merely to be in a process that can never be ended. The means to that goal are the great books, the high points in the history of man's search for himself. The intended result is that each individual, by recapitulating that search, will better know himself.

The question that arises is whether or not these ideals are actually put into practice in the particular "community of learning" that is St. John's. The answer is a qualified affirmative. There are many facets of the program which are at best only partial successes and which lose the flavor of dismal failures only when compared with similar endeavors at other contemporary institutions of learning. Pedantry is not unknown at St. John's. But on the whole, the goal of the college (which Barr and Buchanan and many others consider to be the only relevant goal of education) is actualized. The means to this goal are and must remain experimental, however, until the best of them are found.

The elements of this experiment—the students—are notoriously unconventional. Many are transfers or drop-outs from other colleges who were unable or unwilling to function in what is today considered a "normal" college atmosphere. Their backgrounds are extremely different, and they retain their individuality after they come to St. John's. There are no fraternities or sororities, no organized activist groups, and only an embryonic student government. Because of the size of the student body, cliques, if there are any, are necessarily amorphous. Conversation, intrinsic to the program, is the basis of all student-

student and student-administration confrontations. In keeping with this, both the students and the administration are extremely responsive. Problems are always handled on an individual basis; dogma for its own sake is a natural enemy of the college, both ideally and in actuality. Because of the experimental flavor of the program, and because it is felt that individual progress cannot be measured by any arbitrary or commensurate system, grades are given only for transfer purposes. It is not necessary for a student even to know what his grades are—they are only given to him if he asks for them. What takes their place is a "don rag." Each tutor gives an account of the student's contributions to his class, the matter is discussed to determine a fair and complete picture, and then the student is allowed to comment and question what he likes. The absence of a conventional testing and grading system means that the student must decide how to participate in class, as well as how to evaluate his performance. This requires an extraordinary amount of sustained self-motivation, which is often wearying. St. John's is not necessarily for those who are smart; rather, it is for those who are willing to commit themselves fully to the ideal of a liberal education.

One student reflected, "Regular people regularly graduate from the college. I doubt if the students are 'unconventional.' I think only their education is unconventional, extremely demanding, and perhaps—and only perhaps—fulfilling."

St. John's students must want to go to the college because its rewards are highly personal. Four years of classics do not prepare a student for any specific career. Moreover, the college radically influences the student's values. And while agitation of the soul may be good for the speculative mind, it's murder on the practical mind. Those who know what they want to do in life should avoid St. John's, for they will be teased to distraction by people who want to know "why?"

ST. JOHN'S UNIVERSITY

Location: Collegeville, MN 56321
Campus: rural
Undergraduate enrollment: 1900 M
Total enrollment: 1950
Expenses: $4750
Financial aid: 66%
Library: 280,000 volumes

Student-faculty ratio: 18–1
Transfer students: 100
Median SAT: 500 V, 560 M
Median ACT: 25
Fraternities: NA
Application deadline: June 1

St. John's University is one of the few all-male schools left in the nation. St. John's is a small liberal arts college, located seventy miles northwest of the "Twin Cities" on Route I-94. The campus is set on 2400 acres of rolling hills, woodlands, and lakes.

Although St. John's is an all-male university, it is affiliated with the College of St. Benedict, an all-women's school just five miles away. Students may attend classes on either campus, and all social activities are coed. A bus service is provided that runs between the two campuses for all classes and activities. The "Johnnies' " and "Bennies' " social life centers around movies, dances, lake parties, and activities in St. Cloud, a city of 45,000 people, twelve miles from St. John's.

St. John's liberal studies program places it among the top schools of its size in the nation. St. John's has a four-one-four semester program. Between the normal fall and spring terms is a "January term," when students study one subject in depth, choosing it from over 150 classes and studies abroad. St. John's has foreign exchange programs in Ghana, Tokyo, and Austria, and a strong career placement program.

The library, the science center, three of the dormitories, and the church were designed by architect Marcel Breuer. The church has been called the most striking piece of architecture in Minnesota.

On-campus housing is satisfactory. The newer dormitories, with large spacious rooms, are more expensive.

The food at St. John's is good and the St. John's Abbey is known for its grain bread, which is considered America's best.

Although "Little Notre Dame" is a relatively small university, its athletic programs resemble those of a major institution. The Warner Palaestra houses an indoor track, an eight-lane swimming pool, racquetball courts, a sauna, and other gym facilities. St. John's athletes have won major divisional MCAA titles.

The forest area that surrounds the St. John's campus has many trails on which students hike, jog, cross-country ski, and experience the true beauty of nature. The entire community of St. John's and St. Benedict's has an atmosphere of friendship and sharing. If Minnesota winters don't bother you, a quiet, peaceful, and pleasant existence can be yours here.

ST. LAWRENCE UNIVERSITY

Location: Canton, NY 13617
Campus: rural

Student-faculty ratio: 16–1
Transfer students: 35

Undergraduate enrollment:　　Median SAT: 515 V, 560 M
　1200 M, 1100 W　　　　　　Fraternities: NA
Total enrollment: 2350　　　　Sororities: NA
Expenses: $6185　　　　　　　Application deadline:
Financial aid: 60%　　　　　　　February 1
Library: 260,000 volumes

The traditional St. Lawrence University "Larry" is in his death throes. For many years during the postwar period, the upstate New York university acquired a reputation as the ideal spot for the type of student who desired nothing more than to swim complacently in a sea of academic otiosity. This is an image which both students and faculty have been working to dispel over the past few years, with increasing success.

The intellectual atmosphere has traditionally tended to be light but during the past few years has thickened. There is an odor of the incipient cutthroat in the air. But the small classes and the clean air of the rural setting help keep St. Lawrence relaxed.

The administration, from its board of trustees on down, is increasingly farsighted. Although in the past it exhibited tendencies toward institutional rigidity, it is now involving itself admirably in a liberal response to demands by students and faculty. A tripartite university government is experimenting in a rather enlightened program of mutual community respect and shared power. These changes were not occasioned without student pressure, but all parties of the university community look with some pride upon the reasonable manner in which students are being given a greater voice in campus decisionmaking.

Not all is joyful in Canton, New York, however. The problem is that the town is two-and-a-half hours from either Syracuse or Montreal. Even Mohawk Airlines is twenty miles away. The college has attempted with some success to convert this debit into an asset by offering a wide range of recreational activities over the 1000 rural acres of the campus. A golf course, beach, ski slope, riding stable, and ice-skating arena are all present. It is still not Hollywood or even Albany, however, so some students still flee toward New York City on the weekend.

Others flee even further on one of the university's foreign study programs in England, France, Austria, Spain, and Kenya. A three-two engineering program lets students spend three years studying the liberal arts at St. Lawrence and then two years elsewhere studying engineering. After five years, the student receives an engineering degree. Similarly, a four-plus-one M. B. A. program with Clarkson

College requires four years at St. Lawrence in economics and a year of graduate study at Clarkson. Programs such as these get those tired of rural scenery out of Canton.

There is a reasonable amount of social activities for the many students who remain. Bars outnumber churches by a score of thirteen to eight and draw proportionately. Sometimes there are "big weekends," which are buttressed by the fraternities and sororities. They feature entertainment in their houses or in nearby barns rented for this purpose.

Relationships between fraternities and independents have a general tendency toward politeness, mainly because over the past two decades the influence of the Greeks has significantly diminished. Houses still have large memberships, however, and the chances for their survival are favorable.

The popular myth describes the St. Lawrence student as socially centered—no wonder, considering the golf course, beach, and other recreational facilities. The stereotype is an exaggeration, though. Problems occasioned by the low New York State drinking age and the university's allowance of alcoholic beverages on campus have been minimal. We are told that this is because the students are "mature," which is also the reason why student interest in sex is "neither inordinate nor perverted."

A new four-one-four academic calendar is yet another indicator of how St. Lawrence is changing with the times. The university has embarked on an extensive building program, which will ensure modern facilities for years to come. St. Lawrence is also expanding along other less-tangible lines in order to revitalize and rebuild itself as it faces the balance of the twentieth century.

ST. LOUIS UNIVERSITY

Location: St. Louis, MO 63103
Campus: city center
Undergraduate enrollment:
  2600 M, 2130 W
Total enrollment: 10,364
Expenses: $5600
Financial aid: 65%
Library 1,000,000 volumes

Student-faculty ratio: 12-1
Transfer students: 1100
Median SAT: 485 V, 520 M
Median ACT: 23
Fraternities: 7%
Sororities: 3%
Application deadline:
  July 1

St. Louis University is a medium-sized, academically uneven, Jesuit institution, set in one of the less-safe portions of St. Louis. It now ranks as one of the better Catholic colleges, but St. Louis University has a long way to go before it can assume rank as a major American university.

Academically, St. Louis "needs quite a lot," in the words of one former student. Departments vary in quality, and the differential between stronger and weaker departments grows greater all the time as the better faculties win fat research grants and the weak sisters languish from inattention.

Every aspect of the school's academic life is plagued by financial troubles, a situation that is not alleviated by the conservative set of contributors. President Paul Reinert designed "Project SEARCH," which is intended to bring thoughts from business, government, education, labor, and community groups on how to best finance private higher education. The practical results of this program—the number of dollars SLU can rake in—hold the key to St. Louis's future.

And St. Louis University cannot rely, as many other schools can, on nonacademic factors to offset its curricular weaknesses. The school is composed of a majority of commuters, plus a contingent of out-of-towners who have generally come because of specific St. Louis departments. School life and extracurricular activities are at a fairly low ebb. Fraternities and sororities do exist, but they have no buildings, and their activities are hence much curtailed. Students from out of St. Louis reside either on campus or, often, in nearby apartments. The bulk of the commuters socialize at home, and there is relatively little sense of identification with or attachment to the school.

Although half of the student body is Catholic, you'd never know the school's Jesuit attachment—except for a little required theology. Although on-campus liquor consumption is restricted to those over twenty-one, complete dorm intervisitation is allowed, unless dorm residents decide otherwise.

Sports, never really strong at St. Louis, are growing in popularity as the teams are improving. In fact, the school introduced hockey just as the engineering school was phased out for lack of funds, which caused a furor among those who still look to the institution for an education. The soccer team, of course, is legend and is perennially near the top of the NCAA.

All in all, St. Louis University is something of a hodgepodge, and not an overly attractive one at that. Its academic bumpiness and its serious lack of community spirit offset its genuine academic virtues in a number of departments. And the financial problems don't make the picture any brighter for the future.

UNIVERSITY OF SAN FRANCISCO

Location: San Francisco, CA 94117
Campus: city center
Undergraduate enrollment: 1450 M, 1550 W
Expenses: $6000
Financial aid: 60%
Library: 550,000 volumes

Student-faculty ratio: 17–1
Transfer students: 800
Median SAT: 490 V, 520 M
Fraternities: 3%
Sororities: 2%
Application deadline: March 1

USF is a small Jesuit University located almost exactly in the geographic center of San Francisco, which is a great city in which to spend four years. USF has a magnificent view of the Pacific Ocean, San Francisco Bay, and downtown S.F.

The Catholic affiliation of the school still has a visible impact on USF. While a core curriculum has been revised and more electives are available, twelve units on "man's search for meaning," comprising anthropology, philosophy, and theology, are required.

The college of business administration has become the most popular college and recently underwent an expansion. The school of nursing is excellent, as is the college of science. Small classes are still the rule in the college of liberal arts; the education is above average.

The administration has no trouble filling the dorms on-campus. The convenience can't be beat, but the crime rate in the surrounding area is not among the city's lowest. A good two-thirds of the students commute, which precludes the development of a unified campus social life.

The student body has changed greatly and now includes a large contingent of international students. Students from Asia, Africa, South America, and the Middle East give the school a cosmopolitan atmosphere.

Those with a taste for travel may spend junior year in Ireland, Italy, Japan, or Spain, and special summer travel programs cater to more limited urges for adventure.

The student body includes both liberals and conservatives, but somehow the conservatives seem to be in control. Students' conservatism extends to many matters, including sex. An atmosphere of stability prevails.

USF is not the place to go for a self-directed, flexible education. The school is a little too nice-and-quiet to proivde all the personal and intellectual challenges that make college life what it should be. But, after all, distinctly unquiet San Francisco is right nearby, and San Francisco is an education in itself.

SARAH LAWRENCE COLLEGE

Location: Bronxville, NY 10708
Campus: suburban
Undergraduate enrollment:
  175 M, 575 W
Total enrollment: 1000
Expenses: $8750
Financial aid: 35%
Library: 143,000 volumes

Student-faculty ratio: 9–1
Transfer students: 100
Median SAT: 550 V, 550 M
Fraternities: 0%
Sororities: 0%
Application deadline:
  February 1

Sarah Lawrence is alternately known as the most progressive college in the country and as the most pleasant open-air sanatorium in New York State.

Those who call Sarah Lawrence the most progressive college in the country are referring to the amazing academic reforms which Sarah Lawrence has instituted and which many other colleges may never see. For one thing, Sarah Lawrence students don't get grades. The teachers simply write out short reports on the students' progress, and these reports remain confidential. Furthermore, there are no specific requirements for graduation, no majors, and no examinations. Students take three year-long courses and most of their work is independent. Projects range from traditional research papers to internship in the New York area.

Sarah Lawrence is able to do all these things primarily because of its small size, which allows for a great degree of personal attention and communication between individual students and teachers. And although some freshmen have difficulty ordering all this newfound freedom, the system seems to work beautifully. It may even be worth going to Sarah Lawrence just to take advantage of these reforms. The faculty includes many distinguished writers and scholars, but they are at Sarah Lawrence primarily to teach. Each student has a personal adviser with whom he or she has regular conferences about any personal or academic problems. The final educational result appears to be satisfactory—as indicated by the fact than an increasing number of Sarah Lawrence students are going on to highly rated grad schools.

Those who call Sarah Lawrence an open-air sanatorium are referring, of course, to the people who go to school there. They are all very interesting, alive, experienced, and intelligent, but no one will deny that most of them are somewhat neurotic and a few quite crazy. For one thing, Sarah Lawrence students often come from wealthy families (almost half come from private schools) and from an unusual array of family backgrounds.

We should probably add that there are some Sarah Lawrence students who are perfectly normal, apple-cheeked, homespun types. Contrary to their popular image, not all Sarah Lawrence students are neurotic, and probably not more than two-thirds of them are crazy.

After many years of experience with strange women, the school went coed about eight years ago and immediately acquired a name for itself as a refuge for strange men. As happened at Vassar, the first male class to enter the formerly all-female institution was suspected of homosexuality. Certainly Sarah Lawrence is no stranger to female homosexuality, and the males have been at least as unconventional as their female counterparts. Students can relieve the social problem by taking the junior year abroad or at almost any accredited college in the country, provided their curriculum has been previously approved by the administration. After a year away, returning seniors express a renewed enthusiasm for the unique Sarah Lawrence College academic system.

One would expect Sarah Lawrence's administration to be very progressive. And it is. To add to the reforms already instituted would be difficult; coeducation was an impressive and necessary step, and there just isn't that much more that needs reforming.

The campus is very small, depressing in the winter, and beautiful in the spring. It is very close to New York, and most people get into the city often enough to absorb quite a bit of the local color and to keep up with the arts scene. There is little campus life.

If you require a highly structured academic plan and a ready-made social life, apply somewhere else. Independence, creativity, and an outgoing personality may be prerequisites for a positive experience at Sarah Lawrence College.

SIMMONS COLLEGE

Location: Boston, MA 02115
Campus: city center
Undergraduate enrollment:
　1600 W
Total enrollment: 2664
Expenses: $6844
Financial aid: 40%
Library: 189,000 volumes

Student-faculty ratio: 12-1
Transfer students: 150
Median SAT: 480 V, 500 M
Sororities: 0%
Application deadline:
　March 15

Simmons was founded in 1899 as a combination of a liberal arts college and a professional/vocational training school for women. You won't find much "pure" scholarship here. But the school's size, location, and philosophy of education make it a good place to spend four years preparing for a career.

Simmons is demonstrating a renewed interest in the liberal arts, though by no means to the exclusion of career education. The college insists that students become "well rounded" by fulfilling English, foreign language, and other distribution requirements. The school has many other offerings, and it is possible to combine courses from several areas to create a new concentration to meet the student's special interests. There is a self-designed program called "OPEN" (Option for Personalized Educational Needs), and the faculty is always helpful in working with students on individual programs. Health sciences, management, and communications are especially strong.

One hallmark of a Simmons education is independent study in the form of field work and internships. This gives the student "real life" experience while helping her to focus her career plans. Students in the nursing and physical therapy programs do clinical work in the institutions with which the college is affiliated. Government majors can work with legislators and get valuable exposure to practical politics. Where could you find more opportunities than in a large city like Boston?

Boston, as we all know, is a great place to go to school. Within a three-mile radius of the Simmons campus, there are more than two dozen colleges and universities, all of which add to the social activities of the Simmons women. And the Simmons women are socially active. MIT and Harvard are still old favorites, and Babson is becoming increasingly popular, too. Any student with a little initiative can have as many dates as she can handle. But the fact that Simmons itself is all-women makes it difficult to establish casual, platonic relationships with guys.

There is no chance that Simmons will go the coed route of so many other single-sex colleges. The school was founded on the idea of educating women to realize their full potential. The students agree that going to a women's college brings out qualities of leadership, initiative, and assertiveness.

The Simmons campus is split into two parts. The residence campus (about sixty percent of the undergraduates live there) has nine traditional dorms, the dining hall, health center, auditorium, and a craft/multipurpose building. It is a five-minute walk from the academic campus, which is currently undergoing renovation and rebuilding. The pub, which is the place to go on Thursday nights, is in the basement of one of the dorms. Parties are sometimes held on-campus, but facilities are somewhat limited. Students constantly venture outside of Simmons and explore Boston city life. The Simmons ID card will get students into other schools, whether it be for special activities or to attend classes.

Simmons is situated in the midst of museums, concert halls, libraries, science centers, and theaters. The transit system, which is easily accessible, takes students anywhere they want to go, and right now that seems to be directly into the Boston community. More than ever, students are becoming involved with community volunteer work—everything from teaching underprivileged children to working on campaigns in local and state government.

But all the involvement does not take place off-campus. Traditional activities, such as Friday afternoon teas, Father-Daughter Weekend, Freshman Orientation, and May Breakfast, are still alive. And students are becoming more aware of and concerned with school policies, although the student government is plagued by fluctuations in both student interest and administration receptiveness. There is a full range of small organizations and clubs at Simmons; the accent is on what the student chooses to make of the opportunities available.

Everything at Simmons centers around the individual student. The faculty and most administrators are remarkably accessible. Even in the admissions process there are no set standards; applicants are looked upon as individuals. The stereotyped Simmons student is a preppie, but the student body is relatively diverse; a healthy percentage of students are on some form of financial aid.

Dean's lists and grade point averages are nonexistent, but there is still a strong sense of competition among the highly motivated, ambitious student body. Students have the option of taking courses on a pass/fail basis. An honor code prevails throughout the college. Exams are unproctored and may be taken any place the student wishes; many are take-home.

It certainly is not the physical appearance of the campus that attracts students to Simmons. Some of the buildings are old, and even though some renovation has taken place, much more needs to be done. Physical education facilities are completely inadequate.

What is the attraction, then? One factor is the positive, mutually supportive feeling that the people in the Simmons community generate. Another is that Simmons's pragmatic, career-oriented approach to education is remarkably well suited to an era of feminism and painful economic times ahead. My, how those founders in 1899 were farsighted!

SIMON'S ROCK EARLY COLLEGE

Location: Great Barrington, MA 01230
Campus: rural
Undergraduate enrollment: 210
Expenses: $6380
Financial aid: 43%
Library: 45,000 volumes
Student-faculty ratio: 8–1
Transfer students: NA
Fraternities: 0%
Sororities: 0%
Application deadline: None

Simon's Rock Early College, administered by Bard College since 1979, holds to the premise that many sixteen-year-olds are ready for college work. That means that those who have completed tenth, eleventh, or twelfth grades may apply to spend four years at Simon's Rock.

Over 200 students attend the school. Of those who begin as freshmen, only thirty percent remain to graduate. A four-year B. A. or two-year associate's degree is granted. The A. A. allows a student to attend two more years at a regular four-year institution to earn a B. A.

Simon's Rock is unique in gearing itself to sixteen-to-twenty-year-olds. Special faculty counselors work with a testing, academic, and social profile of each student.

Athletics, the arts, and publications are among the encouraged extracurricular areas. Campus unity is further encouraged by the small size and small town location. No drinking is permitted and there are no frats or sororities.

Lots of us remember thinking we were ready to leave high school and go to college early, but we couldn't. Today, Simon's Rock makes it possible.

SKIDMORE COLLEGE

Location: Saratoga Springs, NY 12866
Campus: city outskirts
Undergraduate enrollment: 500 M, 1500 W
Total enrollment: 2000
Expenses: $7400
Financial aid: 20%
Library: 260,000 volumes
Student-faculty ratio: 12–1
Transfer students: 190
Median SAT: 520 V, 530 M
Median ACT: 25
Fraternities: NA
Sororities: NA
Application deadline: February 1

Located in Saratoga Springs, former mecca of horseracing and mineral-bathing, Skidmore College seems to reflect the Saratogian notion that the past is a greater thing than the future. Skidmore, once considered equal to the "Seven Sisters," has suffered a significant drop in its academic reputation.

But if the work load and the quality of education have declined (still leaving it a pretty good school), Skidmore's campus has gone through some pretty jarring changes, which may or may not indicate a return to lost glory. The year 1977 saw the official phasing out of the "old campus." Long considered the charm of the college, this relic of the past will probably serve the college no longer than two more years. The "new campus," begun in 1965 and still under construction, has recently added a large classroom/administration building, a small gymnasium, a theater, and a fine arts center. Future plans include more housing and a huge sports complex.

The buildings themselves are pleasing to the eye, but the college does little to provide shrubbery or to replace trees which the new buildings eliminate, and the result has been a somewhat stark, depressing landscape. Spring helps an awful lot, though, and Skidmore even lays claim to some ivy on the dorms.

Several departments are outstanding. English is superb; several of the faculty are nationally acclaimed writers. An unfortunate blow to the dance department was the resignation of prima ballerina Melissa Hayden, but the department is still of high caliber. Philosophy and art are also excellent. The business department will be putting out CPAs soon, and a five-year engineering program is offered by the chemistry and physics departments in conjunction with Dartmouth. The faculty is generally young, bright, liberal, and friendly.

Students have very few social and academic restrictions. With the housing problem resulting from the shut-down of the "old campus," more and more students are being allowed to live off-campus, but to keep students on-campus the administration is putting some freshmen into triple rooms. There are no parietals, and dorm living, especially in the south quad, is easy and loud, and a general partying atmosphere prevails.

Student interest in policy-making is on the rise. College governments come and go, with a slight increase in notability each year. Tenure has received a great deal of attention, and a standardized student evaluation form has evolved after years of relative indifference in that area. College elections seem to be drawing more voters every year. Administrators are accessible, but student initiative is the prime mover behind any communication.

"Skiddies" are much-appreciated in a town which boasts 150 bars (more per capita than any other town in New York), and the downtown scene is hectic and fun. Caroline Street, the "Greenwich Village of Saratoga," is still popular, though Harold J's, a disco on the other side of town, resembles the proverbial can of sardines on weekends. Still going strong is Cafe Lena, where Dylan, Don MacLean, and others performed years before they made the big time.

Skidmore's elitist past lives on in the student body. Male "coeds" aside, the typical "Skiddie" often combines the bohemianism of Isadora Duncan with the special grace of Amy Vanderbilt—refined, restrained, but hip and sexually liberated. Clothes are still important, and top-siders and rugby shirts are "in." The prep crowd can be avoided though, and plenty of other types are now in evidence at Skidmore.

Alcohol and pot are very popular, but other drugs are rare. Campus security is lax, and Saratoga police rarely make a bust, and then only in cases of the harder stuff.

With a predominantly female enrollment, Skidmore still welcomes visitors from men's colleges with open arms. Williams, Hamilton, Colgate, Union, and Dartmouth males are prevalent in bars, mixers, and winter term courses. A man's status is still on the minds of many

Skidmore women, but it is slowly becoming absent from their conversations. And when the men don't come to the women, the women go to the men. Weekends are still "suitcase time."

The "artistically oriented" male is still coming to Skidmore, but the new wave of men seems to fall into every conceivable category of college students. They are active (perhaps disproportionately so) in sports, government, clubs, and resident positions. Though the Colgate man can still find a place between Skidmore sheets, normal relationships between Skidmore men and women are on the rise. The question of furthering coeducation is on everyone's lips, and the school is making every effort to attract more men by implementing new programs and enlarging departments and sports facilities.

The transfer rate at Skidmore of about a third of each class has not decreased much in the last few years.

Although the social life may be monotonous, the interests of the students are refreshingly varied. There are worse places to lead a monotonous social life.

SMITH COLLEGE

Location: Northampton, MA 01063
Campus: city center
Undergraduate enrollment: 2500 W
Total enrollment: 2800
Expenses: $7800
Financial aid: 33%
Library: 854,000 volumes
Student-faculty ratio: 10–1
Transfer students: 75
Median SAT: 600 V, 600 M
Sororities: 0%
Application deadline: February 1

The bookstore at Smith College does a brisk business in multicolored T-shirts which proclaim boldly across the chests of Smith students, "A century of women on top, Smith College, 1875–1975." As a pioneer in the higher education of women, Smith has been alma mater to generations of brilliant and motivated women. The school is proud of its tradition and is reflective upon its role as the largest independent women's college in the country.

While the school's administration prefers to think that the present student body came to Smith primarily because it was a women's college, students do not generally agree. Most chose Smith because of its fine academic reputation, some no doubt came because their mothers and grandmothers did, and others because they were rejected at primarily male Ivy schools.

Smith is educationally appealing. The small size, diverse curriculum, and absence of any course requirements make Smith a place where the student can structure her own education and be in close contact with faculty members. English, art history, and government are the largest and most popular departments on campus. Because of the convenient Five College exchange, students may take courses at Amherst, the University of Massachusetts, Hampshire, and Mount Holyoke. Given the offerings of these five institutions, an outstanding education can be found in almost any field. Arranging to take a course at another school is reasonably easy, although difficulties with credit transfer may arise. Free buses run regularly between the schools.

While men from the other Pioneer Valley schools are often on the Smith campus for courses, the number of male "coeds" spending a semester or year at Smith from other schools has dropped recently. The drop in exchange interest is not reciprocal. The competition is heated for Smith students applying for the year at another school or on a foreign program. While many students choose a specific program for their year away, others simply wish to attend a coed college.

The environment for meaningful relationships with men is clearly not ideal. The closest source of males is the Five College area. Cultural and social offerings can provide companionship for anyone who is outgoing and enjoys dating. Being already involved does help make the social realm more bearable, because the mixer scene can become pretty tiresome, and so can Amherst frat parties and Saturday night movies and theater productions. There are, however, parties almost every weekend. It is up to the individual student—and many opt for the library or for "hanging out" in Davis Student Center, where beer, wine, food, and frequent weekend entertainment are offered. Whether or not students find an active social life with men does not appear to affect their feelings about their friendships with women. Friends that you make at Smith and the relationships that you have with those friends are far better than can be found at other colleges.

Smith is located in Northampton, a small city of 30,000. Many cosmopolitan types never overcome their initial shock at the small, specialty-shop downtown area and choose to ignore the city. Things aren't really as bad as they seem, though. The government, psychology, and education departments conduct programs in interaction with the community, while Northampton is historically valuable, and the geographical area is prime for exploration by geology students. Many students do volunteer work in the community at hospitals, schools, and Hispanic-American centers.

Smith retains its "house" system whereby students live in mostly old, ivied houses with fewer than eighty students and eat in house dining rooms with the same number. With twenty-four-hour parietals and no rules against drinking or drug use, the houses are autonomous. The use of alcohol and pot is widespread; anything stronger is hard to find.

The prim-and-proper tradition that visitors always anticipate is maintained only in superficial customs like tea one afternoon a week, linen napkins (paper are also available for the less genteel), and candlelight Thursday dinner, a meal to which faculty members are often invited. Head residents, who are seniors, handle emergencies and procedural details, practicing a "hands off" policy for anything else. The house system fosters a decentralized campus mood which makes the successful running of campus-wide student activities very difficult. There are many opportunities for students to become involved in various types of extracurricular activities, although the workload prevents many from immersing themselves totally. Interhouse sports competition is heated in many houses.

For students wishing alternate housing, there are two cooperate houses where students cook and clean for themselves. In addition, the Friedman complex provides apartment-type living on-campus. There are major renovations underway for an addition to the library which should be completed in 1982.

Like most college campuses today, Smith is experiencing a resurgence of activism. Spirits are high. Still, students are concerned with grades and graduate school or jobs. Smith students, typically derided as being too passive, are now questioning their role as women. Some are interested in pioneering into new fields; others contemplate the reconciliation of marriage and family with occupation and self-fulfillment; and some search for rich husbands so that they may perpetuate the country-club-and-tennis legend. The most important changes that could be made at Smith, the students feel, are the introduction of vocationally oriented courses and a greater spirit of community.

There is no push for coeducation at Smith. Women are on top and enjoying it, with no intention of being subjugated or rolling over.

UNIVERSITY OF THE SOUTH

Location: Sewanee, TN 37375 **Student-faculty ratio:** 10–1
Campus: rural **Transfer students:** 25

Undergraduate enrollment: Median SAT: 550 V, 600 M
600 M, 400 W Fraternities: 65%
Total enrollment: 1060 Sororities: 25%
Expenses: $6280 Application deadline:
Financial aid: 46% March 1
Library: 435,000 volumes

Sewanee is a refuge for tradition and legacy in the true spirit of the old South. The school relies to a great extent on alumni connections and the Episcopal dioceses that own and operate it for applicants and financial backing. Sewanee might suffocate in its own aristocratic provincialism were it not for the quarter of the student body which hails from outside the South, and the few nonconformists the school attracts who enjoy defying the norm.

Though many argue, often over too many bourbons and water, that Sewanee, (situated on a 10,000-acre tract of wooded land atop the Cumberland Plateau in southeastern Tennessee) is as close to heaven as one might get, Sewanee is not a paradise. Indeed, two areas of great concern to administration and students alike are the low (sixty percent) retention rate of a freshman class graduating from Sewanee in four years and the ubiquitous fog. Efforts are underway to alleviate both problems, though some pessimists feel more success will be had with the latter.

In line with inherent tradition, the English department is a typical representative of the strength of the liberal arts: *The Sewanee Review* has long stood in the forefront of the nation's literary reviews. A revamped natural resources department is more comprehensive in its offerings than before, and yet fails to live up to its reputation for what resources the vast campus domain has to offer. Classes are, on the average, quite small, with both student-faculty ratios and relationships exceptionally good. The Bachelor of Science is a particularly rigorous and more rewarding program, with a high percentage of graduates pursuing postgraduate education.

Perhaps the stiff distribution requirements are a factor in the retention problem, as a 300 level (literature) foreign language course is the nemesis of a few; but then, Sewanee, as elsewhere, is a breeding ground for general student apathy. Newcomers must make a gregarious effort to participate in the school's extracurricular offerings.

Sewanee's social life likewise defies stereotyping. Only now is there a rough split in the male-female ratio of entering students, as coeds were first admitted in 1969. Social functions revolve predominantly around the fraternity system, with the bulk of the partying scheduled for three weekend (week-long?) binges. Sororities have recently entered the scene, further contributing to the social stratification and providing southern belles with an outlet for their feminism. The purist independent can find needed solace from the Greeks in the well-equipped library weeknights or in the campus pub on weekends.

Unique to the University of the South (a pretentious name not commonly used on the campus per se) is the close bond with Oxford University in England. Many archaic Sewanee traditions are directly tied to Oxford, including the donning of black gowns by professors and those students with the prerequisite academic average. The architectural style, also borrowed from Oxford, serves as surrogate to the northern ivy-covered pedagogical towers which Sewanee students sometimes feel they are attending.

Athletics supply the usual release from academic frustrations, with greater participation and enthusiasm going to intramurals than to the varsity program. However, Sewanee is fairly competitive on the varsity level, and the "Tiger" spirit is only truly witnessed in the autumnal pigskin contests.

The administrative hierarchy has undergone a near-complete change in personnel through the last few years. Able and receptive men have stepped in, and the university's attitude toward student opinion has been reflected in the inclusion of students of diverse backgrounds on the various search and task force committees.

Relief from the fog and isolation is sought by many and found by few in occasional weekend treks to the nearest metropolitan areas of Nashville and Atlanta (roughly eighty and one hundred-sixty-five miles away, respectively). Daily newspapers can be found there, along with the culture shock of traffic and more than the one stop light found in Sewanee.

Sewanee might pretend to be for everyone, but realistically, the Sewanee experience is appreciated by a slight majority of those who actually matriculate there.

Sewanee overflows with creative energy, and when it is channeled in a constructive direction, i.e., publications, student government, art, and occasionally academia, the whole community benefits.

UNIVERSITY OF SOUTH CAROLINA

Location: Columbia SC 29208
Campus: city center
Undergraduate enrollment: 7500 M, 7000 W
Student-faculty ratio: 18–1
Transfer students: 2500
Median SAT: 446 V, 474 M
Fraternities: 13%

Total enrollment: 24,842
Expenses: $2200 (in-state),
  $3200 (out-of-state)
Financial aid: 50%
Library: 2,000,000 volumes

Sororities: 13%
Application deadline:
  December 1

USC is one of the oldest state universities around, and tradition still rules a strong hand there. Dr. James Holderman, the university president, is trying to upgrade the fraternity/football image. The school is making strides toward heterogeneity. USC, we're told, is much better than people give it credit for being. The journalism and business schools are excellent, while the English department boasts some top-notch professors. Faculty members run the gamut from an "old guard" that wishes it had fought with Robert E. Lee to more liberal "young turks" who might have been on the students' side of the barricades a decade ago.

The university has a wide range of undergraduate programs. The college of business administration enrolls the plurality of the students. Academically, South Carolina probably ranks on a par with other state institutions, primarily because state legislators' sympathies lie with the "good ole boys" who play football and hate Commies, and educational funds are appropriated accordingly. The faculty is nowhere near as strong as it should be, but there's enough money to house the football players in an opulent new dormitory reserved for them.

Athletics, in fact, are probably the main reason why South Carolinians continue to spend money on the university. A few years ago, they went out and hired top-flight Paul Dietzel to coach the football team. While "Pepsodent Paul" somehow never quite attained the national success that he seemed destined for, a hustling basketball team provides some consolation for the sizable number of students who major in spectator sports at South Carolina.

Carolina's reputation as a party school may be slightly exaggerated. Alcohol is ever-popular, with pot coming in a close second. Hard drugs are relatively rare, especially in the fraternities. Despite occasional agitation, the frats still have big rushes, and Greek Day (a quaint tradition when sorority girls wrestle in lard and slap each other with a dead fish) is still an invulnerable campus institution.

The city of Columbia caters to USC students. There are many good bars and clubs. It is something of a joke that on Saturday nights the bars have to close at midnight because of South Carolina's blue laws. The state of South Carolina is something else, but, like the school, it is improving.

USC has quite a number of students from New York, New Jersey, and other northern states. Northerners have varied reactions to Carolina: some really love it, others can't stand the slower pace.

If you like a relaxed, beer-drinking way of life with a chance to get a good education if you seek it out, then Carolina's for you.

UNIVERSITY OF SOUTH DAKOTA

Location: Vermillion, SD 57069
Campus: rural
Undergraduate enrollment:
   2213 M, 2149 W
Total enrollment: 5734
Expenses: $2300 (in-state),
   $3100 (out-of-state)
Financial aid: 60%
Library: 300,000 volumes

Student-faculty ratio: 17–1
Transfer students: 300
Median ACT: 21
Fraternities: 30%
Sororities: 30%
Application deadline:
   August 15

Senator George McGovern used to answer assailants' charges that he was a "far-out radical" by feigning a slightly exaggerated Midwestern twang to say, "The people of the state of South Dakota do not have the habit of sending wild-eyed radicals to the Senate of the United States." These same downhome folk don't send "wild-eyed radicals" to their state university (often their alma mater) at Vermillion, either. USD remains a quiet, peaceful place, albeit a few years more advanced than it used to be.

Signs of awareness are coming to the Vermillion campus, slowly, but surely. After years of enforcing curfews for women as part of its *in loco parentis* duties, the university has finally removed all curfew regulations. Visitation hours at both male and female dorms remain limited—due more to a stuffed-shirt board of regents than to college administrators. And drugs are becoming increasingly accepted, even if absolute usage lags behind that at a majority of colleges.

If a placid solitude still permeates USD social life, the students are clearly hampered by their environment. We can think of any better spots to have fun, but the kids at South Dakota do the best they can with the situation they face, which is Vermillion. The town of 9,000 is more or less a welfare patient of the university, and the depressing burg drags the college down with it. To escape for entertainment, students travel to Sioux Falls, S. D., or Sioux City, Iowa, which gives you some idea of the social desperation of Vermillion.

Most students participate to some extent in campus life, but some sixty percent have cars, and many students depart for home on the weekends. A fairly new four-dorm complex with alternate male and female floors and a common dining hall has been well received at USD and is stirring up interest in on-campus life. Students are unenthusiastic about sports. Jocks would be happier at more sports-minded South Dakota State.

The student senate is the most powerful of any in the state—which means absolutely nothing. Although dominated by Greeks and ignored by everyone else, the senate has been able to influence some faculty decisions of late—including the establishment of some pass/fail courses.

USD can claim one relatively unusual political movement on campus—the American Indian Movement, which was responsible for the occupation at Wounded Knee. Vermillion is the biggest hotbed of American Indian politics in the nation, and an Institute of Indian Studies was formed at USD.

Grass is increasingly common. Drug users are cautioned, however, that narcs remain nearly as numerous as dealers (where a "law enforcement program drags in the biggest rednecks in the state," according to one student).

Recently added redeeming programs include computer science and Afro-American literature. An honors program in the college of arts and sciences is one more lure to good students.

UNIVERSITY OF SOUTHERN CALIFORNIA

Location: Los Angeles, CA 90007
Campus: city center
Undergraduate enrollment: 7406 M, 5330 W
Total enrollment: 26,907
Expenses: $7980
Financial aid: 60%
Library: 1,950,000 volumes
Student-faculty ratio: 14–1
Transfer students: 2500
Median SAT: M: 494 V, 573 M; W: 470 V, 503 M
Median ACT: 25
Fraternities: 18%
Sororities: 18%
Application deadline: May 1—priority deadline January 1

The University of Southern California is the kind of school that 1950s TV child stars Ricky and David Nelson must have attended.

Football remains the biggest thing on campus, most students matriculate with definite career objectives (to become a doctor or lawyer or to take over Dad's business), and the Greek system has a stranglehold on social life that would make even Idi Amin envious.

However, USC, one of the biggest and oldest private institutions in the West, remains the place to go for future success in the southern California area. The SC game is the tried and trusted one of alumni contacts, and the "Trojans" of yesteryear control Los Angeles and the surrounding suburbs in overwhelming proportions. USC students know this, but more importantly, their parents know it—and that is why the kids are there. For obvious reasons, then, the decision of which fraternity or sorority to pledge is often more important to the typical "Trojan" than the selection of a major.

Yet, the University of Southern California is more than just an employment agency for ambitious Greeks. The preeminence of USC alumni in southern California positions of influence is not merely the result of a well-oiled patronage system, but also a reflection of the most respected graduate and professional schools in the nation, particularly in medicine, dentistry, business, and law. Many a "Trojan" willfully undergoes four years of stale beer and old Beach Boys records with the overriding goal of getting into USC Law or USC Med, and for many the strategy pays off.

The undergraduate college seems to take a back seat to the prestigious graduate schools in budgetary matters, and at a school molded in the corporate ethos of "balanced budgets or else," this can prove unsettling for those who dispute the profit-loss approach to education. USC is a prime example of an outstanding graduate division coexisting with an improving undergraduate school.

Expanded undergraduate courses, study abroad pass/fail courses, an honors program, and semesters at other schools or cities are among USC's better contributions to undergrad education.

Journalism is outstanding among undergrad programs. USC gears its professional program to combining majors in specific fields with general education.

As for life there, alcohol is forbidden on campus but allowed in housing. Dorms are open for visits by friends at all hours.

But even if Ricky and Dave and Wally Plumstead and their buddies down at the frat would fit into the USC of today rather nicely, Mr. and Mrs. Nelson might have just the slightest hesitation about sending them there. The SC campus is located in what has become one of the roughest areas of the L. A. ghetto, and the incidence of student rapes, muggings, and even murders has risen in recent years. Some of the on-campus socializing would not get past prime-time censors, either.

The non-Greek social life at USC happens off-campus—at home. Many USC students spend their weekends commuting to their homes in suburbia to visit high school honeys, mow lawns, and escape central L. A. Sports remain popular, with the well-funded "Trojan" athletic teams at the top of the nation in virtually everything.

The mass exodus to the friendly confines of home is not all that surprising, for many USC students borrow heavily from their parents in life-style. Many would like nothing better than to get a split-level house in suburbia complete with garden and three-car garage. That's not to say USC grads are cloned, though.

John Wayne went to USC and it wasn't his education that made him famous. So did Art Buchwald and he's made it on factors other than his academic credentials. Fame and fortune are exclusive of a USC education. But then again, you, too, could become an illustrious alumnus.

SOUTHERN ILLINOIS UNIVERSITY/CARBONDALE

Location: Carbondale, IL 62901
Campus: city outskirts
Undergraduate enrollment: 10,600 M, 6500 W
Total enrollment: 22,550
Expenses: $3000 (in-state), $4000 (out-of-state)
Financial aid: 50%
Library: 1,500,000 volumes
Student-faculty ratio: NA
Transfer students: 2275
Median ACT: M: 20.3, W: 19.2
Fraternities: 6%
Sororities: 4%
Application deadline: none

Southern Illinois University is the "one real cultural center" in southern Illinois, according to novelist John Gardner. That's only half the story. SIU, with major campuses at Carbondale and Edwardsville, is also a notorious party school.

The largest campus is at Carbondale, and it epitomizes Southern. The school has a rule against open drinking on campus that is enforced with only slightly more regularity than the state drinking age in Carbondale: never. As one student put it, "There's nothing to do in Carbondale but drink." Rather than curse their misfortune, the city fathers have done their best to accommodate the students. Every Friday and Saturday night, officials block off the main drag where the bars and discos are located and allow the carnival atmosphere to spill out in the streets. Booths are set up; inhibitions are at a minimum. The students circulate among the bars during the week, too.

But although beer and alcohol are still preeminent, drugs have made inroads into Southern's social scene; smoking dope in the dorms is not very smart.

Other aspects of social life are typical of large campuses. Frats are going broke, interdorm sports are big, and support for the basketball team is enthusiastic. The male-female ratio is a bit lopsided. Road trips to nearby St. Louis are common, with a pilgrimage to the temple of Anheuser-Busch usually included. Prominent national figures lecture frequently, two or three rock concerts are sponsored each semester, and touring companies present ballet and theater performances.

The environs of the Carbondale campus are beautifully wooded, centering around the aptly named "Lake-on-Campus." The lake provides recreational activities, such as boating and ice skating in season. (The weather in Carbondale is either very warm and humid or very cold and windy.) Buildings such as the Morris Library and the high-rise residential halls have been tastefully designed. Many students find the dorms only "passable" and cite the expense and restrictiveness of dorm living. In fact, the recent trend has been to move into house trailers. Despite the tendency of trailers to blow over in storms, and despite the sardine-like conditions (including having to sleep standing up, occasionally), they are the most popular housing alternative.

We are told that a "pompous, unfeeling administration and board of trustees" is a major problem at SIU. Parking spaces are at a premium, and police officers don't hesitate to tow away cars parked illegally. Fines are high.

When the parties subside, it's time (sometimes) to consider academics. Liberal arts are emphasized, and chemistry is strong. The school of journalism is rated one of the best in the nation, and the student-run *Daily Egyptian* recently won two national awards. General requirements take up freshman and sophomore years and are designed to give the usual "broad educational base," although some students feel that spending sixteen hours a quarter for two years, meeting requirements, is a less than optimal use of time. The first two years are almost certainly spent in large lecture courses and in seminars taught by graduate students.

One senior told us, "Southern's a gas, but surprisingly, you really do learn." It does seem surprising, but maybe Southern Illinois is just the right blend of books and booze. After all, they're pretty good at mixing things at Southern.

SOUTHERN METHODIST UNIVERSITY

Location: Dallas, TX 75275
Campus: suburban
Undergraduate enrollment:
 2744 M, 2737 W
Total enrollment: 8677
Expenses: $6200
Financial aid: 35%
Library: 1,500,000 volumes

Student-faculty ratio: 15–1
Transfer students: 450
Median SAT: 500 V, 550 M
Fraternities: 37%
Sororities: 44%
Application deadline:
 April 1

Southern Methodist University counts Bob Hope among its big contributors. Bob is famous for surrounding himself with attractive women on stage, and his money is perpetuating a campus that could probably supply him with more beautiful, healthy faces than he'd ever wish for. Word of mouth has it that SMU girls are part of the pride of the South.

SMU has the potential to become the pride of Dallas, Texas. Its residents would like a good university and SMU could fit the bill if the administration continues to upgrade. SMU has long been characterized as a party school, but some changes are being made. Old ideas of SMU must be revised somewhat.

SMU has built a new University Library, Fine Arts Center, Law Library, and all-sports complex in the past few years. In fact, most SMU buildings were very recently constructed.

SMU has long had a faculty that its students didn't necessarily deserve. The school's best offerings come in art, theater, and business. Courses that teach "marketable" skills are popular, especially among the large commuter population, many of whom are professionals aiming to move ahead in their fields. The university has begun several new programs, including an independent reading program that allows selected students to skip lectures in the humanities. Needless requirements (two semesters of physical education and twelve hours of special humanities courses) do still exist. SMU's greatest academic problem comes from the students themselves—many kids are there just to have a good time. Greek leaders driving around campus with a loudspeaker to urge "all those freshman girls to blow off the first day of class and come over to the house to get together and drink some beer" give you a feel for the problem.

Nevertheless, dating, drinking, and sports are still the unholy trinity for many SMU students. As one student said, "While SMU is a place to go through your own changes at your own speed, too many people use the isolation and the nice weather and all the comforts of home away from home to vegetate for four years."

Another SMU problem is location. It is not located in Dallas proper (which is not a bad city) but rather in an enclave consisting of two island cities (University and Highland Park) with an extremely conservative population and repressive police force. These two communities provide low taxes for their citizens, but their main purpose is that they have their own school system—solid white.

SMU has done away with all curfews (even for freshman women), but visiting is still limited and the rules are enforced. Greek life is tremendously important in upperclass years. Some students now claim that they join because it's easier to get dope through a fraternity, but in any case the Greeks with all their initiations and "fun" are still active at SMU. Some women still drop out when they don't get into the sorority of their choice.

One reason for the lingering party atmosphere is probably the affluence of the SMU student body. Difference between admission to privately run SMU and Texas state schools is largely financial. SMU's endowment is not large enough to permit it to offer many scholarships, so its student body remains rich, largely Texan, certainly highly Southern, and quite suburban.

SMU is a school to watch.

SOUTHWESTERN/MEMPHIS

Location: Memphis, TN 38112
Campus: city center
Undergraduate enrollment:
 504 M, 488 W
Total enrollment: 1024
Expenses: $6075
Financial aid: 52%
Library: 175,000 volumes

Student-faculty ratio: 11–1
Transfer students: 45
Median SAT: M: 538 V, 588 M;
 W: 545 V, 550 M
Median ACT: M: 26, W: 25
Fraternities: 50%
Sororities: 50%
Application deadline:
 February 1

While Southwestern is a small, academically oriented liberal arts college located in midtown Memphis, Tennessee, the atmosphere and competition are not unbearable. A few slip through and we're told most of these are jocks who contribute to the school in their own way. Professors are readily accessible—meetings over a beer in the pub are common.

Communication lines between students and administrators are reportedly wide open. Of course, certain rules remain unbent, but drinking, cars, and dorm intervisitation remain permissible.

Social life is adequate. The Greeks, who compose half the student population, offer many open events. In addition, the dean of students' office helps insure the availability of a social life. A pool, sports events, frequent movies and plays, teas, beer busts, bands and intramural athletics are big.

A student center houses the pub, snack bar, a fairly overpriced bookstore, and a helpful counseling center.

Memphis is a pretty decent place to live. It's friendly and offers good old Southern hospitality. Southwestern's location across from Overton Park makes the park, art gallery, art academy, zoo, and golf course accessible.

Then again, all this is difficult to take advantage of as Southwestern follows a rather unique schedule of three terms (twelve-twelve-six hours). Breaks don't coincide with those of other schools and two classes are crammed into that six-week third term. It has its good points, though—studies abroad and scientific field trips fit well into six weeks.

Like many schools, Southwestern is swinging back toward conservatism. Greeks and independents form cliques that are avoidable. Preppies are few but their style is catching on.

Academically, the school is not dominated by its Presbyterian affiliation. Courses in religion are not required, though we're told "man in the light of history and religion" is an excellent freshman course.

While schedules and programs are flexible, the frosh are sometimes closed out of classes. Independent study and job internships are popular.

Southwestern's honor code is accepted and respected by students and faculty, with a few exceptions. Those rare abuses are handled by the student council.

The beautiful campus, full of Gothic "serenity and seriousness," hosts a spring Renaissance Festival and other cultural outdoor events.

Things in the South are no longer backward, we're told. Southwestern adds a bright spot of civilization to Memphis, Tennessee.

STANFORD UNIVERSITY

Location: Stanford, CA 94035 **Student-faculty ratio: 10–1**
Campus: suburban **Transfer students: 300**

Undergraduate enrollment: Median SAT: M: 620 V, 690 M;
3792 M, 2846 W W: 620V, 630 M
Total enrollment: 12,618 Median ACT: NA
Expenses: 8700 Fraternities: 15%
Financial aid: 53% Sororities: 10%
Library: 4,364,000 volumes Application deadline:
January 1

Stanford is not all it seems to be. While this may be obvious, it is important to think twice about the statistics that appear above these sagacious words and in the various public-relations booklets the university distributes to its prospective undergraduates.

First of all, don't be deceived by the median SAT score. Maybe half the students scored 650 or above, but that doesn't mean you should expect to discuss Hemingway or Nietzsche over dinner. Or anytime, for that matter. The general tone of the school is anti-intellectual and consciously so. After all, this is sunny California, and it would be downright irresponsible for people to have a genuine interest in what they are studying. And besides, what is more important, getting some sun ("bagging rays," as it is called here) or talking about some dude who has been dead for years? You can guess how most Stanford students answer this question.

Stanford is a very athletic school. It boasts a good football team, fields a top water polo squad, and in general pays a great deal of attention to its varsity players. Not so the underfinanced and understaffed junior varsity program—if you haven't been recruited, chances are slim, too, that you'll make the varsity team.

Sports at Stanford tend toward the intramural and the casual—a volleyball game after dinner with people in the dorm, or a run through the hills behind the campus as the sun is setting. Such informality is far more characteristic of sports at Stanford than a date-laden football weekend. Sure, Stanfordites are proud of their team and care about the rivalry with UC/Berkeley across the bay, but it's not the obsession it is at USC or other "football schools."

And while the administration claims that the athletic department does not control the admission of the coaches' choices, it often becomes painfully clear in some of the classes that most football players did not have the stellar academic records many others had to have to get in.

This reflects the admissions office's standard policy more than any out-and-out lying on its part, since the admissions policy is weighted toward capable students who have taken part in many extracurricular activities. If your SAT total was 1000, but you were editor of your school newspaper and a four-year member of the student council, don't be deterred from applying. On the other hand, if you boast a 3.95 average and double 800s, you stand a good chance in any case. Money probably won't help—the admissions office people will insist till they are blue in the face that financial aid information is not available to them until the admissions process is complete.

The claim that fifty-five percent of Stanford students are on financial aid, though, is in itself misleading. A very large proportion of the people you encounter at Stanford will be somewhat snobbish, upper-middle to upper class and will spend their summer and winter vacations at various exotic resorts. This Stanford is by no stretch of the imagination a plebian university, and for someone not used to the monied life, it can be somewhat frustrating.

You may also expect frustration if you are a liberal arts major. Stanford often seems to be more of a professional or vocational school for premeds and engineers than an eclectic university. Some statistics may be in order here. Nearly half of the class of '78 majored in the premed subjects (biology, chemistry, human biology, and medical microbiology), engineering, and economics.

Things are changing, though. In 1980, Stanford announced the instatement of a required one-year course in "western literature" to be followed by one course in each of seven broad subject areas spanning literature, philosophy, math, natural sciences, technology and social thought. These new distribution requirements, which include one course concentrating on a non-Western culture, are Stanford's answer to rounding out their students' educations.

Even though many students are science-oriented, many social sciences and humanities departments are very strong, notably psychology, English, and history.

For students with motivation and initiative, professors are approachable and willing to spend time with students. Even the "big names" conduct both lectures and seminars for undergrads.

The strength of the academics, though, may not make up for the fact that because of their pre-professional outlook, many Stanford students place undue emphasis on their grades and too little stress on what they are actually learning.

Through judicious use of the Stanford housing system, one can add a great deal of learning experience to life outside the classroom. Besides the traditional multihundred-resident dorms (all of which are coed, some by floor, some by room), there are quite a few smaller houses (centered around such themes as political change through nonviolence; American studies; alternative life-styles; French, Italian, and Central

European culture; and some luxurious houses that some say are based on hedonism). There is not enough housing on-campus to accommodate everyone who wants it, so many students are forced to spend one of their four years off-campus.

San Francisco is usually quoted as not being very far off-campus, but the thirty miles that separate the two might just as well be 300 to judge by the way many students neglect the opportunities it has to offer.

Once you look beyond the façade of numbers at Stanford, you get a different picture of the realities. Different from an East Coast school in its climate and academic emphasis, Stanford offers a unique college experience. Don't come to Stanford expecting to find a Harvard, but don't worry—it's not a USC, either.

STEPHENS COLLEGE

Location: Columbia, MO 65201
Campus: city center
Undergraduate enrollment: 1400 W
Expenses: $6000
Financial aid: 42%
Library: 125,000 volumes

Student-faculty ratio: 11–1
Transfer students: 110
Median SAT: 466 V, 470 M
Sororities: 20%
Application deadline: none

Until recently, Stephens College's claim to notoriety has been its reputation as one of the last Southern finishing schools—a "Proper School for Young Ladies." The school has moved beyond the horse-and-buggy era in recent years, and four-year B. A.s and B. F. A.s now far outnumber two-year associate degrees.

The women's studies program established in 1974 has heightened the students' awareness of their history and problems as a group. Many professors teach from a feminist perspective. And most students feel that Stephens's biggest strength is the excellent faculty. This group is concerned with individual needs and progress. Faculty members are willing to sacrifice time to students. Most colleges and universities cannot claim such a dedicated faculty.

Stephens's social life centers more around the nearby Missouri University campus than its own. *Sports Illustrated* once described Columbia as the only nonghost town in America with an arcaded main street and hitching posts in front of all the stores. There are a lot of bars and discos, though, and the town is suprisingly liberal when you consider what state it's in. Also, concerts are frequent at both Missouri

U and Stephens, for the more culturally inclined. Nevertheless, students at both schools concur that one of the best things about Columbia is leaving it. Only forty-seven percent of the student body claimed to be satisfied with their social experience.

Despite the limited social environment, today's "Stephens Suzies" point out that their liberal education helps make up for it. Some fancy the school the "Sarah Lawrence of the Midwest," but we're not sure that Sarah Lawrence would consider an A in "food preparation" as respectable as an A in "chemistry." Stephens's most popular departments are fashion, equestrian science, television-radio-film, theater, and dance. English and social science are also strong.

For the politically minded, there are groups such as the Young Democrats, Stephens Feminist Caucus, Martin Luther King Scholarship Committee (for black students), Lesbian Underground Railroad, and Student Government Association. Community volunteer organizations are also available.

The Stephens campus is beautiful and spacious. The brick buildings represent a mixture of old and new architecture. A new visitors' center, to be completed this year, will be Missouri's second solar-heated commercial building. The college owns a lot of land, including a lake, golf course, stables, and woods.

No one can deny that there is a Stephens "type." She is white, Protestant, middle to upper-middle class and from the South or Midwest. But administrators are trying to restructure their institution with the contemporary American woman in mind. In the process, Stephens is changing from a glorified rich girl's finishing school to a good place for a woman to develop her own brand of feminism. And for those whose interests are a bit less twentieth-century, rest assured that there are still some "Stephens Suzies" whose main topics of conversation are clothes and dates.

SWARTHMORE COLLEGE

Location: Swarthmore, PA 19081
Campus: suburban
Undergraduate enrollment:
　681 M, 593 W
Total enrollment: 1289
Expenses: $7100
Financial aid: 35%
Library: 480,000 volumes

Student-faculty ratio: 9–1
Transfer students: 5
Median SAT: 640 V, 680 M
Fraternities: 10%
Sororities: 0%
Application deadline:
　February 1

Swarthmore College sits on 300 acres of meadows and trees along Crum Creek, ten miles west of Philadelphia and ten miles east of wide-open farmland and country auctions. It it weren't for the dank Philadelphia weather, the location would be a reason for anyone to want to go there. And even despite the weather, the location is an asset.

The campus is groomed by a endowed horticultural foundation which puts tags with Latin names on all the fancy trees and shrubs. The spring flowers, although undeservedly emphasized in most descriptions of the campus, are pretty neat unless you have allergies.

Is the school the academic pressure cooker they say it is? Probably not. At any given moment, half the people in the library are blissfully sleeping on those plush carpets. The students are, however, more motivated ("driven," if you will) than other student bodies we've seen.

That's good and that's bad. When it's good, people like their work and do a lot of it. When it's bad, it can be a bummer. In its most perverted state, it leads an insecure student to go bananas under the "academic pressure" you've probably heard about. In the next worst state, people just go through the motions (which do involve busting your ass pretty regularly) without even internalizing the motivation which makes them do it. They complain a lot and wear dissatisfaction on their faces; they're being "driven" by an external force.

Some call it pre-professionalism, but that's no different from the drive of many students on many other campuses.

The most probable reason for that is that superearnest "Sweatmore" College tries to educate eighteen-year-olds in an atmosphere intense enough so that many people ought to be twenty-three or so before they jump in. Then again, many eighteen-year-olds (and you may be one of them) are ready for the place.

The students are taught in seminars and Swarthmore regards its method highly. The faculty is cautious about off-campus study and work-study programs but offers study abroad usually through other institutions. They are very flexible about time off from school. If you want it, they figure, it's probably what you need.

Swarthmore's moderately famous honors program, now under open review by students and faculty, is perhaps best described by a recent freshman handbook, in the glossary under T. P.:

T. P. (Toilet Paper)

You're probably familiar with the role that toilet paper has played in your life up to now, but there's more in store. Scott Paper Co. owns this college. Furthermore, every toilet stall in the college has two rolls. And some frustrated artist has invariably come along and scrawled "coarse" over one roll and "honors" over the other.

The college's educational program is patterned after the two-T. P. roll system, and it offers "course" and "honors" to upperclassmen. Students in "course" continue taking classes all along and face comprehensive examinations in their major near the end of their senior year. Students in "honors" spend their last two years sleeping till noon and taking two double-credit seminars two afternoons per week. They don't get graded or tested (except informally) during those two years. A couple of weeks before graduation, a team of outside examiners comes in to make sure they really know all about their field. In return for worrying about the outside examiners for two years, "honors" students are given preferential treatment which keeps "course" students mad at the discriminatory system.

Of course, some departments are better than others. Engineering, physics, and math offer a scandalously good student-faculty ratio, and they (like every department) have some awfully sharp faculty members. On the other hand, all the drones who major in English, biology, economics, and political science keep the classes in those departments crowded. The only really good way to major in many of the more populated departments is in "honors." Though the number of music majors is small, the facilities are excellent and are used by students from all disciplines.

If you're not on a first-name basis with many of your teachers by virtue of tuning their cars, house-sitting for them, or simply meeting them socially, you may just be antisocial. Most faculty housing is arranged around the campus.

Ninety percent of the students live on-campus. Until recently, this was because the deans told them to. Now the deans have a housing shortage and a more liberal policy, but most students would rather live on-campus than hassle with the world of landlords. Everyone who lives on-campus eats in the college dining hall, and faces soon become very familiar.

Except for the arts building and women's gym, physical facilities are excellent. Several intensively used public transportation routes criss-cross the campus, making mobility painless and cheap.

Swarthmore has no serious financial problems—a refreshing change from most other colleges. Students agree that the college's financial aid program is generous, and part-time, on-campus jobs are available for virtually anyone who wants one. The school is also able to maintain an extremely low student-faculty ratio.

Extracurricular activities and campus ambience depend in large part on what individual students are doing. The place is small enough to notice the presence or absence of a few people who spearhead a given activity. You, too, can be a spearhead at Swarthmore.

Student musical organizations and theatrical productions are numerous and varied. The student newspaper is definitely a small-time operation, but interest in creative writing is high, and outlets are provided by student-run literary publications and college-sponsored competitions. Art facilities exist but are modest, and student interest fluctuates. Other active organizations include a women's center, World Hunger group, Political Action Committee, and Gay Liberation group. Interestingly enough, the largest campus organization, with over a hundred participants, is the radio station. The student council has little influence on big-time college policy, although Swarthmore students constantly attempt to make the administration listen to their opinions.

Athletics occupies the bodies of many Swarthmore students but the souls of few. The school's philosophy of athletics is soundly proparticipator and antispectator. Teams like football and basketball that depend upon a large talent pool are generally poor at Swarthmore. On the other hand, men's soccer and tennis and women's swimming are strong, and outstanding competitors are never absent from an entering class.

The position of minority students in the small, secluded, wealthy Swarthmore environment is difficult. But the Afro-American Student Society has taken an increasingly active role in student affairs, and the Black Cultural Center coordinates a variety of concerts and colloquia. The college has slightly improved counseling facilities for minority students, but the general philosophy of the administration seems to be to downplay the special problems minority students face and to regard a student as a student.

The social life at Swarthmore is casual. The small size of the school facilitates contact with other students. There is the usual quota of weekly dances, parties, and movies, but most students find the vital part of social life in ordinary interchange with the surprisingly diverse students in the dorms, library, and dining hall. But no prospective applicant should be fooled into thinking that small size makes Swarthmore an instant "community." The student body is stubbornly individualistic.

We're told that the prevailing student feeling is "We're people trying to do a hell of a lot, knowing that we can't do it all well." Thus, it's rare that any extracurricular effort comes off with big-university polish. Swarthmore's priorities are elsewhere. Is that a great loss? Yes, if you want to be a professional photographer on the basis of what you'll learn working for a flashy yearbook. But to most "Swarthies," including many who develop professional interest in spite of Swarthmore, it's a loss well worth tolerating. If you don't mind a student body too small to permit even a modicum of anonymity, Swarthmore is one of the most intense and highest-ranked of the nation's small colleges.

SWEET BRIAR COLLEGE

Location: Sweet Briar, VA 24595
Campus: rural
Undergraduate enrollment: 700 W
Expenses: $6200
Financial aid: 18%
Library: 170,000 volumes

Student-faculty ratio: 9–1
Transfer students: 20–25
Median SAT: 500 V, 500 M
Sororities: NA
Application deadline: March 1

Although Sweet Briar girls have been labeled certain sobriquets like "Rose Thorns" and "Briar Bitches" in the past, they have no standard nicknames today other than "roadies." If there are any others, they aren't being said to Sweet Briar faces.

SB girls admit that they are still, in part, a conservative finishing school. We were told, "If you are conservative and desire a certain polish, then this is the place. (You'd better bring along your khakis, kilts, clogs, knee-socks, Izods, and button-downs to fit in with the general mode of things.)"

Liberal arts prevail at Sweet Briar, and with a broad range of specific requirements, even pre-professionals get a full helping of liberal arts studies. "Art history" and "European civilization" are challenging courses, not to be taken to raise one's grade point average. Although competence in a language is required, the foreign language department needs to be updated and expanded. Keeping in mind the size of enrollment, though, the departments are small. However, this size permits personal rapport between students and faculty.

The "junior year abroad" program is one of the best features of ol' SBC. More than one-third of the junior class each year takes off for Europe, but the program can send you just about anywhere. After freshman year, you are eligible to spend winter term pretty much "as you please," either taking the term off, doing internships, participating in special studies, or in intensive study on-campus. Departments are helpful in program planning.

The social life is what you make it. SBC girls used to socialize with the Washington & Lee frat rats. Today, the trend favors the Hampden Sidney and the University of Virginia boys, all of whom are within a one-hour road trip. The action most certainly centers around fraternities. Occasionally, the Greeks "roll up" to Sweet Briar's gates. Count on spending weekends off-campus—academic pressures are diminishing the Wednesday night road trips.

The food is average as college food goes. However, contained within the sprawling 3,300 acres of Sweet Briar is the famous Sweet Briar dairy, which produces fresh milk and yogurt daily. The dairy is also responsible for daily doses of cow smell and a special brand of entertainment: "Cow tipping" which is a "must" for every drunken bash. (If you are not familiar with the sleeping habits of cows, they sleep standing with knees locked—and, boy, do they go down with a big thud!)

With the largest indoor riding ring in the country, the equestrian set has a great program which continues to produce nationally-ranked riding teams. SBC has beginner programs and provides horses, but you can bring your own.

There is a physical education requirement that may be satisfied by anything from canoeing to yoga. Varsity competition is offered in basketball, swimming, golf, tennis, lacrosse, field hockey, and riding.

Sweet Briar has a variety of traditional clubs and some unique traditions which they tell us "have to be seen to be believed (after the initial shock, they really can be a scream").

Generally, traditions play a big part in Sweet Briar life. The honor code is the most revered. A pledge is signed at the beginning of your freshman year which gives you an amazing amount of freedom during your stay at the college: unless you abuse it. Students are trusted with take-home exams. "Big Brother" is *not* watching you!

Culture, in small doses, hits the campus and an artistic commune known as Mt. San Angelo, a Sweet Briar affiliate, is located across the road, making writers and artists available for lectures and exhibits.

We are told that hard drugs are almost nonexistent, alcohol is king, and marijuana users are discreet. No-doze and Vivarin are the most abused.

Alumnae can be found in high places, a factor all the more encouraging, as Sweet Briar presents a challenge in academics and social life. Ol' SBC turns out some fairly well-educated young milkmaids.

SYRACUSE UNIVERSITY

Location: Syracuse, NY 13210
Campus: city center
Undergraduate enrollment: 11,000
Total enrollment: 15,000
Expenses: $7500
Financial aid: 70%
Library: 2,000,000 volumes
Student-faculty ratio: 15–1
Transfer students: 1000
Median SAT: 500 V, 540 M
Fraternities: 17%
Sororities: 17%
Application deadline: February 1

Syracuse University is a college that belonged to the Sixties. While it is neither the sports haven nor the fraternity school of yore, Syracuse, a big university in a fairly large city is rebuilding both aspects of its former identity. With the construction of a 50,000-seat domed stadium (the only one of its kind in the East), a recent invitation to the 1979 Independence Bowl, and a record as a perennial NCAA contender, spectator sports are on the upswing. The Greeks are coming back to life—houses that folded in the Sixties are recolonizing and the more stable houses are once again exercising selectivity at pledge time. Frats provide a viable alternate life-style to many SU students.

Syracuse has a large number of students. Most of them tend to come from Long Island, New Jersey, or central New York and the city itself has a significant representation in the student body. Alums cite this as a plus—rides home are easy to get and friendships are easier to maintain. So much for diversity, though there are many foreign students.

Living conditions in the dorms are understandably crowded, and off-campus housing may mean chasing one apartment after another while the city and the urban renewal people pursue their own business. But if population density isn't an annoyance, then the living quarters aren't too bad. Most of the dorms are modern, and virtually all are centrally located. The university also provides apartment housing at Skytop, a luxurious and overpriced community for upperclassmen. Student legal services and Alteracts help students with landlord and other lease problems, as funded by the student fee (no addition charge is passed on to students).

Most of the students at Syracuse either love it or are bored by it. Everything seems computerized, from registration to library checkout, and it's not unusual to feel a little lost in the crowd. But parties abound and academic pressure is at a minimum. You don't have to work very hard at Syracuse to get a degree, and if you do want to put time into your education, some facilities are there. There are some excellent people on the Syracuse faculty and a few stellar departments.

While the liberal arts college is weak, strength attracts students to the Maxwell School of Political Science, the SUNY School of Forestry, and the Newhouse School of Communications.

But don't expect a minor Ivy League. Syracuse has two major libraries, the Carnegie for natural sciences and the relatively new Ernest Stevenson Byrd library for everything else, and that includes socializing for lack of a "student union." The book collections are adequate, not impressive. And although Syracuse hires good individuals for teaching, the admissions policy is very lax. Syracuse's reputation is that of an expensive private university, and it tends to take virtually anybody with average grades who can pay the cost. If you're looking for stimulation from fellow students, it's more likely to be found in the honors program, the creative writing workshops, or some of the more esoteric fields of endeavor.

Syracuse's extracurricular activities are improving. Fraternities, sororities, and student organizations take on most of the planning. Five film societies show films, the concert board stays busy, and rumor has it a folk dancing club meets out under the stars when the weather's good. *The Daily Orange* is the Syracuse paper. The student union sponsors rock concerts and a few dances, and there are always various events in music and art either on campus or nearby. The Everson Museum is downtown, and the Syracuse Repertory Theater is within walking distance. Student theatrical presentations are fairly good but are usually the province of drama majors and those involved in the department. Skiing is good for many months of the year and the city does an efficient job at handling snow removal.

Location is a negative factor. The weather's usually grim. Even when it's not, the university's not a place to walk around at night. Thornden Park, which is near the campus, is pretty but a smaller version of Central Park for safety. Convenient Marshall Street is both fun and characteristic of the university's past. Filled with little bookstores, clothing shops, and record boutiques, Marshall Street used to be the hangout for radicals and freaks. Now it tries to be a one-block Greenwich Village.

If you're going to spend four years at Syracuse, bring skiis and a frisbee. The academic demands on you won't be very great.

TEMPLE UNIVERSITY

Location: Philadelphia, PA 19122 **Student-faculty ratio: NA**
Campus: city center **Transfer students: 4400**

Undergraduate enrollment:
7000 M, 7000 W
Total enrollment: 35,000
Expenses: $4680 (in-state),
$6070 (out-of-state)
Financial aid: 60%
Library: 1,501,025 volumes

Median SAT: M: 464 V, 517 M;
W: 477 V, 473 M
Fraternities: 5%
Sororities: 5%
Application deadline:
June 15 for fall,
November 15 for spring

For close to a century, Temple has provided an education for those who could not afford to attend the more expensive institutions or who were victims of racial or religious discrimination. In order to maintain tuition levels as low as possible, it has become a state-related institution in the last decade. Beyond that, however, Temple has always been interested in serving the needs of the public—and those generally run to commercial and technological training.

The upshot of this meritorious activity and ambition is that Temple is archly democratic, lacking in prestige, and enormous. In certain respects, however, Temple's prevailing reputation is unfair. The school provides a solid education for those of its students who care to work. The university has a strong English department and boasts a fine medical school as well; moreover, according to a recent survey, the department of biochemistry is one of the best in the country. Also, the departments of theater and radio-television-film are highly regarded.

Eighty-five percent of Temple's students commute, and the complaint most often heard from all is that the students lack cohesiveness. Not that they would be susceptible to radical organizing—although Republicans are extremely rare, most students reflect solidly middle-class aspirations and values. By and large, most students, many of whom have part-time jobs, go about their studies in a businesslike way.

The biggest problem that Temple faces is a lack of money. The state legislators in Harrisburg are busy dreaming up ways of running the state without exacting new taxes, and one of their favorite solutions has been to trim university appropriations. As a result, low-cost, high-quality education is becoming a near-impossibility. There is a pervasive feeling at Temple that the students are being reduced to the lowest common denominator. Although the university attempts to give them an education responsive to their needs (especially in such areas as business administration), it seems at the same time that there is nothing to write home about, which is just as well, since most students live at home anyway.

A passage in last year's yearbook referred to Temple's dorms as a place "in which the maximum number of people are forced to live in the minimum amount of space with the least degree of privacy and lowest quality of food." Opinions vary about dorm life at the school, but most agree that one gets used to it. Not much better but easier to live with are the Yorktown Apartments, literally across the street from the university. While the rents are high, the rooms adequate at best, and the service marginal, most residents prefer them to the dorms. Decent, fairly inexpensive housing can be found near the University of Pennsylvania campus. For the really ambitious, apartments in center-city Philadelphia are great, but expensive.

The neighborhood surrounding the college is decayed. A massive fund-raising effort has netted several million dollars recently for campus improvements. For those who would like to get away from the campus for a while, the branch campus in center-city has expanded to include a number of course offerings, day or night; it is now possible to obtain a degree there without ever going to the main campus. If you crave a rural setting, there's the Ambler campus with its surrounding trees, lakes, and hills.

Since most of the student population is gone by three-thirty P.M. (at two o'clock on Fridays, the school resembles a ghost town), not much is offered in the way of campus activities. However, there are loads of intramural sports, clubs, and free movies. Speakers and music groups are practically nonexistent. But the place is not a vacuum—if you look hard enough, you can almost always find something to do, and the campus is only a few minutes away from the heart of revitalized central Philadelphia, which is loaded with shops, theaters, museums, bars, and restaurants.

Although a Temple graduate will always be grateful for the opportunity the university has provided him, at the same time he will probably be eager to see his own children go to Penn.

TEXAS A & M UNIVERSITY

Location: College Station, TX 77843
Campus: rural
Undergraduate enrollment: 17,000 M, 9400 W
Total enrollment: 32,000
Expenses: $3400 (in-state), $4480 (out-of-state)
Financial aid: 35%
Library: 1,168,584 volumes

Student-faculty ratio: 13–1
Transfer students: 3300
Median SAT: 486 V, 550 M
Fraternities: NA
Sororities: NA
Application deadline: July 31

The A & M in Texas A & M University stood for "agriculture and mechanical" back in the old days when the school was a strict military training lab for Texas farm boys. But the last decade has seen a widening of A & M's scope, and the school is now predominantly civilian, though still not a party-time insitution.

A & M has the largest engineering enrollment in the country and tough agriculture, vet medicine, and forestry courses. It offers oceanography in Galveston at the Moody College, which produces maritime officers who live on shipboard; a new med school; and a 2000-strong coed cadet corps, isolated in its own part of the campus. Many cadets, we are told, do not want military careers but participate for the tradition and fraternal atmosphere in Army, Navy, Air Force, and Marine units.

The corps tries to maintain a sense of its own identity, aided no doubt by a mounted cavalry, militia school band, and mascot—a collie named "Reveille."

Academics are very important at Texas A & M, and class attendance affects a student's grades. While the stronger departments are engineering, agriculture, forestry, veterinary medicine, environmental design, and sciences; the liberal arts, which are not as strong, provide a communications department that gives hands-on training on the public radio and TV station KAMU, and the student newspaper, *The Battalion*.

When A & M's population doubled within six years, the cities of Bryan (47,000) and College Station (42,000) began to burst at the seams. There is little excitement outside the walls of the university, and students look to Houston (eighty miles away) or Austin (ninety miles away) for solid nightlife.

Social events in the fall revolve around one thing: football. "Aggies" support their team religiously, and weekends are filled with concerts, spirit-building "midnight yell practices," and, of course, the game. Around Thanksgiving, all hands are out gathering any available wood for the traditional seventy-foot-high bonfire which symbolizes the "Aggies'" undying desire to "beat the hell" out of the University of Texas.

The spring semester is highlighted by formal balls, beer blasts, basketball, and baseball. Dances usually include a few Country & Western tunes for "kicker dancing" aficionados. And on Thursday nights, the cowboys come out in their boots, jeans, and western shirts to shuffle across the floor of local country dance halls. A coffeehouse features regional talent.

An active student union compensates for the cultural blandness of central Texas by providing speakers, performers, theatrical shows, movies, and other events at a minimal charge for students. And more than three hundred university organizations will gladly accept "Aggies' " free time and services.

Liquor flows in Brazos county, but the strongest campus beverage is coffee: the A & M campus is dry. Fortunately, the nearby area is not, and "Aggies" are prodigious beer drinkers. Dope is available on-campus despite the generally mild-to-conservative student outlook. It's just not as common as alcohol.

While they sip from their long-neck beer bottles at night, "Aggies" will listen to progressive country, rock, blues, and anything else that's passing through town. In good weather, students will probably be outside participating in team sports. This seems to beat partying for free time activity. A & M's intramural program is huge and popular, and club sports do well in state competition. Though it rarely snows in winter, springs are often cold and wet. A & M is not good country for hay fever, either.

Housing for students varies, because many apartment houses are shoddily built and may be disintegrating soon. The vast majority of students opt for off-campus housing. Parking on-campus is scarce, but parking tickets are not.

A & M's physical plant is basically up-to-date and includes an expanded football stadium, a new basketball stadium, and a cyclotron, nuclear reactor, and wind tunnel.

A & M has an attitude toward fraternities that is quite unusual for a Southern school. Greek frats and sororities are not well accepted and receive no recognition from the administration. Fellow students resent the Greeks as antiegalitarian. Nevertheless, the eleven frats and nine sororities are growing, with national membership in the Interfraternity and Panhellenic Councils.

The predominantly white student body is bound by traditions that transcend its origins (usually Houston or Dallas). The students of Texas A & M are proud to be considered the "Fightin' Texas Aggies."

TEXAS CHRISTIAN UNIVERSITY

Location: Fort Worth, TX 76129
Campus: suburban
Undergraduate enrollment: 2070 M, 2430 W

Student-faculty ratio: 15–1
Transfer students: 500
Median SAT: 480 V, 580 M
Median ACT: 22
Fraternities: 35%

Total enrollment: 6121
Expenses: $4700
Financial aid: 67%
Library: 940,000 volumes

Sororities: 35%
Application deadline: rolling

Texas Christian University suffers from two principal handicaps, and both are implied in its name. To begin with, TCU is located in Texas, one of the most conservative and anti-intellectual places in this great nation of ours. Moreover, it is heavily influenced by Fort Worth, which has a reputation as middle-middle-class, much less sophisticated, affluent, and culturally inclined than its neighbor, Dallas. As if location were not enough, however, TCU is Christian, and people don't come any more Christian than they do in Texas. Moral absolutism, evangelical fervor, and the thoroughgoing embodiment of the Protestant work ethic prevail.

As a result, TCU is an extremely conservative school. Religion and restrictions (no alcohol on campus, limited intervisitation in men's and women's dorms) are the standard answers at TCU to almost any problem (all of the chancellors have been ordained ministers), and the intransigence of the administration is so well known that most students who could change things have given up trying.

There are some good reasons to go to TCU. For one thing, the school has a good athletic reputation, and the trustees have just built a new memorial tennis center and varsity dressing rooms. Academically, if you're interested, TCU is strong in the basics, particularly English and math. The journalism department is small but highly regarded, and its rapid turnover is the result of a succession of better job offers to nearly everyone in the department. And the ballet department is tops. There are also a few good professors in other departments, but it takes a while to find them. The student-faculty ratio, while good by Texas standards, is high in comparison to many other schools, and still no one raises much of a ruckus. Moreover, few people complain, at least publicly, about all the required courses, including (of course) religion.

Only fifty percent of the student body comes from Texas. One feels their presence when the university offers such special programs as "ranch management." Only half of your freshman class at TCU will ever graduate, but some added transfers make up for some of the loss.

Fraternities retain their traditional strength, although independent housing is on the upswing. There are even coed dormitories (sex-segregated by wing). But things are still generally rigid on social intercourse and may be for a while.

Major leisure activities continue to include "raising hell," building floats, and riding oil jacks. Sports are also popular. Culture is not. The entertainment committee does a sloppy job of publicity and no one comes, but as befits TCU, in all likelihood no one would come to concerts anyway.

TEXAS TECH UNIVERSITY

Location: Lubbock, TX 79409
Campus: city center
Undergraduate enrollment:
  11,110 M, 8890 W
Total enrollment: 23,129
Expenses: $2700 (in-state), $3780 (out-of-state)
Financial aid: NA
Library: 1,500,000 volumes

Student-faculty ratio: 19–1
Transfer students: 1700
Median SAT: 460 V, 450 M
Median ACT: 20
Fraternities: 5%
Sororities: 5%
Application deadline:
  thirty days before registration

The former mayor of Lubbock used to boast that Texas Tech had a "high moral climate." He proudly told Texas parents that their daughters would be safe at Tech. Except for an occasional midnight panty raid (which actually still does occur at Lubbock), the mayor may well have been right.

Until fairly recently, Tech had some of the strictest curfews for women's dorms in the country, reminiscent of boy-girl relations in earlier years (i.e., the backseat during the drive-in era). Tech has loosened its dorm policies slightly (some students even live in coed dorms), but visitation rights are still quite limited by today's standards. Of course, on a campus where the men's and women's dorms were built by design on opposite sides of the campus, what can you expect?

Students at Texas Tech do not have to work hard. The quality of education varies from department to department but rarely exceeds mediocrity and often doesn't even reach it. The one noteworthy exception is the engineering department, which ranks second only to Rice's as the area's finest. The schools of home economics and business administration attract quite a few students.

Texas Tech does have required courses—English, American government, political science, American history, phys. ed. science, and mathematics—and a wide range of majors (with a campus of over 2000 acres, it's no wonder one of them is "park administration").

With so little time needed for the pursuit of knowledge, there is generally a great deal of energy left over for the pursuit of pleasure. The problem is finding something to do in Lubbock besides drinking and watching wind—and sandstorms. And even the former cannot actually be done in Lubbock, a devoutly dry prairie town which closes at 10 P.M. (In fact, the late movie begins at eight-thirty.) The social life, if that's what you choose to call it, centers around "the Strip," a half-mile stretch of bars and liquor stores outside the city limits. Football and basketball, enthusiastically supported and sluggishly played, round out the school's fun pastimes.

Texas Tech and Lubbock might be a nice change for someone from the big city; at any rate, it's one of the few places where you can find a vacuum within a vacuum. Probably because they are so similar, the school and the town get along quite nicely. Lubbock businessmen, aware of the importance of student spending, gladly give Tech students ten percent discounts at local department stores (and even at McDonald's). Religion, particularly the Baptist faith, is big—both on- and off-campus. Political fervor is not. Liberalism is an anathema to Lubbock.

Most students are content to let a few fraternity boys try to run the student government. Its power, however, is limited by the same factor which limits everything but booze and football at Texas Tech—the overpowering, ubiquitous apathy.

UNIVERSITY OF TEXAS/AUSTIN

Location: Austin, TX 78712
Campus: suburban
Undergraduate enrollment:
  18,143 M; 15,556 W
Total enrollment: 43,095
Expenses: $3500 (in-state),
  $4580 (out-of-state)
Financial aid: 25%
Library: 4,000,000 volumes

Student-faculty ratio: 23–1
Transfer students: 3500
Median SAT: 500 V, 550 M
Fraternities: 30%
Sororities: 30%
Application deadline:
  July 1

Located in the center of Texas hill country, the University of Texas is the fourth-largest institution of higher learning in the U. S. and the second-wealthiest, preceded only by Harvard. In fact, some people like to compare UT to Harvard—but don't listen to them; they've either never been to Harvard, or they've never been to UT.

Austin, the home of the university and the capital of Texas, is a perfect college environment. Boasting one of the few women mayors of a major city, a semiprogressive city council, and forty-nine swimming holes, Austin combines the advantages of a metropolitan area with a small-town atmosphere. And it is fast becoming the mecca for progressive country music with the "Armadillo World Headquarters" being Austin's answer to Nashville's "Grand Ole Opry."

The university is huge, and we mean Texas-sized. If you start as a freshman, you'll walk miles. If you transfer here as an upper-division student, you may never see half the campus. (Fortunately, there is a shuttle-bus service.) In fact, many feel that the board of regents' motto is, "When in doubt, build." In the last three years, UT has added an Olympic swimming complex, a baseball stadium, and an immense special-events arena, and has just remodeled the student union. Needless to say, UT is into sports—especially football ("Hook 'em, 'Horns,' y'all").

The university has an outstanding academic reputation in Latin American studies, civil engineering, business administration, and journalism/radio-TV-film. The law school is reportedly the finest in the Southwest, and the L. B. J. School of Public Affairs, housed in the Lyndon Baines Johnson Library, is one of the few of its type anywhere. The library system is the tenth-largest in the country and has a very fine art collection.

The political atmosphere at UT has its ups and downs. A few years back, students and faculty held a general strike and rallied in protest when Dr. Lorene Rogers was appointed president against their disapproval. On the other hand, the students elected an "absurdist" student body president and vice-president who ran on the "Arts & Sausage" ticket and whose campaign slogan was "Money Talks."

The Daily Texan, the country's largest student paper, has impressive facilities and poses stiff competition for the city paper. It is the training ground for all the aspiring "Woodsteins" in the journalism school and emphasizes national, state, and local news over campus news.

Academic orientation at UT is distinctly pre-vocational, in contrast to the "liberal education" orientation of the prestigious private schools. The individual student is largely responsible for the quality of his or her education at UT. Most teachers are mediocre, although some are excellent, but the student must take the time to find them. For example, Lady Bird Johnson's former press secretary, Liz Carpenter, teaches a course in the journalism department, and economics professor Dr. Ray Marshall was named secretary of labor by President Carter. There are even rumors that when Walter Cronkite retires, he will teach here. An outstanding teacher in the English department is

John Trimble, author of *Writing with Style,* a new "bible" on the subject.

Not surprisingly, the UT bureaucracy is large and unwieldy. Most requirements are rigidly enforced. Particularly annoying is the rule that prohibits freshmen and sophomores from taking upper-division courses. Fortunately, the advanced-placement policy is liberal, and it is possible to bluff your way around the rules occasionally if you are familiar with the system.

God forbid, though, you should lose your tuition receipt.

Developing a social life in a community as large and diverse as the University of Texas can be a problem. Fraternities and sororities are one alternative for solving this problem. They have increased in popularity here (as elsewhere) in recent years, probably because Greeks provide consistent (if not always meaningful) interaction with a manageable group of people. Ironically, though, two fraternities have been put on probation by the administration recently for illegal hazing practices.

Co-op living is another alternative. There are about fourteen cooperative houses (including an exclusively women's co-op) which house about one thousand students. Also, many students still associate with old high school friends. Of course, there are enough discos and bars to keep loneliness at bay.

The community as a whole has also developed a cultural environment in response to student demand. There are at least two dance events a month, local and traveling theater performances, occasionally an opera, and an ever-present and abundant film selection. Galleries and museums are growing.

Since Austin is close to Mexico, marijuana is plentiful. A lid can be had for anything from ten dollars to thirty-five, depending on quality.

UT is probably ideal for the self-motivated student who wants a good pre-vocational education at minimal expense and who will enjoy—but not be distracted by—Austin's extremely amiable surroundings. But don't forget, UT is in Texas, the land of such contradictions as atheist Madalyn Murray O'Hare and the "Living Proof" Southern Baptists. What else can we say about a school that gave us both Walter Cronkite *and* Farrah Fawcett?

UNIVERSITY OF TORONTO

Location: Toronto, Ontario M5S 1A3

Student-faculty ratio: NA
Transfer students: NA

Campus: city center
Undergraduate enrollment: NA
Total enrollment: 48,900
Expenses: $6015 (foreign students)
Financial aid: NA
Library: 5,000,000 volumes
Median SAT: NA
Fraternities: NA
Sororities: NA
Application deadline:
April 1 for professional divisions,
June 30 for arts and sciences

The University of Toronto, with an enrollment of almost fifty thousand, is Canada's largest and one of its most prestigious universities. It's conveniently located in downtown Toronto, the largest Canadian city. (Metro Toronto's population is well over two million.)

Although U of T's academic reputation may not be familiar to Americans, it is usually rated one of the best schools in North America. Besides offering undergraduate courses in everything from actuarial science to zoology, U of T has a wide variety of excellent graduate facilities. Its many reputable professional faculties include law, medicine, engineering, pharmacy, education, forestry, and architecture.

Competition in the school of arts and sciences, really the college of U of T, can be unbelievable. "Bio 110," for example, a standard premed course, usually has a total enrollment of over two thousand. There are, of course, many sections of the course, but the pressure to beat out your fellow undergrads is still there. Just try getting notes for a class you missed from someone you don't know. Commerce and finance is another tough route for undergrads.

Generally speaking, other arts and sciences departments have smaller classes and offer more personal contact with profs. The largest undergrad department is political economy, which includes political science, economics, and commerce and finance. English, the second largest department, is the most renowned. It has long been considered one of the finest in North America, and its professors include Northrop Frye and Marshall McLuhan. The French department is excellent for literature and so-so for grammar. A large department, it wields power in the university system and has managed to avoid major cutbacks. History, boasting two leading Canadian historians, Careless and Bliss, is also a large department.

Undergraduates in "Skule," the faculty of applied science and engineering, claim to have both the heaviest course load in the university and the most school spirit. Yearly Oktoberfests, human chariot races using forty-five-gallon oil drums, and the Lady Godiva Memorial Band are among "Skule's" claims to fame. Their "brute force committee" organizes the pranks which include reassembly of an Austin Mini in the office of the university president and filling the student council offices with 800 pumpkins on Halloween.

Canadian universities used to offer Americans a bargain education: tuition was less than at most state universities. Times have changed and the administration caught on. Students on a visa must pay extra.

U of T has three campuses: one downtown and two in the suburbs. The downtown campus is made up of seven "colleges," each offering a different atmosphere. One of the seven is for evening courses. The other six offer some housing for students—only 2500 of the over 30,000 students live in-residence—and three are more or less affiliated with a particular religion: Catholic, Anglican, or United.

Residence life is different at each college, so it is impossible to generalize about its quality. One very important part of student life is lacking at U of T: unity. The university is very large, and many people move off-campus into apartments or co-ops after a year or two in residence. Rents start around $90, depending upon how close the apartment is to the campus. Toronto has an excellent transit system employing trains, buses, and subways, so commuting is usually easy. There are also frats and sororities around which provide rooms; they are not as prominent at U of T as in the U. S., though.

U of T offers many services to students, among them a Career Counseling and Placement Center, a decent health service, an International Student Center, and a students' administrative council, which oversees the funding of many student activities.

The campus currently lacks good eating facilities, but the problem is slightly alleviated by excellent restaurants found in nearby parts of the city. Drinking spots on campus are few and far between, so bring your own.

Admittedly, U of T students are not interested in political demonstrations, but they are very active in campus government and a healthy selection of clubs, theater groups, newspapers, and journals. Students do enjoy a great deal of power in the university's governing bodies.

One area where U of T ranks at the bottom of the list is in athletic facilities. The university has the top ice hockey and field hockey teams in the country and a football team that continues to dominate Ontario. The teams have been so successful in spite of antiquated facilities. A new sports complex, however, was completed in 1979.

The main library, completed several years ago, is fourteen stories tall and, if you like modern architecture, a nice-looking complex of concrete and glass. There are countless other specialized libraries scattered throughout the campus in different buildings.

Perhaps the biggest drawback at U of T—as in most of English-speaking Canada—is the absence of group spirit among Canadians. Canadians are certainly not unfriendly, but they are often less outgoing or gregarious than Americans. One thing that never fails to alienate Canadians is American ignorance, so try at least to remember that the capital of Canada is Ottawa.

If you can overcome the feeling that you're nothing more than a nine-digit number, and you think you might enjoy going to school in a different country that is really just a stone's throw away, consider the University of Toronto.

TRINITY COLLEGE (CONNECTICUT)

Location: Hartford, CT 06106
Campus: city outskirts
Undergraduate enrollment:
 950 M, 750 W
Total enrollment: 2100
Expenses: $7600
Financial aid: 30%
Library: 600,000 volumes

Student-faculty ratio: 12–1
Transfer students: 10
Median SAT: 570 V, 610 M
Fraternities: 25%
Sororities: 0%
Application deadline:
 January 1

Beautifully nestled deep in Hartford, Connecticut, insurance enclave of the east, Trinity College provides its 1700 students with the unique opportunity to experience the traditional "liberal arts" education. Trinity is green and Gothic, with a chapel that juts above the Hartford skyline.

The student body now enjoys the freedoms of open curriculum. However, administrators, students, and faculty are reviewing the curriculum to establish whether or not required courses and distribution requirements should be reinstituted. (You all know, of course, that Harvard recently revised its own core curriculum; hence, it is quite likely that Trinity will follow suit.)

Facilities at "Trin" are clearly limited in many respects. The most dramatic example of this is the complete absence of a student center. The unfortunate consequence of this is that the newly renovated and expanded library has become the central meeting place for student social functions. As one student complained, "Can you imagine! Seven through nine-thirty P.M. is cocktail hour, and unless you arrive early enough, it's difficult to get to the bar, let alone study. When cocktail hour is over, there may be an occasional quiet moment in which to work, but one must be sure not to disturb those who are socializing." And, we're told most students head for the pub by ten-thirty.

Academics can be quite good at Trinity and the low student-faculty ratio points to greater faculty contact with students. The most-respected departments are clearly history, biology, economics, philosophy, and religion. The least-respected departments are sociology and psychology. Education used to be a department at Trinity, in fact it was quite a good one, but the administration felt that gym was more important so they just dissolved it. Still, such programs as freshman seminars are administration-supported.

Some of the better professors include Simmons in biology—he's dynamic and definitely outrageous; Smellie in chemistry, who is "simply brilliant"; and Gettier in religion, who receives A+ student evaluations and standing ovations.

The quality of education, at the level of the classroom remains high. Despite criticisms of grade inflation and plummeting SAT scores, academic standards have not been totally compromised and most students feel quite comfortable in meeting their requirements successfully.

Trinity's Rome campus and junior year abroad are among popular alternatives to four uninterrupted years on the Hartford campus. Others include internships and credit for work in such places as Connecticut Public Television.

On campus, a newspaper, radio station, and student government take up the more involved students' time.

The quality of Trinity social life is another matter entirely. Culture is generally absent from campus, though this is not the fault of the theater, music, or art departments. They do their best, considering the severely limited funding they receive and the antiintellectual, apathetic student body with which they have to deal. Films are popular entertainment—cinestudio is great procrastination from work. The city of Hartford doesn't add much to the situation. Culturally, it offers the Hartford Stage Company, the Bushnell Memorial Theatre, the rebuilt Hartford Civic Center, and the city morgue. Women are not advised to walk unescorted at night, since the college is immediately bordered by a rather rough area.

Frats provide a significant amount of Trinity night life since the Iron Pony Pub, known to some as the "Pube," is inadequate. The six frats at least provide an atmosphere where students congregate en masse to inhale beer (there isn't much air at frat parties), swallow live goldfish, or rate girls for their weekly minutes. (One fraternity admits females.)

The Pub, actually the dining room with red lights, provides watered down beer, long lines, and music whose amplitude makes conversation fairly difficult. Still, students congregate there.

For those who choose not to participate in the fraternity life of brotherhood or the pub life of boredom, there's always New York, Boston, or "The Tap", a terrific little neighborhood bar on New Britain Avenue where the immediate community and Trinity's rather small bohemian population mingle.

Diversity in Trinity's student body is a questionable characteristic in many minds. While the "black house," located on Vernon Street, (where the frats are) provides a center for black cultural, social, and intellectual activity, many students find the preppie presence overbearing.

One cynical student complained to us that "The Trinity student population is comprised of about sixty percent hard-core preppie and thirty-eight percent white public school graduates. Of the thirty-eight percent nonpreppie population, a solid twenty percent are trying their hardest to become what they're not, preppie, and in so doing reduce the white nonpreppie figure to approximately eighteen percent. In case you're wondering about the remaining two percent of the population, well they represent Trinity's nonwhite, nonpreppie student body . . . the minorities, including black, Puerto Rican, Middle Eastern, South American, Chinese, Korean, and Japanese. Trinity has put together a rather nice collection—one of each—and that's a generous estimate, most assuredly." His account is exaggerated, and yet it demonstrates a significant point of view—Trinity still needs to get away from its old golden days of elitism.

The dorms are being renovated, new dorms have been built, and the university's athletic offerings are growing yearly. Trinity has a lot of potential. It offers the advantages of a small liberal arts college and you can get a fine education there. Many students really get to like it.

TRINITY COLLEGE (WASHINGTON, D. C.)

Location: Washington, DC 20017
Campus: city outskirts
Undergraduate enrollment: 600 W
Total enrollment: 1000
Expenses: $6425
Financial aid: 52%
Library: 150,000 volumes

Student-faculty ratio: 10–1
Transfer students: 30
Median SAT: 545 V, 528 M
Median ACT: 24
Sororities: NA
Application deadline:
   rolling—March 15
   recommended

The stereotype of the rich, intellectual, finishing school-polished girl is dying, and in its place is a hard-working, tough-thinking woman. For Trinity has psychoanalyzed itself and discovered that the old educational vitamin pills are impotent. Although Trinity (alma mater: "Our hearts are loving you") is rooted in traditions once meaningful to the small college with a strong sense of community, the ways of the past, in a manner reminiscent of Ozymandias, are fading away.

There are still class days with fun and frolic, singing and seniors in academic gowns, and good food in the dining hall (which in itself makes the tradition valuable). But perspectives are changing as the Trinity woman studies in the Library of Congress, tutors in the inner-city, becomes politically involved, and holds a part-time job. However, the basic tradition of academic excellence remains, more than ever before, the hard core of the college generally recognized as the top Catholic women's college in the United States.

Trinity is a women's college, and finding a datable male is an art in itself. Blind dates abound, and there is always the weekly "cattle auction with lots of bull," alias the mixer. If these fail, civilized barhopping is the usual alternative.

Sad to say, many students live on books, books, books. The opportunity for intellectual stimulation exists, owing greatly to the high faculty-student ratio, the political and cultural advantages of the city, and the student's intellectual potential. But, to be blunt, you don't actually need a knife to cut through the intellectual atmosphere. Although a morning smoker session might solve the Middle East's problems, elect a black president, or rewrite *Humanae Vitae,* an evening smoker scene may concern such earthshaking questions as whether or not to have your hair frosted, what was the name of Cosmo Topper's dog, or who is going to jaunt over to McDonald's. The causes of this vacuum are numerous. Simply, there is just not enough time. There is definite academic pressure, and as a result, the competition can kill.

However, as in many other areas of campus life, change is imminent. In the past, curricular regulations were made strictly in the inner sanctum of the administration and, to some degree, the faculty. Course requirements were extensive, and aside from honors courses and seminars and the college-sponsored sophomore year at Oxford, the major advantage was that classes were (and still are) small—often fewer than a dozen students. But a recent combination of openness on the part of the administration and the gradual encroachment by the students into the realm of curricular legislation has effected numerous important academic innovations. Most notable among these is the experimental freshman pilot program, which waives all course requirements, including even the pursuit of a formally declared major. Trinity, in conjunction with Harvard, has also established a graduate program for training inner-city teachers. In general, the emphasis of the new academic philosophy is on an interdisciplinary approach, geared toward forming a liberally educated student.

Certainly, Trinity is no utopia of intellectual, emotional, sexual, and/or spiritual fulfillment; but in general, yes, a girl from Flying Arrow Creek, Iowa, as well as a girl from Westchester County, can find happiness—not often ecstatic bliss, mind you, but happiness—someplace at TC in the "Big City."

TUFTS UNIVERSITY (WITH JACKSON COLLEGE)

Location: Medford, MA 02155
Campus: suburban
Undergraduate enrollment:
 2327 M, 2249 W
Total enrollment: 5545
Expenses: $7770
Financial aid: 30%
Library: 377,940 volumes

Student-faculty ratio: 14–1
Transfer students: 50–100
Median SAT: 580 V, 620 M
Fraternities: 10%
Sororities: 15%
Application deadline:
 January 15

Tufts is the ideal school for the good-to-excellent student who is looking for either a good education or a place near Boston to spend four years, or both. The quality of student has improved steadily at Tufts in the last few years, partly as a result of stiffening competitions at the Ivies. There seem to be three types of Tufts students: very bright ones who didn't get into their Ivy League first choices, bright ones for whom Tufts was their first choice, and not-so-bright ones who were lucky to be accepted. The last category is rapidly disappearing.

"Growing" aptly describes the way Tufts students see their school today. New course offerings, newly constructed buildings, projects in the works (such as those for a sorely-needed student union), and an ambitious university president are adding some expectations for good days ahead. Unfortunately, Tufts also suffers from a limited endowment, high and rising tuition, overcrowding, and other problems common to institutions grappling with skyrocketing maintenance costs.

Nutritionist Jean Mayer, Tufts president since 1976, is working to revitalize much of the university. Academics have expanded to include a new Nutrition Institute, and international relations major, and expanded interdepartmental offerings that will ideally exploit graduate resources for undergraduate use.

Life in Medford gives the Tufts student plenty of opportunities to get away to the country in New Hampshire and Vermont. Ten minutes away from the culturally rich Cambridge and Boston, Tufts is located on a suburban hill that can be pleasant and attractive in the right weather. In short, Tufts and its coordinate sister Jackson (the two are usually not distinguished) give you the best of city and country. (Nearby Somerville, Mass., is the home of Steve's Ice Cream, famous and so popular in the area that students line up around the block for its "mix-ins" of sweets and munchies. The proximity to Steve's is one of Tufts's little-mentioned strongpoints.)

But Boston aside, Tufts offers fine educational resources, along with the freedom to take as much or as little advantage of them as you wish. The student body is large enough to allow flexibility in course planning, and the administration has guaranteed that no one will be bored by the alternatives. Tufts boasts fine child study, political science, drama, European history, and philosophy departments. Tufts's "experimental college" offers perhaps the most popular of all Tufts courses. Qualified undergrads may receive two credits for teaching a course in the "experimental college."

The graduate programs—high-caliber medical and dental schools, the Fletcher School of Law and Diplomacy (the finest of its kind), and the new Nutrition Institute—offer many advantages to undergraduates.

The faculty is generally competent and sparkles with occasional superstars like German professor Sol Gittleman, whose courses on ethnic roots, films, and cultural values have earned him the distinction of being one of the Boston *Phoenix*'s ten most popular professors in Boston.

Tufts social life, which has been uneven in the past, has improved in the last few years with the establishment of a pub, the renovation of a small student center, the growth of organizations promoting concerts, lectures and parties, and the increase of cultural societies. The male-female ratio is about even, making the atmosphere a good deal healthier than on the Smith-Mount Holyoke circuit. But Boston and the surrounding colleges siphon off some of the social life, although indications are that this is changing and that students are trying to create a college community feeling.

Life-styles are varied and quite liberal, with no questions asked about living arrangements and very few about drugs. Most dorms are coed.

Political activities on campus reflect the national trend toward student indifference. A women's center is active. The Afro-American Center serves the campus with resources, lectures, and programs.

Many freshmen we are told become affiliated with the Afro-American Center and later drift off, leaving a certain crowd of blacks whose life is tightly centered around it. The Leonard Carmichael Society coordinates community work in Boston. Campus activities like WMTU, the twenty-four-hour FM radio station, the high-quality weekly *The Tufts Observer*, and musical and dramatic groups have grown in both participation and campus influence.

The worst thing about Tufts is the inadequacy of its physical plant. Gym facilities are sorely lacking and the dorms range from "at least clean" to sometimes quite comfortable. But they are overcrowded and maintenance is just not keeping up well with the wear and tear. The eleven fires that gutted Tufts buildings in the Seventies have led, at least in the case of Barnum, to a beautifully rebuilt dorm. Unfortunately, that fire destroyed the stuffed remains of P. T. Barnum's elephant, "Jumbo," the school mascot.

Even with improving dorm situations (Mayer planned a new dorm opening for 1980), upperclassmen find good housing off-campus. The area's off-campus resources, most notably Boston, tend, in general, to be better used by upperclassmen than by frosh and sophs. That is not to say that campus life goes sour after two years; on the contrary, all we've heard points to some good times in Medford.

Despite all the opportunities at Tufts, the school makes no pretensions to competing with nearby Harvard or MIT. Many students we heard from take pride in having avoided an Ivy League existence, others have found happiness at Tufts despite Ivy rejection. It is possible to float along at Tufts on easy times, though the nature of the students is becoming more serious academically. It may not be easy to shine, but once into Tufts, it's fairly easy to stay. And you'll probably want to.

TULANE UNIVERSITY (WITH SOPHIE NEWCOMB COLLEGE)

Location: New Orleans, LA 70118
Campus: city outskirts
Undergraduate enrollment: 3100 M, 1700 W
Total enrollment: 7500
Expenses: $7000
Financial aid: 25%
Library: 1,000,000 volumes
Student-faculty ratio: 13–1
Transfer students: 470
Median SAT: M: 530 V, 580 M; W: 531 V, 541 M
Median ACT: 25
Fraternities: 50%
Sororities: 47%
Application deadline: February 1

There are more good reasons to spend four years at Tulane University than simply to be able to experience Mardi Gras four times. Tulane is a good example of what is commonly referred to as the "New South." Located in a residential section of New Orleans, it offers a cosmopolitan atmosphere as well as an opportunity for academic achievement.

The school—along with the South—has undergone a transformation during the past decade. Prior to that time, it ranked with other Southern gentlemen's schools like Virginia, Duke, and Washington and Lee. But, along with Duke, Tulane escaped the bonds of its Southern heritage and became a national institution with much to offer.

Although about fifty percent of its students still hail from the South, the school is represented by students from other regions. And the atmosphere at Tulane's coordinate "better half," Sophie Newcomb, is even more cosmopolitan. Despite the fact that almost half the students at Tulane and Newcomb still join the twenty-seven fraternities and sororities which exert a major influence over life at the schools, it is now possible for independents to make a place for themselves. In former times, the schools were virtually run by the Greek-letter groups, which had more influence at Tulane than at most Big Ten schools.

Tulane is a coeducational university with two single-sex undergraduate divisions: the men's college of arts and sciences and the women's Sophie Newcomb College. Women in the colleges of engineering and architecture are required to live in Newcomb housing. Freshmen must live in the dorms, while upperclassmen can choose between single-sex or coed dorms and off-campus living. About twenty percent of Tulane men live in frat houses. The sororities do not provide housing.

No discussion of Tulane is complete without mention of New Orleans. One of the most progressive cities of the South, it offers undergraduates a bounty of extracurricular activities, ranging from Bourbon Street and its pseudodecadence to a professional football team. Tulane itself is located in a residential section of the city, but downtown New Orleans is easily accessible via public transportation. Many students own cars, too, so getting around New Orleans is no problem.

The academic environment at Tulane is a secondary consideration for those who go there, and the school, even with its progress, is not a giant of higher education. However, it's quite possible to get a fine education, since the school does boast a good faculty and many dedicated students. An attractive Tulane "scholars and fellows program" offers top students honors courses and such options as an individualized curriculum, junior year abroad, and participation in graduate courses.

Newcomb is one of the best women's colleges in the country. It can hold its own against the "Seven Sisters" of the East. Newcomb has its own faculty, curriculum, and schedule of extracuricular activities, but functions largely in the university milieu. The emphasis is on the arts and sciences, with few professional or vocational majors available.

Both Tulane and Newcomb must be given high recommendations for students seeking a college with a congenial atmosphere in an urban environment. For outstanding high school scholars, Tulane should receive serious consideration as a "safe" school backing an Ivy League choice. Women would do well to look elsewhere for their "back-up" school, but are encouraged to apply to Newcomb as a first choice. The social life at both schools is outstanding, and anyone who goes to New Orleans for college will spend four years in a happy school which maintains just enough Southern charm to make it a nice place to live in as well as to visit.

UNIVERSITY OF TULSA

Location: Tulsa, OK 74104
Campus: suburban
Undergraduate enrollment:
  2500 M, 2200 W
Total enrollment: 6300
Expenses: $4105
Financial aid: 45%
Library: 930,000 volumes

Student-faculty ratio: 16–1
Transfer students: 700
Median SAT: 489 V, 529 M
Median ACT: 22.7
Fraternities: 25%
Sororities: 20%
Application deadline:
  none

The University of Tulsa offers the best program in the world in petroleum geology. The school was built on oil money, and now the trustees are returning the favor. If you're the son of a know-nothing Arab who struck it rich in the backyard (many are), or even of a Texas or Saudi Arabian tycoon, or if you'd like to be an oil tycoon yourself, Tulsa is the place to go to school.

On most other grounds, though, we wouldn't recommend Tulsa too highly.

The University of Tulsa is certainly improving, and some of its academic opportunities are of surprising depth. The social life is relatively good for a commuter school, and the cultural offerings of Tulsa—the stopping-off point between Dallas and St. Louis—are much better than one would imagine possible in Oklahoma. But if the University of Tulsa is much, much better than it used to be, still it isn't really good.

Probably the best image of Tulsa is its library. The building is air-conditioned and plushly carpeted, but it doesn't house anywhere near enough books. A new, aggressive librarian is working to change the situation (and has met with some success), but for the time, at least, the prognosis is "getting better, but a long way to go." The same could be said of just about everything else at the university.

There is a surprisingly good arts department, especially in music, filled with promising students who didn't quite make Juilliard or Oberlin, or who couldn't stand the politics there. The talented faculty doubles as the heart of the Tulsa Philharmonic. The painting and sculpture program, too, is fine, with new headquarters in a converted downtown building, now dubbed the Living Arts Center. At the center, each student has his own nine-by-twelve living and working studio, with the net effect a creative workshop à la Bauhaus.

In other fields, anthropology and criminal justice—the latter once called "police science"—are moderately distinguished. English at the college is a beer "gut," and philosophy students who learn there's more to life than contemplation of sand fleas usually switch majors to political science.

The social life at the school—as opposed to the pursuits in town—centers on the sororities and fraternities. Men's houses have always been residential, and starting in 1969, the women have had live-in halls. The two-block area in which the buildings stand bustles with renewed activity.

Most of the Tulsa students come, of course, from Tulsa. About two-thirds live off-campus, and most of these commute from home. The campus, therefore, is pretty dead at night, and the social regulations for those who remain are somewhat strict.

Drugs and sex are popular at Tulsa, as they are everywhere. But, as one might expect in an Oklahoma college, drugs are not really abundant on campus (at least, not as abundant as at a Tulsa high school), and sex is most often accompanied by genuine enthusiasm for marriage.

Sports, as at any Southwestern school, are big stuff at Tulsa. The basketball, football, and baseball teams have all been in bowl games or national tournaments within the past few years. Most students find sports events entertaining, and the athletes—while not often headed for professional careers—regard sports as a job which pays the bills. (A few football players actually do go on to the pros.)

UNION COLLEGE

Location: Schenectady, NY 12308
Campus: city center
Undergraduate enrollment: 1363 M, 684 W
Expenses: $8000
Financial aid: 75%
Library: 383,430 volumes

Student-faculty ratio: 13–1
Transfer students: 100
Median SAT: 556 V, 623 M
Fraternities: NA
Sororities: NA
Application deadline: February 1

Union College is one of New York State's best-kept secrets. However, within New York, Union has earned a high reputation as an academically competitive college with a remarkable graduate school acceptance record.

With the overwhelming majority of students coming from upper-middle-class New York and more specifically, upper-middle-class Long Island, diversity has been replaced by homogeneity and intellectual creativity has been superseded by a general affinity for "grinding." These traits, all the more noticeable in such a relatively small college, are the school's greatest drawback.

Devoted to teaching rather than research, the faculty is Union's greatest asset. Their enthusiasm for their subjects and for working closely with the students really offset the other problems one encounters at Union. Among the professors most highly revered by the students are Chang in electrical engineering, Shanebrook in mechanical engineering, and Brown and Nichols in political science. These professors make their departments the strongest in the school. Other good departments are biology, history, and chemistry. All classes at Union are kept to very small enrollments. Term-abroad programs are quite extensive.

Political and social activism has waned at Union except for a small, but ardent group of antinukers. Student political input was greater in past years. One particular source of involvement followed the phenomenal success of Union's hockey team under Ned Harkness. A recruiting "scandal" ensued which involved the school's president. Ironically, this incident probably precipitated the greatest publicity in Union's long existence.

The athletic program at Union is popular. The soccer team is perenially powerful, while hockey is gaining force. The women's volleyball and field hockey teams are state powerhouses. Participation in club sports, such as rugby and the newly reorganized ultimate frisbee team, is also common.

Fraternities are without a doubt the center of the social life at Union. The social events which they organize, though, are usually dependent upon alochol—drinking to excess is a favorite activity. Pot is another, with cocaine a distant, expensive third. The Pub has a full bar in a sedate atmosphere while the Rathskeller, or so-called "Skeller," offers football, pinball, cheap beer and food, and rowdiness. Males at Union perceive the guy-girl ratio to be very poor and many of the females are considered to be "undesirables." However, the admissions office's trend towards admitting a larger percentage of women began with the Class of '83. This new policy has definitely diminished the number of males who find it necessary to "go north" to Skidmore in search of females.

In recent years, seniors who normally lived off-campus have found that dorm or fraternity housing is more suitable. Consequently, there has been some crowding on-campus, forcing many unfortunate freshmen to live in dorm rooms refitted for occupancy by an extra person.

The beautiful campus was designed on a one-hundred-acre hill in the early 1800s by the French architect Ramée. The school's showpieces are twenty acres of formal gardens and the only sixteen-sided building in America, which is the focal point of the campus. Regrettably, the 100-acre hill overlooks the city of Schenectady. Schenectady is the bane of the students at Union. The city offers nothing in the way of cultural entertainment, nor does it even have any good night-spots. Students therefore find staying on campus the best pursuit. Thankfully, the drama and arts departments are active although small.

Since 1798, academics at Union have had a long tradition of excellence. Hundreds of judges, governors, college presidents, and other dignitaries have passed through its pearly gates. Although people learn much in the classrooms and will probably be accepted into good grad schools, it is too bad that so many of the students at Union choose to allow their studies to get in the way of their education. Hopefully, this prevailing attitude will soon disappear as the secret of Union College is passed on and out of New York.

UNIVERSITY OF UTAH

Location: Salt Lake City, UT 84112
Campus: city outskirts
Undergraduate enrollment: 9900 M, 6900 W
Student-faculty ratio: 22–1
Transfer students: 2500
Median ACT: 21
Fraternities: 15%
Sororities: 10%

Total enrollment: 21,400
Expenses: $2700 (in-state),
  $3800 (out-of-state)
Library: 1,600,000 volumes

Application deadline:
August 1

Q: What's in Salt Lake City?
A: The home base of the Church of Latter-Day Saints and the Mormon Tabernacle Choir.

Guess again, because all this is correct, but you have left out the University of Utah, probably the largest almost-dry state-run commuter university in the country.

The University of Utah, one of the few institutions of higher learning in a geographic area not noted for intellectual excitement, consists of 25,000 hardy souls, of whom about half are Mormon. But though the university cannot escape the Mormon influence much more than any other place in the state of Utah, it has managed in recent years to win independence from the ultrastraight environment and philosophy of the Latter-Day Saints. Of course, this spirit of liberalism is somewhat lost on the mammoth campus that in reality includes all of the Salt Lake Valley. Only about seven percent of the students live in dorms, another fourteen percent in fraternities, sororities, and off-campus apartments, and the rest commute home to Mom and Pop in time for lunch. In short, it's a highly fragmented community with very little sense of unity or common identity among students.

Nevertheless, the school, like any other, has some real strengths. Good business and technology preparations are to be found here. The university has one of the top computer science programs in the nation, one of the West's better law schools, and a competent medical school adjoining a medical center now gaining worldwide recognition, especially for its research. The history, English, and language departments are also strong. Advanced ballet classes regularly attract applications from out-of-state.

Other than the above, however, the school provides a solid but undistinguished education. For those who look to the town to unveil what the gown conceals, Salt Lake City may be a bit disappointing. Liquor by the drink is illegal in Utah, and bars can serve only 3.2 beer. Nightclubs don't exactly abound, but their numbers are rapidly increasing. Memberships are reasonably priced and easy to obtain (if you're twenty-one or older, since that's the legal drinking age here). The nightclubs are definitely on the rise and owe their popularity, in large part, to university students. Surprisingly, drugs are moderately popular among certain groups of people and are not terribly difficult to get.

But Salt Lake City is not as culturally deprived as one might assume. Most of the activities are university-centered and they tend to be quite good because they don't have to meet conventional commercial pressures. The Ballet West, based in Utah, has a top reputation in the Intermountain area. The Utah Symphony, ensconced in a fabulous new piece of architecture appropriately named Symphony Hall, is highly regarded, as are a number of amateur theater groups, including the Theater 138 for improvisational, off-beat stuff, and the university-based Pioneer Memorial Theater. Salt Lake regularly attracts major rock/pop/jazz performers, but the town sports little if any decent local talent along these lines.

There's an even greater variety of activities if you're interested in the outdoors. The Salt Lake Valley is tightly girdled by mountains of awesome beauty which house the Alta, Snowbird, Brighton, and Park City ski resorts; all are about thirty minutes' drive from campus. The school has some of the best skiing in the nation, Thanksgiving to May. There's also plenty of opportunity for hiking, mountain climbing, camping, hunting, and similar back-to-nature activities.

Yet possibly the best summary of the University of Utah is the most obvious one—it is in Utah, and there are forty-nine other states from which to choose.

VANDERBILT UNIVERSITY

Location: Nashville, TN 37212
Campus: city center
Undergraduate enrollment:
  2761 M, 2764 W
Total enrollment: 9025
Expenses: $7800
Financial aid: 33%
Library: 1,400,000 volumes

Student-faculty ratio: 9–1
Transfer students: 100
Median SAT: 568 V, 611 M
Fraternities: 50%
Sororities: 50%
Application deadline:
  February 15

Nurtured in a decidedly unacademic region, Vanderbilt can boast an outstanding faculty and one of the more intellectually gifted student bodies in the South. Vanderbilt's main difficulties stem from its identity crisis: its distinct Southern tradition continually clashes with the waves of Northerners and Westerners who go there to get their sheepskins. Probably the only distinguishing feature the students have in common is their high socioeconomic status.

The board of trust and the chancellor, Alexander Heard, made a concerted effort in the late Sixties to imbue Vanderbilt with a highly national flavor. The result has been an upgrading of academic standards with a simultaneous disruption of social traditions.

Among its recent improvements, Vanderbilt boasts an increase in freshment SAT scores, a new $150 million fundraising campaign, a $10 million renovation of its stadium, and the absorption of George Peabody College for Teachers.

Unfortunately, there are certain things Vanderbilt seems locked into: the faculty is so heavily tenured that new blood looks elsewhere, and the prospects of sex are as elusive as single-digit inflation.

The conventional campus wisdom has it that there are no easy departments at Vanderbilt. The academic load in all three schools (arts and science, engineering, and nursing) is rigorous. While the nursing and engineering schools have been forced to lower their admissions standards, there have been no compromises in what is expected of the students. Many Vanderbilt students would sell their souls for a high grade point average. Academic pressure is dangerously high, and real learning is often sacrificed.

Yet, Vanderbilt students are as competent as any in the country. The chemistry, English, and philosophy departments have outstanding faculties. The acceptance rate into med and law schools is high; graduate and professional schools regard a Vanderbilt degree very positively.

The Vanderbilt social scene is dominated by a strong fraternity system (fifteen frats and nine sororities) that miraculously survives despite high dues. Almost half of the students are involved; it often seems much higher. Archaic dating methods are still in vogue, and it is widely rumored that sororities still insist on having members take chastity pledges. Only one sorority house allows drinking inside. Non-Greek social life is centered around the Saratt student center, where movies, a pub, game rooms and party rooms keep the other half happy.

The small group of blacks at Vanderbilt generally feels unwelcome in the fraternity houses. Blacks operate on the outskirts of the social scene, and alienation runs high. When *Time* magazine recently asserted that there is subtle hostility between the white fraternities and the black students, the various Greek chapters treated the situation with benign neglect.

Campus politics are clearly tilted to the right. The right-wing Young Americans for Freedom have conducted a hysterical vendetta for the past few years against the bold and progressive campus newspaper, *The Vanderbilt Hustler*.

Student government is still very much in the hands of the fraternities. Student leaders tend to be affable fellows whose main accomplishment is to accumulate a long list of extracurricular activities to send to their prospective graduate schools. The fact that half the committees they list never meet doesn't seem to bother anyone.

Athletics have been a major topic of controversy for the past three years. Intramurals are popular. Vanderbilt's determination to compete with Alabama and Georgia, two of the Southern powerhouses, has created significant campus tension because the only way Vanderbilt is currently able to field a football team is by not allowing them to attend Vanderbilt. Through an ingenius "arrangement," the athletes (ninety percent of them) attend less-demanding Peabody College down the road. With a new stadium, the administration seems to be helping out.

Campus housing at Vanderbilt is expensive and in short supply; football players, though, are guaranteed on-campus housing. Nevertheless, the majority of students live on-campus.

Vanderbilt's Nashville location has its advantages. The surrounding countryside is at worst breathtaking, and downtown Nashville has a surprising amount to offer. There's plenty of good music (not just country), and the once-hostile relations between town and gown have been cooled. The area is also among the most inexpensive in the country for food, gasoline, and clothes.

Vanderbilt is a place where students work hard, Greeks run the show, and when it's all over, the diploma is worth quite a bit.

VASSAR COLLEGE

Location: Poughkeepsie, NY 12601
Campus: city outskirts
Undergraduate enrollment: 900 M, 1350 W
Total enrollment: 2387
Expenses: $7500
Financial aid: 35%
Library: 500,000 volumes

Student-faculty ratio: 11.5–1
Transfer students: 50–75
Median SAT: 605 V, 610 M
Fraternities: NA
Sororities: NA
Application deadline: February 1

"Whatever Happened to Vassar?" asked a 1979 *New York Times Magazine* article. Outsiders have always looked upon Vassar in a variety of critical ways. "Old hands around here will remember how we were denounced as a nest of Communists in the Fifties, a seducer of virginity in the Sixties, before we became a refuge for homosexuals in the Seventies. It's the price we pay for fame." Former President Alan Simpson thus brushed aside certain magazine articles which portrayed the college as a Saturday Night Orgy Club and a home for gays. This myth was based on the fact that Vassar men, rather than women, have been called "coeds" since their arrival in 1970 at the most liberal of the "Seven Sisters."

We hear that Vassar is alive and well and doing just fine nowadays. The college is successfully emerging from a bumpy period of transition marked by extensive student demands for change. The college has, on the whole, met those demands and continues to satisfy a wide range of individual needs.

The student body is a diverse and interesting group. There is no "typical Vassar student." The school is not dominated by prep-school WASPs, nor overrun by way-out gays. About fifty-five percent of the students come from public schools, and a quarter are Jewish. The gay population, which was greater and more outspoken during the early years of coeducation, is probably equal in size to that of most colleges. Since Vassar encourages individuality, students are not forced to conform.

Nobody doubts that Vassar is still attracting top-notch women but, in the words of one coy female student to her hometown newspaper, "Why would any man want to go to a school without an engineering department or a football team?"

The answer is Vassar's considerable academic flexibility (although the school is expanding athletics to attract more males). Students may design an independent major in a field such as computer-assisted psycholinguistics, combine a penchant for geology with the security of a prelaw/poli sci major, or spend a junior year in the Paris bustle or the Dartmouth backwoods.

But Vassar is a tough place to take courses. The faculty maintains a standard of quiet excellence and remains accessible while continuing to do research and publish. The low student-faculty ratio assures the success of tutorials and provides for independent study projects without lonely floundering. Most faculty members are qualified enough to be teaching at Harvard or Yale, and some do commute to New Haven, teaching part-time there. The work load is heavy, and for a few students, especially those working on senior year theses, the library is the hub of social life. During exams, speeding is not uncommon. About three-quarters of those who apply to medical school are accepted. Art history, English, psychology, biology, and political science are the most popular departments, though not necessarily the best. Other departments, like history and philosophy, are small but excellent.

The Vassar orientation which turned out independent free-thinking women in the Thirties is still at work encouraging individuality in the Eighties.

Emphasis on individuality carries over to housing, where every available free space has been converted to a single. (Some are closet-size, but nontheless it's a place of your own.) For those who want to live off-campus, but with the comforts of "Mother Vassar," the college has built townhouses and terrace apartments ten minutes from the heart of campus. Generally, they comprise five bedrooms, a kitchen, and a living room.

The campus is idyllic—1000 green acres with small hills and ponds, a cider mill, and golf course—and both New Haven and Manhattan are an hour-and-a-half road trip away. (Poughkeepsie itself, a depressing 750,000-person attempt at urban renewal that failed, is not worth mentioning—except for a few bars and grinder shops.)

Very few students have phones in their rooms, so contact is maintained by small-town-style visits. It's not uncommon to stop to see two or three friends on the way to the library.

Perhaps because of Poughkeepsie's dearth of restaurants and clubs for students, Vassar's social life is based on-campus. On weekends, there are movies, dances, student plays, and coffeehouses. The campus bar, named Matthew's Mug after the school's founder, has half-hour to two-hour lines even on weekdays. Formals are held at least once a semester. Drug use is average: if you like to smoke, you can find friends who smoke too, and if you don't, you can find friends who don't. Alcohol is popular, while a few of the more exotic drugs are not as readily available.

Because Vassar is a small school, names and faces become familiar after a few months (although you may never meet the person they belong to). It is also true that friendships exist outside academic interests. Relationships at Vassar tend to be either short-lived and many or long-lived and few. Relations between the sexes are still a bit strained, though the male-female ratio is evening out. Schoolwork is complained about, not discussed.

Vassar is like a mature (albeit 114-year-old) liberated woman who is exploring new life-styles before selecting the one best suited for her. Unlike other coed schools, however, this "Sister-on-the-Hudson" has sufficient endowment and academic excellence so that her reputation remains unscathed throughout massive changes. Innovations are based on student needs; an impressive new biological science building now meets the needs of the growing influx of premeds. The recent $50-million "capital campaign" has converted an old powerhouse into an experimental theater, constructed a new track and soccer field, financed a student center to house the newspaper, radio station, club offices, bookstores, and "Retreat" restaurant, and provided for the construction of an addition to the already outstanding Main Library.

Vassar provides a friendly, supportive environment in which intellectual exploration need not be limited by arbitrarily set course guidelines. Its isolation is offset by the beauty of the campus. Student participation in administrative decisions is welcomed, and the exciting possibility of creating your own curriculum is surpassed only by the chance to create a "New Vassar."

UNIVERSITY OF VERMONT

Location: Burlington, VT 05405
Campus: suburban
Undergraduate enrollment: 3600 M, 3900 W
Total enrollment: 8850
Expenses: $3800 (in-state), $6200 (out-of-state)
Financial aid: 25%
Library: 750,000 volumes
Student-faculty ratio: 13–1
Transfer students: 400
Median SAT: 530 V, 580 M
Fraternities: 15%
Sororities: 15%
Application deadline: February 1 for fall, December 1 for spring

The University of Vermont is probably best-known for its location. The small town of Burlington is nothing to speak of. But the ski hills that surround the town are. And this fact explains why almost half the school is from out-of-state. Students flock to UVM from New York, New Jersey, and Massachusetts, not so much to get an education as to be in close reach of some of the best ski slopes in the Northeast.

This is all not to say that UVM is a poorly disguised ski resort. It certainly is not. There is increasing competition to get in, and one must work to stay in. Just how much one must work is another question entirely.

Students at UVM consider it a party school. Fifteen percent of them are in frats and sororities. The Greeks join with the dorms in sponsoring the ongoing beer blasts. Pot is rarely in short supply. A large amount of partying occurs in Burlington. Despite its boring character, it maintains fifty-three bars—quite a formidable record for a town of 40,000!

The housing is tight at UVM. Although some students live in the frathouses, most spend two years in the dorms (coed or single-sex), and then move off-campus.

Hockey is undoubtedly the school's biggest sport. But the lesser jocks find satisfaction with the high-powered intramurals.

Business is the most popular major at UVM, followed perhaps by education. The engineering department is strong due largely to the state's desire to have a large supply of trained professionals. Many do remain in Vermont. UVM certainly has the resources for one to fashion either a solid liberal arts education or a comprehensive premed program.

So, if you are looking for a decent education and a range of diversions, and you can deal with an isolated environment, UVM may be the school for you. And who ever complained about coming home for spring break with a deep winter tan?

VILLANOVA UNIVERSITY

Location: Villanova, PA 19085
Campus: suburban
Undergraduate enrollment: 3600 M, 2400 W
Total enrollment: 10,000
Expenses: $6000
Financial aid: 60%
Library: 482,000 volumes
Student-faculty ratio: 14-1
Transfer students: 225
Median SAT: M: 488 V, 559 M; W: 488 V, 517 M
Fraternities: NA
Sororities: NA
Application deadline: February 15

The visitor to Villanova today will find it hard to believe that the school was founded 136 years ago. Although the school's expansive (200 acres) campus was obviously acquired before property values on Philadelphia's "Main Line" started skyrocketing, most of the buildings are relatively new (not striking or even modern—just new). Yet it is a fact that Villanova was founded by Irish Augustinians in 1842.

Villanova's college of commerce and finance has a growing reputation, and the science, engineering, and nursing programs are well established and first-rate. In the school of arts and sciences, the university maintains a somewhat traditional and restrictive policy. There are limited intervisitation hours, and alcohol, by Pennsylvania law, is illegal for those under twenty-one. Drugs are used discreetly and dorm counselors are reasonable.

Antagonism flared in the spring of 1974 over a questionable search of dorm rooms and the subsequent suspension/expulsion of several students. A later demonstration for students' rights led to more disciplinary action and resulted in a student suit against Villanova in the federal courts.

The outcome was inconsequential for the students at the time, but it caused university administrators to re-evaluate their approach to student life. The benefactors of the year-long controversy are the new students who will live in a more liberal atmosphere.

Philosophically, the university has natural, deep Catholic roots. High administrative positions are traditionally filled by Augustinians. The Eastern headquarters of the Augustinian Order has its home at Villanova. Courses in religious studies and philosophy are required in all undergraduate programs. A vibrant energetic aspect of Catholicism is evident in the campus ministry and related groups.

Big Five basketball, a moderately successful varsity football program, and nationally outstanding performances in track, swimming, and weight-lifting head a wide athletic program. Women's varsity sports are gaining a foothold, also. A year-round intramural program provides good competition for semiserious athletes of both sexes.

With an impressive tradition and an ever-widening openness to contemporary advances, Villanova has the time and space to provide a fine education for a fairly reasonable tuition.

UNIVERSITY OF VIRGINIA

Location: Charlottesville, VA 22903
Campus: suburban
Undergraduate enrollment: 5000 M, 5000 W
Total enrollment: 16,000
Expenses: $3400 (in-state), $4500 (out-of-state)
Financial aid: 25%
Library: 1,750,000 volumes

Student-faculty ratio: 10–1
Transfer students: 500
Median SAT: 590 V, 615 M
Fraternities: NA
Sororities: NA
Application deadline: February 1

Located in bucolic Charlottesville, the University of Virginia is a study in contrasts. Founded, designed, and built by Thomas Jefferson, today's UVa is caught in an inherent conflict between hallowed tradition and the forces of progress. Thomas Jefferson still haunts the campus, from the architecture of "the Lawn" (the main quadrangle) to being cited as precedent for almost everything. While tradition is important, recent changes in the honor system, and in the admission of women and blacks, are evidence of a trend toward progress. Clearly, UVa blends the best of both worlds.

Among the "Ivy League of the state schools," UVa boasts a top-notch faculty, excellent students, and strong departments. The history, English, religion, government, and economics departments (the latter, quite conservative) compete with the best in the country, and practically every faculty member teaches undergraduates. There are many stimulating lecturers, with a large number of seminars offered. After first year, class sizes usually diminish. UVa's library system is highly rated and thorough; the manuscript room bears mention for its tomes of historic documents.

UVa is based on a six-college system at the undergraduate level. Prospective students may apply to the college of arts and sciences, which is the largest, or the smaller architecture and engineering schools, all of which are difficult to get into. After two years at UVa, a student may apply to the other three schools—nursing, commerce, and education. Ease of transfer between schools varies. Transferring into UVa is very difficult; recent programs to aid transfer students in their adjustment to university life help ease the transition.

While there are some students at UVa who seem to do nothing but write papers and read volumes of British literature, and others who seem to spend every waking hour partying at their favorite fraternity, most students fall somewhere in between the two extremes. A heavy emphasis on fraternities and some emphasis on newly formed sororities means that much of the social life is centered on Rugby Road, home of many of UVa's thirty-three fraternities. While Virginia has come a long way from the days of F. Scott Fitzgerald's orgiastic parties complete with brown-bagged bourbon, and while big party weekends are less structured than in earlier years, vestiges of UVa's rating as a party school still remain. Still, there are many other ways to have fun.

Small nightspots on "The Corner" and around Charlottesville, while not providing the nightlife of a large city, are ideal places to listen to a band or folk singer and drink a pitcher of beer. Posters and flyers around "grounds" (UVa's term for campus) advertise enough movies, speakers, coffeehouses, and dances to fill anyone's social calendar, and several big-name concerts are also scheduled during the year. While UVa has long been called the drinking school of the East—full of such "professional" drinkers that they defied ranking in *Playboy*'s list of top drinking schools—the administration is trying to deemphasize the role of alcohol in dormitory and fraternity functions on grounds. They are also trying to deemphasize drugs, which are a part of university life at UVa.

All first-year students (so-called, instead of freshmen) are required to live in dormitories, and are "guided" through their first year by a highly selective staff of resident assistants. After, the first year, however, students are on their own to find housing, and although the university has several on-grounds housing units for upperclass students, the majority must seek off-grounds housing, which is often expensive. A recent controversy at UVa centers around the question of housing: those who favor expansion want to build a residential college on a tract of land two miles from the center of the university; traditionalists argue that moving students so far away from Jefferson's "academical village" of "the Lawn" and surrounding buildings would be detrimental to the function of the university; still others argue that such a move would be impractical and inordinately expensive.

Other evidence of change at UVa includes the honor system. Once thought to be a sacred institution that prevented all students from lying, cheating, and stealing, the system has come under close scrutiny in past years with the resignation in 1978 of the honor committee's chairman after allegations of misconduct, and the controversy over a student's stealing a one-dollar bill. Just this year, students approved an historic reform when they voted to allow for a mixed jury option—instead of trials being heard solely by elected honor committee members, accused students can now opt for a panel of one-third committee members and two-thirds randomly selected students.

In the spring of 1979, political activism hit UVa when 2500 students demonstrated on "the Lawn" to protest the oppressive and insensitive practices of the school's governing body, the board of visitors. This was the first show of political activism since a 1970 strike against the Vietnam War.

Women and blacks are recent additions to the university. UVa was the last state school to admit women, but coeducation is now firmly and happily entrenched. The black population is not faring as well, though, and several recent displays of racism have made the situation less-than-ideal for UVa's black students, who make up approximately twelve percent of the student body.

Charlottesville and its environs will suit the scenery lover; they also draw a heavy tourist trade each year, which leads to somewhat high prices throughout the town. But UVa has an atmosphere shared by very few other schools in the country. Many see it as combining the best parts of an academic and social life that is disappearing elsewhere. It is a college where finding your niche isn't difficult, and if that sounds good to you, you too may thrive on Charlottesville air.

WAKE FOREST UNIVERSITY

Location: Winston-Salem, NC 27109
Campus: city outskirts
Undergraduate enrollment: 1800 M, 1250 W
Total enrollment: 4500
Expenses: $5400
Financial aid: 65%
Library: 675,167 volumes

Student-faculty ratio: 14–1
Transfer students: 120
Median SAT: M: 545 V, 592 M
W: 570 V, 600 M
Fraternities: 35–40%
Sororities: 0%
Application deadline: February 1

Wake Forest is a small, private, Southern, church-related, liberal arts college. If some of those adjectives sound a little contradictory to you, then you've taken the first step toward understanding a very contradictory school. Wake Forest has long been dedicated to offering an excellent liberal arts education and had been associated with the North Carolina Baptist State Convention, a powerful antiliberal and antiintellectual institution.

In 1978, after four turbulent years of infighting, the all-North Carolina Baptist board of trustees removed all mention of the Baptist State Convention from the university charter. In January of 1978, the Baptists put the approximately $1 million allotment to Wake Forest into escrow. Negotiations over the amount of money the school would receive and the composition of the board followed. It is unlikely that the board will remain exclusively North Carolinan or Baptist in the future. Wake Forest has dramatically begun the transition from a parochial school to a fine liberal arts university with a national student body. Yet the Baptists still provide a healthy sum for the school's operating expenses and more moral guidance than any college needs or deserves. Wake Forest, though, transcends its parochial heritage with an educational program that emphasizes solid and personalized instruction. The school maintains a low student-faculty ratio—a distinctly un-Southern characteristic—yet it is Southern in practically every other sense of the word.

The campus itself, which is filled with organized, stately, and uninspired Georgian architecture flanked by 470 rambling acres of meadows, woods, and gardens, is one of the school's greatest assets. One of the prettiest in the South, it was once the estate of the Reynolds tobacco magnates who lured the college to Winston-Salem in 1956 after 122 years in the hamlet of Wake Forest, N. C. The campus is located in a suburban area, miles from the rest of the city, and students have little contact with the city. We are told Winston-Salem "is a cultural giant for cities of its size. Joan Mondale brought McIntire to visit and *Smithsonian* magazine ran a piece on Winston's pacesetting." There are a few cultural offerings, including those at the North Carolina School of the Arts. Winston-Salem's approval of liquor-by-the-drink sales has improved nightlife. There is better entertainment to be found on-campus than off.

Wake Forest's academic standards are rigid, and the faculty is excellent. Indeed, with its relatively low tuition, Wake Forest is one of the best academic buys in the country. Primarily geared to the undergraduate, Wake Forest also includes the Bowman Gray School of Medicine, the Babcock Graduate School of Management, and a once-reactionary law school whose character seems to be changing. The undergraduate school's professors, however, are liberal—far more liberal than the predominantly Southern student body. Even the best faculty members teach introductory courses, and no classes are taught by graduate assistants. Wake Forest traditionally has prepared its students for careers in law, medicine, and the ministry; not surprisingly, its strongest departments are English, history, and biology.

There is an optional January term which shows no signs of either dying or becoming mandatory as it once was. The overseas jaunt and one-month immersion into a subject (Freud, Faulkner, space and time) options make the scheduling options worth the hassle.

The school owns houses in Venice and London which hold groups of twenty to thirty students each semester, and its sponsors semester-long foreign study programs in Dijon and Madrid. The Fine Arts Center has the rare distinction of having won architectural awards despite being only two-thirds built. Ground has still not been broken on the music wing. The university's music department still inhabits part of the chapel.

Wake Forest's conservative social and political atmosphere reflects the status, background, and occupations of the students' parents. Conservative thought dominates political discussion and the school's social policies. As a result, fraternities retain a stronghold on the male population, and those who don't join fraternities often participate in events sponsored by the "men's residence council," a sort of poor man's fraternity for men who can't cope with the traditional Greek system. The women do not have sororities, so they have created "societies" which serve the same purpose without the frills. Fraternities, however, have changed with the times, and frat men handle most of the limited drug trade on campus. Beer remains the favorite means of escape, though.

Women at Wake Forest enjoy a three-to-two male-female ratio, a fact that sends many men scurrying to nearby Salem College or the University of North Carolina at Greensboro. Male-female dormitory visitation regulations still provoke heated arguments between administrators and students, and though violations are often overlooked, archaic policies severely hamper social interaction on the campus (where a large majority of the students reside). Social improvements will depend upon the willingness of the board of trustees to grant students the kind of social freedoms which would match the institution's academic open-mindedness. Since the break with the Baptists, progress seems likely.

Wake Forest is big enough for the individual to melt into the crowd, but small enough for him to forge his own education. Student participation in extracurricular activities is extensive and enthusiastic, with student publications on the upswing, though many students respond to the fairly intense academic pressure by spending long hours in the library. The excellent faculty and pleasant atmosphere, however, lift Wake Forest into the first-rank of Southern schools.

It should be mentioned, perhaps with a sigh, that despite its size, Wake Forest, school of Brian Piccolo and Arnold Palmer, is a member of the ACC. This means much athletic hype, terrible football, excellent basketball, and the best gold record in the nation for the last ten years. For many students, this is an important facet of life.

Wake Forest is tough to get into, especially for an out-of-state woman. Don't use it as a back-up school to Mt. Holyoke, Duke, and UVa—the others may let you in before "Wake" does.

WASHINGTON AND LEE UNIVERSITY

Location: Lexington, VA 24450 **Student-faculty ratio: 11–1**
Campus: rural **Transfer students: 25**

Undergraduate enrollment: 1400 M
Total enrollment: 1750
Expenses: $5860
Financial aid: 20%
Library: 350,000 volumes

Median SAT: 550 V, 600 M
Fraternities: 60%
Application deadline:
February 15

Chances are that if former Washington and Lee president Robert E. Lee ("Saint Bob") saw what's going on at the university these days, both he and his faithful steed, "Traveler," would roll over in their graves and bring the campus chapel tumbling down around them.

Long gone are the days when W & L's stately brick buildings provided sanctuary for well-heeled Southern gents who were content to put up with a "liberal education" simply because it was the thing to do. A liberal education at Washington and Lee today also means liberal ideas and a liberal life-style (although drug use for a campus of this size is minimal), and if you're looking for that sort of thing, the school boasts a more than adequate supply of what the town rednecks call "hippies."

Unfortunately, W & L also attracts quite a different breed, best described as "Southern gentleman gone sour."

Among them, the "Hell, buddy, let's go get drunk" syndrome reaches epidemic proportions, and an education (they shun anything to do with the word "liberal") is still something to put up with because it's the thing to do.

Somewhere between these two extremes, however, lie the majority of W & L students: a solid group of hard-working (and playing) males who, despite an outwardly conservative manner, are surprisingly open in their views. This liberal-conservative balance (for once, the two terms are reasonably applicable) is, in fact, the real strong point of the school, for although many campuses boast well mannered and manicured student bodies and an equal number possess a flavor of social and political awareness, there are few that combine the two as effectively as W & L.

Social activity is still largely centered around frat parties, big college weekends, and car trips to the five prestigious women's schools which circle the campus (they say "Virginia is for lovers," you know), but a progressive administration has encouraged active programs of lectures, cultural performances, and projects of a political nature.

The traditional mock political convention held every four years for the party out of power is the best example of the school's *savoir faire,* for the event draws a number of active political leaders and wide publicity. Although the students' judgment is not always accurate, the convention represents an unusual learning experience.

For those with the means of getting there (and that means a car), that Shangri-La of culture, Washington, D. C., is within easy access, and well-known resorts like White Sulphur and The Homestead provide excellent recreational facilities throughout the year. Lexington provides little of anything.

While W & L academics are nothing to get ecstatic about, their programs offer good, solid opportunities for improving one's faculties in an imaginative manner. The school is small enough to pursue close student-faculty relationships, and a geographically diverse student body (drawn from all fifty states) makes for a lively classroom atmosphere.

Beyond the walls of W & L classrooms, students can spend a junior year pursuing academic and social activities on an exchange program with Hampden-Sydney, Hollins, Mary Baldwin, Randolph-Macon, Sweet Briar, and Randolph-Macon Woman's College (some of which are all-women's schools).

Back on campus, the college ambiance—with everyone part of the community despite variations in life-style preferences—originates from the days of Robert E. Lee. An effective honor system, run entirely by the student government body (which includes representatives from W & L's law school) encourages the easy going mutual respect common among the students.

Washington and Lee has, in many ways, integrated the best of two worlds with a deep feeling of innovation that bubbles beneath a warm and friendly spirit. Like the state of Virginia itself, the school has one foot in the North, one in the South, one in the past, and one in the future. The sum is for many a collegiate paradise and not a split personality.

WASHINGTON STATE UNIVERSITY

Location: Pullman, WA 99164
Campus: rural
Undergraduate enrollment: 7425 M, 6000 W
Total enrollment: 16,525
Expenses: $3400 (in-state). $5400 (out-of-state)
Financial aid: 25%
Library: 1,000,000 volumes

Student-faculty ratio: 16–1
Transfer students: 1500
Median SAT: NA
Fraternities: 24%
Sororities: 22%
Application deadline: May 1

Years ago, students at Washington State University (then known as Washington Agricultural College) sounded off at rallies with "Farmers! Hayseeds! Pumpkins! Squash! W.A.C.! By gosh!" The yell has faded with the years, but the spirit lingers.

The essential fact to remember about WSU is that it is in Pullman, Washington, which would hardly exist without the university, and proclaims its isolation by being surrounded by eighty miles of wheat fields (until you hit Spokane). The hassled city dweller who longs to get away from it all will have a great opportunity to find an alternative life-style in Pullman—if he can keep from yawning. The active "Cougar" must learn to content himself with outdoor recreations such as horseback riding, tennis, cycling, hiking, camping, and skating. The university owns a ski resort forty miles from campus. Drinking takes place in student rooms, not in public areas of dorms.

The sports field provides the masochistic "Cougar" an opportunity to find his own variety of thrills. WSU competes athletically with the tough Pacific Eight, which annually produces more national championships than any other conference in the nation.

Academically, WSU students find a situation similar to most other large state universities. Undergrads are taught largely by grad students and junior faculty. Lower-level courses are mostly large lectures, and seminar courses are difficult to get into, even if you do find one. Much of this can and should be avoided by enrolling in the honors program. True to its heritage, WSU remains strong in agriculture and animal sciences. The college of agriculture offers sixteen different undergraduate majors, and the school of veterinary medicine is highly rated. Engineering is also becoming increasingly strong.

Unfortunately, an uncooperative legislature has allowed faculty salaries to slip so low that it is hard for the school to retain top faculty. The liberal arts have suffered the most. As a land grant school, WSU gives top money to ag and sciences.

WSU is on the semester system. Because many Western schools are on the quarter system (in particular, the University of Washington and Eastern Washington State College), WSU students desiring to transfer must face the prospect of losing credit in the process. Many are stuck in Pullman for four years against their wishes.

Despite the school's rural location and orientation, a significant number of students from western Washington and out-of-state find their way to Pullman. According to some WSU students, the nonlocals boost the campus atmosphere. WSU had its own series of racial protests a few years ago. And the hand-rolled cigarettes that the students are smoking may not be made with Half-and-Half tobacco.

Fraternities and sororities are still viable forces on campus, although their strength has diminished in recent years. Not too many years ago, an independent at WSU was doomed to social oblivion; now the sharp distinction between the Greeks and independents is blurring. Houses are having trouble filling themselves, and a few have folded. The prestige of belonging to a house is gone, and just about everybody knows it. Upperclassmen, although they still may belong to a house, have been moving off-campus in search of a more individualized life-style.

A hefty eighty-five percent of WSU students are in-staters. Less than half who begin here remain to graduate. If the "Great Northwest" intrigues you, Pullman might be the place to get some exposure or overexposure.

WASHINGTON UNIVERSITY

Location: St. Louis, MO 63130
Campus: suburban
Undergraduate enrollment:
　2400 M, 1600 W
Total enrollment: 8000
Expenses: $7050
Financial aid: 40%
Library: 1,700,000 volumes

Student-faculty ratio: 14–1
Transfer Students: 250
Median SAT: 570 V, 630 M
Median ACT: 27.5
Fraternities: 12%
Sororities: 12%
Application deadline:
　February 1

Washington University, contrary to popular opinion, is in neither the state of Washington nor the District of Columbia. It's in St. Louis, which, as one wit commented, is a city of "Northern charm and Southern efficiency." Luckily, environment has not prevented Washington University from attaining a richly deserved academic reputation.

A locally-based school for its first one hundred years or so, Washington established a top-notch national reputation after its search for students nationwide in the late Fifties and early Sixties. The faculty is outstanding and the student body highly motivated.

Most of the people who attend Washington seem to fit in well with the studious atmosphere. Many of the men, for example, are Ivy League rejects, and at Washington they try to recreate what they might have missed at Harvard, Yale, or Princeton. The result is a serious, no-nonsense academic attitude, often surpassing that of their more prestigious, but less motivated Ivy League counterparts. In the past, however, academic purpose has been synonymous with political apathy, and the campus has all too often become a refuge for those seeking escape from the rougher neighboring community. Fortunately, Washington's ivory tower may be crumbling somewhat, as its students become concerned with both local and national issues.

But if a student wants to settle into a scholarly career, one can hardly blame him for doing so at Washington. Washington University's five undergraduate divisions offer a wide range of academic options. Although the university doesn't really have any "bad" departments, especially strong areas within the college of arts and sciences are Germanic languages and literatures, biology, physics, English, history, and political science. Engineering strengths include chemical engineering, computer science, and mechanical engineering. Accounting and finance are stand-out departments in the school of business administration. The school of fine arts offers excellent programs in graphic communication and painting. In addition to general quality, the school of architecture excels in urban design.

There is a very strong interest in the natural sciences (especially premedical studies) among Washington University students, with about twenty percent of the student body eventually majoring in natural science departments. Large gifts from locally based companies, like McDonnell-Douglas and Anheuser-Busch, have enabled Washington University to develop some of the finest scientific research facilities in the midwest, many of which are made available for research use by undergraduate as well as graduate students. Washington University is also a recipient of many federal and private foundation grants to promote research in diverse academic areas.

The university has recently been making a special effort to enrich the social sciences and humanities. An innovative interdisciplinary approach to the freshman year is the "focus plan," which involves interrelated freshman seminars on specific themes. Further, the university has established liaisons with eight foreign universities to expand students' curricular and experiential options beyond the boundaries of the campus.

Whatever your field of interest, come to Washington University prepared to learn a great deal, but to work hard. The professors are usually willing to get to know their students in and out of academics. This is facilitated by the sparing use of teaching assistants in the classroom. While some introductory lectures are rather large, the vast majority of classes are on the smaller side. For example, Pulitzer Prize and National Book Award-winning English professor Howard Nemerov teaches a literature course to a class of fifteen freshmen. Faculty as well as administrators make a concerted effort to be available to students and include them in many important phases of the university decision-making process. For example, no major decisions about curriculum matters can be made without the approval of separate faculty and student councils.

You may well want to spend four years studying molecular biophysics, but sooner or later, you will have to surface from the lab for a refresher. Washington is sadly lacking when it comes to "rest and recreation."

Intramurals are popular, but varsity sports are out of the question—potential jocks would do better to stay in the Big Eight. The newspaper, *Student Life,* is slowly improving, but the generally "terrific" yearbook is gone, the victim of a shrinking staff.

If you're looking for a party school, you will probably be sadly disappointed at Washington, even though it is the home of Masters and Johnson. As one student commented, "It's not the place to send a girl who wants to have a good time." This is not to say that Washington women don't have good times—most seem very satisfied but appear determined to go on to graduate school rather than just get married. And then again, with a male-female ratio in their favor, the women can afford to be somewhat selective in their relationships.

Because of its central location, the university's student body is unusually diverse: geographically and religiously, as well as socioeconomically. When Washington University began recruiting students from outside the St. Louis area, it built a series of dormitory complexes known as the "South 40" to accommodate residential students. The dorms have become an increasingly popular place for students to live, which has led some upperclassmen to move off-campus. Fraternities and sororities are gaining in popularity, but they are by no means a dominant force in the social life. The increase in popularity of on-campus living has had a positive effect on the number of activities available on weekends and evenings. Students can no longer legitimately complain about not having anything to do on-campus. The Mallinckrodt Student Center, for example, has recently added a delicatessen and a student-run coffeehouse, in addition to Edison Theater, which brings nationally known performing artists to Washington University.

Even though liberal political activist Barry Commoner is on the faculty, don't interpret this as a reflection of student consensus. Students' attitudes are less liberal than their Eastern counterparts but certainly not right wing. Consequently, activist groups on issues like antinuclear energy have only managed to rally a handful of followers. Like most institutions, the school is no longer the activist hotbed it was in the Sixties. Students are frequently so engrossed in their studies that they forget that a world really does exist beyond the ivory tower of the Washington University campus.

In sum, if you're self-contained and generally academically oriented, you will probably find a great deal of tranquility at Washington, despite its changing image. If your main goal in college is to party every night and take only an occasional "work break," then Washington University is definitely not for you. However, if you are seriously interested in obtaining a superb education (and willing to work for it), then Washington University should be given serious consideration when making your college plans.

UNIVERSITY OF WASHINGTON

Location: Seattle, WA 98105
Campus: city center
Undergraduate enrollment: 35,500
Total enrollment: 36,249
Expenses: $4410 (in-state), $6115 (out-of-state)
Financial aid: NA
Library: 3,063,041 volumes
Student-faculty ratio: 16–1
Transfer students: 4000
Median SAT: 505 V, 547 M
Median ACT: 25.0
Fraternities: 10%
Sororities: 10%
Application deadline:
    May 1 for freshmen,
    July 1 for transfers

The University of Washington is a school in transition. There are going to be some changes, but nobody knows for sure what they will be. Newly hired President William Gerberding faces a front line riddled with administrative holes. In 1979, several important deanships were vacant, including those of the schools of business administration, law, and dentistry. The plague of resignations has been attributed to a growing independence of faculty from administrative leadership and the increasing reluctance of the state legislature to provide adequate funding for the West Coast's largest campus.

Academically, Washington is regarded as one of the premier research institutions in the nation—always ranking near the top in federal and private grant money. The undergraduate, however, can sometimes get lost at the university where even the social sciences suffer from "publish-or-perish" paranoia. Large lectures are often supplemented with graduate teaching assistants, who may or may not know what they are talking about. Even some smaller classes are taught by such assistants.

Because it is a state-supported school, the university enrolls many of the area's top high school graduates, as well as a fair number of students with modest abilities and goals. Tuition is fairly low—set at twenty-five percent of costs—and because of the health of the state economy, an increase this year is unlikely.

The marine sciences, oceanography and fisheries, are well funded and well respected. Seattle's geography is a natural for the university's status as a national "sea grant" college. The research ship, *Thomas G. Thompson*, offers students practical experience available at only a few other institutions.

Business administration, especially at the graduate level, is highly rated among the top publicly-supported programs in the nation. The health sciences, with U. S. Senator Warren G. Magnuson as protector, has become one of the nation's best equipped, and includes schools of medicine, dentistry, and nursing.

The main threat to the university's stature as a leading school is state funding. Washington state, progressive in other ways, suffers from a regressive tax system. Capital construction, however, funded with revenues from timber sales and rent on downtown property, is moving ahead, and several new buildings threaten what is left of open space on campus.

The university is located in a natural setting on the shores of Lake Washington and Lake Union. Canoeing and sailing are popular pastimes. The Cascade Mountains to the east and the Olympic Mountains to the west provide nice views for the stay-at-homes, and hiking, climbing, and skiing facilities for those willing and able.

The campus, despite the proliferation of brick, remains striking. Varied architectural styles, some of which are constantly ridiculed, keep the campus from appearing too Gothic.

Because of its location in the heart of the Seattle metropolitan area, the university remains a commuter school, although some 7000 live in dorms either as a learning experience or out of necessity. There are no rules in the dorms, however, a refreshingly uncommon trait for a state university. Fraternities and sororities also provide shelter and social life for 4000 of "the chosen." Off-campus housing is either expensive or dehumanizing, or both. Apartments and houses close to campus fall into the slum pattern of deterioration and rack renting. Parking for commuters is being discouraged by an administration that is feeling community pressure against the daily onslaught of cars. Seattle, however, has one of the nation's best mass-transit systems, so students can easily commute from the better housing several miles away.

Because of its size, the university tends to be impersonal. Undergraduates can spend a large part of their beginning years in lectures of 500–700 students, where it's difficult to meet people. Washington has never been known as a big party school. If you want to get drunk by yourself, you must face the highest liquor prices in the nation.

Seattle's location, way up in the corner of the country, attracts people who are running away from every other area. The climate, which for a large part of the year features a constant gray drizzle, tends to depress students who are from places with the change of seasons. Living in the area, however, is supposed to be good for the complexion.

Seattle was hit hard by the decline in the aerospace industry a decade ago, but that same industry has now turned it into a boomtown. The influx of job seekers has dropped the housing vacancy rate below two percent; thus, rents are up all over town.

The vitality caused by the billions being pumped into the local economy has caused a lot of hip restaurants and bars to spring up. Two of our informants commented, "They cater to the young, well-dressed, sophisticated people, who are well represented on campus, even though everybody hates their guts." There is an equally large contingent of earthy, wool-clad whale-saving types.

Birth control is cheap and readily available in the university area. The biggest venereal disease on campus is herpes, and as a result, the largest herpes study program in the nation is based on-campus. Medical care in Seattle is nationally renowned.

From its peak of activism of a few years back, the university has swung so far back the other way that it's hard to get fifty students together for anything other than a sports event. Jesus people are abundant but not too obnoxious, and the radical fringe still holds court in the Husky Union Building. Seattle is an excellent location for the more-cultural and less-political set. The university offers dance and drama. The city provides plays, symphonies, opera, movies, and is the starting point for most big-name rock concert tours.

If University of Washington starts getting you down, the great outdoors is right in your backyard. And with organized sports making a resurgence, you might expend your energies for the good of the team. There's a lot to do at UW, and you can't beat the breathing room of the Northwest.

WAYNE STATE UNIVERSITY

Location: Detroit, MI 48202
Campus: city center
Undergraduate enrollment:
　7200 M, 7474 W
Total enrollment: 34,337
Expenses: $1119 (in-state),
　$2274 (out-of-state)
Financial aid: 40%
Library: NA

Student-faculty ratio: 18–1
Transfer students: 5000
Median ACT: 21
Fraternities: 2%
Sororities: 2%
Application deadline:
　August 1

Wayne State may have the unique distinction of being the largest commuter school in America. Its students make the daily trek from home or from the city's low-rent housing areas. The problems of all commuter schools are present at WSU on a grand scale. Students tend to lack unity or interest in the school because they're too busy working to meet their college expenses, which have been rising steadily.

Wayne State is as diverse as *urbana Americana* itself—and then some. The students run the socioeconomic gamut from inner-city "Project 350" kids to those from fashionable Grosse Pointe and Birmingham. Given Detroit's reputation as a hot-bed for the "Motown Sound" and racial conflict, WSU's whopping twenty percent black enrollment is natural. It is actually not as spectacular an enrollment as it may first appear, since Detroit itself is sixty percent black and the immediate WSU area is eighty percent black. The Association of Black Students indicates an active, but not necessarily well-organized, membership. For the black studies student, more classes are in order. Surprisingly enough for a commuter school, Wayne State has hundreds of foreign students who are lured by an aggressive foreign student office.

Diversity, however, cannot be equated with community. Because the majority of students pack up and go home every night, the time for free exchange of ideas between them (also known as "bull sessions") is severely limited.

In an attempt to dispel arguments labeling Wayne State as dormant, WSU's administrators are quick to point out that over 6500 students participate in the school's endless array of student activities (over two hundred). Although impressive at first glance (perhaps), these statistics lose significance given the total size of the enrollment and the all-encompassing vagueness of the "student activities." No more than twenty percent of the WSU student body participates in anything—

which includes fraternities (professional, social, and honorary), political groups, religious and ethnic organizations, film clubs, theater groups, and the traditional extracurriculars. We must admit, though, that the WSU administration is trying—where else could you find such groups as "The Friends of the Farmworkers," "Jewish Defense League," "Society for Creative Anachronism," "Society for Students of Objectivism," and "Moo Dok Kwan Tang Soo Do" listed as official student activities?

WSU is not regarded as a major sports power in the state but has put together a strong program. Men's football and fencing and women's basketball have had many successful seasons.

WSU is located in Detroit's Cultural Center, a fairly safe area. Included in this area, adjacent to the WSU campus, are the renowned Institute of Arts, the main branch of the Detroit Public Library, the Detroit Historical Museum, the multimillion-dollar Renaissance Center, Society of Arts and Crafts, Meyer L. Prentis Cancer Center, and the Detroit Institute of Musical Arts. In the immediate vicinity of the campus is the Fisher Theater, which hosts many Broadway shows and other popular plays. The Michigan Opera Theater is also nearby.

In academics, Wayne State ranks below the shining example of the University of Michigan. Most undergrads consider their education good but not necessarily hard-won. The schools of engineering, pharmacy, and mortuary science (yes, we said mortuary science) are higly regarded. The required course hassle which hampers most state school students surfaces here also. WSU students must face sixteen hours of a foreign language, along with other courses that most of them could not care less about.

One final word about Wayne State. If it's what you're looking for, apply. It isn't likely to change much in the near future.

WELLESLEY COLLEGE

Location: Wellesley, MA 02181
Campus: suburban
Undergraduate enrollment: 2000 W
Expenses: $7860
Financial aid: 45%
Library: 600,000 volumes

Student-faculty ratio: 10–1
Transfer students: 86
Median SAT: 608 V, 603 M
Sororities: NA
Application deadline: February 1

Wellesley is an all-women's college where women have traditionally gone to get a good liberal arts education without having to deal with domineering male peers. Today's more assertive feminists might not agree that a woman is at Wellesley to avoid domineering men, but rather to expose herself to "an environment that encourages women" in their own right. The fact that Wellesley is all-women and quite small should be considered before making a four-year commitment. Not everyone would find that an attractive arrangement.

The three things you've probably heard about Wellesley are that it is superior academically, that it is referred to as "The Country Club," and that its students occupy the more elite (translation: "snobby") strata of society. The first two are true, the third only true in part.

Contrary to what some people would like to believe, the primary qualification for admission to Wellesley is a strong academic record, and not social standing and/or family wealth. The college was founded more than one hundred years ago on the premise that women could and should perform on a par with men, and thus should receive an education of equally high quality. Since then, the college's administration, faculty, alumnae, and students have been careful to do nothing that would tarnish that ideal.

As far as academics are concerned, Wellesley is tops. Grading is stringent and the workload heavy. But professors are generally helpful, which makes it all seem more like a challenge than a burden. The art history, English, and economics departments are all extremely popular. The sciences are strong not only because of the addition of a multimillion-dollar science center but also because Wellesley has cross-registration with the Massachusetts Institute of Technology. The small astronomy department boasts fine facilities in its own right.

No department is notoriously weak, but some are small, so the potential applicant should check out the course offerings in her prospective major. Many students also take advantage of internship opportunities in the Boston area. Physical education is required for about one year, but the program is varied and loose enough that even nonjocks can enjoy themselves. Generally, student-faculty relations are good, especially on a one-to-one basis.

It is probably impossible not to do a fair amount of work. The workload is intense, even relentless. Academic pressure can become a student's permanent companion if she is not careful. There are very few As, but on the other hand, very few flunk out. Most students work fairly hard during the week and then take a day or two off during the weekend. Reading period and exam week are killers, but during the regular semester students try to both work and play hard. Many spend their junior year elsewhere in order to relax, recover, and enjoy a different environment.

Besides having the chance to study at MIT, Wellesley students can spend one or two semesters at the other colleges participating in the Twelve College Exchange program: Williams, Wesleyan, Smith, Mount Holyoke, Amherst, Dartmouth, Bowdoin, Trinity, Vassar, Wheaton, and Connecticut College. The Williams program at Mystic Seaport, Connecticut, is also popular, as are programs in England, France, Spain, and Geneva, Switzerland.

There are fifteen dorms in all, grouped for the most part in four major complexes. Each has a distinctive life-style and character, with architecture ranging from American Gothic to "postwar box." Most dorms average around 120 inhabitants; the largest, Tower Court, houses about 250 people, while Simpson houses only a dozen. Five dorms are completely student-staffed; the others have part-time heads-of-house to perform administrative duties. All dorms, with two exceptions, have their own dining rooms which add to student life. Wednesday afternoon tea, a long-standing tradition, offers a chance to wind down.

The Wellesley campus *is* a country club. Without stepping off its more than 550 acres, students can play nine holes of golf, squash, tennis, soccer, field hockey, lacrosse, swim in the Olympic-sized indoor pool or beautiful Lake Waban, or practice ballet, jazz, or modern dance in Wellesley's fantastic athletic facilities.

Wellesley has a high percentage of students involved in nonacademic activities. On campus, they publish the college newspaper and two literary magazines, form several singing and drama groups, and covet student government and residence positions. Students are members of virtually every committee, although their effectiveness varies. Many students work part-time both on and off-campus. Some work for government offices or politicians in Boston; the area probably offers every kind of activism a student could want.

If you simply have to escape Wellesley, it's as easy as hopping the "MIT bus" (so-called because it shuttles students who take courses as part of the MIT-Wellesley exchange program). It runs approximately every hour between Cambridge and Wellesley, with additional weekend stops in Harvard Square. Once there, you can hobnob with the "clubbies" at Harvard or fraternize with the fraternity brothers at MIT. Boston's reputation as a "college town" doesn't rest solely on the MIT-Wellesley-Harvard triangle, however, for there are over one hundred other institutions of higher education in the area. If you're just tired of the college scene in general, though, you can stop at Faneuil Hall Marketplace, the hottest spot in the city, since its multimillion-dollar renovation. There are also numerous cultural offerings, including listening to the Boston Symphony Orchestra, Pops, and Opera Company, or watching the Boston Ballet.

Social life? It's the same old story—you've got to make it on your own. The fact that Wellesley is a women's college means that to get your "jollies" you've got to get to Boston. Boston won't come to you (or if it does, you'll want to send the part that comes right back). If you're a stay-at-home type, not interested in the intrigue that the "Big City" has to offer, don't worry. You can always go to Schneider Student Center, which sponsors a lot of parties, as well as serving beer and wine. Once there, you can pick up the Harvard man of your dreams or the MIT man of your nightmares.

A word about drinking at Wellesley and its environs: the "legal" age was recently raised to twenty, and has put a light damper on dorm-sponsored parties, although there is a "what you do in your own room in your business" policy. This new law, combined with Wellesley's technical status as a "dry" town, explains in large part why much socializing is done off-campus. (In fact, two of the four establishments in town which do have liquor licenses are on the college campus: Schneider Student Center and the Wellesley College Club.)

The traditional honor code is alive and well at Wellesley—students self-schedule their final exams. Traditions culminate with the annual springtime hoop-rolling contest (your "Big Sister" hands down her hoop after this last event of her Wellesley career). Legend has it that the winner of this spirited competition will be the first of her class to marry. Nowadays, graduating seniors seem to have bigger and better things on their minds.

WELLS COLLEGE

Location: Aurora, NY 13026
Campus: rural
Undergraduate enrollment: 500 W
Expenses: $6500
Financial aid: 50%
Library: 190,000 volumes

Student-faculty ratio: 9–1
Transfer students: 25
Median SAT: 550 V, 550 M
Sororities: NA
Application deadline: March 1 recommended

Wells College is one of the East's bastions of stuffiness. The prevalent campus theory (among administrators, anyway) seems to be that abstinence breeds intellect; in practice, that means that there is so much work that some of the less-abstinent pursuits are shuffled aside.

Of course, other things contribute to Wells's general lack of excitement. Its location in Aurora, New York—that is to say, the middle of nowhere. Women can spend their time climbing trees, rolling in the grass, having a beer at the Fargo (once off-limits), hustling pinball, singing with the juke box, or just listening to the mosquitoes. They can also spend time leaving, and they do: to Cornell, Hamilton, Hobart, and Colgate.

Wells is not without its little changes, though. Most of the required courses have been dropped, although the prelaw-premed grind goes on much as before. And "Calvin Cornell" can now stay all night in his damsel's dormitory room, rather than signing out at two A.M. and sneaking back in a window. Married students (doubtless with Cornell premed husbands) are even allowed to live off-campus. Dope is plentiful, cocaine available, and speed welcomed at exam time but, for many, only NoDoz could be considered a dietary supplement.

It is rumored that Cayuga Lake freezes over in winter only if all the freshmen are virgins. It froze this year. Actually, students today claim the frozen lake signifies that none of the freshwomen are virgins—so much for tradition.

Nevertheless, most of the heat that keeps that water unfrozen comes from intellectual, not sexual, exertion. The college has a high academic reputation and seems bent on preserving it. The small lectures and discussion groups allow for considerable contact between students and faculty and emphasize individuality. Also, Well's four-one-four program allows for January exchanges with other schools and places emphasis on internships and independence.

In addition to the twenty-five majors offered, students may combine courses from different departments for their major work, participate in the new management training program, or spend their junior year abroad with various programs in all the European capitals. At home, students are allowed to enroll in one class per semester on a pass/fail basis, and all but freshmen may take one independent-study course each semester. Finals, grades, and theses and comprehensive exams for seniors still persist. Liberal arts in general, and languages in particular, are well taught. The addition of a new fine arts complex has stimulated interest in the creative and performing arts.

The rapport between administration and students is good. There are many close ties between faculty and students. Few professors are without at least a couple of devotees. The "stuffy" respect visible in the classroom and at afternoon tea becomes camaraderie during late nights in the academic buildings or at the Fargo, and, later, affection when faculty are discussed by students back at the dorm. Nicknames and initials are the common form of reference to faculty members: "Dirty Rags," "Chippy," and "The Little Daddy."

The social situation revolves around dorm get-togethers and a few local (very few, and very local) night-spots, or trips to other colleges. The only thing all Wells students have in common is their sex. For the most part, though, they are fairly straight and friendly and concentrate on academics. The adjective "snobbish" is occasionally applied to those women who have grown cynical from contact with frequent male visitors from nearby campuses. Most students enjoy the large, cold library for hide-and-seek and pick up ten to fifteen pounds freshman year from the fantastic (for college) food. Beer has also found its way into the student union.

Politics just float by most Wells students, most of whom view current issues with an I-don't-have-time attitude. Often students realize in December that they haven't seen or heard any national news in three months.

We don't agree with the student who wrote us, "All's well that ends Wells."

President Frances "Sissy" Farenthold, a former Texas congresswoman, has brought change to Wells. An avid proponent of ERA, she is trying to raise the feminist consciousness of Wells. Confident and competent, and having experienced less of the discrimination their mothers and Sissy experienced, it has been said that Wells women are tough-minded students. A spirit of camaraderie can make life in Aurora more tolerable, and student involvement in activities is high. Whether Wells's fortunes can withstand the academic crunch is yet to be seen.

WESLEYAN UNIVERSITY

Location: Middletown, CT 06457
Campus: suburban
Undergraduate enrollment: 1225 M, 1200 W
Total enrollment: 2550
Expenses: $8680
Financial aid: 43%
Library: 900,000 volumes

Student-faculty ratio: 10–1
Transfer students: 90
Median SAT: 630 V, 650 M
Fraternities: 15%
Sororities: NA
Application deadline: January 15

Wesleyan is a marvelous anomaly—an old prestigious school which is not constricted by tradition. People at Wesleyan are individuals: they dress, act, and choose their courses and major to suit themselves, blending any variety of the many delightful academic, social, and cultural choices available. That sense of individualism can breed isolation. Wesleyan has no center, spiritual or geographic, which might demand conformity. There is no overpowering school spirit to smother loneliness. Instead, there is a humorous confusion caused by the dozen or so institutions in the country which share the use of John Wesley's name. For those students who believe that education demands individual activity, responsibility, and therefore some hardship, and for those who are anxious to make their own contributions and are willing to sacrifice some of the security of conformity, Wesleyan offers a unique choice.

Wesleyan provides the perfect academic setting for a personal exploration of ideas. Special programs such as the Center for Humanities, attract top names to the campus and the native faculties are almost uniformly excellent, enjoyable, and unusually accessible. The departments in religion, economics, history, English, and the sciences are especially outstanding. Five graduate programs add to the flavor of the academic offerings, as does the well-equipped but oversubscribed art program.

The academic program at Wesleyan is indicative of a basic faith in imaginative thinking, and is not restricted by the narrow compartmentalization rampant in academia these days. Majors are offered in interdisciplinary "colleges" of letters, social studies, and science in society. A selective "freshman intergrated program" of seminars is offered, and the tantalizing course catalogue includes many surprising cross-listings and "university courses." The popular option of group or individual tutorials provides the ultimate mechanism for personal exploration, indicates the faculty's genuine concern for teaching, and contributes to an atmosphere which fosters rich personal relationships between professors and students.

Wesleyan students are given the responsibility of deciding for themselves how to take advantage of the academic program. Liberal pass/fail and late course-withdrawal policies insure a tremendous degree of freedom to experiment with different fields of study without being punished, for instance, for an overly ambitious course schedule. The predominant activity remains the Wesleyan brand of grinding, known as "squidding." (The term derives from the resemblance of the late-night "grinds" to little bug-eyed squid contained in the aquariumlike Science Library.)

The freedom to make individual academic choices becomes significant in light of the amazing diversity of students at Wesleyan and their willingness to be innovative and original. Well-heeled preppies and watered-down freaks, aspiring jocks and let-me-be-creative artsy types live together in mellifluous counterpoint, if not beautiful harmony.

The diversity of students provides for an unusually lively political scene on-campus, often reminiscent of the Sixties' style of activism. Wesleyan stays true to its form of giving students responsibility by placing them on faculty, administration, and even trustee committees.

Although there is no animosity between social groups, there is also less regular contact between them than one might wish. Dorms are commodious and offer single rooms but are spread out over the many corners of the campus. Upperclassmen can easily stick to their own circle of friends and become consumed by their individual interests, since many live in comfortable houses surrounding the campus. Unfortunately, no central dining facilities exist to offset this fragmentation, except for freshmen. Middletown doesn't help, either—halfway between Hartford and New Haven and between Boston and New York—it is not a college town, though it is a city of 40,000. There are community service opportunities, though few take part, and the surrounding countryside is beautiful and dotted with marvelous cafés and parks.

The concern about isolation at Wesleyan does not mean it is a socially moribund school. A steady stream of outside attractions offers adequate diversion. The modern Center for the Arts is an incredible extravanganza of concert halls, galleries, cinema, theater, and studios and provides the setting for unique experiences with enthnomusicology—don't miss the Javanese "Gamelon" concerts! Or, if you choose, you can roll or pour your own entertainment very easily. Sports at Wesleyan are not incredibly serious, but lots of people participate or attend the important events and seem to have fun doing so.

The admissions office seeks students with something truly special to offer. The large applicant pool allows for that luxury. The standard superior credentials of high SATs, grades, and a few clubs may not be sufficient to guarantee acceptance. A student should try to prove that he is special and intellectually curious—the essay and interview may be the best way to do so. An active minority recruitment program meets with mixed success, with that portion of the student body unfortunately keeping to itself. The general recruitment program is not sufficient to offset Wesleyan's name confusion, let alone proclaim what is special about the place.

In 1980, trustees at Wesleyan endorsed a five-year plan to boost enrollment and reduce faculty positions. The announcement of a tuition, room, and board jump of $1000 for the 1980–81 school year, to $8,680, and reduction of dependence on endowments were among the more drastic changes. The trustees voted to continue "aid-blind" admissions as long as nonuniversity support amounts to at least thirty-five percent of scholarship costs.

The concept of individualism is at the heart of Wesleyan University. It provides the basis for the educational program, one of the finest in the country. People learn to think for themselves at Wesleyan, and no doubt independent thinking can be difficult and distressing, but also exciting as hell.

WHEATON COLLEGE

Location: Wheaton, MA 02766
Campus: rural
Undergraduate enrollment: 1275 W
Total enrollment: 1300
Expenses: $7415
Financial aid: 52%
Library: 200,000 volumes

Student-faculty ratio: 10–1
Transfer students: 20
Median SAT: 500 V, 500 M
Sororities: none
Application deadline: February 1

Wheaton College is located in Norton, Massachusetts. The Wheaton catalog describes Norton as a beautiful rural setting which is only one hour from Boston. The setting may be beautiful, but it is also miles from anything. Wheaton has helped resolve the problem by providing a bus that travels to and from Boston several times daily, and it has purchased two vans which are available to students for cultural, academic, and athletic activities.

The old worn-out phrase that "College is what you make it" can be directly applied to the Wheaton College experience. At any college, it is up to the student to reap benefits from the institution, but at Wheaton, the need for special motivation prevails.

The academics at Wheaton are strong. Wheaton students have a great deal of academic course work, and the quality of this work becomes increasingly fine. Academic pressure, however, is self-inflicted. Most classes are small, and professors are easily accessible. The overall atmosphere is rather relaxed, so the classroom is not always as dynamic as the professors and students might hope. The upper-level classes are the most stimulating. Wheaton offers combined majors, dual degrees, and 5-year programs. "Urban studies" is one of the new departmental additions.

The fact is that Wheaton has a lot to offer if you're willing to grab for it. There are plenty of opportunities for campus leadership positions. If students choose not to pursue leadership positions, they usually become involved with some of the many fine programs that the college offers.

There is an excellent career-planning program that truly makes every effort to prepare women for the business world. The program directors stress that is is rather timely to be attending a women's college, and they make it almost impossible for students to escape involvement in career-planning. Workshops are offered in all areas of career preparation and there is a fabulous January internship program that offers practical job experience. Wheaton graduates pursue careers in all major fields. A strong "old girl network" provides valuable alumnae contacts in most major cities.

There is also a campus fellowship program which selects students to act as administrative interns in the various offices on-campus. This is one of the programs which emphasizes student involvement in administrative affairs.

When rustication in Norton becomes a bit too much, students can participate in the Twelve College exchange program with Amherst, Bowdoin, Connecticut College, Dartmouth, Mount Holyoke, Smith, Trinity, Vassar, Wellesley, Wesleyan, and Williams. Along with the junior year abroad program, Wheaton women have only to take advantage of the chance to spend part of college away from their campus.

The major drawback of Wheaton can be the social life. Brown, Harvard, MIT, Babson, and BU men make regular trips for weekend partying, but cocktail parties and mixers are often disappointing. We might add that the Providence animal, the Brown man, has lost a bit of his on-campus appeal. Recent irresponsible and damaging rowdiness led to Wheaton College's polite dictum that certain Brown men are no longer welcome on campus. It should be stressed that the social life is not for everyone. The Wheaton woman must learn to be assertive and not sit back complacently waiting for "Prince Charming." Women who have friends in the area fare well socially, and there are quite a few women who meet men through friends and private parties.

The beautiful, well-manicured campus is one of the most attractive features of Wheaton. The idyllic setting is often a sanctuary after jaunts to the city. Wheaton is no longer a "suitcase school," but adequate transportation to Boston and Providence is available and widely used. The two nearby cities offer endless cultural and social opportunities.

Efforts are being made to keep the "Wheaties" at home. A new student pub, the Loft, is consistently packed and sports programs are expanding. New paddle tennis courts, a rugby team, and a soccer team add to an active program of organized sports. Greater emphasis on drama, dance, and music performances are among the campus offerings.

Despite the shortcomings pointed up by the efforts at change, Wheaton can be the perfect college for some women. A new, expanded library indicates a recognition of the growing seriousness of Wheaton academics. If a student wants a solid, liberal arts education and doesn't mind the friendly but rural campus, she should seriously consider Wheaton.

The college is on the upswing, growing to keep up with the advancement of women. Still, for a more high-powered intellectual atmosphere, check out Wellesley, Smith, or Bryn Mawr.

WICHITA STATE UNIVERSITY

Location: Wichita, KS 67208
Campus: city outskirts
Undergraduate enrollment: 5300 M, 5250 W
Total enrollment: 16,000
Expenses: $2500 (in-state), $3500 (out-of-state)
Financial aid: 65%
Library: 700,000 volumes
Student-faculty ratio: 20–1
Transfer students: 1500
Median ACT: 19.5
Fraternities: 7%
Sororities: 5%
Application deadline: one month before semester begins

"Where in the hell is Wichita?" This question is often asked by people who are not tremendously familiar with Midwestern geography. Wichita is centrally located, close to nothing. It is the largest city in Kansas and, among other things, it is the home of one of the fastest-growing universities today. Exactly why it is one of the country's fastest-growing insitutions is unknown. Wichita, a citadel of Middle Americanism, is the ideal place to raise a family, with its wholesome and unpolluted environment. But it can be stifling for college students.

In what can only be viewed as ironic tragedy, most of the people who attend WSU are native Wichitans who lack either the money or the foresight to seek the liberalizing experience of four years away from the hometown. More than any others who attend Wichita State, the natives are invariably unsatisfied. They usually live at home, and all too often fail to expand their social circle beyond their high school group, which makes for a rather cliquish atmosphere.

In fact, WSU is known unaffectionately by many as "Hillside (Avenue) High" for both social and academic reasons. Wichita attained state affiliation in the mid-Sixties (after years as a city-supported school), and is struggling to overcome its image as the weak sister of Kansas's "Big Three"—WSU, the University of Kansas, and Kansas State University. The legislature has consistently channeled more funds to KU and KSU than it has to WSU, but changes in this trend can be seen.

WSU is a rapidly expanding institution; the enrollment has doubled in the past five years. WSU's administration is now pursuing an aggressive building program. Among the recently added buildings are the Life Science Building, the Ulrich Museum of Modern Art, and new structures for both the health-related sciences department and the engineering department.

Wichita State's course offerings are generally mediocre at best. However, the school can boast a nationally recognized logopedics department, the state's top poli sci department, and a solid fine arts faculty. WSU administrators like to brag about the serious-minded nature of their student body. And WSU students are relatively sober because a majority of them must work to foot the college expenses. Nearly seventy percent of the students here will be employed while attending college, and nearly half of them will hold down fulltime forty-hour-a-week jobs. The average age of students is twenty-seven, and at last count there were approximately 3300 students who were thirty-five or older. These factors, coupled with others, reinforce the practical bent of WSU's curriculum. Many night courses are offered along with an emphasis on job-producing skills.

For the adventurous, a social life is possible in Wichita, but for the most part there is little to do. Beer drinking remains the biggest pastime (especially for the solidly middle-class fraternities and sororities) as 3.2 beer is the only alchoholic beverage available to students younger than twenty-one. Drugs are obtainable, but pot smoking is not generally accepted in the community and students must take care.

In sum, if you're from Wichita, do your best to go elsewhere to school. If you're from anywhere else, ranging from a rural Kansas town to Long Island, and are willing to really work for an education, you could find a passable one at an inexpensive price in WSU's unpressured atmosphere.

COLLEGE OF WILLIAM AND MARY

Location: Williamsburg, VA 23185
Campus: suburban
Undergraduate enrollment: 1976 M, 2483 W
Total enrollment: 6364
Expenses: $2836 (in-state), $4284 (out-of-state)
Financial aid: 16%
Library: 650,000 volumes

Student-faculty ratio: 15–1
Transfer students: 215
Median SAT: 580 V, 610 M
Fraternities: 33%
Sororities: 33%
Application deadline:
    February 1 for fall,
    December 1 for spring

The College of William and Mary in Virginia (the correct title) epitomizes the "Old South." Located on the edge of restored Colonial Williamsburg, the college manages to cross the time gap between colonial tradition and modernity. A newly completed library serves this college, which claims as its own the founding of *Phi Beta Kappa* and the honor system.

Fortunately, the "Old South" has taken on some trappings of modernity. The students of W & M are still well groomed, predominately Christian, and politically moderate, but no longer are coats and ties for men and dresses for women *de rigueur*. The college still attracts its share of patrician types (by state law, seventy percent must come from Virginia), but the bourgeoisie is not unheard of. The college and the town of Williamsburg are still exceedingly popular with tourists, but W & M draws its share of serious scholars as well. And finally, although W & M is still a college by name (the charter dates to 1693), it is in fact a university.

Even the physical layout of the campus is indicative of the change that has swept over it. The architecture is neatly divided into three styles: Old Colonial, Georgian, and modern. The old campus, including the President's House and the famous Christopher Wren building, is filled with magnolias and Revolutionary War cannons. The Georgian area, built in the 1920s, comes complete with sunken gardens and herringbone brick walls and forms the major part of the campus. And finally, the modern campus, including a new library and math building, is sprouting up beyond the college's Colonial limits.

An experienced observer of W & M might even hazard a comparison between the campus's physical attributes and the attitudes of the student body. There are a few conservatives who spend their time thinking of magnolias, a large majority of the students who are politically moderate in a Georgian style, and a number who are looking for newer solutions. The over-riding principle, of course, is moderation— the basic outcome of an admissions recipe of a majority of Virginians and a sprinkling of Northeasterners, mixed carefully in an old Colonial setting.

The natural sciences, especially physics, and a graduate marine biology program are good. So is early American history—not surprising considering the school's location. There are broad course requirements, some good pre-professional programs, and experimental and combined programs with other universities.

Varsity sports run the gamut from basketball to fencing, from lacrosse to track and field. Intramural programs are also offered.

W & M students follow an honor system and are given further chances for displaying independence in the self-determination of residence hall governance. Drinking in public areas is prohibited. Frats are the center of social life.

W & M students face rigorous grading but the academics can pay off. W & M provides highly competitive admissions and a solid diploma.

As for the "Old South," well, it seems to be increasingly confined to the tourist traps of Old Williamsburg across the road.

WILLIAMS COLLEGE

Location: Williamstown, MA 01267
Campus: rural
Undergraduate enrollment: 1100 M, 875 W
Total enrollment: 2075
Expenses: $7150
Financial aid: 30%
Library: 500,000 volumes

Student-faculty ratio: 12–1
Transfer students: 30
Median SAT: 625 V, 650 M
Fraternities: 0%
Sororities: 0%
Application deadline: January 15

"So you go to Williams? Williams and Mary? That's in Virginia, isn't it?" Williams students are painfully familiar with that well-meaning response, and they all cringe at the lack of fame their beloved college has achieved. But for those in the know in graduate school admissions offices and around the East Coast business establishment, a degree from Williams carries as much weight as one from any Ivy League school.

Located in a rural setting in the Berkshires of northwestern Massachusetts, Williams clearly is not at the hub of the urban scene. Nonetheless, for the frustrated urbanite, Boston and New York are each a three-hour drive away, and the college attempts to provide enough entertainment to keep the students occupied during the hours when they're not "grinding" in the library. Williamstown offers far more than gorgeous fall foliage. The beautiful and continually expanding Clark Art Museum—an excellent private museum housing one of this country's finest collections of Renoirs, a recently added new wing, and a library—is enough to put the town on the map.

In the past decade, Williams has undergone a series of major changes that have made it a somewhat more cosmopolitan institution than it was during its first 170 years. Foremost among these changes was the decision to admit women for the first time in 1971. Williams was not immune to the typical adjustment problems associated with coeducation, but relations between the sexes have mellowed a great deal since then, and recent incoming classes have approached numerical parity. There are still conflicting opinions on how well coeducation is working. Most would agree that it is infinitely better than a single-sex insitution, but the social situation is not without some problems. Many students cite the overbearing work load as the main hindrance to greater socializing.

The second major change that has affected life at Williams dramatically is the abolition of the fraternity system in the early Sixties, in the interest of promoting "diversity" among the students. The frat houses were taken over by the college and converted into living and eating units known as "row houses," which form part of Williams's residential house system. The residential houses tend to be closely knit as a result of organized social events, competition in intramural sports, and simply living together. And the accommodations at Williams allow student to live in relative luxury. Virtually all rooms are singles. Very little of Williams's housing is of the rooms-off-the-endless-corridor variety found at so many colleges. Rather, it is organized on the basis of groups of students, which creates a more congenial atmosphere. Freshmen are housed separately from upperclassmen and, therefore, develop a strong sense of campus unity.

Williams students are usually serious about their academic pursuits, and the college provides an environment for learning that is different from that at many other high quality schools. As colleges go, Williams is very small and very good. You can be assured of never being one of a class of 400 taught by a professor on a television screen. Economics, art history, and physics are considered the strongest departments. Of the others, only biology and the languages are weak.

Though academics may be the students' major concern, sports are far from peripheral. Williams students are a highly athletic bunch (intellectual jocks abound), and they are always eager to cheer on their varsity teams. The highlight of sports in the fall is always the annual football contest against arch-rival Amherst. The women's varsity program is relatively strong and diverse.

The Williams campus and surrounding area constitute an oasis for the sports-minded. Some of the finest skiing in the Northeast is within an hour's drive. The Outing Club is a heavily subscribed campus organization that provides equipment for forays into the nearby wilderness. This small New England college is also the home of the William Golf Course, reputed to be the third-best college course in the country. The Lansing Chapman Rink is the scene of brutal hockey contests in the winter and is converted into an indoor tennis court in the spring and fall, in order to supplement the numerous outdoor clay and composition courts. The college also has one of the finest squash facilities in the country.

Williams is not lacking in academic facilities, either. Fairly recent additions to the campus resources are the Bronfman Science Center, the Sawyer Library, and a new music facility. The college has also just installed a new computer.

In years past, Williams has been condemned as a preppie, rich man's college. Although the student body is now more heterogeneous, the stereotyped image is definitely a campus concern; recent faculty-student panels have explored such questions as "What is Diversity?" and "What Is the Value of a Williams Education?"

Despite the fact that President James Garfield is Williams's most illustrious alumnus, the quality of the students there is very high. They regularly pull in a disproportionate share of Rhodes, Fulbright, Woodrow Wilson, and other big-name fellowships and prizes. If Williams were a little larger, it might have become as well known to the general public as Harvard or Yale. But the combination of superior academics, small size, and pastoral setting is one that does not exist in the Ivy League and that makes Williams a very special place. Life in the purple mountains can be very enjoyable.

UNIVERSITY OF WISCONSIN/MADISON

Location: Madison, WI 53706
Campus: city center
Undergraduate enrollment:
 13,816 M; 12,095 W
Total enrollment: 39,430
Expenses: $3292 (in-state),
 $5426 (out-of-state)
Financial aid: 50%
Library: 3,200,000 volumes

Student-faculty ratio: 13–1
Transfer students: 4700
Median SAT: NA
Fraternities: NA
Sororities: NA
Application deadline:
 March 1 for freshmen,
 April 15 for transfers

Set on beautiful Lake Mendota, the University of Wisconsin/Madison campus is so huge that you might need a map at first just to find your way around. But once you've gotten your bearings, you can settle in for four enjoyable and even educational years. Lots of out-of-staters do.

Living conditions around campus range from comfortable communities to slum neighborhoods. First-year students are advised to try out the dorms, though dorm residence is not required. Since space is limited, many students are forced to find off-campus housing, which most upperclass and graduate students prefer.

"Alternative living" is a Madison specialty; there are many living cooperatives and a few grocery, eating, book, and bicycle co-ops.

Madison is no longer the radical mecca of the Midwest (its claim to fame in the Sixties). The campus mood has become more conservative—though still well informed; political rallies continue to be numerous. Students are less likely to be active participants in political parties than in just plain parties.

Social life can range from a visit to a bar or party to art openings, organized camping with the "Hoofers," or just hanging around at the student union, where one is sure to find something to help kill time. And with the many film groups, you can be assured of a few good one-dollar movies each night.

A lot of student couples live together. The pressure to have a formal "relationship" that one finds at a college one-tenth the size of Wisconsin is not present at this friendly campus.

The Wisconsin athletic program boasts a diverse selection of intercollegiate sports. Big Ten football games are a tradition, complete with all the rowdiness and revelry of a major celebration—regardless of the score. Ice hockey commands much student attention, especially since the "Badgers" clinched the 1976–1977 NCAA championship. The women's sports program has received substantial financial support.

Wisconsin attracts many out-of-staters, and many Eastern-types who are there for the education. Students at Wisconsin become increasingly intense about their studies, and as a result, competition for grades has become tougher. Stricter writing requirements are being enforced. We are told that the attrition rate is higher during the first two years, the usual time when premeds are especially weeded out. Studying seems to be most crucial during junior and senior years. Even when the bars are crowded on a Saturday night, you can be assured that the libraries will also be packed.

The school of journalism is ranked among the top five in the nation, and humanities, foreign languages, and the medical school also enjoy respectable ratings. A healthy graduate and research program complements the rest of Wisconsin's impressive curriculum.

You may not be more than a number at Wisconsin, though. Students often complain that more money is spent on the graduate departments and that the undergrads are regarded as transients. Lectures average between two hundred and four hundred students. Most of these large classes are supplemented by smaller discussion sections conducted by teaching assistants.

If you can't take the cold, don't even bother applying to Wisconsin. Winter can arrive as early as late October and often does not leave until March. After the thaw, though, the spring and summer weather are so enjoyable that they almost make up for the long, hard winter months. Almost.

What definitely do make up for the Wisconsin winters are the academic excellence of the school and the diversity of the student body. No matter what part of the country you're from, the University of Wisconsin is definitely worth a close look.

UNIVERSITY OF WYOMING

Location: Laramie, WY 82071
Campus: small city
Undergraduate enrollment:
 5100 M, 3800 W
Total enrollment: 8921
Expenses: $2649 (in-state),
 $3935 (out-of-state)
Financial aid: 85%
Library: 650,000

Student-faculty ratio: 11–1
Transfer students: 1200
Median ACT: 20.3
Fraternities: 10%
Sororities: 15%
Application deadline:
 one month before
 semester begins

"Oh, give me a home where the buffalo roam, where the deer and the antelope play. . . ." The state of Wyoming, home of some beautiful peaks is most noted for its clear air, wide-open spaces, and spellbinding natural beauty. The square boundaries of the cowboy state had, at one time, been reflected in the attitudes of its only four-year university, the University of Wyoming. Times, they are a-changing.

Young, progressive professors have injected a breath of vitality into the UW atmosphere. Colleges such as "commerce and industry" and "arts and sciences" are recognized on campus as two of the finer departments and are continuing to grow. The philosophy and political science departments are struggling to attain a measure of respectability. The school has a dynamic ecology program, an important development in one of the few states that still has an environment worth preserving. The pharmacy school is quite good. Physics, geology, botany, zoology, agriculture, and civil engineering are also among the university's relative strengths.

The university is constantly improving its physical plant. A new law building and an addition to Coe Library were recently built. Having recently completed additions to Half-Acre Gym, the University of Wyoming is now building a multimillion-dollar arena adjacent to Memorial Stadium and fieldhouse. A new power plant will make the university self-sufficient with regard to energy.

Still, the university has problems. The heavily criticized administration seems directionless and indifferent, though the new president Edward Jennings's door is open to all students. While communication between administrators and faculty is somewhat limited, student-faculty relations seem quite healthy.

The most glaring problem at UW is its overemphasis on athletics. Year after year, the Wyoming legislature appropriates a large amount of money to the UW athletic department. Football is king, and all the state residents are its subjects. Cowboy football draws alumni from all corners of the state—yet the record UW football crowd is barely over twenty-five thousand. So what did the legislature approve? A new and costly addition to the stadium. In addition, a $14,000 fence around the football practice area created some controversy.

The alumni have a strong hidden voice in campus policymaking. Organizations such as the "Cowboy Joe" booster club and the stuffy board of trustees seem to be holdovers from the days of "I Like Ike."

Laramie, with about 25,000 inhabitants, is a peaceful, safe community that is dependent on the university. Local businesses have discarded their negative "love it or leave it" attitude and now have a more friendly and considerate attitude toward the university community. A lot of folks say that Laramie is in the middle of nowhere, but that depends on where your somewhere is. The town is a scenic two-hour drive from Denver and all of the "Mile High City's" advantages. Most Laramie residents and students, though, are satisfied with the easy-going, laid-back atmosphere the town has to offer.

Campus "action" is widespread. Sex is pretty big up here among the flowers and mountains. Fairly romantic, one might say.

For other kicks, students go skiing and rock climbing in the mountain ranges east and west of Laramie. Drinking and partying are also popular. Especially drinking. The bars are always hopping, seven nights a week. Drug use (*shhhhh* . .) is also common, though prices for dope and harder drugs are a little high.

Dorm life at UW is similar to most university scenes. Freshmen under nineteen are required to live in the dorms, a rule which keeps those structures filled and active. And, of course, the cafeteria food is mediocre but laced with enough calories to get one through the day.

Sure, UW is far from God's gift to college students, but give it time, folks, give it time. It appears to be moving slowly in the right direction.

YALE UNIVERSITY

Location: New Haven, CT 06520
Campus: city center
Undergraduate enrollment: 5150
Total enrollment: 9179
Expenses: $9000
Financial aid: 39%
Library: 4,393,000 volumes

Student-faculty ratio: 10–1
Transfer students: 25–150
Median SAT: 660 V, 680 M
Fraternities: NA
Sororities: 0%
Application deadline: January 2

Yale is probably one of the finest undergraduate colleges in the country. The traditional Yale-Harvard rivalry, brought to the height of intensity at the annual Yale-Harvard football games, extends to academics—though most "Yalies" will now boast a superiority to Harvard in both undergrad and many professional schools. Though teaching assistants assume a good-sized role in the discussion sections of larger lecture courses, Yale, as opposed to many big universities, considers the teaching of undergraduates to be the most important job of the faculty. Yale College is and always has been the *raison d'etre* of Yale University. It combines the emphasis on undergraduate education with all the tools and facilities that only a university can provide.

Yale has one of the lowest student-faculty ratios in the country, and the faculty is generally excellent. Yale goes out of its way to attract top professors in many fields, although sometimes at the expense of sacrificing an excellent but untenured junior faculty to a big-name scholar from the outside. Nevertheless, Yale boasts a good chunk of those big names. In the English department, one of the nation's finest, professors like Harold Bloom teach seminars to undergrads. The history department, which is losing some of its most established and distinguished faculty to retirement, is at the nation's top.

The natural sciences at the upper levels are also excellent at Yale. The biology and molecular biophysics and biochemistry departments feature stars like Clement Markert, a pioneer in cloning research, with his hexiparental mouse (a checkerboard rodent with six parents). While many of the older biology faculty prefer their research to their teaching, the dedicated junior faculty members are strong in both teaching *and* research. Economics is the standout in the social sciences.

For the student who enjoys interdisciplinary work, Yale has one of the nation's best American studies programs. Near Eastern, British, and a future Judaic studies program are among the best cross-over departments. Yale offers some unique combined programs in economics and political science, as well as psychobiology (a psychology track in the bio department) and biopsychology (a biology track in the psych department). Yale is decidedly flexible—double majors and independently constructed majors are very popular. The "scholar of the house" program allows selected seniors to spend a year pursuing an independent project, receiving full credit without having to go to any classes. A special freshman humanities program allows a group of about eighty frosh to take a series of interrelated courses discussing the evolution of Western society, with an emphasis on primary sources.

Special seminars in Yale's twelve residential colleges normally start as suggestions by students. Outside experts are frequently brought in to teach the residential college seminars; in the last two years, for example, Howard Cosell led a seminar on bigtime sports in America, Tom Brokaw taught a course in TV news in America, and Gordon Lish conducted a workshop in fiction writing. Because of Yale's liberal arts emphasis, more pre-professional courses tend to spring up as seminars. In the spring of 1980, a record 240 applicants vied for twenty spots in an advertising seminar.

The residential college system must rank beside the faculty as one of

Yale's biggest assets. The twelve colleges, modeled after those at Oxford and Cambridge, are the center of a "Yalie's" life. Every undergraduate and every faculty member is affiliated with a college, and eighty percent of the students live and eat in their colleges. (Off-campus living is not very popular because reasonably nice neighborhoods in New Haven are very expensive and fairly distant from campus.) The residential college system divides the undergraduate population into units of manageable size. Each college has its own resident dean and master, usually senior faculty members. The main disadvantage of the closely knit social life within each residential college is that the environment sometimes takes on a resemblance to "Peyton Place." Similarly, the college system reduces the sense of unversitywide unity. (Yale has no central student center except for a small, sterile coffee lounge in the library, though one is in the planning stages.)

Life in the residential colleges derives its richness from the incredible variety of students attracted to Yale. There is no such thing as a "typical" Yale student, but it is worth noting that most "Yalies" are very bright and achievement-oriented. Ever since the reign of Dean of Admissions Inslee Clark in the mid-Sixties, Yale classes have had more ethnic diversity, more public school graduates, and fewer alumni children.

Conversation is the essence of Yale—especially at meals (which are considered the best in institutional "cuisine"). It is there, over the oak dining hall tables that friendships can flourish between people of different countries and states, with vastly different backgrounds. Yale values diversity, and it's next to impossible to predict what the admissions office is looking for when it selects the freshman class.

Most freshmen live on the "Old Campus" in dormitories affiliated with their residential college. "Old Campus" dorm rooms, after a recent renovation, are among the most luxurious on campus. Overall, Yale is a bit overcrowded, but a wide range of housing is available in the colleges, ranging from three-room quads to spacious singles. Rooms usually boast fireplaces and wood paneling.

There is unlimited variety in the extracurricular activities. Publications are popular and the *Yale Daily News* (the oldest college daily) and the *Yale Banner* (the oldest college yearbook) are the flagships for two thriving families of publications. A renaissance of humor, political, and literary magazines in the 1979–80 school year points to a resurgence of student involvement and outlets.

Many students are also attracted to theatrical productions. The Yale Dramat (again, the oldest group of its kind) presents two professional-quality plays each year. Other plays are produced by groups in the residential colleges; there is a performance of some type nearly every week during the year. Film societies show at least one movie every night, and as many as five or six on weekend evenings. Thanks to the presence of the Yale School of Music, musicians also thrive at Yale; musical groups—vocal and instrumental, with repertoires ranging from medieval to avant-garde—are numerous and varied. Men's and women's singing groups give many formal and informal concerts and go on tours. The Yale "Whiffenpoofs," for example, sing around the world. And Yale's Harkness Tower carillon players have their own society. Because most of these activities demand an intensive commitment, people specialize. It is impossible to be the leader of everything; there is no such thing as a "Big Man on Campus" at Yale.

"Yalies" have a distrust of traditional collegiate ways of doing things, and this is reflected in the political situation at the school. The college council is a low-key group which is most effective in appointing students to joint committees with the faculty and administration; it has little power and attracts little interest. The Yale political union, once a haven for Eli politicos, now concentrates on sponsoring speakers and debates for its members. In general, issues of immediate campus importance—like controversial tuition hikes or faculty appointments—generate more student interest at Yale than national or international issues.

Athletics are an important part of the extracurricular scene. The huge Payne Whitney Gym offers facilities for just about every sort of sport. Yale also owns indoor tennis courts, a hockey rink, and an excellent golf course. Organized athletics include residential college teams in a variety of sports and a strong varsity program. Unfortunately, cutbacks in the Yale budget threaten the future of many smaller teams and are proving the nemesis of the track team, which is in desperate need of a new indoor track.

Yale has traditionally been a football power in the Ivy League—The "Bulldogs" won the 1979 championship. Coach Carm Cozza, one of the winningest coaches around, is highly respected. Basketball bounced back from a dismal decade in 1980 and finished with its best record since 1967. Both men's and women's crew teams are powerhouses; the crew competed in England's Henley Royal Regatta only last summer. "Yalies" may work hard, but they certainly do play hard also.

Yale has the second largest university library in the country and a fine campus of beautiful collegiate Gothic, Georgian, and modern buildings. Excellent laboratories, two large computer systems, the oldest university art gallery in America, a huge rare book and manuscript library, and the world's largest indoor gymnasium are some of the facilities available to undergraduates. The Yale Center for British Art is the most recent and probably the most impressive addition to the Yale facilities. A gift of Paul Mellon, the center contains the most complete collection of British art outside of Great Britain. (Paul Mellon also supports a Mellon Center for the study of British Art and Architecture in London. Students can apply to spend a summer semester there.)

There are some drawbacks to the school, however. First, Yale is located in New Haven, Connecticut—"the Gateway to New England," say P.R. men—whose streets are noisy, polluted, and sometimes dangerous. Campus crime is on the rise and the security force has been beefed up. Students are learning to lock their doors. On the other hand, the city is catering more and more to young people since the opening of some good new restaurants, bars, and night-spots. Downtown New Haven is undergoing much renovation and city cultural life is on the upswing. Most of the cultural events are provided by Yale, especially by its excellent Repertory Theater. New Haven is the last stop of many plays on their way to Broadway, and Broadway itself is only ninety minutes away by Conrail. Boston is about two-and-a-half hours away in the opposite direction. If you have a car (keeping one in the city can be difficult and expensive), New Haven is a major hub of interstate highways to everywhere.

To escape from the city, you can always head into one of the quiet college courtyards. Escaping from your work is a bit more challenging. A good proportion of "Yalies" want to go to law, med, or business school and they're competing for grades against one of the brightest student bodies in the nation. "Yalies" tend to spend more time complaining about how much work they have than they spend doing it. Although not everyone, by virtue of brains or laziness, studies all the time, a good-sized minority of "weenies" does. Yale is definitely not a party school, though most Yalies know how to have a good time. Some still think that as many undergrads can be found in the library as in the Yale Bowl on Saturday afternoons in the fall. "Yalies" must learn a special self-discipline to avoid studying all the time. It can be done.

Unfortunately, too many people at Yale are socially unhappy. The students themselves cite academic pressure as the villain. Then again, with so much to do on a campus that is unusually self-contained, a "Yalie's" lack of social success is usually a direct function of his or her personal initiative.

In 1979, Yale celebrated a decade of coeducation. Women are now integrated into all aspects of university life; they find themselves at home. *The Yale Daily News* elected its first female editor-in-chief to its 1981 editorial board. Women (and minorities for that matter) have their own dean. "Yalies" are increasingly taught by women. However, Yale still has a way to go in filling its tenured positions with women. Women's sports excel, women's singing groups are extremely popular, and "women's studies" courses are offered. A grievance committee has been established to investigate cases of sexual harassment and the recognition of women's vulnerability to city crime has led to an expanded minibus system. Women are now admitted to Mory's and one senior society boasts its first female president.

Finally, Yale is very expensive. With just tuition, room, and board set at $9110 for the 1980–81 school year, it is one of the most costly universities in the nation. With rising tuition and increased faculty cutbacks, Yale is struggling to retain its integrity. Yale offers a "tuition postponement option," in essence a learn now, pay later (for as many as thirty-five years later) scheme. Still, many students, even with large amounts of financial assistance, remain wary of such a commitment.

A Yale education is a major investment. "Yalies" rightfully expect a lot and generally speaking they get it. Yale faculty members expect a lot from their students and they get it. Mutual respect between students and teachers is one of Yale's greatest assets. Yale imposes virtually no rules (except for a distribution requirement which most students do not find confining), preferring instead to let students order their own lives and studies. Most "Yalies" can find a happy balance between work and play. If you want an undergraduate education that is among the best that American dollars can buy and you are willing to work very hard for it in a stimulating campus atmosphere, Yale could be for you. It offers four years of intensity and a gilt-edged diploma that puts you in the league of a very strong Yale network.

YESHIVA UNIVERSITY
(WITH STERN COLLEGE FOR WOMEN)

Location: New York, NY 10033
Campus: city center
Undergraduate enrollment:
  740 M, 483 W
Total enrollment: 3000

Student-faculty ratio: 9–1
Transfer students: 85
Median SAT: 540 V, 590 M
Fraternities: 0%
Application deadline:

Expenses: $6000   **April 15**
Financial Aid: 75%
Library: 770,000 volumes

Yeshiva University, founded in 1886, is America's oldest and largest university under Jewish auspices, and it is unique in its attempt to achieve "synthesis"—that is, to combine both religious and secular studies into a unified academic program. Yeshiva College for men is located in the Washington Heights section of Manhattan, while Stern College for Women is in midtown's Murray Hill section.

Yeshiva offers three Jewish studies programs which cater to students from varying religious backgrounds. The average full-time student spends between thirty and forty hours in class each week, dividing his time almost equally between the two realms of study. The physical science departments, once the backbone of Yeshiva's academic offerings, are slipping in quality, but Yeshiva grads remain competitive with students from other universities. Yeshiva's students are professionally oriented, with the majority either premed or prelaw. The acceptance rate to graduate schools is impressive.

Yeshiva offers a pass/no credit option to upperclassmen, as well as a junior year in Israel program, honors, and independent study.

Extracurricular activities, of course, are limited by the double curriculum, but the limit is one of time rather than opportunities. There is a full schedule of intercollegiate and intramural athletics. Three newspapers—including one in Hebrew—are published by the student body, and there are the usual clubs for those with special interests. Students may also participate in any of the student councils governing the Jewish studies programs and life in the undergraduate college, or in the university senate composed of students, faculty, and administration. There are always the offerings of New York City.

There are no fraternities or sororities at Yeshiva. In fact, their purpose—to bring together students of similar backgrounds and interests—would be wasted on the Yeshiva campus. At YU almost everybody has the same background and interests: all are committed orthodox Jews.

Although Yeshiva's unique atmosphere may prevent the "broadening of one's horizons" that is expected to occur at college, it allows the development of extremely close relationships among students. In fact, the high level of student involvement in school affairs can be traced to Yeshiva's close-knit atmosphere.

Social life for all-male Yeshiva centers on its sister college, Stern

College for Women. Although the two schools are a forty-five-minute subway ride apart, an intricate network of "friends who know friends" makes it easy for anyone to get a date.

Yeshiva is certainly not for everyone. But for the religious Jew interested in learning about his religion and at the same time receiving a good secular education and making a lot of friends, it's the place to go.

Index

A

Adelphi University, 18–19
University of Alabama, 20–21
The American University, 21–23
Amherst College, 23–25
Antioch College, 25–27
Arizona State University, 27–28
University of Arkansas, 30–32
Auburn University, 32–33

B

Ball State University, 33–35
Bard College, 35–37
Barnard College, 37–39
Bates College, 40–42
Baylor University, 42–44
Beloit College, 44–46
Bennington College, 47–49
Boston College, 49–52
Boston University, 52–54
Bowdoin College, 54–56
Bowling Green State University, 56–58
Brandeis University, 58–60
Brigham Young University, 61–62
Brown University, 62–64
Bryn Mawr College, 64–68
Bucknell University, 68–71
Butler University, 71–72

C

California Institute of Technology, 72–74
California State University and College System, 74–75
California State University/Long Beach, 76–77
California State University/San Francisco, 77–79
California State University/San Jose, 79–80
University of California System, 80–81
University of California/Berkeley, 81–83
University of California/Davis, 83–85
University of California/Irvine, 85–86
University of California/Los Angeles, 86–88
University of California/Riverside, 88–90
University of California/San Diego, 90–91
University of California/Santa Barbara, 92–93
University of California/Santa Cruz, 93–95
Carleton College, 95–97
Carnegie-Mellon University, 97–100
Case-Western Reserve University, 100–102

Catholic University of America, 102–103
University of Chicago, 103–105
University of Cincinnati, 105–106
The City College/City University of New York, 107–108
The Claremont Colleges, 108–111
Claremont Men's College (with The Claremont Colleges), 108
Clark University, 111–113
Colby College, 113–115
Colgate University, 115–117
Colorado College, 117–118
Colorado State University, 119–120
University of Colorado/Boulder, 120–122
Columbia College of Columbia University, 122–124
Connecticut College, 124–126
University of Connecticut, 126–128
Cornell University, 128–131
Creighton University, 131–133

D

Dartmouth College, 133–135
Davidson College, 135–137
University of Dayton, 137–138
University of Delaware, 139–141
Denison University, 141–143
University of Denver, 143–144
DePaul University, 144–146
De Pauw University, 146–147
University of Detroit, 148–149
Dickinson College, 149–151
Drake University, 151–153
Drew University, 153–155
Duke University, 155–158
Duquesne University, 158–159

E

Earlham College, 159–161
Emory College, 161–163

F

Fairleigh Dickinson University, 163–166
Florida State University, 166–167
University of Florida, 167–168
Fordham University, 168–170
Franklin and Marshall College, 170–172

G

Georgetown University, 172–174
George Washington University, 174–176
Georgia Institute of Technology, 176–178
Georgia State University, 178–179
University of Georgia, 179–181
Goucher College, 181–183
Grinnell College, 184–186

H

Hamilton College (with Kirkland College), 186–188
Hampshire College, 188–190
Harvey Mudd College (with The Claremont Colleges), 108–109
University of Hartford, 190–192
Harvard University (with Radcliffe College), 192–195
Haverford College, 195–198
Hobart and William Smith Colleges, 198–200
Hofstra University, 200–202
Hollins College, 202–203
The College of the Holy Cross, 203–206
University of Houston/Central Campus, 206–207
Howard University, 207–209

Hunter College/City University of New York, 209–211

I

Idaho State University, 211–212
Illinois State University, 212–214
University of Illinois/Champaign-Urbana, 215–217
Indiana University, 217–219
Iowa State University, 220–221
University of Iowa, 221–222

J

Jackson College (with Tufts University), 438–440
Jacksonville University, 222–223
Johns Hopkins University, 224–226

K

Kalamazoo College, 226–227
Kansas State University, 228–229
University of Kansas, 229–231
Kent State University, 231–233
University of Kentucky, 233–234
Kenyon College, 234–236
Kirkland College (with Hamilton College), 186–188
Knox College, 236–238

L

Lafayette College, 238–240
Lake Forest College, 240–242
Lawrence University, 242–244
Lehigh University, 244–246
Louisiana State University/Baton Rouge, 246–247
University of Louisville, 247–249

Loyola University of Chicago, 249–251

M

Macalester College, 251–253
University of Maine/Orono, 253–255
Manhattanville College, 255–257
Marlboro College, 257–258
Marquette University, 259–261
University of Maryland/College Park, 261–263
Massachusetts Institute of Technology, 263–266
Massachusetts State College System, 266–268
University of Massachusetts/Amherst, 268–269
McGill University, 269–271
Miami University, 271–273
University of Miami, 273–275
Michigan State University, 276–278
University of Michigan, 278–281
Middlebury College, 281–284
Mills College, 284–286
University of Minnesota, 286–288
Mississippi State University, 288–290
University of Mississippi, 290–292
University of Missouri/Columbia, 292–294
University of Montana, 294–295
Morgan State University, 295–297
Mount Holyoke College, 297–299
Muhlenberg College, 299–300

N

University of Nebraska/Lincoln, 301–302
University of Nevada/Reno, 303–305

New College of the University of South Florida, 305–308
University of New Hampshire, 308–310
New Mexico State University, 310–312
University of New Mexico, 312–313
State University of New York/Albany, 313–315
State University of New York/Binghamton, 315–317
State University of New York/Buffalo, 317–319
State University of New York/Stony Brook, 319–320
New York University, 321–323
University of North Carolina/Chapel Hill, 323–325
Northeastern University, 325–327
Northwestern University, 327–329
University of Notre Dame, 329–332

O

Oberlin College, 332–334
Occidental College, 334–336
Ohio State University, 336–338
Ohio University, 338–340
Ohio Wesleyan University, 340–343
Oklahoma State University, 343–345
University of Oklahoma, 345–346
Oral Roberts University, 346–348
Oregon State University, 348–350
University of Oregon, 350–352

P

Pennsylvania State University, 352–354
University of Pennsylvania, 354–356
University of Pittsburgh, 356–358
Pizer College (with The Claremont Colleges), 109–111

Pomona College (with The Claremont Colleges), 109–111
C. W. Post Center of Long Island University, 358–359
Princeton University, 359–362
Purdue University, 362–364

Q

Quinnipiac College, 364–366

R

Radcliffe College (with Harvard University), 192–195
Randolph-Macon Woman's College, 366–367
Reed College, 367–369
Rensselaer Polytechnic Institute, 370–371
University of Rhode Island, 371–374
Rice University, 374–376
University of Rochester, 376–379
Rutgers College of Rutgers University, 379–381

S

St. Bonaventure University, 381–382
St. John's College, 382–385
St. John's University, 385–386
St. Lawrence University, 386–388
St. Louis University, 388–390
University of San Francisco, 390–391
Sarah Lawrence College, 391–392
Scripps College (with The Claremont Colleges), 109–111
Simmons College, 393–395

Simon's Rock Early College, 395–396
Skidmore College, 396–398
Smith College, 398–400
Sophie Newcomb College (with Tulane University), 440–442
University of the South, 400–402
University of South Carolina, 402–404
University of South Dakota, 404–405
University of Southern California, 405–407
Southern Illinois University/Carbondale, 407–408
Southern Methodist University, 409–410
Southwestern/Memphis, 410–411
Stanford University, 411–414
Stephens College, 414–415
Stern College for Women (with Yeshiva University), 494–496
Swarthmore College, 415–419
Sweet Briar College, 419–420
Syracuse University, 421–422

T

Temple University, 422–424
Texas A & M University, 424–426
Texas Christian University, 426–428
Texas Tech University, 428–429
University of Texas/Austin, 429–431
University of Toronto, 431–434
Trinity College (Connecticut), 434–436
Trinity College (Washington, D.C.), 436–438
Tufts University (with Jackson College) 438–440
Tulane University (with Sophie Newcomb College), 440–442
University of Tulsa, 442–443

U

Union College, 444–445
University of Utah, 445–447

V

Vanderbilt University, 447–449
Vassar College, 449–452
University of Vermont, 452–453
Villanova University, 453–454
University of Virginia, 454–457

W

Wake Forest University, 457–459
Washington and Lee University, 459–461
Washington State University, 461–463
Washington University, 463–466
University of Washington, 466–468
Wayne State University, 469–470
Wellesley College, 470–473
Wells College, 473–475
Wesleyan University, 475–478
Wheaton College, 478–480
Wichita State University, 480–482
College of William and Mary, 482–483
William Smith College (with Hobart College), 198–200
Williams College, 483–485
University of Wisconsin/Madison, 486–487
University of Wyoming, 487–489

Y

Yale University, 489–494
Yeshiva University with Stern College for Women, 494–496